Wilfred Thesiger

The Life of the Great Explorer

~

By the same author

Speke, and the Discovery of the Source of the Nile
A Tower in a Wall: Conversations with Dame Freya Stark
Robert and Gabriela Cunninghame Graham
The Highland Year (illustrated)
Wild Thyme and Saladelle (illustrated)
Wilfred Thesiger: My Life and Travels (editor)
Wilfred Thesiger: A Life in Pictures

Wilfred Thesiger

The Life of the Great Explorer

~

ALEXANDER MAITLAND

THE OVERLOOK PRESS
New York, NY

This edition published in hardcover in the United States in 2011 by

The Overlook Press, Peter Mayer Publishers, Inc.
141 Wooster Street
New York, NY 10012
www.overlookpress.com
For bulk and special sales, please contact sales@overlookny.com

First published in Great Britain in 2006 by Harper Press

Cataloging-in-Publication Data is available from the Library of Congress

Manufactured in the United States of America
ISBN 978-1-59020-163-3
2 4 6 8 10 9 7 5 3 1

For Margaret

CONTENTS

List of Illustrations   ix
List of Maps   xiii
Family Tree   xiv
Introduction   1

 1 The Emperor Menelik's 'New Flower'   5
 2 Hope and Fortune   9
 3 Gorgeous Barbarity   21
 4 'One Handsome Rajah'   29
 5 Passages to India and England   43
 6 The Cold, Bleak English Downs   51
 7 Eton: Lasting Respect and Veneration   63
 8 Shrine of my Youth   70
 9 The Mountains of Arussi   83
10 Across the Sultanate of Aussa   101
11 Savage Sudan   122
12 The Nuer   162
13 Rape of my Homeland   196
14 Among the Druze   220
15 The Flowering Desert   237
16 Palestine: Shifting Lights and Shades   250
17 Prelude to Arabia   257
18 Arabian Sands   263
19 Marsh and Mountain   307
20 Among the Mountains   334
21 A Winter in Copenhagen   370

22 Camel Journeys to the Jade Sea   385
23 With Nomadic Tribes in Other Lands   402
24 Kenya Days   436

    Epilogue   455
    Acknowledgements   465
    Notes   469
    Bibliography   501
    Index   511

ILLUSTRATIONS

Unless otherwise indicated, all photographs are from private collections.

Wilfred Thesiger's grandfather, General Frederic Augustus Thesiger, 2nd Baron Chelmsford (1827–1905), who commanded the British force during the Zulu War in South Africa in 1879.

Captain The Hon Wilfred Gilbert Thesiger DSO, c. 1902.

Thesiger's mother, about 1919.

The thatched *tukul* in the British Legation compound at Addis Ababa, where Wilfred Patrick Thesiger was born on 3 June 1910. (*Pitt Rivers Museum, University of Oxford*)

Billy, as the baby Wilfred was known, with Susannah, his Indian nurse-maid, on the Legation lawn, Addis Ababa in 1911.

Susannah's successor Minna (Mary Buckle) in camp during a trek in Abyssinia, about 1915.

Wilfred Gilbert Thesiger and Ras Tafari on the steps of the British Legation at Addis Ababa.

Part of the victory parade on Jan Meda, Addis Ababa, following the Battle of Sagale in 1916. (*Pitt Rivers Museum, University of Oxford*)

The four Thesiger brothers in Bombay, 1918.

Thesiger's uncle Frederic John Napier Thesiger, first Viscount Chelmsford (1868–1933), Viceroy of India 1916–21.

The widowed Kathleen Thesiger with her four sons.

Pierre, a Breton fisherman, and his thirteen-year-old *mousee* at Sable d'Or, Britanny, in 1929.

Thesiger, aged twenty-two, at the Villa Cipressi, his stepfather Reginald Astley's house on Lake Como, in 1932.

Val ffrench Blake, a friend of Thesiger's at Eton.

The Milebrook in the Teme Valley, Radnorshire, which Kathleen leased from 1921 to 1942.

Thesiger photographed at the time he left Eton, in 1928.

One of a series of boxing photographs taken in the early 1930s.

A unique photograph of Thesiger boxing for Oxford University.

Thesiger's caravan near the Awash Station in December 1933, at the start of his 1933-34 expedition to trace the Awash river to its mysterious end in the unexplored Sultanate of Aussa, Abyssinia. (*Pitt Rivers Museum, University of Oxford*)

Omar Ibrahim, Thesiger's headman, with the members of the Awash expedition.

Crossing the Awash at Bilen. (*Pitt Rivers Museum, University of Oxford*)

A party of Danakil warriors near the Mullu waterholes midway between Afdam and and Bahdu, Abyssinia, on 10 February 1934. (*Pitt Rivers Museum, University of Oxford*)

Guy Moore at Wasi Tini, Sudan, 1938.

Idris Daud of the Kobe-Zaghawa tribe, who joined Thesiger at Kutum, Northern Darfur, in 1935.

Idris and Zaghawa tribesmen with a lioness Thesiger had shot. (*Pitt Rivers Museum, University of Oxford*)

Bab Segma, Fez, November 1937.

Kilwal, Upper Nile, Sudan. Nier tribesman watch as a hippo is harpooned. (*Pitt Rivers Museum, University of Oxford*)

Tibesti, August–November 1938. (*Pitt Rivers Museum, University of Oxford*)

Thesiger's bodyguard, Abyssinia 1941. (*Pitt Rivers Museum, University of Oxford*)

Thesiger and Haile Selassie at Khartoum in 1940. (*The War Office.*)

Colonel Dan Sandford presenting a silver salver to Haile Selassie.

The column of Thesiger's capture Italian troops extended for a mile. (*Pitt Rivers Museum, University of Oxford*)

Faris Shahin, who served with Thesider in the Druze Legion.

Colonel David Stirling wearing the badge of the SAS. (*Courtesy of the Imperial War Museum*)

A patrol jeep, similar to the vehicle Thesiger used on SAS raids in North Africa. (*Courtesy of the Imperial War Museum*)

Crossing the Rub' al Khali, the Empty Quarter, the great sand desert of southern Arabia. (*Pitt Rivers Museum, University of Oxford*)

Salim bin Kabina of the Rashid, brining fodder for the camels from the lee side of a dune. (*Pitt Rivers Museum, University of Oxford*)

Salim bin Ghabaisha of the Rashid, who accompanied Thesiger on his journeys in southern Arabia. (*Pitt Rivers Museum, University of Oxford*)

Bin Kabina and bin Ghabaisha in Oman, 1950. (*Pitt Rivers Museum, University of Oxford*)

Muhammad al Auf, Thesiger's Rashid Guide, in 1947. (*Pitt Rivers Museum, University of Oxford*)

Thesiger photographed by bin Kabina in the Empty Quarter. (*Pitt Rivers Museum, University of Oxford*)

Thesiger in Arah dress, 1950 (*Ronald Codrai*)

Nasser Hussain, Thesigers companion and guide in the Iraqi Kurdistan in 1950-51. (*Pitt Rivers Museum, University of Oxford*)

A narrow waterway between tall reedbeds in the Iraqi marshes. (*Pitt Rivers Museum, University of Oxford*)

Bani Lam tribesmen with a wild boar Thesiger had ridden down and shot from the saddle in tamarisk scrub near the Tigris in June 1958. (*Pitt Rivers Museum, University of Oxford*)

Thesiger's *tarada*. (*Pitt Rivers Museum, University of Oxford*)

Taradas and other craft at a market in the Iraqi marshers. (*Pitt Rivers Museum, University of Oxford*)

Interior of a mudhif, or guest house, nearing completion. (*Pitt Rivers Museum, University of Oxford*)

Suaid herdboy. This image was used for the frontispiece for the first edition of The Marsh Arabs, 15 November 1961. (*Pitt Rivers Museum, University of Oxford*)

Kandari nomads coming down from Lake Shiva to the plains, 1965. (*Pitt Rivers Museum, University of Oxford*)

Thesiger in Copenhagen while he was writing the The Marsh Arabs, 15 November 1961. (Helge Ralov)

Thesiger and Kathleen, about 1961.

Jan Verney, Kathleen and Thesiger on holiday in Portugal in June-July 1961.

Thesiger's portrait, painted in 1965 by Derek Hill. (*Derek Hill*)

Outside the Travellers Club, Pall Mall, in 1973. (*Anglia Television*)

Thesiger and David Niven at the Royal Geographical Society. (*Anglia Television*)

Aboard the *Fiona*, the 42-foot ketch on which Thesiger and Gavin Young sailed for five months round the Indonesian islands in 1977 in search of Joseph Conrad's eastern world. (*Gavin Young*)

Thesiger and Gavin Young at Thesiger's flat in Chelsea, 1977.

Thesiger and Lokuyie, a Samburu *moran*, in northern Kenya. (*Pitt Rivers Museum, University of Oxford*)

With Frank Steele on the Uaso Nyiro river, Kenya, in 1970.

John Newbould with a pelican on the shores of Lake Natron.

Kisau, Thesiger's devoted companion, who died in 1974.

Lawi Leboyare. (*Pitt Rivers Museum, University of Oxford*)

Laputa Lekakwar, in whose house Thesiger lived during his last years at Maralal.

Ewoi Ekai, known as 'Kibiriti,' in his garden near Maralal.

Thesiger and Erope on safari. (*Pitt Rivers Museum, University of Oxford*)

Looking out from 'The Viewpoiint' on the edge of the escarpment at Malossa, near Maralal.

Thesiger stroking the nose of 'Africano,' greatest of the bulls on Robert Vavra's farm near Seville, in July 1996. (*Robert Vavra*)

Wilfred Thesiger leaving for Buckingham Palace with Alexander Maitland, on 2 November 1995. (*Julian Barrow*)

MAPS

Abyssinia and Sudan	25
The Danakil expedition, 1933–34	92
The Rub' al Khali, or Empty Quarter	276
The marshes of Iraq	314
Afghanistan and Pakistan	336
Chitral and Hunza	339
The Hazarajat and Waziristan	347
Nuristan and Badakhshan	362
Iran and Iraq	403
The Yemen	413
Kenya	419

(The marking of international boundaries is not authoritative)

THESIGER FAMILY (1722-2005)

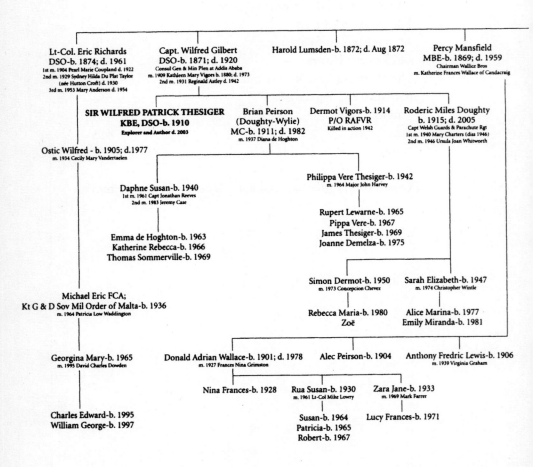

Lt-Col. Eric Richards
DSO-b. 1874; d. 1961
1st m. 1904 Pearl Marie Coupland d. 1922
2nd m. 1929 Sydney Hilda Du Plat Taylor
(née Hutton Croft) d. 1930
3rd m. 1953 Mary Anderson d. 1954

Capt. Wilfred Gilbert
DSO-b. 1871; d. 1920
Consul Gen & Min Plen at Addis Abeba
m. 1909 Kathleen Mary Vigors b. 1880; d. 1973
2nd m. 1931 Reginald Astley d. 1942

Harold Lumsden-b. 1872; d. Aug 1872

Percy Mansfield
MBE-b. 1869; d. 1959
Chairman Wallice Bros
m. Katherine Frances Wallace of Candacraig

SIR WILFRED PATRICK THESIGER
KBE, DSO-b. 1910
Explorer and Author d. 2003

Brian Peirson
(Doughty-Wylie)
MC-b. 1911; d. 1982
m. 1937 Diana de Hoghton

Dermot Vigors-b. 1914
P/O RAFVR
Killed in action 1942

Roderic Miles Doughty
b. 1915; d. 2005
Capt Welsh Guards & Parachute Rgt
1st m. 1940 Mary Charters (diss 1946)
2nd m. 1946 Ursula Joan Whitworth

Ostic Wilfred - b. 1905; d.1977
m. 1934 Cecily Mary Vandertaelen

Daphne Susan-b. 1940
1st m. 1961 Capt Jonathan Reeves
2nd m. 1983 Jeremy Case

Philippa Vere Thesiger-b. 1942
m. 1964 Major John Harvey

Emma de Hoghton-b. 1963
Katherine Rebecca-b. 1966
Thomas Sommerville-b. 1969

Rupert Lewarne-b. 1965
Pippa Vere-b. 1967
James Thesiger-b. 1969
Joanne Demelza-b. 1975

Simon Dermot-b. 1950
m. 1973 Concepcion Chevez

Sarah Elizabeth-b. 1947
m. 1974 Christopher Wintle

Rebecca Maria-b. 1980
Zoë

Alice Marina-b. 1977
Emily Miranda-b. 1981

Michael Eric FCA;
Kt G & D Sov Mil Order of Malta-b. 1936
m. 1964 Patricia Low Waddington

Georgina Mary-b. 1965
m. 1995 David Charles Dowden

Donald Adrian Wallace-b. 1901; d. 1978
m. 1927 Frances Nina Grimston

Alec Peirson-b. 1904

Anthony Fredric Lewis-b. 1906
m. 1939 Virginia Graham

Nina Frances-b. 1928

Rua Susan-b. 1930
m. 1961 Lt-Col Mike Lowry

Zara Jane-b. 1933
m. 1969 Mark Farrer

Charles Edward-b. 1995
William George-b. 1997

Susan-b. 1964
Patricia-b. 1965
Robert-b. 1967

Lucy Frances-b. 1971

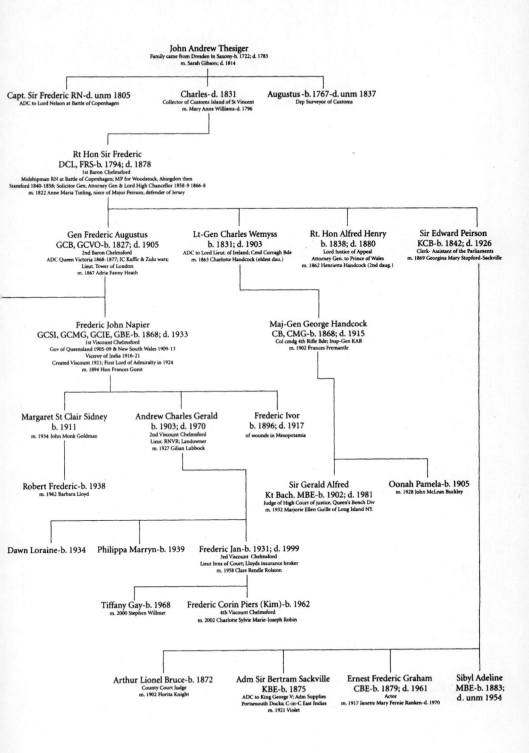

John Andrew Thesiger
Family came from Dresden in Saxony-b. 1722; d. 1783
m. Sarah Gibson; d. 1814

Capt. Sir Frederic RN-d. unm 1805
ADC to Lord Nelson at Battle of Copenhagen

Charles- d. 1831
Collector of Customs Island of St Vincent
m. Mary Anne Williams-d. 1796

Augustus -b. 1767-d. unm 1837
Dep Surveyor of Customs

Rt Hon Sir Frederic
DCL, FRS-b. 1794; d. 1878
1st Baron Chelmsford
Midshipman RN at Battle of Copenhagen; MP for Woodstock, Abingdon then
Stamford 1840-1858; Solicitor Gen, Attorney Gen & Lord High Chancellor 1858-9 1866-8
m. 1822 Anne Maria Tinling, niece of Major Peirson, defender of Jersey

Gen Frederic Augustus
GCB, GCVO-b. 1827; d. 1905
2nd Baron Chelmsford
ADC Queen Victoria 1868-1877; IC Kaffir & Zulu wars;
Lieut. Tower of London
m. 1867 Adria Fanny Heath

Lt-Gen Charles Wemyss
b. 1831; d. 1903
ADC to Lord Lieut. of Ireland; Cmd Curragh Bde
m. 1863 Charlotte Handcock (eldest dau.)

Rt. Hon Alfred Henry
b. 1838; d. 1880
Lord Justice of Appeal
Attorney Gen. to Prince of Wales
m. 1862 Henrietta Handcock (2nd daug.)

Sir Edward Peirson
KCB-b. 1842; d. 1926
Clerk- Assistant of the Parliaments
m. 1869 Georgina Mary Stopford-Sackville

Frederic John Napier
GCSI, GCMG, GCIE, GBE-b. 1868; d. 1933
1st Viscount Chelmsford
Gov of Queensland 1905-09 & New South Wales 1909-13
Viceroy of India 1916-21
Created Viscount 1921; First Lord of Admiralty in 1924
m. 1894 Hon Frances Guest

Maj-Gen George Handcock
CB, CMG-b. 1868; d. 1915
Col cmdg 4th Rifle Bde; Insp-Gen KAR
m. 1902 Frances Fremantle

Margaret St Clair Sidney
b. 1911
m. 1934 John Monk Goldman

Andrew Charles Gerald
b. 1903; d. 1970
2nd Viscount Chelmsford
Lieut. RNVR; Landowner
m. 1927 Gilian Lubbock

Frederic Ivor
b. 1896; d. 1917
of wounds in Mesopotamia

Robert Frederic-b. 1938
m. 1962 Barbara Lloyd

Sir Gerald Alfred
Kt Bach. MBE-b. 1902; d. 1981
Judge of High Court of justice, Queen's Bench Div
m. 1932 Marjorie Ellen Guille of Long Island NY.

Oonah Pamela-b. 1905
m. 1928 John McLean Buckley

Dawn Loraine-b. 1934

Philippa Marryn-b. 1939

Frederic Jan-b. 1931; d. 1999
3rd Viscount Chelmsford
Lieut Inns of Court; Lloyds insurance broker
m. 1958 Clare Rendle Rolston

Tiffany Gay-b. 1968
m. 2000 Stephen Willmer

Frederic Corin Piers (Kim)-b. 1962
4th Viscount Chelmsford
m. 2002 Charlotte Sylvie Marie-Joseph Robin

Arthur Lionel Bruce-b. 1872
County Court Judge
m. 1902 Florita Knight

Adm Sir Bertram Sackville
KBE-b. 1875
ADC to King George V; Adm Supplies
Portsmouth Docks; C-in-C East Indies
m. 1921 Violet

Ernest Frederic Graham
CBE-b. 1879; d. 1961
Actor
m. 1917 Janette Mary Fernie Ranken-d. 1970

Sibyl Adeline
MBE-b. 1883;
d. unm 1954

INTRODUCTION

'Even now, after so many years, I can still remember Wilfred Thesiger as he was when I first saw him,' was how Thesiger suggested I might begin his biography. To this he had added: 'The rest is up to you.'[1]

I met Thesiger for the first time in June 1964 at his mother's top-storey flat in Chelsea. He was then aged fifty-four. He was sunburnt, tall, with broad shoulders and deep-set grey eyes. As we shook hands I noticed the exceptional length of his fingers. He wore an obviously well-cut, rather loose-fitting dark suit. I remember clearly that he smelt of brilliantine and mothballs. He spoke quietly, with an air of understated authority. His voice was high-pitched and nasal; even by the standards of that time, his rarefied pronunciation seemed oddly affected. He had a distinctive habit of emphasising prepositions in phrases such as 'All this was utterly meaningless *to* me'. He moved slowly and deliberately, with long, ponderous strides; yet he gave somehow the impression that he was also capable of lightning-fast reactions. Later, I heard that he had been a source of inspiration for Ian Fleming's fictional hero James Bond. Whether or not this was true, Thesiger, like Bond, was larger than life; and like Bond, he appeared to have led a charmed existence.

He introduced me to his mother, Kathleen, who had retired early to bed. Cocooned in a woollen shawl and an old-fashioned lace-trimmed mobcap, she lay propped up on pillows, with writing paper and books spread out on the bedcover within easy reach. Thesiger left us alone for a few minutes while he carried a tray with a decanter of sherry and glasses to the sitting room. It was then that his mother offered me the unforgettable advice: 'You must stand up to Wilfred.'[2]

Thesiger preferred to sit with his back to the window, in the dark

1

shadow of a high-backed chair. At intervals he fingered a string of purple glass 'worry beads' that lay on the small table at his elbow. He talked energetically and fluently in reply to enquiries, but he himself asked few questions, and instead of taking up a fresh theme he sat quietly, staring at me, until I questioned him again. When I could think of nothing to say, or to ask, he reached again for the purple beads. Meanwhile he scarcely had touched his thimbleful of sherry.

His mother's flat, to which Thesiger returned for two or three months every year, was like a *catalogue raisonnée* of his life and travels. Danakil *jilis* in tasselled sheaths hung beside framed black-and-white Kuba textiles from the Congo. There were silver-hilted Arab daggers and ancient swords in silver-inlaid scabbards. Medals honouring Thesiger's achievements as an explorer and, in his youth, as a boxer were displayed in velvet-lined cases. A portrait of Thesiger painted in 1945 by Anthony Devas hung on the right of the sitting room fireplace. On the wall opposite, three tall glass-fronted cabinets held part of his collection of rare travel books devoted to Arabia, Africa and the Middle East. His mother had brought the cabinets to London in 1943 from their former home in Radnorshire. Thesiger commented proudly: 'I can't begin to imagine how my mother knew they would fit into this room. It was remarkable how she did this. But, there again, my mother is a very remarkable person.'[3]

In a cupboard in Thesiger's bedroom were stored the sixty or more landscape-format albums of black-and-white photographs which he often described as his 'most cherished possession'.[4] As far as I remember he did not produce these albums during my first visit, but over the years I became very familiar with the wonderful images they contained. Only some time later did he show me his collections of travel diaries, note-books and annotated maps describing his journeys. Not until some years after she had died did he encourage me to read letters he had written, many from outlying places, to his mother, who to her eternal credit preserved them with care, as she had preserved those Wilfred's father had written a generation before.

One memory stands out from the vaguer recollections of that first visit. To my surprise, as I was leaving Thesiger took out a pocket diary, consulted it for a moment and said: 'If you've nothing better to do next

Sunday, why don't you come along and we'll cook ourselves supper. My mother's housekeeper is away for the night, but we can heat up some soup and scramble an egg or two.' He grinned and added: 'That'd be fun.'[5] This unexpected invitation marked the beginning of a friendship that lasted for almost forty years.

I have heard it said that Thesiger was very straightforward, uncomplicated, easy to get to know and to understand. To some people he may have appeared like that; and of course, everyone who met him (whether they knew him intimately or hardly at all) received a slightly different impression. But even his oldest friends, who had known him since his schooldays, could not quite agree about certain seemingly paradoxical aspects of Thesiger's character and temperament. Most of them, however, accepted that he was a veritable maze of contradictions; and, if the truth be told, in some ways his own worst enemy. Like the Bedu of the Arabian desert, he was a man of extremes. He could be affectionate and loving (for example towards his mother), yet he was capable of spontaneous, bitter hatred; he was either very cautious or wildly generous with his money and possessions; he was normally fussy and meticulous, but he could be astonishingly careless and foolishly improvident; he relished gossip, yet was uncompromisingly discreet; his touching kindnesses contrasted with sometimes appalling cruelty. He denied being possessive and criticised others who were, including his friend the writer T.H. White, and his own mother, who was by nature possessive – as indeed he was himself. Being possessive, and yet desperately needing to be possessed, was part of Thesiger's chronic sense of insecurity, which resulted from traumas he suffered during his childhood in Abyssinia and England. His vices were fewer, less extreme and yet more conspicuous than his many virtues. The greatest of these – immense and selfless bravery, compassion, determination, integrity and creative energy – enabled him to achieve his outstanding feats of exploration and travel, and to record them with a matchless brilliance in his photography and in his writing.

Thesiger's craggy features and tall, gaunt frame were a gift for the painter or sculptor. His earliest adult portraits were sketched in pencil on menu-cards by (probably inebriated) friends at Oxford's 'bump suppers'. Gerald de Gaury drew him in 1943, and Anthony Devas painted his portrait in oils at the end of the Second World War. In 1953 Fiore de Henriques sculpted Thesiger's head in bronze, a powerful image, like Devas's excellent portrait, which nevertheless romanticised him. In contrast, three portraits painted by Derek Hill in 1965 showed Thesiger, then aged fifty-five, very much as I had first seen him, and indeed as he really was. Although he portrayed the man who had survived dangerous journeys through Abyssinia, the Sahara and Arabia, a decade hunting African big game, and four years' intense fighting in the war, Hill also captured a defensive, shy, vulnerable side of his sitter's complex personality, a side that Thesiger normally kept hidden.

In old age Thesiger was painted, sculpted and photographed by artists and photographers fascinated by his achievements and his weathered features, whose creases, folds and crenellations by then resembled ancient tree-bark, or elephant's hide, or rock, more than the surface texture of an ordinary human being. These later portraits celebrated him as the patriarch of modern exploration and travel, and as a living legend to which they gave substance. Only when his visitors were greeted by a grey-haired, elderly gentleman in a dark suit or country tweeds did many of them realise how, in his books, Thesiger had been frozen in time, like the age-defying images of tribal men, women and children he had photographed more than half a century before. Although Thesiger's last portraits cast him in old age, the finest bridged a widening gap between his wander years and the present; and to his increasingly iconic status they paid due and worthy homage.

ONE

The Emperor Menelik's 'New Flower'

In 1901 an English traveller, Herbert Vivian, described his recent journey through Abyssinia in a book which included impressions of the capital Addis Ababa as he first saw it, less than a decade after the Emperor Menelik II had established the town. 'I looked round incredulously, and saw nothing but a few summer-house huts and an occasional white tent, all very far from each other, scattered over a rough, hilly basin at the foot of steep hills. That this could be the capital of a great empire, the residence of the King of Kings, seemed monstrous and out of the question.'[1] More than twenty pages of Vivian's book *Through Lion Land to the Court of the Lion of Judah* were devoted entirely to Addis Ababa, whose name in Amharic means 'New Flower'.[2] Vivian described the remote setting; the tents and primitive thatched huts of the British Agency (as he called the Legation) in its mud-walled compound; tribesmen arrayed in striking costumes; the huge marketplace, trading in exotic spices and other varied produce, brass and silver ornaments, livestock and weapons, which reminded him of an Oriental bazaar or conjured up images of medieval England. 'To appreciate Addis Ababa,' he wrote, 'it is necessary to realise that this strange capital covers some fifty square miles, and contains a very large population which has never been numbered. Streets there are none, and to go from one part of the town to the other you must simply bestride your mule and prepare to ride across country. Three-quarters of an hour at least are necessary for a pilgrimage from the British Agency to the Palace, and as much again to the market. On either of these journeys you must cross three or four deep ravines with stony, precipitous banks and a torrent-bed full of slippery boulders.'[3]

Lord and Lady Hindlip visited Addis Ababa in 1902, during their big game hunting expedition in Abyssinia and British East Africa. In his book *Sport and Travel*, Hindlip wrote: 'The squalor of native African towns and villages is apparent everywhere … Menelik's capital is nothing but a collection of huts … surrounded on nearly three sides by mountainous country.'⁴ Hindlip's scathing remarks were echoed in 1905 by Augustus B. Wylde, a former Vice-Consul for the Red Sea: 'The place cannot be called a town but a conglomeration of hamlets and huts with hardly a decent house to be seen anywhere. The whole area is nearly tree-less and very disappointing.'⁵

In his autobiography *The Life of My Choice*, published in 1987, Wilfred Thesiger conjured a rather more vivid and more sensual image of his birthplace, which had changed apparently very little by the time his father and mother arrived there, only a few years after Vivian, the Hindlips and Wylde, in December 1909. He did this very skilfully, introducing his parents and placing them at the centre of the stage, sketching the embryonic, sprawling township of Addis Ababa, its wild surroundings and multicultural population, and the social and political chaos into which Abyssinia had lapsed, from 1908, after Menelik had been incapacitated by the first of several strokes.

Thesiger wrote:

Addis Ababa consisted of a series of scattered villages grouped on hillsides with open, uncultivated spaces between. Menelik's palace crowned the largest hill; nearby a jumble of thatched huts and some corrugated-iron-roofed shacks clustered round the large open market. Nowhere were there any proper roads. [In his north Abyssinia diary, dated 1960, Thesiger commented on 12 May: 'Menelik's gibbi [palace] was on a small isolated hill below the present town.' And on 13 May: '[It occupied] a surprisingly small area on the top of the hill … He used to sit under a tree and watch his cattle being watered, with a telescope.'⁶ When Thesiger visited the site of Menelik's palace in 1960, he had found 'almost no sign of it'.⁷]

Abyssinians of any standing travelled everywhere on muleback, followed by an armed mob of slaves and retainers, varying in number according to the importance of their master. Galla, Somali, Gurage, people from the subject kingdom of Kaffa, negroes from the west, mingled on the streets with their Amhara and Tigrean overlords; but it was these latter who dominated the scene, imposed their stamp upon the town and gave it its unique character. Wrapped in white toga-like shammas worn over long white shirts and jodhpurs, they set a fashion which over the years was copied by an increasing number of their subjects.

The clothes, the buildings, the pitch and intonation of voices speaking Amharic; the smell of rancid butter, of red peppers and burning cow dung that permeated the town; the packs of savage dogs that roamed the streets and whose howling rose and fell through the night; an occasional corpse hanging on the gallows-tree; beggars who had lost a hand or foot for theft; debtors and creditors wandering round chained together; strings of donkeys bringing in firewood; caravans of mules; the crowded market where men and women squatted on the ground, selling earthen pots, lengths of cloths, skins, cartridges, bars of salt, silver ornaments, heaps of grain, vegetables, beer – all this combined to create a scene and an atmosphere unlike any other in the world ...[8]

Almost certainly, Thesiger's detailed descriptions of Addis Ababa were not based entirely on childhood memories, but on notes and recollections of visits he made later, between 1930 and 1966, no doubt clarified by reading his father's correspondence and the many books about Abyssinia he had collected over the years. Having painted this colourful backdrop to his life story, Thesiger gave a perceptive résumé of the Abyssinians' character: 'Encircled by British, French and Italian territories, they were intensely proud of their age-old independence and very conscious that their forefathers had been among the earliest converts to Christianity. Consequently they were both arrogant and reactionary, while the past three hundred years had made them suspicious and obstructive in dealing with Europeans. As a race they had an inborn love of litigation and suffered from inherent avarice. Yet they were naturally courteous, often extremely intelligent, and always courageous and enduring.'[9]

A year after Menelik's first, paralysing stroke, 'Conditions in Addis Ababa and in the country as a whole were already chaotic ... They were soon to become very much worse. In and around Addis Ababa murder, brigandage and highway robbery increased alarmingly; in restoring order, public hangings, floggings and mutilations had little effect. The town was filled with disbanded soldiery from Menelik's army, and on the hills outside were camped the armies of the various contenders for power.'[10]

Here, at the heart of Menelik's remote African empire, threatened by anarchy and bloodshed, Thesiger's father took up his official duties at the British Legation in December 1909. He and his young bride, who was four months pregnant, adjusted to married life in these primitive surroundings as they waited anxiously and eagerly for the birth of their first child the following year.

TWO

Hope and Fortune

In March 1911, nine months after the birth of their eldest son, Wilfred Thesiger's father wrote in a romantic mood to his wife, who was then in England and pregnant for the second time: 'What a wonderful thing it is to be married and love like we do, and all has come because you once said "yes" to me in a hansom and gave yourself to me.'[1]

Captain the Honourable Wilfred Gilbert Thesiger was aged thirty-eight and Kathleen Mary Vigors was twenty-nine when they married on 21 August 1909 at St Peter's church, Eaton Square, in the London borough of Westminster. The ceremony in this fashionable setting was conducted by the Reverend William Gascoigne Cecil, assisted by the Reverend Arthur Evelyn Ward, whose marriage to Kathleen's younger sister Eileen Edmée took place in November that same year. The Thesigers made a handsome couple on their wedding day. Kathleen's slender build and radiantly healthy complexion, set off by luxuriant waves of auburn hair, perfectly complemented Wilfred Gilbert, who stood over six feet, and was lean and muscular, with broad, sloping shoulders. His gaunt, rather delicate features, still sallow after two years' exposure to the African sun, were clean-shaven except for a heavy moustache, and his dark-brown hair was brushed from a centre parting. Like his late father, General Lord Chelmsford, Wilfred Gilbert Thesiger was reliably discreet, formal and pleasantly reserved.

Wilfred Gilbert and Kathleen's was the third wedding uniting two generations of their families. Handcock sisters, who were first cousins of Kathleen's mother, had married distinguished younger sons of the first Lord Chelmsford. In 1862 Henrietta Handcock married the Honourable Alfred Henry Thesiger, a Lord of Appeal and Attorney-General to the

9

Prince of Wales. The following year, Henrietta's elder sister Charlotte Elizabeth married Alfred Henry's elder brother, the Honourable Charles Wemyss Thesiger, a Lieutenant-General in the Hussars. In August 1909, witnesses to the Thesigers' marriage included Kathleen's widowed mother Mary Louisa Helen Vigors, Wilfred Gilbert's elder brother Percy Mansfield Thesiger, and Count Alexander Hoyos, a Secretary at the Austrian Embassy and a friend of the bridegroom. In his autobiography, Wilfred Thesiger portrayed his father as 'intensely and justifiably proud of his family, which in his own generation had produced a viceroy, a general, an admiral, a Lord of Appeal, a High Court judge and a famous actor. Intelligent, sensitive and artistic, with a certain diffidence which added to his charm, he was above all a man of absolute integrity.'[2]

Wilfred Gilbert painted in watercolours, wrote verse and also played the cello.[3] By his early thirties he had already had a distinguished career in the Consular Service, and had been awarded a DSO in the Boer War. Perceptive studio portraits by Bertram Park, a society photographer in Dover Street, London, highlighted these compatible yet contrasting facets of his life and character. On the one hand, Park captured the thoughtful, determined expression of a soldier and administrator accustomed to authority; on the other, he evoked the introspective, wistful gaze of an artist and a poet.

Thesiger described his mother Kathleen as attractive, brave and determined, a woman who had dedicated herself to her husband 'in the same spirit shown by those great nineteenth-century lady travellers Isobel Burton and Florence Baker ... ready to follow [him] without question on any odyssey on which he might embark'.[4] 'A photograph of my mother at that time [also taken by Bertram Park] shows a beautiful, resolute face under waves of soft brown hair ... Naturally adventurous, she loved the life in Abyssinia, where nothing daunted her. She shared my father's love of horses and enjoyed to the full the constant riding. Like him, she was an enthusiastic and skilful gardener ... Since she was utterly devoted to my father, her children inevitably took second place. In consequence in my childhood memories she does not feature as much as my father; only later did I fully appreciate her forceful yet lovable character.'[5]

When he wrote about his father's family, Thesiger saw no reason to include the generations of ancestors before his grandfather, the famous general and second Lord Chelmsford. He defended this, saying: 'The Life of My Choice was about me and the life I had led. My father and, later on, my mother were tremendously influential and I was fascinated by what my grandfather had done. These things affected me, but I can't have been affected by relatives living at the time of Waterloo. To suggest that I might have seems, to me, utter nonsense. It would never have occurred to me to spend months studying my ancestors, to see whether or not there might be any resemblance between some of them and myself.'[6]

Whereas later generations of Thesigers have been well-documented, little is known about Johann Andreas Thesiger who emigrated from Saxony to England in the middle of the eighteenth century and in due course established the Thesigers' English line. According to family records, Johann Andreas, now usually known as John Andrew, was born in Dresden in 1722. He married Sarah Gibson from Chester, and fathered four sons and four daughters. John Andrew died in May 1783,[7] and was survived by his wife, who died almost thirty-one years later, in March 1814. John Andrew was evidently intelligent, amenable and hard-working. Although the young Wilfred Thesiger scoffed at efforts to prove similarities between his remote ancestors and later generations of his family, John Andrew's sons, like their father, had been clever and diligent. His great-grandson Alfred Henry, who became a Lord of Appeal and Attorney-General, was described as 'extremely industrious', while Alfred Henry's nephew Frederic, the first Viscount Chelmsford, was known to work 'very hard', as was Frederic's younger brother, Wilfred Gilbert Thesiger.

In The Life of My Choice, Wilfred Thesiger underlined his father's tireless capacity for hard work: 'By December 1917 my father badly needed leave. The altitude of Addis Ababa, at eight thousand feet, was affecting his heart. He had been short-handed, overworked and under considerable strain.'[8] As for Thesiger himself. He was once described by his lifelong friend John Verney as 'the world's greatest spiv'.[9] Yet when writing a book he often worked for as many as fourteen hours a day, and even in his eighties his powers of concentration and his ability to work long hours for weeks at a time appeared to be undiminished.

From the time he arrived in England, John Andrew Thesiger earned his living as an amanuensis or private secretary to Lord Charles Watson-

Wentworth, the second Marquess of Rockingham, who led the Whig opposition and twice served as Prime Minister, in 1765–66 and again in 1782, the year he died. As well as his native German, John Andrew evidently spoke and wrote fluently in English, and possibly several other languages besides. His eldest son Frederic, we know, understood Danish and Russian.

We can only guess what John Andrew might have looked like. It is tempting to picture him as above average height, thin and wiry, with lantern jaws and a prominent nose. These characteristics recurred in later generations of Thesigers: for example General Lord Chelmsford, the actor Ernest Thesiger, and Ernest's first cousin Wilfred, whose large, skewed, three-times-broken nose became his most famous physical hall-mark. But the assumption that John Andrew's looks and build were inherited by his descendants may be quite wrong. His eldest son, Frederic, who appears life-size on one of the four cast-bronze memorial panels at the base of Nelson's Column in Trafalgar Square, bears no obvi-ous resemblance to other male Thesigers descended from his younger brother's family. Neither Frederic's looks nor build matches the gaunt, hawkish Thesiger model. He has a rounded face, a thin, expressionless mouth and an inconspicuous straight nose. He is neither stout nor very lean. It is difficult to judge his height, which seems about the same as Nelson's; but the sculptor, J. Ternouth, may have exaggerated Nelson's height to achieve a more dramatic effect.

Before he enlisted in the Royal Navy, Frederic served with the East India Company's fleet in the Caribbean. He rose to Acting Lieutenant aboard HMS *Formidable*, commanded by Admiral Rodney, at the Battle of Saintes, off Martinique, in 1782. Praised by Rodney as 'an excellent and gallant officer', he later served with the Russian navy during the war between Russia and Sweden. The Empress Catherine II (Catherine the Great) awarded him an Order of Merit and, in 1790, a knighthood of the Order of St George. He became adviser to the First Sea Lord and was promoted commander, then captain. In 1801 Frederic served as ADC to Lord Nelson at the Battle of Copenhagen, when his knowledge of Danish enabled him to translate Nelson's letter, accompanying a flag of truce, which Frederic presented to the young Crown Prince of Denmark. The bronze relief in Trafalgar Square shows him handing Nelson the Danes' letter of surrender. Whilst the Royal Navy had profited from Frederic's experience in the Baltic, no further offer of an active command was forthcoming. There appear to have been no obvious reasons for this. Depressed, disillusioned, without prospects or a wife and family of his own to console and distract him, Captain Sir Frederic Thesiger committed suicide at Plymouth on 26 August 1805, two months before Nelson was fatally wounded at the Battle of Trafalgar.

Sir Frederic's younger brother Charles and his London-born wife, Mary Anne Williams, had six children, including two boys who died in infancy. Frederic, the third son – the late Sir Frederic's nephew and namesake – witnessed, as a thirteen-year-old midshipman, the seizure of the Danish fleet at Copenhagen in 1807. He resigned from the navy, having become heir to his father's estates in the West Indies, and afterwards studied law. He was called to the Bar in 1818 and recommended to King's Counsel in 1834. In 1844 he was appointed Solicitor-General and was knighted. As a Member of Parliament he represented Woodstock, Abingdon and Stamford. Having twice served as Attorney-General, on 1 March 1858 Sir Frederic Thesiger QC was created the first Baron Chelmsford of Essex.

Sir Frederic's noted attributes – 'a fine presence and handsome features, a beautiful voice, a pleasant if too frequent wit, an imperturbable temper, and a gift of natural eloquence' – must have stood him in good stead as a barrister and a politician. In any case, the Thesigers' progress in less than three generations, from the arrival in England of their gifted German ancestor to achieving an English peerage, had been by any standards remarkable, and amply justified the optimism and ambition implicit in their family motto, *Spes et Fortuna*, 'Hope and Fortune'.

Lord Chelmsford's son and heir, the Honourable Frederic Augustus Thesiger, was born on 31 May 1827. After serving in Nova Scotia, the Crimea, India and Abyssinia, as General Lord Chelmsford he commanded the British force during the Kaffir and Zulu wars. In South Africa he earned a lasting notoriety when over 1300 of his troops were massacred by the Zulu army at Isandhlwana on 22 January 1879, known afterwards to the Zulus as 'the Day of the Dead Moon'. Thesiger wrote in *The Life of My Choice*: 'In the Milebrook [the house in Radnorshire, now Powys, where he and his brothers lived from 1921 with their widowed

mother] were assegais and other trophies brought back by my grandfather after he had shattered the Zulu army at Ulundi in 1879 – but I
never begrudged those peerless warriors their earlier, annihilating victory
over a British force on the slopes of Isandhlwana.'[10] Despite having
'shattered the Zulu army'[11] and won the war, Chelmsford was blamed for
misleading intelligence and confused orders which had led to the
massacre. He consequently returned to England with his reputation
permanently tarnished. Thesiger wrote in 1940: 'I have just finished the
book about my grandfather and the Zulu war. [This was *Lord Chelmsford
and the Zulu War* (1939) by Major the Hon. Gerald French DSO, which
Percy Thesiger, Wilfred's uncle, had given him in November 1939.] I
found it most interesting. It seemed to be a very complete justification of
his strategy in that war and a vindication of his generalship ... I had not
realised that the criticism had been so personal and so venomous. What
does emerge very clearly is that he was a great gentleman, and that he
won the respect and affection of those who served under him. He must
have been a great and charming man and I wish I had known him.'[12]

Fascinated all his life by his grandfather's controversial role in the Zulu
war, Thesiger, at the age of eighty-six, visited Isandhlwana and saw for
himself where the massacre had taken place. In South Africa he met the
Zulu leader Chief Mangosuthu Buthelezi, who presented him with a Zulu
knobkerrie, a shield and a spear. Thesiger said afterwards: 'I found
Buthelezi impressive. It moved me to have met him like that more than a
century after Isandhlwana. There we were: Buthelezi, the grandson of
Cetewayo, the Zulu king; and myself, the grandson of Lord Chelmsford,
whose army Cetewayo's warriors half-destroyed, and who finally
destroyed them at Ulundi.'[13]

On 9 April 1905, while he was playing billiards in the United Services
Club, Lord Chelmsford died of a heart attack at the age of seventy-seven.
Thesiger said: 'My grandfather and my father died instantaneously, so
that they could have felt nothing. When it's my turn to push up the
daisies, that is how I should wish to die.'[14]

Wilfred Thesiger's father, Wilfred Gilbert, was the third of Lord and
Lady Chelmsford's five sons. He was born at Simla on 25 March 1871,
four years after Frederic Augustus Thesiger married Adria Fanny Heath,
the eldest daughter of Major-General Heath of the Bombay Army. Their

eldest son, Frederic John Napier, was appointed Viceroy of India from 1916 to 1921; in 1921 he was created the first Viscount Chelmsford. Harold Lumsden Thesiger, their fourth son, died in India, aged only two and a half months, in 1872.

'For some reason,' Thesiger wrote, 'my father was educated at Cheltenham [College], whereas his brothers [Frederic, Percy and Eric] were educated at Winchester.'[15] Wilfred Gilbert had twice failed the Winchester entrance examination, despite receiving extra tuition at a crammer in Switzerland. As a boy he had been delicate. Above average height, he was handsome and slender, and his expression was wistful, perhaps melancholy. In 1889 and 1892 he was examined at Francis Galton's Anthropometric Institute in South Kensington, which was equipped and supervised as part of the International Health Exhibition. Galton's laboratory measured 'Keenness of Sight and of Hearing; Colour Sense, Judgement of Eye; Breathing Power; Reaction Time; Strength of Pull and of Squeeze; Force of Blow; Span of Arms; Height, both standing and sitting; and Weight'.[16] A student of 'hereditary talent and character', and founder of the Eugenics Society, Galton espoused the theory of 'right breeding', which the high achievers produced by successive generations of Thesigers appeared to confirm.

An illness, possibly rheumatic fever, had drained Wilfred Gilbert's energy and left him with a permanently weakened heart. Though he was a 'well conducted boy', his school reports describe him as 'languid and unattentive'[17] – failings conspicuous in the younger Wilfred Thesiger, who confessed to having a limited attention span and who wrote that he had proved 'an unreceptive boy to teach, disinclined to concentrate on any subject that bored me'.[18] Wilfred Gilbert's poor performance in French and German (which had once been his family's first language) prompted a master's opinion that he 'was not a linguist by nature'. While at Cheltenham he began to write poetry. His poems suggest that he was prone to depression or melancholy. Many are preoccupied with death, and evoke a sense of futility which later seemed at odds with his private and public roles as husband, father and staunch representative of the Crown.

Wilfred Gilbert's career in the Consular Service began in Asia Minor, where he served at Lake Van from 1895 to 1898 'as a secretary to Major [later Colonel] W.A. Williams RA, Military Vice-Consul' at the time of the Armenian massacres. He earned a mention in despatches and wrote letters which were keenly observed and often vivid. Many of them presaged others written years later by his son Wilfred, on topics that included hunting, photography and travel. In July 1896 Wilfred Gilbert wrote: 'I want very much to see more of the country ... a good pair of ibex horns still haunts my dreams.'[19] And in April that same year: 'If ever I come out here again I shall certainly bring a camera.'[20] Romantically careless of time and place, he wrote on 'the 20 somethingth of August 1896' from Garchegan, 'somewhere in the mountains': 'It is a glorious life this, living in tents and moving from place to place.'[21] Of the conflict between Armenians and Turks he saw nothing worse than a skirmish, like 'a music hall battle', in front of the consulate. Once an Armenian banker who lived nearby 'sent over to say some revolutionists were in his garden and were going to murder him'.[22]

Wilfred Gilbert spent much of his time at Van gardening, sketching, reading, riding and shooting. He learnt Turkish, and took charge of the household. Thesiger wrote: 'My father made a number of watercolour sketches of [Kurdish tribes in their 'spectacular garb'] that fascinated me as a boy but have since disappeared. At Van he was very conscious of past greatness, when kings of Assyria ruled, fought and fell among these mountains.'[23] Wilfred Gilbert remarked in a letter: 'even a short description of these districts written by a certain Marco Polo, which we have here, is perfectly up to date'.[24]

After Van he had been nominated Vice-Consul at Algiers, but he was posted instead to Taranto in southern Italy. There he monitored exports of olive oil and red wine, and compiled an encouraging report on Calabria's mother-of-pearl industry. Having written poems inspired by the sea, at Taranto Wilfred Gilbert became a keen yachtsman. He also took up fencing. According to Signor Ferri, his fencing master: 'Correctness, thundering attack, and the highest intelligence, distinguish him on the platform.'[25] Even if 'thundering attack' was overdone, it sounded better than Cheltenham's less flattering comments that Wilfred Gilbert was 'not of much power' in the classroom and 'lacked scoring power at cricket'.[26] Thesiger did not share his father's fencing talent: at Oxford he 'was noted as much for the extraordinary and often furious contortions of his blade in fencing – a pastime at which he was never an adept – as for his lightning successes in the ring'.[27]

'During the Boer War,' Thesiger wrote, '[my father] joined the Imperial Yeomanry as a trooper, but was soon commissioned and later promoted to [temporary] captain. He fought in South Africa from March 1900 until October 1901 and was awarded the DSO.'[28] Wilfred Gilbert's DSO was for general service, not, as in his son Wilfred's case, for an outstanding act of bravery. After the war he considered becoming a District Commissioner in the Transvaal, but instead rejoined the Consular Service. In 1902 he was sent as Vice-Consul to Belgrade. The following year he was left in charge of the Legation when the Minister was withdrawn after the brutal murder of King Alexander and Queen Draga by an anarchist group known as the Black Hand.

King Alexander's successor, Peter I (like Wilfred Gilbert's father), suffered from 'a sort of shyness and inability to make small [impromptu] remarks to everyone'.[29] Wilfred Gilbert understood this difficulty, yet could not resist describing, tongue-in-cheek, preparations for the coronation: 'the king has been practising in the palace garden how to get on horseback in his robe and crown with his sceptre in his hand, for he is to ride back in all his glory; and the ministers are having little loops sewn on their best clothes in anticipation of the orders they expect to receive ... For two days it has drizzled and all the Serbian flags are gradually fading into limp rags in which the red, blue and white have run into each other to such an extent that by Wednesday they promise to be little more than mere smudges of colour not of the cleanest.'[30]

After Belgrade, Wilfred Gilbert was posted to St Petersburg, where, to his relief he was not 'bothered with too many social duties'.[31] He looked forward to playing golf at Mourina, an hour's drive from the city, and reassured his now widowed mother: 'I am awfully lucky in servants, having just got a treasure in the way of an office boy and with a jewel of a cook and Collins [his former batman in the Imperial Yeomanry] am really in clover.'[32] This was fortunate, since Wilfred Gilbert's later postings, in the Congo and Abyssinia, were to prove very stressful; and, at Addis Ababa, potentially dangerous.

Like his father, Thesiger grew up to be 'justifiably proud' of his family. By this he meant proud of the Thesigers. He adored his mother and got on well with her relatives, but her family did not greatly interest him. He said: 'The Vigors were landed gentry with estates in Ireland. They achieved nothing of consequence, whereas every generation of my father's family produced somebody who was outstanding.'[33]

Whenever Kathleen Mary Vigors thought of Ireland, she pictured Burgage, her childhood home near Bagenalstown and Leighlinbridge, in County Carlow, where she had been brought up with her sister and brothers until she was eight. Some photographs of Burgage taken in June 1939 show the house and part of the estate, with meadows that slope from terraced lawns down to the River Barrow. Supposedly written at Burgage, Cecil Frances Alexander's popular hymn 'All Things Bright and Beautiful' praised the 'river running by' and the 'purple-headed mountain' – possibly Mount Leinster, which could be seen from the 'Butler's Terrace'. Thesiger said: 'When we came back from Addis Ababa [in 1919], we went to Burgage and we were there for a bit. Burgage was desperately important to my mother. There was this love of Ireland and the Irish. She was passionate about Ireland, and yet she had seen so little of it.'[34]

The Vigors originated either in France or Spain, and were among the many Protestants who fled to England in the sixteenth century. The Irish branch of the family originated with Louis Vigors, who became vicar of Kilfaunabeg and Kilcoe in County Cork in 1615. In the family records it is said that Louis Vigors's son Urban served as chaplain to King Charles I. A later Vigors, Captain Nicholas Aylward, contributed important papers to the Linnean Society and published an essay titled 'An Enquiry into the Nature of Poetic Licence'. Though severely wounded in the Peninsular War, he won distinction for his 'scientific attainments'. Together with Sir Stamford Raffles he helped to found the Zoological Society of London in 1826, and served as the first of its secretaries. Nicholas Vigors's stepbrother, General Horatio Nelson Trafalgar Vigors, was born in 1807, two years after the battle which his forenames celebrate so comprehensively. He served for some years in the 1850s as the acting Governor of St Helena, having previously commanded the island's tiny regiment.[35]

In *The Life of My Choice* Thesiger sketched his Vigors grandparents briefly: 'My maternal grandmother was an undemonstrative and rather prudish woman, whereas my grandfather was rather a rake, a confirmed gambler and obviously excellent company. My mother remembered him with affection all her life.'[36] Thesiger later explained that he described Thomas Vigors, his grandfather, mainly from Kathleen's reminiscences. He recalled: 'When I was a boy, my Vigors grandmother seemed to me a formidable, rather frightening figure. I think, in fact, she was very attached to my mother. They got on well and Granny [Vigors] was always kind to us.'[37]

Kathleen's father, Thomas Mercer Cliffe Vigors, was born in 1853 at Perth in Western Australia. Her mother, Mary Louisa Helen Handcock, was the elder daughter of Colonel the Honourable Robert French Handcock, a younger son of Lord Castlemaine of Moydrum Castle, County Westmeath. Thomas Vigors married Mary Louisa Handcock on 4 April 1877 at St Stephen's church in Dublin. He inherited the Burgage estate in County Carlow when his bachelor uncle John Cliffe Vigors died in 1881. Kathleen, her sister Eileen Edmée and their brothers Edward and Ludlow Ashmead were brought up at Burgage until their parents separated about 1888. The comfortable Georgian house, with ivy-covered walls surrounded by large gardens, fields and woods, gave them a childhood as idyllic as Wilfred Thesiger's early years at Addis Ababa. By coincidence Kathleen's upbringing at Burgage ended when she was eight, the same age Thesiger would be when, to his dismay, he found that 'we were leaving Abyssinia for good, that we should not be coming back'.[38]

The difference was that Thesiger's father and mother were happily married, whereas Kathleen's parents had been hopelessly incompatible. The strained relationship between Thomas and Mary Louisa deteriorated until a separation became inevitable. When Mary Louisa found Thomas in bed with one of the housemaids, he excused himself laconically: 'If one is going to appreciate Chateau Lafitte, my dear, one must occasionally have a glass of *vin ordinaire*.'[39] Taking her children with her, Kathleen's mother went to live in England. She divided her time between Roe Green House at Hatfield in Hertfordshire, and the Vigors's London flat, 18 Buckingham Palace Mansions, where Thesiger and his brother Brian stayed occasionally as schoolboys. Kathleen, Eileen, Edward and Ashmead had been born in London. They continued to visit their relatives in Ireland, including their father, who died in January 1908, the year before Kathleen's wedding.

19

We do not know how or when Thesiger's parents first met; but they were already corresponding, rather formally, by the time Wilfred Gilbert arrived at Boma, in the Belgian Congo, in December 1907. For some reason Thesiger avoided this subject, although in private he would discuss, quite openly, other more sensitive aspects of his life. Being so close to her eldest son, it seems inconceivable that Kathleen did not tell him anything about her courtship with his father. He could have written much more than he did about his parents (and, indeed, about himself) in *The Life of My Choice*. But instead he devoted many of its pages to less personally revealing themes, such as Abyssinian history, in a book that his publisher's editor described as 'magnificent, yet strangely impermeable'.[40] Wilfred Thesiger had often been described as 'enigmatic'. His autobiography merely confirmed this, and at the same time encouraged readers to speculate about the undisclosed details of his private life.

THREE

Gorgeous Barbarity

On 2 November 1909 Thesiger's father and mother arrived at Jibuti on the coast of French Somaliland, after a week's voyage from Marseilles aboard the Messageries Maritimes steamer *Tonkin*.[1] From Jibuti they travelled by train to Dire Dawa in eastern Abyssinia, and onwards to Addis Ababa by mule caravan across the Chercher mountains. They were accompanied by Captain Thesiger's manservant Collins, his faithful batman in the Imperial Yeomanry, and Susannah, an Indian nursemaid from Zanzibar. At Dire Dawa the task of checking and distributing the vast quantities of baggage occupied the Thesigers for several days. 'They had brought all that they would require in Abyssinia: provisions, clothes, books, pictures, furniture, tents, saddlery. There were scores of boxes and crates, all to be checked and loaded before they left Dire Dawa.'[2] In *The Life of My Choice*, Thesiger recalled how his mother told him that 'the only thing that dismayed her was sorting out their incredible mass of luggage, making sure things went by the right route and that nothing was left behind. The heavier loads were being sent to Addis Ababa on camels by the desert route, where the Danakil, always dangerous, were said to be giving more trouble than usual.'[3]

Thesiger did not mention that, as well as several crates having gone missing, the trunk containing his mother's wedding trousseau had been broken open and looted on the way from Jibuti. Exasperated and indignant, Captain Thesiger commented: 'the railway can hardly back out of the responsibility. What on earth a Somali can do with ladies' lace trimmed underclothes is a wonder, but it was probably looting for looting's sake.'[4]

The journey across the mountains took twenty-nine days, including a brief official visit paid by Captain Thesiger to the legendary walled city of Harar. To her lifelong regret Kathleen felt too exhausted by the two-thousand-foot climb from Dire Dawa to the Harar plateau to accompany him. Harar seemed unchanged since the Victorian traveller Richard Francis Burton saw it in 1855 and described it in his book *First Footsteps in East Africa*. When the younger Wilfred Thesiger visited Harar in December 1930, he imagined that even then, 'except for a few corrugated iron roofs, it still looked the same as when [Burton] had been there'.[5]

Neither Thesiger nor his father mentioned Harar's links with the French poet, and gun-runner, Arthur Rimbaud, who lived at Harar and was photographed in 1883 in the garden of its first Egyptian Governor, Raouf Pasha's, residence. Thesiger said: 'I knew who Rimbaud was, I suppose, but I knew nothing of his poetry or what he did in Abyssinia. The one that interested me was [the French traveller Henri] de Monfreid. When I was twenty-three I read his book about pearl-diving in the Red Sea and, for a while, I longed for the same sort of adventurous life.'[6]

Wilfred Gilbert Thesiger's visit to Harar had been officially requested by the Governor, Dedjazmatch Balcha. A favourite of Menelik, Balcha 'had a well-merited reputation for ruthlessness, brutality and avarice, and was hated and feared by his subjects'.[7] Thesiger's father was met by Balcha and some hundreds of soldiers with green, yellow and red banners and chiefs in silver-gilt crowns, red and blue robes and lion- and leopard-skin capes, armed with rifles, spears and shields. Wilfred Gilbert wrote: 'It was very picturesque, the brown rough stones of the town and crumbling loopholed gateway and ... narrow streets where only two mules could walk abreast ... The palace was a whitewashed building, European of a bad style with quaint lions in plaster on the roof ... Afterwards I walked round the bazaars and narrow street market, thronged with wild, white-clothed Abyssinians, Gallas and Somalis ... The only thing one could compare it with are descriptions of the old Aztecs. Gorgeous barbarity such as one could nowadays meet with nowhere but here.'[8]

Describing their marches from Harar along the top of the Chercher mountains, Wilfred Gilbert wrote: 'We are having a splendid journey and Kathleen is better than I have ever seen her.'[9] He thought she looked 'very smart and neat in her khaki astride costume and helmet', and the scenery 'beautiful' with 'thick forests of enormous juniper and wild olive trees full of mountain clematis, jessamine, briar roses and other unknown flowers ... and looking for all the world like Switzerland or Norway'.[10] Kathleen observed impatiently: 'I do not think we needed to spend so long on the journey but we were accompanied by the Legation doctor [Wakeman] ... a half-caste Indian [who] ... liked to take life leisurely.'[11]

They reached the outskirts of Addis Ababa on 10 December, where they were met by the retiring Consul, Lord Herbert Hervey, with an escort of Indian *sowars*, troopers, in full dress uniform, an Abyssinian Ras and various ministers of state. Later, in an undated memoir, Kathleen described her first impressions of the British Legation, her home for the next nine years:

> The Legation lies on a hillside outside the town with vast and beautiful views of the surrounding mountains. I was told that the Legation compound is the same size as St James's Park. In 1909 the large and imposing stone building in which we later lived in such comfort did not exist and we arrived to a settlement of thatched huts or 'tukuls'. Each room was a separate round mud hut joined to the next one by a 'mud' passage and the whole built round a grassed courtyard with a covered way down the middle. [This accommodation had been planned by Wilfred Gilbert's predecessor, Captain (later Sir) John Harrington, and was being constructed when the writer Herbert Vivian arrived at Addis Ababa in 1901.]
>
> The servants' quarters – kitchens etc., stood at the back. The sowars' quarters and the stables stood higher up on the hillside and the native 'village' where the Abyssinian servants lived lay in a hollow beneath them. 'Mud hut' is not really at all descriptive of those charming round thatched rooms; always cool in summer and warm in winter. They were wonderfully spacious and most comfortable to live in, although at that time our furniture was very primitive. The [ceiling] was not boarded over, but rose with thatch to a point in the centre and the supporting laths of wood were inter-wound with many gay colours. The effect was enchanting ... I shall never forget our first meal that evening. Roast wild duck I most particularly remember! Our head servants were Indians and we had an excellent Goanese cook ...[12]

In the first draft of her memoir Kathleen recalled that the furniture 'was mostly made from packing-cases but we had some very handsome "pieces" and a few comfortable beds'.[13] Wilfred Gilbert wrote to his mother: 'Kathleen is making cushion covers and table-cloths ... the effect of a circular room is rather good only one does miss the corners.'[14] He eulogised the Legation's compound, with its

> masses of glorious big rose bushes smothered in blossom [and] a bed of scarlet geraniums ... rather tangled and wild, but very pretty. Tall Eucalyptus trees make an inner boundary and our compound is a square about a quarter of a mile each way. A big field serves for grazing and hay making and will allow a little steeple chase course all round. There is a good tennis court [and] a regular village of little stone circular houses for the servants ... All round are highish hills broken and covered with scrub and to the East a big plain with mountains all round ... the evening lights are very beautiful ...[15]

During the week before Christmas 1909, Captain Thesiger had his first formal audience with Menelik's grandson, Lij Yasu (or 'Child Jesus'), who was attended by the corrupt Regent, Ras Tasamma. Thousands of Abyssinian soldiers riding horses or mules escorted Thesiger's parents to the Emperor's palace, the *gibbi*, which crowned the largest hill at Addis Ababa. 'At that first meeting,' Thesiger wrote, 'my father can have had no idea of the troubles this boy would bring on his country.'[16] The previous year Menelik had appointed Lij Yasu, then aged thirteen, as his heir. By 1911, when Lij Yasu seized power, the government of Abyssinia had begun to crumble. Five years later, Captain Thesiger would report to the Foreign Office that 'Lij Yasu ... has succeeded in destroying every semblance of central government and is dragging down the prestige of individual ministers so that there is no authority to whom the Legation can appeal.'[17]

The Thesigers, meanwhile, each recorded impressions of that first audience: 'a big affair and a wonderful sight',[18] wrote Wilfred Gilbert, while Kathleen found it 'magnificent beyond my wildest dreams'.[19] Wilfred Gilbert continued:

24

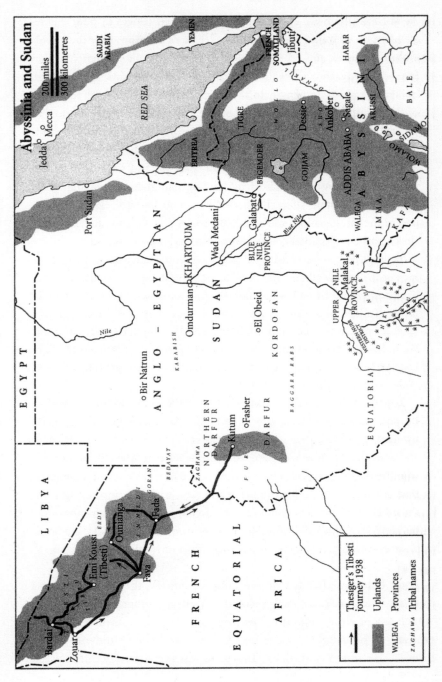

25

As at Harar the big men wore their crowns with fringes of lions' mane standing up all round and the skins of leopards and lions over their gold embroidered silk and velvet mantles, an escort of Galla horsemen in the same dresses, each with two long spears rode on either side on fiery little horses and added immensely to all the movement ... We circled the walls of the palace to the far gate and here there was a great rush to get into the inner court on the part of the Abyssinians and various gorgeously dressed chiefs told off for the purpose, but right and left with long bamboos to keep out the unauthorised, they did not spare the rod. One chief in full dress hit over the head missed his footing and rolled down the steep entrance to my mule's feet. I expected he would hit back, but it seemed part of the game, get in if you could, but accept blows if you can't. Another stick smashed to splinters on the head of a less gorgeous official ...

Inside a large courtyard lined with soldiers a brass band play[ed] a European tune for all they were worth, others with long straight trumpets, like those played by angels in [stained] glass windows, negroes with long flutes all added to the din ... We passed into another court by an archway ... and came to the central one where the walls were lined by chiefs only. We rode into the centre and dismounted and formed our little procession. I went first with the interpreter, then Kathleen, Lord Herbert [Hervey], Dr Wakeman, and behind them the escort on foot ...

I went on alone up the steps to the foot of the throne in front of which Lij Yasu sat with all his big officials and after being introduced ... I read my little speech and then handed it over to the interpreter to be translated and when he had finished I handed over the letter to Menelik to Lij Yasu who then read his speech which was interpreted by the court dragoman. I then asked leave to present Kathleen and went back to bring her up with the others ... It was a very impressive ceremony. The hall is an enormous building very dimly lighted with pillars of wood on either side, the floor ... strewn with green rushes and a long carpet down the centre.[20]

Later that day, after the presentation ceremony, the Thesigers met Lij Yasu again at Ras Tasamma's residence. Wilfred Gilbert praised Lij Yasu: 'a nice boy of clear cut Semitic features and very shy ... when something amused us he caught my eye and laughed and then suddenly checked himself'. He added cautiously: 'Everyone was very friendly but at present

I am only on the surface of things.'[21] Kathleen wrote that for the occasion 'Wilfred was wearing full diplomatic uniform and I my smartest London frock [her 'going away' dress worn after her wedding] and a large befeathered hat. To the European eye we surely would have presented an amusing spectacle more especially as the "diplomatic mule" [ridden by Wilfred Gilbert] was also in full dress with gaily embroidered coloured velvet hanging, and tinkling brass and silver ornaments.'

Kathleen's candid account of the feast that followed might have been borrowed from James Bruce of Kinnaird's *Travels to Discover the Source of the Nile* (1790), a work whose descriptions of alleged Abyssinian customs, such as eating raw meat cut from live oxen, had been dismissed as nonsense by critics following Dr Johnson, who doubted that Bruce had ever been there:

Course after course, one more uneatable than another and served by very questionably clean slave women. This feast lasted quite interminably, or so it seemed to me. But at last it ended … and the curtains surrounding the daïs [where we sat] were suddenly drawn back and a vast Hall was revealed below us crowded with thousands of soldiery. An incredible number of them packed like sardines and all wearing the usual white Abyssinian 'Shamma'. They sat on benches stretching into the far distance, and between these benches there was just room for two men to walk in single file. These men carried a pole on their shoulders which stretched from one to the other, and from this pole was suspended half the carcase of a freshly killed ox. Each man, as it passed him, pulled out his knife and skilfully cut for himself as large a piece of bleeding meat as possible and this he proceeded to eat pushing it into his mouth with his left hand and with his right cutting off a chunk which I think he gulped down whole – and so on until all was finished. Eventually the soldiery filed out somehow and I shall always remember our exit, because, for some reason we went out by the door at the end of the great Hall and to do so we had to pick our way through the bloody remains of the Feast.[22]

In *The Real Abyssinia* (1927), Colonel C.F. Rey described a 'raw meat banquet' on this scale, marking the Feast of Maskal, when 'no fewer than 15,000 soldiers and 2000 or 3000 palace retainers were fed in four relays in the great hall'.[23] The way of life Kathleen Thesiger had left behind in England must have appeared at that moment incredibly remote. Yet it would be events such as the Regent's feast that gave her eldest son Wilfred his craving for 'barbaric splendour' and 'a distaste for the drab uniformity of the modern world'.[24]

England and home were brought suddenly into sharp focus by the death of King Edward VII in May 1910, news of which affected the Thesigers almost like a family bereavement. Captain Thesiger wrote to his mother on 14 May: 'What a terrible blow the King's death has been ... We had heard nothing of his short illness to prepare us. Even now it seems impossible to believe and realize it.'[25] Edward VII died four weeks before the younger Wilfred Thesiger was born. The King's death signalled the waning of an era, which the First World War would finally end. In the microcosm of Addis Ababa's British Legation, 'everything [was] ... put off, polo, races, gymkhana and lunches'. To Wilfred Gilbert and Kathleen it seemed 'as tho' everything had suddenly come to a stop'.[26]

FOUR

'One Handsome Rajah'

In the heart of the British Legation's dusty compound at Addis Ababa, Wilfred Patrick Thesiger was born by the light of oil lamps at 8 p.m. on Friday, 3 June 1910, in a thatched mud hut that served as his parents' bedroom. The following day his father wrote to Lady Chelmsford, the baby's grandmother: 'Everything passed off very well and both are doing splendidly. He weighs 8½lb and stands 1ft 8in [corrected in another letter to 1ft 10in] in his bare feet and his lungs are excellent ... He is a splendid little boy and the Abyssinians have already christened him the "tininish Minister" which means the "very small Minister". We are going to call him Wilfred Patrick but he is always spoken of as Billy. He has a fair amount of hair, is less red than might have been expected and has long fingers.'[1]

On 12 July Thesiger was christened at Addis Ababa by Pastor Karl Cederquist, a Swedish Lutheran missionary. Count Alexander Hoyos and Frank Champain were named as godfathers; his godmothers were Mrs John Curre and Mrs Miles Backhouse, the wives of two British officials. Captain Thesiger reported proudly: 'The man Billy [whom he called 'a jolly little beggar'] grows very fast and puts on half a pound every week with great regularity. I think he is quite a nice looking baby. He has a decided nose and rather a straight upper lip, his eyes seem big for a baby and are wide apart.'[2] Frank Champain had accepted his role as the baby's godfather with reluctance. He would write to Wilfred in 1927: 'Sorry to have been such a rotten Godfather. I told your Dad I was no good ... I can't be of much use but if I can I am yours to command.'[3]

Thesiger's good looks, inherited from his father, were strengthened by his mother's determined jaw and her direct (some thought intimidating) gaze. As a baby he was active, alert and observant. His adoring parents took photographs of him at frequent intervals from the age of one month until he was nine. They preserved these photographs in an album, the first of four similar albums they compiled, one for each of their sons. Some of the earliest photographs show Billy cradled in his mother's arms or perched unsteadily on his nurse Susannah's shoulder, grasping her tightly by her hair. Susannah, a dark-skinned Indian girl, stayed with the Thesigers for three years, working for some of the time alongside an English nurse who proved so incapable and neurotic that Wilfred Gilbert felt obliged to dismiss her. To the devoted, endlessly patient Susannah, little Billy could do no wrong. 'When my mother remonstrated with her,' Thesiger wrote, 'she would answer, "He one handsome Rajah – why for he no do what he want?"'[4] Thesiger may have heard his mother tell this story, mimicking Susannah's broken English.

Though he walked at an unusually early age, Thesiger admitted that he had been slow learning to speak. He said his mother told him that his first words were '"Go yay" which meant "Go away" and showed an independent spirit'.[5] One day the Thesigers found Billy in Susannah's hut, lying on the earth floor surrounded by the servants, who bent over him performing a mysterious rite. Susannah reassured the astonished couple: 'We were just tying for all time to our countries.'[6]

The child's birthplace, a circular Abyssinian *tukul* of mud and wattle with a conical thatched roof, like an East African *banda* or a South African *rondavel*, could scarcely have been a more appropriate introduction to the life he was destined to lead. Thesiger realised this, and used to talk about being born in a 'mud hut', which implied that the circumstances of his birth were more primitive than they had been in reality. He also liked to stress any extraordinary adventures during childhood which helped to explain his longing for a life of 'savagery and colour'[7] In his early fifties Thesiger confessed that he had probably exaggerated his preferences and dislikes – his resentment, for instance, of cars, aeroplanes and twentieth-century technology foisted on remote societies he called 'traditional peoples'. He wrote in *The Marsh Arabs*:

Like many Englishmen of my generation and upbringing I had an instinctive sympathy with the traditional life of others. My childhood was spent in Abyssinia, which at that time was without cars or roads ... I loathed cars, aeroplanes, wireless and television, in fact most of our civilisation's manifestations in the past fifty years, and was always happy, in Iraq or elsewhere, to share a smoke-filled hovel with a shepherd, his family and beasts. In such a household, everything was strange and different, their self-reliance put me at ease, and I was fascinated by the feeling of continuity with the past. I envied them a contentment rare in the world today and a mastery of skills, however simple, that I myself could never hope to attain.[8]

Thesiger did not experience this sense of easy harmony among remote tribes at Addis Ababa, nor indeed for many years after he first left Abyssinia. Throughout his childhood and his teens, even as a young man in his early twenties, he lived in a European setting, with European values imposed by his family. He had felt instinctively superior by virtue of his background, education and race. Until the 1930s, he admitted, he was 'an Englishman in Africa, travelling very much as my father would have travelled'.[9] He fed and slept apart from the Africans who accompanied him. In 1934 in Abyssinia he read Henri de Monfreid's book *Secrets de la Mer Rouge*, and afterwards sailed aboard a dhow from Tajura to Jibuti. Sitting on deck, sharing the crew's evening meal of rice and fish, Thesiger realised that this was how he wanted to live the rest of his life. During the next fifteen years he accustomed himself to living as his tribal companions lived, in the Sudan, the French Sahara and Arabia. Meanwhile, reflecting on his influential childhood in Abyssinia, he said: 'When I returned to England [with my family in 1919] I had already witnessed sights such as few people had ever seen.'[10]

Aged only eight months, early in 1911 Thesiger was taken by his parents on home leave. Carried in a 'swaying litter between two mules',[11] the baby travelled three hundred miles from Addis Ababa to the railhead at Dire Dawa, and from there by train and steamer to England. A few months later this long journey was repeated in reverse, following the same route Thesiger's parents had taken in November 1909. 'The water for his baby food on these treks had to be boiled and then strained through gamgee tissue; his nurse hunted out the tent for camel ticks before he went to bed at night.' Once, when Thesiger's nurse had carried him a short distance from camp, they found themselves face to face with a party of half-naked warriors. 'But she need not have worried, the warriors were just intrigued by a white baby; they had never seen such a sight before.'[12]

In 1911, to avoid the hot weather, Thesiger and his mother, escorted as far as Jibuti by an official from the Legation, travelled to England ahead of his father, who arrived there on 15 June with members of an Abyssinian mission representing the Emperor at the coronation of King George V. The second of Wilfred Gilbert and Kathleen's sons, Brian Peirson Thesiger, was born at Beachley Rectory in Gloucestershire on 4 October 1911. Wilfred Gilbert had bought the house, with its large overgrown garden overlooking the Severn estuary, to provide his expanding family with a home of their own in England. Billy and Brian became inseparable. Sixteen months older, Billy dominated his younger brother, who seemed content to follow his lead. Those who knew the two elder Thesigers affirmed that this continued for the whole of Brian's life. Whereas Wilfred Thesiger and his youngest brothers, Dermot Vigors (born in London on 24 March 1914) and Roderic Miles Doughty (born in Addis Ababa on 8 November 1916), had inherited their parents' looks, Brian bore little obvious resemblance either to the Thesigers or to the Vigors. From his mother's side no doubt came his reddish fair hair and his freckled, oval face – colouring and features which set him apart from Wilfred, Dermot and Roderic. In his late twenties Brian's face showed more bone structure, but even then he bore little resemblance to his brothers. Lord Herbert Hervey's successor as Consul at Addis Ababa, Major Charles H.M. Doughty-Wylie, nicknamed Brian 'carrot top' because of his red hair.[13] Roderic Thesiger was named after Charles Doughty (who had changed his name to Doughty-Wylie before he married, in 1907, a rich and 'capable' widow, Lily Oimara ('Judith') Wylie).

Thesiger's childhood recollections from the age of three or four were clear, lasting and vivid. He remembered his father's folding camp table with *Blackwood's Magazine*, a tobacco tin and a bottle of Rose's lime juice on it. He remembered, aged three, seeing his father shoot an oryx, the mortally wounded antelope's headlong rush, and 'the dust coming up as it crashed'.[14] How many animals he saw his father kill for sport we don't know. The only others he recorded apart from the oryx were two Indian black-buck, 'each with a good head',[15] and a tiger his father shot and wounded in the Jaipur forests in 1918 but failed to recover. Such sights as these had thrilled Thesiger as a boy; they fired his passion for hunting African big game, most of which he did in Abyssinia and the Sudan between 1930 and 1939. He continued to hunt after the Second World War in Kurdistan, the marshes of southern Iraq and in Kenya. By the time he arrived in northern Kenya in 1960, however, his passion for hunting was almost exhausted, and he only shot an occasional antelope or zebra for meat.

In 1969 Thesiger told the writer Timothy Green how as children he and Brian sat up at dusk in the Legation garden, waiting to shoot with their airguns a porcupine that had been eating the bulbs of gladioli. 'Before long Brian, who was only three, pleaded "I think I hear a hyena, I'm frightened, let's go in." "Nonsense," said Wilfred, "you stay here with me." Finally, long after dark, when the porcupine had not put in an appearance, Wilfred announced, "It's getting cold. We'll go in now."'[16] Thesiger's conversation shows how, aged less than four and a half, he was already taking charge in his own small world. He went on doing so all his life. A born gang leader, Thesiger dominated his brothers, just as, as a traveller, he would dominate his followers.

He was aware of this tendency, and in later years he strove to play it down. In *My Kenya Days*, he stated: 'Looking back over my life I have never wanted a master and servant relationship with my retainers.'[17] A key to this is his instinctive use of the term 'retainers': literally 'dependants', or 'followers of some person of rank or position'. Throughout his life he surrounded himself with often much younger men, or boys, who served him and gave him the companionship he desired. Many of them, initially, owed Thesiger their liberty, or favours in exchange for financial assistance he gave them or their families. These favours affected their relationship with him, in which the distinction between servant and comrade was frequently blurred.

As a child Thesiger had ruled over his younger brothers, even using them as punchbags after he learnt to box. The 'fagging' system at Eton encouraged his thuggish behaviour, which was tolerated only by friends who realised that he had a gentler side, which he kept hidden for fear of diluting his macho image. It was characteristic of him, from his mid-twenties onward, that he would choose 'retainers' younger than himself, over whom he exerted an authority reinforced by the difference between their ages, as well as by his dominating personality and his position or status – for example, as an Assistant District Commissioner in the Sudan, and in Syria an army major ranked as second-in-command of the Druze Legion. In contrast, Thesiger's relationships with his older followers were seldom as close or as meaningful. The same applied to his young companions in Arabia and Iraq after they became middle-aged and, in due course, elderly men. Thesiger reflected: 'I don't know why it was. They were just different. We had travelled together in the desert and shared the hardships and danger of that life. When I saw them again, thirty years later, they lived in houses with radios and instead of riding camels they drove about in cars. The youngsters I remembered had grey beards. They seemed pleased to see me again, and I was pleased to see them; but something had gone ... the feeling of intimacy, and a sense of the hardships that once bound us together.'[18]

At the Legation, Thesiger's parents encouraged the children to play with pet animals, including a tame antelope, two dogs and a 'toto' monkey his mother named Moses. Kathleen wrote: 'Altho' we kept [Moses] chained to his box at times, we very often let him go and then he would rush away and climb to the nearest tree top, only to jump unexpectedly from a high branch on to my shoulder with unerring aim. Every official in the Legation loved my Moses and he was so small that they could carry him about in their pockets. He was accorded the freedom of the drawing room [in the new Legation] and I must confess that I still have many books in torn bindings [which] tell the tale.'[19]

Thesiger remembered Moses and the tiny antelope wistfully, with an amused affection. He commented in *My Kenya Days*: 'My father kept no dogs in the Legation,'[20] but this was a lapse of memory. Later he remembered: 'Our first dog in Addis Ababa was called Jock. The next dog had to be got rid of because Hugh Dodds [one of Wilfred Gilbert's Consuls] thought it was dangerous. This was about 1916 ... As a child, I was afraid of nothing but spiders ... When we were at The Milebrook, the first dog I owned was a golden cocker spaniel, and it died of distemper. I had only had the dog for about a year.'[21]

In *The Life of My Choice* Thesiger pictured his childhood at Addis Ababa against a background of Abyssinia in turmoil. This was the chaotic legacy of the Emperor Menelik's paralysing illness and his heir Lij Yasu's blood-lust, incompetence and apostasy of Islam. The turbulent decade from 1910 to 1919 gave the early years of Thesiger's life story romance and power, and enhanced the significance of his childhood as a crucial influence upon 'everything that followed'.[22] As a small boy he was no doubt aware of events he described seventy years later in *The Life of My Choice*, however remote and incomprehensible they must have appeared at the time. In reality his life at Addis Ababa had little to do with the Legation's surroundings – except for its landscapes, including the hills (Entoto, Wochercher and Fantali) and the plain where Billy and Brian rode their ponies and went on camping trips every year with their parents. On these memorable outings Mary Buckle, a children's nurse from Abingdon in Oxfordshire, accompanied the family. Mary, known to everyone as 'Minna', had been engaged in 1911 to look after Brian. Thesiger wrote in 1987: 'She was eighteen and had never been out of England, yet she unhesitatingly set off for a remote and savage country in Africa. She gave us unfailing devotion and became an essential part of our family.'[23] Just as he idealised his father and mother, Thesiger idealised Minna, whom he admired as brave, selfless and indispensable. He wrote affectionately in *The Life of My Choice*: 'Now, after more than seventy years, she is still my cherished friend and confidante, the one person left with shared memories of those far-off days.'[24] This statement was literally true. Thesiger, a confirmed bachelor, respected strong-willed, practical women, mother figures whose common sense and devotion tempered their undisputed authority. Thesiger's occasional travelling companion and close friend Lady Egremont later remembered visiting Minna with him at Witney in Oxfordshire. She watched as he smoothed his hair and straightened his tie, 'like a twelve-year-old schoolboy on his best behaviour',[25] as they waited for Minna to open her front door.

Every morning after breakfast, Billy and Brian would find their ponies saddled and waiting with Habta Wold, the Legation *syce* (the servant who looked after the horses), who usually accompanied them. The boys had learnt to ride by the time they were four. They rode most mornings, and sometimes again in the afternoon. On a steep hillside five hundred feet above the Legation there was a grotto cut into the rock. From there Billy and Brian had tremendous views, to the north over Salale province and the Blue Nile gorges, southward to the far-off Arussi mountains. There, one day, Billy would follow in his father's footsteps and hunt the mountain nyala, a majestic antelope with lyre-shaped horns. Aged four, he had been photographed with a fine nyala trophy head.

After their morning ride Billy and Brian did schoolwork, which consisted of reading, writing and arithmetic; sometimes they drilled with the Legation's guard. After lunch they rode again or tried to shoot birds in the garden with their 'Daisy' airguns. Thesiger wrote: 'Had it not been for the First World War I might have been sent to school in England, separated indefinitely from my parents, as was the fate of so many English children whose fathers served in India or elsewhere in the East. I must have had some lessons at the Legation, though I have no recollection of them, for I learnt to read and write.'[26] The idea of very small children being sent away to school did not appeal to Thesiger, who spoke out strongly against it; but he approved of preparatory boarding schools and, of course, segregated public schools, for older children.

Because he was so obviously fond of children – and, indeed, very good with little girls and boys – he was often asked why he had never married and had a family of his own. In his autobiography, the phrase *The Life of My Choice*, selected for the book's title, occurs in a paragraph where Thesiger affirms his attitudes to marriage and other 'commonly accepted pleasures of life'. He wrote: 'I have never set much store by them. I hardly care what I eat, provided it suffices, and I care not at all for wine or spirits. When I was fourteen someone gave me a glass of beer, and I thought it so unpleasant I have never touched beer again. As for cigarettes, I dislike even being in a room where people are smoking. Sex has been of no great consequence to me, and the celibacy of desert life left me untroubled. Marriage would certainly have been a crippling handicap. I have therefore been able to lead the life of my choice with no sense of deprivation.'[27] He later added: '*The Life of My Choice* was the right title for the book I wrote about myself. It gave you everything. I had lived as I wanted, gone where I wanted, when I wanted. I travelled among peoples that interested me. My companions were those individuals I wanted to have with me.'[28]

Thesiger's impossible dream had been to preserve the near-idyllic life he had known as a boy in Abyssinia. He viewed change dismally, as a threat to the tribal peoples he admired, and to himself as a self-confessed traditionalist and romantic who 'cherished the past, felt out of step with the present and dreaded the future'.[29] Such a reactionary outlook had been doomed from the start, and Thesiger knew it. And, of course, without a sword of Damocles hanging over it, the life he dreamt of would have been spared the impending threat of corrosive change, perhaps of annihilation – a fate later exemplified by the destruction of the marshes in southern Iraq. He took an aggressive pride in being the 'last' in a long line of overland explorers and travellers, a refugee from the Victorians' Golden Age. In a romantic fit of self-indulgent melancholy, he yearned for an irretrievable past summed up by the robber-poet François Villon's poignant query: 'Où sont les neiges d'antan?'[30] – 'Where are the snows of yesteryear?' Ironically, from Thesiger's bachelor-explorer viewpoint, this quotation, taken from 'Le Grand Testament: Ballade des Dames du Temps Jadis', lamented not the vanishing wilderness or its tribes, but the sensual, white-bodied women Villon had slept with during his dissipated youth, in fifteenth-century Paris.

Thesiger's father and mother were supremely important figures during his early childhood, and took pride of place in his idealised (and romanticised) memories of those halcyon days. He wrote of his father: 'Inevitably at Addis Ababa he was busy for most of the day, writing his despatches, interviewing people or visiting his colleagues in the other Legations ... it was perhaps in the camp where we went each year from the Legation for an eagerly awaited ten days that I remember him most vividly. I can picture him now, a tall lean figure in a helmet, smoking his pipe as he watched the horses being saddled or inspected them while they were being fed; I can see him cleaning his rifle in the verandah of his tent, or sitting chatting with my mother by the fire in the evening.'[31]

The camp's setting was remote, perfect: 'an enchanted spot, tucked away in the Entoto hills. A stream tumbled down the cliff opposite our tents, then flowed away through a jumble of rocks among a grove of trees. Here were all sorts of birds: top-heavy hornbills, touracos with crimson wings, brilliant bee-eaters, sunbirds, paradise flycatchers, hoopoes, golden weaver birds and many others. My father knew them all and taught me their names. Vultures nested in the cliffs and circled in slow spirals above the camp. I used to watch them through his field glasses, and the baboons that processed along the cliff tops, the babies clinging to their mothers' backs. At night we sometimes heard their frenzied barking when a leopard disturbed them. Several times I went up the valley with my father in the evening and sat with him behind a rock, hoping he would get a shot at the leopard. I remember once a large white-tailed mongoose scuttled past within a few feet of us.'[32]

Thesiger's lifelong interest in ornithology dated from visits to this 'enchanted' enclave among the hills. As a boy he continued to shoot birds, and went on shooting them for sport and scientific study; but from then on he began to see and to recognise birds not as mere targets, but as living things that were fascinating as well as beautiful. The juvenile diaries he kept in Wales and Scotland between 1922 and 1933 contain detailed observations on local birdlife. During his Danakil expedition in 1933–34, Thesiger shot and preserved no fewer than 872 bird specimens, comprising 192 species, and three sub-species new to science which were named after him.

The chubby, smiling baby grew up as an extremely good-looking if rather sombre child who, his father noted, seemed very shy in the company of adults other than his parents.[33] As a boy of six he had thick brown hair tinted with his mother's auburn, and large, expressive eyes. His mouth, like Kathleen's, was wide, with small, slightly uneven teeth shielded by a long upper lip (like Wilfred Gilbert's) which were hardly seen except when he was speaking energetically or laughing. In those days his nose was long and quite straight. Only after being broken three times did it acquire the misshapen, craggy character that led his oldest friend, John Verney, to describe him as 'a splendid pinnacle knocked off the top of a Dolomite'[34] Although they went about protected from the hot sun by large sola topees, Billy and Brian must have had permanent tans which no doubt set them apart as creatures secretly to be envied by the pale-skinned little boys at their English preparatory school. The healthy outdoor life they led made the brothers fit and strong, with muscular arms and legs, and without an ounce of spare flesh on their lean brown bodies.

The Emperor designate, Lij Yasu, was one of three Abyssinian boys who, then and later, played roles of varying significance in Thesiger's life. The other two were Asfa Wossen, the baby son of Ras Tafari, Abyssinia's

Regent after 1916 and the country's future Emperor; and a nameless child, nine or ten years old, who had fought with Tafari's army at Sagale. Abyssinia's political chaos worsened from 1911 when Lij Yasu, aided by Menelik's commander-in-chief Fitaurari Habta Giorgis, seized the palace and took control of the country. Lij Yasu was never crowned. This had been impossible during his grandfather's lifetime, and after Menelik's death in December 1913 a prophecy stating that if he were crowned he would die may have discouraged him. Lij Yasu meanwhile embraced Islam, and lived for long periods with the warlike Danakil (or Afar) tribes, hunting and raiding villages for provisions. An arrogant, cruel youth, he took pleasure in watching executions and floggings. To satisfy his blood-lust he massacred Shanqalla Negroes on the Abyssinia–Sudan border, and slaughtered three hundred Danakil, including women and children, in Captain Thesiger's opinion 'simply because he liked the sight of blood'.[35] Besides these atrocities Lij Yasu was rumoured to have himself killed and castrated a page at Menelik's palace; and according to one of his officers, when a girl refused to have sex with him, Lij Yasu sliced off her breasts after watching her being gang-raped by his soldiers.

The Life of My Choice – described by Thesiger as 'a fragment' of auto-biography[36] – tends to bury its subject under an avalanche of impersonal details. Though absorbing, these details are far more comprehensive than the often meagre infill of Thesiger's life history requires. As well as exploiting its historical context to the full, Thesiger used the wealth of factual information about his life to produce a 'treasure galleon' of a book, written 'with much distinction and honesty',[37] yet offering few noteworthy revelations about its author. Nowhere in The Life of My Choice is this more apparent than in the opening chapters, describing Thesiger's background and his early upbringing in Abyssinia and England.

In 1913–14 Thesiger's father trekked from Addis Ababa to Nairobi to discuss with the Governor of British East Africa (later Kenya) border issues created by Abyssinian slavers, ivory raiders and the large populations of Boran and Galla tribesmen who migrated to East Africa from Abyssinia after Menelik had conquered their territory. Wilfred Gilbert Thesiger noted in 1911 that the Abyssinians had occupied the Turkana territory in British East Africa and Karamoja in Uganda, although the Abyssinian frontier established in 1907 lay to the north of these territories. In his teens Thesiger was fascinated by books such as Major H. Rayne's *The Ivory Raiders* (a fourteenth-birthday present) and Henry Darley's *Slaves and Ivory*, which provided an exciting background to his father's mission. As a boy of three and a half, however, he remembered only vaguely the journey with his parents and Brian to the Awash station, the next railhead that replaced Dire Dawa until the Chemin de Fer Franco-Ethiopien's line from Jibuti had progressed as far as Addis Ababa, its ultimate destination. Almost fifty years later he wrote in *Arabian Sands* that his attraction to 'the deserts of the East' might lie 'in vague recollections of camel herds at water-holes; in the smell of dust and of acacias under a hot sun; in the chorus of hyenas and jackals in the darkness round the camp fire'. Such 'dim memories'[38] as these derived from this and other journeys with his parents. They suggest that even as a child Thesiger was unusually observant and receptive to the sights, scents and sounds of the African bush and of the Abyssinian highlands where he lived for almost nine incomparably happy years. In 1914 Kathleen, who was pregnant once again, returned to England, and by the time Wilfred Gilbert joined her there at the end of March, the Thesigers' third son, Dermot Vigors, had been born.

On his way to Nairobi Captain Thesiger wrote to Billy and Brian in London from camps at Laisamis and the Uaso Nyiro river, places which the younger Wilfred would often visit during his travels in Kenya. He treasured his father's letters, written in pencil on coarse grey paper, illustrated with lively drawings of giraffes, lion and warthogs. Wilfred Gilbert may have got the idea of illustrating his stories with thumbnail sketches of big game from Sir Percy Fitzpatrick's South African classic *Jock of the Bushveld*. First published in 1907, the book was illustrated with hundreds of drawings, and many half-tone plates, by Edmund Caldwell. The earliest impressions of *Jock* had Caldwell's uncorrected sketch of a dung beetle pushing a tiny ball of dung with its front, instead of its back, legs. Wilfred Gilbert and Kathleen each owned a first edition of the book, and Thesiger remembered his father reading from it in the evenings, sitting on the entrance steps of the Legation. Later, Wilfred Gilbert gave Billy his copy, which the little boy inscribed proudly in pencil: 'W P Thesiger – from Daddy Adiss-Ababa – Abysinia'. (In 1995 Thesiger sold his mother's copy, inscribed by her, rebound, with more of his child's pencilling erased from it, but still perfectly legible.)

Thesiger often emphasised how his father never talked down to him, but instead gave him 'a happy sense of comradeship' and 'shared adventure'.[39] His father's letter from Laisamis, he said, 'could have been written to a boy of seven; I was only half that age'.[40] This was a harmless exaggeration, like Thesiger's suggestion that he alone had been the recipient of the letter; whereas it was addressed, using the children's euphonic pet names, to both Billy and Brian. The Laisamis letter began:

My dear Umsie [Billy] and Wowwow [Brian]
Daddy has been having a very good time hunting ... daddy shot [a rhino] in the shoulder & he turned round & wanted to charge but we shot him again and soon he was quite deaded ...[41]

As she read Wilfred Gilbert's letter aloud, Kathleen must have pictured her husband in his khaki shirt and riding breeches, smoking his pipe in the shade of his fly-tent or under a shady tree; writing with meticulous care on official paper ruffled now and then by the wind; sketching wild animals he described to bring his words alive. His account of shooting a female rhino clearly illustrates the dramatic change in our attitude to wildlife since the days when big game hunting was viewed uncritically (indeed, was strongly justified and admired) as sport. Nor was the episode by any means untypical of hunting adventures at that period. 'Last night,' he wrote, 'two of our soldiers were out at night & they were attacked by an old mummy rhino which had a baby one with her and they had to shoot but they had not many cartridges & did not kill her & then they had to whistle for help & we all took our guns & ran out & daddy shot her and she fell but got up again & we all fired again until she was deaded & then we chased the baby one in the moonlight & tried to catch him but could not as he ran too fast.'[42]

As a small boy Thesiger was thrilled by stories such as these. As he grew older he memorised tales of lion hunts and of fighting between warlike tribes told by his father's Consuls. Arnold Wienholt Hodson, a Consul in south-west Abyssinia, hunted big game including elephant, buffalo and lion. Aged six or seven, Thesiger pored over Hodson's photographs of game he had shot, and listened spellbound to his stories. Later he read Hodson's books *Where Lion Reign*, published in 1927, and *Seven Years in Southern Abyssinia* (1928). Introducing *Where Lion Reign*, Hodson wrote: 'In this wild and little-known terrain which it was my mission to explore, lion were plentiful enough to gladden the heart not only of any big game hunter, but of all those whom the call of adventure urges to seek out primitive Nature in her home among the savage and remote places of the earth.'[43]

By then Wilfred Thesiger was at school in England. As a teenager yearning to return to Abyssinia, his birthplace and his home, he drank in like a potent elixir Hodson's words, which defined precisely the life he aspired to, the life he was determined one day to achieve.

FIVE

Passages to India and England

When war was declared in August 1914, Thesiger's father was still on leave in England. 'An accomplished linguist, fluent in French and German,' Thesiger wrote, 'he was accepted by the Army, given an appointment as captain in the Intelligence Branch, and sent to France, where he arrived on 23 September. This posting was a remarkable achievement ... He was attached to the 3rd Army Corps, and while serving in France he earned a mention in despatches.'[1]

Wilfred Gilbert's four-month posting was indeed 'remarkable', not only because he had been commissioned (in the British Censorship Staff), whereas many regular officers of various ages, anxious to serve, had failed, but also because his language skills had improved vastly since Cheltenham, where his masters judged he was 'not a linguist by nature'. His position as British Minister on Foreign Office leave from Addis Ababa perhaps led to his acceptance by the army as a temporary recruit for non-active service. Furthermore, he had evidently been passed as fit, with no mention of the heart problem that affected him as a boy, and would cause his premature death in his late forties.

In May 1914 Wilfred Gilbert had given Kathleen a specially bound Book of Common Prayer. Dedicated to her and to their children, he wrote in it a prayer of his own which ended: 'Give us long years of happiness together in this life, striving always to do Thy will and content to leave the future in Thy hands.'[2] In January 1915, at the end of his Foreign Office leave, Wilfred Gilbert, Kathleen and their three sons went back to Addis Ababa. By then Kathleen was pregnant for the fourth time. On 8 November Roderic Miles Doughty Thesiger was born at the British Legation. Susannah having returned to India in 1913, an elderly nurse,

43

known to the children as 'Nanny', had been engaged in England to look after one-year-old Dermot and, in due course, baby Roderic.

At Addis Ababa, Captain Thesiger felt concerned that the still-uncrowned Lij Yasu dreamt 'of one day putting himself at the head of the Mohammadan Abyssinians, and of producing a Moslem kingdom' that stretched far beyond the boundaries of Abyssinia's 'present Empire'.[3] Lij Yasu confirmed this fear when, at the Eid festival in Dire Dawa, swearing on the Koran, he professed himself a Muslim. When this was proclaimed to a meeting of chiefs at Addis Ababa there was a riot and shooting that resulted in many dead and wounded. A second meeting proclaimed Menelik's daughter, Waizero Zauditu, Empress, and the Governor of Harar, Dedjazmatch (later Ras) Tafari, as heir. Thesiger dedicated his autobiography to Tafari's memory, as the late Emperor. He had admired Tafari unreservedly, despite his wish to modernise Abyssinia, of which Thesiger surely could never have approved. Meanwhile, Tafari marshalled opposition to the deposed Lij Yasu, whose father, Negus Mikael, led the revolt aimed at restoring him to power. Had the revolt succeeded, Islam might have become the official religion of Abyssinia, where there were already Muslim tribes. Thesiger wrote in 1987, 'Lij Yasu's restoration would at least [have constituted] a considerable propaganda success for [Muslim] Turkey,' and might have brought Abyssinia into the First World War on the side of Britain's enemies, 'at a time when we were fighting the Germans in East Africa, the Turks in Sinai, Mesopotamia and the Aden Protectorate; and the Dervishes [led by the 'Mad Mullah'] in Somaliland'.[4]

As a six-year-old boy, Thesiger remembered seeing Ras Tafari's baby son, Asfa Wossen, being carried into the Legation in a red cradle for protection. This 'most embarrassing proof of their confidence' created an enduring bond between the Thesigers and Tafari which, directly and indirectly, influenced profoundly the course of Thesiger's future life. Standing at the Legation's fence, Billy and Brian saw Tafari's soldiers stream across the plain below, on their way north to Sagale. 'It was an enthralling, unforgettable sight for a small, romantically minded boy.' A few days later, during a morning ride, the brothers heard firing. Galloping home, they were told of Tafari's decisive victory on the Sagale plain, sixty miles north of Addis Ababa, which ended the revolt of Negus

Mikael. 'Forty-four years later,' Thesiger wrote, 'I visited the battlefield and saw skulls and bones in crevices on the rocky hillock where Negus Mikael had made his final stand.'[5]

The victory parades before the Empress Zauditu on Jan Meda field impressed Thesiger enormously. He devoted two pages of *The Life of My Choice* to his father's letter describing them and the sight of Negus Mikael led past, humiliated, in chains. Thesiger wrote: 'Even now, nearly seventy years later, I can recall almost every detail.' He remembered, and clearly envied, 'a small boy carried past in triumph – he had killed two men though he seemed little older than myself'.[6] Thesiger said he had been reading *Tales from the Iliad*, and in Ras Tafari's victory over Negus Mikael and Lij Yasu he could envision 'the likes of Achilles, Ajax and Ulysses' as they passed 'in triumph with aged Priam, proud even in defeat'. This was a piece of dramatic invention. Although H.L. Havell's *Stories from the Iliad* was published in 1916, the same year as the Battle of Sagale, Thesiger was given the book only five years later, in July 1921, as an examination prize by R.C.V. Lang, his preparatory school's headmaster.

More important than this, the 1916 Jan Meda parades inspired Thesiger as a boy to pursue without compromise the adventurous life he would one day lead as a man. He wrote: 'I believe that day implanted in me a lifelong craving for barbaric splendour, for savagery and colour and the throb of drums, and it gave me a lasting veneration for long-established custom and. ritual, from which would derive later a deep-seated resentment of Western innovations in other lands, and a distaste for the drab uniformity of the modern world.'[7]

In February 1917 Waizero Zauditu was crowned Empress of Abyssinia. Lij Yasu, meanwhile, supported by Ras Yemer, one of Negus Mikael's officers, raised a force and occupied Magdala, north of Addis Ababa in Wollo province. Confronted by an army from the province of Shoa, he and his followers escaped, only to be defeated in battle, with heavy losses, near Dessie. From there he fled once more into the Danakil country. Having been detained at Fiche for fourteen years, he again escaped before he was finally captured in 1932 and imprisoned at Harar, where he died 'a physical wreck' at the age of thirty-seven.

By the end of 1917 the effort and strain of the previous two years had begun to tell on Wilfred Gilbert, whose heart was further weakened by the effects of Addis Ababa's altitude of eight thousand feet. In December the Thesigers and Minna Buckle travelled to Jibuti, by the now-completed railway linking Addis Ababa and the coast. From Jibuti, Kathleen, Minna and the children sailed along the coast to Berbera, where they stayed with Geoffrey Archer, the Commissioner of British Somaliland, and his wife Olive. Captain Thesiger meanwhile went on via Aden by HMS *Fox* to Cairo, for talks with the High Commissioner, Sir Reginald Wingate, about the political future of Abyssinia.

Thesiger wrote: 'Geoffrey Archer ... a real giant ... six foot four and broad in proportion ... lent Brian and me a .410 shotgun and took us shooting along the shore, and when we got back told his skinner to stuff the birds we had shot; I was thrilled by these expeditions.'[8] Archer recalled years later how, 'Firing at the various plovers and sandpipers ... skimming close inshore over a placid sea, the children could observe exactly where their shot struck.' Although Wilfred Gilbert noted that Billy and Brian 'each shot several kinds of birds', Geoffrey Archer remembered, 'Heartrending were the scenes when Brian, the younger ... reported to his mother with tears flowing that he had not succeeded in hitting a single bird, while Wilfred, showing signs of a prowess to come, had bagged at least half a dozen.'[9]

On 3 January 1918 the Thesigers crossed from Berbera in very rough seas to Aden. Wilfred Gilbert, exhausted by his journey to and from Cairo, had been ill in bed for four out of six days at Berbera. During the crossing, he wrote, 'we were all ill'. In cooler weather at Aden they soon recovered. In *Desert, Marsh and Mountain* and *The Life of My Choice*, Thesiger told how the Resident, Major-General J.M. Stewart, took Wilfred Gilbert, Billy and Brian to Lahej in the Aden Protectorate, where they saw British troops shell lines of Turks who had invaded the Protectorate from Yemen. Thesiger's memory of the trenches and the puffs of white smoke from exploding shells remained clear, but earned him a reputation as a little 'liar' at his preparatory school.[10] Strangely, none of his father's letters from Aden mentioned this event. Instead, Wilfred Gilbert wrote: 'There seems to have been a week's cessation of hostilities for Christmas. Our men had sports etc while the Turks took the occasion to celebrate a big wedding on their side of the lines. I wanted to take the two eldest boys out this morning to see the aeroplanes working and our guns firing but they were too tired yesterday and it means an early start from here.'[11]

Wilfred Thesiger's childhood photograph album, annotated by his father and mother, shows the Archers' garden with palm trees and their large, dimly-lit drawing room with its tiled floor, Indian carpets and big game trophies on the walls. There are photographs of Billy and Brian riding camels, and one of a small figure in a sun helmet (perhaps Billy) retrieving a shot bird from the sea.

On 3 January the Thesigers sailed from Aden on board a P&O steamer for Bombay. Wilfred Gilbert assured his mother: 'Kathleen and the children are all well and I think their month at Berbera has done them good altho' they rather lost their colour.'[12] The children had their portraits taken in a photographer's studio in Bombay. With his thick brown hair carefully brushed and parted, Billy looked very composed in a plain shirt, silk tie and tiepin.

In *The Life of My Choice*, Thesiger gave a vivid description of the months he and his family spent in India in 1918 with Frederic Chelmsford, Wilfred Gilbert's eldest brother. Appointed Viceroy in 1916, Chelmsford had a reputation for hard work, a lack of originality, and prejudices which, one senior official observed, appeared to originate in ideas 'other than his own'.[13] Meeting his uncle for the first time in the awe-inspiring surroundings of Delhi's Viceregal Lodge, Thesiger recalled that he found Frederic Chelmsford impressive and magnificently remote. Since the government buildings designed by Lutyens were not yet complete, the Thesigers lived in 'palatial tents luxuriously carpeted and furnished, and were looked after by a host of servants'.[14] To the seven-year-old Wilfred Thesiger, camping out on this grand scale, amidst 'pomp and ceremony', waited on by elaborately turbaned, splendidly uniformed Indian retainers, gave the still seemingly unreal experience added theatrical glamour.

According to Thesiger, the highlight of the visit came when he and Brian joined their father for a tiger shoot in the forests near Jaipur. Here again, Thesiger's versions, published sixty or seventy years later, do not quite correspond to Wilfred Gilbert's contemporary description. In his autobiography Thesiger wrote:

Soon after breakfast we set off into the jungle. We saw some wild boar which paid little attention to our passing elephants, and we saw several magnificent peacock and a number of monkeys; to me the monkeys were bandar log, straight out of Kipling's Jungle Book. It must have taken a couple of hours or more to reach the machan, a platform raised on poles. We climbed up on to it; someone blew a horn and the beat started. After a time I could hear distant shouts. I sat very still, hardly daring to move my head.

A peacock flew past. Then my father slowly raised his rifle and there was the tiger, padding towards us along a narrow game trail, his head moving from side to side. I still remember him as I saw him then. He was magnificent, larger even than I had expected, looking almost red against the pale dry grass. My father fired. I saw the tiger stagger. He roared, bounded off and disappeared into the jungle. He was never found, though they searched for him on elephants while we returned to the palace. I was very conscious of my father's intense disappointment.[15]

In 1979 Thesiger had written: 'I shall never forget sitting, very still, in a *machan*, hearing the beaters getting closer. Then a nudge [from my father] and looking down to see the tiger, unexpectedly red, move forward just below us.'[16] In 1987 he wrote: 'Two days later we went on another beat, this time for panther, but the panther broke back and we never saw it. However, a great sambhur stag did gallop past the *machan.*' He added for emphasis: 'Scenes such as this remained most vividly in my memory.'[17]

Describing the tiger shoot in a letter to his mother written on 12 March 1918, Wilfred Gilbert commented: 'This went wrong unluckily as the tiger stopped in front of the wrong machan at 50 yards and then came to mine and showed just his head out of the grass at 130 yards. It was no good shooting at that and I only got a moving shot at the same distance, hitting him but not badly. He gave a roar and went on and everyone fired without effect. We followed up on elephants and found blood tracks but unluckily he got clean away. The Maharajah [of Jaipur] promised me another but the beat was a failure and he broke back through the line and we never got a glimpse of him. The same happened with a panther drive which was doubly bad luck.'[18]

The Maharajah's *shikaris* had located a sambhur stag in the nearby hills, and after a 'good climb' Wilfred Gilbert saw through his binoculars the sambhur's horns and one ear 'twitching to keep off the flies'; the rest of the animal was hidden by grass and scrub. Risking a shot from two hundred yards, across a ravine, Wilfred Gilbert wrote: 'I had to guess where his chest would be ... and dropped him stone dead. This bucked us up a bit ... but it was very hard that the only shot I missed at Jaipur was the tiger.'[19] 'Billy and Brian ... had the time of their lives. They came blackbuck shooting in bullock carts. I got 3 quite good heads [Thesiger remembered only two]; pigsticking also when they and Mary [Buckle] followed us on elephant.'[20] Nowhere, however, did he mention Billy being with him on the *machan*, tense, motionless, waiting for his father to shoot a tiger.

In view of the fact that Thesiger's recollections, which even as late as 1987 were so vividly detailed, so precise, were yet different from his father's, it seems he may have combined a vaguer memory of Wilfred Gilbert's stories with his own much more recent sightings of tiger at Bandhavgarh, Bhopal, in 1983 and 1984. When Thesiger saw these tigers he was writing *The Life of My Choice*, and was able therefore to describe a (perhaps partly imagined) scene from his childhood as clearly as if it had only just occurred.

The 'opulence and splendour' of Jaipur's court seemed to equal if not surpass the viceregal splendours of Delhi. To Thesiger as a boy what mattered was 'the all-important hunting'; he admitted he was too young to appreciate the gorgeously ornate palaces, the Maharajah's courtiers in sumptuous robes. Far more appealing to Billy and Brian was the return crossing from Aden to Jibuti on board HMS *Juno* after their voyage by P&O liner from Bombay. A Marine band played and the captain fired one of the ship's guns 'after [the children] had been given cotton wool to stuff in [their] ears'.[21]

Six months later, Captain Thesiger was recalled to London by the Foreign Office to report on Abyssinia. He returned to Addis Ababa in December 1918 via Paris, Rome, Taranto and Cairo. The worldwide epidemic of Spanish influenza that claimed more victims than the war itself had struck Cairo, causing many deaths. At Jibuti, Wilfred Gilbert found letters from Addis Ababa. He wrote: 'Poor Kathleen must have had an awfully anxious time. 4 doctors out of 6 dead, besides a lot of other Europeans and some 13–20,000 Abyssinians. They died like flies and at last ceased even to bury their dead. Billy, Roddy, Dermot and Mary had had it and the compound [was] all down so that they had at times practically no servants.'[22] Thesiger wrote in 1987: 'Ras Tafari sickened. His detractors might well ponder what would have happened to the country had he died.'[23] Thesiger remembered his mother had been reading to him *A Sporting Trip Through Abyssinia* by Major P.H.G. Powell-Cotton. 'We had got to where Powell-Cotton was at Gondar, trying to shoot a buffalo, and his servant came running down the hill and frightened the buffalo away. My mother thought I looked a bit flushed. She took my temperature and she popped me into bed.'[24]

By the end of the year, Wilfred Gilbert Thesiger's duties at Addis Ababa had come to an end. In April 1919 the family travelled together to England for the last time. For Billy, their final exodus from Abyssinia was bewildering; more than a sad occasion, it had been totally incredible: 'Until almost the last day I could not believe that we were really leaving Abyssinia for good, that we should not be coming back.'[25]

SIX

The Cold, Bleak English Downs

Wilfred Gilbert and Kathleen Thesiger, their four children and Mary Buckle (now twenty-seven) arrived back in England in May 1919. To Billy especially England seemed a foreign land, which he remembered only indistinctly from his second visit in 1914 when he was little more than a baby. In his seventies, he said: 'I had imagined England was like India. I was very disappointed when my father told me that, in England, there were none of the animals or birds I knew. No hyenas, no oryx, no kites. I thought it sounded a deadly, deadly dull country to live in.'[1] Thesiger often quoted his writing in conversation, and presumably phrases that originated in his conversations found their way into his books. In his autobiography he had written that, as a child, 'I thought what a dull place [England] must be.'[2]

Since the former rectory Captain Thesiger had bought at Beachley in 1911 had been requisitioned by the navy, the family spent the summer in Ireland. They stayed with Kathleen's relatives at Burgage, before moving to Ballynoe, a rented house fourteen miles from Burgage on the River Slaney. Wilfred Gilbert wrote: 'there is good fishing ... also rough shooting. The house is very well kept with pretty gardens.'[3] Billy shot his first rabbit at the Dyke on the Burgage estate. At Ballynoe he went ferreting. Later that year, at Okehampton on Dartmoor, 'much to his joy',[4] he shot his first running rabbit, with a double-barrelled Purdey .410 shotgun he and Brian had been given in 1918 by Wilfred Gilbert's brother Percy. (Wilfred Gilbert had brought the gun back with him from England to Addis Ababa, where the boys used it to shoot pigeons that perched on the roof of the Italian Legation.) Billy enjoyed watching his father paint, or fish for salmon in the Slaney. He 'became enthusiastic' when Wilfred

Gilbert 'tried to teach [him] to sketch'[5] and thought the boy's first efforts showed promise.

Friends came to stay, including Billy's godmother Mrs Curre, and Hugh Dodds who had served under Wilfred Gilbert as a Consul in Abyssinia. At Burgage, Wilfred Gilbert had to 'stay in bed for breakfast and rest after lunch and in general [take life] very easily'. He continued to rest at Ballynoe, untroubled except by a shortage of water from the well due to an unusually dry summer.[6] His posting after Addis Ababa as Consul-General in New York had to be delayed until his health improved. In a 'private letter' the Foreign Office had proposed to raise Wilfred Gilbert's allowances, making his official income £5000 a year, enough to pay for 'a good deal of entertaining' and 'to keep a motor car', which he emphasised would be 'essential'. He wrote, 'Kathleen is quite pleased with the idea of New York now that I am to keep my rank and the pay is to be increased. It is not yet decided how we shall manage affairs but probably I may go out first while she stays over the boys' first holidays [from school] and would then come on with the babies.'[7] Everything depended, however, upon a significant improvement in Captain Thesiger's health.

In September the family visited Dublin to buy school uniforms for Billy and Brian, and to enable Wilfred Gilbert to consult a heart specialist, who found him 'perfectly sound and with very low blood pressure'. Wilfred Gilbert wrote: 'I suppose [this] accounts for the breathlessness and general slackness and he says I must take things quietly. I have I think put on nearly a stone in weight which is probably to the good but it is a long and tiresome business getting fit again ... Dr Moorhead ... said there was nothing wrong with me organically but that the heart muscles are weak and blood pressure still very low and he added that it would take some time to get over the general strain. He had seen many younger men from the War in the same state and found that it usually took about a year to put right ... It is no use trying to go to New York until I am really fit as I should only break up and ... might then get a dilation of the heart, whereas if [I] wait and get fit now there won't be the smallest chance of anything.'[8]

After leaving Ireland, Wilfred Gilbert and Kathleen arranged to stay with Geoffrey and Olive Archer at Horsham in Sussex, then to spend a month or six weeks in Brighton, 'having a perfectly quiet time', until

Wilfred Gilbert had recovered enough to take up his consular posting in New York. But any hopes of starting work were finally dashed by the Archers' doctor, who confirmed that Wilfred Gilbert must rest for a year, or risk damaging his heart. Wilfred Gilbert wrote: 'All the doctors say the same thing so one must accept it. I have told the [Foreign Office] I will come and see them.'[9] The Thesigers rented rooms with sea views at number 4 Marine Parade in Brighton, a few minutes' walk from the beach. Kathleen's mother, who kept a flat nearby, became a frequent visitor.

In September 1919 Billy and Brian began their first term as boarders at St Aubyn's, a preparatory school in the village of Rottingdean, three miles along the coast, due east from Brighton. Their parents had visited the school, where some of Wilfred Gilbert's relatives had been educated, and met R.C.V. Lang, the new headmaster. Thesiger said: 'My father and mother were evidently impressed by him and this convinced them we should go there. I remember my father took us to Eton about that time. I asked him: "Is this where I am going?", and he replied, "Yes, one day." We saw boys rowing on the river and I remember the boats banged into one another and one of the boys hurt his hand.'[10]

In those days St Aubyn's 'Sunday' uniform, worn by boys travelling to the school and on special occasions, consisted of a three-piece worsted suit and a bowler hat. In these adult clothes Billy and Brian looked very odd indeed. Boys of their age certainly looked, and no doubt felt, more comfortable in the more practical everyday uniform, consisting of grey shorts and a matching grey jersey. When Thesiger visited the school sixty years later, he wrote: 'Time seemed to have stood still. The boys wore the same grey shorts and jerseys; the band was practising, marching and countermarching on the playing field. I attended morning chapel and neither the seating nor the service had altered.'[11]

Until the 1970s, during visits to London Thesiger still wore a three-piece suit and a bowler hat, clothes more appropriate for a civil servant than a desert explorer. More to the point, these old-fashioned clothes made him increasingly conspicuous, something he disliked, and claimed he had always avoided. In *A Reed Shaken by the Wind*, Gavin Maxwell described Thesiger as he first saw him in London in 1954: 'He was very unlike the preconceived theories I had held about his appearance ... The bowler hat, the hard collar and black shoes, the never-opened umbrella, all these were a surprise to me.'[12] Thesiger's response was very reasonable, though predictably tart: 'When I'm in London I put on a dark suit and I know I'm wearing the right clothes for lunch at The Travellers, or for going out somewhere in the evening. I use an umbrella like a walking-stick and, besides, it's useful if it rains ... I admit, I gave up wearing a bowler because no one else wore one. As for not looking like an explorer: I'd be very interested to know just what an explorer is supposed to look like. Surely I'm not expected to turn up at my club wearing shorts and a bush shirt!'[13] Thesiger did concede, however, that Maxwell's description worked as a literary device by creating a contrast between his appearance in two different worlds: England and the Iraqi marshes.

On his first day at St Aubyn's, Thesiger tells us that he went round shouting, 'Has anyone seen Brian?' instead of 'Thesiger Minor'. He added: 'I was not allowed to forget this appalling solecism.'[14] His upbringing in Abyssinia had left him quite unprepared for the busy communal life of an English private school. Yet he maintained: 'You would be quite wrong saying I was desperately unhappy at St Aubyn's. It was more a feeling of being isolated. They did gang up on me rather ... at night in the dormitory. I don't mean in a physical sense. I could take care of myself that way. It was being out of it all, being isolated. You were only by yourself at night after you went to bed, and getting yourself up in the morning. There were always people, boys, in your room. It's probably true that I was used to sleeping by myself at Addis Ababa ... at St Aubyn's I didn't like sleeping in a dorm with the others.'[15] 'My father and mother used to visit us at weekends. Not every weekend, of course, but pretty frequently. They'd watch us playing games and so on, and we rather wished that they wouldn't'.[16]

Soon after the brothers first arrived, they had been questioned about their parents and their home life. Thesiger wrote: 'At first I was a friendly, forthcoming little boy, very ready to talk, perhaps to boast about journeys I had made and things I had seen. My stories, however, were greeted with disbelief and derision, and I felt increasingly rejected.'[17] (He remembered boys exclaiming: 'Have you heard what Thesiger Major says? He says he was in the trenches in the War.'[18]) 'As a result I withdrew into myself, treated overtures of friendship with mistrust, and was easily provoked. I made few friends, but once I adapted to this life I do not think I was particularly unhappy. I could comfort myself, especially at night, by recalling the sights and scenery of Abyssinia, far more real to me than the cold bleak English downs behind the school.'[19] Billy grew quarrelsome and aggressive. He fought in the gymnasium with a boy named Lucas, grasping him by the throat until he sank down unconscious: 'This did not increase my popularity.'[20] While he remembered being thrashed for various minor offences at St Aubyn's – and later, at Eton, being caned or birched for idleness – his attack on Lucas apparently went unpunished.

Thesiger's cousin, the actor Ernest Thesiger, described his own very similar experiences at a private school in his 1927 autobiography, *Practically True*. Like Wilfred, being outspoken was a major cause of Ernest's problems. Unlike Wilfred, he was bullied. Ernest wrote: 'I had never been a particularly happy child. At my private school I had been bullied by my contemporaries and disliked by my masters, both, probably, for the same reason, namely that I possessed a somewhat unbridled tongue combined with an uncomfortable knack of finding out people's weak spots. This does not make for popularity, and should be held in check by those not physically strong enough to protect themselves.' Ernest added: 'To be unusual or unconventional was the one sin not forgiven by the British schoolboy.'[21]

In the conventional atmosphere of St Aubyn's, Wilfred's boastful repetition of strange events in his unusual childhood, and his almost complete ignorance of established rules of schoolboy behaviour, and of games like football or cricket, earned him a reputation as 'a liar and a freak'. While other boys thought him weird, to the staff he seemed quaint, sometimes unexpectedly amusing. A letter from E.M. Lang, the headmaster's sister, gives a taste of the boy's precociously waspish humour: 'Wilfred was too funny at dinner the other day. Miss Edwards told one of the boys not to shout so. She then left them for a few minutes and heard Wilfred say to the same boy, "Oh, do shut up. You make as much noise as the Queen of Abyssinia!"'[22]

From December to early January 1920 the Thesigers took what was destined to be their last holiday together as a whole family, at Dartmoor House, near Okehampton in Devon. At Brighton on 31 January 1920, two months short of his forty-ninth birthday, Wilfred Gilbert Thesiger collapsed from a heart attack while he was shaving, and died, cradled in

Kathleen's arms. His last words were: 'It's all right, my dear.'[23]

According to Thesiger, his father's sudden death had come as a 'devastating shock' to his mother.[24] Although to an extent Kathleen must have been prepared for the worst, she had now, not yet forty, been left a widow, with no home of her own, no income, and four children between the ages of four and nine to care for. Thesiger said: 'When my mother told me my father had died I felt sad, but this feeling didn't last for more than a few weeks. It doesn't when you are very young. In contrast when I heard the news that my first spaniel had died, I was grief-stricken. About four days [another time Thesiger said 'a fortnight'] before my father died, a strange thing happened. I dreamt that he had died. I remember how distressed I felt [after] I had woken up. I never mentioned this to my mother, nor have I ever mentioned it to anybody else since then, but this strange coincidence always remained in my mind.'[25]

The sudden death of Thesiger's father was the third crisis in his young life in less than a year. He was still disorientated and homesick after leaving Abyssinia. The enormous contrast between the freedom of his early upbringing at the Legation, with few lessons and endless opportunities for riding and shooting, and the crowded, regimented world of St Aubyn's made his preparatory school seem like a prison. As if exile in England and the confinement of school were not enough, his father's death robbed him of a parent, friend and role model. He had become very close to Wilfred Gilbert while at Addis Ababa, whereas Kathleen had been a remoter figure whose attention was focused mainly on her husband. As a boy he had known nothing about Wilfred Gilbert's failing health, about which his mother must have felt increasingly anxious. No doubt his parents had been careful to hide any concern from their young children. Although he always insisted that after a few weeks he ceased grieving for his father, besides anxiety for his mother, Thesiger felt his father's loss more keenly than he would admit. He showed deeply affectionate concern for Kathleen, writing to her as 'My Precious Little Mummy' and assuring her, 'I will be good to you in the holidays.'[26] Typically, he never referred to Wilfred Gilbert's death in his letters, unlike Brian, who was more inclined to disclose his feelings, writing to his mother on 30 January 1921: 'It is tomoro [sic] one year since Daddy left us.'[27]

The death of Wilfred Gilbert had another, unforeseen result, which was first revealed in Timothy Green's profile of Thesiger published in 1970. Despite the favourable impression R.C.V. Lang had made on Billy's parents, and the reassuring letters he wrote, according to Thesiger, St Aubyn's headmaster was 'a sadist, and after my father's death both Brian and I were among his victims'.[28] Thesiger went on: 'The school motto was "Quit you like men: be strong", an exhortation not without relevance to some of us boys. [This was a motto quoted often by the mother of Jim Corbett, whose books, including *Maneaters of Kumaon*, were among Thesiger's favourites.] He beat me on a number of occasions, often for some trivial offence. Sent up to the dormitory, I had to kneel naked by the side of my bed. I remember crying out for the first time, "It hurts!" and Lang saying grimly, "It's meant to." For two or three days after each beating, I was called to his study so that he could see I was healing properly.'[29]

Such was Thesiger's version of Lang's beatings in *The Life of My Choice*. He had written in an earlier work, *Desert, Marsh and Mountain*, how 'on the slightest excuse, such as making a noise in the passage or not putting our shoes away properly, he beat us with a whip with a red lash. I carried the marks for years. These early beatings certainly hardened me, so that later at Eton, where I was beaten repeatedly and deservedly, I regarded the conventional "tannings" and even the occasional birchings almost as a joke.'[30] The young Billy dreaded Lang's brutal beatings, and another punishment 'more suited to the Foreign Legion than to an English preparatory school': in hot weather, being forced by the drill-sergeant to run round and round the asphalt yard. To one writer, Thesiger described Lang as 'a homosexual sadist who flogged me with a steel shafted riding whip until I bled all over the place'. His interviewer wrote: 'He carried the marks of the beatings for more than ten years.'[31] Lang's thrashings were exceptionally vicious even by the extreme standards of that period, when caning and birching were regarded as normal punishment. Whipping a naked boy of nine or ten until he bled was the action of a pervert and a sadist. No less perverted or sadistic was Lang's habit of summoning to his room boys he had thrashed, ordering them to undress, and examining the wounds he had inflicted to make sure they were healing.

Although Thesiger claimed that neither he nor his brother ever told their mother about these beatings,[32] Brian had written to Kathleen, 'You will be sorry to hear I had a canning [sic] on Friday, 3 strokes [with] a bamboo cane';[33] and again, 'I had a caning for not doing some corections [sic]. Mr Lang gave it to me with a stick like your swichy [sic].'[34] By 'swichy' Brian could have meant a thin cane, but more likely he meant a long tapering riding whip, or switch, like the steel-shafted whip with a blood-red lash Thesiger described to an enquirer in 1969. In his eighties, Thesiger disclosed further shocking information which supported his claim that Lang was a 'homosexual sadist'. Once again, Thesiger (but apparently not Brian) had been among Lang's carefully chosen victims.

In a letter to Captain Thesiger in December 1919, Lang had shown an optimistic concern for Wilfred, writing: 'Billy has made a very good start and has quite settled down to the spirit of the school, and I do not think we shall have any trouble with him. As you know, I was afraid at the beginning that he might kick against the discipline, but since he has been excellent … He is quick tempered and that makes it harder for him, but he controls himself well.'[35] This certainly conflicted with Thesiger's bitter memory of his rejection by other boys, of lonely nights when he lay in bed picturing the Legation's garden and surrounding hills, and his furious attack on Lucas. By 'discipline' Lang presumably meant St Aubyn's unfamiliar regime. Writing to Kathleen Thesiger on 20 March 1920, two months after Wilfred Gilbert's death, Lang assured her: 'I will do all I can for your boys, especially now. They have the making of fine characters … [Billy] will probably want careful treatment to train him to be master of himself, and that is where a Father will be missed: but I think I know his good points and his failings and I promise you that I will do my very best to start him on the right path in life.'[36] In a letter written a few months later, Lang was more explicit: '[Billy] is working better than he was earlier in the term, and his behaviour is certainly much better: it has done him good to know that there is always a last resource!'[37] Lang described Billy as 'very backward'.[38] He wrote: 'I have report of each of them every day from their form-masters, and they know that if it is not good, they will get punished. They are like a good many other boys, who are inclined to let their attention wander from their work, and have to be kept up to the mark: they are certainly getting plenty of discipline … Wilfred … has lost

58

that attitude of being "against authority" … Brian occasionally gets fits of obstinacy.'[39]

Such candid letters did not hide the fact that Billy and Brian were punished, though of course Lang gave no details. His letters indicated that he was a strict disciplinarian, but gave no hint of other sinister motives, which possibly had as much to do with Lang himself realising that he had strayed from 'the right path in life' as his missionary desire to guide wayward small boys along it. Whipping boys until they bled may have been for Lang an 'externalised' form of self-chastisement that expurgated his sense of guilt for his perverted sexual desires, yet was still viewed by him as a justifiable punishment.

In a sense he was right in describing Thesiger as 'backward'. But Billy's letters, littered with mis-spellings, were often amusing and, like his father's, well-observed and always deeply felt. For instance, describing to Katheen St Aubyn's school 'maxagean' (magazine), he wrote: 'It allso says about the charwoman [a play on 'chameleon'], and how they have a pretective colouration of dirt which is a very true statement, and allso how they have a prehensile tongue. This is allso very true, because they are always jabering all the time. You ought to come and see us play rugar. It is my favourit game because if you are collared you can hit the person away and can do practicly what ever you like.'[40]

As well as looking after her brother, E.M. Lang (who like Lang had never married) supervised the welfare of St Aubyn's boys. It is just conceivable that she did not know her brother viciously abused certain children. Lang, presumably, never discussed the subject with her; and laundrymaids, who washed the boys' bloodstained underclothes and pyjamas, no doubt felt it wise to keep such damning evidence to themselves. Possibly for effect, Thesiger claimed he did not resent Lang's beatings; and he even went as far as to suggest that they prepared him for the many hardships he endured years afterwards as an explorer and traveller. Before making further disclosures about Lang, Thesiger said: 'Obviously, at the time, I had no idea that he was homosexual. After all, I was a boy of just nine or ten … It wasn't just Lang telling me to get undressed, and kneel down naked by my bed while he thrashed me. It was the way he examined us afterwards in his study. Once or twice he came into the bathroom and said: "You've been playing with yourself, boy, let me look at you." He made me stand up in the bath and examined me pretty thoroughly.' Thesiger added: 'I am sure he only beat or tampered with boys like myself, and another boy, whose fathers had died.'[41] He denied being upset by Lang examining and touching him: 'In fact I was playing with myself on those occasions. All small boys do this sort of thing. I just felt embarrassed being caught at it by the headmaster.'[42] Thesiger also confirmed that when Lang touched him, he had not resisted. This is not really surprising, since Lang was a large, 'imposing' man who not only symbolised ultimate authority, but also enforced it. As headmaster, in those days he had commanded unquestioning respect. Besides, Lang was not the sort of individual many small boys would have thought of contradicting.

The beatings ended after 'about three years' when Arnold Hodson, who had been a Consul in southern Abyssinia, visited the Thesigers in Radnorshire during the school holidays. 'One evening he said jokingly, "I don't suppose you get beaten at school nowadays, not like we were in my time." Neither Brian nor I had told our mother about these beatings but now, incensed, I pulled up my shorts and showed him some half-healed scars. Years later I learnt that Hodson went down to Sussex and told the headmaster that if he beat either of us again he would have him taken to court.'[43]

In his late sixties, Thesiger gave a less dramatic, more plausible, version of the story. According to this, Hodson glimpsed the scars when he took Billy and Brian to the seashore. In both versions, the outcome is the same. 'Repetitions of this savagery were at last halted by a friend of the family, who took Wilfred to the beach and noticed the marks. When they returned to the school on the Sunday evening, the friend sought out the headmaster and warned him that if he ever touched the boy again he would be faced with prosecution.'[44]

It may seem strange to modern parents that Kathleen Thesiger, apparently knowing that Lang beat her sons, never saw their scars and so had no idea how severe the beatings were. A former pupil of St Aubyn's, who boarded there soon after Billy and Brian, commented: 'We never told our parents about being beaten.' He confessed he was afraid of Lang, who despite Hodson's warning went on thrashing boys as mercilessly as before. When Thesiger visited St Aubyn's in May 1981, he found that after sixty years 'the school had hardly changed in outward appearance; what was profoundly different was the relationship of headmaster and boys. Between them I sensed affection, confidence and trust.'[45]

Contrary to Thesiger's statement that 'I certainly learnt next to nothing at St Aubyn's,' according to school reports he achieved moderately good marks. In July 1922 he was placed fourth out of ten boys in the Lower Remove, ahead of the Campbells, twins who he complained had 'dominated' him. Having known almost nothing about football, he enjoyed 'soccer or rugger'. Later, at Oxford, he insisted he 'loathed' cricket, yet in January 1942, proposed by his cousin the 2nd Viscount Chelmsford, he became a member of the MCC.[46]

Lang had warned Kathleen that public school entrance examinations were becoming harder and more competitive. Billy (now known as Wilfred) failed the examination for Eton, but after two terms at a crammer he passed at his second attempt, 'a whole form from the bottom of the school'. When Wilfred left St Aubyn's for Eton in 1923, Brian was taken away and sent for a year to Dermot and Roderic's preparatory school, Beaudesert House at Minchinhampton, near Stroud in Gloucestershire, where Mary Buckle's presence as a matron gave the children support and homely reassurance.

In 1920 Kathleen and her two youngest sons moved from Brighton in search of a permanent home elsewhere. Kathleen lodged for some months with friends and family at Horsham in West Sussex, at Roughton in Norfolk, with her brother Ashmead in Hatfield, and at various addresses in London. Thesiger wrote: 'When a kind and affluent sister-in-law offered to buy her a house in the suburbs of London, she asked, "What will my boys do there?" The reply was, "We'll get them bicycles and they can learn to ride them."'[47] The affluent, kindly, but misdirected sister-in-law had been Percy Thesiger's wife Katherine. Kathleen did not accept her offer, but Katie and Percy gave crucial assistance later, when Wilfred and Brian went to Eton, paying the boys' school fees until their grandmother, Lady Chelmsford, died in 1926. Lady Chelmsford had inherited a large sum of money in 1905, when her husband died. She left Kathleen a comfortable legacy: an annuity of £400 to Wilfred, and an income to each of his three younger brothers.

In 1920 Kathleen rented Titley House, a dilapidated, remote farmhouse at Titley in Herefordshire, and in 1921 she leased The Milebrook, a six-bedroom house in the Teme Valley, Radnorshire (now Powys), which gave her and her sons a home for more than twenty years. Wilfred 'identified [himself] completely' with The Milebrook, which became as important to him as the Legation at Addis Ababa. From 1922 until 1933 he kept a detailed diary of life there during his holidays from school and university, with careful notes describing the bird and animal life of the country around the house. The diary's three volumes were bound expensively in leather, and each secured with a brass lock and key. In England, as at Addis Ababa, Wilfred took charge of his brothers and minuted their activities in his diary. On 8 August 1922 he wrote: 'A rabbit was seen in the fruit bushes by WP Thesiger esq. BP Thesiger esq was also present but failed to see it. A Council was immediately held and steps were taken, all holes drains and burrows blocked up. One large hole was found by pond under the tall tree. A Hunt will be held before Saturday.'[48] His entry on 26 August the same year gave a hint of things to come: 'Took tea up Stowe [Hill]. Mr Hodson, Miss Handbury, Mrs W Thesiger, Miss Buckle, W Thesiger esq, BP Thesiger esq, D[V] Thesiger, RMD Thesiger (names of members of the expedition). Climbed the rocks (Stowe).'[49]

SEVEN

Eton: Lasting Respect and Veneration

Thesiger's first term at Eton began in September 1923. In *The Life of My Choice* he devoted several pages to describing Eton: the layout of buildings; numbers of boys known as Oppidans and Scholars; the house prefect system; and school prefects, whose long-established society was known as Pop. In contrast to St Aubyn's, at Eton Wilfred settled in quickly and made friends with other boys, among them Harry Phillimore, Ronnie Chance and Desmond Parsons, who like himself were boarders at McNeile's House.

He drew parallels, and very clear distinctions, between St Aubyn's and Eton. Among the seventy boarders at St Aubyn's he had been lonely, but he was almost never alone. At Eton he had his own room, with his own carpets, furniture, books and framed drawings by *Jock of the Bushveld*'s illustrator Edmund Caldwell, bought by Kathleen. His room gave him the 'inestimable sense of privacy' he had known at the Legation.[1] At St Aubyn's, Billy and Brian had each had a little garden with crocuses, daffodils and strawberries.[2] Their gardens were their private domain, with which they identified. Wilfred's room at Eton likewise meant more to him than privacy: 'The privacy idea of Eton meant a sense of ownership. It was my room, with my pictures. I always get these words wrong. When I said "privacy" in the book, I meant "ownership", something that belonged to me.'[3] He always felt that the life of Eton could not be understood by outsiders. 'I wrote about Eton in *The Life of My Choice* for people like Val [ffrench Blake] who had been there and who knew what it meant to me. Those who hadn't been to Eton would simply skim over this ... If you took an afternoon off and went down there, you'd get an impression of St Aubyn's or even of Magdalen and Oxford. But Eton is different. It would take longer to get to know. And anyone who hadn't been to a public school, even ... couldn't begin to understand what the life there is like.'[4]

In *The Life of My Choice*, he wrote: 'I have many memories of Eton: services in College Chapel, especially in winter when the lights were lit ... the Field Game on winter afternoons while mist crept across the grounds; the lamps on the High Street and crowds of boys hurrying back to their houses before "lockup".'[5] Here again, Thesiger's Eton images were of lamplight and winter. Late in life he looked back on the school with a romantic nostalgia that tempered his harsher memories. As a scholar, he was 'barely moderate', 'just good enough at games to become Captain of Games in an athletically undistinguished house'.[6] This qualified him as a member of the 'Library', a house prefect. The Library was among the Eton traditions for which he acquired 'lasting respect ... and veneration'.[7] At Eton, he wrote in his late seventies, 'I learnt responsibility, the decencies of life, and standards of civilised behaviour'[8] – virtues people usually acquire at home.

Despite the improving atmosphere of Eton, Thesiger's masters and fellow pupils thought him 'boorish'. When Brian joined him at the school, the brothers were shunned as 'a couple of thugs'. Wilfred's friend Val ffrench Blake recalled: 'People gave them a wide berth. Wilfred had a gentler side and he could be very nice when you got to know him.'[9] Thesiger's thuggish reputation had been earned by his behaviour in and out of the classroom, and by his 'murderous' proficiency as a boxer. He was notorious for his powerful knockout punch, which once broke an opponent's jaw; his boxing attainments won him respect but not friendship.

At Eton, as at St Aubyn's, Thesiger was lonely and given to day-dreaming about Abyssinia, where he was determined to return and live like one of his father's Consuls, hunting big game and travelling among wild tribes. He admitted freely: 'My experiences at Eton should have been far richer than they were. However, I remained wary of strangers and I lacked self-confidence. It wasn't being thrashed and fondled by Lang that harmed me at St Aubyn's. It was being rejected by the other boys. Being shunned by them as a liar and made to feel an oddity like some exotic specimen in a zoo. I never got over it – I mean, properly – and this sense of rejection and of being somehow different affected me for the rest of my life.'[10] Thesiger said that he neither disliked nor resented R.C.V. Lang; indeed, he said that he felt elated and proud when Lang 'patted my head and told me I had done well'.[11] Yet he despised his Classics tutor at Eton, 'Cob' Bevan, who never laid a hand on him, whose only failing was being a bore.[12]

In Addis Ababa as a child, Thesiger had been at the centre of his world, an absolutely secure world which revolved around him. St Aubyn's destroyed not only his precious self-esteem but his all-important sense of belonging. From then onwards he sought and strived continually for acceptance, an essential ingredient of life he could no longer take for granted as he had in the past, but felt he had to 'win'.

Of the friendships Thesiger made at Eton, that with Val ffrench Blake was one of the most significant. Three years his junior, ffrench Blake was intelligent and practical, a gifted musician with a precocious mastery of classics. Thesiger struggled with Latin, which his Classics tutor, C.O. Bevan, 'a stolid red-faced clergyman without wit or humour ... made [him] loathe'. He wrote that 'as a result of his tuition Latin verse remained incomprehensible to me. Bored stiff by him, I paid little attention: he retaliated by having me birched for idleness on three occasions, but these attempts to drive Latin into me from the wrong end proved equally unproductive.'[13] In a school report Bevan commented: 'He writes unintelligible English and then eats it.'[14] This apparently referred to Thesiger's curious habit of chewing bits of paper.

Val ffrench Blake helped Thesiger with Latin, and became invaluable to him. It was this image of ffrench Blake as a round-faced, studious boy of fourteen that Thesiger 'carried with [him]' for years. It remained: overlaid by images of fourteen-year-old Idris Daud, his Sudanese gunbearer; of sixteen-year-old Bedu, Salim bin Kabina and Salim bin Ghabaisha; of Amara bin Thuqub, a Marsh Arab in his mid-teens from south Iraq.

By now Thesiger had already developed a bitter hatred of 'mechanical transport', such as cars and aeroplanes, which he saw as a threat to the remote tribal worlds he planned to explore. While contemporaries at Eton found speed exhilarating and longed to own powerful cars, Wilfred immersed himself in books about African big game hunting and travel, or reread old favourites, including John Buchan's novel *Prester John*, which he said later had been given to him by Brian at St Aubyn's.[15] Some letters to his mother contained wish lists of the books he longed for as presents for birthdays or for Christmas. In February 1924 he wrote telling her: 'Mr McNeile lent me The Ivory Raiders by Major Rayne. It is very good and quite true. It is all about the Abyssinian Raids into Kenya Colony.'[16] A list of 'African Books owned by W Thesiger' included *The Ivory Raiders* and the 1790 first edition of Bruce's *Travels to Discover the Source of the Nile*, which he bought for ten shillings at a shop in Eton. He had inherited some of his father's books, among them Major P.H.G. Powell-Cotton's *A Sporting Trip Through Abyssinia* and *In Unknown Africa*, and *African Nature Notes and Reminiscences* by the famous hunter Frederick Courteney Selous. Of the fifty titles he collected while at Eton, one of the most influential was T.E. Lawrence's *Revolt in the Desert*, a popular abridgement of Lawrence's privately printed *Seven Pillars of Wisdom*. In September 1935, a few months after he had first arrived in the Sudan, his mother sent him a copy of the first 'trade edition' of *Seven Pillars*, and in 1964 he was able to buy from the antiquarian book dealer Maggs Bros a magnificent copy of the rare 1926 subscribers' edition.

The Eton masters Thesiger remembered were C.A. Alington DD, the headmaster; Thesiger's housemaster, A.M. McNeile, known to his forty-seven boarders and other boys as 'Archie'; George Lyttelton, 'whose published letters to Rupert Hart-Davis have given pleasure to many',[17] and whose son Humphrey became famous as a jazz musician; and, of course, Thesiger's *bête noire*, 'Cob' Bevan. Dr Alington symbolised absolute authority, an 'Olympian figure in a scarlet gown', reminiscent of Wilfred's uncle Frederic Chelmsford when Viceroy of India, resplendent in state robes, who seemed to his highly impressionable nephew to be 'more than human'.[18]

Thesiger was confirmed at Eton College Chapel in November 1926: 'I had been brought up in a conventional Church of England family. In this sense, I was nominally a Christian. By the time I was confirmed I had found it impossible to believe in the divinity of Christ, or to accept God as a benign, all-powerful Being.' He accepted that Christian beliefs he had grown up with, and had never questioned, might have been undermined by the traumas he experienced aged only eight or nine: being uprooted from Abyssinia, 'pitch-forked' into a school where he was shunned and physically abused, losing the father he adored and worshipped, an ultimate role model who would not be 'coming back'.

He said: 'I didn't believe that Man was made in God's image, but that God was made in the image of Man. The words I stood and mouthed at my confirmation service were, by then, already meaningless to me.'[19] Aged thirteen, he had written to his mother: 'We had two very nice services today and a lovely hymn, "God is working his purpose out, that which shall surely be"', whose fatalistic message was chillingly underlined by news that one of the boys had found a man 'who had committed suicide (hanged himself from a tree down by Cuckoo Weir)'.[20] He later told an interviewer how during those services his mind used to wander, picturing the Epiphany ceremony of Timkat in Abyssinia, and the priests in their white robes dancing before the Ark of the Covenant. In another letter to Kathleen he praised the Bishop of Buckingham, who had preached 'a very clever sermon on the Christian religion'. 'Do you know,' he added, 'that now in Zanzibar stands the Cathedral [where there] was not long ago the slave market and where the altar now stands several years ago was the whipping post.'[21] Giving a wintry description of his room, he wrote: 'I am at the moment ... roasting chestnuts in front of a blazing fire. It is freezing here. Our milk for tea was frozen and all the trees are covered with frost which makes them look wonderful and very beautiful. I am very warm at nights and if I feel cold [he was troubled by poor circulation for much of his life] can put my dressing gown and great coat on my bed.'[22]

During his first summer term, in 1924, Wilfred's mother took him with her to London, where they had been invited to tea at Albert Gate by Ras Tafari, the Regent of Abyssinia, shortly before Tafari's thirty-second birthday. This was the account Thesiger gave in his autobiography in 1987, although in a letter he wrote from Eton in July 1924 he spoke of Tafari '[coming] to tea with us'.[23] Tafari Makonnen was born on 23 July 1892. In 1910, five years after his father, Makonnen Walda-Mikael, had died, he was appointed Governor of Harar. In 1917, following the Empress Zauditu's coronation, he became Abyssinia's Regent. *The Life of My Choice* opens with a description of this intimate occasion in 1924, which for the fourteen-year-old Wilfred Thesiger had a defining importance. Two things emerge from his account of the meeting. First, his impressions of Tafari were mainly visual ones; this is understandable, since the conversation between Tafari and Kathleen Thesiger would have involved Wilfred very little. He had plenty of time, therefore, to study Tafari carefully, and take note of his clothing, his appearance, his dignified manners. Second, he attached a particular significance to the meeting because of its 'defining importance' for himself. Apart from Ras Tafari's condolences for Captain Thesiger's death, and his appreciation for his help at a 'critical' period, the only conversation Thesiger recorded took place between him and the Regent. As on other occasions, it seems he relied on his mother's memory. Almost certainly Kathleen would later have repeated to Wilfred Tafari's flattering remarks about his father, which he no doubt reworded when he wrote *The Life of My Choice*.

According to this account, Ras Tafari received Kathleen and her eldest son in the Abyssinian residence at number 2 Albert Gate, in Knightsbridge. Thesiger wrote: 'Wearing a black, gold-embroidered silk coat over a finely-woven shamma, he came across the room to greet us, shook hands and with a smile and a gesture invited us to be seated. He was very small but even then to my mind his slight body and lack of height emphasised his distinction, drawing attention to the sensitive and finely moulded face ... We spoke in French, the foreign language in which he was fluent.'[24] As a girl, Kathleen Thesiger had spent holidays with her mother on the French Riviera, and she spoke French reasonably well. But while Wilfred had received good marks for French at St Aubyn's, it is unlikely that he could have followed easily, or taken part in, a lengthy conversation about mutual friends or events in Abyssinia such as the 1916 revolution. Thesiger's generalised remark 'We spoke in French' can only have referred to his mother and Ras Tafari. As the Thesigers were leaving, Wilfred seized the opportunity to blurt out how he 'longed above all to return' to Abyssinia. Tafari was evidently moved by the boy's sincerity and passion. His reply – 'You will always be very welcome. One day you must come as my guest'[25] – was more than a polite courtesy, as Thesiger would discover a few years later.

From Eton, Thesiger wrote to Kathleen: 'Wasn't it fun seeing the Ras ... send me any cutting you see in the Papers about [him] ... Tell me whether it was [a] live elephant, lion or gilt cup Tafari gave us [as a present] ... I wonder what Ras Tafari thought of the Bank of England

and Houses of Parliament. I saw in the papers that he seldom smiled, which gave him his kingly dem[ean]our but when he came to tea with us he smiled quite a lot. I expect Brian and Dermot will love seeing him.'[26] Nowhere did he refer to Tafari's invitation.

In another letter, Thesiger confirmed that he had already decided on a career that would get him back to Africa – specifically to Abyssinia. He acknowledged that it was unusual for a boy to have such a clear and definite plan for his future, as well as the determination to achieve it. He later recalled: 'I'd already decided by the time I was fourteen, earlier perhaps, that I wanted to join the Sudan Political Service. There were several good reasons for this. The Sudan bordered on Abyssinia. I felt that serving there would help me get back to Abyssinia, whereas being somewhere like Nigeria wouldn't. Besides, I had read books such as Abel Chapman's *Savage Sudan* and J.G. Millais's *Far Away up the Nile* and I was attracted to the Sudan by the prospects for hunting and getting among tribes that lived on the Nile. It was the hunting and tribes, and being close to Abyssinia, made me feel the Sudan was the right place for me.'[27]

EIGHT

Shrine of my Youth

Thesiger spent almost three months in France in 1929: from early May until the end of June he stayed with a French family at Fontainebleau to improve his French, studying with fifteen other boys under a tutor, Commandant Lettauré; and for most of July he was on holiday at Sable d'Or in Brittany, where he often accompanied an elderly Breton and his assistant or *mousse*, aged thirteen, fishing for lobsters, conger eels and mackerel. The old fisherman, Pierre, had been a *pêcheur d'Islande*, one of a hardy breed celebrated in Pierre Loti's famous novel of that name. His stories of 'the weeks at sea, the gales, the great hauls of fish', gave Thesiger the idea of working aboard a Hull trawler off Iceland, in 1931, during his long summer vacation from Oxford.[1]

Thesiger went up to Magdalen, 'perhaps the most beautiful of Oxford colleges', in the autumn of 1929. Compared with St Aubyn's and Eton, his four years at Magdalen were fulfilled and happy. The 'cold bleak English downs' and the 'bitterly cold and damp' Thames Valley stood as wintry metaphors for the two schools, whereas in *The Life of My Choice* he wrote: 'My memories of Oxford ... are summer ones.' A marvellous paragraph summarised these memories in a vivid collage of sensual imagery: 'the tranquil beauty of the High Street in the early morning before the traffic; May morning and the choirboys singing on Magdalen Tower; reading in a punt on the river beneath overhanging willows; the water meadows beyond Parsons' Pleasure, and the sound of corncrakes; sailing with Robin Campbell on Port Meadow and then tea together at the Trout Inn; dinner parties in my rooms, with evening light on the College buildings and the scent of wallflowers from the President's garden'.[2]

At Oxford Thesiger read military history, although his chronic 'inability to cope with Latin' prevented him from taking the Crusades as his special subject. He admired and envied T.E. Lawrence's groundbreaking research on the military architecture of the Middle East, and his thesis, *Crusader Castles*, published in 1936, a year after his death, a copy of which Thesiger eventually owned. To his regret they never met during Lawrence's brief visits to John Buchan at Elsfield Manor, near Oxford, where Thesiger was sometimes invited to lunch or tea. Thesiger and Lawrence had much in common. Both had Anglo-Irish backgrounds, both studied history at Oxford and both became Fellows of Oxford colleges. Neither drank nor smoked, bothered about food or took an interest in women. Both needed to be liked and appreciated. Lawrence claimed he was 'sexless', while for Thesiger sex was 'of no great consequence'.[3] They held similar views about money and work, and the 'separateness' of friendships. While they were truthful, both tended (in varying degrees) to gloss over plain facts with a romantic veneer. Both practised self-discipline, yet were not averse to self-promotion in the sense of 'backing into the limelight'. As for differences between the two, Thesiger was tactile, whereas Lawrence hated to be touched; and, of course, Lawrence revelled in speed – speedboats and powerful motorcycles – while Thesiger viewed the invention of the internal combustion engine as a catastrophe. Lawrence was the most famous British Arabist of his day; Thesiger was a great Arabist in the making. With John Buchan as a mutual friend and a catalyst, it is difficult to believe that they would not have got on well together. As for the other Lawrence, David Herbert, with whom Thesiger has never been compared, and whom he would almost certainly have disliked, they nevertheless shared strong views on 'the close tie of male to male'[4] and the mechanised materialism of Western nations, 'ready for an outburst of insanity [throwing] us all into some purely machine-driven unity of lunatics'.[5] In 1928, despite his professed loathing of cars, Thesiger had learnt to drive. He said: 'At the Titley farmhouse and at The Milebrook, until my mother bought a car, we got about using a pony and trap. The small open car I got after I left Eton extended the range of my brothers' and my social lives very considerably.' Thesiger used to park this car outside Magdalen, a practice, he wrote, 'people thought was rather undignified'.[6]

His history tutor, J.M. Thompson, gave tutorials which were diverse and 'always stimulating'[7] but, for Wilfred, lacked the real-life excitement of the wild victory parades at Addis Ababa in 1916, or of seeing the Zulu assegais and other trophies his grandfather had brought back from the Zulu War. Nothing Thesiger read at Oxford's history school compared with the books he read about the Zulus, including Rider Haggard's African novels, or about Abyssinia or Dervishes in the Sudan. In the same way, the buildings and people he saw in London or Paris had failed to stir his imagination like the colourful crowds, mosques and tombs he remembered in India as a boy.

Thesiger avoided Magdalen's 'communal life' and organised sports: 'I did not drink, and for such festivities as Bump Suppers celebrating success on the river by the College eight I had no taste.'[8] In May 1931 he did attend a Boat Club supper, and that month someone pencilled on his college menu: 'I've never seen you inebriated before, and I hope I never do again ... !!!' In fact Thesiger drank very little, and unlike his parents and his brothers, he never smoked. Out shooting in Wales or fishing off Brittany, he would drink cider. He enjoyed sweet liqueurs, and used to pour a generous measure of dark, sweet sherry into his favourite oxtail soup or minestrone. Beer and spirits he never touched.

For four consecutive years Thesiger boxed for Oxford, and captained the university in his final year. Three wins against Cambridge, he wrote modestly, 'gave me a certain standing in the College'.[9] Thesiger first learnt to box at Addis Ababa, encouraged by Count Arthur Bentinck, a member of his father's staff. A First World War veteran who had been badly wounded in France, Bentinck was appointed Captain Thesiger's Military Attaché in 1917. Thesiger wrote: 'One day at the Legation he had produced boxing gloves, and instructed Brian and me to put them on. He always maintained that our later success was due to his initial coaching. He alarmed us as children – he had a gruff manner, a game leg and a pronounced cast in one eye. Later he became a close family friend.'[10]

At St Aubyn's and Eton, boxing had won Thesiger respect but not friendship. In his male-orientated world, boxing equated with assertiveness, controlled aggression and strength of character. It was an exclusively male pursuit which signalled virility and courage. Boxing, even when the contestants fought tirelessly and hard, channelled and curbed aggression.

However brutal they might appear, the matches were never brutish, and the rules and art of boxing maintained a proper division between the controlled aggressive spirit of the ring and an uncontrolled violence 'improper in the affairs of men'.[11] In this sense the sport suited Thesiger's ethos as well as big game hunting and bullfighting. In each of them, the appeal for Thesiger was the same: to master uncertainty, to win decisively, always facing the possibility of defeat (as a boxer) or of death (from a dangerous African animal such as a lion or a buffalo).

Thesiger said: 'I had the heavy punch whereas Brian was stylish in the ring. Brian fought hard, right to the end. Of the two of us, he was probably the better boxer.'[12] During Thesiger's year as Oxford captain his brother Dermot wrote in *Isis*, the university journal: 'A kindly fortune favoured him with the means of practising and ripening his fistic ability. It entrusted him to the care of an Indian ayah, who devotedly assured him that there was no reason why he should do anything other than he pleased. Further, it produced a self-willed child of six with three brothers smaller than himself, thus mitigating the danger of an embryo boxer being sadly battered in the early stages of his career.'[13]

At Eton Thesiger had boxed as a flyweight in 1925, a bantamweight in 1926, a lightweight in 1927 and a welterweight in 1928.[14] At Oxford, 'Finding it difficult to get down to middleweight, I decided to fight as a light-heavy in the University trials.'[15] For his height, almost six foot two inches, this weight – with an upper limit of twelve stone seven pounds – was not excessive. He was broad-chested and broad-shouldered, with sinewy arms, massive biceps and muscular legs which figured prominently in the photograph of him with his guard up, published originally in the *Illustrated London News* and later in *Desert, Marsh and Mountain*. He wrote: 'Boxing was the only sport I was any good at, but I often wondered, sitting with gloves on waiting for the fight before mine to end, why on earth I did it. Yet, once I had started, I felt a savage satisfaction in fighting. I was never conscious of pain, even with a torn ear, a broken nose and split lips, but I do remember occasions of desperate tiredness, and of effort to keep my hands up or stay on my feet.'[16]

In his summer holiday in 1930, for the nominal wage of a shilling, Thesiger worked his passage as a fireman aboard the tramp steamer *Sorrento*, through the Mediterranean as far as Istanbul and Constanza in the Black Sea. When he returned home at the end of a 'rewarding' month, he found two letters waiting for him: an invitation from Ras Tafari to attend his coronation as the Emperor Haile Selassie in Addis Ababa following the death of the Empress; and, from the Foreign Office, confirmation of his appointment as Honorary Attaché to HRH the Duke of Gloucester, who was to represent his father, King George V, at the ceremonies.

The Duke of Gloucester's party left London by the boat train from Victoria on 16 October 1930. From Marseilles they sailed to Aden aboard the P&O liner *Rampura*.[17] From Aden they crossed to Jibuti on HMS *Effingham*, and travelled by train from there to Addis Ababa. Apart from Thesiger, the Duke's mission included the Earl of Airlie, Captain Brooke, Major 'Titch' Miles from Kenya, Mr Noble from the Foreign Office and Major Stanyforth. Aged twenty, obliged to wear a morning suit that contrasted dully with his companions' dress uniforms and decorations, Thesiger felt conspicuous and ill at ease. The arrival of Sir John Maffey, who led the Sudan delegation that accompanied the mission, helped. Maffey had served as Frederic Chelmsford's private secretary when Thesiger's uncle was Viceroy of India; Wilfred and Brian had stayed in Scotland, near Loch Naver, with him and his family for ten days in 1929. Lord Airlie was also kind, 'But,' Thesiger wrote, 'it was the natural kindness of the Duke of Gloucester himself which helped me most.'[18] Seeing Maffey again reminded him of an encounter with one of his daughters in Sutherland the previous year. Thesiger said: 'I felt tremendously attracted to her. But then I thought: I must stop this or it will wreck the rest of my life.'[19] It is not known whether his feelings were reciprocated, although his way of telling the story implies that they were. The experience was probably unique. In 1933 Dermot Thesiger wrote definitively in his *Isis* article: 'as to [Wilfred's] normal pleasure, it would appear that women have no part therein'.[20]

Wonderful as it was, the Emperor's coronation meant less to Thesiger than the adventure of returning to Abyssinia. He jotted in his diary: 'Felt thrilled to be back.'[21] He stared, fascinated, from the train windows at the arid Danakil desert, empty save for tiny dik-dik antelope, baboons and lesser bustard. In a letter to his mother he described the ceremony quite briefly, with here and there amusing, observant touches that brought the occasion alive. 'The actual coronation was held in a canvas building added onto St George's Cathedral ... The Emperor and Empress (who is to have a child in a month's time and consequently has the European midwife as lady-in-waiting) had had an all-night vigil in St George's ... The Empress and Prince were also crowned, with rather awful European crowns ... The Abyssinian diplomatic corps wore European clothes and cocked hats, which was a pity ... Tafari [now Emperor] was to have left in his state carriage, but the horses were unmanageable ... After the ceremony the Abyssinian air force flew over the building (they have crashed two planes [out of a total of six aircraft in working order] in the last fortnight) ... I went to the reception afterwards. There was a tremendous selection of fireworks, but unfortunately an accident occurred and they all went off at once.'[22] In *The Life of My Choice* Thesiger gave a more polished version, with only a brief mention of the prematurely exploding fireworks. Even this incident he managed to dignify, adding: 'This must have been a bitter moment for Haile Selassie, but once again he gave no indication of his feelings. He stood for a while, watching the pyrotechnic chaos in the yard below, then moved slowly back into the banqueting hall.'[23]

Thesiger wrote to Brian: 'The Coronation was the most stirring and impressive show I have ever seen. You could easily imagine yourself back in the days of Sheba. I suppose there never will be such a scene again. It was held in a building added onto St George's church. The robes were magnificent. The chiefs were present in their lions mane crowns and velvet cloaks and the priests in every coloured robe and crowned with glittering crowns. The main church was filled with the rest of the priests, and throughout the ceremony the thudding of their drums and the rise and fall of their chanting came faintly to our ears. I went in and saw them dance. A wonderful sight. The church was surrounded by the other Rases and chiefs in themselves a sight never to be forgotten ...' Lost for words, he signed off: 'I have so much to tell you and you can't even try to describe such scenes as I have seen in a letter.'[24]

Two days after the ceremony, Thesiger had a private audience at the palace. The new Emperor was 'extremely gracious'. Their conversation (as usual in French) was very like that Thesiger reported in London. In *The Life of My Choice* he wrote: 'He received me with grave courtesy and enquired after my family. When I expressed my appreciation of the honour he had done me by inviting me to his coronation, he replied that as the eldest son of his trusted friend, to whom he owed so much, it was proper that I should be present. I told him how happy I was to be back in his country. "It is your country. You were born here. You have lived here for half of your life. I hope you will spend many more years with us," was his answer. As he spoke I was very conscious of the smile which transformed his usually impassive face. It was twenty minutes before he terminated the interview. That evening I received two elephant tusks, a heavy, ornate gold cigarette case, a large, colourful carpet and the third class of the Star of Ethiopia.'[25] He wrote on 10 November telling Kathleen: 'We were all decorated the other day and I got the Star of Ethiopia second class [sic].'[26] He added, as if to play down this honour: 'A thing you hang round your neck.' He noted: 'If my father had lived, he and my mother would have met Tafari in London, during his State Visit, and they would have attended his coronation. Instead, I represented my father. Seeing the Legation again, where I was born and brought up, the old servants and their affection for my parents – all of this mattered desperately to me ... If I hadn't been invited like that, by Haile Selassie, none of it would have happened.'[27]

Other letters give ample proof of Thesiger's intense attachment to the Abyssinia of his childhood. In books he wrote from middle-age onwards he returned continually to the theme of his youth at Addis Ababa and its 'crucial influence' on his life. This was no mere literary device; yet childhood were memories perfected by a rose-tinted lens. In his letter in 1930 he described how he had climbed a hill behind the Legation which he frequented as a boy. He called this place 'Shrine of my youth'. High places, giving wide and distant views, were important to him. The hill behind the Legation at Addis Ababa; Stowe Hill near The Milebrook, where he and his brothers went for walks or went shooting as teenagers; a sheer precipice near Maralal in northern Kenya – Malossa, which he referred to always as 'The Viewpoint'. The mountain 'shrines' were quite personal, and were not to be confused with merely fine mountain views of Morocco, the Middle East and western Asia, where he travelled between 1937 and 1983. Thesiger invariably rejected attempts to explain the significance to him of hills and mountains, saying only that they had 'always attracted' him. Any analysis of his emotions he condemned as 'rubbish': 'It's been fashionable for years to analyse Lawrence, to denigrate him, to probe into his childhood, his friendship with Daoud. I hate all of that. The last thing I'd want is someone probing about in my life. But, after I've kicked the bucket, I suppose, they can do as they please.'[28]

From Addis Ababa, Thesiger wrote: 'I got a horse and went to the old ruined church behind the Legation ... then on to the little wood and home through the plains. Great fun and I loved it.' The church, originally built of mud and thatch, may have been the same building Wilfred Gilbert Thesiger described in the October 1913 issue of *Man*, the Royal Anthropological Society's monthly record. Of his old home, Thesiger wrote: 'The Legation is terribly the same and yet horribly different ... It brings back the days we were here rather painfully.'[29] He met no fewer than '15 old servants and syces, including Hapta Wold, Ratta and Mahomet and they are very pleased to see me and bursting with enquiries about you all'.[30] The British Minister, Sir Sidney Barton, became very involved with Wilfred and his journeys in Abyssinia in 1930, and again during 1933 and 1934. Thesiger wrote discreetly of Barton and his family: 'I have not yet formed an opinion of the Bartons. The whole place is overrun with daughters and wives ... I don't think they care about [the horses] though the daughter is keen. Lady B said "The Sowars were the raison d'être of the stables." All terribly different.'[31] Wilfred enjoyed the banquet given by Sir Sidney Barton in honour of the Emperor. Despatched from London in October, according to the *Birmingham Post*, a cake produced for the occasion, stood five feet five inches high, on a gold base twenty-two inches in diameter, and weighed more than one and a half hundredweight.[32] Many years later, he acquired seven volumes of press cuttings reporting events in Abyssinia from 1929 to 1942. The collection had belonged to Sir Sidney Barton, and among other things it included very full coverage of Haile Selassie's coronation.

Thesiger admitted that his view of history was 'romantic' rather than 'objective'. He might have added 'selective'. Whereas his description of the coronation in *The Life of My Choice* was dignified and sombre, his letters from Addis Ababa in 1930, though no less admiring, had a lighter touch. Of the Duke of Gloucester's stay at the old palace, he wrote: 'They are having an odd time at the Gibbi. About a score of courses for every meal, and most of the servants seem to have disappeared. HRH does not treat things seriously and sees the funny side of it.' The Italians, he noted, were angry after being refused the *gibbi* as their quarters, since 'the palace was engaged'.[33] Thesiger later dismissed such anecdotes as inappropriate for an autobiography dedicated to the Emperor's memory. He felt annoyed and depressed by 'intrusions' from the West into the old Abyssinia he had known as a boy. 'Already it was slightly tarnished round the edges ... the bodyguard now wore khaki, some of the palace secretaries were in tailcoats and top hats. There were cars in the streets and brash, noisy journalists crowded round hotel bars competing for sensational stories to wire to their papers. On ceremonial occasions they thrust themselves forward with their cameras.'[34] He remembered being elbowed aside by someone shouting, 'Make way for the eyes and ears of the world!'[35] Evelyn Waugh, reporting for the *Graphic*, joined Lady Ravensdale, a 'hopelessly loquacious' American, at the unveiling of a memorial statue to the Emperor Menelik. Waugh wrote: 'One photographer, bolder than the rest, advanced out of the crowd and planted his camera within a few yards of the royal party; he wore a violet suit of plus-fours, a green shirt open at the neck, tartan stockings, and particoloured shoes.'[36] Thesiger, in turn, mocked Waugh's grey suede shoes, his floppy bow tie and his fashionably wide trouser legs: 'he struck me as flaccid and petulant and I disliked him on sight'.[37] During the 'preposterous Alice in Wonderland fortnight'[38] at Addis Ababa, Waugh gathered enough material for two books: the satirical novel *Black Mischief* and *Remote People*, a prime specimen of his 'impeccable' acid-etched prose, which Thesiger praised, yet thought was wasted on descriptions of trivia such as the red flannel underclothes worn by Haile Selassie's temperamental German house-keeper.[39] His dislike of Waugh was confirmed by Waugh's disparaging references to the new Emperor in *Remote People*: 'Haile Selassie (Power of the Trinity) ... is the new name which the emperor has assumed among his other titles; a heavy fine is threatened to anyone overheard referring to him as Tafari. The words have become variously corrupted by the European visitors to "Highly Salacious" and "I love a lassie" – this last the inspiration of a RAC mechanic.'[40]

Sir John Maffey discouraged Thesiger's plan to hunt big game in the Sudan after the ceremonies were over. Thesiger wrote: 'I talked it over with Sir John, and he said if there was a chance of a shoot here take it, as a Soudan shoot would be terribly expensive. A licence costs £50 and I could not have got round it.' He declined Sir Sidney Barton's proposal that he should join his and Lord Airlie's hunting party in the Arussi Mountains, insisting that he needed to hunt by himself to gain confidence and experience for the future.[41] Colonel Dan Sandford, who served under Wilfred Gilbert Thesiger in 1913 and had become a friend of the family, advised Wilfred to hunt in the Danakil country; owing to the Danakil tribes' murderous reputation it was avoided by Abyssinians, and game was plentiful. Thesiger delighted in recounting Barton's solemn warning: 'He said: "Don't go further down the Awash than Bilen. If you get yourself cut up by the Danakil, it would rather spoil the effect of the show [the coronation]."'[42] Presaging his later style of travel and exploration, Thesiger wrote: 'I am taking camels for transport as there are two longish marches over the desert.'[43] His godmother Mrs Backhouse, herself a keen hunter, lent him her .318 Westley Richards magazine rifle. From Colonel Sandford at Mullu he borrowed a double-barrelled .400 Jeffery, a more powerful weapon than the .318, in case he decided to hunt (or else encountered) buffalo in the extensive reedbeds at Bilen. Sandford also lent him one of his most trusted employees, a Somali named Ali Yaya who was 'a first class headman', together with 'their 2nd cook and a boy'.[44] The Abyssinian government provided four armed *askaris* as an escort. Thesiger wrote: 'I am naturally hopelessly excited at the idea. It is what I have always longed to do above all things, and the Hawash [sic] is the best shooting left in Abyssinia.'[45]

Before he left Addis Ababa Thesiger met Major R.E. Cheesman, who had served as Consul at Dangila in north-west Abyssinia from 1925 to 1929. In 1926 Cheesman published a book of his travels, *In Unknown Arabia*. His account of Lake Tana and the Blue Nile followed ten years later. Cheesman remembered talking on the steps of the Legation to Thesiger, who said: '"I want to do some exploring. Is there anywhere I could go?" I told him he was rather late in the field; that areas round the North Pole and the South Pole were all that had been left. He said he was not interested in cold countries. I then reminded him that there was a nice hot spot down in the Danakil desert and that nobody had explored it to find out where the Awash river went to.'[46]

On 15 November he wrote to Kathleen: 'I am off tomorrow ... The Government decided our activities were to be confined to 3 heads apiece. (The Minister [Sir Sidney Barton] and Airlie are also going on a safari). Abyssinian humour ...' Lord Airlie and Barton planned to hunt nyala in the Arussi mountains with the Duke of Gloucester, who also hunted in British Somaliland, long before popularised by Captain H.G.C. Swayne's *Seventeen Trips Through Somaliland* (1895) and *Two Dianas in Somaliland*, written by Agnes Herbert in 1908.

From Sade Malka, roughly halfway to Bilen, Thesiger wrote: 'Everything is going very well ... So far I have shot one Soemering's gazelle and one oryx with a good head, also a bush pig.' He shot and wounded other game, but missed eight shots at a long-necked gerenuk antelope. Three attempts to shoot a buffalo in the reedbeds at Bilen also failed. At target practice with the .318 his shots went high, perhaps due to its brass cartridges being overheated by the sun, or the deceiving effect of strong sunlight when judging distances.

Thesiger's much-scarred Danakil *shikari*, Moussa Hamma, wore an earring indicating he had killed ten men. This 'most pernicious custom' at first shocked Wilfred, yet it also excited him: 'I accepted the fact that among the Danakil a man's status depended on the number of other men he had killed. They castrated their victims, and this I also accepted. I've always believed ... killing is natural to men.'[47] By killing and castrating other men, Danakil warriors demonstrated their maleness and superiority. Robbed of its symbolic virility, a castrated corpse was no longer the corpse of a 'true man'. In Thesiger's view, the Danakils' savage ethos comprised nothing more or less than the survival of the fittest, and the triumph of will over adversity or weakness. He acknowledged that, judged by Western standards, the Danakil style of killing appeared cowardly and totally dishonourable. Warriors had no qualms about murdering an unsuspecting victim. They made no distinction between warriors they killed in a skirmish, and unarmed men they stalked like animals in the bush and shot in the back. Thesiger said: 'It wasn't up to me to judge them. What mattered to me was the danger; the excitement; the challenge. I sensed it at Bilen, where Itu Galla raiders had killed a man just before we arrived. Then there was the river ...'[48] He wrote in *The Danakil Diary*: 'At Bilen I had watched the Awash flowing northwards through the desert to its unknown destination. Ali, my headman, had constantly made enquiries on my behalf, and had told me that the local Danakil said that the Awash ended against a great mountain in Aussa, where there were many lakes and forests; this however was hearsay. I had felt then the lure of the unknown, the urge to go where no white man had been, and I was determined, as soon as I had taken my degree, to return to Abyssinia to follow the Awash to its end.'[49]

Thesiger recalled in 1996: 'Back at Oxford I thought incessantly about that month I had spent among the Danakil. I had gone down there to hunt, but this journey meant far more to me than just the excitement of hunting. The whole course of my life was to be permanently affected by that month. There had been the constant and exciting possibility of danger ... with no possibility of our getting help if we needed it. The responsibility had been mine and, even though I was only twenty years old at the time, men's lives had depended on my judgement. I had been among tribesmen who had never had any contact with a world other than their own.'[50] He often spoke of that 'decisive' month's hunting on the Awash, yet it had been Cheesman's suggestion that he should explore the river to its unmapped end that fired his imagination. But, to spare his mother needless anxiety, he refrained for the time being from mentioning in his letters his life-changing discussion with Cheesman. Thesiger realised how Kathleen missed his father; how, despite bringing up four sons and leading a busy social life at 'The Little Mile', she often felt lonely. He knew that if he were to die, the loss would break her heart. Yet he sensed that his mother would understand, ultimately, better than anyone, what the possibility of exploring the Awash river meant to him.

Despite 'the constant and exciting possibility of danger'[51] from wild animals and wild tribes, Thesiger's safari to Bilen had involved a lesser risk than the exploration of the unmapped Awash. The trip to Bilen had been a necessary, 'wonderful experience'.[52] It was an all-important step that made the stuff of Thesiger's boyhood dreams reality. Everything in his young life from the age of three, batting an empty cartridge case at birds in the garden,[53] to nineteen, stalking red deer in Sutherland, seemed like a preparation for the thrilling moments when he shot his first African animals (a jackal and a Soemering's gazelle 'with quite a good head'[54]) on 17 November 1930, near the Awash station.

81

Thesiger's safari ended on 11 December at Afdam, in the Galla country east of the Awash, on the railway line from Jibuti to Addis Ababa. Among the Galla he had 'an unpleasant feeling ... of being in a hostile country ... constantly being watched from the hilltops'[55] by tribesmen who vanished as the safari approached. He spent most of 9 December hunting. In failing light he fired at what he thought was a greater kudu, screened by thick bush; instead he wounded a male lesser kudu that dashed away before dropping dead after a hundred yards. A greater kudu, with its impressive spiralled horns, would have made a perfect trophy, a perfect end to the adventure; the lesser kudu, though the best he had killed, seemed like an anticlimax.

He rounded off his month's safari by visiting C.H.F. Plowman, the British Consul at Harar. 'The Ploughmans [sic] have offered to send a horse to Dire Dawa for me to ride up to Harrer [sic] on the way home if I like. I should love to see Harrer.'[56] In *The Danakil Diary*, he wrote: 'Rode round Harar in the evening ... the town has a chocolate appearance. It is situated on a small hill ... The Harari people are quite different from the surrounding Galla and are much lighter in colour ... The women look very bright in their Harari clothes. Red, yellow and orange are the favourite colours.'[57] 'It is incredible, however, the number [of people in Harar] that are blind in one eye.'[58]

NINE

The Mountains of Arussi

Haile Selassie's coronation, and the shooting safari that followed, added glamour to Thesiger's forbidding reputation as a boxer. Among strangers, without some coaxing, he still felt reluctant to talk about his experiences. Within his circle of family and close friends, however, he proved to be an excellent storyteller. He was also an attentive listener. While his stories were often amusing, he never told jokes. He said: 'I don't begin to understand this fascination by humour and, besides, I always think I've got none. Things people tell me make me laugh. When I see them written down I don't find them so funny.'[1] Thesiger's high-pitched, throaty cackle exposed his gums and his small, discoloured teeth. When he laughed, his whole face lit up, his eyes glittered, his bushy brown eyebrows arched expressively. Yet some people who met Thesiger for the first time found him bloodless and distant. One visitor described him as 'rather blank, with penetrating eyes that look as though they haven't seen much to laugh about'.[2] This impression was accurate, but it portrayed only one aspect of his personality.

Meeting Robin Campbell at Oxford helped to bring Wilfred out of his shell. In this new, unfamiliar setting, Campbell, who was two years younger than him, filled a void in Thesiger's emotional life. Thesiger told an interviewer: 'He was one of the gilded youths of Oxford. He had the looks and the charm of Rupert Brooke. Everyone was trying to get hold of him and the fact that this most sought after person actually liked spending time with me, brought out my self-confidence. After that, I assumed, for the first time really, that people could like me.'[3] In his seventies, Thesiger recalled his feelings in more detail: 'It was love ... I wanted to hold him in my arms ... But I always feared any advances would spoil a very close friendship. My feelings for Robin were romantic feelings, whereas Val ffrench Blake was interesting to talk to.' He added, somewhat unjustly, 'Perhaps there was not much more to Robin Campbell than his looks.'⁴

Furtive embraces and voyeuristic encounters set a pattern for Thesiger's sexual life from then on. His photography expressed this very clearly. He viewed his male subjects as forbidden objects of desire, signalling his feelings for them by his choice of pose and his sensitive handling of light and shadow. The beauty of his images derived in part from the unconscious revelation of these suppressed feelings to the viewer, as much as from Thesiger's skilful composition and his intuitive ability to capture and record what he called 'the exact moment caught or lost forever'.⁵ When he wrote, 'Sex has been of no great consequence to me, and the celibacy of desert life left me untroubled,' he meant exactly that. He insisted that the concept of physical sex, with men or women, revolted him: 'I should have liked to have children. It was what I needed to do in order to get children that put me off.'⁶

Thesiger never explained, or may have been unable to explain, why he was revolted by the physical act of sex. He dismissed most attempts to analyse his motives and thought processes as 'rubbish' and saw no point in discussing or exploring the source of this revulsion. It may have originated in Lang's abusive bathtime inspections, in being made to feel ashamed for 'playing with' himself, or perhaps from embarrassingly bungled experiments in lovemaking while he was in his teens. He dealt with it by spurning physical sex, by channelling his energy and emotions into dangerous, self-testing pursuits: big game hunting, exploration, remote travel. Boxing gave him 'savage satisfaction'; broken bones and torn lips were tangible reminders of his Danakil *shikari* Moussa's scarred arms and body.

On 30 September 1929 Thesiger had been elected a member of the Travellers Club in Pall Mall, proposed by his uncle Edward Vigors and seconded by Sir Ralph Verney, and as part of his blossoming social life at Oxford he joined clubs including the Raleigh, Vincent's and the Gridiron. He described this period in *The Life of My Choice* as 'getting over the feeling of rejection instilled into me at St Aubyn's' and discovering that 'most people were only too willing to be friendly if I gave them a chance'.⁷

In the summer of 1931 he sailed with a Hull trawler to fishing grounds off Iceland's southern coast. They skirted the Faroes, 'an awe-inspiring sight, with the sea thundering against great black precipices and hurling scattered sheets of spray high up the face of the rock; above this turmoil a host of wheeling, screeching sea birds showed white against the cliffs'. Of the gruelling labour, Thesiger wrote: 'I remember the brief darkness at midnight when the arc lamps lit the decks; the interminable hours of daylight; the unceasing work with men too tired to talk; the hurried meals; the luxury of sleep when we were moving from one fishing ground to another.'[8] These wonderful descriptions recalled memories of hours spent in the *Sorrento*'s bunkers the previous year, 'hard, hot, dirty, choking work' shovelling coal, and would be echoed in later memories of his first desert journey, across the French Sahara: exhausting, marvellous days ending in 'tired surrender to sleep'.[9] As a memento of his trip to Iceland, Thesiger kept a letter written on 28 July 1931 by R.P. Ross of the steam trawler owners, F. & T. Ross, West Dock Avenue, Hull: 'Just a line to let you know we have sent this morning two haddocks, two lemon soles, and one halibut to ... The Milebrook ... Hoping you are feeling no ill effects from your voyage ... PS The Pelton [Thesiger's vessel] landed 578 kits [i.e. barrels] and made £380.'[10]

On 8 October 1931, Kathleen Thesiger remarried at the age of fifty-one. Her second husband, Reginald Basil Astley, was sixty-nine. Astley was a childless widower whose first wife, Caroline Douglas Stewart, had died in 1921. A cousin of the twentieth Baron Hastings of Melton Constable, Norfolk and Seaton Delaval, Northumberland, he was an Old Etonian. He owned a villa on Lake Como and the Weir House, Alresford, Hampshire, whose tranquil setting included a trout stream and closely mown lawns shaded by ancient cedars. According to the Weir House visitors' book, Kathleen Thesiger had been a fairly frequent guest there since at least 1927.

In his 1931 Milebrook diary Thesiger mentioned only briefly his mother's engagement to this elderly, white-haired gentleman of leisure, whose dilettante interests included art, architecture, the lineage of noble families and, of course, trout fishing. Thesiger wrote on 20 August 1931: 'Mrs T's engagement to R Astley made public.' This was a mistake; between 'made' and 'public', Thesiger scribbled hastily, 'not yet'. The following day he wrote firmly: 'Mrs T's engagement made public. [Wilfred's godmother] Mrs Backhouse ... arrived for tea. W[ilfred] and B[rian] shot pigeons in the afternoon.'¹¹ Thesiger 'never thought it odd' that Kathleen announced her engagement to Astley on the anniversary of her wedding to Wilfred Gilbert Thesiger. To some the engagement seemed ill-timed, but it is conceivable that, by overmarking one anniversary with another, Kathleen intended to signal that her life had moved on. Whether or not this was the case, her memory of Wilfred Gilbert never faded, nor did her love for him diminish.

Thesiger wrote nothing about the wedding in his diary. On 6 October Kathleen left for London by the mid-morning train.¹² Wilfred took the same train the following morning.¹³ By coincidence, Kathleen had married Thesiger's father at St Peter's church, Eaton Square, and her second marriage took place at another St Peter's (as it was then), which stood almost next door to her brother-in-law Percy Thesiger's porticoed, red-brick London house, number 25 Cranley Gardens in South Kensington.

To begin with, Thesiger and his brothers had regarded Reginald Astley as a joke; later on, they realised his qualities as a man and an amateur historian. At The Milebrook, Thesiger said, 'Reggie had his own room, opposite mine. It was a marriage of companionship. My mother dominated him, but not unpleasantly. She was a stronger character ... that's all it amounted to.'¹⁴ Thesiger knew how lonely his mother had been, and felt relieved that she had found a congenial companion for her old age, when her sons had left home. But later he would reflect that the marriage 'didn't in fact work very well'.¹⁵ Of the four brothers, Roderic got on best with their new stepfather. Not only did he share Astley's fascination with pictures and architecture,¹⁶ but, being the youngest, he had almost no recollection of Wilfred Gilbert, whereas Wilfred inevitably made comparisons between his father and stepfather that did not always favour Astley.

Kathleen endeavoured always to be fair in her treatment of her sons. She loved them all and showed no obvious favouritism, although Thesiger later said that in those days she had felt closest to Dermot, with whom she shared a passion for horses. Thesiger had ridden since early boyhood, but by his late teens his passion for shooting took precedence over everything else. He came to regard horses as 'silly creatures, and inferior to camels'.¹⁷ Whilst Dermot had adored his horses, Thesiger would claim that no animal he ever owned, not even his beloved spaniels, meant as much to him as Faraj Allah, the beautiful Bisharin female camel he acquired in the Sudan.[18]

For a blissful fortnight in the summer of 1932, Thesiger and six friends from Oxford stayed at the Villa Cipressi, Reginald Astley's house on the shore of Lake Como. The party included Robin Campbell, Harry Phillimore, Edward Ford, Bill Peat, Tony Rumbold and John Schuster. All were Etonians, except for Campbell, who had been educated at Wellington. They swam in the lake, waterskied and sunbathed naked on the lawns among flowering magnolias. 'After dinner,' Thesiger wrote, 'we would sit looking out over the three arms of the lake and talk until, drowsy with sun, swimming, food and wine, we went off to bed.'[19] It all seemed perfect, yet this vacation marked a waning of Thesiger's once-inseparable friendship with Robin Campbell. Forty years later, Tony (then Sir Anthony) Rumbold invited the two men to lunch, hoping their lapsed friendship might be revived. To Rumbold's disappointment (and Thesiger's), nothing came of this. Rumbold said: 'It didn't go very well. Their old friendship had gone and the atmosphere was rather a cold one. I thought it was sad. Robin had been wounded and had his leg amputated during the war. I think this affected Wilfred, who wanted to remember Robin as he was when we were all young. Perfect – you know, like a Greek god.'[20]

After Brian Thesiger's godfather, Major Charles Doughty-Wylie, was killed in Italy in 1915, his widow Judith 'constituted herself' as Brian's godmother.[21] Rich and manipulative, Judith later promised Brian that, if he changed his name to Doughty-Wylie, he would inherit her money. Thesiger said: 'Like my father before me, I grew up to be proud of my family. Nothing on earth could have induced me to do this. My mother, however, told us: "You mustn't interfere. You must allow Brian to do as he wishes ... It is up to Brian to decide."'[22] When he left Oxford, Brian joined Doughty-Wylie's regiment, the Royal Welch Fusiliers, and on 26 September 1933 he changed his name by deed poll from Thesiger to Doughty-Wylie. Wilfred and Brian remained as close as before, yet Thesiger admitted that he had found it difficult to understand, or approve of, his brother's decision: 'Brian was still Brian, but I suppose, in a way, I always resented what he had done.'[23]

The two brothers had been inseparable since they were small children. As Thesiger never tired of repeating, everything connected with his early childhood at Addis Ababa was vitally important to him. His first nine years, he firmly believed, influenced the whole of his life. He had enshrined those halcyon days and years, obliterating from his memory anything that might have tarnished their unalloyed perfection. Nothing he remembered of his upbringing in Abyssinia was less than idyllic. To achieve this, Thesiger needed to separate the wheat from the chaff, and to do so fairly ruthlessly. Like everyone, he saw as much as he wanted to see, and turned a blind eye to anything he preferred to ignore. But he tended to carry this normal self-protective process to an extreme. He came very close on occasions to reinventing his early boyhood years in order to harmonise them with the idealised, almost mythical, decade which inspired his extraordinary adult life as a world-famous explorer and traveller. Everything that Thesiger said or wrote about his early life was true. But he did not always tell the whole story, and the fascinating detail he chose to reveal was viewed through a rose-tinted lens, from his determinedly self-orientated, exclusive and sometimes quixotic perspective. Thesiger's father, his mother, his younger brothers, his nurse Susannah, his 'cherished confidante' Minna Buckle, the Legation servants and staff, his father's Consuls scattered across the length and breadth of Abyssinia, even animals and birds in the garden and the hills round his home, became indispensable cast members in this childhood drama. When he left Abyssinia in 1919, the first chapter in his life had closed. In a real sense, as well as metaphorically, his selective memories of those years were sealed off and preserved forever, embalmed and perfectly incorruptible.

The person closest to Wilfred in age, who shared these experiences, was his brother Brian. While Brian had featured in many of the juvenile episodes recorded in *The Life of My Choice* and *Desert, Marsh and Mountain*, Thesiger erased him from other events, including adventures with his father such as the viceregal tiger-shoot at Jaipur, at which both boys had been present. Thesiger said: 'The books I wrote described my life and the things I'd done. When we were children, Brian and I went everywhere together ... almost everything we did then, we did together ... We were together at St Aubyn's ... later at Eton, and at Oxford ... It's true, we were very close, and yet Brian was so different from me. He wasn't affected by our life in Abyssinia in the same way I was ... He was always wasting his time, chasing about after girls.'[24] Thesiger's mother and father had hoped for a daughter, yet his mother told a visitor, years afterwards: 'If I'd had a daughter, I'd have drowned it at birth!'[25] Kathleen had been joking, of course, unlike T.E. Lawrence's mother when she made her jealous remark: 'We could never be bothered with girls in our house.'[26]

During his fourth year at Oxford, Thesiger spent more and more time with his brother Dermot, who was by then an undergraduate at Magdalen. He wrote: 'Roddy did not go up to Oxford until the year after I had left. Dermot and I had been together at Eton but then Dermot was one of the Lower boys who came when I shouted "Boy". Now we were grown up and the difference in our ages was immaterial.'[27] Dermot was tall, slender and handsome. His memories of Abyssinia were at best very vague. Travelling abroad did not appeal to him – he used to say he never wanted to go further than Dover. Highly intelligent and witty, Dermot followed in his great-grandfather the first Lord Chelmsford's footsteps and was called to the Bar after he left Oxford. Like his great-grandfather he had his heart set on a political career: 'his dream [was] to become Prime Minister'.[28]

Thesiger sometimes took Dermot with him to tea at Elsfield Manor, John Buchan's house near Oxford. Buchan was President of the university's Exploration Club, and Wilfred wrote to him in 1931 asking for advice. He had read Buchan's novels as a boy, starting with *Prester John* at St Aubyn's. In 1969 he remembered: 'I became a passionate John Buchanite, I read every one [of his books] as it came out and I tried to emulate his style. I never tire of his books and I can read them now with pleasure at every moment.'[29] Twenty years later, Thesiger's opinion of Buchan's writing was still high, but more critical: 'Reading *The Thirty-Nine Steps* again, I enjoyed it. But it does feel dated. I don't mean the story and the settings, but the writing – just a bit.'[30] When he described John Buchan, Thesiger might have been describing his own father: 'I can still picture him as I knew him, his sensitive ascetic face etched with lines of pain but lit by his innate kindliness, his lean body in comfortable country tweeds. Although a man of many and varied accomplishments, he remained a countryman at heart.'[31] Thesiger's uncle, Frederic Chelmsford, had been cast in a similar mould as 'a patrician in the Roman tradition, cultured, erudite, civilised'.[32] Chelmsford was a keen fisherman and shot who spent his summers at Otterburn and Wark, in Northumberland, whose 'wild black moors' his brother Wilfred Gilbert had celebrated in verse. Thesiger recalled the thrill of catching a fifteen-pound salmon there, in a racing river swollen by torrential rain. He wrote in 1987: 'No excitement in my life has ever quite equalled the tense fifteen minutes during which I was connected to that fish.'[33] This was an apt metaphor for Thesiger's relationships with his younger companions. Much of the excitement and interest lay in the first contact and his gaining absolute control.

During his years at Oxford, Thesiger often discussed his plans to explore the Awash river with his mother, his brothers, friends and relatives, including John Buchan and his uncle Lord Chelmsford. In April 1933 his uncle collapsed and died, like Wilfred's father and grandfather, of a sudden heart attack. Since he had first stayed at Otterburn at the age of seventeen, Thesiger's feelings of alarm and awe in his uncle's presence had gradually been replaced by increasing affection. Chelmsford became a father figure, and when he died Wilfred felt 'a sense of desolation'.[34] He wrote: 'My uncle intended to contribute to the cost of my Danakil expedition. In *The Life of My Choice*, I said my aunt insisted I should receive the sum he had meant to give me. This, in fact, wasn't quite right. Aunt Francie was well-off, but she was – you know – very careful, and she only gave me half of the money that Uncle Fred had promised to give me.'[35] Thesiger partly funded the expense of the Awash expedition by selling some gold rings which Haile Selassie's son and heir, the Crown Prince Asfa Wossen, had given him during a visit to London. The rings made £400. The President of Magdalen, George Gordon, donated £50 on behalf of the college. Thesiger also received a grant of £125 from the Royal Geographical Society; and another of £250 from the Linnean Society's Percy Sladen Memorial Trust. The British Museum of Natural History in South Kensington promised to buy any suitable specimens of birds and mammals he had collected, and from various firms he acquired provisions, cartridges, medicines and supplies of film, either at a discount or free of charge. Definitions of the purpose of the expedition altered, it appears, according to the sponsor's agenda. A letter from Dr S.A. Neave, Assistant Director of the Imperial Institute of Entomology, stated that Thesiger was 'undertaking a zoological expedition to Abyssinia ... His primary object will be to collect material for the British Museum (Natural History), and he also hopes that he may be able to obtain data for this Institute, which is officially recognised by all countries in Africa as the international centre for receiving and coordinating information respecting migratory locusts.'[36] Predating by more than a decade Thesiger's famous investigations of locust outbreak-centres in Arabia, Dr Neave observed that in the Danakil country beyond the end of the Awash river, 'it is possible that breeding areas of the desert locust ... or other migratory species occur there'.[37]

At Thesiger's request, Sir Sidney Barton, the British Minister at Addis Ababa, obtained the Emperor's permission for the expedition to follow the Awash to its end. Barton informed Thesiger that 'permission could not be obtained for your expedition to leave Aussa via the French Somaliland frontier, so I am afraid you will have to be content with the Hawash section ... fever in the [Awash] valley is very bad in October and ... it is not really safe to start until the beginning of December – after which it is alright up to May. Conditions in the lower valley are presumably worse, so if you want to avoid mortality among your followers I think you should bear this in mind.'[38] Barton's approach to Haile Selassie was backed by a letter from the Secretary of the Royal Geographical Society. Instead of geographical discovery (as might have been expected), the Society's letter, like that from the Imperial Institute of Entomology, emphasised that Thesiger's main objective was 'to study the distribution and life history of locusts'. The letter nowhere mentioned exploration, but only stated vaguely: 'These travellers wish to undertake surveys and photography.'[39] Thesiger was unable to clarify why the purpose of his expedition had been described (quite distinctly and separately) as zoology, entomology, surveying and photography instead of his own definition, 'to follow the Awash river into the fabulous Sultanate of Aussa and discover how and where it ended'. Rather than collecting birds, insects, mammals and plants, it was the 'lure of the unknown' and the challenge 'presented by the murderous company of the Danakil and the physical difficulties of the journey [that had proved] irresistible'.[40]

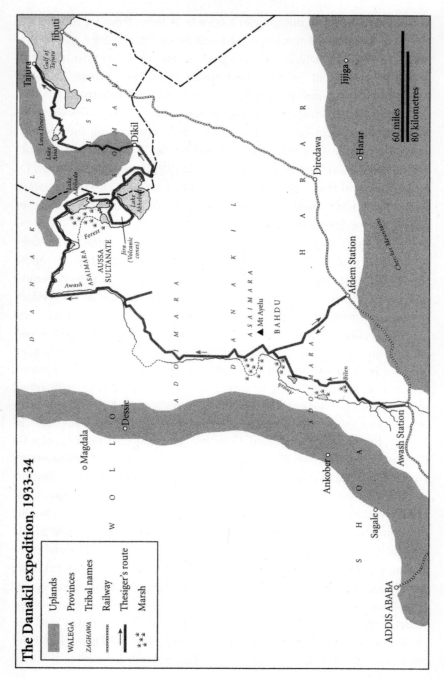

The Danakil expedition, 1933–34

Uplands
WALEGA **Provinces**
ZAGHAWA **Tribal names**
Railway
Thesiger's route
Marsh

60 miles
80 kilometres

Tajura

Jibuti

Gulf of Tajura

Lake Desert

Lake Asal

Dikil

Lake Adaibada

Lake Abhebad

Forest

Jira (Volcanic cones)

ASAIMARA

AUSSA SULTANATE

Awash

D A N A K I L

A D O I M A R A

D A N A K I L

A S A I M A R A

Mt Ayelu

BAHDU

Awash

Bilen

A D O I M A R A

Dessie

Magdala

W O L L O

Ankober

Sagale

S H O A

ADDIS ABABA

Awash Station

Afdem Station

Diredawa

Harar

Jijiga

H A R A R

Cherchet Mountains

I S S A

S O M A L I S

92

Once again, Colonel Dan Sandford helped Wilfred to assemble his caravan, while Kathleen gave her son encouragement as well as practical support. Thesiger said: 'My mother was a naturally possessive woman. She knew very well what the dangers were, and the risks I was running. Yet, in spite of this, she did all she could to help me – getting in touch with people, everything.'[41] Kathleen knew that an Egyptian army commanded by Werner Munzinger had been annihilated by Danakil tribesmen in 1875, between Tajura and the eastern border of Aussa. In 1881 Giulietti and Biglieri's expedition was massacred, and in 1884 a second Italian party led by Bianchi, Diana and Monari suffered the same fate. She and Wilfred had discussed these massacres, and also Ludovico Mariano Nesbitt's account of his Danakil expedition, published in October 1930 in the *Geographical Journal*. Although Nesbitt had escaped with his life, only to die in a plane crash in 1935, three of his servants were murdered during the journey he later described in his book *Desert and Forest*, which Thesiger reviewed favourably after he had returned from his 1933–34 expedition.

Understandably, Kathleen insisted that her son must find a companion. It was the last thing Wilfred wanted, but for his mother's sake he agreed. Evelyn Waugh had asked 'at second-hand' if he could accompany him. Thesiger dramatised his refusal in *The Life of My Choice*: 'Had he come, I suspect only one of us would have returned.'[42] Apart from mapping the river's end, among his other tasks Thesiger intended to collect as many bird specimens as possible from the Danakil country. Preferably, the companion he chose needed to be a skilled ornithologist, and to be able to shoot any specimens they required. Thesiger approached Peter Markham Scott, son of the Antarctic explorer, a gifted field naturalist, an ornithologist, a painter of birds and portraits who had trained at the Royal Academy Schools and would exhibit at the Royal Academy from 1933 onwards. Nine months older than Thesiger, Scott had graduated from Trinity College, Cambridge. Thesiger said: 'Peter's mother, Lady Kennet, invited me to tea. She asked me a lot of questions: why I wanted to discover where the river ended; who the Danakil were; was there any danger involved, and so on. Well, there it was … I said, yes, it would be dangerous … and that was the point of doing it. Then she said: "I am sorry, Mr Thesiger, but in view of the risk I cannot possibly consent to my son coming with you." Well, if my mother had said that about me, I'd have been absolutely furious.'[43]

Robert Robertson, a young Scotsman, had hoped to accompany Thesiger, but his father Sir William Robertson opposed the idea – like Lady Kennet, on the grounds that it was too dangerous.[44] In the end, Thesiger agreed that David Haig-Thomas should join him. Haig-Thomas's credentials, in every respect, seemed ideal. His chief interests included ornithology and photography, and he had boxed at Eton as a bantamweight in the school's annual competition in March 1925. Perhaps his most important contribution would be persuading Thesiger to buy a Leica II 35mm miniature camera. As a beginner, Wilfred had previously used an old Kodak box camera that once belonged to his father. He took this simpler camera with him to Abyssinia and used it together with his brand-new Leica, unaware that it was faulty, as a result of which many of its negatives were cropped.

David Haig-Thomas's family contributed £250 to the cost of the expedition, raising Thesiger's credit balance to £1075. In addition, from his late uncle Lord Chelmsford's estate he received £50, £30 from Brian, £25 from Kathleen's brother Ashmead Vigors, and a further £20 from Magdalen College. In a letter from Addis Ababa, dated 23 December 1933, Thesiger stated that the expedition had cost £1500; this meant either that he and his mother between them must have added a further £300 of their own money to the other contributions, or else that he had managed to save this from the annuity left to him after his grandmother, Lady Chelmsford, had died.

While Thesiger continued to read for his final examinations at Oxford, and to raise funds for the Awash expedition, Colonel Sandford commuted between his farm at Mullu and Addis Ababa, arranging temporary accommodation, permits, baggage animals, men and supplies. The letters he wrote between June and August indicate how much trouble he had taken on Wilfred's behalf. A letter from Addis Ababa dated 8 June 1933 discusses important details of the forthcoming expedition. Having helped to organise Thesiger's first safari, in 1930, Sandford knew his strengths and weaknesses. He wrote: 'I came here from the farm yesterday largely in order to get going with your preparations. I saw Barton who told me that ... you would get your permits to explore from the Hawash

Station to the point where the Hawash disappears into the ground ... Sir Sidney ... has taken a great deal of trouble for you, and so long as you don't take too much for granted (which old birds like us resent) he will do all he can to help. That is just a word of warning in season, so don't get hot under the collar!!' Assuming that the expedition's primary objectives were 'Survey and birds', Sandford proposed that Thesiger should also collect 'blood slides, lice, ticks, and so on' for the Tropical Diseases Hospital, or for the former head of medical services in the Sudan. While accepting that fever was 'pretty virulent' in the Awash valley, he reassured Wilfred that if he was careful, carried a good supply of 'the right medicines' and learnt how to treat his followers properly for malaria, 'especially in giving injections', he 'needn't be greatly afraid of it'. Sandford's headman, Umr, would buy '20 good camels' for £70 and 'ten riding mules' costing $80 (Abyssinian thalers) apiece – 'efficient', 'handy' transport for Thesiger, his interpreter, cook, tent boys and any sick whom 'you cannot leave ... on the roadside'. As for the headman and interpreter, Sandford wrote: 'I don't think you will do better than take Umr Wadai ... He is a Somali and was headman to Sir G[eoffrey] Archer and Duke of Gloucester. He is expensive but worth the money. He wanted $120 to $150, but I have cut him down to $100 per month plus rations ... I am looking around for a suitable No 2 to him – a man with knowledge of the Hawash valley and of all the languages there. Umr speaks English, Amharic and Galla perfectly but doesn't know the Danakil language.'[45] Thesiger noted: 'Umar had been with [the Sandfords] since he was a boy.'[46]

Colonel Sandford added a rough estimate of the cost of the expedition for the first four months, not counting provisions, camp equipment, weapons, ammunition and travelling expenses between England and Abyssinia: 'I should think £300 would cover your expenses in this country ... But I am not prepared to be called to book if it costs more! You may have to pay for game licences – say $100 each person, but this is not yet fixed.'[47] In fact, Thesiger was charged no less than 680 Abyssinian thalers for game licences. Either Sandford's estimate had been low, or, more likely, six licences were issued: one each for Thesiger, Haig-Thomas and four of their men.

On 13 July Sandford wrote to Umr instructing him to buy eight riding mules, including three 'good strong animals for the personal use of Mr Thesiger and the gentlemen with him', and fifteen 'first class baggage camels suitable for work in the valley of the Hawash',[48] complete with baggage saddles and other equipment, and a man to look after them. As protection against 'the Hawash type of "malignant" malaria', a Dr Lambie recommended Atebrin, Plasmocin and Plasmocin C, Emetin and Yatren for dysentery, and Neo-Salvarsan for tick or relapsing fever. Thesiger had enquired about free railway passes in Abyssinia, and the possibility of hunting along the Abyssinia–Sudan border. Sandford replied: 'I don't think you'll get a free railway ticket, but I'll enquire whether reductions are ever made to scientists!' As for 'trekking along the Sudan border in search of game', he doubted that this would be worthwhile.[49] By the end of August, Thesiger decided that he and Haig-Thomas would delay starting the expedition to avoid the Awash's worst malarial season, and would spend two months hunting nyala and other game in the Arussi mountains.

The mountain nyala, a large antelope that resembled the greater kudu, was only found in the highlands of Arussi and Bale, where the hunter-naturalist Edward North Buxton had discovered it as recently as 1910. Since then, few had been shot by sportsmen. On 23 November 1933, David Haig-Thomas's father Peter, who had himself hunted in the Arussi, wrote to Kathleen, who had sent him one of Wilfred's letters from there: 'Many thanks for letting me read such an interesting letter. They evidently went further South than I did in the Arussi Mts. I saw 73 female nyala but never a male.' Such numerous sightings were evidently exceptional. Thesiger wrote in 1996: 'few Europeans had ever seen a mountain nyala, so Haig-Thomas and I were naturally eager to secure one'.[50]

Aware of his obligations to the Natural History Museum, Thesiger wanted to shoot specimens of k'ebero (or cuberow), also known as the Abyssinian wolf, as well as the blue-winged geese needed to expand the museum's collection, which at that time consisted of a single specimen brought back in 1868 after Napier's Magdala expedition.

Having been awarded a third-class degree in modern history, Thesiger returned from Oxford to The Milebrook. In the third and final volume of his Milebrook diary, his last entry, dated 18 April 1933, describes a fine day's birdwatching in the Elan Valley. He might have been describing a scene at Addis Ababa: 'Saw two kites. Both came out of oak trees on hill side. Very good view. Can this be one of the old ... ones and a new mate[?] Am certain there was only one there till now. Very exciting. Hunted round together. Ravens very demonstrative. A good afternoon.'[51]

On 24 August 1933 Thesiger and David Haig-Thomas travelled by train and ferry from London to Marseilles, and from there by the MM *Chermonceaux*, third class, to Jibuti. Apart from the £300 Sandford calculated they would need in Abyssinia, Thesiger had spent £389.3.11 equipping the expedition in England. The most expensive item had been foodstuffs, purchased in style at Fortnum & Mason at a cost of £208.8.10. Thesiger and Haig-Thomas each brought guns and miniature rifles (.22s firing lead bullets or dust-shot) for collecting birds, and big game rifles to shoot meat for their caravan, as well as trophies. Their large, comfortable tents were equipped with verandahs, and they would dine off folding tables laid with tablecloths, cutlery and glass, shaded from the sun by a parasol with fringes like an enormous lampshade. Thesiger commented: 'I travelled then as my father had travelled in the past, like an Englishman in Africa.'[52]

They were met on 8 September at Addis Ababa by Sandford and Frank de Halpert, a banker who knew Thesiger and his family. Umr Wadai, 'a tall, powerfully-built, middle-aged Somali',[53] was with Sandford. Umr was to be Thesiger's loyal, trusted companion for the next nine months. The Sandfords provided Wilfred with an excellent cook, Habta Mariam, who was elderly, frail, yet very sturdy. The first supper Habta Mariam prepared, from ducks shot at Mojjo, 'tasted delicious, a happy augury for future meals'.[54]

Guided by Umr, they engaged two Somalis, Abdullahi and Said Munge, as gunbearers, and, as head *syce*, and later assistant to Umr, a middle-aged Amhara named Kassimi. Goutama, Kassimi's assistant, had worked as a young *syce* at the Legation when Thesiger was a boy. He was a devout Christian, of slave origin, and very dark-skinned. The camels Umr had already purchased, and their Somali camelmen, awaited Thesiger and his party at the Awash station.

After an audience with the Emperor at Addis Ababa on 22 September, Thesiger and Haig-Thomas spent a week with Dan and Christine Sandford in their charming, mud-walled, thatched farmhouse at Mullu.

On the Mullu river they shot six fat blue-winged geese. In *The Danakil Diary* Thesiger noted: 'we obtained several specimens for the museum'.[55] According to his unpublished 'Notes on the Blue Winged Goose', however, between September and November they shot twenty adult geese – including the six at Mullu – and two goslings of this little-studied species, which, Thesiger observed, was 'a very silent bird for a goose'.[56]

The Arussi trek had scarcely got under way when a brigand, or *shifta*, stole a rifle from one of their followers. Thesiger described the incident briefly in *The Danakil Diary*, but an unpublished version taken from Haig-Thomas's diary is more detailed. To Thesiger the theft was of little consequence; to Haig-Thomas it had been an adventure: 'I was behind the caravan collecting birds but grabbed a rifle and followed by Said and Joseph raced along towards the shouting ... Having clubbed a Galla [the *shifta*] had seized his rifle and made off and was only a short way in front. WT being in front ... fired over his head and he dived into thick bush. I soon came up, and we gave up thinking he would escape through the bush. [Thesiger stated that he 'Followed him, very ticklish work as thick scrub and I thought he would fight.'] Umr and our syce kept him in view, got to close quarters and after firing close to his head he surrendered. He was bound all the time muttering "here you have me bound, if only I had some cartridges and was in the bush I could shoot you like rats" ... He had been a shifta for 9 years and had shot several men.'

In his version, Thesiger discreetly omitted to mention that they found on the *shifta* letters to a Fituarari: as Haig-Thomas wrote, 'a high personage in A[ddis] A[baba] saying "I am sorry I have not got you anything for so long and hope to get you something soon." He told us he had friends not far, and that they had been spying on the caravan the night before.' He added, maybe nervously: 'It is possible they may try to raid the camp tonight for a hostage.'[57] Later, at Chelalo, Haig-Thomas recorded graphically, they 'saw a man hanging from a tree, far from fresh. The hyenas could reach his legs and had eaten them. Umr says he was a shifta. I wonder why nature usually so beautiful has not evolved a more pleasant method of ridding herself of unwanted boddies [sic]?' He remained optimistic, however: 'we may see nyala tomorrow?'[58]

In a large, steep-sided valley at Mount Chelalo, they heard two k'ebero calling to one another across the valley east of the mountain. The animals made 'a most weird noise, faintly resembling a baboon's bark'.[59] On 6 October they shot a female k'ebero in heathland on the edge of a forest of causo trees. Haig-Thomas sighted two that were hunting for moles. The k'ebero were 'unafraid and curious', sometimes 'passing leisurely by within 20 yards'. In these highlands, Thesiger noted, k'ebero were 'quite tame', and 'evidently plentiful from the number of droppings seen'; the animals went about either singly or in pairs.[60] As well as birds and mammals, in Arussi Thesiger collected seventy-six plants and flowering shrubs, including cacti, yellow daisies, pale-blue and dark-blue delphiniums, and a 'round green ball [with an] orange flower [protruding] out of it' supported on a single stem, which was perhaps a marigold or a dahlia.[61]

On 8 October, by mistake David Haig-Thomas tracked and shot two nyala. Thesiger wrote in *The Danakil Diary*: 'He jumped one in thick bush and saw it hide soon after in another patch of thick heather. Stalked it and shot at it, when it apparently bolted. Fired four more shots and killed it. Found the head very much smaller than he had thought. When Umar arrived with the mule, he found another one – the original one – lying dead where first shot at. A great nuisance as David only paid for one on his licence.'[62] Haig-Thomas observed ruefully: '[Umr] had arrived and found a nyala dead where I had first shot ... They must have been lying side by side and I should think the first nyala must have fallen on the second?'[63]

A few days later Thesiger saw through binoculars an 'extremely fine' bull nyala lying in the open, four hundred yards away. After an hour, the bull got up and started to graze. Thesiger made a careful stalk, on all fours, to within a hundred yards of the nyala, which now faced him. The moment it turned side on, he fired. The bull staggered, then recovered. Two more shots killed it. The nyala's horns measured forty-nine inches, 'an unofficial record'. For Haig-Thomas, this was a defining moment; a 'real triumph' for Thesiger, who noted with relief in his diary, 'I am so glad I did not take another indifferent head.'[64]

Travelling through the Arussi mountains gave Thesiger the opportunity to assess his followers and make any necessary changes before the Danakil expedition started. It also gave him and Haig-Thomas a chance to find out how they would fare as travelling companions, even though the hardships and stresses of their Arussi journey were slight compared with the dangers they would face in the Danakil. The high plateau felt bitterly cold. Thesiger's pony grew listless and died. The baggage mules sickened, due to fever or to bad grazing, and their stomachs distended. One had to be shot. Thesiger wrote: 'As long as they are kept on the move they keep alive, but die as soon as they are allowed to lie down.'[65]

By mid-November, David Haig-Thomas had developed painful ulcers on one leg and an abscess in his throat. Prickly grass seeds picked up in his socks caused Thesiger's right foot to itch and swell. Haig-Thomas's ulcers got worse. A doctor he met on a coffee plantation lanced the abscess, but soon afterwards he developed tonsillitis in both tonsils. Thesiger wrote: 'Four days after we had left the Daro [river] he decided to push on ahead with Kassimi, on our two best mules, in order to catch a train from the Awash Station to Addis Ababa for medical treatment.'[66] He continued: 'We reached the Awash Station on 25 November. Haig-Thomas was at the railway rest house. He had returned from Addis Ababa two days before, apparently cured, but his throat had now flared up again.'[67] Unable to speak, hardly able to walk, Haig-Thomas returned once more by train from the Awash station to Addis Ababa on 28 November. The following day he sent Thesiger a telegram: 'Cannot come.'[68]

Thesiger wrote in *The Danakil Diary*: 'I was content to be on my own, glad that I should have no need to accommodate myself to a fellow-countryman, that any decisions in the days ahead would be entirely mine. Haig-Thomas had been cheerful and good natured, and never once had we quarrelled. No one, indeed, could have been more easy-going; but we never got on close terms or found much in common during the four months we had been together since leaving England. I did not feel I should miss his company, and the fact that I should have no fellow-countryman with me to take charge if I fell sick or was wounded did not worry me, since I had every confidence in Umar.'[69]

In July 1934 David Haig-Thomas left England to spend a winter in the Arctic, as the ornithologist attached to the Oxford University Ellesmere Land Expedition led by Dr Noel Humphreys.[70]

TEN

Across the Sultanate of Aussa

David Haig-Thomas must have been bitterly disappointed when his health prevented him from rejoining the expedition. Thesiger's slightly ambivalent postscript to the Arussi journey and Haig-Thomas's departure published in *The Life of My Choice* was reprinted afterwards in *The Danakil Diary*. As usual, he wrote exclusively from his personal viewpoint, and did not mention either Haig-Thomas's disappointment or Kathleen's alarm when she heard the news that Wilfred would have to continue his expedition without Haig-Thomas as a companion. To Thesiger's dismay, Haig-Thomas arrived back in England before Kathleen received the letter Wilfred had written explaining David's departure. He said: 'When my mother learnt that David was back in England, she was absolutely horrified. He came down to The Milebrook and explained what had happened. My mother thought David hadn't behaved very well and that he shouldn't have left me, like that, on my own. I'm sure she was angry, and this was only to be expected. Anyhow, I felt rather relieved after he'd gone. In many ways he couldn't have been nicer, but he was odd ... I mean, he never brushed his teeth or took a bath. I don't think he ever read a book and, after a few days, we had nothing left to talk about.'[1]

Judging by his 1933 diary, Haig-Thomas had no idea how to spell, yet his descriptions were clear, sometimes vivid, and written in honest, unvarnished prose. Thesiger, it seems, made little or no effort to persuade him to rejoin the expedition after having his leg and throat treated at Addis Ababa. In his account of the journey published in *Desert, Marsh and Mountain* in 1979, Thesiger gave his view of Haig-Thomas very precisely: 'when we reached the railway he decided to go back to England.

101

I was glad to see him go, for though we had never quarrelled I found his presence an irritant and was happy now to be on my own. This was no fault of his, for he was good-natured and accommodating. Like many English travellers I find it difficult to live for long periods with my own kind.'²

Regardless of his feelings, Thesiger could not afford to remain camped at the Awash station until Haig-Thomas's leg and throat were cured. 'My immediate anxiety was that the authorities might forbid my journey, since the Asaimara of Bahdu had recently renounced their allegiance to the Government.'³ The Asaimara inhabited the Bahdu plain below Ayelu, one of the Danakils' three sacred mountains. Of the two main Danakil (or Afar) groups, the Asaimara, or Red Men, of Bahdu were more ferocious than the Adoimara, or White Men, who inhabited the rest of the country. Possibly Thesiger had used Haig-Thomas's afflictions as a convenient excuse to be rid of him. The two did not get on well enough to stand the strains of a difficult and dangerous journey; besides which, Thesiger would have been reluctant to share with Haig-Thomas, or anyone else, the 'discovery' of the Awash river's end. He later distanced himself from his indispensable headman, Umr, writing:

even for Omar [sic] I had felt no authentic friendship, regarding him rather as a trusted subordinate. He in turn expected me to distance myself from my followers, which he accepted as proper for an Englishman. For instance, he would have been upset if I had shared a meal with the camelmen. As a child at the Legation I had never known the intimate relationship with ayahs and bearers which many children in India had experienced. I had grown up accepting our servants as subordinates, distinct in colour, custom and behaviour. I undoubtedly had a feeling of superiority, since my father was the British Minister and I was his son. This feeling, however, certainly did not include colour prejudice, which is something I have never felt. Aesthetically, I regard white as the least attractive colour for skin.⁴

While Thesiger paid a handsome tribute to Umr, 'He and he alone had made possible my seemingly unattainable goal,'⁵ he added a proviso: 'Umr carried out my instructions, kept my caravan together and negotiated with the Sultan in Aussa. But I had been the driving force behind the expedition.'[6]

At Bilen, during his hunting trip in 1930, the Adoimara Danakil had informed Thesiger that the Awash river ended in a lake near Mount Goumarri, in the legendary Sultanate of Aussa, a forbidden territory which remained until then unexplored. The Sultan or Amoita, Mohammed Yayu, was an all-powerful despot who, it was said, hated Europeans. In 1928 Ludovico Nesbitt, the author of *Desert and Forest*, met the Sultan, who refused him permission to enter Aussa. While the river's end remained unexplored, Nesbitt confirmed that the Awash flowed into Aussa.

From the Awash station, Thesiger wrote to his mother on 26 November: 'We arrived here rather late … but David, who has had some boils on his leg, rode on in front to get to Addis Ababa by the train and sent a telegram to you from me. I thought you might be getting anxious about our delay. We got hung up by a customs post in Bale, my fault for misreading my pass and entering a district not mentioned in it … I am buying more camels, and awaiting the arrival of 10 soldiers [in fact he was allocated fifteen] who are to go with us. This morning I gave out the rifles lent us by the Legation, and we are extremely well armed. Almost every man has a rifle and ammunition. David had returned from Addis Ababa and was waiting for us here when we arrived.'[7] In contrast to his account in 1979, in which he described Haig-Thomas's presence as an 'irritant', Thesiger added: 'I am very glad to have got him back as he is an excellent companion on trek, taking everything very smoothly.'[8] While this was doubtless intended to reassure his mother, Thesiger would write to his brother Brian two months later: 'Have you seen David since he returned? It was rotten luck on him. He was a delightful companion with a temper which nothing could ruffle. I do hope he enjoyed the Arussi trip, though I feel he would have enjoyed this one even more. His absence handicaps me badly with the birds.'[9]

On 27 November Wilfred had written to Dermot: 'Don't let [mother] worry about me. It is the one thing that makes me unhappy, to think that she is probably worrying.'[10] Yet he described a lion hunt to Kathleen as 'exciting while it lasted', the excitement of following fresh tracks, even without sighting any lion, and the thrill of anticipation as he 'crawled along clutching the trusty .450 you gave me'.[11] Perhaps his feelings towards Haig-Thomas changed dramatically over the years; or perhaps, aware that his mother and his three brothers shared all the letters he wrote to them individually, he did not wish to upset Kathleen by suggesting there had been any ill-feeling between him and Haig-Thomas, still less appear to criticise her insistence upon him having an English companion. In this respect the contrast between Thesiger's reaction to Haig-Thomas in 1933 and the way he documented their relationship years later is paralleled by his much-publicised rows with Gavin Maxwell in the Iraqi marshes in 1956.

The prelude in Arussi, Thesiger wrote, had been 'a great and valuable experience to me, and very much increased my self-confidence ... We are now camped just outside the Hawash Station and shall be off down the Hawash in 4 days I hope. I am pleased to be back among my beloved Danakils again. They are an attractive race'.[12] Reginald Astley had written him a long letter, full of news. Wilfred noted: 'I am so pleased that the Weir House is sold and that question is settled, but I am sorry for Reggie.' The sale, he felt, was 'a cartload off [Kathleen's] mind'.[13] Perhaps Astley had suggested that the family give up their tenancy of The Milebrook and move to the Weir House. Selling the Weir House eliminated this possibility.

Before Haig-Thomas's departure, Thesiger had assured Kathleen: 'Darling mother, I cannot tell you how often I think of you, and how very much I wish you were with me. You are such a prop to the four of us, and you have given us what no other boys seem to get from their homes. Those who have never had a Milebrook can never know what it means, and by far the greater part of the world never has. I always feel sorry for David when the mail comes. In place of stacks of letters for me from you all he may perhaps have one odd one. I shall always value this close bond which unites the five of us above everything, and it must be the one thing which never gets broken.' (He did not include his stepfather in this 'close bond'. Instead of replying to it himself, he had asked his mother to thank Astley for his long letter, adding how much pleasure it had given him; but one suspects that he never counted Reginald Astley as part of the family.) 'As long as we have each other we need nothing else. In the years to come even if separated by distance we must keep this priceless unity, and never slowly drift apart. You must always remember, mother dear, that it is you who have given it to us.' On 27 November he added a significant post-script: 'I am keeping a most detailed diary of every occurrence however trivial. If I write a book [about the Danakil expedition] it will be indispensable.'[14]

Thesiger's revealing letter of 26–27 November makes it clear that he was keeping a journal of the Danakil expedition with the intention of writing a book about it, even though he later described his books and photographs as mere 'by-products' of his travels. In this respect his approach reminds us of Freya Stark, a prolific letter-writer whose vast correspondence served as her diaries. Unlike Freya, Thesiger didn't keep carbon copies of letters he wrote, and unfortunately he preserved very few letters from his mother and his brothers, so his archive of fascinating travel letters gives only his side of their correspondence. Thesiger's father had written a great many letters during his sojourns abroad, and these his parents had kept carefully. Kathleen took great care of Wilfred Gilbert's correspondence, which was housed in specially made linen-covered boxes. She also kept all Wilfred's juvenile essays and letters from 1917 until 1973, when she died. Besides his letters, Thesiger wrote diaries of all his journeys; and from 1930 onwards he took photographs, which in due course became his preferred method of recording his travels. As the postscript to his letter of 26–27 November 1933 suggests, though he never at any time travelled in order to write an article or a book, or wrote articles or books to pay for his journeys, he recorded his journeys with a view to publishing the diaries and letters he wrote about them, illustrated by the photographs he took. While *The Danakil Diary* was being edited in 1996, he recollected that he 'had been asked to write a book' about his exploration of the Awash river. He did not mention, and perhaps had forgotten, the book that he himself had planned to write. When he reviewed Nesbitt's *Desert and Forest* in the RGS *Journal* in 1934, he praised the book's 'vivid and distinctive prose, and many passages ... of great beauty'; but his criticism of the 'vague' zoology and 'misgivings about the scientific exactitude of Mr Nesbitt's observations' clearly implied that he felt there was room for a more accurate and precise work describing the Danakil tribes and the previously unknown fate of their mysterious river.[15]

Thesiger's hunting trip in 1930, and his journey to the end of the Awash river in 1933–34, set a pattern for most of his subsequent travels. From then on he travelled on foot with tribal companions and baggage animals, almost never accompanied by another European. All his important journeys were done in this 'traditional' manner. During his 'lesser' travels in the Sudan, Syria, Palestine, Morocco, southern Iraq, India, Jordan, Kenya, Tanzania and Ladakh, he was joined sometimes by other Englishmen. Despite his reservations, he enjoyed their company:

> People like George [Webb], Frank [Steele] and John [Newbould] were all interesting to talk to. They were interested in their surroundings ... interested in everything that went on. George spoke a number of African dialects and languages. He was very intelligent and very witty. He helped me get permission to travel in northern Kenya. In 1962 we climbed to the top of Mt Kilimanjaro. Frank had been a District Officer in Uganda, where he did quite a lot of elephant hunting and hunted other big game. After that he served as Vice-Consul at Basra. I met him there, in southern Iraq, when I was living among the Marsh Arabs. Frank used to join me for a few days in the marshes; and afterwards we travelled together in Jordan and Kenya. John wanted to come with me to Nuristan, but he couldn't get a permit. Later on, while he was down at Ngorongoro, we did a fairly long journey together with mules, in the Serengeti, across the Masai steppe. Gavin Maxwell and Gavin Young both wrote books about their journeys with me in the Iraqi marshes. Gavin Maxwell wasn't a bit like David [Haig-Thomas] and yet he was ... He knew a lot about birds, and he could be fascinating to listen to; but, in the marshes, I found him exasperating ... Gavin Young, on the other hand, was easy-going and very popular. Amara and my other canoemen, and their families, were always delighted to see him.[16]

Thesiger's caravan set off from the Awash station on 1 December, and arrived in his old hunting grounds at Bilen on the fifth. He wrote from there telling his mother: 'Everything is going splendidly and my camp is happy and contented. I left the Hawash as soon as the soldiers' camels arrived and did a night march almost to Sade Malka. We then came on slowly from there, and I have now given the men and camels 3 days rest.

I am anxious not to hurry as I don't want to tire my camels.' Of the habits of buffalo at Bilen, he wrote: 'They are astonishingly wary as they are never persecuted. They never come out till after dark and are back again in the reedbed before dawn. I very nearly got two today, but they got my wind at the last moment, and plunged off making a great noise as they galloped [away].' In a paper read to the RGS on 12 November 1934, Thesiger commented: 'I marched down the river ... stopping for several days at Bilen in order to try and obtain a specimen of the buffalo which inhabit the reed-bed there ... I failed to get a buffalo ... They were astonishingly wary ... I have never heard of one being shot, which makes their extreme shyness difficult to explain. From the tracks which I saw I think the herd consists of only ten individuals.'[17]

In his introduction to 'Birds from Danakil, Abyssinia', published in *The Ibis* in October 1935, Thesiger outlined his journey to the end of the Awash, whose object he described as following its course 'in order to solve the problem of the river's disappearance':[18] 'The Awash rises in the mountains near Addis Ababa and enters Danakil in its south-western corner. Mr David Haig-Thomas['s] ... return to England ... handicapped me severely, since I was now single-handed, and I had not myself studied the birds of this region before leaving England.' Having described the purpose of the expedition and offered an apology for 'a number of gaps in the collection' of birds, he went on: 'I left Awash Station on 1 December, 1933, but on reaching Bahdu was compelled to return to Afdam owing to trouble between the Abyssinian Government and the Danakil tribes. I arrived at Afdam on 22 December. Many weeks were wasted before I could obtain permission to start again on my journey. I left Afdam on 8 February, and this time I was successful in tracing the river to its end in Lake Abhebad. I then crossed the lava deserts of French Somaliland to Tajura, where I arrived on 20 May.'[19]

Writing to his mother, he described his camp at night, surrounded by hyenas – 'No one can pretend they are musical but I am glad to hear them again' – and the marvellous light at daybreak and dusk. A lyrical mood evoked memories of his father's descriptions of misty 'light and colour'[20] on the Somali coast: 'I cannot tell you how lovely the dawns are here [at Bilen]. They are indescribably beautiful, and as I always try to get off early we see it every morning. It is more lovely than the sunset, though for some reason I prefer the evening stroll round to the morning one. I suppose this is because the day's work is then over, and you come in to a hot bath and a large supper. In the evening the Mohamedans nearly always chant round their fire, and this sounds most attractive.' He returned to more practical themes: 'I try to practise my Arabic on them but most of them speak it worse than I do, using an indiscriminate mixture of Arabic, Somali, Amharic and Galla. Despite this I can usually make myself understood.' More troublesome than the hyenas that 'swarm everywhere' were 'swarms of Dankali [sic] round the camp, begging for flour'. He added as an afterthought: 'I am afraid I shall not be able to get another letter back to you. We are on the edge of a tribal boundary [between the Adoimara and Asaimara Danakil], and the people here and in Asaimara are hereditary foes. They would certainly kill an Asaimara if I tried to send him back with a letter.' A postscript – 'Could you keep the Times, Foreign News Editor, informed of my movements' – presaged articles he later wrote for that newspaper.[21]

The Adoimara at Bilen had assured Thesiger that his party 'would certainly be massacred if [they] attempted to enter Badhu'. Having come safely through the 'ill-famed' pass of Mataka, they emerged onto a fertile plain, a mile wide, between the hills and the river, where cattle, sheep, goats, ponies and donkeys grazed on rich grass, and giant fig trees grew in clusters along the riverbank. At Beriforo, the caravan was confronted by 'a large gathering of armed warriors [about two hundred of them] ... and their reception ... was far from friendly. They were inclined to force a quarrel, declaring that my Somalis were Essa, with whom they were then, as always, at war. But references to a non-existent machine-gun [contained in one of Thesiger's rifle cases] helped us to reach an understanding.'[22] In *The Life of My Choice* he wrote: 'The tension, however, eased after Omar managed to get hold of some elders. Over many cups of tea, he succeeded in convincing some of them that I was an English traveller on my way to visit the Amoita in Aussa. He persuaded them that I was not employed by the Government, explaining that I was under the Emperor's personal protection, which accounted for my escort of soldiers. Even so, I felt by no means certain that the elders would be able to prevent their refractory warriors from attacking us after dark. We spent an apprehensive night. At intervals I wandered round the camp, flashing my powerful torch into the darkness. I doubt if anyone slept.'[23]

At a nearby village where they camped among the huts 'in the centre of a most malarious bog', a letter addressed to the headman of the armed escort arrived from the government. The letter had been passed along from village headman to village headman, and its contents by then were common knowledge. It ordered Thesiger to turn back, since the country ahead was too dangerous. Should he refuse, the soldiers were to return without him and inform the Danakil that the government was no longer responsible for Thesiger's safety.

Thesiger wrote: 'I very reluctantly decided that to continue after losing half my rifles, and when the Dankali knew that the Government had refused to be responsible for our lives, was to invite certain massacre for myself and for my men.'[24] He later recalled: 'Our greatest risk was when we were in Bahdu that first night. That was when things hung in the balance ... At Bahdu I wasn't afraid. [What I felt] was excitement.'[25] By the time the government's letter had arrived, Thesiger told his mother, 'We were through the place where any trouble might have been expected, and I have not the least doubt that I should have reached the end of the river from where I was without difficulty.'[26]

Thesiger 'wasted' six weeks at Addis Ababa until the Abyssinian government allowed him to continue his expedition from the Afdam station, where he had left Umr in charge of the caravan. Soon after he got to Addis Ababa he wrote to Kathleen, on 23 December, telling her: 'Everything has crashed at the moment, but I hope to be able to pull things round ... However nothing can be done for a day or two and I shall go out to the Sandfords for Christmas. I had hoped to spend it at the end of the river ... Darling mother, I suppose it is good for the soul but it is bitterly disappointing to be baulked like this. It makes it more bitter when it is not your fault that you have failed, and you believe that except for this you could have done it. I have staked such a lot on this venture, not only money, though there is £1500 of that, but everything. However I shall fight desperately to get back there.'[27] At Addis Ababa Thesiger stayed with Frank de Halpert. He wrote asking Kathleen to buy a new or second-hand copy of Lydekker's *Game Animals of Africa* from Rowland Ward's, and send it to de Halpert as thanks. De Halpert had admired a well-used copy Thesiger had taken with him on the Awash expedition;

Thesiger had used this book on safari in 1930, and kept it with him for reference in the Sudan between 1934 and 1939.

After some lengthy discussions with Sir Sidney Barton and Dr Martin, the Governor of Chercher province, Dr Martin allowed Thesiger to resume his expedition. In return for fifteen armed soldiers as escort, he wrote a letter to Dr Martin absolving the Abyssinian government of all responsibility for his safety. (Dr Martin's officials lost the original letter soon afterwards, and Martin wrote to Thesiger in February 1934 asking him for a copy of it.)

Thesiger's caravan already numbered forty men, most of whom had been armed with rifles. He wrote: 'They have increased my escort some-what. I deliberately prevented them doing so too much, however, as that only adds [to] instead of lessening the risk. If you went down to the Hawash with 100 soldiers you would certainly have fighting. Such a number would frighten the Dankalis who are a jumpy people, and they would probably attack you as a means of protecting themselves against the supposed danger of your presence. The number I have got, about 40 rifles, is just right. Too strong to be an irresistible temptation and yet too few for them to be made nervous.'[28]

As Thesiger's caravan was leaving Bahdu in December, Umr had brought over the adopted son and nephew of Miriam Muhammad, an important chief and *hangadaala*, or spiritual leader, of the Bahdu Danakil. Miriam Muhammad and his nephew, Ali Wali, had been imprisoned at Asba Tafari as hostages for the Asaimara Danakil's good behaviour. When Miriam Muhammad refused to guarantee Thesiger's safety among the Asaimara at Bahdu, Thesiger had been recalled to Addis Ababa. From Afdam in January, at Ali Wali's suggestion, Thesiger telephoned Dr Martin and secured his uncle's release. Ali Wali and another Danakil chief, Ahamado, were ordered to accompany the caravan as far as Aussa. Meanwhile Miriam Muhammad's presence ensured the safety of Thesiger's party when they returned to Bahdu.

Thesiger wrote to Kathleen: 'I have also got permission from both the Abyssinians and the French to cross the frontier and go to Jibuti ... it will be interesting going across that country, and will save my having to go back on my tracks which is always a pity ... I expect to arrive at Jibuti at the very beginning of May. I might then ... take a dhow from Jibuti to

Port Sudan. It would be most interesting to see that coast from the sea, and also the Arabian barrier reefs. This was David's idea and I have stolen it. I think it would be cheap and only take a short time. Have you read de Monfreid's books? They are in French. They would make anyone anxious to see a bit of that coast.'[29]

Though Umr was effectively responsible for the caravan, Thesiger not only shared, but took, decisions day by day. He devoted time to photographing the country and the people, mapped the course of the river, wrote a diary, recorded detailed descriptions of Danakil customs, shot meat to feed himself and his party, and collected specimens of birds, plants, animals and insects – tasks which absorbed and occupied him from daybreak until nightfall. He wrote: 'I always fortify the camp with a defence made of flour sacks and chop boxes ... We always refer to Olive's gun case [and its gun lent by Lady Archer] as the machine-gun and wave it about when there is an opportunity. [The Danakil] certainly think it contains one. The search lights too give a great sense of security at night.' Again he underlined his motive for this journey: 'without a risk the game would lose its fascination, and it has an enormous fascination, nor would it be worth doing ... It makes you do all in your power continuously. You cannot be slack and slovenly here, and there is a satisfaction in being pitted against a difficulty. How sententious!'[30] He acknowledged the danger to his caravan: 'There unquestionably is a great risk for any of my men who straggle or get separated from camp, but I have warned them repeatedly about this, and we are careful always to march in a solid body. If a camel needs reloading we all stop, and I have elaborate advance guards and rear guards.'[31]

Collecting bird specimens proved fascinating, but very time-consuming, work. He wrote from Afdam on 5 February:

Yusuf the bird man bolted and left 2 months wages behind, rather than go down the Dankali country again. I always said he was a rotter, and should have parted with him long ago but for David's entreaties. I have had a busy time trying to train someone to take his place. The cook's boy and head camelman both show promise[32] ... I have got over 100 birds since I have been here, and there are about 50 different specimens [he presumably meant species], and I have nothing like got them all. This is arid desert

111

without a drop of water except at the bottom of deep wells. You can imagine the numbers [of birds] in the forest along the river. It gives me a lot to do. I can only trust the men to skin, and have to sex, stuff, pack and label each specimen myself. But it is great fun and I have them all out in my spare moments to admire them. I now have four men who can skin, and so we can get through a lot in a day. But a large part of the day has to be spent collecting them especially when you already have the common ones. Some are very lovely.[33]

Thesiger kept a running total of the birds in his expedition diary, which filled almost two large notebooks. By the end of the journey he had collected no fewer than 872 specimens, comprising 192 species or sub-species. Three new sub-species – an Aussa rock chat, a Danakil rock sparrow and a Danakil house bunting – had Thesiger's and the ornithologist Mark Meynell's names attached to them, acknowledging Thesiger, their 'discoverer', and Meynell, who worked out the collection in England.

Thesiger's earliest photographs did little more than visually record the Danakil and their forbidding landscapes. He scribbled impatiently: 'I am anxious to hear what my photos were like. I do hope there were some successes. [He had sent some of his exposed film to England with Haig-Thomas.] I am taking a lot here, and think that the light is easier. It varies very little. The big camera [his father's Kodak] certainly is a lovely one to use.'[34]

Apart from meeting the Sultan of Aussa, Thesiger's most treasured memories of the Awash expedition included an encounter with a young Danakil named Hamdo Ouga, or Ahamdo Ugo, chief of the Badogale, son of the last Sheikh of Bahdu. Hamdo Ouga, who was related to the Sultan of Aussa, had 'much power in the land'.[35] When Thesiger first met him he had returned from the Issa frontier, having killed three men. Hamdo Ouga was killed soon afterwards by raiding Adoimara. He was 'a most attractive boy', Thesiger recalled.[36] 'He looked about eighteen, with a ready, friendly smile and considerable charm … He struck me as the Danakil equivalent of a nice, rather self-conscious Etonian who had just won his school colours for cricket.'[37] This description invariably amused and delighted audiences at the talks Thesiger gave in his later years at the Royal Geographical Society. The double-focus image of a teenage

Danakil chief who had killed three men had a vulnerable charm that revived Thesiger's idealised memories of Eton, and appealed widely to less critical admirers. Aged six, Wilfred had envied and identified with a boy soldier who fought at Sagale in Ras Tafari's victorious army. At twenty-three, he again identified himself with a warrior role model, one from 'a strange people' whose 'main object in life [was] to kill and mutilate someone else'. He wrote to George Gordon, the President of Magdalen College: 'I met one youth of about 12 years old who had just killed, followed round by a crowd of admiring children. It is these enterprising young men who are a menace to our stragglers.'[38]

In contrast to the ferocity of the Asaimara Danakil, the game in their 'gaunt and desolate'[39] country seemed excessively tame. Thesiger wrote to Brian from Afdam: 'I did not do very much shooting in the Danakil country partly as in places it is too risky, and also chiefly because the animals are so tame it is but little sport. I have seen oryx feeding with my mules 150 yards from my tent door, and you can often pass within 50 yards of them.'[40]

Between Afdam and Aussa, the wild but hospitable Danakil gave Thesiger's forty-strong caravan two hundred sheep and thirty oxen, besides 'hundreds of skins of milk'. Six weeks later they reached Galifage, on the north-west border of Aussa, where they camped on the fringes of thick forest. 'The tall trees were smothered in creepers; the grass was green and rank; little sunlight penetrated to my tent. It was a different world from the tawny plains, the thirsty thorn-scrub, the cracked and blackened rocks of the land through which we had passed.'[41] In a letter, Thesiger described Aussa as

an extraordinary oasis shut in all round by sheer precipices of black rock. The Hawash flows round it on 3 sides seeking an exit ... Coming here we have passed through a veritable land of death. Black volcanic rock tumbled and piled in every direction and not a sign of life or vegetation except on the very river's edge. If my photos come out I shall have some good ones. Then suddenly the mountains open out and you find yourself on the edge of Aussa. This is roughly square in shape and the whole place is wonderfully luxuriant. Half of it is dense forest, with clearings where they graze their flocks and cultivate some durrah. The other half is extensive swamp. There are five lakes varying from 5 to 18 miles in length ... There is one horror here and that is the tarantulas, large, hairy and 4″ across. They scuttle round camp as soon as the sun sets. Last night we killed 12 ... In my dreams they assume the most nightmare proportions.[42]

Thesiger's meeting with the Sultan of Aussa in a moonlit forest clearing might have been an episode in a novel by John Buchan or Sir Henry Rider Haggard. The earliest version Thesiger wrote immediately afterwards in his Danakil diary; later versions, much abbreviated, were included in letters to his mother and to Sir Sidney Barton; after that came articles for *The Times* and a paper he read to the RGS in November 1934 with a fuller description of the encounter, which became the basis for more polished accounts in *Arabian Sands, Desert, Marsh and Mountain* and *The Life of My Choice*.

He told Barton and Kathleen that he had met the Sultan twice, 'in itself rather a feat'. 'We had a moonlight meeting in a big clearing surrounded by the silent forest ... He has given me the silver baton without which it is impossible to move a step.'[43] Thesiger wrote to Sandford, telling him he had finally met the Sultan after '3 weeks getting into touch'.[44] To Kathleen he wrote: 'I cannot hope to describe anything in a letter and am reluctant to spoil what I have to tell you by a bad description ... It has been wonderful, in very truth a dream come true.'[45] The 'silver baton' was 'a stout bamboo bound round with engraved silver bands which gives to the bearer the authority of the Sultan'. Thesiger received this some days before the meeting. At Gurumudli on 29 March,

we heard the sound of distant trumpets. The forest was sombre in the dusk, between the setting of the sun and the rising of the full moon. Later a messenger arrived and informed me that the Sultan was waiting to receive me. We followed him deeper into the forest, along twisting paths, until we came to a large clearing. About four hundred men were massed on the far side of it. They all carried rifles, their belts were filled with cartridges. They all wore daggers, and their loin-cloths were clean – vivid white in the moonlight. Not one of them spoke. Sitting a little in front of them on a stool was a small dark man, with a bearded oval face. He was dressed completely in white, in a long shirt with a shawl thrown round his shoulders. He had a silver-hilted dagger at his waist. As I greeted him in Arabic he rose, and then signed to me to be seated on another stool [a chair Umr 'had had the forethought to bring for me'⁴⁶]. He waved his men away. They drew back to the forest's edge and squatted there in silence.

On the way to Aussa, Thesiger wrote, 'I had been faced with conditions of tribal anarchy, but now I was confronted by an autocrat whose word was law. If we died here it would be at the Sultan's order, not through some chance meeting with tribesmen in the bush.' Thesiger's account in *Arabian Sands* is the best-written, even though some details, such as the family provenance of the Sultan's silver dagger and a purring of nightjars that flew overhead, are excluded:

He spoke little and never smiled. There were long intervals of silence. His expression was sensitive, proud, and imperious, but not cruel. He mentioned that a European who worked for the government had been killed by tribesmen near the railway line. I learnt later that this was a German [named Beitz] who was working with the Ethiopian boundary commission. After about an hour he said he would meet me again in the morning. He had asked no questions about my plans. I returned to camp without an idea of what the future held for us. We met again next morning in the same place. By daylight it was simply a clearing in the forest with none of the menace of the previous night. The Sultan asked me where I wished to go and I told him that I wanted to follow the river to its end. He asked me what I sought, whether I worked for the government, and many other questions. It would have been difficult to explain my love of exploration to this suspicious tyrant, even without the added difficulties of interpretation [via Umr]. My headman was questioned, and also the Danakil who had accompanied me from Bahdu. Eventually the Sultan gave me permission to follow the river through Aussa to its end. Why he gave me this permission, which had never before been granted to a European, I do not know.⁴⁷

In this version, written in 1957, Thesiger made it clear that while the danger was very real, the atmosphere of menace was created by the moonlit gloom; even more, perhaps, by the silence, because African forests at dusk are seldom silent. Thesiger's abrupt, rhetorical ending, 'I do not know', very effectively snapped the tension of this brief, enormously important description of the Sultan's interviews, which it seems had been carefully planned and expertly stage-managed by the Sultan, Mohammed Yayu, and his advisers.

From the barren heights of Mount Kulzikuma, Thesiger saw, 'far nearer than I had expected, set in a limitless waste of volcanic rock ... a great expanse of water, sombre under threatening storm clouds. That was where the Awash ended. I had come far and risked much to see this desolate scene.'[48] The moment when he confirmed that this was the Awash's end appeared, both in his diary and his books, as an anticlimax. On 27 April 1934 he wrote: 'It was satisfactory to have established conclusively that the Awash did end in [Lake]Abhebad.' That day he had tramped for six hours to the lake's south-eastern extremity, where a chain of pinnacles, sinter formations, some of them thirty feet in height, 'covered with the most delicate tracery',[49] rose above the surface: 'We passed through a country as dead as a lunar landscape; the heat was tremendous, making us sick and giddy. Throughout the hottest hours we crouched among the rocks, our heads swathed in cloths, wondering if we should have the strength left to return.'[50] Here the blinding sun was fiercer than Afdam, where Thesiger had never found the heat intolerable; far more intense than the Awash valley, where the dry breeze had for him 'a very powerful call, and I felt at home when I first came down off the tableland and felt the unmistakable warm evening wind of the desert'.[51]

At the French fort in Dikil, Thesiger obtained permission to cross the desert north-east to Tajura, permission which had previously been refused. The long-awaited spring rains now broke, filling the watercourses and the waterholes ahead. Yet in this harsh wilderness they found nothing to feed the camels, except two acacia bushes in full leaf near Lake Assal which saved the lives of the stronger camels and enabled Thesiger's party to reach the coast. Of his eighteen camels, fourteen died of starvation. Thesiger wrote: 'It was heartbreaking, for I knew them all so well: little Farur, Elmi, Hawiya, and the great-hearted Negadras ... It took us three days to pass round [Lake Assal] ... and we dragged the dying camels by main force from one sharp-edged block of lava to the next.'[52] At the

Dafare waterhole they hired replacements for the dead camels from Aizamale tribesmen camped there.

Almost a fortnight after leaving Dikil, six months after he had first entered the Danakil country, Thesiger and his caravan arrived on 20 May 1934 at Tajura. Thesiger had shown Umr how to use a camera, and three days before they reached Tajura Umr photographed him standing with a rifle across his shoulders, bearded and moustached, in a sheltering khaki topee. Thesiger had achieved his ambition, and accomplished 'a thoroughly good piece of work in really dangerous country'.[53] He looked confident and defiant. Yet according to Colonel Sandford, the expedition had taught him 'to be patient and diplomatic as well as to "thrust" '. Sandford had told Thesiger he was 'winning golden opinions [perhaps 'pinions'] – which remark never failed to goad him to fury',[54] and confided to Kathleen: 'Between ourselves Sir Sidney Barton told me when I last saw him that Wilfred had greatly impressed him – he thought he had developed a great deal since he was last out here.'[55] 'I think Wilfred has shown himself to be thoroughly sensible in his dealings with the natives, and he is not likely to bring down trouble upon his head.'[56] As to the young man's future, Sandford commented generously and perceptively: 'I am not sure that his heart is really set on the Sudan Civil [i.e. Political Service] – but if they get him they will in my opinion get good value.'[57]

However much it went against the grain, Thesiger had learnt to balance determination with patience and tact, especially when dealing with his elders. He had at last begun to master his temper, although he never managed to suppress his sudden, violent rages. He acknowledged this weakness, and the much-needed assurance Umr Ibrahim's 'imperturbability' had given him.[58] He felt proud and satisfied at having achieved the objectives of his journey: having traced the mysterious river to its end; having collected so many birds; having taken 'hundreds' of good photographs and gathered 'enough information for an interesting book on the Dankalis'. Writing to Kathleen, however, he found it impossible to resist patronising David Haig-Thomas's efforts at ornithology and photography. N.B. Kinnear observed in 1934 that whereas Haig-Thomas 'had taken the trouble to make himself acquainted with the birds of the country', Thesiger 'readily admit[ted] that he did not know much about Abyssinian birds'.[59] Thesiger confirmed his scant knowledge, writing: 'I have got ... probably 350 different kinds [in reality the figure was 192] ... [though] David [apparently over-cautious] told me that we should not get 50 different kinds of bird in the whole of this trip.' As for photographs, he remarked: 'I am so glad that my Arussi photos are good. It makes me hope that the hundreds I have taken on this trip will also come out. Poor David, he is unlucky. He took such a lot of trouble with his light meter etc. Probably he would have done better just to snap as I did. I wonder if any of the ones I took on the mountain at Chelalo came out. It was so cloudy that I took time-exposures by guess work.'[60]

A few days after arriving at Tajura, Thesiger sailed on an Arab dhow across the bay to Jibuti. During the expedition he had been reading French-language paperbacks by Henri de Monfreid, including *Secrets de la Mer Rouge*, *Aventures de Mer*, *La Croiserie de l'Hashish* and a controversial book, *Vers les Terres Hostiles de l'Ethiopie*, which 'got him expelled from Abyssinia'.[61] De Monfreid was a French Catalan from the Roussillon. His father Daniel de Monfreid, a painter and art dealer, had been Gauguin's representative in Europe during the artist's last years in Tahiti and the Marquesas. The younger de Monfreid grew up to be anti-establishment and anti-British. With his upper-middle-class origins and a foot in both camps, de Monfreid's background paralleled Thesiger's, just as his renegade lifestyle appealed to the determinedly conventional yet free-spirited Thesiger, who respected his family's and his country's traditions, yet empathised strongly with the Zulus after Isandhlwana, admired the Dervishes at Omdurman and followed anxiously, enthusiastically, the fortunes of the rebel Abdel Krim and his forces in Morocco.

At Aseila, on the way to Dikil, Thesiger met Fara, who had been de Monfreid's devoted cook. Thesiger wrote: 'I had hoped when I got to Jibuti to meet de Monfreid. He had however gone on a visit, I think it was to France, but his dhow, the Altair, was anchored in the bay. I went on board her and met his crew. From his books I already knew their names. I heard he was selling the Altair. I thought fleetingly of buying her and leading a life resembling his, but reality took charge.'[62] A paper enclosed in Thesiger's original manuscript diary may have been written by de Monfreid. It gives a detailed breakdown of the running costs of the *Altair* for any prospective purchaser, suggesting that Thesiger had made serious enquiries about the vessel. But the eldest son of the former British Minister at Addis Ababa was never destined to live like de Monfreid, a social outcast 'fishing for pearls off the Farsan isles and smuggling guns into Abyssinia through Tajura'.[63]

In February 1933, six months before Thesiger left for Addis Ababa, de Monfreid sailed round the 'hallucinating landscape'[64] of Gubet Karah on the Red Sea with a party of prehistorians, Pierre Teilhard de Chardin, Dr Paul Wernert and the Abbé Henri Breuil. From there they trekked to Lake Assal. On the Harar plateau, Wernert examined prehistoric art in the Porc-Epic grotto; at Sourré, Breuil copied rock paintings of cattle, wild animals, herdsmen and hunters as he perched on scaffolding high above a ravine. In 1959, the year Thesiger's first book, *Arabian Sands*, was published, the ageing de Monfreid set off to the island of Réunion in the Indian Ocean (where Abdel Krim had once lived in exile), in search of treasure said to have been buried in 1730 by Olivier le Vasseur, an eighteenth-century pirate. Empty-handed, still driven by his insatiable craving for adventure, three years later de Monfreid returned to his old haunts in Ethiopia, the former Abyssinia.[65] In *The Danakil Diary*, Thesiger noted that de Monfreid, whom he hoped to meet at Jibuti in 1934, was not there.[66] Having chaperoned the prehistorians to the Red Sea coast and Harar, he had returned to France to be with his wife and young family.[67]

Saying goodbye to his men in the railway station at Jibuti 'deepened [Thesiger's] depression ... All [the remaining twenty-two] ... had proved utterly reliable, often under conditions of hardship and danger. None had ever questioned my decisions, however seemingly risky, and I had never doubted their loyalty.' The following day he left Jibuti, travelling third-class aboard a Messageries Maritimes steamship en route from Indo-China to Marseilles. Umr was there to see him off. Reliving the moment in 1996, Thesiger wrote in his concluding chapter of *The Danakil Diary*: 'As I watched him descend the gangway I was more conscious than ever how much of my success was due to him.'[68]

On 8 August 1934, Umr wrote Thesiger a flattering letter, giving his address merely as 'Omar Ibrahim, Addis Ababa, Ethiopia':

Dear Sir

... since you left me and the other servants we have all been wondering about your safety and health. We are also very anxious – as per promised – to see the Photographs that you intended to produce as well as the several newspapers which may contain an account of your trip through Ethiopia. After your departure I was called by the Secretary to the British Minister [Sir Sidney Barton] who told me that he expected two gentlemen from England about two months hence, and I will be called upon to carry out the same duties as I did with you. I rather think, however, that the trek will not be as good with them as it was in your case. Please, Sir, send me some word of your plans as I am almost daily bothered by the other servants who are eager to get a word or two from you. I am also hoping that your entire collection of birds reached England quite safely. I, in common with the others, will always be grateful to you for the innumerable acts of kindness that you had so frequently extended to us.

Obediently your servant, Omar Ibrahim.[69]

Soon after he returned to England, Thesiger's mother and stepfather gave a dinner party for him at Claridge's, which John Buchan attended as guest of honour. On 12 November 1934 Thesiger read a paper entitled 'The Awash River and the Aussa Sultanate' to the Royal Geographical Society. Introducing him, the Society's President, Major-General Sir Percy Cox, stated unequivocally that Thesiger's 'primary object' had been to solve the mystery of the Awash river's end: 'A secondary object was the collection of natural history specimens, especially birds and mammals.'[70] Thesiger took up Cox's theme early in his lecture: 'Unfortunately Haig-Thomas fell ill ... This handicapped me badly with the collecting, but I succeeded in my main objective, which was the thorough exploration of the river ... I also collected 880 specimens of birds.'[71] While this was true, he might have paid a warmer tribute to Haig-Thomas, who had contributed a substantial sum of money to the expedition, as well as shooting several specimens of blue-winged geese for the Natural History Museum. He could also have mentioned Haig-Thomas's extensive preparations for the journey, notably his research into the country's birds, which was acknowledged by N.B. Kinnear after Thesiger read his paper. Instead, Thesiger appeared to treat the consequences of Haig-Thomas's illness as a testing challenge that he had faced alone, and had successfully overcome.

Perhaps Thesiger had felt more sympathy for Haig-Thomas than he showed outwardly, and realised how hard it must have been for him to abandon the expedition before it got properly under way. Haig-Thomas's decision was surely no less traumatic than Thesiger's brother Dermot's decision to withdraw from a boxing match at Oxford knowing the odds were hopelessly against him, of which Thesiger approved: 'I think Dermot was extremely sensible over the boxing. It takes a courage which few people possess to do what he did. It is far easier to enter and be smashed up entirely, than to face facts and not give a damn for other people's remarks. I admire him more than ever for this.'[72]

The mystery of the disappearing Awash had been solved. Closing his narrative in *The Danakil Diary*, Thesiger wrote: 'I had come far, overcome many difficulties and risked much, but I had achieved what I had set out to do.'[73] Yet the 'lure of the unknown' remained an irresistible enticement to adventure. He declared: 'I had no desire to go back to civilisation, and wish[ed] I was just starting out from the Awash station with the whole Awash river still before me to explore.'[74]

ELEVEN

Savage Sudan

For twenty-three-year-old Wilfred Thesiger, the Danakil expedition had been a life-defining experience. Even more than his month hunting big game along the Awash in 1930, the journey through Bahdu and Aussa to the Red Sea coast realised Thesiger's boyhood dream of adventure. Above all, it proved that the life of 'savagery and colour' he had longed to lead was attainable.

The successful Danakil expedition helped to bolster Thesiger's still fragile self-esteem, which had been almost totally destroyed at St Aubyn's and only superficially restored at Eton. His almost undefeated record as a boxing Blue, and his near-mythogenic status as a guest of the Abyssinian Emperor who hunted alone among the Danakil, had helped to rebuild Thesiger's self-confidence at Oxford. He had found himself admired and liked, enviably sought after by Robin Campbell, the 'golden youth' who exemplified what Thesiger called Oxford's 'decadent' era.[1] But for the rest of his life he found it difficult to trust completely more than a handful of people outside his immediate family circle. Even those who eventually did win his trust (or as much trust as he felt he could bestow) often discovered that Thesiger seemed continually to be preparing himself for the inevitable disappointment of being let down. He enjoyed many friendships over the years, but had few close friends. Deep down, Thesiger believed that even the best of friendships could not possibly last.[2] His instinctive mistrust and chronic wariness, he claimed, had resulted from being treated as a liar and a misfit at St Aubyn's.[3] No doubt this was true. Moreover, he had been uprooted from his home in Abyssinia and its 'extraordinary freedom'. This was replaced by the friendless, unfamiliar, brutal regime of his preparatory school (although in his autobiography he claimed he was not 'particularly unhappy' at St Aubyn's[4]). As a result he felt deprived, disorientated and lonely. Not least, he was affected by the tragedy of his father's sudden death. Again and again, he emphasised that he had very soon got over this, adding: 'children are like that'[5] but (like the death of his spaniel) it taught him an unforgettable lesson: that all things come to an end. From then on Thesiger had become wary of 'overtures of friendship',[6] and instinctively mistrustful. If and when he decided to trust someone, he set almost unattainably high standards of commitment on their part. He described those he trusted as 'identifying completely' with him, yet almost never did he identify with someone else, except in general terms with tribal peoples. In a futile gesture, he took from friendships as much as he could; he was edgy and frustrated with those he could not control or steer.

Once he remarked: 'I suppose I've spent my life searching for permanence.'[7] As a child, as a youth, Thesiger filled this void by imagining big game hunting adventures among wild tribes, in which he emulated or even surpassed his father's life and achievements. The 1933–34 Danakil expedition not only brought his boyhood dreams alive, it fired his ambition to 'win distinction as an explorer and a traveller'.[8] Thesiger was elected a Fellow of the Royal Geographical Society on 12 November 1934, the same day as his lecture; on 24 November the RGS acknowledged his payment of £45, the fee for life membership.

Before leaving Oxford in 1933 Thesiger had applied to join the Sudan Political Service, and had been advised by their agent that he need not attend an interview until he returned to England the following year. Four articles he wrote about his Danakil expedition were published daily by *The Times* between 31 July and 3 August 1934. A fortnight after the articles appeared, Thesiger was interviewed by the Sudan Political Service's Board, at Buckingham Gate. He said later: 'I think the dangerous journey I had just done at the age of only twenty-three, and the articles in *The Times*, helped to get me accepted. There again, even if I hadn't explored the Awash or written anything at all, they would probably still have taken me. A member of the Board did ask me why I wanted to join the Service, and I very nearly said, "Because I want to shoot a lion." It was on the tip of my tongue. He was a self-important little man and I could hardly resist the temptation to provoke him. I'm sure the other members of the Board would have approved of that reply, but he certainly wouldn't. Anyhow, I stopped myself just in time and gave him a rather dull answer that seemed to satisfy him. I've no longer any recollection of what it was I actually said.'[9] All his life Thesiger took himself and his activities very seriously, and tended to prefer people who did the same. He always made a clear distinction between those who were serious about themselves and their work, and others who were merely sententious or pedantic. Thesiger remembered that the name of the member of the Board who asked him why he wanted to join the Service was Hall.[10] This may or may not have been correct: it is possible that Thesiger associated him with Julian Hall, his fag master at Eton, whom he regarded as pompous, and had disliked intensely ever since Hall had caned him for forgetfulness on an evening when he was due to box for the school. He was knocked out in the second round – the only time this ever happened at Eton or Oxford. Thesiger blamed Hall for his defeat, and sixty years later he still felt bitter, writing: 'I never forgave Hall.'[11] At Jibuti, three months before the Board's interview, Thesiger had been reprimanded by the Governor, Chapon-Baissac, for bringing Abyssinian soldiers into his territory and for not handing over his weapons at Dikil. He may have been reminded of this 'corpulent, pompous, short-tempered little man'[12] when he felt tempted to provoke his interviewer at the Sudan Agency, whose arrogant manner threatened to bring out the worst in Thesiger, perhaps to test him.

The Sudan Political Service had been founded by Evelyn Baring, the first Earl of Cromer, British Consul-General in Egypt and author of a two-volume study of modern Egypt, who controlled the Egyptian government from 1883 to 1907. In 1877 Muhammad Ali's grandson, the ruler of Egypt, had appointed General Gordon as Governor-General of the Sudan. After Gordon was killed by the Mahdi's dervishes at Khartoum in 1885, the Mahdi's Caliph ruled for thirteen years until he was defeated by Kitchener, and the Sudan was reconquered by Britain. In 1930, after a lengthy tour of the Sudan, the writer Odette Keun commented: 'The success of the Sudan experiment is due to the quality of its British civil administrators ... The little body of alien men that governs this country has alone made it what it is. But how this body of men manages to be so indisputably first-rate is a mystery which I cannot solve. They are all drawn from British Universities. They are all appointed when they are very young. The Commissioners of the Sudan who examine them personally in England make a point of knowing their athletic record, and their physique is taken into consideration. (Many of these Civil Servants were rowing Blues in their time, or well-known cricketers or football-players.) Their moral reputation is investigated.' Keun added the measured caveat: 'Still, such enquiries are at best only precautionary measures and involve no guarantee that the candidates will turn out well.'[13] She outlined some of the responsibilities and tasks facing any young recruit, such as Wilfred Thesiger, when he arrived in the Sudan:

His governing of [the Sudanese] includes the dispensing of justice – and to be just he has not only to assimilate a hitherto unheard-of legal code, but to understand impulses and mainsprings of emotions which he cannot possibly feel himself, and motives of behaviour and conceptions of morality which have nothing to do with his own experience. He is obliged to learn a very difficult language in a very short time, often with no other instructor than a text-book ... He is forced to turn his hand ... to every sort of ... work that crops up in lonely far-away understaffed places ... He has to be well-groomed and dignified in his person pour l'exemple; cheerful and helpful in the society of his equals, who sum him up with great quickness and acumen; unselfish professionally – not out for personal kudos, but falling readily into teamwork – tenacious to overcome obstacles, stoical to resist the material discomforts and dangers of the climate and the special colonial temptations of drink, drugs and bodily neglect; sexually austere (that is to say, continent, when he is unmarried, for some nine months out of twelve – until his leave comes – for there are no free unattached women of his own kind established in the Sudan and the English social code, poles apart from the Latin, vetoes liaisons with native women pitilessly). In short [the new recruit] has to become one of an order of Samurai. And he becomes one of these Samurai![14]

Many of the issues raised by Odette Keun had a particular significance for Wilfred Thesiger. His powerful physique had been developed and tested as a boxing Blue at Oxford, and again during his Danakil expedition. His determination to join the Sudan Political Service, however, was not matched by a determination to acquire classical Arabic. He became fluent years later in Arabia, but among the tribes in Darfur he had great difficulty in making himself understood. As for his tastes and lifestyle: unlike either his parents or brothers, he had never smoked, and he drank little. From his teens he had empathised with 'races other than [his] own'. He took his code of personal discipline and moral integrity from his father, his ultimate role model, whose memory he treasured.

All his life Thesiger took infinite care to dress in exactly 'the right clothes for the occasion'.[15] At Kutum in Northern Darfur, where he was posted, he wore khaki-coloured knee-length woollen stockings his mother had ordered at his request from Fortnum & Mason.[16] His khaki uniforms were made in London by well-known military tailors; the Khartoum firm of Abdi Awad tailored his elegant cream cotton three-piece suits.

According to his autobiography, Thesiger had felt 'untroubled' by living for long periods of time without a sexual relationship. Although sexual liaisons with native women were frowned upon, they were not unknown. Thesiger remembered: 'Once, in the Nuer country, I walked into a hut and trod on the DC [Wedderburn-Maxwell] who was on the floor with a woman. Apart from my intrusion, he wasn't very pleased that I'd trampled on his bottom.'[17] Some writers have asserted Thesiger was 'asexual', which is untrue. He himself wrote: 'Sex has been of no great consequence to me, and the celibacy of desert life left me untroubled. Marriage would certainly have been a crippling handicap. I have there-fore been able to lead the life of my choice with no sense of deprivation.' This published statement was a modified version of an earlier draft: 'For me sex has never been of any consequence, a diverting but trivial pleasure. Marriage would have been a crippling handicap in my life, a bond I could never have tolerated, the same demanding fem[ale] morning, noon and night.[18]

Judging by his remarks, Thesiger (like van Gogh) regarded sex as a necessary function of personal 'hygiene'. He never talked about physical sex as an expression of love, or even of affection. His attitude to sex was perfunctory, immature and selfish. He firmly declared that he had no sexual relationships during his years in the Sudan, suggesting instead that he had channelled his sexual energy into other 'diverting', physically demanding pleasures such as hunting dangerous game and arduous desert journeys by camel across Northern Darfur and the Sahara. Sex, for Thesiger, was something one dealt with, rather than enjoyed. Once, when asked if he thought T.E. Lawrence had been actively homosexual, he replied: 'I don't know. But if he was, and it bothered him, he should have slept with half a dozen of 'em and got the damned thing out of his system.'[19] In a revealing memo, he defined his view of women as remote functionaries rather than objects of desire: 'I have lived among men in a society in which women did not intrude. They stayed [on the] other side of the curtain, busy with household tasks.'[20] He wrote approvingly of Mrs Dupuis, who joined her husband, Darfur's Governor, at a tribal gathering in 1935: 'In this male society she was never obtrusive.'[21]

Colonel Sandford had been right in assuming that Thesiger's heart was not set on the Sudan Political Service, insofar as Thesiger viewed the Service as a means to an end, rather than a long-term career. His choked-back retort to the Board's interviewer – that his reason for wanting to join was to shoot lion – was over-simplistic, yet very near the truth. Thesiger's lack of interest in administrative duties, his addiction to travel and his passion for big game hunting, culminating in a dangerous, gladiatorial obsession with hunting lion, did not pass unnoticed either by his peers or by his superiors. The Sudan's Civil Secretary from 1939 to 1945, Douglas Newbold, wrote to Thesiger's District Commissioner, Guy Moore, in May 1939: 'Your picture of WT is very accurate. He now realises he is a misfit, but a misfit only in a Government and owing to excess of certain ancient virtues and not because of any vices – a brave, awkward, attractive creature.'[22]

Before he left for the Sudan, Thesiger should have completed an Arabic language course at the School of Oriental and African Studies in London. But he neglected this, and instead worked on his maps and diaries, preparing his autumn paper on the Awash for the Royal Geographical Society. He also wrote the introduction and field notes for a thirty-three-page report on 'Birds from Danakil, Abyssinia', published by the British Ornithological Union's journal *The Ibis* in October 1935. He 'always regretted this missed opportunity to become proficient in classical Arabic'.[23]

While Thesiger was busy planning his 1933 Danakil expedition,

Kathleen had helped him by contacting influential people on his behalf.
Now, even before he had left England, he met one of the Sudan's
Governors, who made it his business to find out where Thesiger had been
posted and, having done so, arranged for him to be relocated to an area
that catered to his adventurous spirit and his passion for big game
hunting and travel. Thesiger wrote: 'When I reported to the Civil
Secretary's Office, the day after my arrival in Khartoum, I was delighted
to learn that I had been posted to Kutum in Northern Darfur, generally
regarded as one of the three most coveted districts in the Northern
Sudan. I learnt later that I owed this posting to Charles Dupuis, Governor
of Darfur, whom I had met at a friend's house in Wales shortly after I had
been selected for the Service.'[24] Describing Dupuis, Thesiger might have
been describing his father: 'a lean, weathered man of forty-nine, attentive,
courteous and unassuming'.[25] Although he implied in his autobiography
that he had met Dupuis by chance, it is probable that Thesiger or his
mother contrived this important invitation by their neighbour Mrs J.M.
Gibson-Watt, at whose home Dupuis was staying. (Ironically, Mrs
Gibson-Watt's late husband was a great-grandson of James Watt, the
inventor of the steam engine, who helped to pave the way for the
Industrial Revolution. Watt's invention prefaced two centuries of
technological progress and social reformation which the romantic,
traditionalist Wilfred Thesiger utterly deplored.)

More significantly, Mrs Dupuis and Wilfred's cousin, Sybil Thesiger,
were close friends who planned to travel together across Africa from east
to west by lorry in April 1935. With this connection, and since he had
already been accepted by the Sudan Political Service, it was inevitable that
he should have been invited to meet Dupuis while he was staying near
Thesiger's home. Thesiger made his hopes and intentions clear to Dupuis
at this first meeting. In *The Life of My Choice* he recalled: 'We had a long
and, for me, enthralling talk, mostly about Darfur. I sensed at once that
his heart was in that remote province. Apparently, on getting back to
Khartoum from leave he had enquired and been told that I was being sent
to Wad Medani, a sophisticated cotton-growing area on the Blue Nile,
with the intention of breaking me in to routine office work. Dupuis told
Gillan [Sir Angus Gillan, the Civil Secretary, whose wife Thesiger had
already met, and danced with, at The 400, an exclusive nightclub in

Mayfair[26]] he was certain I would resign if I was posted there, and persuaded him to send me to Darfur instead.'[27]

Thesiger wrote from Khartoum on 14 January 1935: 'I should have picked Darfur every time as the place I should like to have gone to from among the Northern provinces, but I thought there was not the least hope of being sent there.'[28] As for Khartoum itself, he wrote: 'I hate this place ... God forbid that I should ever be stationed here. I really could not bear it.'[29]

In his foreword to *Game Animals of the Sudan* (1931) by the country's former Chief Game Warden, Captain H.C. Brocklehurst, John Guille Millais, a son of the Pre-Raphaelite painter, wrote evocatively and from the heart that 'Sudan offers many wonderful scenes and hunting trophies to the man of grit who can cut out a line for himself and go off the beaten track into that vast Africa which still holds an abiding fascination to the man of imagination and courage ... There are many spots in Sudan where the white man has not been, and to youth and enterprise the gate is still open.'[30] Praising the Sudan's administration, Millais echoed Odette Keun: 'nowhere [in Africa] have I seen natives, whether Arab or Bantu, give more willing and friendly service to the white man as they do in Sudan. This is, of course, entirely due to the skilful handling of those in supreme authority and the personality of the District Commissioners and lesser officials of the outposts.'[31] Thesiger's imagination was fired by Millais's challenging description of the Sudan's unexplored game fields, just as he had read with feverish excitement the artist-naturalist Abel Chapman's *Savage Sudan* (1921) and Millais's own well-illustrated account of a long safari with his son Raoul, *Far Away up the Nile* (1924).

Although in Kenya (formerly British East Africa) by the early 1930s big game hunting had been organised commercially on a large scale for more than three decades, there was at that time no equivalent in the Sudan. Thesiger said: 'I am always thankful that I got to the Sudan before the days of professional hunters and their clients had started.' In contrast to Kenya, 'In the Sudan, you bought your licence ... hunted by yourself, with your gunbearer and trackers. I did all of my hunting on foot, except when I "galloped down" lion, on horseback.'[32] Galloping down lion had been a popular sport in East Africa before the war. In *A Game Ranger's Notebook* (1924), A. Blayney Percival, the first Chief Game Warden of

Kenya, described it as 'the finest sport in the world': 'From the moment the quarry is afoot till he is dead there is no cessation of excitement. The first sight of the stealthily moving animal sets the pulses tingling, and the race over country after him stirs the blood as no stalk can possibly do.'[33]

On 13 January 1935 Thesiger arrived in Khartoum from Egypt, where he had stayed in Cairo with John Hamilton (a former District Commissioner in the Sudan), and afterwards in Luxor, which he remembered at dusk, lit by 'the sun setting in a blaze of colour behind the lifeless hills across the river'. Onward from Aswan, Thesiger travelled upstream to Wadi Halfa by paddle steamer, 'the ideal way to see the Nile, the proper way to approach the Sudan'. From there, insulated in a comfortable first-class carriage, he crossed 'the challenging starkness' of the Nubian desert by train to Khartoum.[34]

Among Thesiger's personal baggage were the rifles he had brought with him from England to shoot big game. His brother Brian had given him as a present a .350 Rigby Magnum magazine rifle. He also had the more powerful double-barrelled .450 Rigby Nitro-Express his mother had given him in 1933, a twelve-bore shotgun and a .22 rimfire rifle he had used to collect the smaller birds of the Danakil country. Before he continued his journey to Kutum in Northern Darfur, his base for the next two years, he visited the Chief Game Warden's office in Khartoum, where he purchased his general licence and enquired about hunting conditions in the Darfur region. He recalled: 'I met Pongo Barker, the Game Warden, at his office in the zoo. I gathered he had done very little hunting, unlike Brocklehurst, his predecessor, who wrote a book about big game in the Sudan.'[35] When he realised I was keen on hunting and going to Northern Darfur, Barker told me I could hope to get addax, white oryx and Barbary sheep, all highly prized trophies. I asked about lion; he said there were plenty in the district but I was not likely to get one; no one had yet managed to shoot a lion at Kutum. I had every intention of doing so.'[36] (Captain Brocklehurst devoted barely four pages to lion in *Game Animals of the Sudan*. He quoted experiences of lion in Mozambique and Tanganyika; in the Sudan, he recorded lion spoor north of Wadi Howar.)

Thesiger arrived at Kutum, after being driven for three days in a lorry, to find that the District Commissioner, Guy Moore, was away on trek: 'Moore ... and I would be the only two British officials in the district [which was the largest in the Sudan, covering sixty thousand square miles]. Kutum, the District Headquarters, had no wireless station, and mail arrived fortnightly by runner from Fasher, the Provincial Headquarters. Well-meaning people warned me that Moore travelled incessantly about his district, covered extraordinary distances with his camels, never bothered about meal times, and ate – when he did eat – at the oddest hours, and would expect me to do the same. I welcomed the prospect of serving under such a man.'

Thesiger wrote to his mother: 'Everyone here says [Moore] is one of the nicest men in the Service,'[37] and after six months he was able to confirm that 'Moore is one of the nicest men I have met. He is extraordinarily like Arthur Bentinck in some ways, a person whom you feel is absolutely straight. He also has got the same hot temper and inability to suffer fools gladly. He is a most sympathetic person with a very great share of natural kindness. I have got a very great respect for him, but fear that my next DC will probably fall short of the mark in consequence, but I hope they won't transfer me for some time. When I do get moved I want to get right south to Mongalla.'[38] He wrote in *The Life of My Choice*: 'Two servants, a *sufragi* or butler and a cook, had been engaged for me before I arrived; both were from Berber, the home of professional Sudanese servants. I have forgotten their names; neither lasted very long.'[39]

Thesiger was 'immediately captivated by Kutum',[40] which he described to his mother as 'a most attractive spot on the side of some very strange boulder strewn hills looking out over a green Wadi to bush country and endless peaks in the distance'.[41] Before he left Kutum in February, Reginald Dingwall, the Assistant District Commissioner whom Thesiger was to replace, showed him round, helped him to settle in and sold him riding camels and odds and ends of furniture. Thesiger wrote that he would be sorry to see Dingwall go: 'I like him very much, and he has been endlessly helpful to me.'[42] The house he vacated was 'really very nice – A large thatched house with mud walls and a verandah round outside. It has one vast room about as big as the drawing room at Stanage [home of the Rodgers family, who owned the Stanage estate at Knighton, including The Milebrook] as a sitting room and a dining room, a bedroom and a number of other small rooms which you can use as store rooms and bathrooms. It has got a cement floor which is invaluable as it saves things from the white ants which swarm in the walls so that you can leave nothing touching them or it gets eaten at once. There is a fireplace in the big room. I took over some of Dingwall's chairs and small tables, and with the rugs which I have bought I have made it extremely comfortable ... I expect my establishment will slowly increase in numbers until I have about a dozen retainers, though there is not much for them to do.'[43]

Ever since his childhood Thesiger had needed a permanent home as well as the colourful, savage, unburdened life he craved. In his eighties he repeated that one motivation for his journeys had been a desire for peace of mind, and for somewhere to settle. His need for comradeship had been inseparable from his need for a gathering point: in other words, for a home. Thesiger idealised the people and places that fulfilled this need at different stages in his life: his parents and the Legation at Addis Ababa; his mother and The Milebrook; Idris Daud, his Zaghawa servant, and Kutum; the flat in Chelsea which he shared for thirty years with his mother, and which remained for a further twenty-five years his 'haven' or his 'little shell'. After his mother died, Thesiger increasingly regarded as his home the simple wooden houses at Maralal, in northern Kenya, which he built and shared with his Samburu adoptive sons and their families. His rooms at Eton and Oxford had given him a sense of 'ownership' and the privacy he needed.[44] His parents' rented flat in Brighton, even the rundown farmhouse Kathleen rented for a year at Titley in Hereford-shire, mattered because they were associated with his father, his mother, his brothers – and his old nanny Minna Buckle, to whom he now referred occasionally as 'Bucks' in letters from the Sudan.

The campfires he shared with his followers in many countries, beginning with Darfur, were also 'havens' and 'gathering points' of memorable significance. Sitting on the ground by a fire, 'feeding with [his] tribal companions',[45] gave Thesiger the sense of comradeship and involvement he desired, and the satisfaction that he was accepted. He treasured the memory of sailing in a dhow to Jibuti after his Danakil expedition, and the unforgettable sharing of the crew's evening meal of rice and fish. In Northern Darfur, Guy Moore encouraged Thesiger to travel light, and to treat his followers not as servants but as companions. Camped beneath the stars, 'in the heart of the desert, on the naked rind of the planet, in an isolation like that of the beginnings of the world', Thesiger and the tribesmen with him 'built a village of men'.[46] He embraced this unencumbered style of travel, which gave him everything he wanted. By then he had discovered that 'it wasn't necessary to burden one's life with too much weight, with too many things to do'. This allowed him to live as a bachelor, more easily than if he had had to face the normal difficulties of life. Thesiger's 'best work'[47] may have been the way he used his time: that is to say, by living the adventure of being himself. In 1967 he told an interviewer that sitting on the ground, feeding with local tribal chiefs, although it gave one 'a sense of common humanity with them – doing this in the Sudan I confess I felt rather condescending'.[48]

At Kutum, Thesiger arranged his house and waited for Guy Moore to return. The marvellously evocative descriptions of Kutum in *The Life of My Choice* are really more polished versions of letters in which he sketched the house whose thatched roof and mud walls recalled his birthplace. In 1987 Thesiger wrote in his autobiography: 'I covered [two bedsteads] with colourful Fezzani rugs and leather cushions, and used them as divans in the sitting room. I put other rugs on the floor and eventually some lion skins ... I later decorated [the mud walls] with spears, swords, throwing-knives and the horns of animals I shot. In the bookcase I put my complete sets of Conrad and Kipling, Blackwood's *Tales from the Outposts*, Gibbon's *Decline and Fall of the Roman Empire*, Frazer's *Golden Bough*, Lawrence's *Revolt in the Desert*, Doughty's *Arabia Deserta*, Churchill's *The River War* and a number of other books, mostly historical. I soon made the house comfortable and, despite its lack of amenities, infinitely preferred it to the characterless bungalows in Fasher.'[49]

As a Christmas present, Thesiger asked Kathleen for the first 'trade' edition of Lawrence's *Seven Pillars of Wisdom*, published shortly after Lawrence's death in May 1935. He added pragmatically: 'The 1st edition will be valuable.'[50] But Thesiger collected books first and foremost in order to read them, and had no qualms about exposing a scarce, valuable work such as Churchill's *The River War* (which he sold for £1200 in 1995) to the pervasive climate or destructive insects at Kutum. He sometimes read merely to pass the time when Moore was away on trek, leaving him in charge. When he was 'all alone',[51] with no one to talk to, his books helped him to endure the solitude.

In July, after the rains had broken, he wrote begging Kathleen: 'If you have any books which you have finished with do send them out ... Don't buy books and send them out, but every now and again when you have one you have finished with do post it to me.'[52] 'If the others want to know later on what I want for Christmas tell them I want the complete set of Conrad, and if they would send me a volume or two of it I can gradually collect it all. I could get along very happily with a complete set of Conrad and Kipling. There are no other two writers to touch them and you can read them time and time again.'[53]

Guy Moore became one of the most important influences in Thesiger's life. Thesiger had expected 'a tall, spare, weather-beaten man of few words; in fact he was short, tubby, talkative, with a red face, very blue eyes and an explosive temper which he generally controlled. He had been in the Flying Corps during the First World War and won an MC. After the war he had served as an Intelligence Officer among the desert tribes in Iraq, where he learnt fluent Bedu Arabic.'[54] Serving at Kutum under Moore, Thesiger found himself in a world that resembled an adult version of his childhood in Abyssinia. He conceded, to an extent, that Moore represented a father figure, whom he remembered as 'never pompous', 'never dogmatic', compassionate and generous. Together they visited a big tribal gathering at Fata Burnu, north-west of Kutum, where the spectacle of massed tribesmen (Thesiger originally wrote in a letter that there were five thousand of them, changed this to six thousand,[55] and gave their number as ten thousand in The Life of My Choice[56]) and their chiefs could hardly have failed to remind Thesiger of the Sagale victory parades he witnessed at Addis Ababa in 1916: 'Mounted on horses and camels, they brandished swords and spears, and shouted their war songs to the thunder of drums ... The chiefs were resplendent in coloured robes, their turbans wrapped across their faces hiding all but their eyes; many of their followers, especially among the Zaghawa, wore brightly-coloured jibbas. As they surged past I noticed a few in coats of mail, which were reputed to date from the time of the Crusades, as was the pattern of their long, straight swords. I found this parade, at which the tribes honoured their Governor, a thrilling introduction to Northern Darfur.'[57]

Among those present were Lieutenant-Colonel G.K. Maurice, the doctor, and Major R.J. Audas. Audas, Dupuis and Maurice, whom Thesiger called 'The Darfur Holy Trinity',[58] had served in the district for many years and were inseparable friends. Audas shared Thesiger's passionate enthusiasm for big game hunting. He advised Thesiger where to look for Barbary sheep, and how to sit up for lion at night over a bait, although Thesiger said: 'In fact I never shot a lion at night, nor did I ever use bait.'[59] (A cabinet in the Mammal Department of the Natural History Museum in South Kensington, containing the skulls of forty-nine lion presented by Thesiger in 1938 and 1945, also contains lion skulls from the Sudan presented to the museum by Major Audas.[60])

Moore encouraged Thesiger to trek all over Northern Darfur using camels. He sent him to the Tagabo Hills, which gave Thesiger his first memorable experience of camel-riding. 'Next day,' Thesiger wrote, 'I was so stiff I could hardly move, but after another six hours in the saddle I loosened up and never again felt stiff from riding a camel.'[61] He thought it was 'rather fun provided you don't let him walk when it is the most uncomfortable thing which I know. But at first it catches you in a whole lot of unsuspected muscles in your back and thighs. I am just beginning to fancy that I have got a rather good seat, and to talk wisely, or so I think, about humps and bosses. On the strength of it I have bought myself a new riding camel. A very small and rather attractive animal which I have named Habib or Beloved in Arabic. He can go very fast and ... Moore who really does know something about camels approved of him.'[62] Describing Habib to Kathleen, Thesiger wrote: 'My new one ... is a fascinating animal, as small as a female camel and rather young but fast and I hope a stayer. He is much more the Arab type of racing camel. Moore approves of him and says he will give me a certificate for him. You are allowed to have 2 ponies and 6 camels on a certificate at Kutum. This means that if they die or you have to sell them on leaving the district the Government refunds you the price you paid for them. You can also draw an allowance to cover your syce's wages, and their fodder bill.' Although Thesiger could be extravagant, he was usually careful with money: 'Another thing which is very pleasant is that you can draw an extra 5/- a day travelling allowance for every night you spent out of your station, even if it is only in Fasher. I get £4 for this trek [to Tagabo].'[63]

When Thesiger got back to Kutum from the Tagabo Hills he found two tiny lion cubs, offspring of a lioness which local tribesmen had speared that morning, lying on the newly flayed skin of their mother outside his house. He successfully reared the cubs, which 'made the most delightful pets'[64] and often lay on his bedstead on the verandah. Whereas the lion cubs were decorative and exotic, some mongooses left in Thesiger's care by Charles Dupuis proved useful. Thesiger went 'ferreting with them, visiting all the most snaky places [near his house], with the mongeese running round all day. They also eat all the beetles and bugs of every sort which I mind far more than snakes.'[65] At Maralal, in his eighties, Thesiger killed small vipers in the garden by stamping on them, then grinding them under the heel of his shoe. At Kutum he used a 'walking stick gun' to shoot a furiously angry puff adder which the mongooses, lightning-fast, had kept at bay.[66] In May, when the cubs were three months old, he reassured Kathleen: 'Don't worry about the lions. I promise not to keep them when they begin to grow up. At the moment they are only the size of large cats.'[67] The cubs gave him company and continual amusement: 'They have taken to stalking the chickens which they do very skilfully, but lose their nerve and bolt at the last moment when the terrified chicken gives a squawk.'[68] He shot the cubs when they were nine months old. Thesiger said: 'Some people criticised me for this, but the Khartoum zoo didn't want any more lion and I was often away from Kutum. If I'd turned the cubs loose they would have become maneaters. I knew I had no alternative but to shoot them, but I hated doing it all the same.'[69]

Thesiger's reasons for shooting the cubs were perfectly valid, but the act dismayed some of his staunchest admirers. When his spaniel died the young Thesiger had been grief-stricken, and in letters to his mother he would beg for news of the family's dogs and horses. In Kenya, however, he alternated affection for his one-eared cat and Juno, a mongrel bitch, with cruelty, kicking the dog or hitting it with his stick, and seizing the cat by the neck and hurling it away. He wrote to his mother in December 1935: 'I also got the very sad news of poor old Bobs. Dear old dog, I was very fond of him and his death is a sad blow. I shall miss him so at the Milebrook, as I know you are [missing him] now. However one had got to expect it, and the poor old dog had aged a great deal of late. I have just shot my two lions which I hated doing as I was very fond of them. The house seems very forlorn without them and I keep looking round to see where they are. But it was either that or chaining them up, as they had taken to killing sheep of late. You cannot think how attractive they were.'[70] (Moore kept a pet cheetah called Norah, whose fate is unknown.)

To an extent, Darfur was 'an ideal prelude' for Thesiger's Arabian years.[71] The Northern Darfur tribes, like the Bedu in Arabia, were largely nomads, their lives spent wandering on the southern limits of the Sahara. He wrote of the three months in 1938 he spent travelling to and from Tibesti in the French Sahara: 'For me this journey in the heat of summer served as an apprenticeship to the five years I would later spend in Arabia. It so conditioned me that even under the worst conditions there, with thirst and hunger my daily lot, I would never wish I were elsewhere. On this Tibesti journey, I had in fact suffered neither thirst nor hunger, but I was never again to ride for such long hours, day after day, for weeks on end.'[72]

His journey to the Tagabo Hills in March 1935, meanwhile, accustomed him to riding a camel and prepared him for a journey in April to the Jabal Maidob, where he and Moore attended a meeting between Sheikhs of the Kababish and Maidob tribes. In letters to his mother and Brian he described the new riding camel he had bought, at Moore's suggestion, from a Kababish Sheikh. A Bisharin from the Red Sea Hills, it was named Faraj Allah: 'It has charming manners, and lets you do anything you like with it.'[73] In Thesiger's view 'There was certainly no other camel to equal it in Darfur, and few west of the Nile.'[74] Such a claim was typical of Thesiger, who asserted that his family's achievements had been unrivalled, that his upbringing and adolescence at Addis Ababa and The Milebrook had been incomparably happy, that his schools were the finest in England.

Faraj Allah's previous owner, Sheikh Ali Taum of the Kababish, the Sudan's largest camel-owning tribe, was a 'desert aristocrat' who had restored his people to 'pre-eminence' after the British occupation.[75] Thesiger got on extremely well with Charles de Bunsen, the tribe's administrator, 'a most charming person' aged about thirty who 'revelled in his nomadic existence'[76] and had a similar outlook to Thesiger's own.[77] The dramatic arrival of forty Kababish, led by their Sheikh, left a thrilling impression: 'a fine sight as they came across the desert towards us at a fast trot. The Arabs were turbaned and dressed in white, while their camels, extended at this pace, displayed an unexpected grace of movement.'[78] Most important of all, he would later write: 'This was my first encounter with an authentic Bedu tribe, the first time I heard the inimitable speech of the Arabian desert, very different from the Arabic used as lingua franca in Darfur.'[79] The Maidob gave him his crucial introduction to the real desert.

Charles Dupuis had asked Thesiger to report on the Barbary sheep in Jabal Maidob, which gave him an excuse to shoot one as a trophy. While Moore returned to Kutum, Thesiger 'spent a blissfully happy week, shooting all over the ['sheep jabals'] – very hard work but I was glad to find myself fit, and left the Jabal never having felt so well in my life. I got a sheep with an excellent head the first morning I was out. The first one I saw. They are lovely animals and very much larger than one expects. It takes three men to move one. They are a deep chestnut rufous and have a large fringe down their chests. They have heavy back curving horns. Mine are 28¾" [Brocklehurst's book gave 27¾" as a record for the Sudan]. During the week I saw a number of others but did not shoot another as one only has 2 yearly on one's licence and I did not see one noticeably bigger.'[80] (Thesiger gave his decision a less pragmatic twist in *The Life of My Choice*, stating: 'I had no wish to shoot another.'[81])

With the Maidob chief Malik Sayyah he travelled across the desert as far as the Anka wells: 'It took us five days between water but we managed it pretty comfortably and I loved it.'[82] On the way he shot a male white oryx 'after a hard day's riding of about 50 miles looking for them. [The] solitary bull gave us an exciting chase.' That evening he watched a herd of forty-two oryx with long, scimitar-shaped horns 'as they poured over the skyline close by' in 'a torrent of brilliant white and chestnut'.[83]

This desert journey was deeply influential. For the first time, Thesiger travelled as Guy Moore had encouraged him to travel (and in the style of de Monfreid): 'I sat or slept on a rug on the ground, with my few possessions in my saddle-bags, and enjoyed that easy, informal comradeship that this life and our surroundings engendered. It was my first experience of the infinite space of the real desert, its silence and its windswept cleanness.'[84] When Thesiger returned to Kutum, he told Moore how the desert had fascinated him. In 1987 he relived the moment, using direct speech, something one of his editors later felt he seldom handled convincingly. Thesiger wrote – apparently from memory – that Moore had said: 'When I get back from leave you can go off for a month into the Libyan Desert. I'd like you to do that. I always think of the desert as the High Altar of God.'[85] The version he gave his mother at the time was far more prosaic: 'Moore hopes to get off on leave at the beginning of July. I don't expect to get out much while he is away, but hope, if nothing crops up to stop it, to get off into the Libyan desert for my trek as soon as he gets back, towards the end of October I expect.'[86]

Throughout his life, Thesiger alternated abstinence and hardship with indulgence and ease. He said: 'I have never thought about this; it just happened. I suppose most food tasted better after you'd been starving, just as a drink of clean water is all I dreamt of when I was thirsty.'[87] Travelling across the desert towards Kutum, he and his party fed on dates, or thick millet porridge mixed with vegetable sauce and washed down with cups of strong, sweet tea. In England, he would declare strong tea 'undrinkable'. His friend John Verney portrayed Thesiger in his second volume of autobiography *A Dinner of Herbs* (1966) as 'the sort of man who will happily walk barefoot for months across a waterless desert, subsisting on a handful of dates and occasional sip of camel's piss, but who, back in civilisation, cannot endure the most trivial discomfort. He becomes frantic even if his egg isn't boiled right for breakfast.'[88]

Soon after he returned from Jabal Maidob, Thesiger wrote thanking his mother for some expensive chocolates: '[They] have arrived and I could not have been given anything better. Funnily enough I had been thinking for some days that I must write to Fortnum & Masons and order some sweets. You know the craving for sweets which you get when you have been out on trek for some time. They are delicious and the difficulty is to spin them out and not eat them continuously.'[89] At Kutum – as he had at school and at university – he looked forward to these luxuries. They soothed away other anxieties. Horses were dying. Meningitis was rife. 'Two people have died in the last few days. There is one sad case of a boy of about 11 in the school. He had an abscess in his ear 2 months ago, and then got double pneumonia as the abscess got all right. He got over this and now has got meningitis. The cold water treatment for this has brought back his pneumonia. It is rather heartbreaking to see him. He is wonderfully plucky when he is not delirious. We have also got a man dying in hospital of tetanus, a horrible sight.'[90] Disease and illness haunted Thesiger, who often remarked how useful a medical training would have been during his travels. (Later, in Iraq, he would receive basic training at an American mission and the military hospital in Basra in order to perform circumcisions, dispense medicines and treat wounds.)

In July he wrote to Kathleen: 'I should love the Seven Pillars of Wisdom for Christmas but wonder if it all won't be sold out in advance.' In the same letter he voiced concerns about Mussolini's determination to incorporate Abyssinia into his 'new Roman Empire':[91] 'I am certain that there will be war in Abyssinia. I cannot see how our Government can stop it, especially now that it seems obvious that France and Italy have a secret agreement giving Italy a free hand in Abyssinia. An invidious position for France who must run with the hares and hunt with the hounds.'[92] Thesiger had told Moore that if Abyssinia was attacked he would resign from the Service and fight. Moore sympathised, but advised him not to 'jump the gun'; in the event of war with Italy, Thesiger would get a chance to help defend Abyssinia 'while fighting for [his] own country'.[93] Though he felt 'proud to be English and wished to be nothing else',[94] Thesiger still thought of Abyssinia as 'home' – something even the perceptive Guy Moore had not comprehended fully. Although England had been the Thesigers' adoptive country for six generations, fighting for his 'own country', to Wilfred, meant fighting for both Abyssinia and for England (as he – and many of his contemporaries – commonly referred to Great Britain).

As soon as Moore left Kutum on leave, Thesiger began hunting lion in earnest. His first four attempts – either tracking them among boulders and thorn scrub or 'beating in line, rather like you do for rabbits'[95] – all failed. Instead of saving Seven Pillars for Christmas, Kathleen evidently sent the book as soon as she had bought it. Thesiger wrote on 16 September, thanking her in a long letter which included thrilling accounts of lion hunts with the Bani Hussain tribe, the first near Kebkabia: 'I am delighted with the Seven Pillars I have always wanted to read it, but never expected to have a copy. It will occupy my leisure hours for weeks to come.'[96] By then he had shelved his plan to write a book about the Danakil expedition. Soon after arriving at Kutum, he noted that the expedition diaries he had asked his mother to send 'should arrive here soon'. Despite anticipating that he would be 'very busy this year', he wrote, 'I want to try and get on with a book about the Danakil country.'[97] Instead, he spent the greater part of his time travelling all over Northern Darfur. From September until he left Kutum to serve in the Upper Nile swamps, he was urged continually to come and shoot lion that raided the Darfur tribes' cattle, mauling and sometimes killing herdsmen who went after them. He described his first experiences with the Bani Hussain, two days' journey from Kebkabia, on the way back to Kutum:

I stopped for the night at a village where they said there were lions and sure enough soon after dark we heard them coughing, not roaring, quite close answering one another. I never actually heard a lion roar though I heard them coughing like this several times. Early next morning I sent 3 men out on horses to find their tracks. They came back almost at once saying they had found them in a large wadi close by. We followed them up. The men were Bani Hussain and track marvellously, going along at a steady jog over the most rocky ground. They see a pebble slightly shifted or a bruised stem of grass at once, tracking almost entirely by such signs, only bending down every now and then to examine the ground to make sure they are still on the lion. Most of the time I could not make out any sign of a track. I was ahead with one of them and after we had been going for a couple of hours he suddenly stopped and I saw a three quarter grown cub lying under a mimosa scrub about 40 yards off. He saw us at once, but I did not shoot as I wanted a full grown one.

Next instant a lioness jumped up and I heard the bullet strike. Then we had a breathless minute. As soon as I shot the scrub began erupting lions. I hit and knocked over a cub, and wounded a lioness counting one, two, three, as you do marking birds at a hot corner in a drive. You could hear the bullet strike very plainly. I was shooting as fast as I could work the bolt and should have had another cub, only the first lioness started to charge and I had to give her another shot. This broke her shoulder but she continued to sound and look extraordinarily bloody minded. I finished her off and found the cub lying dead. The other lioness had made off though there was a lot of blood, and two cubs got away free. I let the lioness stiffen while we skinned the other two which took a couple of hours, and then followed her up. Every few yards she had lain down, and bitten everything within reach. We found her in some tallish grass about 300 yards off. She suddenly jumped up with a roar but I hit her before she could charge, and finished her with another shot as she staggered side-ways.[98]

Thesiger later said: 'If you were with people as I was in the Sudan, in Northern Darfur, one of the best ways to get on terms with them was to go and help them kill something. You would go along when they were out spearing lion which had killed their cattle. If you galloped the lion down, jumped off and shot it, you probably saved a couple of chaps from being killed or mauled and you were getting closer to them.'[99] That he should speak of the Bani Hussain as 'chaps' was revealingly, typically inconsistent. In a letter to his mother from Khartoum in 1935 he had criticised 'a man in the Civil Secretary's office' who led a party of twenty visitors round the battlefield at Omdurman. Thesiger wrote scathingly: '[He] gave us a simply incredibly bad lecture, and destroyed any feeling of drama by referring repeatedly to the Dervishes as "blokes" and "chaps".'[100] (Admittedly, there is a difference between an official describing the Mahdi's warriors as 'chaps' on the battlefield at Omdurman, and Thesiger referring colloquially to the Bani Hussain as 'chaps' thousands of miles from Northern Darfur, in the sitting room of his London flat.)

Thesiger had made mistakes during his first encounter with lion; he would make others, fortunately for him (and the men with him) without serious consequences. He wrote:

[At] the next village we stopped at we again heard lions roaring during the night, and the man from the village, these were Fur, found the tracks soon after sunrise. There was a party of about 15 of them and they followed the tracks at a steady jog, very hard on the wind at first. [Among Thesiger's friends in the Sudan his lion-hunting feats became legendary. 'He was so tough,' said one of them, 'that he simply ran after the lion till it gave in from sheer exhaustion. He could outrun it.'] One holds the line and the others fan out sideways picking it up as soon as he gets off it, attracting the others' attention with a few clucks. It was exactly like beagling. The lion was a large one from his tracks. After an hour and a half we found where he had lain up, but had then seen us and made off at a canter. They hate going out of a fast walk however, and he only cantered for a short distance every now and then when we got too close. Our object is to bustle him along and work him into a temper when he will come to bay. After about 3 hours of fast going he suddenly sprang out of a thick patch of scrub and crossed my front about 30 yards away. My sight had somehow dropped in the chase and my bullet only cut him across the shoulder. [Being out of breath, shooting offhand, might easily have spoilt his aim.] He came to bay almost at once, and two dogs we had with us held him very well, keeping just out of reach. We came over a rise almost on top of him, and I shot him through the chest just as he flung out his tail. I had always read that you can tell when a lion is going to charge by this; till he throws it straight out you can see it flicking from one side to the other. He was growling hard, but I cannot remember if he was showing his fangs, a thing I have always meant to note. He was a fine big one with a good mane for the Sudan. The first lions I had seen seemed unexpectedly small until I had shot them [these were lionesses and a three-quarter-grown cub]. This one looked as large as a donkey when he first crossed in front of me. He was very dark all over.[101]

Thesiger had gone to Otash to meet the District Commissioner, Paul Sanderson, in order to map the Bani Hussain tribal boundary and investigate land claims. The night before he joined Sanderson, a lion killed a cow in a nearby village. Thesiger sent his caravan ahead to the meeting place, while he went after the marauder.

This time we had a gruelling day. We put him out of some thick scrub after 2 hours tracking, but I did not get a chance of a shot. Usually they lie up on rocky ground under a few thorn bushes in open country, to get away from the flies and the ticks, which are awful in the long grass, crawling up your legs in scores. When disturbed the lion makes for thick cover along the wadi beds. This one went fairly straight for about an hour, after which he got into very tall grass and thick scrub and began twisting and turning like an eel, crossing his own tracks and ours time after time. You could not help feeling sorry for him, we were so implacably on his heels. Several times we heard him grunting just ahead. He next headed for open country, and some vultures picked him up and wheeled above him, as rooks will over a hunted fox. He kept a steady 300–400 yards ahead here and we could not get a sight of him, though the vultures told us exactly where he was. We then crossed some marsh, it had poured the night before, and several deep channels full of water, coming at last to a large wadi. I shall always remember those enormous pug marks going along endlessly down its sandy bed, just filling with water, and with the water from his coat still wet on the sand, after he had crossed a pool. Every now and then he took to the banks, where he left a track like a buffalo through the reeds. It was killing work, but you felt he must be getting as done as you were. After 4 hours, from when we had jumped him, he began to twist and turn again, taking to the dense grass and scrub. We had an hour of this, until he suddenly sprang out of a thicket with a roar, but I had gone to the other side of it and did not see him. When the excitement had quieted we took up his trail again. Soon afterwards we heard him panting in some thick jungle as we passed beside it. We peered into it for some time before we could make out his shape a dozen yards away. He started to growl and I thought he was getting ready to charge so shot at what I thought was his head, but was actually his back legs. He charged at once, and I got in one more shot when he was about 2 yards off. This made him swerve slightly and he took the man standing beside me. The man thrust his shelagai, a spear with a head 6″ broad, held like a pike, into his mouth, but the lion put both paws on his chest and they went down together. There was then a wild scramble, and it was a second or two before I could finish him off, there being a confused medley of lion, men and spears in a clearing the size of a billiard table. He mauled two of them rather badly on the chest and thighs, and chewed up a third man's hand a bit. The spear which had been thrust into his mouth was twisted into a circle. He was a very big lion but almost maneless. Years before he had had one of his top fangs knocked out and his skull cracked. There was a considerable thickening of the bone along the crack.

I got the wounded into camp by sunset and met Sanderson. We treated the wounds with very strong Carbolic. I had them with me for 10 days and though they all went rather nasty you can expect this from lion wounds, and I finally got them into Kebkabia dispensary well on the way to recovery, I hope. They are wonderful patients and never flinch or utter a sound no matter how deep you probe.

ABOVE: Wilfred Thesiger's grandfather, General Frederic Augustus Thesiger, 2nd Baron Chelmsford (1827–1905), who commanded the British force during the Zulu War in South Africa in 1879.

ABOVE RIGHT: Captain The Hon Wilfred Gilbert Thesiger DSO in army uniform, photographed c.1902 in Belgrade, where he served as Vice-Consul and later with the acting rank of Second Secretary in charge of the Legation.

One of Thesiger's favourite photographs of his mother, about 1919, showing 'a beautiful, resolute face under waves of soft brown hair'.

ABOVE: The thatched *tukul* (mud-and-wattle hut) in the British Legation compound at Addis Adaba, where Wilfred Patrick Thesiger was born on 3 June 1910.

LEFT: Billy, as the baby Wilfred was known, with Susannah, his Indian nursemaid, on the Legation lawn, Addis Ababa, in 1911.

A rare photograph of Susannah's successor, Thesiger's nurse Minna (Mary Buckle) in camp during a trek in Abyssinia, about 1915.

Wilfred Gilbert Thesiger (right) and Ras Tafari, later to become the Emperor Haile Selassie (wearing tinted spectacles), on the steps of the British Legation at Addis Ababa.

ABOVE: Part of the victory parade on Jan Meda, Addis Ababa, following the Battle of Sagale in 1916: 'I believe that day implanted in me a lifelong craving for barbaric splendour, for savagery and colour.'

RIGHT: Photographed in Bombay in 1918, Dermot Thesiger stands behind Brian (left) and Wilfred (right) on either side of Roderic, youngest of the four brothers.

Frederic John Napier Thesiger, first Viscount Chelmsford (1868–1933), Viceroy of India 1916–21. To his highly impressionable nephew Wilfred he seemed 'more than human' when they first met in 1918.

BELOW: The widowed Kathleen Thesiger with her four sons. Clockwise, from the left, Wilfred, Brian, Dermot and Roderic.

ABOVE: Pierre, a Breton fisherman, and his thirteen year-old *mousse* at Sable d'Or, Brittany, in 1929. 'Every morning, before it was light, I crossed the mile-long sands to the cove where the fishermen kept their boats…'

Thesiger, aged twenty-two, at the Villa Cipressi, his stepfather Reginald Astley's house on Lake Como, Italy, in 1932.

BELOW: Val ffrench Blake, a friend of Thesiger's at Eton, who gave him advice, criticism and encouragement in 1957–58 while he was writing *Arabian Sands*.

BELOW: The Milebrook in the Teme Valley, Radnorshire, which Kathleen leased from 1921 to 1942.

Thesiger photographed at the time he left Eton, in 1929.

BELOW: Previously unpublished in the UK, this photograph is one of a boxing series taken in the 1930s. Another photograph from this series appeared in *Desert, Marsh and Mountain* in 1979.

BELOW: A unique action photograph of Thesiger boxing for Oxford University, taken just after he has delivered a knockout punch.

ABOVE RIGHT: Omar Ibrahim, Thesiger's headman, 'a tall, powerfully-built, middle-aged Somali', in turban and shorts, with the members of the Awash expedition.

RIGHT: Crossing the Awash at Bilen.

LEFT: Thesiger's caravan near the Awash Station in December 1933, at the start of his 1933–34 expedition to trace the Awash river to its mysterious end in the unexplored Sultanate of Aussa, Abyssinia.

ABOVE: A party of Danakil warriors near the Mullu waterholes midway between Afdam and Bahdu, Abyssinia, on 10 February 1934.

LEFT: Guy Moore at Wadi Tini, Sudan, 1938. Moore was Thesiger's DC in Northern Darfur. Thesiger dedicated *Desert, Marsh and Mountain* to Moore, 'who taught me to appreciate the desert, its people and their ways'.

Idris Daud of the Kobé-Zaghawa tribe, who joined Thesiger at Kutum, Northern Darfur, in 1935. Idris acted as Thesiger's gunbearer when he hunted big game, accompanied him to the Western Nuer District and travelled with him across the Sahara to Tibesti in 1938.

Though a fatalist, Thesiger believed in chance: 'This lion seems to have destroyed my run of luck, and though after I had left Sanderson I trailed two others I got neither ... The one we did see had a lovely mane which I very much coveted. However 5 lions is as much as one can expect from one trek. My room is carpeted with their skins.'[102]

If Kathleen had worried that her son's lion cubs would become dangerous as they grew older, reading his graphically detailed descriptions of shooting cattle-killing lion at close quarters must have made her frantic. All Thesiger's letters to his mother began and ended affectionately, anxiously reassuring her that she occupied the centre of his universe. 'God bless you Mother Darling,' he wrote on 13 August 1935, 'I love you very dearly and think of you and our little Mile [The Milebrook] a great deal. I wish I had your picture here, but am really glad I have not as it would only spoil.'[103] He ended his letter describing the first lion hunt in the same vein: 'God bless you Mother dear. I love you dearly and think of you endlessly these days and of our happy Milebrook. I long for letters more than you can know. God bless you ...'[104] Sometimes in letters to his brothers Thesiger would urge one or other of them to keep an eye on Kathleen; if necessary, to put her mind at ease by assuring her that he, Wilfred, was fit and well and taking care of himself. Yet in letters to his mother he went on describing hunting adventures with lion and other big game.

After Moore returned from leave on 25 November, Thesiger trekked north to Jabal Maidob, and from there to Bir Natrun in the Libyan desert:

I took no servants, just my two Arab camelmen, 3 guides and 4 police, and no camp kit, sleeping and sitting on my camel-saddle rug and sheep skin. I also dressed as an Arab, wearing a turban, tobe, and going bare footed, and fed with the camelmen. As it was Ramadan our food consisted of one dish of flour porrich [sic] with a seasoning of native sauce at sunset. I found it extremely good and very filling and from about 3 o'clock onwards spent my time looking forward to it. After we had fed we drank endless small cups of very strong tea made syrupy with sugar, and ate dates. We rode hard spending 10 to 13 hours every day in the saddle, leaving an hour before sunrise and riding without a halt till just before sunset. One great advantage of travelling light like this is that there is no time wasted loading up. You just saddle your camel, throw on your saddle bags, with your carpet and sheep skin over the top of all. During the whole 25 days I never once felt properly tired. You breathe a sigh of relief when you leave all the fuss and bother of servants and camp furniture behind, and don't look forward to returning to it. Of course it is necessary in tropical Africa, but the Libyan Desert is Arabia not Africa. What a clean place the real desert is. You feel both your mind and your body being purified every day you spend in it. It makes you realize more clearly than ever that nearly everything that we consider necessary to our life is really superfluous and clogging.[105]

In *The Life of My Choice*, Thesiger clarified some details in this, the earliest account of his journey to Bir Natrun. For the first time he wore 'local dress', a transition he justified by writing that 'European clothes are singularly uncomfortable on camelback'.[106] As a European, he need not have abstained from eating and drinking between sunrise and sunset, but he did so to keep his men company, and to prove to himself and his companions that he could travel all day in desert conditions without food or water. He wrote that he had found this 'no hardship; the weather being cool'.[107] All his life he was sensitive to cold, and in the desert, sleeping under chilly starlight, he was glad of his sheepskin rug and a warm blanket. But he needed little else. A decade later, he was to experience this simple way of life again in Arabia, travelling with the Bedu. 'All they possessed were their camels and saddlery, their rifles and daggers, some waterskins and cooking pots and bowls, and the very clothes they wore; few of them even owned a blanket. They possessed, however, a freedom which we, with all our craving for possessions, cannot experience.'[108]

North of the Wadi Howar, Thesiger wrote, 'we got out into the true desert, bare, rolling, featureless sand for the most part, with every now and then an outcrop of rock. I had an unforgettable first sight of it ... a vast expanse of red sand without scrub or grass extending to the limitless horizon. Subconsciously one caught one's breath as one pushed out into it.'[109]

Two hundred miles from Jabal Maidob and the first of three watering places on the Forty Days' Road – the old slave route from Darfur to Egypt – Bir Natrun provided natron (hydrogenated sodium carbonate) and salt for the Maidob, Zaghawa and Kababish tribes. Goran tribesmen from the Ennedi mountains in Chad watered there before raiding the Kababish, and making contact with these raiders had been the official motive for Thesiger's journey. At Bir Natrun he camped beside parties of Maidob and Kababish. He wrote: 'The salt pans are in very long narrow depressions between outcrops of volcanic rock smothered under the sand dunes. They extend for 6 miles approximately ... There is no great contrast of colours as at [Lake] Assal.'[110] Three of Natrun's four wells, surrounded by palm trees, were brackish. Unfortunately Thesiger failed to get news of the Goran who two months previously had raided seventy camels from the French camel corps. On the return journey, south of the Wadi Howar he shot two addax gazelles, a male and a female. 'It was impossibly difficult to get up to them,' he wrote, 'as the grass was very short and the ground as flat as a football field. I got them both on one day, the second quite 400 yards off. That night we all made pigs of ourselves as we craved for meat. Addax meat is the best meat in the country, very fat and juicy. It is strange that this animal which never drinks and won't live anywhere but on the very edge of the true desert has the best flesh of any animal in the Sudan.'[111] Until then, the only meat they had eaten on the journey had been two large tortoises, cooked in their shells: Thesiger commented wryly, 'not exactly a banquet.'[112]

He arrived back at Kutum in time to drive to Fasher with Guy Moore for Christmas dinner. Describing the Governor's party in *The Life of My Choice*, he wrote: 'I was glad Idris [his servant] had not been brought to help the Governor's servants for I felt embarrassed, wondering what they all thought of the way we Christians were celebrating the birthday of our Prophet. They saw the Governor [Dupuis's successor, Philip Ingleson] dressed up as a prisoner, his middle-aged wife as a schoolgirl, other wives dressed as men, their husbands as sheikhs, troubadours, bull-fighters and God knows what else, and all of them drinking and dancing and getting noisier.'[113] Thesiger had never felt at home with heavy drinking and boisterous behaviour. He told Kathleen: 'I did not enjoy this [party] much. Too much forced hilarity.'[114] Reading between the lines, Moore obviously felt the same. The two men arrived in dinner jackets, since neither wanted to wear fancy dress as their hosts had requested. Thesiger commented starchily: 'When criticised for this, we said that we were parodying Englishmen who dressed for dinner in the jungle.'[115] They did not care that this sounded unconvincing.

After he had returned to Kutum from the lion hunt with the Bani Hussain at Kebkabia and his meeting with Paul Sanderson, during an inspection of the Kutum prison Thesiger noticed among its inmates the Zaghawa boy who would become his closest companion for the next five years. Idris Daud was a fourteen-year-old, with 'unusually negroid features for a Zaghawi', from Tini village on the western border of Darfur and Chad. Thesiger learnt that he had been charged with stabbing another boy to death. He wrote: 'I disliked seeing a boy of his age locked up indefinitely with a crowd of men, so after one of his elders had guaranteed that he would not run away I released him, and told him to go and help in my house.' What he meant was that he hated the thought of Idris being sexually abused by the other prisoners. He added significantly: 'Not long afterwards I had to sack my *sufragi* for pilfering my stores and drinking the whisky I kept for my guests, and a little later I sent the cook back to Khartoum because I wanted local tribesmen with me, not professional servants from the Nile valley.'[116]

Thesiger felt drawn to Idris on sight. By releasing him from prison and arranging for the payment of blood money owed to his victim's family, he ensured Idris's indebtedness to him. Idris's friendship transformed Thesiger's life at Kutum. Close though Guy Moore and Thesiger became, Moore was often away on trek, whereas Idris seldom left Thesiger's side. An object of discreet affection and a trusted friend, Idris ran the Kutum household efficiently, and served reliably as a gunbearer whenever Thesiger hunted big game.

An essential part of Thesiger's ethos was that anyone close to him should be outstandingly efficient. Idris Daud was no exception. Thesiger wrote: 'I soon discovered he was a skilful tracker and utterly fearless. Once, after lion, we found some barely discernible tracks which the Zaghawa with me declared were fresh. Idris maintained they were from the previous day, and was told by his elders not to talk out of turn. However he was right, as we discovered on following the spoor to where the lion had lain up the night before.'[117] More than fifty years later, Thesiger recalled that his young Turkana companion and helpmate Erope would often be consulted by Game Rangers about details of every kind connected with wild animals and the art of tracking them.[118]

Yet, instinctively anxious in case Idris let him down, Thesiger waited for more than six months before mentioning him by name in letters to Kathleen and his brothers. Back from leave in Syria and Palestine, he wrote on 15 July 1936: 'The 14 year old murderer appears to have kept the fort most successfully. I suppose thieves are afraid of someone who is such an adept at opening people up with a knife.'[119] This remark clearly contradicts Thesiger's published statement that Idris had stabbed the other boy 'inadvertently' in a scuffle.[120]

In his childhood Thesiger's brothers had formed a gang of which he was the natural leader, and he remained a gang leader all his life. The teenage tribesmen with whom he lived and travelled after 1935 – starting with Idris Daud – both kept him young and fulfilled his need to assert a sometimes token authority, to dominate even those upon whom he lavished affection and generosity. Often, as with Idris, he initiated relationships based on indebtedness or a sense of obligation. Lawi Leboyare, the first and fondest of Thesiger's 'adoptive sons' in Kenya, faced with Thesiger's ritual refusal of exorbitant demands for money or cars, used to complain (as part of the ritual): 'You picked us from the desert. You promised you will give us all these things. Now, *mzee juu*, you don't seem to care.'[121]

The Samburu at Maralal knew exactly how Thesiger dealt with their petitions. First he would be angry and dismissive; afterwards he would be gentle, forgiving and kind. He often followed his furious outbursts or long sulks with profuse apologies and tactile demonstrations of affection, stroking someone's hand or putting his arm around a shoulder. He had the satisfaction of not giving in too easily, while the supplicant, likewise, found his patience rewarded. In *The Life of My Choice*, Thesiger told how he once lost his temper with Idris, who burst into tears. 'Putting my hand on his shoulder I said, "Forgive me."'[122] He later explained: 'I had written, "Putting my arm round his shoulder", but George [George Webb, Thesiger's friend and literary adviser] thought this appeared too intimate. People might assume a homosexual relationship existed between Idris and myself, so he insisted I change it, which I did. Personally, I didn't think it mattered a damn.'[123]

At a dinner party in Fasher given by the commander of the Western

Arab Corps, Thesiger heard him remark that there were reports that Italians had occupied Bir Natrun. Thesiger said he had just returned from Bir Natrun, but had not seen any Italians. 'You could have cut the silence with a knife. Then somebody said: "It must have been you." Apparently the news had reached London, and forces in the Sudan had been alerted. It caused quite a commotion at the time.'[124] Though he devoted two paragraphs to this story in *The Life of My Choice*, he only mentioned it in passing when writing to his mother on New Year's Eve 1935: 'It has however proved a useful journey, since there were rumours in Khartoum and Fasher that the Italians had occupied Bir Atron [sic] and were using it as a forward base.'[125]

Before setting off for Bir Natrun, Thesiger had refurbished his house and planted his garden – besides attending to his clothes, of which he took great care. Too much watering, he noted, spoilt brussels sprouts and beans. 'Suttons sent masses of seeds ... Last year as no one took any trouble with the garden we got nothing out of it. This year I hope we shall have unlimited vegetables and flowers.'[126] Memorising the garden at the Legation in Addis Ababa had soothed sleepless nights at St Aubyn's, where Wilfred and Brian had tended their own small gardens, a home-making activity Wilfred carried on at Kutum and, after 1978, at Maralal. Among his favourite garden flowers were bougainvillaea, roses and sweet peas; of the commoner wildflowers he liked especially irises and gentians.

Thesiger's liking for brightly coloured flowers contrasted with his preference for line drawings or etchings rather than watercolours or oil paintings, and for black-and-white film instead of colour.[127] The same applied to his taste in carpets: 'I have just bought another Fezzani carpet. I now have four and these with my lion skins and more sombre local rugs, and my heads on the wall, have made my big room, the only one I use, extremely nice so that it is a pleasure to be in it. These Fezzani carpets are expensive and difficult to come by. The Dupuis' had some especially nice ones. They are very bright coloured and woven in intricate patterns.'[128] He asked Kathleen to order a panama hat from Lock's in St James's: 'A good one which will fold up into nothing. I want it a good neutral colour, such as deep straw, so that I can shoot in it. If they have only white ones tell them to dye one. At present when I wear a hat, out of office hours when one wears a uniform topi, I wear my dark brown homburg, a somewhat incongruous head dress. As I have left the band belonging to it in some thorn scrub when looking for lion could you also ask Locks to send another band. The hat is of the usual dark chocolate family colour, like those belonging to the others. I shall want it respectable to come home in. It is a great comfort to find that the sun has absolutely no effect on me. I always doubted if it would have.' The cold was another matter: 'Do you remember the sleeveless pullover you knitted for me at Christmas? It is quite invaluable and lives in my pocket and I use it endlessly both here and on trek. I also find Bucks's [Mary Buckle's] white sweater with OE [Old Etonian] colours invaluable, wearing it every evening. My silk scarf which Dermot and Roddy gave me and my woolly bear coat are endlessly useful. It is very cold in the early morning here and one is very grateful for such extra warmth. They are all going to accompany me into the desert in my saddle bags. One great advantage of riding camels as compared with horses is that each person can carry enough in his saddle bags to become self sufficient.'[129]

Horses and ponies came into their own, though, for galloping down lion with the tribesmen of the Bani Hussain. During Thesiger's first year at Kutum he had shot twelve lion, which he hunted on foot accompanied by local trackers. He described the dangerous sport of lion hunting on horseback in an article he published in *Sudan Notes and Records* in 1939. A typical Bani Hussain hunting party of twenty or twenty-five horsemen would ride in line: 'bare from the waist up and with raised spears, they break into song. First one of them sings two lines and the others then crash in with the chorus, while the lion a stone's throw in front snarls back over his shoulder at them ... When hunting lion they expect to get at least one man mauled or killed. On one occasion a lion mauled twelve Zaghawa before they succeeded in killing him. When with them I have always spoilt the sport by shooting the lion ... After killing the lion the party return home at the gallop, regardless of the distance, singing all the way through any villages they pass ... the refrain of their triumph song "Wali, Wali gab el Kheir Ya Wali".'[130]

Stirred by reading Lawrence, and fuelled by long conversations with Moore, Thesiger's attraction to the Muslim world extended far beyond the boundaries even of a region as large as Northern Darfur. On leave in 1936 he visited Palestine and Syria, and in November 1937, accompanied by his mother, who was then aged fifty-seven, he travelled in Morocco. The following year he made his longest and hardest journey up to then, by camel across the French Sahara to the remote Tibesti mountains.

Travelling by the Orient Express to Aleppo, a town beloved by Freya Stark, he changed for Beirut. In *The Life of My Choice* he remembered: 'I was convinced I was going to dislike Beirut – as indeed I did.'[131] Writing in 1936, he put it more bluntly: 'Beyrout [sic] is a vile spot with nothing to redeem it.'[132] On this journey Thesiger travelled by train, car, lorry, camel and on foot. He wrote: 'I have always enjoyed long train journeys through undeveloped countries.' In contrast to cars, which he 'loathed', and used reluctantly, he considered that 'trains do little to disturb the pattern of life of the surrounding countryside'.[133] He motored to Damascus via Baalbek, which he felt 'cannot compare with the ruins at Luxor, especially Karnak'.[134] Already Syria was 'overrun with cars and the arterial road between Beyrout and Damascus resembles the Oxford bypass'.[135] From Jabal Druze he trekked 150 miles to Amman, completing by lorry the last stage from Azraq to Amman. Azraq, with 'its ruined castle, palms, marshes and lagoons',[136] brought to life Lawrence's description in *Seven Pillars of Wisdom* of his arrival there from the desert.[137] For Thesiger, to have approached Azraq by car would have spoilt its romance. Instead he borrowed a camel and rode it to the town as Lawrence had done.[138]

At Amman, Thesiger stayed with John Bagot Glubb ('Glubb Pasha') and Frederick Gerard Peake ('Peake Pasha'), sharing a house whose garden occupied the site of a ruined Byzantine church in this 'small and still unspoilt Arab town'.[139] He admired both these men, particularly Glubb, who had known Guy Moore in Iraq. C.S. Jarvis, Peake's biographer, wrote of him that 'the semi-Arab state of Trans-Jordan, for the freedom of which he fought under Lawrence of Arabia, and the formation of which, after the armistice of 1918 ... constituted his life's work'.[140] In Trans-Jordan, Glubb was second-in-command of the Arab Legion which Peake had raised and commanded in 1920. Already his prestige was very great among the Bedu. Thesiger wrote: 'No European has ever acquired comparable knowledge ... and understanding ... nor won from these proud tribesmen a like respect.'[141] In a review of *Arabian Sands* in 1959, Glubb returned (or more correctly, pre-empted) the compliment, describing Thesiger as 'perhaps the last, and certainly one of the greatest, of the British travellers among the Arabs'. Like many English travellers in Arabia and the Middle East, Thesiger's sympathies lay with the Arabs. In Palestine, he wrote that 'the Arabs there had been provoked into revolt by the Government's authorisation of Jewish immigration ... I could see no justification for this influx of Jews into an Arab land two thousand years after they had been expelled by the Romans.' Jerusalem's ancient walled city, 'the tragic scene of so much strife and hatred down the ages', appeared to encapsulate the bitter conflict.[142]

On his way back to Kutum, Thesiger met the Sandfords in Cairo. Their farm at Mullu had gone, as well as their entire possessions, after Italy invaded Abyssinia and captured Addis Ababa in May 1936. Dan Sandford's news of the atrocities committed by Italian forces against the Abyssinians left Thesiger angry and frustrated. Like Sandford, he was determined to fight for the freedom of Abyssinia whenever Britain and Italy went to war. At Kutum, Moore and Idris welcomed him. Moore was delighted that he had met Glubb, thanks to whom he had visited a Bani Sakhr camp, and seen for the first time true Bedu of Arabia. After Thesiger returned to Kutum he trekked for six weeks in the Zaghawa country from Tini, Idris's village, as far as the Sindia wells, north of Wadi Howar.

By this time Moore knew Thesiger fairly intimately, and understood that the courageous, sometimes gauche young man was a tough character. To Thesiger's delight, Moore described the Sindia wells to him as 'a hang-out for scoundrels from both sides of the frontier ... just the sort of people who would appeal to you'.[143] But there had been heavy downpours of rain, and with so much water lying everywhere the wells were deserted. Riding his favourite camel, Faraj Allah, Thesiger hunted with Badayat camel-raiders whose camels were preyed on by lion. Using his .450 Rigby he shot two lion: a large male wakened by Faraj Allah's nervous grunts, and another lying up nearby. Both offered easy targets. The same day he killed an oryx, one of an unusually large herd of four hundred; the oryx's roasted meat gave Thesiger and his companions a 'feast'. Accompanied by the faithful Idris, he continued to hunt lion, riding with Bani Hussain or Zaghawi tribesmen. Thesiger wrote: 'It became an obsession. I felt that if I kept on, one day a lion would certainly kill me. But the urge to keep hunting them was too strong to resist.'[144] During five years in the Sudan he shot seventy lion, being charged no fewer than sixteen times. Apart from the lion skulls and hides he gave to the Natural History Museum, he had the collarbones of his seventieth lion mounted in gold by Asprey. One of the bones he gave to his mother, the other to Minna Buckle.

Except for an occasion when a lion charged and knocked him down (Thesiger was never certain whether it collided with his shoulder, or whether he had been knocked down by a man standing next to him whom the lion attacked and wounded), he was never harmed by them. When he wrote about this incident fifty years later in *The Life of My Choice*, his published account did not match exactly the description he gave in a long letter he wrote to his mother soon afterwards, which made no mention of being knocked down when the lion attacked. Thesiger learnt that in five years 120 Bani Hussain had been killed or mauled while hunting lion that raided their cattle.

The next three lion Thesiger faced included an exceptionally cunning, wary animal with a white mark encircling one foot, known to the Fur as Abu Higl, or 'Father of the Bracelet'. An acute sense of smell, Thesiger felt convinced, had enabled Abu Higl to avoid pursuers and survive.[145] He wrote unequivocally soon after: 'standing there with every sense alert I knew they were near, and was very conscious that the last lion I had shot had knocked me down'.[146] He shot two of the three lion, but Abu Higl escaped. In April 1937 he wrote to Kathleen: '[Ain Kora] is the place where [lion] are so bold and forced the natives to evacuate 3 villages completely. One old male lion known as Abu Higl ... is particularly bold. I have been after him for two years but have not yet got him.'[147]

Among the books his mother and brothers sent him, one of those he enjoyed most was Vivienne de Watteville's *Out in the Blue*, an account of her safari with her father in 1923–24 to collect big game specimens for the Berne Natural History Museum. Vivienne de Watteville had known Geoffrey and Olive Archer, which reminded Thesiger of Christmas with the Archers at Berbera in 1917. Not only that, her father Bernard, an enthusiastic hunter, had been killed by a wounded lion near Lake Edward in the Congo. Like Thesiger, de Watteville had hunted lion 'relentlessly'.[148] In the Congo in 1924 he shot twelve; five in a week. Several of them had to be finished off at close quarters, including an angry lioness with a broken jaw. Thesiger found *Out in the Blue* an exciting read, but he must have winced at the account of the horrific mauling that resulted in de Watteville's slow, agonising death.

Tribesmen of the Bani Hussain, Fur and Zaghawa, who hunted down cattle-killing lion for the sake of honour, matched Thesiger's boyhood ideal of 'savagery and colour'. He speculated on the effects upon peoples such as these of a war between Britain, Italy and other European powers. 'I feel increasingly,' he wrote, 'that the rule of the white man in Africa is coming to its close. Perhaps in Morocco the spark will first be lit and the real masters of the land will once again come into their heritage, while Europe lies a poisoned smoking ruin. If a European war does break out we shall not hold Africa as we held it [in] 1914–18. Here it will be boredom which will send them out on the warpath. It is illuminating to talk to the older men. After a bit they admit that the youths are restive and bored. They hear the girls singing of the famous warriors of the past, of battles and of courage and of desperate deeds, all of which are closed to them. When we first came here, and even as late as the [First World] war, they were still tired from the orgy of killing in the time of the Mahdi and Khalifa and desired rest and security. Now they are "drunk on milk" and want troubled times back so that once more courage and strength may come into their own. After all they are fighting tribes. Well, everything is in the hands of Allah.'[149]

Years later, Thesiger used Idris to voice these warlike aspirations: 'Like many young Zaghawa, Idris fretted at security and craved at heart for those wild, lawless days, when the *nahas* beat for war and young men could prove their manhood and win the approval of the girls. He had once said to me, "The only excitement I have had in my life has been riding down lions with you." Listening to him, old men shook their heads, saying that the young these days were suffering from "*sakhr al laban*", were drunk on too much milk.'[150]

In November 1937, Thesiger and his mother travelled together in Morocco. 'I have always wanted to go there,' he had written to Kathleen, 'and it would interest me to see how the French run their best colony. It would be cool there then and so I hope we could go together, even if we did not see much but Fez and Marrakesh. If we do go it would be wonderful if I had some letters of introduction to some of the French officers there. Do you know anyone I could get these from? I am sure you would enjoy it ... I should enjoy it so much if you were with me.'[151] His brother Roderic arranged a letter of introduction from friends to Haj Thami al Glawi, Pasha of Marrakesh, who gave Thesiger and his mother a banquet at Telouet, his spectacular castle in the Atlas mountains.[152] Thesiger did not think of including his stepfather in this trip. He viewed Reginald Astley as his mother's elderly and strictly platonic companion. At The Milebrook she and Reggie slept in separate rooms; he could never replace Wilfred's father in either Kathleen's or her sons' affections; besides, Thesiger wanted to have his mother to himself for a few weeks. He had planned methodically, as always, how to divide his 1937 leave: 'I long to do so much with you [Kathleen] next holidays. The Milebrook, London, Ireland and Morocco, but you must be fit and strong [his mother's back had been troubling her]. Take care of yourself my dear.'[153] When an Oxford chum, John Schuster, invited him to stalk in Scotland that October, Thesiger left it to Kathleen to decide: 'Much as I should enjoy Scotland with John, I am set on Ireland with you.'[154]

Although Thesiger corresponded mainly with Kathleen, he also wrote at frequent intervals to Brian, Dermot and Roderic. He was extremely attached to his three younger brothers, and was more involved with their lives, and thought more about them, than his brief, sometimes superficial remarks in *The Life of My Choice* suggest. Writing to them from the Danakil country or the Sudan, for example, he would share his news or ask them to exchange his letters among themselves and with their mother. Very often he wrote letters to his brothers that were geared to their particular interests: boxing and shooting for Brian, politics and world affairs for Dermot, art and architecture for Roderic. Such topics might rate no more than a sentence or two, and his interest in them was often slight. He had learnt early on in life, however, the art of writing letters with the recipient in mind, whereas he wrote his books to please himself, and shrugged: 'They [his publishers and readers] can make of them what they like.'[155] As for his brothers, Roderic was 'marvellously good', writing to Wilfred twice a week. Dermot and Brian wrote more infrequently,[156] yet they were generous. Though neither wrote to Wilfred for over eighteen months after he left England, Dermot had sent him 'a very handsome present: all Blackwood's *Tales from the Outposts* [published in 1934–36]',[157] in twelve volumes, bound in matching royal-blue cloth, in each of which Thesiger signed his name. Not only did Brian contribute funds to the Danakil expedition, in 1934 he had given Wilfred a beautiful Rigby rifle. Now he sent large, expensive food hampers to him from Fortnum & Mason.

Brian Thesiger Doughty-Wylie, a second lieutenant in the Royal Welch Fusiliers, married Diana de Hoghton on 6 July 1937. 'I got your letter about Brian's wedding,' Wilfred wrote to his mother. 'I do wish I could have been there. It sounds as if it had been a very beautiful wedding.' His own firm decision never to marry did not prevent him adding, as something more than a dutiful sentiment: 'I do hope they will both be very happy.'[158]

In February 1936, at Guy Moore's suggestion, before he went home on leave Thesiger undertook a camel journey from Jabal Maidob to Omdurman, a route traditionally used by Maidob sheep drovers: '[Moore] knew now how I should appreciate making this journey by camel to Omdurman and how greatly it would increase my experience.'[159] Thesiger and his companions rode for up to eighteen hours a day, because, he wrote, 'I could not resist the opportunity to test my endurance.'[160] He needed continually to reassert his strength and staying power, to match the mental and physical demands of the 'all-male' tribal societies among whom his life was largely spent. To deal with his 'disturbing' fascination[161] with young tribesmen such as Idris – 'a pearl beyond price'[162] – he had to be perceived as ultra-masculine, to master his emotions, not only to keep up with his companions but to outperform them, pushing himself and them to greater limits of resolution and physical stamina. Thesiger's need for self-testing never ceased to be important. In his nineties and infirm, he complained only that his sedentary life 'lacked challenge'.[163]

After almost two years in Northern Darfur, Thesiger rode and managed camels very skilfully, had acquired a love of deserts, and had lengthy treks by camel to his credit. He wrote: 'On 3 June 1937 I celebrated my twenty-seventh birthday by riding from Umm Buru back to Kutum, a hundred and fifteen miles, in just under twenty-four hours. I was riding Faraj Allah, accompanied by Idris on Habib ... Neither camel showed signs of exhaustion.'[164] Of course, this was meant to imply that neither Thesiger nor Idris had felt exhausted by their marathon either. Two days later, Thesiger outlined the journey in a letter to Kathleen: 'I spent my birthday trying to get from Umm Buru to here [Kutum] in the 24 hours. It is 110 miles. It would not be difficult in the cold weather and if there was a moon till 3 AM and it is too warm to trot camels in the middle of the day. We just did it. We rode for 16 hours without getting out of the saddle, and again for 7 after a bit of a rest. The camels had already done a month's hard trekking and were not fresh and their feet were worn thin, so that we had to case them where it was stony. However today to look at them you would not know they had been trekked. They are incredible animals. I too am fit and barely felt stiff and not the least tired ... I only took Idris with me.'[165] In a letter to Dermot, Thesiger affirmed: 'I was stiff but not tired.'[166] With Thesiger mounted on Faraj Allah, and Idris and their companions on 'an ordinary scratch lot' of camels,[167] the party trekked the drovers' road from Jabal Maidob to Omdurman, about six hundred miles, in eleven days. Thesiger found the landscape 'flat and uninteresting', the days 'monotonous', and the final stage 'one long slog'.[168] He noted in his official report that 'A good riding camel could do the journey in 9 days.'[169]

At Khartoum in March 1937 he took the prescribed examinations in Arabic and Law. 'I failed in the Arabic getting 256 instead of 300 out of 500. The manuscript and dictation failed me. I passed in Arabic into English, the English into Arabic and the conversation ... I passed in practical Law and failed in the Theory.' He added: 'Not surprising as I had not read any since I was at Oxford.'[170] Although he defended his decision to concentrate on his Danakil maps and lecture at the RGS in 1934, he regretted having done so at the expense of acquiring the rudiments of classical Arabic at the School of Oriental and African Studies in London.[171] From a practical viewpoint, besides, he was already 'fluent' in the coarser Arabic spoken by the tribes of Northern Darfur. In 1977, comparing his Sudanese Arabic with the classical Arabic of Arabia, he observed wryly that, to any cultured Arab, listening to him 'must have been like listening to someone speaking English with a broad Dorsetshire accent'.[172]

In July 1937 at El Fasher, Thesiger was told by the Governor, Philip

Ingleson, that on his return from leave he was to be transferred from Kutum to the Upper Nile. Fearing that he might be posted to the Wad Medani cotton-growing district, Atbara or Khartoum for administrative experience after his examinations, he discussed his future with the Civil Secretary, Sir Angus Gillan. He had told Gillan that he wanted to resign from the permanent Political Service and rejoin as a contract District Commissioner, on condition that he would serve only in 'the wildest and remotest' areas.[173] Gillan at Khartoum, and Ingleson at Fasher, both tried to discourage him. 'They said by resigning I should never become a Governor, and that I'd lose my pension. I told them none of these things mattered to me.'[174]

By transferring Thesiger to the wild and primitive western Nuer district of the Upper Nile, the Sudan Political Service gave him exactly what he asked for. Guy Moore had been with him at Fasher. 'I had a long talk to the Governor with Guy ... and he really was amazingly nice about it. His chief objection was that I threw away my chances of rising above a DC by taking a contract, but I know that I should never have survived the other process, and I am sure that if I eventually proved really to be the man for the job I should get it even in this bureaucratic Government.'[175] Moore had hoped to keep Thesiger at Kutum for at least two more years, as Thesiger too had hoped. Though disappointed at the prospect of losing his most congenial Assistant DC, Moore believed that Thesiger's decision to serve on contract in the wilds was 'probably wise'.[176] From Tini, Moore wrote to Kathleen: 'I am not likely to find anyone again who fitted in so well to this kind of life ... I am old enough now to criticise my superiors: and I think they have done wrong in moving him.'[177]

While Thesiger knew that he would be sorry to leave Kutum, he took a positive view: 'I think that I shall like the south. It will be quite different to here of course, but interesting I am sure and wild and unsophisticated. Yet I regret bitterly leaving now. During the past six months I have felt that I have got into the saddle here. I am now fluent at spoken Arabic, I have mastered many of their customs, and until one has done that you cannot really do anything, as practically everything is settled by tribal custom here, and I have got to understand them and made real friends of many of them. Up till now I have been of very little use to Guy. Now when I might be, I am to be moved to a new country, a new language, a new people, new customs, culture and religion, and an utterly different administrative outlook. I have been very happy here, and very lucky to have been under Guy Moore. I shall miss him badly, he is so human, understanding and sound.'[178] Moore and he had revelled in Wilfred's books: 'We have very similar tastes and talk most evenings till long after midnight.'[179] All this Thesiger had adored, and felt was irreplaceable.

Before he left for England he made a final trek to Jabal Maidob, this time accompanied by Mark Leather, a young Bimbashi (the lowest British commissioned rank in the Sudan Defence Force) from the Western Arab Corps at Fasher. Despite Thesiger's usual misgivings about strangers, he and Leather had a wonderful journey. Leather proved to be 'an admirable companion ... enthusiastic about everything, and desperately keen on his hunting';[180] on Jabal Salur he shot a Barbary sheep, a ram with record horns measuring thirty-one inches that surpassed the magnificent trophy Thesiger had shot in 1935. For his part, Leather found Thesiger a 'most excellent companion ... a real "tough guy" [who] knows how to do things hard'.[181] Thesiger later wrote nostalgically: 'For those days I lived with the Maidob as I love living, moving where we would, sleeping under the stars, at one moment gorged on meat, the next with nothing but some flour with water, and with no barriers between us. We had one unforgettable night when we came across some shepherds and spent the night with them. Everyone so free and natural. They played to us on their pipes round the fire far into the night, lads each of whom looked like Pan.'[182]

Thesiger and his mother travelled from London by train and ferry to Marseilles, and from there they arrived at Tangier on 8 November 1937. Together they travelled to the romantic walled city of Marrakesh, with its surrounding palm groves set against a dramatic backdrop of the snow-covered Atlas mountains. From there they visited Telouet, Taroudant, Meknes and Fez, whose setting amidst encircling hills, Thesiger felt, could only be compared with Istanbul viewed from Pera or Jerusalem from the Mount of Olives.[183]

Thesiger and Kathleen loved every moment of their journey. Having been separated for almost two years, they revelled in each other's company. He looked after his mother with meticulous care, anticipating her needs, making sure she was comfortable, happy, getting the most out of the experience. Despite its increasing popularity with tourists, this was still the Morocco of old. There were no flights from Europe in those days; Marrakesh 'still seemed a long way off',[184] which added to its charm and mystery. Kathleen logged their journey in a copy of the *Guide Général du Maroc (première année)* 1935, illustrated with many photographs and with vivid watercolours by Matteo Brondy, marking with a cross each sight they had seen and adding casual remarks – 'interesting', 'most interesting'; the bland descriptions so often used by Thesiger, which belied a thrill of wonder and of sensual excitement. Thesiger commented in 1987: 'travelling with my mother in Morocco ... I was not disappointed ... she was good company, indefatigable, uncomplaining, interested in all she saw'.[185] Kathleen was by then iconic for Thesiger, a goddess unique in his exclusively male pantheon. During the next thirty-five years they travelled at intervals in Palestine, Syria, Turkey, Greece, Italy, Spain and Portugal, and several more times in Morocco. Some of these expeditions were gruelling, but Kathleen, even in her eighties, undertook them with relish.

TWELVE

The Nuer

In *The Danakil Diary*, Thesiger recalled an evening on his way from England to Abyssinia to attend Haile Selassie's coronation, when he had listened 'with great interest' as Sir John Maffey, Governor-General of the Sudan, told how Nuer tribesmen had killed their District Commissioner, Vere Fergusson, three years previously, in 1927. Maffey 'said that two years earlier he had approved the Sudan Government's takeover of the Western Nuer. This naked, warlike tribe lived out of touch in the swamps of the White Nile. Hitherto they had been left alone, but their repeated raids on the administered Dinka eventually necessitated intervention. The Nuer had resisted fiercely and severe fighting had resulted before they submitted. Now they had killed Fergusson, the District Commissioner, and again taken up arms. While I listened [that evening in October 1930] I never anticipated that seven years later I would be helping their District Commissioner to administer these proud tribesmen in a virtually unknown area of the Southern Sudan teeming with wildlife.'[1]

When Thesiger wrote this sixty-five years later, his memory of the occasion was still clear: 'I eventually got hold of a book about Fergusson, and I read it with enormous interest. He seems to have been a remarkable man. He was utterly dedicated to his work among the Nuer. He spent his own money on them ... doing things for them. His attitude to them was rather like the way I looked upon the Bedu, or the Marsh Arabs, or the Samburu in Kenya.'[2]

As usual Thesiger identified with tribesmen, rather than their administrators: with the Zulus in South Africa, with the Danakil and Galla in Abyssinia, here in the Sudan with the Muslim tribes in Darfur

162

and the Nuer of the Upper Nile. From the Bahr el Ghazal ('river of the gazelle') he wrote to Kathleen:

I like what I have seen of the Nuer so far. In 1920 and thereabouts they were to this part of Africa, what the Masai were once to East Africa, the great fighting tribe who put the fear of God into everyone else. Then this Government in the shape of Fergus[s]on interfered. They tried conclusions with machine-guns on two or three occasions, losing 200 men or more each time, and again when they killed Fergus[s]on they were mercilessly punished. I believe some 400 Nuer were shot after this. Now I think they recognise that it is useless to pit spears against magazine rifles and machine-guns, however brave they may be. It is sad. There is no future that I can see for any of these tribes under European administration. They just atrophy.[3]

On 3 September 1927, three months before his death, Fergusson wrote to his mother: 'What hits me badly is the thought that civilisation must eventually encroach on them, and ruin their fine ideals and customs. I do my very best to keep them unsoiled; but it's a hard and, I fear, hopeless fight.'[4] Despite his implied criticism of Fergusson as an instrument of government, Thesiger understood his viewpoint. Here was no self-serving paternalist jargon, but absolute proof of Fergusson's commitment to the Nuer. The effect of his determination to protect tribes such as the Nuong Nuer from Westernising influences is difficult to judge. They knew only their world, which they saw and experienced as insiders, without the need, means or will to compare it with the 'dismantling, drab western civilisation' Thesiger and Fergusson both deplored.[5]

The country of the Nuer, or 'Nath' as they called themselves,[6] extended over some twenty thousand square miles, its scattered population about ten to the square mile. The Nuer landscape was completely flat, its clay soil thinly wooded and covered with tall grasses in the rains. It was a country of extremes. Every year the great rivers flooded after heavy downpours; when the rain ceased and river levels fell, the land was stricken by drought.[7] For much of the year Thesiger found himself trekking with a line of naked porters, or hunting, thigh-deep in water across the Nuer swamps. He reflected long afterwards on his Sudan years and their contrasting settings – the deserts of Northern Darfur, the swamps of Nuerland – which mirrored in sequence his five memorable years in desert Arabia and his seven years in the Iraqi marshes. Yet this comparison was somewhat contrived. While the deserts of Northern Darfur, Libya and Chad were comparable with the Arabian desert, and while, as in Arabia, tribes such as the Bani Hussain, Maidob and Zaghawa, with whom Thesiger became closely involved, were Muslim, the Nuer were pagans. Their way of life, language, religion and appearance bore no comparison to the Muslim tribes of Darfur.

The Nuer were a Nilotic people, like the neighbouring Dinka and the Shilluk; it may be among the Dinka that the name 'Nuer' originated.[8] The Marsh Arabs, on the other hand, were Shi'ite Muslims with whom Thesiger could communicate, with whose way of life (a complete antithesis of the nomadic Bedu lifestyle in Arabia) he merged easily. Among the Nuer, Thesiger gained their trust by hunting and trekking with them; but his two years' service on the Upper Nile allowed him to acquire only a smattering of their language.[9] 'Kwechuor', Thesiger's phonetic rendering of *kwacuor*, meaning 'an ox speckled white with a white face', was the 'bull name' given to him by the Nuer (for an adult Nuer, 'the ox bearing his name had an almost sacred significance'). In 1987 Thesiger wrote that the name meant 'a black ox marked with white'.[10] But nearer the time he was named, he wrote: 'My bull name is Quoichuor [sic], which means the black bull spotted like a leopard. In reality he is a wretched little bull calf, or so it seems to me who have no eye for a cow, given to me with much ceremony by Garkek chief of the Jakaing [sic] ... I am known by no other name than my bull name.'[11] According to Evans-Pritchard, the Nuer terms *kwe* (white-faced) and *cuor* (speckled) should approximate to *Kwechuor*, and Thesiger's black bull (or ox) spotted like a leopard should be something closer to *kwac* (spotted like a leopard) and *car* (black), which might sound like Kwechuor, depending on the Nuer pronunciation of these words. It is probably too fanciful to imagine that the Nuer simply gave him a bull name which nearly matched their sound-picture of 'Thesiger'.

Idris had come with Wilfred from Northern Darfur. He and Malo, the Nuer interpreter, soon became friends. To Thesiger's proud satisfaction, in due course Idris learnt to speak basic Nuer, and he too was given a bull name, 'Bor Jagey' (a white ox of the Jagei group of Nuer tribes), 'a singular honour for an African stranger'.[12] Hearing that his Nuer porters identified themselves as 'Kwechuor's men' appealed enormously to Thesiger, who would be known in Africa and in Arabia by a variety of names: to the tribes of Northern Darfur he had been *samm al usuud*, or 'lion's poison'; Samburu teenagers at Maralal in Kenya would be known as '*mzee juu*'s boys' (in Swahili *mzee juu* is a term of exceptional respect, meaning 'top elder'); whilst Bedu at a gathering arranged at Abu Dhabi by Sheikh Zayid in Thesiger's honour caused excitement by brandishing their camel sticks above their heads and chanting: 'We are Umbarak's men!' (*umbarak* meaning 'Blessed of God'[13]). All these groups were the adult equivalents or extensions of the juvenile gang of four Thesiger brothers, of which Wilfred always remained the undisputed leader.[14]

As Assistant District Commissioner, Thesiger joined the District Commissioner, H.G. Wedderburn-Maxwell, aboard the *Kereri*, the old wood-burning Nile paddle steamer that served as their mobile headquarters. Thesiger's billet consisted of two small adjoining cabins, one for sleeping, the other for storage. 'Lashed alongside the *Kereri*,' he wrote, 'was a large, roofed double-decked barge ... packed with porters, tribal police, prisoners and a variety of women, as well as our four horses, some sheep, goats and chickens, and any cattle we were transporting: conditions aboard it were crowded and chaotic, but no one seemed to mind.'[15] In effect the *Kereri* was a microcosm of the far more spacious District Commissioner's compound at Kutum, where apart from Guy Moore's thatched mud house, and Thesiger's similar house close by, there were a guest house, a dispensary, an office, a prison, police lines and the houses of the Sudanese officials, in a varied landscape of bush country and mountains.

By comparison, from the *Kereri* the view of water, swamp and scrub was monotonous, stretching as far as the eye could see. On Boxing Day 1937 Thesiger wrote from Malakal: 'The country is absolutely flat ... from here it seems to be one vast swamp, though dry in areas from now on ... We spend practically our whole time on trek, on foot with porters. There are no roads in the district which is nearly all under water.'[16]

Henry Godfrey Wedderburn-Maxwell was fifteen years older than Thesiger, 'a stocky, fair-haired man, in conventional bush-shirt and shorts and Wolseley pith helmet'. He had 'a frank, open face with wide-set eyes, and impressed me at once as friendly and utterly reliable. While we talked he puffed his pipe; during my two years with him he always seemed to be lighting it or smoking it.'[17] Thesiger learnt that he owed this transfer to the Upper Nile to his predecessor having died of blackwater fever. 'Wedderburn, as he was always called ... had now achieved his ambition by being posted to the Western Nuer, and hoped to spend the rest of his service among them. I soon found I was lucky to have him as my DC, for in the cramped quarters of the *Kereri* he was easy to live with, accommodating, good-natured and imperturbable.' Unlike the occasionally irascible Guy Moore, Thesiger never saw him lose his temper.[18]

Like Moore, Wedderburn-Maxwell remained a bachelor during the twenty-five years he served in the Sudan. The outbreak of war delayed his retirement until 1946. Though he knew other areas of Nuerland and spoke their language, he had arrived at Malakal only a fortnight before Thesiger. The two men decided to do nothing but trek and shoot for a year, getting to know the vast district and contacting as many Nuer as possible. Thesiger wrote home: 'one section of them are eating dogs, and this is giving rise to a good deal of anxiety, as it has some mysterious magical significance, dogs being unclean. They seem to flare up pretty easily ... I wonder if I shall ever get fond of them. I will give them a try anyway.'[19] Pining for his mother, he wrote: 'I loved Morocco and shall always treasure my memories of it, and I *loved* being with you.'[20]

To his delight, some of the photographs he had taken in Morocco came out well, and in the western Nuer he photographed scenes of big game hunting – a buffalo he shot, Nuer tribesmen butchering the carcase of an elephant. He also took many beautiful pictures of his Nuer porters, on trek, talking in a relaxed group, forcing their way through papyrus against a stiff breeze. He still used photography simply as a means of recording information, snapshots as alternatives to letters or occasional brief entries in his diary. As yet he took few, if any close-up portraits, although he now began to compose set pieces: his shooting trophies carefully arranged on the *Kereri*'s deck, a naked Nuer tribesman standing unselfconsciously among tall reeds – thrust aside by his outstretched arms – who poses like an actor taking a curtain-call.

For Christmas 1938, Dermot and Roderic sent a new book of photographs, *Seen in the Hadhramaut* by Freya Stark. Thesiger wrote to Kathleen on 8 January 1939: 'Lovely photos. I do wish I could take ones like those.'[21] To Roderic he wrote on 19 January: 'Thank you so much for Freya Stark's book of the Hadhramaut. The photos are very beautiful and it is a book which I shall always be glad that I possess.'[22] *Seen in the Hadhramaut* indeed proved to be very influential. Turning its pages, Thesiger said, he realised for the first time the impact and potential of close-up camera portraits. That his photographs showed a remarkable, sudden improvement after the war resulted from his studying Freya Stark's portrait technique. Some of her photographs were obviously much better than others; none, however, were downright failures. Desert light and wind-carved dunes in Arabia raised Thesiger's appreciation of landscape to far greater heights than before, despite his experiences of desert travel in Northern Darfur, Libya and the Sahara. Yet even among the Nuer, he took advantage of his surroundings. Many of his finest photographs from the Sudan were of Nuer on trek, resting or hunting: 'I thought what marvellous subjects they would make for a sculptor': lean, long-legged men with powerful yet refined musculature, a build favoured by Donatello rather than by Michelangelo, and thus in perfect harmony with Thesiger's preferences, whether of Renaissance sculpture or of living men. Even when he photographed his Nuer porters from the rear as they marched in curving line towards a dead-level horizon, over parched grassland or thigh-deep in water, he captured the smooth symmetry of their loping movements, which contrasted unflatteringly with his own laboriously plodding gait. And yet, out hunting with the Nuer, Thesiger could run as hard and as far as they did, and still aim and fire his powerful rifles accurately enough to stop a charging lion.

Aged twenty-seven, Thesiger had acquired austere good looks, and his broad-shouldered, powerful build defined him as an explorer, big game hunter and hard traveller. His thick, dark-brown hair, clipped short, was shaved almost smooth over his neck and temples, and well above the ears. Usually he was clean-shaven, but on long treks (such as his camel journey from Kutum to Bir Natrun) he grew a ragged beard and moustache like those in the photograph taken by Umr at the end of his 1933–34 Danakil expedition. His face, chest, hands, arms and legs (to above the knees) were deeply sunburnt. The rest of his body was seldom exposed to the sun, and by comparison the skin looked almost white. All his life he needed only brief exposure to the sun to recover the sunburnt, ochre hue with which he would always be identified.

On a month's trek to the Bahr al Jabal, where he planned to rendezvous with Wedderburn-Maxwell and Wedderburn's predecessor, H.A. Romilly, Thesiger shot his first buffalo bull. He wrote: 'we followed [two] ... and some 3 hours later saw them standing under some bushes. I shot the largest behind the shoulder. He went about 100 yards and died. He was huge. I had no idea a buffalo was so large. When I sat on his side my feet only just touched the ground. He had no head, it was worn right down and I did not keep it.'[23]

Thesiger liked both Wedderburn-Maxwell and Romilly. Sketching Romilly in *The Life of My Choice*, he noted: 'Like his close friend Wedderburn, he was a bachelor; this was certainly no life for a married man. Romilly had a strong face, with steady, friendly grey eyes above a lean and leathern body; he also had the curious habit of chewing the end of his handkerchief and I always think of the pair of them, Wedderburn with his pipe, Romilly with his handkerchief. As a self-sufficient man, combining authority with lack of pretentiousness, Romilly put me in mind of Arnold Hodson and those others who used to trek up from their lonely outposts in Abyssinia to report to my father in Addis Ababa. I felt far closer to such men than to my young contemporaries in the Sudan, many of whom, before they joined the Service, had hardly been out of England.'[24] Having been brought up in mainly adult company until he was nine, it was perhaps natural that Thesiger should feel more at home with an older generation than with his contemporaries. More than this, he responded to men like Guy Moore, Charles Dupuis and Romilly, whose character and looks reminded him of the father whose early death had left an irreplaceable void in Thesiger's life. He did not, however, identify Hodson or Romilly directly with Wilfred Gilbert. Even Hodson, the lion hunter whose stories had thrilled him as a boy, he portrayed as a subordinate who journeyed for days 'to report to my father':[25] a significant, carefully judged remark which reminds us of his father's status and elevates Wilfred Gilbert far above and beyond any possible comparisons.

In the dry plains and swamps of the western Nuer, Thesiger hunted big game mainly for sport. He wrote: 'Many DCs, even in the Southern

Sudan, had no interest in hunting. I am sure in consequence they neglected a means of getting on terms with the tribesmen they administered.
This would have been especially so if the quarry were dangerous and the
hunt a joint venture.'[26] Many Nuer told Philip Bowcock, Thesiger's successor, after the war: 'Oh, Kwechuor! He was like one of us.'[27] This
flattering claim was echoed by elderly tribesmen in Northern Darfur,
who still remembered Thesiger the hunter after sixty years.

Though he pined for the deserts and Muslim tribes of Northern
Darfur, Thesiger found the Nuer 'exciting': 'I liked being with the Nuer
and having them grouped round my tent; I enjoyed listening to the sound
of their voices, or watching their perfect physical coordination as they
strode in front of me along a path, seeing them slip through the bush
when we hunted buffalo, or beat across-country when we looked for
lion.'[28] None of these pleasures compensated for the Nuers' lack of
refinement by comparison with Muslim tribes such as the Bani Hussain,
the Zaghawa and the Maidob. Thesiger later confessed that he might have
been content to live among the Nuer had it not been for his years in
Northern Darfur, which focused his ambitions and raised his expectations. The gulf separating Muslim and pagan cultures was defined for
Thesiger when one day he watched a Nuer porter 'grab a handful of
maize from a pot, step a yard aside and stand there urinating while he
fed'.[29]

Idris and Malo shared Thesiger's enthusiasm for big game hunting.
Besides the forty lion he shot in the Upper Nile district, he also hunted
elephant, buffalo, hippopotamus and Nilotic antelopes like the rare Mrs
Grey's kob.[30] He described his hunting adventures in letters to his mother
and brothers, eager to share with his family the raw excitement of life
among the Nuer.

Yesterday I joined the Nuer harpooning hippo. This is quite thrilling.
There were some 35 hippo in a lagoon 4 to 8 feet deep and about 500 yards
across. They cut off small islands of sudd [floating masses of reeds and
weeds] some 8 to 12 feet across and push them out into the lagoon. There
were 5 of these papyrus rafts, each with one to three harpooners on it. I
went on the largest with 3 harpooners, and Idris insisted on coming too.
You are up to your knees in the water, but these natural rafts of interwoven

papyrus roots are remarkably firm. We then drifted and poled down on the hippos driving them into a corner. We kept to the deep water, while other Nuer massed in the shallows. As they feel themselves getting cornered the hippo break past the rafts in the deeper water by trying to swim under them. You can see where they go from the wash and the bubbles. Then the harpooners try and fling their harpoons home. These harpoons are very sharp with a single barb and attached to a strong rope some 30 yards long [in *The Life of My Choice* he reduced this to a more conservative thirty feet]. The other end of the rope is fixed to a dead tree trunk which is driven into the centre of the raft. The harpoon is temporarily fixed to a pole in order to throw it, but this comes away when it strikes. Several times they got a harpoon home but it came away almost at once, and one man got caught in the rope and dragged overboard. However his brother cast the rope loose and he got back on board, but badly cut by the rope. At last the raft next to us got a harpoon well home just above the hippo's eye. The result was simply terrific. He kept flinging himself out of the water, shaking his head, grunting and diving. I had no idea till then how huge a hippo is. He took this raft in tow, while the other rafts attached themselves to it, and tried to get other harpoons home, or stab the hippo with large heavy bladed spears. It was wildly exciting for the hippo was always within 30 yards. Once he came for our raft. He rose out of the water at my feet, a vast cavern of a mouth and two angry pig eyes. I sent my spear home into his mouth and rolled out of reach. I got the spear back afterwards, its 18 inch blade bent into an S. As he rolled beside us I let him have my other spear right behind the shoulder, a very satisfactory blow which got me a lot of praise. Every time he rose after this one could see the blood flooding down his side. Unfortunately just as we were getting him into the shallows the harpoon came out and he got away.[31]

Thesiger apologised that this eight-page letter from Kilwal in the western Nuer seemed 'to be all about shooting', and wrote, 'a lot of it will read dully I am afraid'. This was no more than polite modesty. Yet the pleasant routine of answering his mother's and brothers' letters, he affirmed, enabled him 'to keep a sort of diary'. He began writing travel diaries after the war, some as detailed logbooks, some merely rough jottings which he expanded in occasional letters home; others he composed more carefully. He had recorded the 1933–34 Danakil expedition in three large notebooks, two covering the journey, the third noting observations and reports of Danakil customs. During his five years in the Sudan, however, he kept no diaries apart from in 1938, when brief résumés of lion hunting were followed in the same diary by a daily record of his journey by camel across the French Sahara to the seldom-visited, remote Tibesti mountains. Much as he looked forward to this journey in August 1938, he dreaded the prospect of Idris leaving him soon after they returned. He confided to Dermot: 'He is an extraordinarily nice lad. God knows what I shall do after the Tibesti trip when he goes home. I shall miss him far more than I care to think of.' By April he had already shot ten lion in the western Nuer. He wrote: 'I hope to get 10 more before I go on leave to make 50.' He added that, as a concession to Idris, 'I let [him] shoot a small solitary bull [buffalo] we found a few days ago. He killed him stone dead with one shot and was very triumphant.'[32] In Northern Darfur Thesiger had used riding camels such as Faraj Allah, his pride and joy, to travel any distance. In the Nuer country, except for galloping police horses after lion, he trekked everywhere on foot. He noted wearily: 'my feet are worn out, all raw and blistered so I am glad of a rest. They will get hard soon.'[33]

The size of wild African animals astonished him: the hippo he speared with Nuer harpooners; the buffalo bull shot on the way to Bahr al Jabal; his largest lion, shot on the Upper Nile; elephant in the papyrus swamps which dwarfed the captive specimens he had seen in Khartoum zoo. He shot and photographed a sixteen-and-a-half-foot-long crocodile, whose huge girth made him doubt the tales he had heard of twenty-foot Nile crocodiles. As he retrieved the film from his Leica camera, its spool unwound accidentally, destroying the evidence. Thesiger blamed himself for the loss of these precious negatives: 'Changing the roll I was careless and tore the old one, so that it all came unwound. There were a number of lion photos, and also my leopard and 16½ foot crocodile in this roll. It is most annoying and pure stupidity. I did the same last year with my photos of the Kutum gathering. As they have lost the bottom jaw of my crocodile, I now have little to show for him.'[34]

On 1 April 1938 he wrote: 'I am ... going down to Bahr al Jabal to the S end of the district to try and find an enormous elephant who lives there. He is called Maguer and his name is known right through the Nuer country. I believe without joking that his tusks are exceptional. I should much like to get him.'[35] Perhaps he gave the assurance that he was not joking because he remembered that he was writing on April Fool's Day, but he tartly dismissed this suggestion: 'It wasn't something that would have occurred to me. I would never have thought in those terms.'[36] In *The Life of My Choice* he wrote, possibly referring to Maguer: 'I had hoped to get one with hundred-pound tusks.'[37]

While he was among the Nuer, Thesiger shot four elephant. The best 'had tusks of eighty-three and eighty-one pounds; the others were in the seventies'.[38] He kept a tally of dangerous game he had killed by cutting tiny notches in the walnut stock of his .350 Rigby Magnum magazine rifle. After he sold the weapon to Rigby many years later, the company replaced its defaced stock with a new one. Thesiger remembered vaguely that they gave him back the original stock, but despite searching diligently for it in his London flat, this fascinating memento was never found.[39] In his letters he described adventures with elephant:

I got an elephant with tusks of 74½ and 66½lbs. Good for many parts of Africa, but only moderate for here ... we spotted from an ant heap the back of an elephant in the long grass, looking like a small hill. The grass covered him save for the top of his back and head, so that to see his tusks we had to get to within a few yards. No easy matter in two foot of water and thick reeds when if he heard us he would either bolt or charge. When we next saw him 30 yards off we found that there were two. An extra tall patch of grass had completely covered the other. We could also hear the tummy rumblings of others on our right but out of sight. We worked very slowly right in under them both in turn, where we stood and waited ... Twice when we were very close one of them strolled in our direction necessitating an instantaneous flight as silently as possible ... The mosquitoes were bad. We eventually got a sight of both their tusks but decided to hope for something better.[40]

Thesiger's licence entitled him to shoot two elephant a year, and of course he wanted the heaviest-tusked animals he could find, so he took every precaution to avoid wasting his licence by having to shoot in self-defence any charging elephant with small tusks. Eventually, he wrote, they 'found 4 elephants on some dry ground, with short grass not more than 3 feet high. Large swamps and the river close by. They were all large bulls with decent tusks. We worked slowly in to within 40 yards. The one with the best tusks being the furthest off and partly hidden by another, [we] then waited till he moved. Rather fascinating being so close to elephant when you can see them well. When I could see him I shot at his shoulder. He spun round, surprisingly quickly for his size. I let him have the other barrel and then two more. He looked sick but did not stop. Another shot broke his back leg and brought him crashing down. The light[er] tusk was very much worn. He was a very old bull, with no hairs on his tail.' It was after this that he remarked: 'From seeing them in the Zoo and Museums you get no idea of the size of an elephant, as it appears in the wild, especially when you are pretty close under it.'[41]

Hunting along the fringe of dense papyrus swamps, he wrote, 'I got up to innumerable other elephants ... I spent most of [one] morning within a few yards of them, but never so much as a glimpse of their tusks. One was a very big elephant [that] dwarfed his normal sized brother ... We got right up to the big one, and I think got our heads a bit high trying to see his [tusks]. He suddenly put up his trunk and scratched his head, while he peered at us, exactly like someone in doubt, then turned and lumbered back into the papyrus.'[42]

Thesiger photographed a bull elephant he killed the following day. 'The Nuer soon collected, and in 2 hours the whole of him, except for his skull, had disappeared ... They swarmed all over him, getting right inside him, hacking and slashing with their spear heads, and were soon covered with the elephant's blood and their own, for they all got more or less cut. I was very popular.' On his way to the elephant country he had glimpsed a rare white rhinoceros at sunset, 'so it was no use trying to take a photo', and he later shot a Nile lechwe (Mrs Grey's kob) 'with quite a good head, the Sudan speciality par excellence. Attractive animals blackish brown in colour with a large white patch on the withers and lovely lyre-shaped horns.'[43]

Sometimes Thesiger's descriptions of the Sudan's big game are lightened by touches of humour – for example, his cameo of the huge, bewildered bull elephant – or, like one of the Nile lechwe, enhanced by beauty and precision. He always maintained that he had 'shot selectively and seldom'. Despite the large numbers of animals roaming the country's little-known wilderness, he felt deeply concerned that 'game in the Sudan is going to be wiped out by the natives using their traditional methods ... In the past inter-tribal hostility restricted the range of the hunting parties ... Now they can hunt further and further afield, and have every inducement to do so owing to the high prices the meat and skins fetch. The incentive is commercial.' Yet, somewhat surprisingly, Thesiger believed the exception was 'elephant hunting which is done largely for the renown attaching to a successful elephant hunter'.[44] In this respect he was no different from the Nuer. Killing lion, elephant and other dangerous game earned him admiration and respect at a period when big game hunting was accepted uncritically as a sport, hunters were regarded as manly, and hunting adventures were glamorised by films and popular literature.

After the Second World War Thesiger acknowledged the mass rejection of these atavistic values, but he did not attempt to excuse his enthusiasm for hunting, or to deny the excitement it gave him: 'Hunting dangerous game with a rifle was thrilling; whereas hunting with a camera could never have given me the same excitement. After hours of tracking – when you fired the shot and killed a lion, or a buffalo, or an antelope with a really fine head – you felt a tremendous surge of satisfaction. The shot brought it all to its climax. I should never have felt this, if I'd taken a photograph of an animal instead of shooting it. And I'd have been left wondering whether the photograph had come out, and whether it was a good one.'[45]

Thesiger noted that in 1937 there had been a mass migration of elephant through the district, when Nuer of the 'Bul, Leik, Jekiang, and Jagey' clans 'alone killed between 200–300 of them. They kill [elephant] on foot with throwing spears ... I should greatly like to see them doing it. They say a full grown elephant cannot catch a man if the going is good and he keeps his head.'[46] Though he pined for Kutum and the north – 'part of the Moslem world, and so connected up however indirectly with events in N Africa, Arabia, Palestine, India, Afghanistan, indeed with everywhere which interests me'[47] – he condemned the Arab elephant hunters, armed with ten-foot-long shovel-headed spears, who pursued their quarry on horseback. Because the Arabs were 'very apt to treat the country as their own' (a habit by no means exclusive to them) and disdained the 'black and naked' Nuer,[48] Thesiger persuaded Wedderburn-Maxwell (who he knew disliked Arabs) to treat with 'forbearing' any tribesmen who flouted restrictions he had recently imposed on elephant hunting by the Nuer. Having made elephant hunting more tolerable for the Nuer, despite a looming threat to African wildlife by 'native' hunters, Thesiger agreed with Wedderburn-Maxwell that 'we won't have them spearing giraffe as they are rapidly wiping them out'.[49] By this display of administrative dexterity, Thesiger sought to resolve any conflict between his duty to the Sudan Political Service and his instinctive sympathy for the Nuer and most other indigenous peoples.

Although he found elephant hunting in the swamps 'rather too exciting',[50] lion hunting gave Thesiger more variety. On 7 June 1938 he wrote:

I got about the biggest lion I have ever shot. It rained during the night and so we could easily follow the tracks. We jumped two of them in thickish bush. I broke the back of one, but instead of killing him it only paralyzed him, and he made a fiendish din. The bushes were too thick to allow us to finish him off without moving, and the other instead of bolting stopped just out of sight, and greeted every move we made with a thunder of growls. I have never known an unwounded lion do this before. I got pretty scared as I doubted if I could stop him if he charged, and he sounded as if he was on the point of it every second, and [though] I was not sure if the wounded one could still charge, he sounded as if he would like to. Finally the unwounded one stood up, and threw up his tail which always means a charge. However I could see him and knocked him over, dead I thought. We then finished off the first, and gave the other a bit of time to die in. But we found him gone and no blood. I think I must have stunned him as the tracks showed where from a staggery walk he had started to gallop. Anyway I thought discretion the better part of valour and left it at that.[51]

Thesiger had only recently recovered from a bout of malaria. He wrote, 'I am quite fit again,' but had he felt as well as he claimed, he would probably have tracked the second lion. He admitted: 'Fever certainly knocks one to pieces and for the next month you have no energy at all. I was sick the whole time for 5 days, so that I could keep nothing down and was very weak at the end of it. Atabrin is wonderful stuff ... I am quite recovered now. I am looking forward to my leave in Tibesti.'[52] During his illness he was looked after by the faithful Idris, who in turn 'went down with a sharp go of fever' just as Thesiger had begun to recover.[53] Suggestive of their close relationship, Thesiger wrote, 'however we are both all right again'.

At Malakal in April Thesiger heard that his proposed journey to Tibesti had been approved by the Civil Secretary's office in Khartoum. He had enjoyed his seven months among the Nuer, he wrote, which 'above all ... had amply fulfilled my boyhood dreams of big game hunting'.[54] He had spent most of his time trekking across 'a remote, hardly accessible area of Southern Sudan, among a war-like, barely administered people whom I had grown to like and admire'.[55] This, at least, was the version of events he gave half a century later in The Life of My Choice. But the letters he wrote while he was serving in the western Nuer district show that he had felt frustrated and unfulfilled, despite, as he wrote, having 'become attached to the [Nuer] who had chosen to remain with me as my porters, while Idris gave me the comradeship I required'.[56] The prospect of visiting Tibesti that summer gave him an increasingly necessary objective.

His mother's news that a maidservant had handed in her notice annoyed Thesiger. 'I never cared for her, but am surprised and angry at her ingratitude,' he wrote. 'I don't think it is that her class are necessarily ungrateful, not the older ones anyway, but that it is due to their new education, such as they get today in Stanage school [near The Milebrook] and nearly everywhere else. It makes them aggressive, rude and ungrateful. I wonder what she intends to do. I cannot believe she will get another job which suits her as well, anyway I hope not.'[57] What a world of difference he saw between this perceived ingrate and the formerly lawless, now almost flawless, teenage Kobé-Zaghawa, Idris Daud.

Writing to Kathleen on 5 and 18 May 1938, Thesiger outlined his motives for travelling to Tibesti: hopes of being posted back to the Sudan's semi-desert northern territory or, failing that, of a wandering life in Arabia and the Middle East combined with – of all things – a career as a freelance newspaper correspondent. Underlying his daydreams, Thesiger made no secret of his acute dissatisfaction with life among the Nuer tribes. He had never been seriously ill until then, but after the attack of malaria he now felt anxious about his health. 'I long to get back to the cleanness and fresh air of the desert,' he wrote. 'No one could say this is an attractive country. I am more than ever convinced I don't want to spend my next 6 years here. I am not sufficiently interested in the people to feel it is worth ruining my health at a job in which I have not got my heart. These pagans are too primitive, unsophisticated, and crude to be interesting. I still keep pulling strings to get that job in the Northern Desert created for me even at reduced pay.'[58]

On 18 May he wrote:

I heard yesterday that the French have given me leave to go to Tibesti. I never doubted they would and was more afraid the Sudan Government might object [his Tibesti journey had been approved in early February with a starting date in June, later changed to early August[59]]. The reasons I want to go there are that it is one of the few wild and little known parts left in Africa. That it is an interesting mountain mass with peaks rising to 10,000 and 11,000 feet in desert country inhabited by Tebu and Goran tribes, somewhat like the Zaghawa, who are independent and unruly by nature and I want to see how the French administer them, and that being just south of Libya it might just be important if there was war with Italy. Then too by getting to know something of that part of the world I have an added qualification for the job in the Northern desert I want them to give me. Also it will be an interesting experience in desert camel travel. I shall be away for August, September and October … At present I feel unsettled and uncertain.

I know I am never going to settle to this life, and I have given it a fair trial trying to be unprejudiced. But I find myself tired of these naked, uninteresting, uncompanionable savages, and beginning at times to dislike the sight of them and their country, which is no frame of mind in which to administer them. I have got into a dead end and after 7 years or so of this shall be pretty useless for any other job, besides probably not being too fit. I feel wasted here, and also not justified in taking £600 a year to go on having a big game shoot, all that I am really doing at present. This country and these people have no outside interests and no connections with anyone but their immediate Dinka neighbours, as naked as themselves. At Kutum one was on the fringe of the Moslem world …[60]

He planned to think things over during the journey to Tibesti, and come to a definite decision. 'If I leave [the Sudan Political Service],' he wrote, 'I shall go off probably to Arabia, and spend some time there. If we have trouble [i.e. war] which seems inevitable sooner or later, there will be a use for people with knowledge of things and places off the beaten track, the Yemen for instance and [added as an afterthought] Tibesti. I could have an interesting life collecting intelligence in places which suited me, combined probably with a bit of journalism for the Times if they would take me. I should never make anything financially at it, but would be living very cheap and could always buy a life annuity with some of my capital. I don't think I should ever want much money. I don't know what I should do with it.'[61]

Since 1927, when he read Lawrence's *Revolt in the Desert* at Eton, Thesiger had been attracted by the Arabs and by Arabia. In Northern Darfur Guy Moore had encouraged and stimulated his fascination for deserts and desert tribes. Camel journeys to Jabal Maidob and Bir Natrun had given Thesiger valuable experience, but these would be over-shadowed by the Sahara, and ultimately by Arabia. He confided his passion for desert life to Dermot, using lyrical phrases that recurred, sometimes reworked, twenty years later in the pages of *Arabian Sands*: 'I enjoyed getting back to the clean harshness of the desert [on the journey to Tibesti], the simplicity of desert life, the comradeship of desert peoples, to camels, the vast openness of the sands and the freedom of the mountains ... I was very fit, and appreciated at their full worth the things which we accept as normal, but which were then but rarely come by. A long drink of clean water, meat to eat, a few hours sleep when one is dropping with it, or a few minutes linger over a fire in the cold of the early dawn ... it was good to be free, and to see the dawn come up after a long night march and to feel the cold of evening, and to set one's life by the stages of the moon.'[62]

The German explorer Dr Gustav Nachtigal, the first European to describe Tibesti, approached the area in 1870 from Fezzan. Nachtigal saw 'only a small part of this extensive territory ... continually hampered no less by hunger and thirst, illness and exhaustion, than by the malice and animosity of its inhabitants'.[63] Until the Second World War, Thesiger noted approvingly, 'no mechanised transport had penetrated this part of the Sahara'.[64] French army officers stationed at Tibesti still crossed the desert from Fort Lamy in Chad escorted by a detachment of *goumiers*, or camel corps. In 1913 French forces commanded by Colonel Largeau conquered the Borkou oases; from Borkou, Tibesti was explored by Lieutenant-Colonel Tilho, whose most important military expedition mapped the region in 1925. Among the Badayat of Northern Darfur, Thesiger had heard of mountains, known to them as Tu, that lay in the desert 'many days' journey towards the setting sun'.[65] His elderly Badayi informant, Kathir, joined Thesiger's small party as its guide when they left Tini, Idris Daud's village, on 3 August 1938.

Thesiger's three-month camel journey to and from Tibesti was the longest he had undertaken since he travelled in the Danakil country five years earlier. In 1979 he described the journey in *Desert, Marsh and Mountain*, and again in 1987 in his autobiography, *The Life of My Choice*. He wrote these descriptions based on his letters and a 1938 diary of the journey. Writing from Faya, Thesiger outlined his route from the Sudan's western border to Emi Koussi and Zouar: 'So far the journey has not been difficult, with plenty of wells. Between here and Fada, which is the desert crossing, we had water every 2 days and there seems to be no difficulty about water in Tibesti itself.'[66]

Thesiger had already urged Kathleen: 'don't worry about me. I won't take risks about water etc and have good people with me. Real masters of desert travelling.'[67] Devotedly he wrote: 'Your last two letters made me long to see you again before I started. You mean everything to me my dear ... Don't make yourself unhappy fretting. I will write if I see any prospect of getting off a letter of course, but don't get bothered if one does not come.'[68] Stage by stage, he recounted his route: 'from Tini through Wadai (Oudai in French) across the Wadi Hauash into Ennedi, up to the west of the Basso and those big mountain masses to Fada, thence by Ouaita, Oude and Moussu oases to Faya in Borkou'. Finally: 'I hope now to go NE to Ounianga Kebir, thence West to Gouro, thence to climb to the top of Emi Koussi, and then to go north to Bardai, coming back down the West side of Emi Koussi to Ain Galaka.' The bare outline of the journey thus disposed of, Thesiger extolled the landscapes, the soul-cleansing harshness and pervasive peace of the desert: 'some lovely mountain country round Fada, sandstone plateaux weathered into fantastically upstanding pinnacles, peaks, and buttresses with sand dunes at their feet, and the whole country clean with the cleanliness of the desert. Harsh country, burning and blinding in summer, and swept with biting winds in winter, but a good country since it brings out the hardihood latent in man, and purifies by its serenity.'[69]

At one village, Thesiger noted in his diary, 'they had just fined a lad a sheep for having mixed his tea in mimosa[?] before drinking it. [They] appear to have similar conventions to the Baggara ... about tea drinking enforced by small fines inflicted by a special tea sheikh. Offences: to change hands, support cup underneath with little finger etc.'[70] To avoid the blazing midsummer sun, Thesiger's party, with their twelve camels, travelled across the desert by night. They travelled two thousand miles in the three months available to him, marching or riding for eighteen, sometimes twenty hours at a stretch. (Towards the end of the return journey to El Fasher, Thesiger recollected that 'we had been seventy hours in the saddle out of the ninety-six'[71]). Journeying to and from Faya, Thesiger found that the long hours passed quickly in the company of a young Tedda named Dadi. A Tikah chief's nephew, he did not ride his camel but like other Tedda walked beside it, 'singing interminable lilting camel songs'.[72]

For Thesiger, the Tibesti journey served as an apprenticeship to his five years in Arabia after the war. He wrote: 'It so conditioned me that even under the worst conditions there, with thirst and hunger my daily lot, I would never wish I were elsewhere.'[73] Using Idris to mirror such feelings, he noted that the youth 'had found satisfaction, I think, in the very hardship of this journey, which had given him the chance to match his endurance against the redoubtable Tedda; predictably he got on well with them and was much liked'.[74] Thesiger's comparison between Idris and the Tedda of the Sahara counterpoints, and is counterpointed by, a comparison between Thesiger and the Bedu of desert Arabia. He signals clearly his voyeuristic interest in handsome, long-haired youths like Dadi, Faris Shahin of the Druzes, Salim bin Kabina and Salim bin Ghabaisha of the Rashid, and Amara bin Thuqub, his Marsh Arab canoeman. The 'girlish' good looks[75] and deceptively gentle manner of certain young tribesmen often hid endurance, latent physical strength, even a tendency to violence. Thesiger confessed that he found strongly appealing a mixture of danger and androgynous beauty; features that characterised many of his most successful camera-portraits taken in Africa, Arabia and western Asia.

Sandstone outcrops in the desert had often been weathered fantastically: 'One night we passed along the foot of Jabal Bishgara by moonlight. A narrow valley between the naked rock and a high steep sand dune with a few twisted thorn bushes and sodom apples growing in it. The glistening faces of rock, carved by the wind into queer shapes, towered high above us. It seemed a ghostly place, a fit habitation for jinns, as we passed silently through it.'[76] At Faya, headquarters of the Ennedi *circonscription*, he was much impressed by the hardships under which French soldiers lived and operated. He wrote to Kathleen:

What a blessing it is to be able to speak French, even my ungrammatical variant. It adds tenfold to my pleasure. Thank Heavens you insisted on my learning it. I have always thought that the English lived a reasonably hard life, but the life these Frenchmen live makes the life of a Sudan official appear soft, luxury loving, and lazy in comparison. Their Groupes Nomades spend 3 years continuously on trek, on a war footing, and doing some treks which would appear fantastic to the Sudan, with perhaps one month altogether at the station, with no beds and no luxuries, and a fair share of hard riding after raiders. Even at Faya which corresponds to Fasher, there are no wives, no cars, and nothing which could be described as luxuries (sheets and pillows for example). Against this you can put the life of a Sudan political official, or Bimbashi in the Sudan Defence Force, with a £2000 mosquito proof house, two cars, every luxury including electric light and fans in most province [sic] headquarters. A regular easy office life, with an armchair, whisky and soda on the veranda and abundant female company in the evenings ... I envy the Frenchmen their life. It is the hard man's life which they lead as a matter of course, and not as an exception which in the Sudan is regarded as eccentric, which I envy them. This is the life for a young man. The Sudan for a middle aged man who has retired from the Army. I also envy them their country, which is far finer than the Sudan and wonderfully vast. From the Sudan frontier to the Atlantic, from the Congo to Morocco and Tunisia. Their great mistake is that they won't learn the language and have consequently to rely on interpreters. In consequence they can never get to know the people, and their terms of service in one place are too short, only 3 years.

Thesiger offered as a generalisation: 'Also as a rule I think the best Englishman is better than the best Frenchman at dealing with natives, but am not quite sure about the average. They are totally different but I am not sure that they don't about work out in the end very much the same in value.'[77]

The things he criticised were things he already disliked and rejected: 'soft' living, alcohol, 'intrusive' female company.[78] Though Thesiger's liking for 'the hard man's life' – journeying and feeding with tribesmen, sleeping rough, shooting big game, riding camels, trekking on foot – was viewed by many of his peers as eccentric, it was a life he had craved since boyhood, and had lived with Guy Moore and Idris Daud in Northern Darfur. Close ties between men thrived on this atavistic brand of stoic heroism. Like the 'other' Lawrence, Thesiger 'imagined that for a man to achieve another man's total devotion might be the noblest, most heroic experience of all'.[79]

On 16 August, after sunset, on the way to Faya from Fada, Thesiger's party was caught in a violent sandstorm that blew for three hours. Everything they carried with them lay half-buried by drifts of sand, whose heavy weight squeezed the last drops of precious water from their goatskins. Thesiger found it 'Eerie and unpleasant to lie muffled in a tobe [loose sheet] as [the storm] swept over one for ... hours, and curiously lonely.'[80] He phrased this in *The Life of My Choice*, 'I felt utterly isolated,'[81] which was more emphatic but in a way far more impersonal. 'Almost without water, [he doubted] if the camels would stand another full day in the sun'.[82] Confused by an overcast sky which hid the sun, Thesiger's guide Isa Adam had lost his sense of direction, but using a compass Thesiger managed to guide his small caravan to the Moussou oasis where the skins were replenished.

On his map Thesiger underlined place names in soft pencil, correcting their spelling, writing brief descriptions in the margin. (Like almost all Thesiger's maps, his 'Tibesti' map, ordered from Stanford's in London, had been cut into sections and reassembled, glued to a single folded linen sheet which strengthened the original paper and made it far more durable.)

The 11,000-foot mountain Emi Koussi had been one of his objectives. He described how he first saw it at dawn, 'faint like a cloud upon the desert's edge',[83] and looking north-west, from Kada spring, as 'very faint and high both at sunrise and sunset'. Guided by an elderly Tedda tribesman, Thesiger climbed to the summit of Emi Koussi, accompanied by Idris and Kathir. He described the climb in the RGS *Journal*: 'We struggled along, alternately climbing and descending, but slowly working upwards, until we came to the great gorge of the Mashakezey, 1000 feet or more in depth and so sheer that a stone flung from the top fell clear. A faint track marked with donkey droppings disappeared over the edge. Somehow the camels went protesting down that, while we lay back on tails and saddle ropes, and loosened boulders crashed ahead.' To his surprise, in rain pools among the rocks Thesiger found tiny fish, 'half an inch long, silvery in colour, with crimson tails and back fins'. From Emi Koussi he had 'an awe-inspiring view out across range upon range of mountains and jagged peaks, rising from precipitous shadow-filled gorges'. After a night of bitter cold, camped on the southern edge of the crater, next morning Thesiger and Idris climbed to the summit of the crater's southern wall, 'thus attaining the highest point in Tibesti'.[84] The elderly Tedda being uncertain of the way, a Tibbu herdswoman from whom they had previously borrowed two camels led them back to the Miski valley. 'She strode ahead of us,' Thesiger wrote, 'a wild and impressive figure, with a naked knife in one hand and an oryx horn in the other.'[85] While the hospitality Thesiger received from French officers at the desert forts had been generous – 'almost embarrassing' – a tiny bowl of milk offered to them by the Tibbu herdswoman meant more as it 'must have been her all'.[86]

Riding north-west from Emi Koussi 'across windswept uplands, over passes … through narrow gorges, under precipices and past towering peaks', Thesiger reached Tieroko. Most magnificent of all Tibesti mountains, Tieroko dominated the Modra valley, where a clear, swift stream flowed through 'a bed of high green rushes, with palms'. At Bardai, where Nachtigal had barely escaped from hostile tribesmen with his life, Thesiger copied petroglyphs of human figures and animals carved in the hard rock. As they travelled, he talked to Idris of his family and home, whose setting the young Zaghawa could never have imagined. He wrote to Kathleen: 'Idris is as valuable and companionable as ever, and happy to be on trek again in desert country. Though he has not seen you he has heard much about you and sends his salaams.'[87] 'The men who came with me from Darfur all fell out by the wayside, only Idris remaining to the end. He is extraordinarily enduring. When we got off our camels and I snatched some much wanted sleep, he would set to without a word and make me *assida* [thick maize porridge] waking me a little later to tell me it was ready. God how I am going to miss him. I shall be very lonely without him.'[88]

They travelled by night, or camped in some village, among landscapes made ethereal by the moonlight. At Modra, 'from below [Thesiger's camp] came the music of falling water and the scent of sage and other herbs ... The moon was full and the valley filled with light and shade, while that great mountain [Tarso Tieroko] rose out of it ghostly and awe-inspiring.'[89] Thesiger described the varied clothing worn by the Tedda of Tibesti: 'A white *afalangi* with immensely wide sleeves. Small boys wear this, but with theirs it is very often left unsewn down each side, the length of the sleeve and then from the armpit to the bottom. The men also wear a short sleeved, short skirted *jibba* for working in. Often worn under the other. A white *jalabia* which has rather baggy sleeves fastening at the waist. And for special occasions a cloaklike garment of black silk trimmed with red or occasionally with pale blue, with short but wide sleeves and slit down the neck. Or a similar shaped garment of pale blue cloth decorated at the neck and sleeves with a design in gold thread. They almost invariably wear their *imma* folded across the mouth.'[90]

Thesiger liked the Tedda 'immensely'. Approaching Aouzou from the Tirano pass, a lame Tedda youth named Arami, 'with two most attractive small boys, like Maidobi lads',[91] spent the night at Thesiger's camp. From the 'stupendous' Nanamsena gorge he descended to Aouzou, in a saucer-shaped, sandy valley, with gardens, palm trees, acacias and a square, mud-walled fort, surrounded by bare black hills. The fort's Sergeant had been stationed from 1933 to 1935 at Jibuti. He knew soldiers Thesiger met during his Danakil expedition, and Henri de Monfreid, whose Red Sea adventures had fired Thesiger's imagination.[92]

The 'embarrassingly hospitable'[93] Sergeant took Thesiger and Idris to Erbi, a palm grove where they found a 'veritable Eden. Crystal clear water

… green grass, palms and gardens … Sheep and shepherd boys among the palms and rocks.' Thesiger mused longingly: 'I should like to stay a week.'[94] The 'loquacious Sergeant at Aouzou, the only Frenchman I met in Tibesti whom I disliked',[95] plied Thesiger with wine which, he wrote in 1987, 'I never wanted.' He omitted to mention that while at Erbi, lazing among the palms, he had a bottle of wine as a relaxing accompaniment to the tray of dates brought by three boys whose 'grace and simple courtesy were touching'.[96] That evening a dance was held at Aouzou fort, *tirailleurs* and local women dancing together.

Though outwardly 'extremely hospitable and agreeable', the Sergeant proved to be cruel, racist and uncouth. The previous day he had shot four gazelle with an automatic rifle, and wounded five more. 'He talk[ed] incessantly of *les blancs* and said that when a white speaks it is to them as if God spoke. Curiously complacent and unimaginative [he said] the way to be popular is to tickle the girls at the dance. Undignified and vulgar I wonder[ed] what they really think of him.'[97] In *The Life of My Choice* he sharpened and personalised this rebuke by replacing 'they' with 'Dadi', the mop-haired young Tedda, as the boorish French Sergeant's hypothetical judge.[98]

Thesiger was deeply impressed by the Tedda's spartan lifestyle. 'These Tebu [Tedda] are a magnificent hardy people,' he wrote, 'and very attractive. They depend almost entirely on their dates to keep them alive. Those living with their herds of goats on the mountain tops shelter in caves, leading the life led by prehistoric man, and enduring incredible hardships of cold and hunger.'[99]

At Bardai, on the way to Zouar, Thesiger explored the vast crater of Doon, also known as the 'Trou au Natron': sheer-sided, eighteen miles across and half a mile deep, it was a hard day's climb to the crater bottom and back. Idris found the hot springs at Sobouroun more startlingly impressive: 'a tangle of rocks, red, purple, yellow, white and green in colour and everywhere from them jets of steam escape, so that the place sounds like a railway station', Thesiger wrote, an untypical but effective evocation of this 'strange pestilential place'.[100]

He and his companions approached Zouar through the Forchi gorge, an immense cleft in the mountains, twenty-two miles long and only ten to thirty yards wide, its walls 'one clean, unclimbable face of hard rock' from two hundred to seven hundred feet high.[101] 'In the sandy pools scoured at the base of the larger rocks were shoals of small fish, which we tried in vain to catch'.[102]

On 27 September 1938, at Zouar, Thesiger heard news of the crisis in Europe. 'I happened to arrive ... to hear on the wireless that they were evacuating Paris and digging up London. War seemed quite inevitable so I got on a camel and rode night and day for Faya, where I arrived 6 days later, to find that they had reached a settlement. I wish I had been in England, it would have been intensely interesting.'[103] As a distraction, before Thesiger left Zouar the flamboyant commandant, Captain Mareuge, invested him with a makeshift decoration, that of Chevalier du Maquereau de Teghane, in light-hearted recognition of his recent observations on the 'marine life of Forchi gorge' and his 'touching' admiration of the Tibbu, or Tedda people. Perhaps the tipsy ceremony reminded Thesiger of the drunken Oxford boating parties he had so despised; whatever the reason, he never mentioned it in his Tibesti diary, his letters, or any of his published descriptions of the journey. Sixty years afterwards, however, General Jacques Massu, who had served as a Lieutenant at the Zouar fort, described the occasion:

I well remember Mr Thesiger's passage through Zouar (in Tibesti), in 1938, and his cameleer profile, wearing a soft felt hat. He was coming from Darfur and heading for Europe. The commanding officer of the Tibesti sub-division was Capitaine Mareuge, since deceased, whose second in command I was, pending my taking over from him shortly afterwards. He liked to act as a lord and, as such, he had created a decoration, known as 'le Maquereau de Tegahan' (the Mackerel of Tegahan) from the name of a palm grove near Zouar. On his order, I made the decoration with the tinfoil top of a champagne bottle, shaped as a fish, and hung it on a piece of red ribbon equipped with a pin. At the end of an improved [improvised?] and well washed down meal, Mareuge got up and delivered a toast in honour of Mr Thesiger, who was making a difficult and meritorious solitary trip. Then he pinned his decoration on Thesiger's chest. Thesiger didn't react and left us the next day. He didn't mention our hospitality in the book about his trip [The Life of My Choice].[104]

Thesiger later claimed he hardly remembered this event.[105] He neither shared the commandant's piscatory sense of humour nor considered his play-acting appropriate at this time, when Europe appeared to be on the threshold of war. Discreetly, he wrote: 'That evening, I drank to the Anglo–French entente with him and his lieutenant.'[106]

On his way from Faya to the Sudan border, Thesiger visited the lakes of Ounianga Kebir, whose strikingly lovely colours he noted in the margin of his map. 'Yoa (blue); Ouma (red); Midji (red); Forodone (green).' He described them more thoughtfully in his diary: Yoa, 'of incredible loveliness', was 'a deep Mediterranean blue, with precipices of rose and white rock resembling marble, golden sands, palms, rushes where the springs are …';[107] Ouma and Midji were 'a deep permanganate of potash red'; the long, narrow Forodone was 'a deep vegetable green'.[108] The 1933–34 Danakil expedition had given Thesiger useful practice in mapping, and his marginal pen-and-ink sketches of Tibesti positioned the four lakes more precisely than they appeared in his 1933 edition of Colonel Tilho's survey, printed in Paris by the Service Géographique de l'Armée.

Thesiger and Idris arrived back at Tini on 26 October. Within the space of only four years, Thesiger had achieved two geographical 'firsts'. In 1934 he had been the first European to traverse the forbidden sultanate of Aussa; now, in 1938, he became the first Englishman to reach Tibesti. He wrote to Kathleen:

I arrived at Tini on the morning of the day I had given Guy [Moore] as my date, my camels on their last legs, our flour, sugar and tea finished, and four more days until my leave expired … It is difficult to describe in a letter the many places I have seen and to give you an adequate idea of it all. I have had a wonderful 3 months, living the life I love, in a country which attracts me and among people who appeal to me. Nor can I give you a proper idea of Tibesti … as rugged and mighty as the Atlas but absolutely barren … No Englishman has visited Tibesti before me which is surprising. It is not easy to be the first Englishman nowadays … I have taken large numbers of photos which I am sending you … I have copied a large number of rock drawings, some of them very old … I have also brought back the fossilised bones of a hippo from the plateau above the lakes of Ounianga.[109]

Thesiger and Idris covered the 250 miles from Tini to El Fasher in four days, riding their camels '65 hours out of the 96'.[110] In *The Life of My Choice* he wrote: 'When we reached Fasher on 1 November we had been in the saddle seventy hours out of the ninety-six,'[111] enhancing their formidable achievement still more by this slight exaggeration.

In a moving soliloquy about his journey some years later, he echoed words by Antoine Saint-Exupéry in 1939 in *Wind, Sand and Stars*, who evoked the Sahara's impermeable solitude, where human contact was the 'only true form of wealth'.[112] Thesiger wrote in *Arabian Sands*:

> this was the real desert where differences of race and colour, of wealth and social standing, are almost meaningless; where coverings of pretence are stripped away and basic truths emerge. It was a place where men live close together. Here, to be alone, was to feel at once the weight of fear, for the nakedness of this land was more terrifying than the darkest forest at dead of night. In the pitiless light of day we were as insignificant as the beetles I watched labouring across the sands. Only in the kindly darkness could we borrow a few square feet of desert and find homeliness within the radius of the firelight, while overhead the familiar pattern of the stars screened the awful mystery of space.[113]

The threat of war with Germany had given his journey unforeseen importance. He confided to his mother: 'I heard ... that [copies of my Tibesti report] have been sent to the Foreign Office, War Office, and Embassy at Cairo, and several other places. I have been lucky and my report is opportune. This ... affair has brought Tibesti into the foreground, and as I am the only Englishman to have been there the report is valuable.' He added prophetically: 'If when I leave here I become a traveller this will help, as the authorities will back me when I wish to get off the beaten track.'[114] He gave Roderic a terse appraisal of the Munich crisis as he saw it: 'God knows, everything in Europe seems as bad as it could be. We have averted war for the time being, but if as the price of that we have revolution in France I fear we shall be worse off than ever and if there is a war by losing Czechoslovakia we have lost an irreplaceable ally.' He concluded: 'I suppose what is written will come.'[115]

Thesiger's fatalism was inspired more by Omar Khayyam than the

Koran. He 'desperately' missed the tribes of Northern Darfur,[116] whose Muslim faith and secular traditions he respected, but never for a moment did he consider becoming a Muslim himself. He believed, nevertheless, that 'There is only one way to travel and that is to try and merge into one's surroundings and to be accepted by those one travels amongst. I don't delude myself that I succeed but I get my interest and pleasure trying.'[117]

Idris's uncle, the Sheikh of Tini, gave a feast to celebrate his nephew's homecoming. Feeding with Zaghawa villagers, surrounded by camels, listening to old men's stories of fighting and raiding, Thesiger felt content. But his satisfaction, and his vicarious pride in Idris's achievement, were shadowed by the knowledge that soon he and Idris must go their separate ways. The Sahara's still unspoilt tribes, exotic palm groves, awe-inspiring mountains and remote lakes of brilliant stained-glass colours had left Thesiger elated, and physically and emotionally fulfilled. But he felt depressed now that the desert journey and his three months' leave had ended. Without Idris for company, he dreaded returning to his 'pointless' existence among the Nuer. He had felt melancholy, too, after his Danakil journey ended in 1934, when he feared (quite needlessly) that he 'should never find again the thrilling excitement of unadministered tribes, of deserts, or the lure of some unknown country'.[118]

In November Thesiger wrote to his mother from Khartoum: 'I part today with Idris and feel miserable at doing so. During these 3 years he has been a friend and companion such as I shall never find again. His type are not servants and I was lucky to have got him. He is anxious to get back to tribal life, though he is sad at leaving. If I pressed him he would probably stay, but it is better for him to go. I shall be lonely and forlorn without him. I am paying his expenses to go on the pilgrimage [to Mecca] in a month's time';[119] '... we had hunted together, trekked together, and shared the things we had, so that he was like a son to me'.[120] Idris was the first of many teenage tribesmen whom Thesiger treated as adoptive 'sons'. Five decades later, he described as 'dear to me as a son' the last of these youths, Lawi Leboyare, who 'has been with me for the past fifteen years, ever since he left his village school [in Kenya] at the age of ten'.[121] Thesiger did not like the adjective 'coded', but reluctantly agreed that his use of words such as 'son' and 'comrade'[122] might be interpreted as a code. As a helpmate and an emotional crutch, Thesiger wrote, 'I brought a Fur lad down with me from Fasher. He had been my *syce*'s boy and then acted for a time as cook. When I was in Fasher he came and asked me to take him along with me. He was with Guy as a sort of spare boy. I am glad to have him. I hope he won't get a lot of fever ... The Nuer are worse than hopeless as servants.'[123]

Thesiger had been interviewed by Sir Angus Gillan, the Civil Secretary, after he returned from Tibesti to Khartoum, and again at Malakal by the Provincial Governor, George Coryton, a tall, quiet man, somewhat reminiscent of Thesiger's father and others of the same mould, 'in obviously hard condition', with whom Wilfred had felt immediately 'at home'.[124] He wrote from the western Nuer that this interview 'gave me the chance of telling [Coryton] that I had asked the Civil Secretary for a transfer. I told him that I had come back from Tibesti knowing that I should never settle down in the South, and had told the CS this in Khartoum and that if they could not find me a suitable job in the North it were better I went. It is not fair to Coryton or Maxwell to train me up as a Nuer DC and for me then to leave. Both the Civil Secretary and Coryton have been extremely nice about this and neither of them are anxious for me to leave the Sudan, though they agree that I shall never be any good in the South feeling about it as I do. I have been moved by their sympathy, understanding, and desire to help.'[125]

At Shamba, on the Bahr el Jabal, Thesiger found the last resting place of the murdered District Commissioner Vere Fergusson. Overgrown by rank grass and located in a swamp, the grave mirrored Thesiger's dejected mood; writing to Kathleen on 22 December 1938, he noted that it had looked 'very forsaken and pathetic'.[126] Once the Civil Secretary had read his Tibesti report and returned it to him, Thesiger planned to write a series of articles about the journey for *The Times*. In 1934 *The Times*'s editor, Geoffrey Dawson, had paid Thesiger £100 (equal to a typist's salary for a year) for his four Danakil articles. In 1937 Dawson asked him to write on Morocco, which he did, highlighting Moorish–French relations, social inequality, urban poverty and the upsurge of nationalism, in an anonymous article whose title, 'The Mind of the Moor' (supplied by *The Times*), Thesiger dismissed as 'pretentious'.[127] Thesiger felt sure *The Times* would publish his Tibesti articles: 'I hope they will give me £100, which is what they gave me for the Danakil articles,' he wrote. 'I believe I am the first Englishman to have been to Tibesti so that they won't have had any articles on there before.'[128] Douglas Newbold, who succeeded Gillan as Civil Secretary, liked the articles but doubted if *The Times* would publish them. Newbold proved to be right: 'they [were] a bit long, and not "news" ' in 1939, when Britain was on the threshold of the Second World War.[129]

The rains in 1938 were exceptionally heavy. Confined to the *Kereri* without much to occupy him, Thesiger ate, slept and read voraciously books sent by his mother. He read for the second time *Gone with the Wind*, 'a remarkable book', and, helped by the Arab clerk on board, the *Thousand and One Nights* in Arabic. Long spells of inactivity depressed him. He worried continually, often needlessly, about Kathleen and his brothers, about preserving his letters from the Sudan, his photographs, the precious big game trophies he had left the London taxidermist Rowland Ward to mount and begged his mother to hang in the hall at The Milebrook. That April, Brian and his wife Diana, who had married in July 1937, travelled with Brian's regiment the Royal Welch Fusiliers to India. Thesiger wrote: 'I am glad they have got out of England as it will shake them up. Brian was I think getting too set in his ways.'[130] He wrote again on 3 June (his twenty-ninth birthday): '[Brian] does not sound as if he had settled down to India yet ... I was amazed to see how he finds everything squalid. I suppose it is natural. I am so used to it that I should find it unnatural and artificial if it were not.'[131]

Wilfred's letters to Dermot and Roderic tended to recycle the news he had given Kathleen, but they also reveal affection and concern for his two youngest brothers. By 1938 Dermot was marshalling for Mr Justice Lawrence (Geoffrey Lawrence, later Lord Oaksey, who presided over the Nuremberg trials at the end of the Second World War[132]). Thesiger and Dermot were especially close, and had grown closer during Wilfred's last year at Oxford. He wrote to Dermot after returning from Tibesti, signing off: 'God bless you Dermot dear. I look forward so much to seeing you again. I thought of you often during those long night marches. Write to me.'[133] He fretted that, unlike Brian and Dermot, Roderic was still unemployed: 'It is worrying his just leading a young man about town life. He has not got the money to do it and it is futile, and he is worth such a lot more than that.'[134]

Apart from his 1938 diary, which he had devoted mainly to his journey to Tibesti, Thesiger relied on his letters to document his years in Sudan. He cautioned his mother: 'I hope you keep my letters safe, since as I keep no diary they are the only written record I have. Perhaps sometime you could sort out and file them. It would be worth I think getting a proper file for them. When I was last at home there was a big pile of them but very mixed. When I get home we must also sort out my photos and get them put in [to albums].'[135] He had been anxious about the quality of his Tibesti photographs, which Richard Owen, the editor of *Sudan Notes and Records*, persuaded him to have developed in Khartoum: 'A mistake I am afraid. They seem patchy from the small prints, but if Kodak [in England] take trouble over them separately I think several will be good. It is no good them printing the poor ones ... Let me know how my heads and skins at Rowland Wards have turned out.'[136]

Stormy skies over the Nile, as Thesiger feared, presaged early and very heavy rains in April 1939. By then the talk of war was rife: 'Everywhere preparations'. To Thesiger's delight he was promised 'a body of irregular scouts to patrol the Western Desert. A good life and what I have always wanted.'[137] With a March post came more books – Captain F.H. Mellor's *Morocco Awakes*, Roald Amundsen's *North-West Passage* and selections from Doughty's *Arabia Deserta*. Kathleen wrote that Roderic had got a job, though Thesiger wondered how he would like accounting.[138] The post included a letter from Rowland Ward confirming that the mounted heads and skins were ready. Thesiger noted ruefully: 'I also got a bill for £55 for them which gave me a bad shock ... I don't think Rowland Ward have put [the heads] on shields, just as well or it would have been another £20.'[139] He had felt bewildered and frustrated that his offer to work in the northern desert without pay, had been rejected because it was 'not fair' on him.[140] Years later he found out that Douglas Newbold had judged him 'a brave, awkward, attractive creature' who himself realised that he was 'a misfit' in a government post.[141] Thesiger had said as much in a letter to Kathleen: 'Being so unorthodox and odd, I must be a bugbear to a rather conventional Government, but still they have been very patient.'[142]

Six months before he went on his last leave to England before the war, Thesiger visited Tolodi in the Nuba mountains. The DC, Reggie Dingwall, whom he had succeeded at Kutum in 1935, took him to a village in the hills where al-Liri Nuba celebrated Eid with three days of feasting and dancing. Unlike other naked, pagan Nuba, the al-Liri were Muslims and wore Arab dress; armed with Remington rifles, the men fired them 'about a foot in front and just over the head of your favourite girl as she danced with you'. Thesiger thought the al-Liri boys 'strikingly good looking in an effeminate way'.[143] The Nuba wrestlers, whose powerful bodies 'rippled with muscle', he admired as much as the statuesque, though less 'massively-built', Nuer men.[144] He thought men in general more graceful than women, 'who bulge in all the wrong places'.[145] On trek in the western Nuer district, he wrote from a camp: 'It is not easy to concentrate as the doorway of my tent is filled up by 6 young Nuer women, all chattering and as difficult to drive away as rooks in a corn field. They boast 3 strings of beads between the 6 of them and that is all. It is a pity I don't think them as attractive as they evidently think themselves.'[146] At a Nuer marriage dance in 1939, 'the ... warriors were all stark naked except for a few beads and feathers in their hair ... [and a] very lovely flat bead of Eton blue, of which they often wear a string across the forehead ... They are a magnificently built people and very tall. It is not often that I stand looking up at the people I am talking to. They are not leggy but well proportioned and many of them quite thick set. I wonder if any other people can equal them for beauty of body. They really are like Greek statues.'[147]

Thesiger took no close-up portraits of the Nuer, whom he photographed trekking, hunting among wind-tossed papyrus, butchering elephant he had shot, or conversing together in a group. His photographs reflect a sense of remoteness he felt among them, compared with closer relationships he had achieved with Muslim tribes in Northern Darfur. 'Among the Nuer,' he wrote, 'I lived in a tent apart from my men, waited on by servants; I had been an Englishman travelling in Africa.' It was as if he had taken a gigantic step backwards, from the democratic values he had learnt in Darfur and the Sahara to his 1933–34 Danakil journey, which he likened to his father's style of travel a generation before. Apart from this, Thesiger had not yet acquired the photographic techniques he would exploit so successfully after 1945: getting as close as possible to his subjects for intimate portraiture; kneeling or squatting down and photographing from an upward angle, with the sky as a neutral background.

Among the Nuer he found no equivalent for Idris Daud – a forerunner of other companions with whom he identified and who would inspire many fine photographic portraits. Much of his inspiration he owed to Freya Stark's photographs in *Seen in the Hadhramaut*. Her beautiful images showed Thesiger the possibilities of photography with the Leica, and made him realise how much further he could explore camera portraits, light and shadow, texture and composition.

Kathleen had tried to reassure Wilfred about his future, emphasising his 'exceptional' qualities that appealed to Charles Dupuis and Guy Moore. Thesiger insisted that she was wrong; the Sudan government had no use for 'exceptional people'. Writing from the Civil Secretary's office, Richard Owen endorsed Thesiger's bleak view of the Service: 'I met the new probationers the other day. A nice lot of young men but I began to wonder when instead of asking about rifles and camel saddles they asked if there were tennis courts in their stations and if they could get frigidaires up from Khartoum.'[148] Thesiger wrote: 'As a small boy I grew up on Rider Haggard. What does the present day boy read at his private school? I am out of date and really only a war would recreate conditions in which I could be of any use I fear.'[149] Already he 'enshrined the past, felt out of step with the present and dreaded the future'.[150]

Embittered by Italy's invasion of Abyssinia, dumbfounded by a Munich pact that had ceded the Sudetenland to Germany, he wrote:

one must live from hand to mouth, for who knows what the future holds? I simply cannot understand Chamberlain's policy. It seems the very antithesis of everything which [one] was brought up to admire and to regard as English. A policy dictated by a number of elderly men, who are morally and mentally unstable owing to their sufferings in the [First World] war, to an electorate of nervous war babies. Any private individual who behaved in private life as England has behaved during the past 4 years, would be kicked out of his club and never spoken to again. Materially Europe and England are far, far beyond the Zaghawa and Maidob in progress, morally it seems to me that they have dropped below the level of the most degraded and unpleasant African tribe that it is possible to find.[151]

In October Thesiger and Wedderburn-Maxwell journeyed with the *Kereri* up the Baro river, carrying stores to Gambeila, a Sudanese trading post in Italian-occupied Abyssinia. From the river's confluence with the Sobat, they saw the highlands of Abyssinia in the distance. 'They held my gaze,' Thesiger wrote. 'It was there that I hoped eventually to fight the Italians.'[152]

THIRTEEN

Rape of my Homeland

In July 1939 Thesiger had gone on leave to England, confident he would be posted back to Kutum when he returned to the Sudan. The latter part of his leave, according to *The Life of My Choice*, he had planned to spend travelling with his mother 'in Iraq and Persia'.[1] Just as he always spoke of 'Abyssinia' instead of Ethiopia, throughout his life Thesiger stubbornly referred to Iran as 'Persia'. He said: '"Persia" gives me a sense of continuity with the past – a sense of history. Iran makes me think of cars and of oil-fields, youngsters in shoddy European clothes, hanging about street corners with nothing to do.'[2] His original idea had been for them to spend six weeks in Lebanon, Syria, Iraq, Trans-Jordan and Egypt: 'I should like to go back [to Morocco], but we had better go and see some new country next spring, and Jerusalem and Damascus will please you I know, and all the flowers will be out ... You will love Luxor too. It is very beautiful in the evenings, when the sun is setting behind the Valley of the Kings.' 'I am saving up,' he wrote, 'so that we can do it completely and well. It should be immense fun.'[3] On his twenty-ninth birthday he firmly rebuffed a cautious letter from his mother, who had apparently advised postponing, or at the very least shortening, their journey due to the imminent threat of war: 'I am determined to go to Syria and Iraq. I cannot possibly spend my whole leave in England as you seem to suggest ... Six weeks will give me all the time I want in England.'[4]

At The Milebrook, Thesiger received a telegram ordering him to report to the Canadian Pacific steamship RMS *Montcalm* at Glasgow docks on the River Clyde. He was already aboard on 3 September, when Neville Chamberlain announced that Britain was at war with Germany. This meant that all transfers from the Sudan's provinces were suspended.

The *Montcalm* sailed in convoy from the Clyde to Port Said, making a wide detour into the Atlantic before entering the Mediterranean. Thesiger described the mildly eventful voyage to Dermot as 'an interesting journey out in a large convoy escorted by a battleship and some dozen destroyers as well as an airplane. We had three scares when they dropped depth charges and on one occasion they told us they thought they had sunk a submarine ... It was an impressive sight as we steamed along for we were a dozen big ships and all close together and all zig-zagging together.'[5] In another letter he reassured his mother that the 'probable' cause of one scare had been 'only a large shoal of fish'.[6] Aboard the *Montcalm* were 'nearly half' the officials in the Sudan Political Service, including several Provincial Governors. Had the vessel been torpedoed, Thesiger commented facetiously, 'promotion in the Sudan Political Service might have been spectacular'.[7]

After spending two days in Cairo he travelled to Khartoum, and from there to Malakal. Idris had returned from his pilgrimage, and had waited for Thesiger at El Obeid, on the road to Kutum, but joined him eventually at Kosti on the White Nile, roughly halfway between Khartoum and Malakal. 'It is very good to have him with me again,' Thesiger wrote, and added laconically: 'He seems to have had an interesting time.'[8] At Malakal Thesiger found a letter from Douglas Newbold, the Civil Secretary, offering him a six-week training course with the Cheshire Regiment in Khartoum, which led to a commission in the Sudan Defence Force. As an officer trained for active service, Thesiger realised, he would be despatched to Abyssinia to fight the Italians, for whom he now felt 'a bitter, personal hatred'.[9]

Having accepted Newbold's offer, Thesiger trained at Khartoum with fifteen other volunteers. The course was 'very comprehensive' and 'pretty stiff',[10] he wrote: 'We do drill and PT followed by an icy swim at dawn, and then lectures, demonstrations and instruction in Machine-guns. They teach us well and make it interesting.'[11] Bill Harris, himself a Bimbashi in the Abyssinian campaign, described Thesiger as 'one of those hardy men who seem to take a delight in being as uncomfortable as possible'. Although this was by no means strictly true, Harris supported his contention by describing how he had found Thesiger at Belaya, 'naked in the middle of the stream having a vigorous bath in the freezing water'.[12]

At Belaya, his commanding officer Hugh Boustead recalled: 'He had come straight from ... Sakalla, after living on the country for two months; he could not understand why people travelled with rations. He took a bathe in the icy water of the stream, and then with enormous appetite demolished the last of Bill Harris's stores while we watched in amusement and sympathy for Bill. It was a memorable meal for Wilfred, and in later years he would be reminded of it by his hosts: "It's no good offering you anything, is it, Wilfred? You live on the country," while the marmalade pot would be ostentatiously hidden.'[13] In *My Kenya Days*, Thesiger wrote: 'Thirty years later, when I met Bill ... for the first time since the war, I walked into his room, came to attention, put a pot of marmalade on the table behind which he was sitting, and said, "Repaid."'[14]

In a group photograph taken at the Cheshire Regiment's barracks, Thesiger stands with his arms crossed in the middle row, his height and powerful build matched by the tall, muscular officer cadets on either side of him. He had felt optimistic about joining the Sudan Defence Force, but by January 1940, when Italy had not yet entered the war, he confided to Kathleen: 'I don't know what is going to happen to me ... Yesterday we were asked to write in if we had any strong preferences. I intend ... to write and say that I am most anxious to get away from the Sudan, now that there appears to be no likelihood of war with Italy, and join the army at home. If this is impossible I would rather stay on in my job as DC than join the SDF. To be in the SDF out here would really be intolerable.'[15] At Dessie in Abyssinia towards the end of the war, Thesiger would find himself in a similar predicament, feeling marginalised, ineffective and remote from Europe during the last decisive months before Germany's defeat by the Allied armies.

In March Thesiger wrote telling Kathleen that Douglas Newbold had promised that he would not be posted back to Malakal, and had instead offered him a job administering an unoccupied territory in the neighbourhood of Lake Rudolf, later renamed Lake Turkana. 'We are going to start administering this, since it was twice used last year as a jumping off place for two big raids on the Turkana, in one over 70 people were killed and some 10,000 head of stock driven off, at least according to Kenya. This would be interesting work in country in which I have always been interested.'[16] Thesiger had heard this area described by his father, and had read about the wild tribes and wild country around the lake in books by Captain C.H. Stigand, Major Henry Rayne and Lieutenant Ludwig von Höhnel. A birthday present from Brian, his copy of Stigand's *To Abyssinia Through an Unknown Land* (1910) had belonged to 'Minna' Buckle, who presumably gave it to Brian, and Rayne's *The Ivory Raiders* (1924) had been a fourteenth-birthday present from his mother. Not until much later did he acquire von Höhnel's scarce two-volume *Discovery of Lakes Rudolf and Stefanie* (1894), describing the expedition led by Count Samuel Teleki von Szek in 1888.

The war put paid to Newbold's suggestion; yet Thesiger's fascination with northern Kenya and its warlike, nomadic tribes such as the Turkana and Rendille, never waned. Two decades later, in November 1960, he fulfilled a long-standing ambition, trekking with camels across Kenya's Northern Frontier District to Lake Rudolf. This was the first of many journeys in northern Kenya he made on foot, with baggage animals, between 1960 and 1978; after that he was to spend nine months every year living among the pastoral Samburu, at Maralal.

After returning to Malakal, Thesiger paid a second visit to the Nuba tribes near Tolodi in Kordofan with Reginald Dingwall. Though he rarely photographed subjects in movement, among the Nuba he took photographs of wrestlers in their natural amphitheatre of boulder-strewn hills. These pictures succeeded artistically and technically, but they were less impressive than photographs of Nuba wrestlers taken in 1949 by George Rodger, or during the 1960s and seventies by Leni Riefenstahl, 'a marvellous photographer, a marvellous observer of scenes',[17] whose superb colour images illustrated her books *Last of the Nuba* (1972) and *People of Kau* (1976). While Thesiger admired Riefenstahl's work, he remained sharply critical of her methods: 'I am told she persuaded the young men to paint their bodies, and let her photograph them, by offering them ridiculous sums of money. Of course, they demanded the same from everyone else who went down there afterwards, and this wrecked it ... I have never paid anyone to let me photograph them. I've never needed to do this, and I wouldn't do it, anyway.'[18]

Six weeks later he was back at Khartoum on attachment to the Essex Regiment, which meanwhile had replaced the Cheshires. On 24 April

1940 he received a Governor-General's temporary commission, number 443, with the rank of Bimbashi. An impressive parchment, printed in both Arabic and English, dignified this outmoded rank of Turkish derivation. Bimbashi was the lowest British commissioned rank in the Sudan Defence Force and originally equivalent to Colonel in the Egyptian Army.

The Sudan Defence Force was dedicated to overthrowing the Italian army of occupation in Abyssinia, and restoring Haile Selassie to his throne. In terms of manpower and weapons, the Italians were far superior. Their forces comprised a quarter of a million soldiers, with heavy armaments and air support, whereas the British had only two battalions together with the SDF, and no artillery. The SDF was made up of the Eastern and Western Arab Corps, the Equatorial Corps and the Camel Corps, under the overall command of General William Platt. Thesiger was posted in April 1940 to No. 3 Eastern Arab Corps, under Bimbashi Arthur Hanks, at Galabat on the Sudan's east frontier opposite the Italian-held fort of Metemma.

After Italy invaded Abyssinia in 1935, the Sandfords had left their farm at Mullu and returned to England to live in Surrey, where Dan Sandford was appointed treasurer of the still-unfinished new Guildford cathedral, designed by Edward Maufe. Having been recalled by the Commander-in-Chief, Middle East, General Sir Archibald Wavell, for active service, in August 1939 Sandford conceived and took command of 101 Mission. This tiny insurrectionist force, which included five British officers, was divided into three sections: the first, led by Sandford himself, would pave the way for the invasion of Gojjam and raise Abyssinian guerrilla forces to fight the Italians; the second section was led by Arthur Bentinck; and the third by Lieutenant Arnold Wienholt, an Australian-born Old Etonian cousin of Arnold Wienholt Hodson, who had served as a Consul under Wilfred Thesiger's father.

Among the official hierarchy in the Sudan, feelings towards Haile Selassie and the impending invasion of Abyssinia by British forces were mixed. To many, there was no moral distinction between an Italian administration in Abyssinia and British rule in the Sudan. Some feared that re-invading Abyssinia, inciting revolt and restoring the exiled Emperor to power, might ignite a Sudanese uprising against the British. Sandford's insistence that Haile Selassie, as a symbolic presence, should lead the invading force on its march to Addis Ababa caused deep concern and embarrassment to the Sudan's Governor-General, Sir George Stewart Symes, a friend of the dashing and popular Duke of Aosta, the Italian Viceroy of Abyssinia. Apart from Symes, Douglas Newbold, the Civil Secretary, had once fought with General Rudolfo Graziani against the Senussi in Libya.

Thesiger disagreed profoundly that British rule in the Sudan was comparable with that of Italy in Abyssinia. 'The Italians under Mussolini committed horrific atrocities and acts of barbarism the like of which the British Empire would never have condoned. There is almost no equivalent for Italy's brutal treatment of the Abyssinians – civilians as well as soldiers. I say "almost" none, because of what took place at Amritsar in India, in 1919, while my uncle was Viceroy. General Dyer ordered his men to fire into a crowd, gathered in an enclosure. Almost four hundred people were massacred and many more were wounded. Though it was unpardonable, this was an isolated event; whereas the atrocities carried out in Abyssinia were part of a ruthless policy to crush opposition and force the Abyssinians to submit to Italy.'[19]

Early in May 1940 Thesiger arrived at Galabat as second-in-command of Arthur Hanks's company. He came from nearby Gedaref, where he had found an attractive mixture of troops from Abyssinia, Nigeria and the Sudan, men he felt he would 'prefer to lead ... rather than white troops if there is fighting'.[20] His only complaint had been about 'a breed of monstrous spiders ... Loathsome animals with big fat bodies some 4" or more across.'[21] Thesiger had detested spiders since his childhood, and his intense dislike of them, bordering on a phobia, haunted him throughout his life. He said that while his mother was pregnant with him she had been frightened by a spider, and he sometimes pondered whether this might be connected with his incurable dread of spiders.

The SDF official diarist at Galabat noted that Idris, Thesiger's 'personal servant', was 'a reprieved murderer and quite a charming chap if a shade wilful'.[22] The diarist's shrewd portrayal of Idris was eclipsed by Thesiger's eulogy in The Life of My Choice: 'He had made his pilgrimage ... a tremendous experience ... Idris described it all, and said, "God reward you for sending me." He was a Haj, but on account of his youthfulness he deferred the assumption of that title. He now accompanied me everywhere and I was glad to have him; with his easy unassuming nature he was readily accepted by the troops. He was a good shot and Hanks issued him with a service rifle and a bandolier.'[23]

Thesiger made no secret of Idris's indebtedness to him. He described Idris using the same stock expressions – 'accompanied me everywhere', 'I was glad to have him', 'readily accepted' – that he would use later when describing other relationships with 'close companions' from tribes in Africa, Arabia, Asia and the Middle East. Idris remained with Thesiger until December 1940, when at his father's request he went back to Tini, his home village. Thesiger never saw Idris again. Soon after, Idris was replaced by Muhammad, an orderly with the SDF's Eastern Arab Corps who proved a satisfactory companion. Thesiger wrote: 'I remember Muhammad beside me, silent as usual, attentive and helpful as always.'[24] Yet on the eve of the Abyssinian invasion – thinking perhaps of their adventures hunting lion, buffalo and elephant, or travelling together to and from Tibesti – Thesiger confided: 'I would have given much to have had Idris with me.'[25]

News that Italy had entered the war was broadcast by the BBC on 10 June. The diarist noted that Thesiger did 'a savage war dance'[26] before he and another Bimbashi, a former DC, Ran Laurie, celebrated this news by firing their machine-gun into the Italians' frontier positions. Some hours later they received a circular forbidding any offensive action without permission from headquarters. Thesiger's version of events has since been questioned, and it has been suggested that no firing occurred until Hanks unleashed a fusillade of some eight thousand rounds against Metemma fort. However, Thesiger commented: 'We never got a reprimand for our precipitate action, and it has always given me satisfaction that I fired the first shots in the Abyssinian campaign.'[27]

Thesiger's part in the re-invasion of Abyssinia began at Galabat, where he first patrolled the frontier with a platoon based at a crossing on the Atbara river. He had no radio communication with SDF headquarters at Gedaref, and he enjoyed being on his own with men he liked and had got to know personally. In this sense, his first experience of war closely resembled his preferred method of travel. Even the Arab immigrants from Arabia who watered their camels near this camp on the Sudan border were a pleasant reminder of the Northern Darfur tribes, and their presence signalled the direction Thesiger's travels were to take after the war. Of a local tribe, 'Gurmuz, real Shankalla [or black men]', Thesiger wrote scathingly: 'one cannot help feeling that they really are not fit to be anything but slaves. They are like stupid animals.'[28] He had no sense of colour prejudice (except that, aesthetically, he preferred dark skin to white), and he was certainly not a racist, yet he saw nothing wrong in describing Gurmuz as 'stupid animals'. Once in northern Kenya, in a fit of temper he alarmed his English companion by cuffing about the ears a feckless Turkana whom he cursed as 'an oaf' and 'an ape'.[29]

On 3 June 1936 Thesiger, who was on leave from the Sudan, had been among a small party of friends who, together with a Foreign Office representative, met the exiled Haile Selassie at Waterloo station on his arrival in London, Thesiger's twenty-sixth birthday. According to Christine Sandford, the Emperor 'was received with acclamation by a large crowd'.[30] Thesiger wrote more explicitly in 1987: 'No official reception awaited him ... To avoid the crowds assembled to welcome him, he was driven by back streets to his Legation in Queen's Gate.'[31] When Haile Selassie received Thesiger and his mother two days later at the Abyssinian Legation, Thesiger recalled: 'He looked worn and tired but otherwise unchanged since I had last seen him at Addis Ababa in 1934 ... as we sat there looking on Hyde Park, he evinced no bitterness, gave no sign of the despair he must have felt. Only when he spoke briefly of the horrors he had seen was I conscious of his unutterable sadness.'[32]

To Thesiger's disgust, the money Haile Selassie had invested in Britain was handed to King Victor Emmanuel II of Italy, whom Mussolini titled 'Emperor of Ethiopia'. As a result, Haile Selassie was left 'destitute' and 'an unwelcome refugee' in a country he had always admired and trusted.[33] What he perceived as the British government's degrading treatment of the Emperor affected Thesiger more deeply because of the absolute trust that Haile Selassie had placed in Thesiger's father, both as an individual and as a representative of the British crown. Thesiger told an interviewer in 1969: 'It was the one great emotional cause of my life. [Abyssinia] was my home, the country of my childhood being raped – and England did nothing. It was heartbreaking.' He was quoted writing to a friend in 1937: 'It does not look as if any of my generation are going to have a future. We certainly don't deserve it after Abyssinia.'[34]

On 27 June 1940 Haile Selassie arrived by aeroplane in Khartoum. To the Governor-General Sir Stewart Symes, who disapproved of Sandford's invasion plans and favoured peaceful co-existence with the Italians, the Emperor's presence was an unwelcome embarrassment. Thesiger had been angered by the Emperor's lukewarm reception in London in 1936, and he again felt outraged that Haile Selassie had been given 'the ridiculous and humiliating pseudonym of "Mr Smith" by officials who viewed his presence as "an embarrassment"'.[35] This obviously referred to Symes. Yet in 1935, before leaving Khartoum for Northern Darfur, Thesiger recalled: 'I was invited to dinner by Sir Stewart Symes, the Governor-General; I had met him at Haile Selassie's coronation when he was the Resident at Aden. I enjoyed the evening … it was a friendly family party in the impressive setting of the palace, rebuilt on the site where Gordon had kept his lonely vigil.'[36] To Kathleen he wrote unequivocally: 'You will have heard on the wireless that HS is out here in the Sudan and that work is going ahead to give him back his own. Here we are in contact with a certain amount of it and most interesting it is. I love meeting any Abyssinians who pass through. Most of them have been in the field for 6 years and now at last they are to get their reward. It must have taken great courage and determination to go on resisting during those years, when no one gave them an encouraging word, nothing indeed but discouragement and advice to accept the inevitable. Well I hope there are better days ahead for them.'[37]

A photograph taken at Khartoum in 1940, published in the *Sphere*, showed Thesiger in craggy profile, identified only as 'an officer', talking to Haile Selassie. Both are wearing sun helmets; the Emperor is dressed in full khaki uniform, while Thesiger is in regulation army shorts and short-sleeved khaki jacket. 'I saw HS and his two sons,' Thesiger wrote to his mother from Khartoum on 11 October.

I had lunch with him the other day and enjoyed it greatly. He was I thought looking very well. Much better than when we saw him in London. I had tea with the elder son [Asfa Wossen], and am taking him round Omdurman this afternoon. HS was full of enquiries about you and the others, and asked about you not once but repeatedly. Most of the people I met at the Legation in Addis Ababa and elsewhere seem to be collecting in here. Arthur B[entinck] was quite close to us and I talked to him on the telephone but was unable to get away and see him … I saw the prolific D[an] S[andford] twice. He is very much in charge here but out of touch now. Steer and Chapman Andrews [Haile Selassie's Political Officer, who had flown to Khartoum with the Emperor] and Cheesman are all here so I get plenty of opportunities to talk about Abyssinia.[38]

At dawn one day early in July 1940, Thesiger and his platoon occupied an undefended hill at Metemma, across the dry riverbed from Galabat, and fired on the Italian camp. The border forts of Galabat and Metemma stood on facing hills in a wilderness relieved by stark trees, which the War Office artist Edward Bawden painted very vividly. Captioned 'Frontier No-Man's Land' in an official 'Story of the Conquest of Italian East Africa', Bawden's landscape captured the stark Galabat–Metemma lines which were 'for two months the scene of artillery duel, patrol and skirmish'.[39]

Two days later the RAF bombed the Italian camp, and one of the five attacking planes was shot down by small-arms fire. A newspaper report stated that 'a major of the Sudan Defence Force … had a message passed to him that cries had been heard some distance from the burning aircraft. The major, despite machine-gun fire, at once went to the spot where he found [the aircraftsman, W.J. Davidson] conscious although mortally injured.'[40] The 'major', in fact, was Bimbashi Thesiger, who described the incident graphically in a letter to his mother:

He was burnt all over, a really terrible sight but quite clear headed. I gave him some morphia but could not get him to sleep. Never have I imagined such courage. Our troops were quite amazed and spoke of it for days. He asked first what had happened to the pilot and then what sort of show they had made of it. After that he talked of his home in Yorkshire, while we sat there with the machine-gun bullets flicking through the bushes. Our troops were splendid and as gentle as women with him. He never complained even when we carried him, just saying, 'OK carry on,' though there was hardly a piece of unburnt skin on him and his eyes were gone. I got down to the pilot who was lying on a very exposed bit of ground, but found him dead. He had jumped for it I think and was terribly broken …

I tried to drag him back up the hill, but he was very heavy and in full flying kit, and [the Italians] soon saw me and opened on me with their machine-guns. I went back to try again later after we had got the one wounded up to the fort, but as soon as they saw me they opened terrific machine-gun fire on me so as he was dead I left him to be got in after dark. The aircrafts-man died at dawn next day ...[41]

He was buried with full military honours.[42] In *The Life of My Choice* Thesiger mentioned this incident only very briefly, writing: 'five of our Wellesley aircraft bombed Metemma, and one was shot down by heavy small-arms fire'.[43]

Galabat fort was captured by Italian forces on 27 July, the day after the RAF bombed Metemma. That same day the Italians captured Kassala, further to the north. A fortnight later, Colonel Sandford, commanding his section of 101 Mission, crossed the Abyssinian frontier near Galabat to organise resistance forces in Gojjam. Bands of guerrilla fighters, according to Haile Selassie's wish, were now described as 'Patriots' instead of 'rebels'. 101 Mission, comprising five British and five Abyssinian officers, had been organised by Special Operations Executive, or SOE, a department, directed by the Ministry of Economic Warfare, concerned with assisting resistance movements. Before entering Abyssinia on 12 August, Sandford (called by the Abyssinians *Fiki Mariam*, or 'Love of Mary') had requested that Thesiger should accompany him,[44] but to Thesiger's bitter disappointment General Platt, a 'dour', 'wiry little terrier' of a man,[45] refused on the grounds that Thesiger needed more experience of 'orthodox soldiering'.[46]

Sandford had left Lieutenant Arnold Wienholt behind to collect what transport he could, then follow him. Before Wienholt left for Gojjam a fortnight later, Thesiger 'often walked over to his bivouac, shared the "dampers" he cooked and the strong tea he brewed'.[47] Wienholt's gaunt, hard frame and quiet manner recalled, for Thesiger, African hunters of the past; it seemed appropriate that he had served with one of the greatest of those hunters, Frederick Courteney Selous, in East Africa during the First World War. Thesiger had read Wienholt's book *The Story of a Lion Hunt* (1922), describing his adventures in the Kalahari desert and the war. The fact that Wienholt was Arnold Hodson's cousin linked him with

Thesiger's crucially important childhood in Abyssinia, just as his quiet manner, spare build and enthusiasm for big game hunting evoked Wilfred Gilbert Thesiger.

Thesiger described Wienholt's departure from Galabat very movingly in *The Life of My Choice*, and before that in a handwritten note he kept in his copy of Wienholt's book. The note reads: 'Eventually he got hold of some donkeys and set off to join Sandford who was at Sakela in Godjam [sic]. He was accompanied by a servant and his donkey boys. I saw him off and it was strikingly reminiscent of Rocky's last departure in Jock of the Bushveld. He was on foot with a rifle over his shoulder and a long stick in his hand. He turned and waved to me just before he went round a corner of the path. He was ambushed and killed a few days later.'[48] Whether or not this romantic sketch of Wienholt bidding Thesiger a last farewell was accurate or partly imagined, it conveys very vividly the threadbare nature of the Abyssinian campaign as it was before Orde Wingate, backed by Wavell, took overall command in 1941 with pledged resources of £1 million sterling.

On 5 November, the day before Brigadier (later Field Marshal and Viscount) William Slim would attempt to recapture the Galabat fort, Thesiger wrote to Kathleen, explaining the importance of this attack and his mixed feelings of excitement and foreboding:

Tomorrow is the day for which we have been waiting all through the rains. We attack at dawn. By the time you get this the result will be old news of course. I feel that it will have results out of all proportion to the forces employed and I hope it marks the turn of the tide. The results of a victory for us will be tremendous really, and should enormously increase Italy's difficulties in Abyssinia. It is extraordinary to contrast this place with what it was six weeks ago. Now it is seething with troops, guns and the endless transport of modern war, whereas then it was just our scanty few, with some mules and camels. They are going to do it in a big way and we are getting heavy air support. I am glad I am here. I should hate to be anywhere else and of everybody our Company has earned the right to a place in the attack. How much fighting we get will depend on circumstances but I think it probable that we shall get plenty. The troops are in great heart, and amazed at what has been moving up here during the past week. They feel that after the toil and weariness of the rains they are at last going to get their chance and that tomorrow will be their day. I hope they will do well and feel sure that they will. They are a fine crowd. I have done a couple of rather exciting night patrols up to the enemy wire these last two nights. It is rather fascinating creeping up in the dark when you can hear them talking close by and yet see only a few yards. The country has dried up tremendously and the grass is very dry. There are big fires in the distance. I am afraid that you will have some anxious days when the news of this fighting comes out on the wireless. I will send off a wire as soon as I get a chance. Poor Mother, I know how dreadfully you worry, and how wearing this war is to you. We get the excitement and thrill of it while you can only sit and wait for news. God bless you dearest. I think so incessantly of you, and of the happy days we have spent together, at the Milebrook and in Morocco. Thank God that we went there together and had that wonderful month. Memories are good things these days ... I am very happy, love this life, and would not be anywhere else for anything. War in Europe I am sure is grim and awful. Here it is old fashioned, and one feels the planes are intruding, and it is a great life and one I thoroughly enjoy, and I have too a crusading feeling for the Abyssinians. I am looking forward [to] tomorrow, though I expect when we move off in the early hours I shall have the empty feeling I used to get before a big fight at Oxford.[49]

Waiting at Galabat for the order to attack, again and again Thesiger's thoughts focused on his mother and his brothers. His letters, always affectionate, now more than ever expressed feelings of anxiety and an almost desperate love for them all. For Kathleen, whom he assured he loved 'so intensely'; for Brian, his wife Diana and their baby daughter; for Dermot, whose ambition was to serve as a pilot-officer in the Royal Air Force; and for Roderic, who had joined the Welch Guards and had also become engaged to be married. He reflected on the years of crisis in Abyssinia: Italy's invasion from Eritrea in October 1935; the Abyssinians' courageous defence of their country, despite being armed with obsolete, sometimes primitive weapons, lacking support and supplies, led by such fearless warriors as Ras Mulugeta, who spurned the guerrilla tactics urged by Haile Selassie and instead fought hand-to-hand with their enemies until sunset, as they had always done in the past. The Italians' use of mustard gas had horrified Thesiger and left him feeling 'murderously angry'.[50]

Such barbarity and cruelty, intended to crush Abyssinian resistance, had been sanctioned personally by Mussolini 'as a last resort', and later 'on a vast scale', together with flame-throwers. Mussolini had advocated bacteriological warfare, but Marshal Pietro Badoglio, who led the invasion, drew a line at the Duce's proposal. In his foreword to Badoglio's account of *The War in Abyssinia*, translated into English in 1937, Mussolini wrote: 'When the enemy is at a crisis, he must never be allowed the chance of recovery: he must be pursued and destroyed to the last man ... We must be grateful to Badoglio for having been daring almost to rashness. But in war one must be daring ... the war which lasted from 3 October [1935] to 5 May [1936] may with full justice be termed a "Fascist" war, because it was waged and won in the very spirit of Fascism: speed, decision, self-sacrifice, courage and resistance beyond human limits.' Thesiger commented savagely on this utterance by the 'posturing and ranting'[51] dictator: 'The only way the Italians went beyond "human limits" in Abyssinia was by their excessive and barbaric cruelty.'[52] It had been Badoglio who ordered his aircraft to drop canisters of mustard gas on Abyssinian troops, in December 1935.

In his characteristics, habits and personal beliefs, Thesiger often appeared ambiguous and inconsistent. Despite everything he said and wrote about his lifelong attachment to Abyssinia, he admitted on various occasions that by 1940 his feelings for the country were less passionate than they had been in the past. By the time he returned to Addis Ababa in 1966, to take part in the twenty-fifth anniversary celebrations marking the victorious campaign, he confessed that he felt 'differently' about the country and its people, somewhat less attached to them, yet he still cherished his memories of all that Abyssinia had meant to him as a boy.[53]

His contempt for Evelyn Waugh was made more bitter when he read the writer's praise for Italy's 'civilising mission' against Abyssinian 'rebels and accomplice populations'. This 'mission', as Thesiger knew only too well, included the mass slaughter of more than four hundred monks and deacons at Debra Lebanos monastery, and other similarly horrific atrocities. Incredible as it seemed to Thesiger, Waugh applauded Italy's efforts to 'spread order and decency, education and medicine, in a disgraceful place'.[54] While he wrote with genuine admiration about Waugh's 'impeccable prose',[55] in private Thesiger referred habitually to him as 'that bastard, Evelyn Waugh'.[56]

Despite an awesome barrage of shell fire in November which destroyed most of Galabat, the Italians' Eritrean battalion, holding the fort, fought courageously, but were ultimately defeated. When Slim moved on to take Metemma his troops were driven back by intensive machine-gun fire from the fort and continual attacks from Italian bombers and fighter planes. Several British fighters were shot down. Without anti-aircraft guns, Slim had no means of protecting his troops on this exposed terrain. Among the Essex Regiment especially, which had advanced on Metemma, casualties were heavy. The Essex retreated, dispirited, in confusion (according to one commentator, they panicked). Writing in 1987, Thesiger concluded a discreet reference to the assault on Metemma: 'Slim called off the attack, and withdrew his troops to the shelter of the woods, from which patrols could dominate Galabat.'[57] By the end of the year, Slim and the Essex Regiment had been withdrawn from the Sudan. Slim would go on to command the reconquest of Burma from the Japanese, and later became Governor-General of Australia.

Soon after the attack on Metemma Thesiger was ordered to Khartoum, having been personally selected by the 'wiry little terrier'[58] General Platt as Sandford's second-in-command in Gojjam.[59] At Khartoum he reported to (then Major) Orde Wingate. His description of Wingate as he first saw him mirrors another by the journalist, politician and cavalry officer W.E.D. Allen, who met Wingate during the Gojjam campaign. Allen remarked on features shared by Thesiger and Wingate: 'pale blue eyes, narrow set ... spare bony figure ... big nose and ... the bony structure of the face'.[60] Thesiger remembered: 'As I came into his office he was studying a map on the wall. He swung round, said, "I've been expecting you," and immediately launched into his plan to invade Gojjam, destroy the Italian forces stationed there, reach Addis Ababa before the South African army from Kenya could do so, and restore Haile Selassie to his throne. While expounding his seemingly improbable plans, he strode about his office, his disproportionately large head thrust forward above his ungainly body, in his pale blue eyes, set close together in a bony angular face, was more than a hint of fanaticism.'[61]

Wingate, then aged thirty-seven, had seen active service only under Wavell in Palestine, where he brilliantly organised and led raids by Jewish night squads against Arab guerrillas, for which he was awarded a DSO. In October 1940 Wavell, as Commander-in-Chief Middle East, put Wingate in charge of organising the Abyssinian Patriot forces, as the rebels were now known, an assignment which made full use of his experience and strategic skill.

Whereas Sandford clearly saw himself as a political adviser, and Wingate as a military commander, Hugh Boustead, commanding the Frontier Battalion – senior to him in rank, more experienced – found Wingate incompatible, irksomely unpredictable and unreasonable. Wingate's mistrust of Boustead worsened the friction between them. During the fighting at Burye, on the road to Addis Ababa in February 1941, Wingate accused Boustead of cowardice when he withdrew from an indefensible position. Thesiger noted: 'Boustead never forgave him.'[62] When Sandford, as Haile Selassie's Chief Political Adviser, was promoted from Colonel to Brigadier, Wingate refused to cooperate with him 'on principle', and General Platt was forced to deliver a 'caustic' reprimand.[63]

Thesiger saw the Abyssinian campaign both as a highlight of Boustead's career and as an outstanding personal triumph for Wingate. He wrote: 'Boustead had indeed had considerable and varied experience of war, but he lacked Wingate's originality of thought, bold imagination and ruthless single-mindedness.'[64] Such attributes had made feasible Thesiger's 'most dangerous journey'[65] to the end of the Awash river, his arduous trek across the French Sahara to Tibesti, and the other journeys involving considerable hardship and risk which he undertook later, in the deserts of Arabia, in the Middle East and in western Asia, after the war. Like Wingate, Thesiger's war of liberation in Abyssinia was both personal and inspirational. Thesiger portrayed Wingate's interview with a disillusioned, downcast Haile Selassie in Khartoum in 1940 as 'a strange and eventful meeting, between the diminutive but indomitable Emperor and the uncouth, inspired soldier who was going to liberate Gojjam for him. Haile Selassie's legendary descent from Solomon and Sheba may have given him special standing in Wingate's eyes: certainly Wingate emerged from this encounter dedicated to the liberation and independence of Abyssinia.'[66]

Just as Wingate had been impressed by Haile Selassie, he was no doubt also impressed by Thesiger's devotion to his birthplace, its Emperor and its people. It is difficult to believe that Thesiger would not have made such feelings clear to Wingate. Certainly their relationship was eased by their shared determination to defeat the Italians and restore Haile Selassie to his throne. Yet only once did Wingate relax his 'self-imposed barrier' and talk openly to Thesiger about himself, 'his stern, puritanical upbringing, his unhappy days at school, his unpopularity at Woolwich, his passion for fox hunting and steeplechasing and his dedication to Zionism'.[67] When Thesiger asked him why he became a Zionist, Wingate replied that this 'dated from his prep school, where he had been mercilessly bullied and the boys had organised what they called "Wingate hunts". He had been brought up on the Bible by devout parents, and in those unhappy schooldays had found in the Old Testament a people who never gave in, though every man's hand was against them. He had accordingly identified them with himself.'[68] Thesiger observed afterwards: 'It was interesting that Wingate said he identified the Israelites with himself, never that he identified himself with them.' He added the self-revealing observation: 'Perhaps in those early days Wingate's character had been permanently warped; yet, perhaps it had been tempered too, and made resolute.'[69]

Thesiger's experiences at St Aubyn's to some extent echoed Wingate's, and may have had a similar lasting effect which both men tacitly acknowledged. That there was a bond between them is made credible by Wingate unburdening himself to Thesiger, both seated appropriately on a rock overlooking 'a great sweep of mountain', like some biblical law-giver and his acolyte. How much of himself Thesiger revealed to Wingate in return, we don't know. Perhaps an opportunity never arose, since Wingate's reflections seemed as much a self-scourging tirade as a serious attempt to confide to Thesiger the deeply personal, character-forming issues that affected his boyhood and youth. Wingate's biographer Christopher Sykes gave a different version of these impromptu revelations, and added that Wingate had given 'a more illuminating account to Frederick Kish. In his earliest days, he said, he had received an injection of the Bible, but the effect only appeared many years later.'[70]

A training manual Wingate had written for the Israeli army, 'The

Soldiers' Ten Commandments', echoed many of Thesiger's deeply-held beliefs: 'Know and love what you fight for ... Abstain from brutality and cruelty ... Always keep your body and equipment in good condition ... Know how to endure thirst and other hardships without complaining, and show restraint in the fulfilment of your needs ... Place the welfare of your comrades before your own.'

As soon as Wingate was confirmed commander of 101 Mission, he renamed it 'Gideon Force', after the Old Testament Hebrew judge who led the Israelites to victory over their Midianite oppressors. Gideon selected his fighting men by observing how they drank from the River Harod: 'And the number of them that lapped, putting their hand to their mouth were three hundred men ...'[71] 'There is no doubt that the thought of this saviour of the Chosen People was constantly in Wingate's mind' as he chose three hundred men for Gideon Force, having observed ten thousand candidates as they fed, 'because they were not gluttons'.[72] Wingate's thesis reflected precisely those traits of nomadic desert tribes that Thesiger valued above all, and to which he devoted paragraphs in his masterpiece, *Arabian Sands*. According to Wingate: 'When a soldier is on a march, then we see his real quality. The man who desires to drink the moment he gets thirsty, the man who becomes ill-tempered and stubborn when he is tired, the man whose self-control and self-restraint weaken when he endures physical effort, he is indeed a bad soldier.'[73] To this, Thesiger might have added: 'and a bad traveller', or 'a bad travelling companion'.

More than forty years later, Thesiger recalled: 'Personally I was fortunate in my relationship with Wingate, and he was never rude to me.'[74] He never went so far as to admit that he actually liked Wingate, and their brief acquaintance during the war, had Wingate lived, would never have extended, like Thesiger's acquaintances with Hugh Boustead, Gerald de Gaury and David Stirling, to years of friendship in civilian life.

Unknown to Thesiger, Sandford had been expecting his arrival at Sakela, on the Blue Nile, for six weeks when Thesiger reached him at last in December 1940, after riding on camels for twelve hours a day across wild, sometimes beautiful country. He spent Christmas night 1940 without food or water at the foot of Mount Balayia. Once, on the open plains, an Italian fighter dived towards them. Thesiger fired five shots at the plane, which flew away. 'I had possibly damaged it,' he wrote.[75] He had wasted no time, and was momentarily disconcerted by Sandford's greeting, 'Hello Wilfred. I must say you've taken a long time to get here,' until he realised that Sandford was referring to the long delay at Khartoum before Wingate had ordered Thesiger to make his own way to Sakela. He wrote, 'I became desperate to join Sandford,'[76] yet he felt grateful for Wingate's order which spared him the 'nightmare' of being parachuted into Gojjam. In 1987, aged seventy-seven, Thesiger stated perhaps too emphatically: 'to get to Gojjam I was willing to jump, even without training'.[77] In 1959, while his memory of these events was still precise, he wrote: 'I am proud to have served in Abyssinia with Sandford's mission which prepared the way for Haile Selassie's restoration, and to have fought in Wingate's Gideon Force which took him back ... to Addis Ababa.'[78] Here he presented Sandford's and Wingate's roles in chronological sequence, and also made his preferences clear, emphasising that he was 'proud' to be with Sandford, but omitting the word in connection with Wingate. This small distinction was very significant. Although Thesiger admired and respected Wingate, Sandford – an old, valued friend of Thesiger's family – meant far more to him.[79]

Accompanied by Haile Selassie, Wingate's Gideon Force advanced steadily from the eastern Sudan border, through Gojjam, to Addis Ababa. There were five thousand men and twenty-five thousand camels; most of the camels died. On 20 January 1941 they raised the Abyssinian flag on Abyssinian soil. On the road to Addis Ababa, Italian-held towns – Bahr dar Giorgis, Dangila, Ingebara, Burye – fell one by one. When the Italians abandoned Burye, they retreated to the fort at Dembecha. Routed from there, they made for Debra Markos, the capital of Gojjam, which became Wingate's next critical objective. Among the Abyssinians, Thesiger observed, 'The diehards who have never submitted, but are ready to fight it out to the end without prospect of help, are enormously encouraged and most of those who had given in are now coming out to join them ... It is remarkable how fiercely they cling to their independence. They possess a burning patriotism which has never been acknowledged, quite unlike that in any other part of Africa. They will fight to the end rather than submit to the foreigner, and Italy by her incredible mixture of stupidity and brutality has roused them to white heat.' Looking ahead to the future, he predicted: 'But when the fighting is over HS will be faced with a terrific task. The old order has been effectively destroyed and most of the leading houses wiped out, and now anyone with a following has taken a title, and though ready to sink their differences while the Italians are still in the country they will be fairly jealous of each other when it is over.'[80]

His thoughts again turned to home and family – and to England – made even more remote by war. To his mother he wrote: 'I do wish I could get a letter from you. I wonder so much what is happening. Have you had any bombers round the Milebrook[?] ... How superb and invincible, the Navy, Army, and RAF have proved to be. I wonder how many of my friends died in Belgium and round Dunkirk ... I do long to hear how Brian, Dermot and Roddy are ...'[81]

The difficulties of the Gojjam campaign were increased by the hopeless incompatibility between Wingate and Boustead. Often Wingate appeared to be cruel and offensive; he hardly bothered to change his clothes, and tore at food with his fingers as he squatted on the ground. Boustead, on the other hand, was 'warm-hearted and sociable'; he wore a clean uniform and dined in comfortable surroundings. Much as Thesiger enjoyed the food he ate in Abyssinian villages, 'it was a pleasant change to be invited by Hugh Boustead to an evening meal. We would sit at a table with a tablecloth and cutlery lit by a red-shaded candle, and eat well-cooked food, and drink the Chianti he had acquired ... Wingate openly despised such luxury.'[82] Wingate's arrogance and intolerance provoked many bitter arguments with his superiors, and made it impossible for him to function except when in command. Thesiger believed 'his aims transcended personal ambition. He was an idealist and a fanatic' who 'needed a cause with which he could identify himself'.[83] Yet, behind his ruthless façade, Wingate had suffered terrible remorse, due to lapses of self-control which according to his thesis on 'The Vices of Soldiers' were the sure sign of 'a bad soldier'.[84]

At Dembecha fort, while Thesiger was supervising Abyssinian troops as they cleared the ground for a runway, Wingate suddenly lost his temper with his interpreter and slashed him repeatedly across the face with a stick. The next day, while Wingate was away from the fort, the interpreter and three other men were horribly burnt when a petrol drum exploded in a shed where they were smoking cigarettes. The dying interpreter screamed in agony for Wingate. Fortunately the dispensary at Dembecha had been left intact by the retreating Italians, and Thesiger discovered a supply of morphia. As there was no doctor present, not even a medical orderly, Thesiger took it upon himself to give each of the men a lethal injection of morphia. He recalled: 'That evening when Wingate returned I told him. He was silent for a while and then muttered, "God, it makes me feel a brute."'

How much Wingate valued Thesiger is shown by two contrasting episodes in the final stages of the Gojjam campaign. In March 1941, on the way from Dembecha to Debra Markos, Wingate sent Thesiger ahead to join Lij Belai Zeleka and his Patriot forces, and with his help ambush the Italian garrison as they retreated from Debra Markos by the Safartak bridge across the Blue Nile Gorge. This important assignment was familiar to Thesiger, whose role consisted at that time of 'leading patrols right round behind the Italians sometimes on foot, sometimes on ponies and sometimes by motor transport. They used to arrange for fires to be lighted round suitable targets so that [the RAF] could bomb them at night and generally put the natives in the right frame of mind.' So Julian Prichard – whose family lived at Knighton, close to The Milebrook – wrote to Kathleen, reassuring her that Wilfred was 'doing a really splendid job and is renown[ed] for the way he has with the Abyssinians'.[85]

Excellent though many of the Patriot fighters were, a number of them, including Lij Belai Zeleka, were flawed by 'petty weaknesses'.[86] Instead of keeping his forces on the move in order to ambush the retreating Italians before they reached the Safartak bridge, Zeleka delayed, using a variety of excuses. On 5 April, to his utter astonishment, Thesiger heard that the Italians had successfully crossed the Blue Nile into Shoa province. When he reported his failure to Wingate and Boustead, Timothy Green recorded that Wingate was furious with Thesiger.[87] Yet in *The Life of My Choice*, Thesiger wrote that 'Boustead was furious with me over this missed opportunity, but Wingate was unexpectedly understanding.' According to Green, Wingate 'had to concede that Thesiger had been powerless to act'.[88] With the benefit of hindsight, Thesiger should have been alerted sooner to Zeleka's treachery. Instead, his faith in the Patriots had enabled Zeleka to deceive him. The reason for Zeleka's refusal to cooperate in the ambush was that the aristocratic Ras Hailu, who had collaborated with the Italians, offered Zaleka his daughter in marriage if he promised not to intercept the Italian garrison as they retreated from Debra Markos.

In 1945 Lij Belai Zaleka and Ras Hailu's son were both executed in public at Addis Ababa, having been recaptured after they killed a guard and escaped from prison. It is possible that Wingate had decided to treat Thesiger with unexpected leniency to spite Boustead. Wingate no doubt guessed correctly that Thesiger had never suspected Lij Belai Zaleka's self-interested motives for delaying his advance to the Safartak bridge. Years later, when Thesiger published his account of these events, he may well have repeated words or phrases he used when reporting to Wingate:[89] 'I supposed he must know what he was doing: it seemed inconceivable that he would miss this chance of a decisive victory, one that would ensure him lasting fame.'[90]

Wingate, against orders, escorted Haile Selassie to Addis Ababa, which they entered in triumph on 5 May 1941, leading what remained of the Abyssinian Patriot Battalion. The 11th Division's casualties in the course of the campaign 'could almost be counted on the fingers of one hand', whereas thousands of the enemy had been killed and some 22,000 captured. Meanwhile Thesiger joined Bimbashi Johnson, Lieutenant Rowe and Major Donald Nott in pursuit of the twelve thousand Italian troops, led by Colonel Maraventano, whose retreat was slowed by the number of casualties they had sustained. Writing in the 1980s, Thesiger had to draw on biographies and eyewitness reports to help him construct his narrative. His war diary was taken from him in London in 1943, and never returned, his letters contained few descriptions of the last days and weeks of the Gojjam campaign, and forty years later his memory of events was sometimes (understandably) incomplete or imperfect. Indeed, the fact that he remembered so many details of the Abyssinian campaign was remarkable. However 'confused', in his modest judgement, were his recollections of pursuing Maraventano's forces over rough mountain tracks, valleys and streams, he would find ways of bringing such distant memories alive. He remembered, for example, being fired on by snipers perched high on the cliffs, and 'the disquiet of frequently looking down the barrels of [Patriots'] rifles, all of which were loaded, most with the safety-catch off'.[91]

Until 14 May, when Wingate arrived in camp near Derra, Thesiger wrote, 'we felt cut off and forgotten'. They were exhausted, short of food and ammunition, and even their recent conquest of Debra Markos had failed to raise their spirits or give them a belief in ultimate victory. Although Wingate was much disliked, his wild, messianic appearance proved inspirational. Thesiger wrote: 'Now for the first time I really appreciated his greatness. Bearded and unkempt, he had got off his mule, stared about him with searching eyes, set face and jutting jaw, then called us together. He wasted no time ... The Italian force from Debra Markos was aimed to strengthen the Duke of Aosta's forces at Amba Alagi. Wingate intended to destroy or capture it within ten days.'[92] Wingate ordered Thesiger to 'get in front' of the retreating Italians and 'inflict at least two hundred casualties'. Thesiger and Rowe, with a small band of Patriots, easily captured Wagidi fort, sited on a sheer-sided plateau east of the Blue Nile. Wagidi lay roughly midway between Derra and Agibar, whose fort was occupied by a large Italian garrison.

In a skirmish outside Wagidi the following morning, Thesiger was wounded in the knee by a piece of shrapnel. Muhammad, his faithful orderly, helped him to limp away to safety. Thesiger told an interviewer in 1969: 'I thought it was a graze from a piece of rock. It was bleeding a bit, so I wrapped a handkerchief round it and ran on for a couple of miles.'[93] In 1987 he modified this description: 'Hobbling back with my arm over Muhammad's shoulder, I felt the two of us offered an obvious target.'[94] In a 'rather disorganised retreat',[95] Rowe was wounded and taken prisoner; he died of his wounds at Addis Ababa. Altogether about thirty men from Thesiger's Patriot force were reported killed or missing. Nevertheless, to Wingate's grim satisfaction – and Thesiger's surprise – he had 'got [his] two hundred [Italian casualties], indeed rather more'.[96]

Soon after, Wingate took Colonel Maraventano's surrender, together with the twelve thousand men he commanded. On 22 May 1941 Thesiger and a band of Patriots forced the surrender of Agibar fort and took prisoner the fort's commandant and its garrison of 2500 troops. Though Wingate's biographer Leonard Mosley asserted that 'Wingate's successes in Ethiopia were the result of bluff and ingenuity rather than the clash of arms' (which described Thesiger's success at Agibar very accurately), W.E.D. Allen noted: 'The spectacular Italian collapse at Agibar was due to the consistent pursuit by Nott and Thesiger rather than to the "bluff" of Wingate, who arrived in time to take the surrender.'[97] Reviewing Mosley's biography of Wingate, *Gideon goes to War* (1955), Allen observed that Wingate's 'victory in Ethiopia was effectively due to Regular officers like Hugh Boustead and Donald Nott', whereas 'his most brilliant military coups … were due to inspired amateurs like Thesiger and Johnson who had little military training'.[98]

In 1934 Thesiger's determined, naturally dominant personality had impressed the Sultan of Aussa enough for him to allow Thesiger to follow the Awash river through a forbidden country to its end. In 1941, by sheer force of personality, Thesiger had convinced the Italian commandant at Agibar to surrender the fort. It is tempting to imagine that Thesiger shared some of his cousin, the actor Ernest Thesiger's, theatrical talent. Certainly he had a strongly developed sense of occasion, and he could be very persuasive even when imposing his wishes by sheer force of personality rather than common sense or logic. At first Agibar's commandant said his officers would never accept Thesiger's terms, which were unconditional surrender and raising over the fort not the British, but the Abyssinian flag.[99] In *The Life of My Choice*, Thesiger reconstructed from memory his uncompromising ultimatum, using direct speech for dramatic effect:

'Very well,' I said. 'I admire their resolution but I hope they realize what their refusal to surrender to me will entail. Ras Kassa with his army from Shoa, Ras Ababa Aregai from Manz and thousands of Gojjam Patriots are on their way. In a few days' time they will be here. When they storm the fort, expect no mercy. This is your last chance to save your lives. If you surrender now I will escort you to Fiche. If you refuse you will have to fight it out.' The medical officer interrupted me: 'No, no, that is not at all what we want!' The Italian flag came down over the fort, and the Abyssinian flag rose in its place.[100]

FOURTEEN

Among the Druze

At Fiche, north of Addis Ababa, Thesiger reported the capture of Agibar fort and its garrison to Wingate. 'I felt I had redeemed my failure at the Blue Nile Gorge,' he wrote. 'I realised that I owed my success to him. He could easily have denied me another chance, but he had always appreciated my passionate involvement with the Abyssinian cause. Months later I heard that he had recommended me for a DSO.' On 30 December 1941 Thesiger was awarded this well-deserved decoration, 'which for a subaltern', he observed modestly, 'was far beyond my expectations'.[1] On 18 January 1942 he wrote thanking Kathleen for her telegram congratulating him on the honour: 'I must admit I am proud to have got it, even though I could wish it were better merited. I knew that I had been put in for one, and thought I might get an MC out of it, or that it would come to nothing, so did not say anything about it to you; for I had been twice recommended for an MC, which deservedly got no further. I did not wish to disappoint you if I got nothing. One of the chief reasons why I am so pleased is that I know how happy it will make you.'[2]

A parade of the Italian prisoners at Fiche, ordered by Haile Selassie, was followed by a banquet for British officers at the palace in Addis Ababa. Acting on orders from Major Donald Nott, Thesiger informed Colonel Maraventano of the parade. When Maraventano protested at the 'barbarous' humiliation of his troops, Thesiger showed him 'no vestige of sympathy'. Written forty years afterwards, Thesiger's account of his reply once again employs direct speech for dramatic effect, and serves as a chilling reminder of the atrocities committed by the Italians.

'Don't dare to speak to me about barbarous treatment of prisoners,' I
replied. 'You Italians shot Ras Desta, the Emperor's son-in-law, who
commanded the armies in the south, after he had surrendered to Marshal
Graziani. You Italians shot Ras Kassa's sons after they had surrendered to
you. You shot four hundred priests near here in the monastery of Debra
Libanos. Your blackshirts massacred ten thousand men, women and
children in Addis Ababa after you took the town. Now you have the
effrontery to stand there and talk about barbarous treatment of prisoners.
A few days ago in Agibar I found photographs of your officers holding by
the hair the severed heads of Abyssinians, with their feet on the corpses.
Perhaps you yourself took part in the Roman triumph which Mussolini
held in Rome at the end of the war, Abyssinian prisoners were paraded.
Now it's your turn. Tomorrow at ten o'clock you will march past the
Emperor or be driven past him by Ras Kassa's men. I don't care which.'[3]

In contrast to the thrilling parades Thesiger remembered after the
Battle of Sagale in 1916, the parade at Fiche was 'quiet and orderly', 'a
necessary manifestation of victory'[4] and yet a 'sombre and rather sad'
occasion. Only Wingate's absence in Cairo from the officers' banquet
spoilt what had been, for Thesiger, a 'fitting and memorable conclusion
to the Gojjam campaign'.[5]

The day after the banquet, Thesiger was posted to Cairo with orders to
join Glubb Pasha's Arab Legion in Trans-Jordan. In Cairo he learnt that
this post had already been filled; instead he was told to rejoin the Sudan
Defence Force in Abyssinia. Since this did not appeal to him, he asked his
interviewer, an 'obviously sympathetic' Major, if he might be posted to
Syria, where British forces had met with unexpectedly stubborn Vichy
French resistance. He mentioned that he had travelled in Syria in 1936,
and knew Jabal Druze. 'This proved to be a fortunate remark.'[6] The
following day he was posted to Mafraq in Trans-Jordan, as second-in-
command under Colonel Gerald de Gaury, who was then raising a Druze
Legion.

By this time Thesiger's khaki uniforms were threadbare. He reminded
Kathleen: 'In my last letter I asked you to get Tetley and Butler to make
me and send out as soon as possible two uniform suits (General Service

buttons), one drill, one rather heavier for winter. Could he also make me one pair of riding breeches. I also want a good Sam Browne belt. At present I have not got a single decent coat or trousers.'[7] A month after arriving in Jabal Druze, he updated his mother in a letter which he ended casually with the news 'I am now a Major.'[8]

In Gerald de Gaury, Thesiger found a kindred spirit. A student of Islamic culture and traditions, elegant, discerning, captivated by Moorish Spain and the poetry of James Elroy Flecker, de Gaury painted in watercolours and collected rare books on the Middle East. Many years later, Thesiger inherited books and manuscripts, including a magnificent Koran three hundred years old, from de Gaury's library. For Christmas 1941 Kathleen sent Wilfred *Valleys of the Assassins* by Freya Stark, a book about her journeys among the Lurs in Persia. Her travels were assisted by (then Captain) de Gaury, who first met her in 1932 soon after she first arrived in Baghdad. She had begun to learn Arabic at San Remo after the First World War, while recovering from emotional strain and typhoid. As a young officer and diplomat convalescing from war wounds, de Gaury studied Arabic for somewhat similar reasons. In *Beyond Euphrates* (1951) Stark described him as 'vague, with … that pleasant easiness of space about him which the mere worker can scarcely understand … I liked him because he lived in a world of imagination, much as I did … the war and the army in 1914 … had turned him from his natural path of writing or painting, either of which might have made him happy.'

It is quite likely that de Gaury encouraged Thesiger to improve his Arabic and move freely about Jabal Druze. Instead of the Legion's headquarters, Thesiger chose to live in a village house looked after by a young Druze orderly; an arrangement which de Gaury willingly accepted.

Thesiger described the Druze as 'an interesting people whom I have always wished to see. In origin their religion is Islam but they have diverged so far that today there is practically no connection. They claim to be Arab but are quite distinct in appearance. There seem to be two types: a dark sallow one, and a blond ginger moustached blue eyed one, but neither type look like Arabs. Nor do they behave like Arabs being far less reserved, and very fond of drinking and singing.'[9] He drew detailed word pictures of Druze houses, gardens and villages built on the site of

Roman towns 'in a very good state of preservation'. He liked their food, 'eaten on the ground in Arab fashion from one big bowl', and recollected the sensual pleasure of an afternoon spent in someone's garden eating mulberries and plums. The only drawback, and 'a strain', was the total lack of privacy: 'Always there are people round you, and even when you sleep the room is full of them, so that when you wake up they are already awake and moving.'[10]

Among the Druze, Thesiger took the opportunity of refining his Sudanese Arabic. He wrote: 'I am living in [Malha] one of their villages ... the one I like best in the whole Jabal. They are a most hospitable people and we spend the whole day being entertained in their houses.' Though 'endless feasting seemed an odd way to wage war',[11] Thesiger gathered useful intelligence; besides, the Legion's presence lessened any risk of rebellion among hostile Druze. 'I like the evenings best for after dinner there is dancing and singing and everyone drops in. They are good mimics and parody the dance of neighbouring tribes and of the French North African troops. Nearly every evening it continues until midnight ... They are great connoisseurs of grapes and most mornings we are invited along to someone's vineyard.'[12]

Thesiger's delight in Jabal Druze was enhanced by his close friendship with his orderly, sixteen-year-old Faris Shahin, a member of the highly respected Hanawi family and a relative by marriage of Captain Fawwaz, Thesiger's Druze second-in-command. In *The Life of My Choice* he described Faris as 'intelligent, literate like all the Druze, well informed and universally popular ... with the almost girlish good looks that characterised many Druze boys. Yet any impression of gentleness was misleading; he had a fierce pride in himself and his family. I once saw him roused when someone referred slightingly to the Hanawis: his hand was close to his dagger and he looked really dangerous.'[13] Temperamentally, Faris was the opposite of Thesiger at sixteen, whom Val ffrench Blake described at Eton as 'a thug', a 'murderous' boxer, yet 'very nice' behind his macho image, 'with a gentle side he kept hidden'.[14] Standing beside Thesiger and John Verney for a photograph taken in 1941, Faris barely came up to Thesiger's shoulder. His short stature made him look younger and far less mature than he was in reality.

Throughout his life, Thesiger cherished the idealised image of his father. In consequence he attached great importance to relationships between his tribal companions, such as Idris Daud and Faris Shahin, and their fathers or grandfathers, whom he often portrayed as charismatic and influential. Idris's grandfather, Hamid, had been *malik*, or king, of the Kobé-Zaghawa, and Idris's father had rescued Hamid when he was wounded during a battle. Blind and sweet-tempered, renowned locally as a poet, Faris's father, with his fine voice, 'swept his audience into the past with him' when in the evenings he recited historical verse-narratives he had composed. Thesiger, whose Arabic was not yet fluent, confessed that he understood little of Shahin's poems and had 'to be content with their rhythm'.[15]

Although he claimed to be tone-deaf and unable to derive much enjoyment from listening to music, Thesiger could appreciate the rhythm of certain hymns, jazz, classical and popular melodies. Among the latter, 'Bye-Bye Blackbird' and Noël Coward's 'A Room with a View' remained lifelong favourites which he associated with summer recollections of Oxford.[16] Thesiger enjoyed marches played by military bands, and tribal music played on stringed instruments, flutes and drums. He admitted that he found music by Beethoven or Mozart 'nothing but a meaningless jumble of noises';[17] yet listening to the throb of African drums and the rhythmic stamping of bare feet gave him enormous pleasure. In a letter to Kathleen, he described a performance by Whirling Dervishes in Damascus:

We went to the house of Emir Abd al Kadar [sic], the grandson of the Emir who defended Algeria against the French, and after coffee there to the house of the Dervish sheikh ... When we arrived at the house of the Dervish sheikh they were praying. We were ushered into a room looking out on the courtyard and given coffee. After half an hour we were asked to come into the courtyard, and sat round the walls. The dervishes were lining two sides of the courtyard. The sheikh beat on a tambourine and the rest chanted together while a small boy kept time on cymbals. Three men then came in, in long white robes tight at the waist and very full skirted and a small boy in similar robes in green. All four wore very tall felt caps. They clasped their hands on their chests and whirled round in a circle, their skirts rising up round them. Their faces were absolutely expressionless. Slowly they raised their arms over their heads, and then stretched them out sideways. They must have done 60 turns to the minute. They would go on for some 10 minutes, then, when the music stopped, bow to their chief and walk slowly off without a trace of giddiness. One of them went on whirling for over half an hour without a stop. The music grew wilder and wilder and the lines of dervishes bent and swayed in time to it, while these expressionless white clad figures whirled like tops. It went on for an hour and a half.[18]

He recalled in *The Life of My Choice*: 'Even as a spectator I had been carried out of myself. Now I came slowly back to earth.'[19]

After the Vichy French surrender on 14 July 1941, the Druze Legion became part of the occupying force in Syria under a British administration. When de Gaury was transferred to Cairo, Thesiger commanded the Druze Legion until Colonel Butler from the Trans-Jordan Frontier Force took over. Thesiger remained with his cavalry squadron until it was replaced by a camel squadron, which he commanded. 'I have gone over to a squadron mounted on the animals which I have always preferred,' he wrote. 'I was very happy with the cavalry but would rather have these … I am 2nd in command of the whole show.'[20]

In November 1941 the Druze Legion was transferred to Palestine, after it was decided that the Free French should administer Jabal Druze. Although Thesiger had enjoyed his peaceful interlude among the Druze, he had grown bored with inactivity. Hoping to fight in the Western Desert, he applied to SOE for a transfer. Instead, he was instructed to remain behind and make preparations in case the German invasion force in Russia should enter Syria from the Caucasus. Before joining an explosives training course at Latrun in Palestine, Thesiger spent ten days' leave travelling to Petra in Trans-Jordan. He wrote to his mother on 25 November:

I went to Amman and thence to Maan, sitting in a goods train for a monotonous 10 hours. I then hired a car to the Wadi Mussa and went on from there to Petra by horse. I would have given anything to have had you with me, but whenever I do a trip I feel it is getting to know the ground, so that when we come out here after the war, I shall know the best places to take you to. It is difficult to describe Petra. It is an astonishing place and parts of it are lovely and all very strange. You get there by winding down a very narrow gorge about 8 feet wide, and cliffs 200–300 feet high on each side. Then suddenly framed in front of you in the cliff opposite is the 'Khazna' or Treasure house. When I saw it the sun was not on it but the reflected light made it glow, a rose pink. I have never seen anything as beautiful. You must have seen photos of it. Many of these buildings reminded me of Canterbury quad in the House [at Oxford]. I slept in a cave at Petra and next day climbed up to the Dair which is another of these impressive temples carved in the face of the rock near the top of the mountain. It is a long climb up and most of the way by a staircase cut in the mountain. You get a superb view from the top out over the Wadi Araba.[21]

Forty-five years later, when Thesiger described Petra in *The Life of My Choice*, he was by then familiar with the explorer Jean Louis Burkhardt's journeys, and 'could imagine Burkhardt's awe on first seeing it in 1812, his excitement as he wondered what further marvels awaited his discovery'.[22]

Earlier in 1941 de Gaury had moved his headquarters from Mafraq to Bosra eski Sham, where he and Thesiger were based in a huge castle built by the Saracens around a Roman amphitheatre. Thesiger remembered his excitement at seeing this castle in the distance as he rode towards it across Jabal Druze. At Bosra eski Sham they were visited by Arab Sheikhs and their retainers, among them a grandson of the famous Audah Abu Tayyi of the Huwaitat, who (as Thesiger knew having read *Revolt in the Desert* and *Seven Pillars of Wisdom*) had served in 1918 with Lawrence of Arabia.

Months later, travelling with Lieutenant Edward Henderson throughout Syria and Lebanon, Thesiger visited many of the great fortresses described by Lawrence in his scholarly thesis *Crusader Castles*. Of them all, Thesiger felt, 'Krak des Chevaliers was the most impressive and best preserved. Some Arab families were then living within its walls,' which gave 'a sense of continuity'.[23] 'I am now required for another job,' he explained, 'which I shall greatly enjoy, and which should enable me to see most of Syria and Palestine. It will be special work not in command of troops.' He told his mother: 'I have been working a certain amount at my Arabic, and the fact that I talk nothing else improves it. It took some 3 months in order to get hold of the local dialect.'²⁴ However seductive he had found 'a paradise of orchards' on the outskirts of Damascus, 'gardens and flowing water, particularly beautiful in spring when the almond and peach trees were in blossom',²⁵ Thesiger never lost his nostalgia for home and family in Radnorshire. He wrote on Christmas Day 1941: 'What I would give to see you all again, and what an immense amount we shall have to talk about when we meet. Somehow I picture it as a winter evening in the drawing room after tea, like it was when we came back from school. A large fire and the blackbirds going noisily to bed in the bushes outside the window.'²⁶

Henderson proved to be 'a happy choice' for Thesiger, and his arrival at Damascus was the beginning of a lasting friendship.²⁷ Thesiger described their visit to Krak des Chevaliers, high up on a mountain ridge halfway between Homs and Tripoli:

> The mists were down, swirling round it, and only giving us glimpses of the water logged valley far below ... The weather added mystery to this extraordinary place. The castle is wonderfully preserved, and the first Crusader castle in existence. It is a great deal more impressive than Windsor castle and in as good a state of repair. The ground falls away very steeply on three sides to the valleys below, where there are many villages. Some of these are Greek Orthodox, some Moslem and the greater part Alomite, the pagan mountaineers who live to the North in the mountains along the coast. We passed a number herding their sheep and cattle in the rain muffled in thick felt cloaks. I should like to see more of them.²⁸

However impressive his surroundings might be, already Thesiger felt deeply conscious that it was people rather than places that most interested him. He wrote in *My Kenya Days* in 1994: 'Ever since my time in Northern Darfur with Guy Moore, it has been people, not places, not hunting, not even exploration, that have mattered to me most.'²⁹ And 'my life ... has always been concerned with individuals rather than the community as a whole. But, for me, these individuals have to be part of their traditional setting.'³⁰

On 27 October 1954 Thesiger returned to Krak des Chevaliers, this time with his mother and Faris Shahin. In large handwriting, which Thesiger joked gave her 'four words to a page'[31] (actually three or four words to the line), Kathleen described the jolting drive by car and Land Rover, 'through open desert country with hills on both sides, but often wide empty spaces' to 'the most magnificent remains of a medieval castle in the world ... Built of golden sandstone it dominates the whole land-scape ... We lunched on the top of the castle from whence you command a most impressive and widespread view in every direction.'[32] A photograph taken by Freya Stark in 1939 shows Krak des Chevaliers in its wild surroundings with high snow-covered mountains in the far distance. The castle had been known as Hisn el-Akrad, 'Castle of the Kurds'; 'Akrad' became 'Krat', eventually 'Krak'.

After Krak des Chevaliers, Thesiger and Henderson visited Homs, Hama, 'a strangely sinister town ... where enormous waterwheels creaked day and night', and Baalbek. Riding on horses, they were able to absorb their surroundings. Even as a boy at Eton Thesiger had resented not only cars but 'every other manifestation of the modern combustion engine', which he firmly believed 'diminished the world and robbed it of all diversity'.[33] He wrote on 27 December 1941: 'Certainly today in a car it is possible to see an immense amount of country in a couple of days, but it is impossible to savour it to the full, as you would going across it with animals like Gertrude Bell did, and travelling in a car somehow establishes a gulf between you and the local people.'[34]

That Baalbek's temples had not impressed him more during his first visit in 1936, he wrote, 'puzzles me ... Today the setting is finer, with the mountains on either side deep under snow. But the ruins themselves are wonderful.' Here he added as an evocative, homely touch: 'The stone from which they are built is a lovely warm colour, like that in the Cotswold villages.' Despite resenting cars, Thesiger anticipated: 'We should have rather a lovely drive through the snow across the Anti-Lebanon [mountains], and I am anxious to see Damascus at this time of year.'[35] (It appears they had exchanged their horses for a car.)

In January 1942 blizzards blocked the roads to and from Damascus. The city's bazaars were shut because of the freezing cold. Thesiger saw 'an astonishing sight': the desert, 'all white and frozen hard with camels moving about over it', like a Christmas card picture. This was fine weather for sportsmen, he noted: 'I met Hugo Meynell [whose brother Mark had helped to identify Thesiger's bird collection from the Danakil country in Abyssinia] again the other day. He had just been shooting, and 6 of them had got some 350 duck and 180 snipe in one day round Lake Hule, a lovely spot under Mount Hermon.'[36]

During 1942, Thesiger and Henderson continued to travel all over Syria and Lebanon. 'We stayed in all the cities,' Thesiger wrote, '… and in villages, and in the tents of the Bedu, and we visited several Christian monasteries. We met a great variety of people, Arabs, Turks, Circassians, Alawites and Druze.' From a hideout among caves in the lava fields of the Laja, in the Hauran, they could observe any traffic using the main road from Damascus, and using Thesiger's recent training in ambush and explosives, acquired at Latrun, 'perhaps do some sabotage'.[37] Writing to Kathleen in January 1942, he described the Laja, where he had lunched 'with the sheikh of a crowd of outlaws' as 'an inaccessible waste of lava known appropriately in Arabic as "The Refuge"'.[38]

After returning from his sojourn in the Laja, Thesiger wrote a long letter to Kathleen, giving marvellous descriptions of the Druze country and its people.

I have just been down in the Leja [sic], North of Jebel ed Druze. It is a lava flow from the volcanoes in Northern Jebel ed Druze. An extraordinary piece of country, full of fissures and caves, and except along a few ill defined tracks impossible to cross except on foot. The Druze live in the Eastern half and the Slut Arabs in the Western half. These Arabs have a bad reputation for treachery and brigandage since for centuries all the wanted men of Syria have found a secure haven here. I actually spent most of my time in the Druze side. It was very lovely down there for the flowers were out, and the grass and small patches of corn were very green. The flowers were scarlet anemones, white daisies, yellow buttercups, and iris. A large dark purple iris, and a dwarf iris of blue and gold. We had some very heavy rain the first day and got properly soaked. The rain turned to snow on the hills and there was a sharp frost. Next morning Jebel ed Druze stood out very white under its mantle of snow, while [Mount] Herman looked incredibly lovely its base hidden in the haze, high up in a very blue sky. The air was sharp and cold and it was very exhilarating riding through this rain-washed world in the sunshine among the flowers.

I like the Druze increasingly. They are so hospitable and friendly, and such fine looking people who have retained their traditional method of life and their own clothing, in a world which is fast becoming drab. They live in houses of Roman origin, or if recent built on the ancient model. The great hall is a great square room supported on two or more Roman arches.

There is a stone seat round the three sides, other than that containing the entrance, and a shallow sunken fireplace in the centre of the room where the brass coffee pots are kept continually full. The floor is flagged, and there are a few rugs and cushions on the seat. This great hall fills up soon after one's arrival in the village; the elders in their tightly bound white turbans, which distinguishes them as initiates into the secret Druze religion, coming to pay their respects, and the youth of the village in headchiefs and cloaks like the Arabs coming along to see who you are.

All the time one is with them, morning noon and night, one is in public. There is never any rest or privacy. You sleep in this hall in quilts which are borne in by the servants as the last guests leave about eleven o' clock, and all the guests who are staying in the house sleep together. Very early in the morning they start stirring, and the room soon fills with smoke as the fire is lighted and they brew the eternal bitter coffee. This coffee is handed round continuously, a few scalding drops in a small china cup without a handle. The Druze are renowned even with the Bedu for their hospitality, and as soon as a guest arrives a sheep is slaughtered. Some 4 hours later the meal is ready. A huge bowl of rice swimming in 'semen' [sic] with the sheep on top. The company then sits down in relays round the dish which is on the floor in the centre of the room, and eats as quickly and as much as possible. The host meanwhile continues to pour scalding semen (fat) [only now did Thesiger realise that his phonetic rendering of the Arabic word 'samin' needed urgent translation] over the food, while reciting the formula of welcome. In Arabic every phrase has its correct answer, whether of welcome, of farewell, or of thanks, and as they are innumerable it is difficult at first to get them right, and it is stupid to get them wrong. The Druze pride themselves on the purity of their Arabic. It is all great fun when one can do it. If one is staying in a village one feeds in a different house for each meal, and each time there is a 'mansaff' or sheep slaughtered for the meal. Quite often there are 70–90 people present so you can get an idea how spacious some of their halls are. Very often they play the 'rubabi' (a single stringed instrument) and sing lilting songs.'[39]

Thesiger acknowledged that Arab ways were sometimes hard for anyone unaccustomed to them. In March 1942 an English officer, Mervyn Phipps, had asked if he could join Thesiger's party, travelling for a week with camels in the desert south-east of Damascus. 'We lived on a bit of rice,' Thesiger wrote, 'what [sic] the Arabs took with them, and though I am inured to the lack of proper food it is hard for the first time. Also to get it into your mouth at all requires a knack in rolling it into a ball. The first time I asked [Phipps] if he had had enough he said "I have not managed to get any in yet" and when they produced a piece of unleavened bread for dinner he said "You are pulling my leg."'[40]

Thesiger and Henderson also visited Circassian and Turkish villages, finding the Circassians 'very hospitable' and glimpsing Turkish life 'as it used to be in Turkey'; 'eating mutton and drinking coffee, in rooms which by contrast with those of the Druze were small, bare, mat covered … with carpets to sit on and cushions to rest against'. Thesiger wrote admiringly of the villagers, 'No one can make you feel as really welcome as these people can, and remember that you come to them as a passing stranger and not as an invited guest, and this year food is scarce.'[41]

They watched a Shammar migration, 'a nation on the move', and visited the Ruallah, living in black tents scattered across the desert, welcomed by their famous Amir, Nuri al-Shalan, whom Lawrence had described more than two decades previously as an old man. Aged as he now was, he was still alert and upright, with dyed-black hair, and his word was law. He epitomised the despotic archetype Thesiger most admired and in ways sought to emulate: 'his merest glance commanded immediate attention'.[42]

Thesiger found the hospitality of these desert Bedu, with whom he spent a night, 'almost annoying': 'In one case we were lunching in some tents, and an Arab from some tents nearby made us promise to stop and drink coffee with them. As we got off our horses they cut a sheep's throat, and then we were committed to another meal, having just eaten, with all the inevitable delay in preparing it … Yet such is their code, and you cannot stop at a Bedu tent and not feed. It is a grand sight in the evening just after dark when the herds come in, and the bells on the sheep's necks tinkle, and the dogs bark, and the children shout as they drive them into their places for the night. Can you wonder that I love being with them.' Anxious that Kathleen should not feel excluded from a way of life which now mattered more and more to him, he hastily added: 'I wish so incessantly that you were here with me. You shall see it all when the war is over, and you will revel in it all just as I do.'[43]

In *Arabian Sands* Thesiger compared himself unfavourably with nomads and villagers in this land where 'the patina of human history was thick along the edges of the desert'. He wrote: 'There I lived among tribes who claimed descent from Ishmael, and listened to old men who spoke of events which had occurred a thousand years ago as if they had happened in their own youth. I went there with a belief in my own racial superiority, but in their tents I felt like an uncouth, inarticulate barbarian, an intruder from a shoddy and materialistic world.'[44]

Thesiger, the 'barbarian', had shot almost a thousand birds in Abyssinia in the cause of science, and he had no scruples about killing reptiles such as snakes. Among the Druze, however, he found: 'The lark and the serpent are held in great reverence by them; and not only the Druses, but the inhabitants of Syria in general pretend that if a person kills or hunts a serpent, the injured reptile will breathe upon him, and the scent of the serpent's breath will remain upon him till an opportunity is afforded to a brother serpent to revenge himself for the maltreatment of his fellow ... The veneration of the Druses for larks is also, as I have said, to be remarked; it is considered a sin for any one to shoot at those aerial songsters, and sooner or later, it is believed, condign punishment will attend the criminal act.'[45] This dire warning was given by George Washington Chasseaud, a resident of Beirut, in his scarce treatise *The Druses of Lebanon*, published in 1855, a copy of which Thesiger finally added to his collection of rare books in 1972.

Thesiger's only setback had been a mild attack of sandfly fever. He assured his mother that it was nothing: 'It makes you feel rather wretched for a few days but does not recur like malaria. In the summer an attack of it is almost inevitable.'[46] More alarming had been Kathleen's news that Reginald Astley's sight had failed, apparently without warning. Thesiger wrote: 'I was ... horrified to hear that Reggie is stone blind ... I am afraid everything must be very difficult for you. Do give him my love and tell him how distressed I am.' With relief, he added: 'I am so glad that Mary [Buckle] is coming back to you. She is so great a standby. I know you need her and that she will never fail you. She is so much one of the family.'[47]

News of his stepfather's blindness had been delayed; only that December did three of Kathleen's letters to Abyssinia reach Thesiger in Syria.[48] Despite his dutiful enquiries, greetings and expressions of sympathy for the 'poor old man', Thesiger clearly felt more anxious about his mother. 'I am afraid you must be having a wearing time,' he wrote, 'with Reggie's blindness and your anxieties over us ... I hope he keeps cheerful ... But I realize only too well what an extra burden has fallen on your shoulders.'[49] As always he ended his letters affectionately, thoughtfully, often reminding Kathleen how much he loved her, how much he owed her, sending more love to Brian, Dermot, Roddy, Reggie and the faithful 'Bucks'.

On 14 May 1942 Wilfred received a telegram from his mother telling him that his brother Dermot had been killed. In *The Life of My Choice* he wrote a paragraph about Dermot in a chapter entitled 'Oxford and The Milebrook', the two places where he had felt closest to his brother. Thesiger wrote: 'Dermot was devoted to England and always maintained that he never went abroad if he could avoid it. Witty, ambitious and idealistic, his ambition was to be elected to Parliament, his dream to become Prime Minister ... After he had been accepted [by the RAF] he trained in South Africa, and was then posted as a Flight Sergeant to Coastal Command. His ineptitude at mathematics delayed his commission, which was finally granted on the day he was killed on an operational flight ... When he was killed Sir Vincent Massey, the High Commissioner for Canada, and Mr Justice Lawrence, the High Court Judge for whom Dermot had marshalled [as a junior barrister], wrote appreciations of him in *The Times*, a remarkable tribute in this time of war to an unknown young man.'[50] Nicolette Devas, whose husband Anthony painted Thesiger in 1944 and 1945, remembered Dermot's last visit to their house in Markham Square, Chelsea: '[He] arrived from his Air Force base green with fatigue and slept all day in an armchair while children played over his knees and the sound of the gramophone echoed round his head with Mahler's heartrending "Song of the Earth". [Dermot] slept through it all. Yet I like to think that it helped him in some way, that perhaps he drew strength from the normality of children playing and women cooking. A few days later he was ... killed.'[51]

Numbed by the 'incredible' news,[52] Wilfred wrote half-rhetorically, searchingly, to his mother:

How can I express what I feel yet you will know, as I know. I feel an empty sense of loss now that he is gone, for he was so very fine. He was so far above the ordinary, so splendid proud and true. Yet with the feeling of great loss I have no sense of waste. He and his comrades have given themselves so freely in a cause which they never doubted. They are the knights of this age ... He, like us, had such a happy life and this he and we owe to you. For it was you dearest Mother, who by never giving in and by shouldering such crushing burdens during those early days in England, gave us the Milebrook, and all that it meant to us, and I think particularly to Dermot ... I am also so glad that I had that year at Magdalen with him, when I saw such a lot of him and learnt to know his worth ... In his last letter he said that if he was killed it would be a proud death.[53]

Thesiger wrote again on 4 June, assuring Kathleen: 'I know only too well how bitterly you must be suffering ... Dearest one you know how much you mean to me, far more than anyone else does or I think ever can. You are really all I have, and I shall never be able to replace you. Realize the utter need which I and the others have for you, and let this help you now.'[54] Thesiger's revealing letter shows that he understood only too well that the closer are family ties and friendships, the greater the loss when they are broken: 'You have given all you had to the four of us, and I know what we have meant to you, and how your sons were all you lived for. We gain and gained much from being such a self contained family but we also pay much.'[55] The death of his adored younger brother left Thesiger feeling isolated and vulnerable. He urged his mother: 'Take care of yourself for you are all I have, and if anything happened to you I should have nothing left.'[56]

Only later did Thesiger learn the details of his brother's death. Dermot had not been killed in action. He was piloting an operational flight off the east coast of England when the aircraft's wing struck the mast of a shipwreck and crashed into the North Sea.[57] There were no survivors. Thesiger agreed with his mother that it was a blessing that Dermot's body was not recovered,[58] writing: 'He has just gone, the way he would have wished'; and 'I was relieved that my mother never saw Dermot with his face all smashed up after his crash. I often think, if he had lived, I might have been the one who was closest to him ... Instead, Dermot stayed there in the sea, nibbled away at by the fish and rotting.'[59] In a moving letter to Wilfred, Roderic had quoted: 'If it be death I shall die for ever unconquered/If it be life I shall rise strong in my pride and free.' Thesiger added: 'This seems to me the perfect epitaph for him. I should myself like a tablet in Stowe Church [near The Milebrook] with that on it. He had made himself so much a part of that piece of country.'[60] These words were quoted by the Reverend Prebendary J. Harrison during a sermon he preached in the parish church at Clun, near Stowe, at the dedication of a memorial to Dermot on Sunday, 29 November 1942.

Dermot's friend Humphrey Brooke wrote an extraordinary letter to Kathleen, which suggested that Dermot had believed he would die young, and had even predicted how he would die: 'I can't help thinking of him as he was on his recent spells of leave – so wholly undeterred by the certainty of death at some near date and radiantly happy in the face of this. You would know how happy he was but I suspect he hid from all of you the conviction he had that he would not long survive. He used to joke about it to me in that inimitable mocking way of his, and he always ridiculed my protestations that intrepid people like him were often lucky. I can hear him saying the last time he was about on short leave less than 3 weeks ago, "No Humphrey, I shall just crash into the sea and as I go down I shall think to myself 'Dermot Thesiger this is a glorious end!'"'[61]

Any threat to Syria of invasion was eliminated when (in Thesiger's words) the German army became 'bogged down' in Russia.[62] Thesiger felt frustrated, having nothing constructive left to do in Syria. He had found intelligence-gathering interesting work, and had gained satisfaction from it and from establishing a base for surveillance operations in the Laja. But he would remember his wartime travels in Syria and the Lebanon more as an opportunity for seeing the country, its impressive monuments and fortresses, and meeting the varied peoples and tribes who lived there. He treasured memories of the Ruallah and their autocratic leader Nuri al-Shalan, of Sultan Pasha al-Atrash, who had led a Druze rebellion against the French in 1924 and had been one of Thesiger's boyhood heroes. 'Now, when I met him,' Thesiger wrote, 'he did not disappoint me ... however, alone among my visitors [at Malha] he professed no allegiance to the British.'[63]

FIFTEEN

The Flowering Desert

On 20 June 1942, at his own request, Thesiger was transferred to Cairo. There, at Grey Pillars, SOE's imposing headquarters, he was told that he would be dropped behind enemy lines in Cyrenaica. Apart from its being 'a special job', he explained to Kathleen, 'I cannot tell you what it is or where, as you will well understand. I expect to be here for about a fort-night and am enjoying the flesh pots of Shepherd's and putting on a "hump" ... I am delighted to have been given this job. It is my line of business and promises to be interesting and exciting. I enjoyed my year in Syria but was getting restive and rather fed up, and had asked for something more active, when I was offered this ... There is only one thing which distresses me and that is that you will be worried again, and I would give such a lot to avoid that. Dearest Mother you have had so much worry and grief and I hate to add to it. I know however that you would be the last to have any of us hang back.'[1]

Thesiger meanwhile explored the old city of Cairo. As a member of SOE, he could dispense with army uniform: dressed as a civilian, speaking Arabic, he felt relatively inconspicuous:

I liked to sit sipping tea in one of the many open-fronted booths that lined the streets, and to watch the passing crowd, while I bargained for a carpet, an old Turkish dagger, a length of silk, an amber rosary, or a piece of silverwork: anything could be found here if one knew where to look. Porters, bowed under heavy loads, shouted 'Balak! balak!' ['Look out!'] to clear a passage; donkey carts, piled high, moved forward through the crowd a few paces at a time; small boys dodged about carrying trays of tea; a group of bearded, turbanned mullahs, wrapped in cloaks and sanctity, entered a mosque; a muezzin gave the long, lingering call to prayer. Here was colour, squalor, dirt, poverty, with good humour swiftly erupting into sudden brawls, and a variety of pervasive smells.[2]

An accurate observer with a sharp eye for detail, Thesiger used word pictures, as he had learnt to use a camera, to portray places, and people in colourful settings which interested him. Yet after days 'rather hanging about with nothing to do', and no definite briefing, even the colourful street life of Cairo left him feeling bored.[3] He wrote on 27 June: 'Owing to a change in the situation here the job which I was called down here for is off for the time being.'[4]

General Claude Auchinleck, in command of the Eighth Army, had halted Rommel's advance at El Alamein, only seventy miles from Alexandria. SOE, faced with the serious possibility that the Germans might occupy Cairo, instructed Thesiger to remain behind, working undercover from a safe house, funding his clandestine activities with sovereigns and uncut diamonds. 'It all seemed highly unprofessional,' Thesiger wrote in 1987, 'as I had learnt to expect from the set-up in Grey Pillars.'[5] As Auchinleck continued to hold the Germans in check at Alamein, the threat to Cairo diminished, and Thesiger persuaded SOE to transfer him to the Red Sea Hills. With support from the 'virile, handsome' Ababdah tribe, he believed he could disrupt German communications should Rommel take Cairo and advance up the Nile. He wrote of the Red Sea Hills: 'They appeal to me greatly for I like the barren austerity of the country ... I like the people too. They are of the "Fuzzy Wuzzie" type.'[6] With almost three years' experience fighting with the Patriots in Abyssinia, and liaising with the Druze and other Syrian tribes in preparation for a German invasion, Thesiger felt well qualified to undertake guerrilla operations in Egypt. Besides, working undercover in Cairo, which he hardly knew, where he felt little affinity for the inhabitants and had neither friends nor even trustworthy acquaintances, did not appeal to him.

He wrote to his mother: 'I have always wanted to have a look at the Red Sea Hills,'[7] which were 'very barren, but in a way that is their charm. I have just had four days on a schooner coming up the coast. It is full of interesting little bays, with coral reefs, so that it is safe to bathe, and I have never had better bathing in my life.'[8] Far away from the claustrophobic alleys of old Cairo, he wrote: 'I am off in a couple of days into the hills on camels, and am very much looking forward to this. They are lovely these hills, of pink granite ... In a car you just motor past, whereas, on a camel you go right into them, and moving slowly have time to explore them, and you visit the wells and see the Ababdah who live here. I shall feel full of new life after a week among them on a camel.'[9] Thesiger had been with Lieutenant Tim Foley, who was mining wolfram, or wolframite, ore used in the manufacture of tungsten. He described Foley as 'a very delightful Irishman, who ... has spent 18 years goldmining in the Red Sea Hills'. He teased Kathleen: 'You would love him, for he is very Irish. He was with Arthur Bentinck too while in Abyssinia, and did the most extraordinary feats blowing up Italian convoys on the Gondar road, slipping down at night onto the road with a party of Abyssinians. The Italians offered a large reward for him dead or alive.'[10]

A visit by the Prime Minister, Winston Churchill, in September 1942 had boosted the army's morale. 'Here we had a very successful battle the other day when Rommel attacked our forces, and seem to have defeated him successfully and thoroughly. I think Churchill's visit did a lot of good. I don't know whether you in England know what he means to us out here. To us he is just England.'[11] In the first week of November, General Bernard Law Montgomery's decisive victory at El Alamein forced Rommel to retreat towards Libya. Egypt was no longer in danger of being invaded, and Thesiger returned to Cairo, hoping for an active posting with the Long Range Desert Group, a commando force comprising young volunteers and trained men that carried out desert journeys hundreds of miles into enemy territory. But his impromptu approach to SOE's Brigadier at Grey Pillars resulted in 'a most surprisingly unsympathetic hearing'.[12] In *The Life of My Choice* he gave a dramatised version of his interview with the Brigadier, which he had described already very effectively in letters to Kathleen:

I asked to be released by SOE if the LRDG accepted me.

'The LRDG would not take you as a major.'

I answered rather shortly: 'I would be content to be a captain, even a lieutenant, if I was with them.'

He replied: 'Anyway, I'm not releasing you. You should not have come up to Cairo without my permission.'[13]

To Kathleen he wrote: 'the job I am on [in the Red Sea Hills] is no longer of value as a result of our victory in the Desert, yet they won't let me go ... I ... am anxious now to get out to something fresh. If I had been trying to get away from the Desert for a safe job at the base they would have been justified in taking up the attitude they did. I have a very good job to go to. It is merely a question of getting quit of my present department.'[14] By 'a very good job' Thesiger meant operating behind enemy lines with the SAS. This he achieved, despite the SOE Brigadier's furious opposition, by a direct approach to Colonel David Stirling, founder and commanding officer of the SAS. Thesiger had also canvassed support from the 'sympathetic' Military Secretary in Cairo,[15] but did not wait for the outcome of a meeting between the Military Secretary and the SOE Brigadier. Needless to say, Thesiger's sometimes bullish and unconventional methods proved unpopular. 'I have met with a good deal of obstruction,' he wrote, 'and I think jealousy.' Had it not been for this, he was convinced, he might have had some role to play at El Alamein: 'I should have liked to have taken a part in this victory, and I know they could have used me usefully. It now looks as if the war will soon be over in the Middle East.'[16] By 21 November, after 'a maddening fortnight in Cairo', Thesiger confirmed: 'I have got released on loan [to the SAS] and am off at once. We should have an interesting time and see a great deal of the country ... I am serving under a Colonel who has won a great reputation already. He is a couple of years younger than Roddy, but is one of the greatest leaders out here. I have just finished getting my things together at their camp in the desert, and we leave tonight.'[17]

A month previously, on 18 October, Thesiger had heard from his mother that his stepfather was seriously ill. Reginald Astley died, aged eighty, on 6 October.[18] Although Kathleen assured Wilfred that she had enough money to live on for the time being, he wrote: 'Don't hesitate to make use of my account if you are in need. I am wondering what Reggie left in his will, and how he left it. Sometimes I feel rather apprehensive about this.'[19] His anxiety was to an extent justified at the time, although Kathleen was actually financially comfortable for the rest of her life.

Thesiger's letters imply that Astley's affairs had been muddled, and the terms of Kathleen's inheritance had to be clarified after his death.

David Stirling soon realised that Thesiger was an ideal candidate for his unit, first named L Detachment of the Special Air Service Brigade, later the Special Air Service, or SAS.[20] The unit had originated when a staff officer, Brigadier Dudley Clarke, had invented a parachute brigade which did not exist, in order to deceive German intelligence. Its badge, a winged dagger, and its motto, 'Who Dares Wins', were devised by Stirling. By 1942, little more than a year after it was established, the SAS detachment had been raised to a regiment. In complete contrast with Orde Wingate, Stirling was courteous, immaculately dressed, and by 'treating his officers and men with consideration and respect, he gained their friendship as well as their admiration'.[21] The SAS motto would have been even more appropriate for Wilfred Thesiger than his family's more speculative 'Hope and Fortune'.

Before he left Cairo for Kabrit, in the Suez Canal Zone, Thesiger met John Verney, whom he had last seen at Jabal Druze in Syria. 'We only saw each other for a few minutes,' he wrote, 'but it was delightful to see him. I am very fond of him. He was just off back to the desert, and I ran into him purely by chance. He looked very well.'[22] Brian Thesiger meanwhile had returned, with his wife and two baby daughters, from India to work at the War Office in London, and Roderic had been sent to an unknown destination. Thesiger worried constantly about his youngest brother, writing: 'I fancy Roddy is in North Africa. I wonder what he thinks of it all. I am sure he is glad to be in it at last. I have admired his determination enormously.'[23] With active postings in Abyssinia, the Middle East and North Africa, Thesiger realised how fortunate he had been. He had 'won distinction', and the war had given him the excitement and challenge he craved.[24] As a contrast, he wrote musingly, 'Brian who is a regular soldier has so far seen nothing of it.'[25] In the event Brian would be awarded a Military Cross at Anzio; after serving in Tunisia in the Parachute Brigade with the First Army, Roderic would be dropped over Sicily, at Primasole Bridge and again at Arnhem, where he was wounded and captured. Both Brian and Roderic would survive the war.

Stirling knew precisely what he was doing when he obtained Wilfred's release from Special Operations Executive. 'I found David Stirling at his brother Peter's flat [in Cairo] ... he listened courteously while I explained my frustrations with SOE. I told him that I had been with Wingate in Abyssinia, was familiar with desert life, and spoke Arabic.'[26] Thesiger told his mother: 'This job promises to be fascinating. I cannot tell you anything about it except that I am going as Arabic speaking officer to a unit.'[27] Here was the key. When Stirling discussed Thesiger's involvement with the SAS many years later, he praised his knowledge of and consummate skill in dealing with desert Arabs. Stirling's all-encompassing remark, 'Wilfred had a real nostril for desert,'[28] answered very concisely the criticism by an SAS Sergeant who had been unimpressed by Thesiger's military knowledge: 'I put him in the same category as other officers invited, but not trained, by the SAS to take part as "observer" ... He fitted well into the team, but I would have called him a "passenger" rather than an "operator".'[29] Thesiger commented drily: 'This was wartime ... the SAS was a small unit with no room for passengers. David Stirling wouldn't have accepted me if he hadn't thought I could be useful.'[30]

On 21 November, Thesiger joined a convoy from the SAS base at Kabrit and drove to Agedabia, past the battlefield at El Alamein.[31] The convoy was made up of the SAS 'B' Squadron and reinforcements for 'A' Squadron, based hundreds of miles to the west, in Cyrenaica. Thesiger remembered sights he found 'immensely exhilarating':[32] the burnt-out wreckage of the decisive battle which changed the course of the entire war, and the 'endless ... moving mass of vehicles'[33] and men they passed, day after day, grinding victoriously under clouds of dust across the desert. Yet inwardly he still felt 'bitter and discontented'[34] for having missed (as he saw it, having been denied) the opportunity of playing some active part at El Alamein.

He described his journey with the convoy, and the events which followed, in a detailed letter to his mother written some months later, on which he based the account of his activities with the SAS in the Western Desert in The Life of My Choice. None of the letters Thesiger said he wrote to his mother between 21 November 1942 and 18 February 1943 appears to have survived, and after David Stirling was taken prisoner in Tunisia in 1943, he confessed that he found himself uncertain about the sequence of events.[35]

By May 1943 Kathleen, aged sixty-three, had left The Milebrook and moved to a bright top-storey flat in Chelsea, where she lived for the next thirty years. In November 1942, after Reginald Astley died, Thesiger had written to her: 'I hope greatly that you will be able to keep The Milebrook on. I am most impatient to get news of this.' By February 1943 he had had time to reconsider: 'I gather from Francis [Rodd, of the RGS] you are leaving The Milebrook. I am sure you are right ... We have been very happy there and it would have been a mistake to hang on. Get a comfortable place in London and don't hesitate to use my money ... I know what a wrench leaving The Milebrook will be, but feel sure it is wise. You would be lonely there, and haunted by memories.'[36]

Without special status or specialised training, Thesiger was regarded as 'just another officer'[37] in his convoy of almost a hundred men transported by jeeps and lorries. Clad in an Arab chemise and headdress, with his pummelled sunburnt features and upper-class drawl, according to one NCO, he seemed 'a most peculiar major'.[38] At Agedabia they left the coast road and skirted the German positions at Agheila. Here the desert was as barren as any Thesiger had ever seen.[39] At Bir Zaltin, a hundred miles south of Agheila, they joined the SAS 'A' Squadron, commanded by Major Blair 'Paddy' Mayne. Attached to one of eight 'B' Squadron patrols, led by Stirling, Thesiger drove a jeep turn-about with Lieutenant Gordon Alston, a more experienced officer, accompanied by two wireless operators in another jeep, about four hundred miles further west, to El Fascia. To escape detection the patrols travelled by night. Thesiger wrote: 'it needed unfailing concentration to avoid getting stuck in a sand drift or damaging the sump on a rock. I had never derived any satisfaction from driving a car and was consequently a bad driver, and I found these night drives interminable, exhausting and bitterly cold.'[40] Thesiger's and Alston's target was the road west of Bouerat, on the Libyan coast. On their first night patrol, Thesiger machine-gunned a German convoy, then blew up some telegraph poles, cut the wires and set land mines. Finding a large tented camp, they drove with headlights on among the enemy vehicles, sprayed several tents with machine-gun fire, and drove away.

Thesiger and Alston carried out more night raids on German camps, but to Thesiger's surprise they were never challenged or shot at. 'I had a comforting delusion,' he wrote, 'that we were invisible.'[41] One night they drove up to a canteen with lorries parked near the tent, inside which men were talking, laughing and singing. Thesiger recalled: 'I fired a long burst into the tent, and short bursts into the engines of the lorries as we drove off. During these operations we must have killed and wounded many people, but as I never saw the casualties we inflicted my feelings remained impersonal. I did, however, begin to feel that our luck could not last much longer.'[42]

Thesiger rejected any comparison between himself shooting unarmed soldiers in their tents, and so-called 'homicidal' Danakil warriors stabbing or shooting unarmed, unsuspecting victims in the back: 'When I was with the SAS, shooting up German camps was part of the job. Among the Danakil, killing a man gave you greater status in the tribe. I disapproved of this at first, but after a while I accepted it. Their standards were completely different to ours. By that I'm certainly not implying theirs were inferior ... besides, I didn't feel that it was up to me to judge them.'[43]

While Thesiger and Alston lay up between night raids at El Fascia, occasionally they heard German armoured cars scouring the desert nearby, no doubt searching for SAS patrols. Once, after Alston and the two signallers had gone to fetch water from the cistern at El Fascia, Thesiger saw a small plane flying in Alston's direction, and heard the noise of heavy vehicles. He hid himself in the open under a blanket he had camouflaged with scattered handfuls of earth and twigs. An armoured car passed less than two hundred yards from the tiny depression where he lay, and stopped for what seemed like an eternity before driving on. Soon after, Thesiger heard several bursts of machinegun fire, and assumed that Alston and the two signallers had been either killed or captured. In fact they turned up safe and sound: the source of the firing was German soldiers in pursuit of a French SAS officer, Lieutenant Martin, and his driver, who caught up with Thesiger and Alston later that day.

The following day, Christmas Eve, Thesiger and Alston found another hiding place in 'a delightful wadi full of trees and carpeted with green grass and flowers'. Thesiger wrote: 'Some Arabs turned up in the morning ... They were very friendly and I found their Arabic comparatively easy to understand. We made them tea and later they fetched us a goat and spent the night with us.'[44]

The writer Virginia Cowles, quoting information supplied to her by Alston, gave a more detailed version of these events in her book about David Stirling, *The Phantom Major* (1951). Describing Thesiger's 'delightful wadi' as 'a valley about a quarter of a mile wide, with steep sides, and a profusion of long bushes which offered good cover', she wrote:

> soon after their arrival an Arab shepherd playing a pipe wandered into the ravine and spotted them. The raiders were not too happy about this. They knew that Tripolitanian Arabs often collected rewards for reporting British soldiers to the enemy. However, Wilfred Thesiger, the Arab expert, knew the ceremonial way to offer tea. He carried an enamel tea-pot and little cups expressly for this purpose. The shepherd seemed friendly enough, and the men were having a discussion whether or not they should move, when a second Arab appeared. This one was more important, for he was dressed in white and rode a donkey. He had a goat on a lead. 'He presented the goat to us,' wrote Alston, 'and Wilfred whispered to me that it should be killed there and then, cooked and eaten and the best bits given to our guest. This would then render us safe for at least forty-eight hours. I looked round in despair but luckily one of the French soldiers did the necessary with a knife and cut the wretched animal up.'[45]

Alston's recollections of the wadi may have been less picturesque than Thesiger's, but Thesiger had a far wider experience of deserts, and any variation of these arid landscapes had peculiar significance for him.

Thesiger's chapter in *The Life of My Choice* titled 'With the SAS in the Western Desert' was based largely on a letter he wrote to Kathleen on 7 May 1943. This was the 'interesting letter' he had promised her in February that he would write when the campaign was over.[46] Thesiger's letters to his mother from May to October 1943 describe in vivid detail everything that happened to him from the time he joined the SAS at Kabrit until he left northern Palestine to serve as a Political Officer at Dessie in Abyssinia. The impact of these unfiltered images is sometimes more powerful than the polished, 'literary' versions he produced for his autobiography. He began the letter dated 7 May 1943:

I left Cairo as you remember on November 21st. I was attached to the SAS Regiment, parachutists operating in 'jeeps', under Colonel Stirling. Our object was to get behind the enemy lines and shoot up his lines of communication. At that time the front was at El Ageila, on the Cyrenaican–Tripolitanian border. The journey up was most interesting. We went through the El Alamein battlefield, littered with destroyed tanks, crashed aircraft and burnt out lorries. An enormous amount of stuff was moving up along the road at the time.

When we got to Agedabia we moved off south and passed round the end of the enemy lines near Marada. From there we moved on towards Zella. The desert here is I suppose one of the most barren in the world. Never a sign of life or of vegetation, just sand and gravel and some rocks. We were a large number of cars, some 100 jeeps and 20 3-ton lorries. Our constant apprehension was that we should be spotted from the air or by patrolling armoured cars, and then bombed. There was nowhere where we could hide if planes came over. Generally we lay up during the day, moving off in the late afternoon and keeping going all through the night. These were cold long tiring drives. We drove with all our headlights on, absolutely necessary in the second half when we got into very stony country cut up by wadis ... We had a brush with enemy armoured cars crossing the Hon–Bouerat road just north of Hon and lost two jeeps. The Italians handled their armoured cars abominably or they would have inflicted heavy losses on us.

We split up on the Wadi Zemzem. The object was to have one small party, shooting up the road, laying mines and cutting telegraph lines, every ten miles between Tripoli and Ageila, where the Germans were trying to make a stand. It was hoped that we should completely stop all night traffic for 10 days, and this we succeeded in doing. I was with Stirling but he left us after the first night in order to go back to Cairo ... to arrange phase two. A young captain called Alston, an Etonian of Roddy's age, and myself operated together in one jeep, armed with two twin Vickers machine guns. We lay up at Fasher or Fasquia, a well on the Wadi Zemzem west of Bouerat ... and for seven days motored off at sunset to the road 40 miles away, and shot it up. It was a murderous business, for the enemy convoys parked along the road were at our mercy. Each night there were more cars, till during the last two there were cars parked everywhere off the road 2 miles deep for mile after mile. We just drove up to one of these convoys, the cars were very scattered for fear of bombing, and having picked out a suitable bunch went up to them as if we were going to park alongside. Having got within 20 yards we stopped and opened up with our machine guns. The moon was full towards the end, but even so the flash of the guns firing incendiary and tracer was quite blinding. It was all a curious experience for quite often we remained, before firing, for a couple of hours in their midst, with them talking and walking about all round us in the bright moonlight.

They never fired a shot back at us. It certainly must have been most unpleasant for them. One night I got into a laager where they were repairing tanks, and within 20 yards of their main mobile workshop with camouflaged tanks and tents all round, and when I tried to fire my guns jammed. It was impracticable to test them after cleaning them in the daytime. I changed the magazines, expecting every moment to be challenged, but as they still would not work had to come away. Next night I found 9 lorries drawn up outside a tent, head to tail, with the drivers getting their orders inside. I cannot have been 30 yards off and riddled both tent and lorries. It was always a tricky job getting back the 40 miles across the desert, on a compass bearing in the dark, sometimes with the stars covered with clouds, and both of us tired, for we had to [find] a small patch of bushes in which the other car with the wireless was hidden.

That night we got back at dawn, and shortly afterwards an enemy reconnaissance plane came over very low, and then we heard armoured cars on both sides. That was an unpleasant day, for there were 3 planes and some 20 armoured cars, combing the ground for us from 8.30 till sunset. Backwards and forwards they went, and individual cars kept turning off their engines and waiting for us to make some sound I suppose, so that one never knew where they were. Twice there was heavy firing within a mile or two. I thought they had found Alston, who had gone down at dawn to the well in the jeep, and was amazed when he suddenly turned up on foot in the late afternoon. He had thought that they were shooting me up, and had come along to try and recover the cyphers [wireless codes]. I don't know who they were shooting up but suspect it must have been a party of ours further North coming in ...[47]

After the war, when Thesiger read an English translation of Rommel's diary, edited by Basil Liddell Hart, he realised that Rommel himself must have been with the armoured cars searching for them that same day.[48]

After Tripoli fell to the British in January 1943, Alston was recalled to Cairo. Thesiger was given permission to join the recently established Greek Sacred Squadron of the SAS,[49] which had been formed 'to emulate the Theban Band of Hellenic times',[50] and operated with a Free French force commanded by General le Comte Philippe François Leclerc. Thesiger spent six weeks at Qasr Rhilana in Tunisia, near the Algerian border, with the Free French force before joining the New Zealand Divisional Cavalry. He wrote to his mother on 7 May 1943: 'We ... took part with them in the Battle of Akarit and the subsequent pursuit to Enfidaville.'[51] Yet in The Life of My Choice he appeared to contradict this, writing: 'We took no part in the battle but as soon as it was over pushed forward with the New Zealand Divisional Cavalry who, in their light tanks, led the advance.'[52]

Reminiscent of T.E. Lawrence, his hero, Thesiger wrote: 'The pursuit was very exhilarating. We drove along across fields carpeted in flowers at 30 mph in jeeps with the New Zealand tanks and carriers. Little as I like things mechanical, moving forward at speed with tanks is exciting and exhilarating.'[53] The terrible carnage and destruction at Akarit was still a clear memory, as vivid as the 'murderous' night raids on German convoys along the Bouerat road. Writing to his mother, Thesiger softened harsh images of death with gentler visions of the reawakened desert landscape. 'Southern Tunisia,' he wrote, 'is a dull country, redeemed however in the spring by flowers, the like of which I had never imagined. There are not patches of flowers but a whole countryside carpeted with them. Red poppies and yellow marguerites, and white daisies mostly, but besides these an infinite variety of other flowers. Never, never, had I believed such flowers existed. We moved all day through a countryside which was one vast flowerbed, and at night lay down to sleep among them.' Tenderly, he assured her: 'You would have loved them.'

Thesiger shared his parents' love of scented flowers, especially roses. Travelling in Iraqi Kurdistan after the war, Wilfred again found himself surrounded by masses of wildflowers. 'In the spring there were ... red or white anemones on the lower slopes, covering whole hillsides with carpets of colour; and among them red ranunculus, yellow marigolds, gladioli, stocks, dark blue squills and irises. High up on the mountains scarlet tulips grew in profusion, scattered tiger lilies flowered in hollows among the rocks, dark blue gentians bordered drifts of snow'.[54] In the highlands of Nuristan in 1965, he camped close to a river in 'a delectable place where the untroubled water idled past, dragging at the overhanging willow in the current; where black cattle, watched by boys with flutes, grazed on rich pasture among banks of lilac primulas, wild roses, purple orchids, asphodel and grass of Parnassus'.[55]

In the heat of conflict, the flowering deserts of Tunisia gave him pause and reassurance: calming sights he shared eagerly with Kathleen. 'Sheets of colour,' he wrote. 'Never have I seen anything so beautiful'.[56] In return, Kathleen had sent Wilfred, as a keepsake from The Milebrook, sprigs of rosemary and wild briar. He thanked her: 'I have put this in a locket and wear it round my neck.' Leaving the house in the Teme Valley, their family home for more than twenty years, had been heartbreaking for Kathleen. It had, Thesiger wrote, been 'such a sunlit little house set in its glorious garden. Nothing can take the memory of it from us, which will remain undimmed as long as I live. My last memory of it is so vivid, picking sweet peas with you [in 1939] in the blazing sunlight just after hearing of the invasion of Poland'.[57]

SIXTEEN

Palestine: Shifting Lights and Shades

From Enfidaville, the Greek Sacred Squadron was recalled to Egypt. Thesiger drove with them from Cairo to a new SAS headquarters at Athlit in northern Palestine. At Janin he embarked on a week's parachute training, which he dreaded; he was taught by the same instructors who taught his brother Roddy, and they remembered him well.[1] One of Thesiger's group, a young Greek, was killed when his parachute failed to open; 'he went into the ground near where I was standing, but this shook me less than I would have expected'.[2] Thesiger gave a toned-down description in a letter to his mother: 'I saw him come down but luckily some way away and did not have to go over to him.' He added: 'I am glad to have done it, for it is always a good thing to have done something which scares you before you start.'[3]

On the way to Athlit Thesiger spent a day in Jerusalem, 'a wonderful city and more lovely each time one sees it'. He thought 'The Dome of the Rock (the chief mosque) ... the finest I have ever seen. It glows like a jewel.' Kathleen, he was certain, would love the old city with its 'jumble of narrow streets' and shafts of subdued light coming down, and the bazaars crowded with people in 'a powerful blend of colour and smells'. He added approvingly: 'The streets are very narrow and cars cannot intrude.'[4]

He was happy to be back in Palestine: 'a lovely country ... its charm grows each time I see it. It has an infinite variety of shifting lights and shades and scenery which is always changing.'[5] A visual allegory for Thesiger's incurably restless nature, 'shifting lights' and 'changing scenery' mirrored the irresistible lure of the unknown, and the incomparable thrill of new and wonderful sights and scenes.[6] Yet, he lovingly reassured his mother: 'I long for the end of the war because it means that

I shall get back to you ... to the one person who will care, and with whom I shall long to make plans for the future.' He stressed, above all, that Kathleen must look forward, not back. Had she remained at The Milebrook, 'memories of it would have been clouded over with later memories of unhappiness and loneliness ... Now you must make a home for us in London to which we can come. Also it will leave you freer to come away with me when I am on leave. We can then go off wherever we wish.'[7] He implored her, meanwhile, to be brave: 'Don't whatever happens cease to care and cease to fight. I know too well how tired and disheartened you must be feeling, and how there seems nothing but anxiety to look forward to, but this war will end.'[8] Thesiger found the sallow-skinned Greeks of the Sacred Squadron an 'interesting and attractive race when one gets to know them, and a very brave one too'. He added, for Kathleen's amusement: 'I have a driver servant called Mercury which is rather smart I think.'[9]

Among the hills, Thesiger visited Arab border villages, where he was made welcome 'despite resentment with the British over Jewish immigration'.[10] He sympathised strongly with the Arabs in Palestine. 'A few years later,' he wrote, 'with the virtual connivance of Britain and America, they were to be driven from their homeland or subjected to the intolerable rule of the Israelis, who claimed the right to a country from which they had been expelled two thousand years earlier. Seldom can a greater wrong have been inflicted on an innocent people with such general approbation, and the seeds of such catastrophic and widespread hatred been sown with so much complacency.'[11]

The fury with which Thesiger described scenes he witnessed in Jerusalem may have been a way of exorcising his demonic, still-raw feelings of grief after Dermot's death at only twenty-eight years of age. In May 1943 he found the King David Hotel in Jerusalem 'full of loud ostentatious Jews, throwing money about in an orgy of vulgarity'. Having got this out of his system, the next day he wrote placidly: 'I had a lovely walk through the cornfields and olive orchards, and then the most heavenly bathe in the sea ... I have a good job and am content and happy.'[12] He said: 'At the time I felt very strongly about these things and in many ways I still do. I hated the Italians for what they did in Abyssinia, but I didn't go on hating them after the war. I enjoyed being in Italy with my mother, meeting our Italian friends. And I wrote most of *The Marsh Arabs* in Florence, living there for months in a *pensione*.'[13]

Towards the end of his life, Thesiger insisted that any biography of him should be as inclusive and as candidly revealing as possible. In *The Life of My Choice* he criticised one of Orde Wingate's biographers, Christopher Sykes, for omitting two incidents that illustrated Wingate's 'ungovernable temper'.[14] Thesiger wrote: 'I think he was wrong to do so, and have included them not to denigrate Wingate, but because I consider he was of sufficient historical importance for every incident that reveals his character to be worth recording.'[15] Aged eighty, Thesiger shrugged aside any remnant of false modesty and asserted (quite rightly) that he too was 'of sufficient historical importance' for the character-revealing incidents in his life to be 'worth recording'.[16]

Thesiger was delighted to find a Druze squadron stationed near Athlit. When he visited them, the first person he saw was Faris, who 'rushed over, shouting to the others [Wilfred] was back'. This was the camel squadron which Thesiger had previously commanded at Malha. The following Sunday he went back with two Greek officers and shared a traditional Druze *mansaf*, mutton stew with boiled wheat. Later, with the squadron's commander, Salih Ma'z, and Faris, Thesiger drove to Arnah, the highest Druze village on Mount Hermon, where there were reputed to be 360 springs. 'Everywhere,' he remembered, 'icy cold water trickles down the mountainside. The village is set in meadows of tall very green grass, poplars, willows, and almond and apricot trees. It is all very beautiful. The Druze here wear baggy blue trousers, and coats of deep red colour with white headcloths ... There was a goat herd, an old man in a red coat, on top of the mountain with his goats. We drank long draughts of fresh goats' milk cooled with snow, while the goats drifted down the mountain among the snow to the music of their bells. Never have I had such nectar. We took 25 minutes to run down what had taken a laborious 2 hours to climb up. In the village the elders were waiting for us, and a great dish of rice and mutton was ready.'[17]

Thesiger admired the villagers' 'fierce pride in being Druze', their tenacious adherence to traditional ways of life and dress, which made them 'look and behave like aristocrats'. The Lebanese, by contrast, were 'an unhappy parody of the French, dressed in unbecoming ill-made

European clothes, living in houses crammed to overflowing with bad furniture and bric-a-brac of the last century, which has drifted out here from Europe, a people with no poise and no culture, super-sensitive and always uncomfortable'. Dismally he prophesied: 'I suppose in time the East will all become like that, much of it already is, in its desperate search for the secret of our success.'[18]

While he was stationed at Athlit, Thesiger took advantage of a fort-night's leave (his first since 1940, apart from a week in Khartoum and another week he spent at Petra) to visit northern Syria, then motor along the Turkish frontier and into Iraq, near Mosul. He told his mother: 'it was a fascinating trip ... I was at a loose end and an officer was going up there so I went along too.'[19] The officer was a young South African, Laurens van der Post, who like Thesiger had served under Wingate in the Abyssinian campaign. Quite by chance, in Damascus Thesiger found Romilly and Wedderburn-Maxwell, with whom he had served on the Upper Nile, and together they wandered all round the city, which 'was crowded, being Ramadan, and looked very lovely by moonlight'.[20] At Qamashlia, amid squalor he found 'a fascinating variety of races':[21] Armenians, Assyrians, Arabs and Circassians, Kurds, Turks and Turkomans. Kurds at Ain Diyar, a village within sight of the twelve-thousand-foot Kurdish mountains, enthralled him as they danced, swaying in the moonlight to 'the beat of drums and the rhythm of their songs'.[22]

Nowhere in letters or The Life of My Choice, did Thesiger mention Laurens van der Post in this context. He had enjoyed van der Post's company in 1943, but he disapproved of books such as Venture to the Interior (1952) and The Lost World of the Kalahari (1958) that van der Post wrote after the war. The mere mention of Venture to the Interior in Thesiger's presence was usually enough to provoke the barbed retort: 'What venture? What interior?'[23] Many years later, Thesiger told an interviewer: 'I've seldom liked anybody more, but there seem to be two contradictory people in him – the one who writes books and the one I met on that occasion.'[24] He and van der Post met again in May 1966, at Addis Ababa, where they attended the twenty-fifth anniversary of Haile Selassie's return to the capital, and were photographed together at a reception. They met occasionally after that, in London. Shortly before Thesiger's eightieth birthday, van der Post wrote to him affectionately: 'I have never thought in terms of birthdays. You have always been the Wilfred I met in the course of the war and with whom I did that strange little foray through Syria and into Armenia ... I would truly love to see you and talk as we used to talk on the road to Lattakia.'[25]

Though he criticised van der Post's writing, Thesiger possessed the same ability 'to develop, and exaggerate',[26] transforming the basic reality of experience into enduring art. There are many examples of this in his writings: in the Sudan, when he claimed to have been knocked down by a lion; in Gojjam, running for 'a couple of miles' after being wounded in the knee; being hunted by Rommel in the Western Desert; standing at the spot where the Greek parachutist was killed. Yet he never intentionally misrepresented facts. Whereas Thesiger devoted seven years to producing a factually precise autobiography, van der Post, according to his biographer J.D.F. Jones, 'went to great pains to camouflage, conceal and recreate the story of his life'.[27]

Beyond the Tigris, Thesiger and van der Post drove past encampments of Shammar Arabs, and spent a day at Jabal Singhar, the Yazidis' holy mountain. Intrigued by customs, Thesiger noted the Yazidis' curious prohibitions: 'they will utter no word beginning with "sh", will never wear blue, nor a shirt open at the neck, will not defecate into water [unlike Sabeans who did this exclusively], nor eat lettuces'. He wrote: 'I was much impressed by their good looks, their dignity and the cleanliness of their dwellings'[28] (this remark is odd, since Thesiger hardly noticed whether or not his surroundings were kept clean, although he took the greatest care of his clothes and his appearance), and described the Yazidis as 'quite extraordinary and very fascinating'. They were 'commonly known as "Devil worshippers", for believing God to be beneficent, they devote their time to placating Satan who is malign ... They dress in white, with high felt caps with turbans twisted round them. Their hair is long and falls to their shoulders in a few thin plaits. They are among the best looking people I have seen. They gave me a feeling of paganism, of strange rites of the sacred groves type, and yet of a friendly ingenuousness. Their houses were spotless like monks' cells. It is impossible to give you an impression of them without showing you photos of them. I took a lot. They are a people I have always wanted to see and they did not disappoint me.'[29] Thesiger vowed he would return; in May 1949 and July 1950 he did so, travelling, either on foot or by pony, the length and breadth of Iraqi Kurdistan.

Thesiger's military service ended 'quite unexpectedly' soon after he returned from leave to Athlit.[30] Haile Selassie, in need of political advisers to help him administer Ethiopia (as Abyssinia was now known*), asked for Thesiger to act as adviser to his eldest son, the Crown Prince Asfa Wossen, whom the Emperor had appointed ruler of the province of Wollo. On 14 October 1943, Thesiger wrote informing Kathleen:

> I am off to Addis Ababa by air for a fortnight tomorrow ... I have been asked for by the Abyssinian Government as personal assistant to the Crown Prince and assistant adviser in his Province [sic] of Dessie. Salary £1200. My first reaction was to refuse as it will mean dropping out of the war, but I am beginning to feel convinced that it is up to me to accept. The Emperor has asked for me personally and it is difficult for him to get the right type who has any sympathy with the Abyssinians. It is a sad fact that nearly all Englishmen who have to deal with them dislike them cordially. I have a sympathy with them and am liked and trusted by them. They have evidently had a row with the previous advisers, and he is now looking round to put in men chosen by himself. The job will be very difficult. Practically everyone will be out to sabotage everything one advises, but it would be interesting and I should like to feel I had helped them to rebuild their country. Here I have talked to various people and gather that HM Government would like me to accept. I am going down there to talk it over with the British Minister and Sandford, and get an idea of how things are before I give an answer. I gather there is a good deal of trouble going on which is an added inducement to accept. I would not take a routine peaceful job, but this promises a good deal of interest and adventure.[31]

Reading these last sentences, Kathleen may have caught a fleeting glimpse of herself at Wilfred's age, and have smiled as she recalled

---

* The name Abyssinia derives from *Habashat*, the name of an immigrant tribe, or else from *habasha*, an Arabic word meaning a medley or a mixture of races. The extinct Ethiop language gave its name to Ethiopia, as Abyssinia was known after World War II. In a speech Haile Selassie made after his return to Addis Ababa in May 1941, he spoke of Ethiopia.

Wilfred Gilbert Thesiger's remark in 1909 after hearing news of riots in Addis Ababa: 'I think Kathleen's Irish blood is stirring at the chance of a ruction.'[32] Thesiger added a cautious afterthought: 'If it proves hopeless I can leave, and the experience will be worthwhile.'[33]

From Addis Ababa, Thesiger flew back to Cairo, and from there to London, where he spent two months' leave with his mother at her flat in Tite Street. En route for London, he had narrowly missed sharing the fate of his brother Dermot: 'I had a low priority for a seat on a plane. Every morning for a fortnight I went to Movement Control to make enquiries. One day the officer in charge said, "Where did you get to last night? We had a cancellation and a seat for you: we rang your hotel but you were out. It was just as well," he continued, "we've just heard the plane was shot down." A few days later I got away and in London I was demobilised.'[34]

SEVENTEEN

Prelude to Arabia

On 9 January 1945, halfway through his two-year contract as Political Adviser at Dessie, Thesiger wrote to the Minister of the Interior at Addis Ababa: 'On my return to Dessie I have discussed the situation with HIH the Crown Prince and it is evident to me that as a result of the restrictions which have been imposed on my movements and activities no useful purpose can be served by my continuing to occupy my present post. I therefore with considerable regret give notice that I am resigning my post as from February 11 1945 up to which date I have served the Ethiopian Government for a full year.'[1]

He had written this with mixed feelings. Uppermost, as he had complained in a letter to his mother of 12 December 1944, were a sense of regret that his posting had been a failure, and a sense of resentment that he had been treated like the 'consul of a suspect power and not like a trusted member of their own government'. He complained that he had been 'informed about nothing, counselled about nothing, and allowed to see nothing' of Wollo, a province with which he was quite unfamiliar. 'Can you wonder,' he sighed, 'that the general feeling on the part of people who have worked in this country is that [the Abyssinians] are hopeless.'[2]

In the same letter Thesiger gave the first brief details of an opportune meeting that was to influence the rest of his life: 'Here I have met a man called Lean, whom I first met in 1933 at the [Natural History] Museum [in London]. He is out here over locust control. He is anxious that I should join them when I have finished here. They are building up an organisation on an international scale, and require experienced travellers who will go on exploring journeys into the Sahara, Central Arabia, the

Yemen and Persia. Rather fascinating work I think ... I should enjoy doing it in Saudi Arabia. I should get endless travel with an object.'³ In the letter Thesiger states that Lean had offered him a job after his contract with the Abyssinian government expired. This offer gave him an even greater incentive to resign from a post he had found increasingly frustrating and unfulfilling. Later versions of these life-changing events are not entirely consistent with the sequence of events reported in Thesiger's wartime correspondence. In *Arabian Sands* (1959) he wrote:

In the last year of the war I was again in Abyssinia, where I was Political Adviser at Dessie in the north. The country required technicians but had little use for political advisers. Frustrated and unhappy I resigned. One evening in Addis Ababa I met O.B. Lean, the Desert Locust Specialist of the Food and Agriculture Organisation. He said he was looking for someone to travel in the Empty Quarter of Arabia to collect information on locust movements. I said at once that I should love to do this but that I was not an entomologist. Lean assured me that this was not nearly as important as knowledge of desert travel. I was offered the job and accepted it before we had finished dinner.⁴

In *Desert, Marsh and Mountain* (1979) Thesiger gave a similar, if shorter, account,⁵ while in *The Life of My Choice* (1987) he wrote: 'in Addis Ababa, at dinner in a friend's house, while I was waiting to leave the country, I happened to meet O.B. Lean ... During dinner he offered me a job, to look for locust outbreak centres in the deserts of Southern Arabia. I accepted at once, without asking about pay or anything else.'⁶ In another version, published in 1994, Thesiger appears to state that he invited himself to a dinner party given by a friend who had mentioned that Lean would be there, and that he was looking for someone to collect information about locusts in Arabia. According to this version, Thesiger had been offered the job and accepted it 'before they had finished the soup'.⁷

A cousin of the film director David Lean, Owen Bevan Lean had previously been employed by ICI, before taking charge of the Middle East Anti-Locust Unit, which was incorporated eventually into the United Nations' Food and Agriculture Organisation. Thesiger's host that evening was David Buxton, a locust specialist whose work in Abyssinia gave him the freedom of movement denied to Thesiger by the Crown Prince.[8]

On 8 January 1945, Thesiger wrote telling Kathleen, 'I am resigning on Feb 11th.'[9] He confirmed to her on 6 February: 'Meanwhile through Buxton here and Lean in Cairo I shall find out a bit more about the locust job.'[10] By now he knew more about the 'locust job's' terms and conditions: 'Good pay, good leave, travel with a purpose in the countries which appeal to me, and opportunities to explore, do natural history work, and study the tribes.' Even so, he urged his mother: 'Don't disapprove of the job till we find out a bit more about it!' (In April he would write: 'They have offered me £800 a year and all expenses paid while travelling.')

Since his teens Thesiger had sought his mother's approval of almost every important decision he made about his life. He was sometimes impulsive and careless when forming snap judgements, yet he could also be surprisingly indecisive. He sought Kathleen's reassurance before making decisions that affected his long-term freedom of choice. After his mother died, he frequently turned for advice to close friends, or to members of his family. Kathleen, no doubt, felt relieved that her eldest son was out of the war, and pleased and proud that he had followed in his father's footsteps as an administrator in Abyssinia. She had been moved by a letter of condolence written to her by the Crown Prince on 28 October 1944: 'It was with profound sorrow that I heard of the death of your beloved son [Dermot] and please accept my deepest sympathy. It has been a great pleasure to see your son Wilfred ...' She prayed that Wilfred would not be hasty, that he would not resign his post without giving it and Haile Selassie's recently liberated, war-ravaged empire a fair trial.

As further evidence that he had not yet accepted Lean's proposal, Thesiger wrote: 'I would not consider any job at the moment if I thought I could get back into a combatant job in the army, but ... I am certain that I should not get a fighting job again. I have been away too long.' He went on: 'Before I can take a job I must get properly out of the army for at the moment I am only on the unemployed list [not fully demobilised, as he would state in *The Life of My Choice*]. Last night I rang up Buxton. He said Uvaroff ['the head of it all in London'] had been in Cairo at a conference ... I gather both he and Lean had been asking about me and that they will offer me the job if I want it ... Anyway I shall keep it in mind but you need not fear that I shall take on anything without consulting you.' As further proof of this, he added: '[Governor-General Sir Hubert] Huddleston from the Sudan is here [at Addis Ababa]. I am seeing him this morning. It is well worth keeping that door open too but I don't really want to go back as a DC ... Sandford dined with the Emperor last night and the Emperor was nice about me and expressed his sorrow that I had not been a bit more patient when things would have come right. However I know that they never would have.'[11]

Looking back on his year as a Political Adviser in Abyssinia, Thesiger contrasted his experiences in the 'antique land' of Gojjam, and later among the Druze and Arabs in Syria, with the lack of courtesy, hospitality and cooperation which made everyday life and work at Dessie so depressing and frustrating. He wrote in *The Life of My Choice*:

> During the campaign in Gojjam I had lived among the Patriots, feeding with them and sleeping in their houses. It had been an enthralling experience to take part in their archaic life, and to witness the customs and courtesies of a bygone age; I often thought how much I should have missed had I been serving with the Frontier Battalion. However, here in Dessie, I had my own house and servants, and I found I was never invited out, except by Asfa Wossen himself. Actually, this was normal behaviour towards Europeans on the part of Abyssinians in the larger towns: even the Sandfords in Addis Ababa were seldom invited to a meal. I inevitably contrasted this treatment with my experience of the Druze and Arabs in Syria. They had welcomed me to their homes, overwhelmed me with hospitality; even strangers, whom I just chanced to meet, had insisted on entertaining me.[12]

Although Thesiger got on well with the Crown Prince, he found Asfa Wossen's evasiveness, endless procrastination and refusal to discuss serious issues both hampering and irksome. 'That year at Dessie,' he wrote, 'was the most frustrating of my life.' Without touring extensively in Wollo province, he felt (quite reasonably) that he could offer the Crown Prince little advice of any practical value. Yet permission for him to travel freely was not forthcoming. On 28 December 1944 Thesiger had an interview with Haile Selassie, which he described in a report summarising the 'Ethiopian Government's refusal to allow [him] to tour the province of Wallo [sic]':[13]

> I said that I had always been anxious to work in the country. I would not have left my regiment which was training to fight with Marshal Tito's men in Jugo-Slavia, at the request of anyone but His Majesty, nor to serve as a civilian in any other country. I would also mention that I had sacrificed my career in the Sudan Political Service to take up my present post, since they had insisted on my resignation before I did so. I had hoped to be of assistance personally to the Crown Prince but had been disappointed over this. My difficulties had arisen over my duties as adviser. I had always maintained, as I did now, that I could not advise on a province about which I knew nothing. Except for Aussa, which I had visited in 1934, I had seen nothing of this province. The roads ran through the lowland, so that in order to acquire a knowledge of the province and its conditions it would be necessary to make several extensive mule journeys ... [Thesiger admitted that he was 'absolutely useless at any form of office work'; travelling about on foot with baggage animals in wild country had a far greater appeal for him, as the Emperor must have known.] In 9 months I had not once been consulted about anything, informed about anything, nor allowed to see anything of the province.[14]

By 1944, the Sultan of Aussa was dead: Mohammed Yayu, who had given Thesiger, the fledgling explorer, permission to follow the Awash river to Lake Abhebad. Ali, his successor, Thesiger noted, was still 'a boy and I gather not much of a personality'.[15]

After Thesiger returned to Dessie from Addis Ababa on 2 January 1945, the Sandfords arrived there, with permission to visit Lalibela and its famous churches hewn like sculpture from solid rock. Thesiger asked the Crown Prince if he might accompany them, but was refused permission to do so. This was the final straw. Thesiger informed Asfa Wossen that he had decided to resign his post; in his typed report, he added that in view of his past treatment he did not consider that he had acted with 'unique haste'.[16]

Thousands of miles away from Ethiopia, Thesiger wrote, 'tremendous events were taking place. In Europe and the Far East, great battles were being fought. The SAS were engaged in the Mediterranean, Wingate was leading his Chindits into Burma, while here was I, stuck in Dessie, achieving nothing. Yet such is the fortuitous nature of events, had I been anywhere else I should never have been offered the chance of exploring the Empty Quarter of Arabia, which was to prove the most important experience of my life.'[17]

EIGHTEEN

Arabian Sands

Before he undertook his first journeys in the Arabian deserts, Thesiger suggested that his mother should read *Alarms and Excursions in Arabia* (1931) by Bertram Sidney Thomas, which described the practically unknown country between the Rub' al Khali, or 'Empty Quarter', and the Indian Ocean. 'I don't think that anyone but Bertram Thomas has visited this area,' he wrote, 'so that it has the attraction of real exploration by camel.'[1] A remark by Thomas in the last chapter of the book must have appealed particularly to Thesiger: 'Liberty is the Badu's darling passion, and this, though it involves a hungry and thirsty existence, he prefers to the comfort and material rewards that go with servitude.'[2]

Writing from Cairo, Thesiger gave Kathleen a résumé of various alternatives open to him, yet left her in no doubt of the life he really longed to lead: 'The war in Europe seems to be over ... I feel that I should volunteer for Burma and the Far East. But I fear getting back into the Army since I so easily may then be given an administrative job somewhere out here or in Europe, and get nowhere near the fighting, and if I cannot get a combatant job I think I am as usefully employed by the locust people and a great deal more interestingly. There are a very limited number of people qualified to do the exploratory work which they want done. If I am back in the Army I lose my freedom of choice.'[3] Echoing Bertram Thomas, he might have added: 'and my liberty'.

Before Thomas began his epic crossing in 1930, the Rub' al Khali was the last extensive area of the world which still remained unexplored, and in that sense 'unknown'. The crossing of this vast desert, Thesiger wrote, 'offered the final and greatest prize of Arabian exploration. Many famous Arabian travellers had dreamed of this achievement but the realisation of the dream was reserved for Bertram Thomas and St John Philby.'⁴ The Empty Quarter was effectively a desert within a desert. The largest sand desert in the world, it covered an area of approximately a quarter of a million square miles. Even after the epoch-making journeys by Thomas in 1931 and Philby in 1932, huge areas of it remained totally unexplored. For Wilfred Thesiger, this was the attraction. He recalled in 1987: 'it was surrounded by a no-man's land of warring tribes. Hitherto I myself had regarded it as inaccessible; now suddenly, utterly unexpectedly, it was within my reach.'⁵ As he contemplated the journey that lay ahead, he once again looked back to his earliest beginnings, where his compelling desire for adventure, exploration and travel originated. 'As a boy,' he wrote, 'I had longed to be an explorer. Early childhood in Abyssinia, and the books I later read, predisposed me to African adventure. Haile Selassie's invitation to his coronation had given me the opportunity to travel in the Danakil country; this had been my introduction to the desert, and my first experience of exploration. Later, during my two years in Northern Darfur and my subsequent journey to Tibesti, I had become increasingly drawn to the desert and to desert peoples. By then, however, the Sahara had been explored, its tribes pacified and administered. During the war, the LRDG and SAS, profiting by the previous experience of [Brigadier Ralph] Bagnold who had explored the Libyan desert by car, had penetrated into its remotest areas: accordingly there was nothing left for me in the deserts of North Africa. Only in Arabia did an enormous tract of desert, which even the Arabs call Rub al Khali, the Empty Quarter, remain largely inviolate, offering the final challenge of desert exploration.' He concluded triumphantly: 'All my past had been a prelude to the years that lay ahead.'⁶

Thesiger was often asked why he had felt compelled to make such dangerous journeys in desert lands, to which he replied that, like the desert tribes, he 'rejected that easier life of lesser men'.⁷ He later refined this statement to 'The harder the life, the finer the person.' To this 'hard and merciless life' shadowed by hunger, thirst, anxiety and fear of attack was added the constant strain of living with 'an alien people who made no allowance for weakness'. Thesiger wrote: 'Often, in weariness of body and spirit, I had longed to get away.'⁸ Yet in his heart he knew that 'it was the very hardness of the life in the desert which drew me back ... the same pull which takes men back to the polar ice, to high mountains, and to the sea'.[9] Though he found it difficult to analyse the motives that drove him to undertake these journeys, or the intangible rewards they brought him, Thesiger considered the 'lure of the unknown', and the continual testing of his resolution and his endurance, absolutely crucial. 'Yet,' he insisted, 'those travels in the Empty Quarter would have been for me a [meaningless] penance but for the comradeship of my Bedu companions.'[10]

Thesiger left Addis Ababa on 17 March 1945, and flew from there to Cairo. In many ways he was sorry to go. He felt sad, too, at parting with Dan and Christine Sandford, who were among his family's oldest and staunchest friends. 'No one could have been kinder to me than they were,' he wrote: '… they are both people for whom I have a profound admiration; they spend all their time doing things for other people and in spite of all the buffetings of fate remain cheerful and kindly.'[11] He outlined for his mother the first journey the Middle East Anti-Locust Unit (MEALU) wanted him to undertake: 'I gather that they wish me to go to Southern Arabia and explore for them a piece of virtually unknown country NE of the Wadi Hadhramaut, between the Rub al Khali and the sea. A really fascinating journey. Bertram Thomas has been across some of it. It would take a couple of months or so and I should start in May and do it by camel. I cannot think of anything I would sooner do … I know you are disappointed that I am not coming straight home but it would be folly to refuse this offer and would probably do in any chance of getting a permanent job with them if I wanted it, and the idea of going there fascinates me.'[12]

News that Douglas Newbold had died in the Sudan upset Thesiger greatly. It was 'a very great blow to everyone who knew him. I feel a great personal loss … for he was a man of great humanity.'[13] His mother wrote that Minna Buckle was retiring as her housekeeper and companion: 'She has been with us all my life,' Thesiger replied, 'but I think that it is probably best.' Closeted in Kathleen's top-storey flat, the two strong-willed elderly women found that living together created unbearable tension. Minna retired to a cottage at Witney in Oxfordshire. She was replaced eventually by Mollie Emtage, a devoted, diminutive middle-aged spinster, of whose 'wonderful food',[14] including her delicious curries, Thesiger 'often thought with longing' when he was alone and starving in the desert.

In April, Thesiger and Vesey Fitzgerald, a locust officer from MEALU, visited Bahrain, Hofuf in the Hassa oasis, Hail and Riyadh. Vesey Fitzgerald taught him something of locusts and their habits. Thesiger had seen locusts in the Sudan, and at Dessie 'had watched swarms rolling across the horizon like clouds of smoke';[15] except for the destruction they caused, until then he had learnt almost nothing about the insects themselves.

Thesiger arrived at Bahrein on 8 May, VE-Day, and stayed with the Political Agent. 'Somehow,' he wrote, 'it is difficult to realize that the war in Europe is over.' Thinking of his brother Brian, who was serving in Burma, he added: 'One can only pray that the war in the Far East won't take too long.'[16] The six-week excursion by car with Vesey Fitzgerald took them right across Arabia from Jeddah, where they stayed with Harold Dickson, the British Agent in Kuwait, at his house on the waterfront where dhows were moored for a mile or more on both sides.[17] Dickson told Thesiger how Bertram Thomas had stayed with them in Kuwait on his way to England on leave before he crossed the Empty Quarter. Dickson knew about Thomas's plan, and could not resist the opportunity to provoke him, saying: 'I'm going to tell you something, but you've got to promise that you won't tell anybody else about it. I've made all the necessary arrangements to cross the Empty Quarter next month.' Thomas rounded on Dickson: 'I should regard that as a very unfriendly action. I have every intention of being the first man to cross the Empty Quarter and to live the rest of my life on the proceeds.' Whenever he repeated this story, Thesiger would add uncritically: 'That gives you another side of Bertram Thomas's character.'[18]

Thesiger mentions in an obituary he wrote of Bertram Thomas for the *Geographical Journal* in 1951 that he had twice met Thomas briefly in Cairo during the war. The Bait Kathir tribesmen with whom Thesiger travelled in the Rub' al Khali in 1945–46 spoke of Thomas, who had been the first European to come among them. Thomas had won their respect, and Thesiger realised that he had been welcomed by them because he belonged to 'the same tribe as Thomas'.[19] To his regret he never met Thomas again. The concluding paragraphs of the third chapter of

Arabian Sands Thesiger reproduced, almost word for word, from his obituary of Thomas. While Thomas had crossed the Empty Quarter 'by the easiest way', his journey was nevertheless a tremendous achievement. Philby's route was 'far more difficult' and the four hundred miles he covered between wells in the western Sands near his journey's end, in Thesiger's view, would 'always be an epic of desert travel'.[20]

Instead of May, Thesiger's first journey along the edge of the Rub' al Khali was put back to October, so following his journey with Vesey Fitzgerald he visited the Assir, bordering north Yemen and the Red Sea. He climbed to nine thousand feet over mountains forested by junipers and wild olives, and found a marvellous profusion of wildflowers – jasmine, honeysuckle, pinks, primulas, and his favourites, wild roses. Here he took about 250 photographs, using the same Leica 35mm miniature camera he had used since 1934. He thought the 'mountain Arabs … a very lovely race … their hair long down over their shoulders with sweet-smelling herbs in it'.[21] Many boys and young men possessed the androgynous looks he much admired, and sometimes described as 'disturbingly beautiful'.[22] In June he visited the hot coastal plain of Tihama, where once again he took 'a great many photos'.[23] He rhapsodised in his field diary: 'I have never seen such a beautiful people. Any individual child or youth would be remarkable elsewhere. They are too lovely to last in this utilitarian age, belonging to "that other Eden".'[24]

Thesiger spent June till September 1945 on leave in London. Of his mother's Chelsea flat he wrote: 'You have created a great thing for me … and I love it. It has exactly the same intimate friendly feel as The Milebrook always had, and I feel sure the Legation had, for you would create it wherever you were, and it is the essence of a home.'[25] Despite the new flat's relaxing atmosphere, Wilfred's almost too-precious relationship with his mother had been temporarily clouded by his apparent indifference to her struggle to recreate a life for herself from the wreckage of grief, loss and upheaval that followed Dermot's death, Reginald Astley's illness and death, and her removal from The Milebrook. By then Kathleen was sixty-five, and showing signs of ageing. She looked gaunt and lined, and suffered from chronic sciatica. Outgoing and naturally gregarious, she had continued to live a varied social life, yet there were times when she felt dispirited and lonely. Wrapped up in himself and his plans, Thesiger appeared not to notice, to be quite unaware how his self-preoccupied silences distressed Kathleen. 'I am sorry,' he wrote, 'if I was often silent and uncommunicative but I loved being in the room with you even when I was reading and you were playing Patience, and strangely it is of those moments that I think, rather than of our parties, for then I had you to myself. You mean so very much to me and it is my misfortune if I do not make you feel this. That is why I hate it when you say you no longer feel that you have anything to live for. The most important thing would have gone out of my life.'[26]

Thesiger's relationship with his mother was affectionate and complicated. He often felt exasperated by Kathleen's attention-seeking and possessiveness, yet he allowed her to manipulate his emotions. He needed her constant approval, was fiercely protective of her, took responsibility for her, admired her in his charmingly awestruck way, loved her unconditionally, and (coached by subtle promptings) never ceased to be grateful to her for all she had done for him and his brothers. In *The Life of My Choice* he described her as 'a sociable person with a remarkable gift for friendship and an immediate understanding of others, especially the young ... Though not intellectual, my mother was intelligent ... She was generous by nature and had an Irish sense of hospitality, combined great pride with high standards and absolute loyalty. She had instinctive good taste, especially in her dress, and whatever the setting she always looked right. Above all, my mother was fun to be with.'[27] Thesiger's own tastes were notoriously conservative and traditional, yet he praised Kathleen's clothes as 'contemporary and elegant'. By comparison he thought his mother's friend Lady Mary Maxwell, mother of Gavin Maxwell, 'looked positively Dickensian',[28] and described Sylvia Pankhurst (two years younger than Kathleen), whom he met at Addis Ababa in December 1944, as 'an indomitable and courageous old lady, but rather shabby in appearance'.[29]

At Kathleen's request, Thesiger sent her from Cairo 'a registered parcel with 2 pairs of Nylon stockings no 9½. I found it difficult to get the right size,' he apologised. 'Plenty of size 9. I hope they will be what you want and the right colour. They seemed alright to me.'[30] In Cairo he met Brian's godmother Judith Doughty-Wylie, who was working as a volunteer at an air force canteen in Heliopolis. To his dismay, she told him that Brian had not written to her 'for months, though Diana has her new address'. Judith 'was very nice about Brian', but Thesiger felt she had been hurt by his failure to write to her. Tactfully, he suggested that Brian must have written to her previous address by mistake.³¹ Thesiger said: 'Brian did ignore his godmother and this upset her. Instead of leaving her money to him, as she had promised she would, she left it instead to his daughters. It was his fault entirely, for paying her so little attention.'³²

Back at Salala after a ten-day journey to the two-thousand-foot-high mountains of Jabal Qarra, Thesiger wrote: 'Last night I tried on all my Arab kit, dagger and all, and really thought that I looked rather well.'³³ In *Arabian Sands* he explained the necessity for doing so, while deprecating the effect of Arab clothing on his appearance. 'To have worn European clothes would have alienated these Bait Kathir at once, for although a few of them had travelled with Bertram Thomas, most of them had not even spoken to an Englishman before. I wore a loin-cloth, a long shirt, and a head-cloth with the ends twisted round my head in their fashion. None of these Bait Kathir wore the black woollen head-rope which is a con-spicuous feature of Arab dress in the north. As this was the first time I had worn Arab dress I felt extremely self-conscious. My shirt was new, white and rather stiff, very noticeable among the Bedu's dingy clothes. They were all small men, and as I am six foot two I felt as conspicuous as a lighthouse and as different from them as one of the RAF [at Salala].'³⁴

Starting from Salala in October, a two-month journey to Mughshin oasis gave Thesiger his first glimpse of the Empty Quarter. He was accompanied by thirty Bait Kathir, ragged-haired tribesmen whose wild appearance evoked memories of Danakil in Abyssinia. He had become fluent in the Arabic dialects of the Sudan and of Syria, where among the Druze he spoke nothing but Arabic for months on end. But these dialects bore little resemblance to the Bait Kathir's: neither to its pronunciation, nor its intonation, nor its often archaic vocabulary. When he recalled his first attempts to converse with the Bait Kathir, Thesiger shrugged aside these difficulties, merely remarking: 'I still spoke Arabic haltingly, for I am a bad linguist.' When he asked them about the Rub' al Khali, 'the goal of my ambitions', 'No one had heard of it. "What is he talking about? What does he want?" "God alone knows. I cannot understand his talk." At last Sultan [of the Bait Kathir] exclaimed "Oh! he means the Sands," and

I realised that this was their name for the great desert of southern Arabia.'[35]

Thesiger wrote to his mother in January 1946 from Salala: 'I got back from the Mughshin trip yesterday and sent you off a wire ... I had a most successful trip, got to all the places I wanted to see and collected a very great deal of information. I went off NW from here to the end of the wadis Mitan and Fasad, where they end against the Sands, then to Mughshin, and NW into Ghanim, and later NE to Sahma almost to the quicksands of Umm es Samin [sic] and back down the Wadi Katibit to Undhur. In all I was away 64 days some 34 of them in the Sands. In all we saw some 50 Arabs, and no one for about 50 days so that it may well be called the Empty Quarter.'[36] He described flat gravel plains that extended '150 miles inland' to the Rub' al Khali as 'a spacious and curiously satisfying country. There the Sands were quite different to what I expected. Great mountainous dunes 300 feet high ... The dunes were sometimes connected by ridges, sometimes separate, sometimes close together and sometimes far apart. The colouring of the Sands was of an indescribable purity and with the richness of a Bokhara carpet. Deep red on white, cream on white, or pink on green gold ... I liked the 30 Arabs who came with me enormously and got on well with them ... The secret is to live like them and with them, and to share your food with them and not keep anything apart for yourself, to show you can go as short of water, walk as far, and ride as far without getting tired, and then they accept you.'[37] He added a shrewd comment: 'Also of course I am paying them very well,' showing he was already aware of the Arabs' 'intense love of money',[38] that contrasted sharply with their readiness to share. 'It is characteristic of Bedu,' he wrote, unconsciously holding a mirror to his own quixotic nature, 'to do things by extremes, to be either wildly generous or unbelievably mean, very patient or almost hysterically excitable, to be incredibly brave or to panic for no apparent reason.'[39] He confided to Kathleen: 'I am now longing to get off again to the freedom of the inner deserts. It is curious how the desert satisfies me and gives me peace. You cannot explain what you find there to those who don't feel it too, for most people it is just a howling wilderness.'[40]

Thesiger had found the country round Mughshin stricken by years of drought. The Bait Kathir told him that no floodwater had reached

Mughshin from the Qarra mountains for the past twenty-five years;. consequently this was not an 'outbreak centre' for locusts. He decided after he returned to Salala to travel from there to the Hadhramaut, westwards along the southern edge of the Empty Quarter, to discover whether floods ever reached there from the Mahra mountains along the coast. 'No European had yet travelled in the country between Dhaufar and the Hadhramaut,' he wrote. 'I had met with one of the Rashid sheikhs, called Musallim bin al Kamam, on my way to Mughshin, and had taken an immediate liking to him. I asked him to meet me with some of his tribe in Salala in January [1946], and to go with me to the Hadhramaut ... The Rashid were kinsmen and allies of the Bait Kathir ... They were as fine-drawn and highly-strung as thoroughbreds. Beside them the Bait Kathir seemed uncouth and assertive, lacking the final polish of the inner desert.'[41]

From January to March he travelled in the Hadhramaut, 'an easy journey since there had been exceptionally good rains in the desert'.[42] Thesiger's party encountered 'a fair number of Arabs', from whom they obtained milk and meat. Despite raids by Dahm tribesmen from Yemen, making 'everyone pretty jumpy', the journey was uneventful. Thesiger wrote: 'I did not get into the Sands on this trip but came along the steppe about 2 days to the south of the Sands by the Wadi Hadhramaut, Sanau and Thamud ... The trip interested me a lot for I am the first person to have been through that area I think ... The existing map is fantastically out, the wadis marked on it being 200–250 miles out of place.' He asked Kathleen to tell Francis Rennell Rodd at the RGS that he had made a 'fairly careful' compass traverse of the whole area he had covered, 'which should get it a bit more exact'.[43] Since his maps were so inaccurate, Thesiger asked his mother to explain to Dr Boris Uvaroff in London that he had found it difficult to be certain of the location of locust breeding-grounds cited in his reports for MEALU. 'I have now sent him off another large collection of insects,' he added, 'and a collection of practically every plant in the area, also a number of fossils.'[44]

'Uneventful' in the sense that it was neither very difficult nor dangerous, the journey from Salala to the Hadhramaut marked a turning point in Thesiger's travels, since it was here he met the first of two youths from the Rashid tribe who became his inseparable companions until he left Arabia. Salim bin Kabina appeared while Thesiger's party were watering their camels at a well on the Wadi Rahazian, a tributary of Umm al Hait. The yield was poor, and for two days they had worked in relays, day and night. Salim bin Kabina helped them, 'Conspicuous in a vivid red loin-cloth, and with his long hair falling round his naked shoulders ... On the second day he announced that he was coming with me. The Rashid sheikhs advised me to take the boy and let him look after my things. I told him he must find himself a camel and a rifle. He grinned and said that he would find both, and did.'[45]

Thesiger felt immediately attracted to bin Kabina, who was perhaps sixteen, 'about five foot five in height and loosely built'. He moved with 'a long, raking stride, like a camel, unusual among Bedu, who generally walk very upright with short steps. He was very poor, and the hardships of his life had marked him, so that his frame was gaunt and his face hollow. His hair was very long and always falling into his eyes, especially when he was cooking or otherwise busy. He would sweep it back impatiently with a thin hand. He had a rather low forehead, large eyes, a straight nose, prominent cheekbones, and a big mouth with a long upper lip. His chin, delicately formed and rather pointed, was marked by a long scar, where he had been branded as a child to cure some illness. His father had died two years before and it had fallen on young bin Kabina to provide for his mother, young brother, and infant sister. I had met him at a critical moment in his life.'[46] In his Rub' al Khali diary, Thesiger wrote on 1 February 1946: 'Water very scarce at 9 feet. Dug holes all over the wadi bed. Considerable numbers of Mahra turned up including Saad bin Tauni, sheikh of the Harawiz section, also Musellim Garad another Harawiz sheikh and a few Bait Imani, including some of my men who went on ahead to change their camels. Salih bin Mubarak among them. Wandered round collecting [fossils] with Salim bin Mohamed [Thesiger later crossed out 'Mohamed' and wrote 'Kabina'] an Imani boy. He is about 17 and is to be circumcised shortly.'[47] The next day Thesiger wrote: 'Collected with Salim bin Mohamed [Kabina] in the morning. Found 2 fossils. Enlisted Salim at 2 dollars a day.'[48] In his letters Thesiger sometimes referred to bin Kabina as 'Bin K' or 'Binkey'.[49]

In *Arabian Sands*, written less than a decade after their first meeting, Thesiger's memory of Salim bin Kabina was still clear and vivid. Even so,

Idris and Zaghawa tribesmen with a lioness Thesiger had shot. Idris holds Thesiger's .450 Rigby, a powerful double-barrelled rifle he used when hunting dangerous game.

RIGHT: In November 1937 Thesiger and his mother made the first of many visits to Morocco. This is his photograph of Bab Segma, Fez.

Kilwal, Upper Nile, Sudan. Nuer tribesmen, against a backdrop of tall papyrus, watch as a hippo is being harpooned.

ABOVE: Tibesti, August–November 1938. 'It was those three months in the Sahara … that taught me to appreciate things that most Europeans take for granted: clean water to drink; meat to eat; a warm fire on a cold night; shelter from rain; above all, tired surrender to sleep.'

ABOVE: Thesiger's bodyguard, Abyssinia, 1941.

LEFT: This War Office photograph of Thesiger and Haile Selassie at Khartoum in 1940 appeared in the *Sphere*, captioned: 'The Emperor wearing a khaki uniform chats to a British officer in the Sudan.'

BELOW: Colonel Dan Sandford presenting a silver salver to Haile Selassie.

LEFT: Patriot fighters at Shoa, Abyssinia, 1941.

ABOVE: The column of Thesiger's captured Italian troops extended for a mile.

FAR LEFT: Faris Shahin, who served with Thesiger in the Druze Legion. This photograph was taken about 1949.

LEFT: Colonel David Stirling wearing the badge of the SAS, the brigade which he founded and commanded.

A patrol jeep, similar to the vehicle Thesiger used on SAS raids in North Africa, fitted with single and twin Vickers 'K' and a .5MG. Each jeep carried at least twenty four-gallon cans of petrol in addition to food and water for a month.

Crossing the Rub' al Khali, the Empty Quarter, the great sand desert of southern Arabia.

BELOW: Salim bin Kabina of the Rashid bringing fodder for the camels from the lee side of a dune. Bin Kabina first joined Thesiger in February 1946.

BELOW LEFT: Salim bin Ghabaisha of the Rashid, who accompanied Thesiger on his journeys in southern Arabia.

BELOW: Bin Kabina and bin Ghabaisha in Oman, 1950.

ABOVE: Muhammad al Auf, Thesiger's Rashid guide, in 1947. 'He gave me an immediate impression of controlled energy, of self-confidence and intelligence.'

LEFT: Thesiger photographed by bin Kabina in the Empty Quarter.

RIGHT: One of the portraits of Thesiger in Arab dress taken by Ronald Codrai in 1950.

Nasser Hussain, Thesiger's companion and guide in Iraqi Kurdistan in 1950–51.

BELOW: A narrow waterway between tall reedbeds in the Iraqi marshes.

BELOW: Bani Lam tribesmen with a wild boar Thesiger had ridden down and shot from the saddle in tamarisk scrub near the Tigris in June 1958.

ABOVE: Thesiger's *tarada*, 'dark and glistening, slim and high-prowed'.

BELOW: *Taradas* and other craft at a market in the Iraqi marshes.

he referred continually to photographs he had taken of him and other Arabs who accompanied his journeys in Arabia, and these camera portraits give his literary descriptions their extraordinary precision.[50] His detailed observations were stimulated by affection, and combined with his sharp memory, they brought images of bin Kabina vividly to life. Thesiger described how they walked together side by side in the early morning, 'a little apart from the others'. How bin Kabina 'strode along, his body turned a little sideways as he talked, his red loin-cloth tight about his narrow hips ... Attentive and cheerful, he eased the inevitable strain under which I lived, anticipating my wants. His comradeship provided a personal note in the still rather impersonal atmosphere of my desert life.'[51]

Thesiger might have been describing Idris Daud, or Faris Shahin, or Dadi, the long-haired Tedda youth who joined him briefly in 1938 on the way to Tibesti. Idris alone did not possess the androgynous beauty Thesiger admired in Faris Shahin, Dadi, the youths of Tihama, Salim bin Kabina – and bin Kabina's friend Salim bin Ghabaisha, who joined Thesiger and bin Kabina in 1947.

Before he returned again to London on leave, Thesiger travelled in the Assir, the Tihama and the Hejaz. From Jeddah he wrote to Kathleen in June 1946, describing 'a wonderful trip in the Hedjaz mountains which took 3 months instead of 6 weeks as I got permission to go wherever I wished and so made full use of my opportunity'. He had travelled from Qunfidha to Abha and from Abha to Dhahran on the Yemen frontier; then to Sabyia, through some very wild country and back to Abha. By donkey he went from Abha along the crest of the Hejaz mountains: 'Lovely country at 9000' covered with juniper forest and wild olive, with jasmine, honeysuckle and maiden hair fern. Very like Abyssinia in places and in others like Palestine ... if I am going to the Rub al Khali in Nov[ember],' he wrote, 'I shall want a spell at home first. I long more than I can say to see you again. Also it will be grand to see Brian again after all these years ... tell [Roddy, whose aesthetic judgement he trusted] I have untold photos for him to sort.'[52] By then Thesiger had outgrown the self-conscious awkwardness he had felt when first trying on Arab clothes at Salala the previous year. He concluded his 1946 Hejaz diary: 'An interesting evening in the suq. Pass[ed] unnoticed in Arab dress.'[53]

Thesiger's descriptions of his journeys, almost invariably, were distilled and refined, first appearing in diaries, then in letters to his mother, then as carefully composed articles or lectures, with meticulous footnotes, printed in the *Journals* of the Royal Geographical Society or the Society for Asian Affairs (formerly the Royal Central Asian Society), finally in the books he wrote sometimes many years later. He did not begin to write *Arabian Sands*, for instance, until seven years after he left Arabia. Some of the journeys he described in *My Kenya Days* had occurred more than thirty years earlier, while *The Danakil Diary*, describing his first expedition in Abyssinia, was published in 1996, sixty-two years after the original account of this journey appeared as a four-part serial in *The Times*.

Thesiger's account of his two epic crossings of the Rub' al Khali, the Empty Quarter, was subjected to this same extensive editing process. When he undertook these journeys, he stated emphatically that he had no intention, nor had he even considered the possibility, of writing a book about them. The many thousands of photographs he took while travelling in the Arabian deserts and in other lands were a visual documentary and *aide-memoire* which complemented his diaries and letters. If we accept that Thesiger never intended to write a book about his journeys in Arabia, the suggestion that he do so was made, unsuccessfully, for the first time in 1947, a decade earlier than has generally been supposed. In that year Laurence Kirwan, then Director and Secretary of the Royal Geographical Society, wrote to Thesiger's mother: 'I have not been idle as regards the subject of our telephone conversation the other day ... I believe that John Murray's are the most appropriate publishers. I have interested John Murray in this idea, and I am quite sure that more will be heard of it. I have in mind that following this book, a further book might be prepared on the Sultanate of Muscat, which is, from many points of view, a little known area, and Wilfred would be in an excellent position to write it ... As regards the first book, I trust that I will have support from you and from Roddy, and as soon as Wilfred comes back I will give a party and introduce him to Jock Murray, who is the most active partner in the firm and a great friend of mine. They have, as you know, published Freya Stark's books for some years, and also Van Der Meulen's books on the Hadhramaut, of which the latest [*Aden to the Hadhramaut*] is shortly appearing.'[54]

It is possible that Kathleen had wanted Thesiger to write a book – not only because his journeys in Arabia were important and their story deserved to be published, but because she saw writing as a means of keeping him near her at a time when she felt, more than ever, alone and vulnerable. Instead of settling in England with his wife and children, Brian had been considering an army posting in Malaya. Thesiger consoled Kathleen: 'I am sorry Brian is restless. I agree with you that if he does go off to Malaya he will probably wreck his home life. He has got a good and interesting job in the War Office and I hope he will find a home and settle down.'[55] Roderic's first marriage, to Mary Rose Charteris, was dissolved in 1946. That year he married Ursula Joan Whitworth, who bore him a son and daughter. Having trained at the Courtauld Institute after coming down from Oxford, Roderic pursued a highly successful career in fine art, first as an assistant in the Tate Gallery; then as expert on modern paintings at Sotheby's, afterwards with Colnaghi from 1955 to 1971, as Director in charge of Old Master paintings and finally as Chairman.

In October 1946, when Thesiger began his first crossing of the Empty Quarter, writing for him was still largely a means to an end, confined to letters and the factual, often prosaic observations he recorded in ink or pencil in the large quarto and foolscap diaries he carried in his saddle-bags. Photography, on the other hand, offered him an emotional and creative outlet; hoping to improve both the technical and artistic quality of his pictures, he bought a new Leica 35mm camera from James Sinclair, the photographic dealers in Whitehall who for years developed and printed his photographs for him. Writing to his mother from Cairo on 19 March 1946, he had remarked: 'I have got some really good photos this time of my journeys. The new camera seems to have been worth it.'[56] It may be that the extreme risks and privations of desert travel in Arabia had also sharpened Thesiger's awareness of his surroundings. As a photographer, perhaps for the first time he began to appreciate the desert's creative potential. He had always preferred drawings or etchings to paintings in oil and watercolours, and he preferred the subtler shadings of monochrome film to colour (he admitted later that this derived from the days when colour film still gave unpredictable results). Instead of features like hills and rivers, the desert offered clean lines, sculpted forms and space. The inspirational effect of space in deserts was

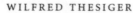

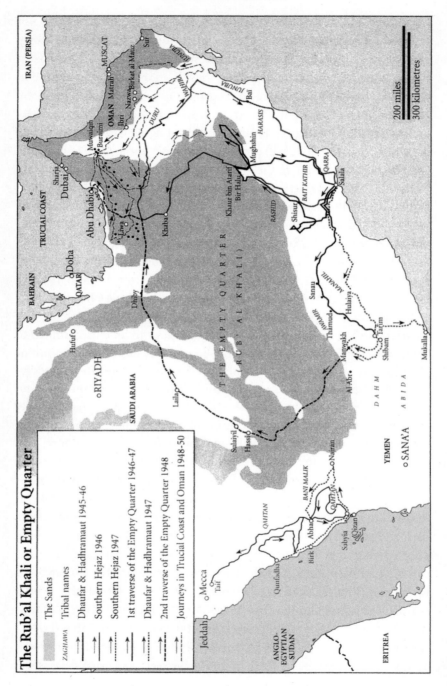

The Rub'al Khali or Empty Quarter

The Sands

ZAGHAWA Tribal names

→ Dhaufar & Hadhramaut 1945–46

→ Southern Hejaz 1946

→ Southern Hejaz 1947

→ 1st traverse of the Empty Quarter 1946–47

→ Dhaufar & Hadhramaut 1947

→ 2nd traverse of the Empty Quarter 1948

→ Journeys in Trucial Coast and Oman 1948–50

200 miles

300 kilometres

similar, indeed, to the spiritual uplift inspired by height and space in a cathedral. As well as taking close-up portraits, Thesiger photographed Bait Kathir, Rashid and other nomadic Bedu tribes in their vast landscapes of wind-carved sand, dominated by immense dunes, to which they and the camels they rode or led added life, movement and a sense of human scale.

Thesiger's photographs of bin Kabina and bin Ghabaisha expressed his attraction to these young Rashid no less eloquently than the word portraits he wrote in *Arabian Sands*; photography complemented his prose, which gave movement, sound and tactile realism to his beautiful images of the Bedu in various attitudes of repose. The photographs which helped him to portray in words his companions and their desert surroundings were informed visual statements, narrative works of art, self-defining visions of Thesiger's desert world. Less impermeable than some of his writing, more openly expressive of his emotions, Thesiger's photographs of Idris, Faris, bin Kabina, bin Ghabaisha and others who lived with him or accompanied him throughout his travels, broke the emotive code embedded in his writing, denoted sometimes by key words such as 'companion', 'comrade', 'retainer', 'servant'. Whatever his feelings towards them as adolescents might have been, Thesiger denied absolutely that they amounted to anything more than an aesthetic appeal. 'They were beautiful,' he said, 'and I enjoyed looking at them.'[57] The need for continence and the mastery of his emotions were nevertheless among the hardest privations imposed by Thesiger's desert journeys with the Bedu. The constant turmoil of emotional frustration, as much as his companions' often maddening generosity to passing strangers, may have provoked his 'withdrawn and irritable' moods, and his occasional, uncontrollable outbursts of temper.[58] He wrote in *Arabian Sands*:

Homosexuality is common among most Arabs, especially in the towns, but it is very rare among the Bedu, who of all Arabs have the most excuse for indulging in this practice, since they spend long months away from their women. Lawrence described in *Seven Pillars of Wisdom* how his escort made use of each other to slake their needs, but those men were villagers from the oasis, not Bedu ... I myself could not have lived as I did with my companions and been unaware of it had it existed among them;

we lived too close together ... Once when we were staying in a town on the Trucial Coast, bin Kabina pointed out two youths, one of whom was a slave, and said that they were sometimes used by the Sheikh's retainers. He evidently thought the practice both ridiculous and obscene.[59]

On 26 February 1947 Thesiger wrote to Kathleen, giving his unvarnished earliest account of his first crossing of the Empty Quarter:

I have got back to Salalah after accomplishing all and more than I had hoped to achieve ... I have just finished what is I think the hardest journey yet done in Arabian exploration and one of the longest ... I went up to Mughshin and from there set off to cross the Empty Quarter across the waterless Eastern half. I started from here 30 strong but only took 10 Arabs from Mughshin, giving the rest a rendezvous 2 months later on the southern coast. We watered next 4 days later in Ghanim where I went last year, and from there set off across the sands on the next waterless 300 mile lap. We expected to find Arabs after 4 days in Ramlat el Ghafa on some grazing there and counted on changing our worst camels. The others came from the steppes to the south, and I soon saw that the vastness and emptiness of these sands was breaking their nerve. It took us 4 days across rather grim country to get to Ramlat el Ghafa, and when we got there, though we found some Arabs, their camels were in very poor condition. I therefore decided to send 4 of my party back.

The sheikh, a man called Sultan, refused to go on unless we all went on, thereby trying to compel me to turn back. The herds boy had added to their alarm by a story of two Arabs on camels in excellent condition and with 4 skins of water who perished trying to get across last year. When it was apparent that Sultan would not come on I asked Mohamed, my guide, and Bin Kabina if they would come with me, and both said 'Yes': so I divided the food and water. Two others were now shamed into coming with me, but the others meant to get back. The five of us therefore pushed on. We had sufficient water for 2 pints each daily, and 40 lbs of flour for 5 of us for a month, but nothing else, for although we had started from Salalah with a great quantity of food, the Bedu had eaten a 3 months' supply in less than one month. You cannot stop them eating when they have food. I was worried about our water for it gave us no margin, but for food we could if driven to it eat one of our camels and anyway could last many days without any.

The sands were unbelievable – mountainous dunes rising 700' high from the gravel floor below so that I had a constant delusion of being among mountains, and the salt flats shone like blue lakes from below. I have never heard of such dunes, over which we had to get our camels. We rode night and day to get across before our camels failed us or our water finished. Yet hard work as it was I loved it, and am more than ever bitten by the sands. They are very wonderful and supremely lovely.

We got across in 15 days to Dhafera where there were wells and Arabs, and keeping well out of sight, for these were the Saudi Arabs and I had no permission to be here and did not wish to be endlessly detained, we went up to the edge of Liwa. This is only 3 days from the Persian Gulf, and here are palm groves, settled Arabs, sheep, donkeys, and merchants. I feel, therefore, that I crossed the Empty Quarter, and by a route which even the Bedu practically never attempt, for they use instead the well watered central route by which Bertram Thomas crossed. I sent Bin Kabina and a local Arab into the settlements to buy food for by now we were desperately hungry. The locals refused to accept our M[aria] T[heresa] dollars, demanding rupees and finally for 100 gave them a small sack of very poor quality dates and some wheat grain.

For the next 20 days we lived on boiled wheat grain with a flavouring of dates crushed in very brackish water. I felt we must be living even worse than the average person in Europe, for of this uninviting fare we only got a cupful each once a day. We went on Eastward across the sands until we got to the Wadi el Ain, all wrong on the map. Here we were among the Duru and I had to conceal the fact that I was a Christian and pass myself off as a Sheikh from Syria on his way from the Saud to the Sultan of Muscat. I spent 8 days in the Wadi el Ain, while Mohamed and 3 other Arabs went up to Ibri and bought food, for we were again starving. I should have liked to have visited Ibri, but was afraid of being detained by the Imani's people there. From el Ain we went by the Wadis el Aswad and Ameiri east to near the Wadi Halfain and then down to the coast near Duqum. All the way from Mughshin and here I had been in country never before seen as far as I know by a European, and I have got I think an accurate map of it. The existing map is hopelessly out. Near Duqum I picked up the rest of my party and returned to Salalah. You can tell Francis [Rodd] where I have been, for now that I have done it, it is no longer necessary to keep it secret.

I am now off in 4 days time to Mukalla through the Mahra country nearer the coast than I went last year, for I am anxious to get this bit filled in. I expect it will take 3 months for I don't want to hurry as it will be hot and the country is very bad going and mountainous. I shall have Ruashid with me, five Bedu of Mohomed [sic] and Bin Kabina's tribe. The Bait Kathir are in disgrace for having deserted me in the sands ...[60]

At an evening meeting of the RGS on 20 October 1947, Thesiger gave a more polished account of his first crossing of the Empty Quarter:[61]

Starting from Salala on the Arabian Sea in October 1946, I travelled until May 1947 across the Rub' al Khali to the settlements at Liwa near the Trucial Coast, then back to Salala by the steppes of western Oman and the Jaddat al Harasis, and from there through the northern Mahra country to Mukalla. This journey of two thousand miles was undertaken for the Middle East Anti-Locust Unit and continued the investigations carried out during my journey in 1945–46 ... It was through country not as yet visited by any European, except between Baï and Salala and Salala and Mughshin where Bertram Thomas had travelled in 1928 and 1929 ... Nothing ... was known of the eastern sands except that the Badu [sic] believed them to be waterless and to consist of mountainous dunes.[62]

He described the 'rather grim country' between Ghanim and Ramlat al Ghafa as 'successive desolate crystalline salt flats (sabkha) enclosed by dune masses 300 to 400 feet in height. They were of a rich red gold, veined with silver and very lovely, but devoid of vegetation other than a few patches of [salt bushes].'[63]

Having set the scene for his audience by sketching the great clockwise arc of his crossing, Thesiger went on to fill in the narrative detail. He had provided the twenty-four Bait Kathir and Rashid who accompanied him as far as Ramlat al Ghafa with almost a ton of flour, five hundred pounds of rice, liquid butter, coffee, tea, sugar and dates, the latter imported from Oman and Basra by dhow. Despite a warning that these rations must feed his party for three months, as he had anticipated, the already half-starved tribesmen distributed a large portion among their families, and themselves consumed much of the remainder.

On 25 October 1946, Thesiger's party left Salala and travelled by way of the Umm al Hait wadi to Mughshin. At Shishur they were joined by Salim bin Kabina, Muhammad al 'Auf, who became Thesiger's indispensable guide, and Sheikh Muhsin bin Khuzai. Muhsin had been badly wounded by raiders two years previously. Nearing the well at Mughshin, his camel stampeded and he was thrown, smashing his thighbone and reopening his old wounds. Thesiger set his broken thigh and gave him an injection of morphine, but was obliged to leave the old man behind in a makeshift shelter, shaded by a ghaf tree. When Thesiger returned to Salala on 23 February 1947, to his delight Muhsin was among the friends waiting there to greet him, having arrived at Salala a few days earlier, 'tied on to his camel'.[64]

In the barren wastes between Mughshin and Ramlat al Ghafa, according to Thesiger, 'It was soon apparent that the Bait Kathir, and in particular Sultan, were losing their nerve. Our water was dangerously short and they were lost and bewildered among these great dunes ... dismayed by the increasing weakness of their camels and by the continued lack of grazing.'[65] Ramlat al Ghafa was 'very beautiful'. Larks rose in song from yellow-flowering tribulus among the great dunes of red sand, 'shot with silver and gold'.[66] When it became clear that Sultan and the Bait Kathir were determined to go no further, Muhammad al 'Auf, bin Kabina, Musallim bin Tafl and Mabkhut bin Arba'in agreed they would come with Thesiger across the Empty Quarter. Years later, bin Kabina confirmed that al 'Auf, who had been their spokesman, had said, 'We're your men, we'll go where you go.'[67]

From Ramlat al Ghafa, Thesiger wrote,

we travelled north-west through mountainous dunes interspersed with white salt flats. Our five riding camels were from the steppes and these steep climbs and long slithering descents frightened them ... The moon was young and we travelled on through the first half of the night, our camels stepping out into the cold across the crackling salt flats beneath the dimly seen, unreal sand dunes, encouraged at times by the full throated roaring of Arab war songs. Beyond Sabkha Takha we came to the 'Uruq al

Shiban [sic], a rose red, mountainous range of sand, very lovely in the light of dawn as it rose in jagged peaks and spurs 500 to 700 feet above the ice-coloured sabkhas. Unexpected cumulus clouds banked up at noon to add to the illusion that we were high among alpine peaks with frozen lakes of blue and green far below. Running north-north-east and south-south-west and only to be crossed in very few places, the 'Uruq al Shiban are almost certainly the highest of the dunes in the Rub' al Khali ... It was cold by day and bitter cold by night. We travelled for two days between barren, sheer-sided dunes of yellow sand, across sterile salt flats whose crusts were cruel to our naked feet. We made good progress, travelling late into the night. Once we were halted by a total eclipse of the moon. My companions showed no uneasiness, singing: 'Allah is eternal/The life of man is short/ The Pleiades are overhead/And the moon among the stars.'[68]

Describing their ascent of the Uruq al Shaiba in *Arabian Sands*, Thesiger wrote how his party had manhandled the 'trembling, hesitating' camels 'upward along great sweeping ridges where the knife-edged crests crumbled beneath our feet. Although it was killing work, my companions were always gentle and infinitely patient. The sun was scorching hot and I felt empty, sick and dizzy. As I struggled up the slope, knee-deep in shifting sand, my heart thumped wildly and my thirst grew worse. I found it difficult to swallow; even my ears felt blocked, and yet I knew that it would be many intolerable hours before I could drink. I would stop to rest, dropping down on the scorching sand, and immediately it seemed I would hear the others shouting, "Umbarak, Umbarak"; their voices sounded strained and hoarse.'[69]

From 'the gentle downs of Ramlat al Kharfiya' and 'the hard red downs of Ramlat al Hamrur', Thesiger's party reached the sands of Dhafra, and on 13 December the Khaba well. Three days later they stopped near Bir Balagh, on the southern edge of Liwa oasis, where Thesiger had hoped that they would be able to buy a goat, but instead they managed only to obtain wheat grain and two small packages of very poor dates that would provide their only food until they reached Khaur Kadri, in the Wadi al 'Ain, on 3 January 1947. In Rabadh, as they struggled across 'an endless sea of crescent dunes', a herdsboy tending his camels led them to a Rashid camp. Here five Arabs armed with rifles received them. Thesiger and his companions sat on the sand and waited until the Rashid asked, 'What is your news?' to which they gave the formal reply, 'The news is good.' The Rashid then gave them coffee flavoured with cardamom, while they exchanged further greetings and information. When the herds were driven in at sunset, they were given bowls of frothing camels' milk, and afterwards feasted on the meat of a freshly slaughtered camel, 'with the princely hospitality of the true Bedu'.[70]

To the east of Rabadh at Khaur Kadri, at the well they encountered a small caravan of Duru', traditional enemies of the Bait Kathir. Though Thesiger found them 'extremely hospitable', these Duru' seemed 'tense and watchful'. His companions were apprehensive of the Duru', and to avoid arousing suspicion, and to enable the Rashid to visit the 'Ibri market for supplies, Thesiger masqueraded as a Syrian travelling from Riyadh to visit the Sultan in Dhaufar: 'news that I was a Christian must not get abroad, since otherwise the Duru' might chase us back into the desert or the Wali [at 'Ibri] send soldiers to detain us ... The dunes and bushes hid me at the hours of prayer and the excuse that I was suffering from fever avoided unnecessary contact with our occasional visitors.'[71] Thesiger's companions assured him the Duru' would never have met a Syrian; besides which, his ragged beard, dark sunburnt skin and travel-stained clothes made his imposture of a Syrian traveller sufficiently convincing. Even Thesiger's unusual height, compared with the smaller Arabs, did not arouse suspicion. He wrote: 'Had I tried to go there from the south the Duru would certainly have identified me with the Christian who had travelled there the year before with the Bait Kathir and held me up. Coming from the north my rather unconvincing disguise passed muster because no one expected me to be a European.'[72]

In the desert, Thesiger and his companions thought incessantly of food; even their frugal evening meal was something to which they looked forward eagerly. Thirst, he discovered, troubled the Rashid less than hunger. The Arabs would eat flesh of almost every kind: 'hares, wild cats, foxes, fennecs, hyaenas, which they call the prophet's ram, hedgehogs, jerboas, jirds, skinks, lizards, and eagles'.[73] What constituted lawful food, he noted, varied from place to place, and 'usually bears little relation to reason'.[74] Only the meat of a wild ass appeared to disgust the Rashid, yet bin Kabina 'was always sickened by lizard-meat'.[75]

Thesiger enjoyed telling, against himself, the story of a hare the Rashid killed near Rabadh:

…Musallim suddenly jumped off his camel, pushed his arm into a shallow burrow, and pulled out a hare. I asked him how he knew it was there, and he said that he had seen its track going in but none coming out. The afternoon dragged on until we reached the expanse of small continuous dunes which give these sands the name of Rabadh. There was adequate grazing, so we stopped on their edge. We decided to eat the rest of our flour, and Musallim conjured three onions and some spices out of his saddle-bags. We sat round in a hungry circle watching bin Kabina cooking the hare, and offering advice. [Thesiger did exactly the same in London or Maralal, urging on whoever was cooking a meal, asking continually how it was progressing and when it would be ready to eat.] Anticipation mounted, for it was more than a month since we had eaten meat, except for [a] hare that al Auf had killed near the Uruq al Shaiba. We sampled the soup and decided to let it stew just a little bit longer. Then bin Kabina looked up and groaned, 'God! Guests!' Coming across the sands towards us were three Arabs. Hamad said, 'They are Bakhit, and Umbarak, and Salim, the children of Mia,' and to me, 'They are Rashid.' We greeted them, asked the news, made coffee for them, and then Musallim and bin Kabina dished up the hare and the bread and set it before them, saying with every appearance of sincerity that they were our guests, that God had brought them, that today was a blessed day … They asked us to join them but we refused, repeating that they were our guests. I hoped that I did not look as murderous as I felt while I joined the others in assuring them that God had brought them on this auspicious occasion. When they had finished, bin Kabina put a sticky lump of dates in a dish and called us over to feed.[76]

The four Rashid returned from 'Ibri after seven days, bringing flour and seven packages of excellent dates. From Khaur Kadri the party rode on beyond the Wadi 'Amairi across the gravel plains of the Hadba to the Wadi Musallim and, two days further on, the Ghaba where ghaf trees grew in extensive woodlands. On 31 January 1947, they reached Baï. 'Old Tantaim' of the Bait Kathir gave them an emotional welcome, 'with tears running down his face, too moved to be coherent', bitterly angry with the members of his tribe who, by deserting Thesiger at Ramlat al Ghafa, had brought 'black shame' upon them.[77]

From Baï they continued south over the Jaddat al Harasis, and three weeks later they arrived back at Salala. Thesiger remained there for a week, writing up his diaries, sorting through his collections of insects, plants and fossils, and arranging with the Rashid the journey from Salala westward to Mukalla that would complete his survey of this area in southern Arabia. He realised that MEALU attached far more importance to his return journey through Oman than to his crossing of the Empty Quarter, which to him had been of infinitely greater significance. He wrote: 'I had come to Dhaufar determined to cross the Empty Quarter. I had succeeded and for me the venture needed no justification.'

At Salala, 'It was a pleasant change talking English instead of the constant effort of talking Arabic; to have a hot bath and to eat well-cooked food; even to sit at ease on a chair with my legs stretched out, instead of sitting on the ground with them tucked under me. But the pleasure of doing those things was enormously enhanced for me by the knowledge that I was going back into the desert; that this was only an interlude and not the end of my journey.'[78] As much as Thesiger revelled in contrast, he craved the stimulus of continual change. Without it, he soon grew restless. In *Arabian Sands* he ascribed to these desert journeys both an aspirational and a spiritual importance: 'The Empty Quarter offered me the chance to win distinction as a traveller; but I believed that it could give me more than this, that in those empty wastes I could find the peace that comes with solitude, and, among the Bedu, comradeship in a hostile world. Many who venture into dangerous places have found this comradeship among members of their own race; a few find it more easily among people from other lands, the very differences which separate them binding them ever more closely. I found it among the Bedu.'[79] The comradeship he found among 'people from other lands', and his attraction to the East, had much in common with the Orientalist painters' formula: colour (embracing a rich variety of costume, customs and surroundings), danger, mystery, romance and, compared to Western Europe, a greater degree of sensual freedom. Due perhaps to the influence of his early upbringing in Abyssinia, Thesiger had an aesthetic preference for dark-skinned peoples. In theory this excluded Europeans, but in practice he was attracted as much by Mediterranean-dwellers such as Greeks and Italians as he was by Africans, Arabs, Afghans and Indonesians.

As for Thesiger's pursuit of 'the peace that comes with solitude', by his own admission he found solitude unbearable. His friend John Verney described him as someone who 'hates being left alone for more than a minute. He may travel in remote parts of the world, but always accompanied by a crowd of tribesmen, porters or whatever and has probably spent fewer hours in total solitude than, like most painters, I'm accustomed to spend in a week.'[80] By solitude, Thesiger appears to have meant something like the 'clean'[81] space of desert undefiled by modern communications or modern transport, and the harmonious traditional life he found among the tribes who lived there. In *Arabian Sands* he wrote how in England he 'longed with an ache that was almost physical to be back in Arabia ... I wanted the wide emptiness of the sands, the fascination of unknown country, and the company of the Rashid.'[82]

Leaving Salala on 3 March, Thesiger's party reached Mukalla on 1 May. In a letter to Kathleen he described the journey there as 'good and easy': '[I] enjoyed it for I had with me many of the Bedu who were with me last year. We travelled easily and lay up in the middle of the day when it was hot. I think it was worthwhile from a geographical point of view for I established the watershed between the wadis flowing inland, which I crossed last year, and those flowing down to the sea. Existing maps are valueless and I shall have got the main features in anyway. I collected a lot of insects for Uvaroff also plants and reptiles for the [Natural History] Museum and a good deal of information on the tribes who are little known.'[83]

By the pool at Aiyun, near the Kismin pass, Thesiger first saw Salim bin Ghabaisha, who became his close companion and whose beauty he extolled in the pages of *Arabian Sands*:

The boy was dressed only in a length of blue cloth, which he wore wrapped round his waist with one tasselled end thrown over his right shoulder, and his dark hair fell like a mane about his shoulders. He had a face of classic beauty, pensive and rather sad in repose, but which lit up when he smiled, like a pool touched by the sun. Antinous must have looked like this, I thought, when Hadrian first saw him in the Phrygian woods. The boy moved with effortless grace, walking as women walk who have carried vessels on their heads since childhood. A stranger might have thought that his smooth, pliant body would never bear the rigours of desert life, but I knew how deceptively enduring were these Bedu boys who looked like girls ... Bin Kabina urged me to let him join us, saying that he was the best shot in the tribe and that he was as good a hunter as Musallim [bin Tafl], so that if he was with us we should feed every day on meat, for there were many ibex and gazelle in the country ahead of us. He added, 'He is my friend. Let him come with us for my sake. The two of us will go with you wherever you want. We will always be your men.'[84]

That evening, bin Kabina suddenly collapsed. Thesiger told his mother in a letter dated 17 May 1947: 'Binkey gave me a bad fright. We were all suffering from colds on leaving Salala and one evening he collapsed after dinner, quite suddenly and unexpectedly and when I got to him was unconscious, very cold with no pulse. Nothing I could do, including half a flask of brandy, would bring him round. I was desperate for I thought him dying.' Frantic with worry, Thesiger could hardly bear to listen while his companions discussed among themselves whether or not the boy might die. When someone asked where they were going tomorrow, Thesiger declared miserably 'that there would be no tomorrow if bin Kabina died'. All that night he lay awake at the boy's side, so close to him that he could feel the moment he relaxed 'and knew that he was sleeping and no longer unconscious'.[85] 'In the morning he could not speak but gradually recovered and by the evening was alright. He left me in Mukalla the owner of a rifle dagger and 4 camels, well deserved for his loyalty and I hope now set up for life.'[86]

Thesiger's letter continued his description of the journey: 'We had no adventures though there were large parties of Daham [sic] 200 strong raiding to the north of us. I offered to take a pursuit party of my own men, who were well armed, and some of the Manahil tribe, who were being badly looted, and try and bring them to bay but they could not give us accurate enough information of the raiders' whereabouts to make it worthwhile. It would have been interesting if we had managed to find them.'[87] Thesiger's language was strongly reminiscent of his letters describing lion hunts in the Sudan. One of his friends has commented: 'This was typical. It was how he described shooting up German convoys during the war. There's no doubt of it, Wilfred had a killer instinct.'

In his RGS lecture Thesiger gave a different version. He stated that Musallim bin al Kamam and old 'one-eyed'[88] Abdullah bin Misad left his party at Habarut wells and went as envoys to demand the return of a hundred camels looted by the Dahm. A month later, as they were nearing the coast, 'Aidha bin Tanas, the Manahil Sheikh, rode up with thirty men and asked Thesiger's party to join him in pursuit of Dahm raiders who were in the vicinity. Thesiger agreed, provided that 'Aidha bin Tanas provided camels and that his information was reliable. They camped at Faughama, near the shrine of Nabi Hud, for three days, but hearing no further news of Dahm raiders, they travelled on to Humum territory, and from there over the Jol and down the Wadi 'Arf to the coast, arriving at Mukalla on 1 May.

Looking back on the journey, Thesiger praised the Rashid whose comradeship helped him to overcome the physical dangers and hardships of the Empty Quarter, and who gave him their loyalty and protection:

I had come among these Badu as a Christian and a stranger, to share a communal life where privacy was unknown, where every word was public and every action seen. Crowded together in the immensity of the desert, we had lived subject to the rigid discipline of their ways ... For six months I had travelled with them, and between us was the bond of hardships we had endured and the comradeship of desert life. The Mukalla townsmen scorned them as wild Badu from the Rub' al Khali, that half mythical land of emptiness and death, while they in turn viewed these glib fat merchants and their crowded sea port with arrogant disdain. In a day or two they would be gone, Muhammad, Mabkhut, and Bin Kabina, Salih bin Kalut, 'Awad, Bin Ghubaisha [sic] and young Musallim bin Nauf, returning across the mountains to the desert and the harsh freedom of nomad life. The biting cold of winter nights, the blinding heat of summer, hunger verging always on starvation, thirst, drought, and the danger of sudden raids, such were the hardships and hazards of their existence and the secret of their character. Often I had been exasperated by their avarice and wearied by their endless discussions, but I had witnessed their courage and self-reliance, their endurance and their pride of race, and I remembered their patience, generosity, and unselfishness.

Thesiger's conclusion underscored his personal tribute to the Bedu with a bleak prediction: 'I know that they and their way of life are an anachronism and will tend to disappear, but I also know that amongst them in the desert I have found a freedom of the spirit which may not survive their passing.'[89]

Between May and August 1947, Thesiger once again travelled in the Hejaz, the Tihama, the Assir and Najran. He spent September and October on leave in England, staying at his mother's flat in London, where he revised the text of his address to the RGS. In March, the Society's Laurence Kirwan had written to Kathleen that 'a fair amount has been done to it since you last read the original manuscript, but I still think it could be improved in places by cutting and by a slightly greater emphasis on the personal aspect'.[90] (When the literary agent Graham Watson of Curtis Brown read the first drafts of Arabian Sands in 1957, he too advised Thesiger to adopt a more personal tone, to 'loosen up' and confide in his readers.)

MEALU had been very satisfied with Thesiger's investigations, his reports and the specimens of insects and plants he collected for the Locust Research Centre at the Natural History Museum. During a discussion which followed Thesiger's lecture in October, Dr Boris Uvaroff commented: 'The journey which Mr Wilfred Thesiger has so well described was only part of a very large programme designed to bring about the control of the desert locust and to discover its main habitats ... In spite of all the difficulties, which Mr Wilfred Thesiger very greatly understated in his paper, we have obtained as a result of his investigation a fairly good knowledge of which areas are dangerous and which are not ... in addition he found time to bring back other data which have increased very materially our knowledge of this part of Arabia.'[91] That same month MEALU offered Thesiger a permanent appointment in the Hejaz, which he declined. 'The Locust Control Centre,' he wrote, 'offered me a new job supervising the destruction of locusts in the Hajaz, with a good salary [at least £900 a year], all expenses paid, and the prospect of permanent employment. But it was not enough ... The Western Sands offered the challenge which I required in order to find a purpose for another journey. To cross them would be to complete the exploration of the Empty Quarter.'[92]

Writing in the RGS *Journal* in June 1949, Thesiger began the description of his second crossing of the Empty Quarter: 'I had travelled in the southern Rub' al Khali in 1945–46 and crossed it in 1946–47 and the spell of that great desert was upon me. Bertram Thomas had travelled across the central sands from Dhufar to the Qatar peninsula in 1930, and the following year Philby had made his great journey from the Hasa southwards to Mamura and thence westward to Sulaiyil. I had crossed the eastern sands from Dhufar to Liwa, near the Trucial coast, and then back to Dhufar by the Oman steppes. Only the western sands still retained the challenge of the unknown.'[93]

As an overture to this expedition, while he waited for bin Kabina, bin Ghabaisha and Musallim bin al Kamam to join him, Thesiger travelled for a fortnight in the little-known Sa'ar country to the north of the Hadhramaut. He wrote to his mother: 'It is interesting country since it had not previously been visited by Europeans and it enabled me to link my map up with Philby's work further to the west ... I went off among them quite by myself with no one with me whom I had ever seen before ... I found them very friendly and cooperative. I am now well known by name to all these tribes.'[94] To the Bedu he was 'Umbarak', meaning 'Blessed of God' (in his eighties he denied that they had called him 'Umbarak bin London', and insisted he was known as 'Umbarak bin Miriam', or 'Son of Mary' – since Mary was his mother's middle name[95]).

He continued: 'Bin Kabina and another Arab arrived in the Hadhramaut a few days after I had started [for the Sa'ar country] and set out to follow me. They had come some 500 miles since getting word that I was here. Bin Kabina's camel went lame before he caught up with me, so hearing that I had made a date with the Arabs to meet down on the edge of the sands in a fortnight's time he stayed up there to rest his camel, sending his companion on to me to give me word of him ... I hope another one, Bin Ghabaisha, may arrive before I leave.' Anxious about a talk describing his first crossing of the Empty Quarter which he had recorded for the BBC that summer, Thesiger enquired: 'Did my broadcast come off and what did it sound like? I wish I had heard it. I hope it did not sound affected.'[96]

The Sa'ar were known as 'the wolves of the desert'. A large, powerful tribe, they were hated and feared by all the south Arabian desert tribes, whom they raided mercilessly. Yet, like the Duru', Thesiger found the Sa'ar 'a pleasant friendly people, virile and upstanding and innocent of the corroding avarice of the Bait Kathir'.[97] In the Sa'ar country he 'covered a lot of ground visiting Raidat es Saar, Manwakh and Tarim and getting their positions more or less fixed and the course of the big wadis flowing north'.[98] On this journey he took several rolls of photographs, which he posted to London, asking Kathleen to have them developed and printed 'picture postcard size. But not ... several of the same person ... to select the best unless there are two or three exceptional ones and not to print any which are not good. They [Sinclair's] might print the small strips of contact prints as guides.'[99] One photograph showed a bin Maaruf Sa'ar camp at Manwakh: 'Small, black, goat-hair tents ... scattered about over the valley. Naked infants romped round them, and dark-clad women sat churning butter or moved about getting sticks or herding goats.'[100]

Thesiger knew his second crossing of the Empty Quarter would have to be a clandestine affair, as it was fraught with risk:

Two years earlier I had thought of doing this journey. King Ibn Saud [of Saudi Arabia] had however emphatically refused permission when our Ambassador had asked for it – and, in any case, it had been too late in the season to go there when I reached the Hadhramaut from Dhaufar. Now I made up my mind to make this crossing. I should be defying the King, but I hoped that I should be able to water at some well on the far side of the sands and then slip away unobserved. I was certain that some of the Rashid would accompany me, and with them I should have the freedom of the desert. I therefore wired to Sheppard [the British Resident] at Mukalla, asking him to send a messenger to bin Kabina at Habarut, telling him, bin al Kamam, and bin Ghabaisha to meet me in the Hadhramaut at the time of the new moon in November. If I kept the party small I could pay for the journey with the money I had saved. The future could take care of itself.[101]

In his RGS lecture on 4 October 1948, Thesiger did not mention that he had begun his journey without Ibn Saud's permission, but this became clear as soon as he described their arrival at Sulaiyil. It had taken sixteen waterless days to cross the Empty Quarter from Manwakh. Each night they groped in the dark for kindling, lit a fire, then baked the wheat-flour cakes they divided between them and ate dipped in butter. Afterwards they drank the bitter black coffee of the Arabs, flavoured with cardamom.[102] This evening meal never varied; in the morning they ate only a handful of dates. The goatskins that held their precious supply of water sweated badly; in consequence they had lost almost half of it by the time they reached Hassi, near Sulaiyil, on the other side of the Empty Quarter, and were forced to ration themselves to a little more than a pint a day. 'This,' Thesiger wrote, 'was however fresh and very different from the brackish foul-tasting water which we had carried the year before from Ghanim across the sands.'[103]

Writing from Laila, Thesiger told his mother:

The land was full of raids and rumours of raids and the Bedu were full of fear ... [The bin Maaruf Sa'ar] charged us fantastic prices for [camels] but this was to be expected for they realised that we must buy them and that we were pressed for time. We had the very greatest difficulty in getting guides for they said that if we met any Arabs, Yam or Dawasir, before we got to Hassi, they would attack us without any question and that we should be too few to escape. Concerned with the problem of getting across the Empty Quarter I underestimated this danger but realise now that if we had met Arabs we should have been finished. Finally I persuaded two of them to guide me across by promising them each a rifle when we were on the other side ... The grazing was poor and for the first four days we found none and then came on a small patch which gave our camels a good feed. After this we found a little grazing but never very much so that we were concerned for the growing weakness of our camels, but they were in good condition to start with and got us across all right. The sands were disappointing at first, flat and dull, but the last 5 days we got into big dunes the highest of which rose 500' above the gravel flats below. I have I think filled in another big blank. When we got near the far side we found the sands full of recent camel tracks but luckily the winter rain to the North had drawn all the Arabs out of the sands though some had been there 10 days before. I found on reaching Sulaiyil that Ibn Saud had loosed his tribes on the Sa'ar, Kerab and other Hadhramaut tribes, giving them orders to raid and kill all they met in retaliation for these recent raids by the Sa'ar on his tribes. Very big raiding parties out to kill all they met from the south were consequently on their way south as we came north, and at Sulaiyil, where I found the Dawasir fanatical and churlish [Thesiger used the same phrase to describe them in his RGS lecture], they said openly, 'Oh, if only we had caught you before you got here,' and vowed that not one of us would have escaped. So we had our share of luck. At Sulaiyil we were detained by order of the King for entering his kingdom without permission, but only for one night, for Philby spoke on our behalf and we were released next day. I then came up here with my Rashid and Philby came down here to meet me and he could not have been nicer or more complimentary. Really it has been the greatest pleasure to meet him again and to get all the latest news.

From here I now plan to go East to Jabrin, thence to Liwa and Abu Dhabi and from there through the Jabal al Akhdar to Muscat.[104]

He asked Kathleen to write to him at Muscat: 'I shall be going through Abu Dhabi in about 1 month's time and if you need to you could probably get a wire to me there through the Political Officer, Trucial Coast. But don't unless absolutely necessary as I want to slip past unnoticed.'[105]

In *Arabian Sands* Thesiger gave a detailed account of his interrogation by the young, gracious Amir of Sulaiyil:[106] 'Eventually the Amir asked me where we came from and why. I explained that I had come from the Hadhramaut, that I had been exploring and shooting oryx in the Empty Quarter and, having run out of water, had come to the Hassi. I told him that the Rashid, who were with me, knew neither the country nor where we were going. He asked me how in that case we had found the Hassi, and I said that Philby had marked it on the map, and that the two Saar who had been with us had known where it was, having visited it from Najran. I said they had gone back when we reached this well. I insisted that I alone was to blame for having come here, and accepted all responsibility.'[107]

Thesiger told how he and bin Kabina were driven by the Amir to another village and left in a bare, dark room in a castle, where 'the wind banged a loose shutter throughout the night'.[108] He feared that if he was taken away to Jeddah he would never know the fate of bin Kabina and his other companions; that their hands might be cut off as a punishment for bringing a foreigner into Saudi Arabia without permission. After being released, he and bin Kabina returned to Sulaiyil, where the others, including bin Ghabaisha, had spent 'a cold night in the stocks'.[109] That night one of two Yam tribesmen dining with the Amir described how he had killed bin Duailan, known as 'the Cat', a famous raider whom Thesiger had met in the Hadhramaut the previous year. Hanging from the dead bin Duailan's neck were a pair of field glasses which Thesiger had given him.

When Thesiger and St John Philby met at Laila, 160 miles north of Sulaiyil, Philby recounted what had happened after Ibn Saud received the Amir's telegram. 'He was absolutely furious. Asked me who you were; then said he would make an example of you that would stop other unauthorised Europeans from entering his country. I tried to put in a word for you, but he wouldn't even let me open my mouth. I was worried what might happen to you and decided the best thing to do was to write him a letter. I gave it to him in the morning, saying as I did so that it was a man's duty to intercede for his friends. He was quite different from the night before; said at once that he would send off an order for your release.'[110] Thesiger wrote this account in *Arabian Sands*, adding that Philby, whom he had met for the first time in Jeddah on 25 May 1947, and after that in London, was by then 'an old friend of mine and I was delighted to see him'.[111]

In letters to Kathleen from Riyadh, Philby gave first-hand news of Wilfred and of Ibn Saud's response to the telegram sent by the Amir of Sulaiyil:

So he has again crossed the Empty Quarter, and obviously along the very line I suggested when we discussed things in your flat that night [in September–October 1947] ... I was beginning to wonder when he would appear on this side of the sands, when on the evening of the 25th [January 1948] the king received a telegram from the Amir of Sulaiyil, announcing the arrival there of a party of Arabs from the Hadhramaut with an Englishman called Thesiger. The king was very angry ... However it was very lucky that I was present that evening: otherwise I might never have heard of the matter. Who is this fellow? asked the king, and nobody present could enlighten him; so I said: As a matter of fact he is a friend of mine, who has been wandering about Arabia a lot of late in connection with the Locust Mission's work; and I expect they ran out of water or food, and were forced by circumstances to make for the nearest wells, without any intention of infringing your immigration laws. In the circumstances, I said, it would be a gracious act if your Majesty would pardon their offence. Certainly not, replied the king; they had no right to come without permission, and if we overlooked their offence, we would have others doing the same thing. As the court was in full session, and the king does not like being argued with in public, I thought it best to drop the matter. Yesterday morning however I wrote a tactful letter, which I handed to the king at his morning session; and last night, when I arrived at the palace for a dinner party, the Deputy Foreign Secretary informed me that the king had instructed him to tell me that my plea for pardon and release of the offending party had been granted by him! ... After dinner I went up to the king to thank him for his kindness; and he replied: It is for you that I have done it. So I thanked him again, and all's well that ends well; and twelve hours of jail is a cheap price for an outstanding success ... I think you will now agree that I did not exaggerate that night in placing [Wilfred] in the highest class of Arabian explorers!

Philby described meeting Thesiger 'in the Amir's parlour' at Laila, and how they

dined together and spent the night together in my tent, while his four men from the south shared a tent with my men. It rained quite hard during the night and they were glad of the shelter ... he was certainly looking very fit after his great journey of 16 days from Manwakh ... on very short rations of food and water for the humans, and only precarious grazing without any water at all for the camels. In colour there was little to choose between [Wilfred] and his swarthy companions: a sort of browny black! But he was in very good spirits, and looking forward to several more months of wandering in the desert. This is the life which suits him perfectly. I was able to give him the news of the world and also some quite recent copies of the Airmail edition of the Times which I had just received before going to meet him. He was able to replenish his meagre supply of necessaries (flour, etc) to some extent at Laila but he travels very light as regards food, and the surprising thing is how his men stand up to such austerity.[112]

Meeting Philby gave Thesiger an excuse to indulge in one of his favourite pastimes: hours devoted to uninterrupted 'hard talking' with a friend. Philby recalled: 'We had about 24 hours together and, as you may imagine, had plenty to talk about, sitting up till well after midnight and resuming again at dawn over our morning tea, and so on to lunch and after till my departure.'[113]

In due course, no doubt influenced by Philby, Ibn Saud's resentment at Thesiger's unauthorised incursion faded. Thesiger wrote to Kathleen from Bahrain on 1 May 1948: 'I am off to Riyadh tomorrow to stay with Philby for a few days and then back here. I hope to see the king.'[114] He wrote again a fortnight later, telling her: 'I had a very successful visit to Riyadh. Ibn Saud insisted on my going up there as his guest, so that I went up at his expense by air and was put up at the Royal guest house, and when I was leaving a servant came round with a gold watch and the traditional Arab clothes as a present from the king. I met the king of course but he is now very old and tired. I wish I could have met him years ago. Still I am very pleased to have met him. Rather like having seen Napoleon, even during his latter days on St Helena, an event never to be forgotten.'[115]

Eight days' journey from Laila, Thesiger and his companions reached Jabrin. He remembered 'riding interminably through a glaring haze-bound wilderness, which seemed to be without beginning and without end. The weariness of our camels added to my own, making it barely tolerable.'[116] Philby and Cheesman had positioned Jabrin on the map by compass traverse. Although these pioneers had been 'meticulously accurate in their work',[117] nevertheless a ten-mile error was possible. Thesiger had found no one at Laila willing to guide them, and there were no landmarks in this desert to warn him if he was going wrong. They carried flour, rice, dates, butter, sugar, tea and coffee, and six skins full of water.

The distance from Laila to Abu Dhabi was six hundred miles. On the eighth morning they saw Jabrin straight ahead of them, 'the splashes of the palm-groves dark on the khaki plain'.[118] Thesiger's companions stripped and bathed in the cold sweet water of the shallow well, but Thesiger 'shrank from this bitter washing'[119] in a chill desert wind.

A further eight days' riding across 'interminable naked sands'[120] brought Thesiger on 22 February to Dhiby well, which Bertram Thomas had located in 1931, at the end of his historic journey across the Empty Quarter. The well lay in a depression to the south of the Qatar peninsula. Thesiger had been uncertain whether he would be able to find it, but his satisfaction was short-lived, since the water, although drinkable by their thirsty camels, was too brackish for human consumption. Fifteen days after leaving Jabrin, within sight of Liwa's 'great mountains of golden sand', they reached the shallow well of Ghadhai, where they found water which, though brackish, was fit to drink. By then, Thesiger wrote, 'we had perhaps two gallons of water left in our skins'.[121]

Thesiger described the final stages from Laila to the coast in a letter to his mother dated 16 March 1948:

I have arrived at Abu Dhabi after a pretty hard journey across from Laila in the Dawasir country where I wrote to you last. They refused to give us a guide to Jabrin and we were so anxious to be gone that we set off without one. None of my Rashid had ever been in these parts so that the task of guiding fell to me. At first my Arabs were a bit doubtful if I could do it, but when we hit the well at Jabrin off to within half a mile and exactly where I said we should they gained confidence. I knew that Laila was accurately placed by Philby and Jabrin by Philby and Cheesman so that it was a comparatively easy job to steer a compass course. At Jabrin we found no one so that I had eventually to guide them to Sabkha Mutti and then to the well we watered at last year south of Liwa. This last bit from Sabkha Mutti [salt flats] to Liwa was more difficult as I had nothing but a rough idea of the distance and direction and we had to make our water from Jabrin suffice to Liwa, there being no drinkable water in this area ... Round Liwa we got back into the mountainous dunes of last year so that I was able to get a lot more photos to replace those burnt last year. I was glad to get to the oases of Liwa which no European had ever seen and to get them down on my map ... Here the Sheikhs of Abu Dhabi have given us a magnificent and very warm welcome and everyone is friendly and charming. What a contrast to our reception among the fanatical Dawasir who cursed us

297

whenever they saw us. It is pleasant to eat as much as one wants again and to taste meat after three months without any and to lie about and be idle. Now I plan to go up to Buraimi in the Oman mountains and stay there for some days with Zaid, one of the Abu Dhabi Sheikhs. I hope to go hunting and coursing and falconing and it will be very pleasant for these Sheikhs are charming. From there to 'Ibri and then up into Jabal al Akhdar and I expect to get to Muscat in June. We shall go slowly now, camping, hunting and collecting in very interesting and comparatively unknown country. From Muscat by sea to Bahrain, thence to Iraq and home at the end of July.[122]

When Thesiger first arrived there, Abu Dhabi was still, he wrote, 'quite a small port on the Persian Gulf and as yet quite unspoilt, but oil surveyors etc are busy in the area and I fear they will find oil and that all this will go. However I have seen it as it was and am glad of that and that I came across Arabia on a camel and not by car or plane.'[123] From Abu Dhabi Thesiger and his four Rashid – bin Kabina, bin Ghabaisha, Muhammad and Amair – rode a hundred miles to Buraimi, a journey of four days. They stayed for a month as guests of Sheikh Zayid at Muwaiqih, one of eight villages in the oasis. On the four-thousand-foot Jabal Hafit, Thesiger became the first European to see the Arabian tahr, an animal that resembled a wild goat. Leaving Muwaiqih on 1 May, escorted by four of Sheikh Zayid's retainers, they rode north-west to Sharja, on the Persian Gulf. Thesiger was mounted on Sheikh Zayid's camel Ghazala ('the gazelle'), which he said was 'the most renowned camel in Oman, and may well have been the finest in all Arabia'.[124]

At the end of his first crossing of the Empty Quarter, Thesiger had reflected: 'To others my journey would have little importance. It would produce nothing except a rather inaccurate map which no one was ever likely to use. It was a personal experience, and the reward had been a drink of clean, nearly tasteless water. I was content with that.'[125] Now, at Sharja aerodrome he felt like an outsider among the English RAF officers drinking in the mess, just as at Laila he had been despised as 'an intruder from an alien civilisation'.[126] He had felt the same alarming sense of dislocation in 1948 among airmen in the RAF camp at Salala, of whom he wrote despairingly: 'They belonged to an age of machines; they were fascinated by cars and aeroplanes, and found their relaxation in the cinema and the wireless. I knew that I stood apart from them and would never find contentment among them, whereas I could find it among these Bedu [the Rashid with whom he planned to travel to Mukalla], although I should never be one of them.'[127] 'I could now move without effort from one world to the other as easily as I could change my clothes, but I appreciated that I was in danger of belonging to neither. When I was among my own people, a shadowy figure was always at my side watching them with critical, intolerant eyes.'[128]

From Sharja Thesiger went to Dubai, where he stayed with an old friend, Edward Henderson, who had served with him in Syria during the war. Henderson now worked for the Iraqi Petroleum Company and lived in a large house overlooking the creek which divided the town. In Dubai, Thesiger noted, 'life moved in time with the past ... people still valued leisure and courtesy and conversation. They did not live their lives at second hand.' Wearing European clothes, he felt 'little better than a tourist',[129] an intruder from another world.[130]

In October, after he returned to Dubai from England, Thesiger explored the Liwa oasis south-west of Abu Dhabi, which in 1946 he had skirted but had been unable to approach because of tribal fighting. As well as bin Kabina, bin Ghabaisha, Amair and bin al Kamam, Sheikh Zayid advised Thesiger to take as guide a Rashid named Sahail bin Tahi,[131] who, Zayid assured him, knew 'every corner and water hole in the desert'.[132] Though now grey-bearded and elderly, bin Tahi was 'heavily-built and obviously very powerful'.[133] Wrestling him for amusement, Thesiger broke a rib, and suffered stabbing pain as he rode the fine Batina camel Zayid had lent him slowly westward through Liwa's palm groves and small brushwood-enclosed settlements.

From Buraimi in January 1949, Thesiger wrote to Kathleen describing a hawking trip with the Trucial Sheikhs.

It was great fun and I enjoyed it greatly. We were hawking bustard and hares and had six hawks with us. At first they were only half trained and missed several chances. We hawked on camel back spreading out to look for fresh tracks which we followed when we found them. The hawks were unhooded, never more than one at a time, as soon as we put up a bustard and would see it as far as half a mile. Usually when overtaken the bustard would land and turn its back to the hawk and spread out its tail. The hawk would then pounce on it and they would struggle and battle sometimes over a distance of 25 yards. We meanwhile would have a wild gallop across the sands to catch them up. Once we found 8 together and got six of them, one after the other, for one of the hawks first saw them on the ground and flew round looking for them without finding them but thereby made them lie close.[134]

Largely from memory, it appears, Thesiger rewrote this episode in *Arabian Sands*, in remarkably clear detail. He described how they watched the birds alight, how they approached slowly and in silence, how the falcons chased and killed the bustard. When the last of the bustard took to the air, a peregrine flew in pursuit but missed it. 'The bustard seemed to be flying quite slowly with unhurried beats of its great wings, yet the peregrine was evidently flying its fastest.'[135]

During these months Thesiger took hundreds of photographs, sending anything from one or two to sixteen rolls of film for James Sinclair to develop.[136] Among these photographs were many beautiful images of Liwa, the dramatic, steep sand-massifs nearby and the palms and settlements of the oasis. A voyage by dhow to Bahrain gave Thesiger marvellous opportunities to record the crew hauling on ropes as they set the vessel's heavy mainsail. Despite having been seasick, he managed to photograph a Kuwaiti boom, magnificent in full sail, sweeping past on its return journey from Zanzibar. Thesiger's finest photographs included some of Sheikh Zayid and his falconers, several of them mounted on camels.

On 15 February 1949, Thesiger became the first European to see the quicksands known to the Duru' as Umm al Samim and – according to his 1948–49 Oman diary – Umm al Samin by the Murra Rashid. He wrote in *Arabian Sands*: 'scattered bushes marked the firm land; farther out, only a slight darkening of the surface indicated the bog below'.[137] In his Oman diary he had written at the time: 'The sabkha sandy coloured rather darker than sand. Especially dangerous after rain or floods in wadis. Even the Duru give it a wide berth except when they collect salt.'[138]

Thesiger recounted to a meeting at the RGS on 17 October 1949 how

'One Duru' told how he had seen a flock of goats disappear, after struggling for a while with their fleeces spread out around them, and they all said that there is no warning of danger until the surface breaks up beneath you.'[139] Ralph Bagnold explained the colour of Umm al Samim, describing it not as a quicksand, but a salt marsh: 'The wind blows dust over the sticky salt crystals and the marsh is usually of a dirty yellow colour.'[140]

The discoveries of Liwa and Umm al Samim, and his exploration of Oman, brought Thesiger's Arabian travels to a close. These journeys were important: not least because of the fanatical hostility of the elderly Imam Abdullah al Khalili, and Oman's townspeople and villagers, towards Europeans at that time, which made penetrating the interior more difficult than it had been when James Wellsted first visited the country in 1835. Thesiger had wanted to explore the Gharbaniat sands of western Oman, 'rose-red dunes and snow-white flats'[141] where he hoped to find oryx. He and his companions found oryx spoor, but being short of water they had to push on instead of lingering there to hunt. Approaching Batha Badiya in the Wahiba sands, they crossed valleys and downs 'the colour of dried blood', and soft sands whose honey colour paled the further north they travelled. In the territory of the hostile Imam, Thesiger pretended to be a Baluch, sometimes a townsman from a distant part of Arabia. 'Badu are all-observing,' he wrote. 'To try to pass among them as a tribesman would be to invite exposure at the first glance, but their world is limited to the desert and its fringes.'[142] In the villages of Batha Badiya, when his companions exchanged news with Arab caravans from the coast, Thesiger 'remained discreetly silent, except for the customary salutations, though always conscious of the silent scrutiny of their dark eyes'. It flattered Thesiger that 'The Duru' in the wadi al 'Ain had told us that they had often speculated about me when I had stayed with them two years before [and masqueraded as a Syrian] but that it had never occurred to them that I was a European.'[143] On the way back to Muwaiqih, Thesiger had a superb view of the Jabal Kaur, 'a huge light-coloured [mountain] scarred and seamed with narrow sheer-sided watercourses'.[144] One of his best-known photographs shows a figure (possibly Thesiger himself) gazing towards Jabal Kaur from the Saifam wadi that runs close under the mountain's southern face. By the time they returned to Muwaiqih on 5 April 1949, Thesiger and his companions had ridden their camels eleven hundred miles since they left Sheikh Zayid's fort on 28 January.

After he returned to the Trucial coast from England in November, Thesiger had hoped to travel to inner Oman by way of the Duru' country, and visit the Jabal al Akhdar, whose 'stark barren precipices', he noted wryly, 'belie the [Akhdar's] name of the "green mountain"'. But bin Kabina warned him that the Duru' had now sworn to kill 'the Christian' if he again entered their territory.[145] From Dubai, Thesiger wrote to his mother on 7 January 1950: 'My plans are still uncertain. Two of the Duru' sheikhs are here and have been with us for several days. I am hoping to persuade them to let me go through their country but at present they are demanding exorbitant presents from me in return. I am not prepared to go down there again without the permission of the Duru' sheikhs and escorted by them, for while one can get away with it once as I did last year it would be folly to attempt to get through again without their permission. I hope that we shall be able to reach a settlement and that they will take me to Jabal al Akhdar. If however I fail to come to any agreement with them I shall go off into the sands with the Rashid for a bit. There is wonderful grazing in the desert this year.'[146]

Aided by Sheikh Zayid, Thesiger enlisted the protection of Huwaishil, a Duru' Sheikh, whose small party accompanied him through the Duru' to Oman. Thesiger's presence caused fierce resentment, and his party was frequently threatened. Besides their hostility to him as a Christian, he found that tribes 'who cherished their own way of life ... were afraid that if they allowed one Christian to pass he would be followed by others in motor cars, looking for oil, who would seize their land'[147] – a concern with which Thesiger felt immediately sympathetic. In the Rabadh, seventy miles east of the Awaiya well, Thesiger and nine of his party suffered a severe attack of influenza, lasting three days, with violent headaches, high temperatures and pains all over their bodies. At 'Ibri, where there had been an epidemic, several people died. To make matters worse, Thesiger's party was by then short of water and, sick as they were, had to ride on, though 'it was difficult to remain in the saddle'.[148]

Meanwhile, the fanatical Imam had not only forbidden anyone to guide Thesiger to Jabal al Akhdar, but had ordered townsmen at Mamur to kill him if he attempted to travel any further into his country. Sulaiman bin Hamiyar, Sheikh of the Bani Riyam, whose tribe inhabited Jabal al Akhdar, was the most influential figure in Oman apart from the Imam. Angered that the Imam had prevented Thesiger from visiting al Akhdar, Sulaiman camped at Mamur, where he gave Thesiger and his party protection until they had withdrawn to safety among the Duru' hills.

Two years previously, travelling in a leisurely manner on board a dhow from Sharja to Bahrain, Thesiger had taken time to reflect on his journeys across the Empty Quarter and his reasons for embarking on them. He wrote: 'For me, exploration was a personal venture. I did not go to the Arabian desert to collect plants nor to make a map; such things were incidental. At heart I knew that to write or even to talk of my travels was to tarnish the achievement. I went there to find peace in the hardship of desert travel and the company of desert peoples. I set myself a goal on these journeys, and, although the goal itself was unimportant, its attainment had to be worth every effort and sacrifice ... No, it is not the goal but the way there that matters, and the harder the way the more worthwhile the journey.'[149]

Writing to Kathleen from Buraimi at the start of his journey to Jabal al Akhdar, he tempered these philosophical reflections on Arabia with canny, down-to-earth reason: 'I expect to be away about a couple of months so that I shall get down to the coast at the end of March and home by the beginning of April I hope. I am sorry to be back rather later than I told you, but by not arriving in England until the beginning of April I shall save a year's income tax for the new financial year begins on April 1st.'[150] By the following morning, however, Thesiger's caring, impetuous *alter ego* showed signs of reasserting itself: 'Just off,' he scribbled in an affectionate, hasty postscript. 'The saddles are on the camels. God bless you dearest one. I love you very dearly. Take care of yourself until I come home.'[151]

Thesiger also made the following mysterious disclosure: 'I have seen the Sultan,' he wrote, 'and have been offered and accepted the job. I am to be his Minister of Foreign Affairs, but in reality to deal with everything. I have taken an instant liking to him, and the job should be interesting, with too much rather than too little to do.'[152] It appears, however, that nothing came of this offer, which would have conferred on Thesiger a status somewhat similar to Philby's at the court of Ibn Saud, and Thomas's role in the Sultan of Muscat's affairs. Thesiger never referred to this matter again in his correspondence.

It seems certain that by 'the Sultan' he meant the Sultan of Muscat, whom he met during the week he spent at Salala in January 1946 after his first crossing of the Rub' al Khali. Evidently he got on well with the Sultan. In *Arabian Sands* he wrote: 'The Sultan, Saiyid Said bin Timur, whom I met for the first time, was very kind to me and gave me every assistance ... He assured me that the restrictions which had been imposed on the RAF did not apply to me, and that I could go anywhere and talk to anyone while I was in Salala.'[153] By 1949, however, Thesiger was 'not at all anxious to encounter the Sultan of Muscat': 'When I had met him in Salala after my first journey through these parts he had been charming. Now after another unauthorised journey [in Oman] I was sure he would be furious.'[154] In 1950 the Sultan demanded that Thesiger's Muscat visa should be cancelled.[155]

From Sheikh Zayid's fort at Muwaiqih, Thesiger, bin Kabina and bin Ghabaisha went to Dubai, where they stayed with Edward Henderson and his assistant Ronald Codrai at their house near the harbour. Codrai, who was a gifted photographer, took several romantic portraits of Thesiger wearing his Arab shirt and headcloth, armed with a dagger and a rifle. During meals, Thesiger wrote, bin Kabina and bin Ghabaisha 'watched carefully to see how we used the knives and forks and managed with singularly little trouble. They were more self-possessed than most Englishmen whom I had seen feeding with their hands for the first time.'[156] Henderson and Codrai were 'endlessly good-natured', especially when bin Kabina and bin Ghabaisha burst into their rooms at dawn, urging them ' "Up and pray! Up and pray!" as they beat the beds with their camel-sticks'.[157]

These vivid snapshots of the young Rashid in an unfamiliar European setting lightened, yet also served to highlight, the pathos of Thesiger's impending final departure from Arabia. Thesiger felt deeply moved by Codrai's remark, as he watched bin Kabina and bin Ghabaisha gathering their few possessions together for the last time, 'It is rather pathetic that this is all they have.'[158] Yet both men knew that to the Bedu of the Arabian desert, everything that was not a necessity was an encumbrance; that besides, the life of towns was 'no life for a man',[159] that for them danger lay 'not in the hardship of their lives, but in the boredom and frustration they would feel when they renounced it'.[160]

In the desert, Thesiger had found the challenges and companionships he desired. But the Saudi government and the Sultan of Muscat refused to believe that he made his journeys without any political or economic motive. Another, and more personal, reason for their growing hostility is suggested in a letter written by C.H. Inge from the Secretariat at Aden in December 1948:

Since your last journey in these parts the Sa'udi authorities have more than once brought your name into correspondence and conversations about tribal raids near the frontiers. The story in brief is that some of your companions, Protectorate tribesmen, carried out a raid in Sa'udi territory. Presumably the raid, if it occurred at all, took place after the men left your company, but unfortunately nothing will persuade the Sa'udis that you are not in some way to blame. Following a series of very large scale raids early this year, in which the Sei'ar, Kurab and allies got badly beaten up by the Yam, Daham, Abida etc., we have had a satisfactory meeting with a Sa'udi delegation and reached agreement on the reconciliation of past scores and on measures for the suppression of raids in the future. Your name came up again in the discussions. I am therefore writing to warn you that the Governor will probably not allow you to travel in the frontier area unless the previous consent of the Sa'udi authorities has been obtained and this is quite likely to be refused.[161]

Without access from the Trucial coast, Oman or Dhaufar, Thesiger knew that it would be impossible to continue his travels in the Empty Quarter. He ended *Arabian Sands*, his testament to those unsurpassable years, at a poignant moment of parting from his companions:

The lorry arrived after breakfast. We embraced for the last time. I said, 'Go in peace,' and they answered together, 'Remain in the safe keeping of God, Umbarak." Then they scrambled up on to a pile of petrol drums beside a Palestinian refugee in oil-stained dungarees. A few minutes later they were out of sight round a corner. I was glad when Codrai took me to the aerodrome at Sharja. As the plane climbed over the town and swung out above the sea I knew how it felt to go into exile.[162]

Concluding *Seven Pillars of Wisdom*, T.E. Lawrence had written: 'and then at once I knew how much I was sorry'.[163] That Thesiger's last words should echo those of Lawrence, the hero he never knew, was surely no coincidence. Like Lawrence, Thesiger paid a heavy price for realising his Arabian dream, since, as Lawrence wrote,

the effort for those years to live in the dress of Arabs, and to imitate their mental foundation, quitted me of my English self, and let me look at the West and its conventions with new eyes: they destroyed it all for me. At the same time I could not sincerely take on the Arab skin: it was an affectation only. Easily was a man made an infidel, but hardly might he be converted to another faith. I had dropped one form and not taken on the other, and was become like Mohammed's coffin in our legend, with a resultant feeling of loneliness in life, and a contempt, not for other men, but for all they do. Such detachment came at times to a man exhausted by prolonged physical effort and isolation. His body plodded on mechanically, while his reasonable mind left him, and from without looked down critically on him, wondering what that futile lumber did and why. Sometimes these selves would converse in the void: and then madness was very near, as I believe it to be near the man who could see things through the veils at once of two customs, two educations, two environments.[164]

NINETEEN

Marsh and Mountain

Travelling back to England from Oman in May 1949, Thesiger made a brief journey through Persia by car, from Bushire to Shiraz, Isfahan, Teheran and Tabriz, and thence from Kurdistan to Baghdad. He wrote telling his mother:

> Isfahan was quite lovely and I took a large number of photos ... Wonderful mosques and large and very interesting bazaars, perhaps the best I have ever seen ... I went across the Elburz mountains and drove down to the Caspian at Chalus ... The mountains themselves are really magnificent, with quite a lot of snow on their tops, and lots of wild flowers, tulips, poppies and delphiniums ... I am now off to Tabriz ... and down to the Iraq frontier by the famous Rowunduz gorge and from there to Erbil and Mosul ... I would give anything to have you with me now for you would delight in this country. It is so pleasant after Arabia for everything there is running water and little oases of green, poplars and willows and flowers. I don't like Teheran, a modern city without character but beautifully situated.[1]

The mountains gave Thesiger 'an uplift of the spirit'.[2] Immediately he felt the urge to return and travel among them. Describing Hendren, above the gorge of Rowunduz, twelve-thousand-foot Helgord, and the snow-flecked Qandil range with its massive precipices a mile high, he wrote emphatically: 'Never had I seen such country.'[3] For Kathleen's benefit, he noted: 'On the Caspian side of the mountains the country is quite different ... It is very well wooded and strangely enough reminded me of Ireland until one got down to the coast and the rice fields.'[4]

He returned to Iraqi Kurdistan for three months in August 1950, and for another five months the following May. During those months, he wrote, few foreigners[5] could have seen as much as he did of this beautiful land: 'There can have been few villages I did not visit, few mountains I did not climb.'[6] Thesiger was accompanied on these journeys by a good-natured, helpful young Kurd named Nasser Hussain, who spoke Arabic. Sometimes they walked, leading a mule or a horse they hired to carry their saddlebags; at other times they rode on borrowed horses from one village to the next.

Thesiger preferred to travel light. He carried spare clothing, a blanket or two in case they camped out, medicines, favourite books such as *Lord Jim* or *Kim*, his Leica camera and a .275 rifle he bought second-hand from Rigby in 1950. Between 1952 and 1965, when he travelled at intervals in the mountains of Pakistan, Afghanistan and Nuristan, he did not bring a rifle. To give some protection against the extreme cold or bad weather he did then carry a small tent, but apart from that his kit remained the same.

In *Among the Mountains* he wrote: 'Without the urge to hunt I should never have seen half the country that I did, nor looked on many a stupendous view. But in all my months in Kurdistan I only shot one bear and one ibex.'[7] He wrote from Kirkuk in 1950: 'I have borrowed a shotgun and have got the rifle I bought in London so I hope to get some shooting. It is a good way to get to know the Kurds who are very keen hunters, and gives me an intelligible reason for climbing about in the mountains.'[8] Yet by 1951 he admitted: 'I find I have lost much of my enthusiasm for shooting and don't really mind if I get anything or not, but looking for bear or ibex is a convenient excuse for climbing about on the tops of the high mountains.' In Arabia he had collected fossils, plants and insects for the Natural History Museum in London. He did the same in Kurdistan. 'I am now off into the mountains near Rowunduz,' he wrote in May 1951, 'and shall be near the tops collecting specimens under the snow line. I have just sent off about 1000 specimens to the British Museum.'[9] This 'immense number of plants' included: 'Iris, gladioli, poppies, lilies, squills, ranunculus, stocks and lots of stuff whose names I don't know.' He hoped that the museum would be pleased.[10]

In October 1950 Thesiger returned to Jabal Sinjar, near Mosul, where he had first visited the Yazidis, the so-called devil-worshippers, for one night in 1943. He wrote to Kathleen: 'I have taken a great number of photos ... At one village there was a large dance going on and everyone was dressed up in their best clothes. Rather attractive dancing with the men and women and children dancing round in a circle hand in hand.'[11] He saw the lovely mountain shrine of Sheikh Adi during the Yazidis' annual pilgrimage, 'a very gay colourful scene' with groups of pilgrims dancing in the courts among the houses and peddlers selling sweets and toys. 'It is a pity,' he wrote, 'that in England we have now lost the spontaneous communal way of enjoying ourselves. It was rather like an old fashioned fair.'[12] When he stayed with the Consul at Mosul the following May, he met the crime writer Agatha Christie and her husband, the archaeologist Max Mallowan, who was in charge of the excavations at Nimrud.[13] He liked them, and hoped to see them again in London. Nimrud, however, failed to interest him: 'Large mounds and to me meaningless holes and trenches and some broken up fragments of ivory statues.' Nineveh, which was outside Mosul, he thought 'impressive by its very size, miles and miles of earthworks and a huge mound'.[14]

Thesiger had been as unmoved by Nimrud's 'meaningless holes and trenches' as he was by much of music, art or architecture. When a visitor in London said he had been studying architecture, Thesiger exclaimed: 'Oh God, you're going to clutter the place with more bloody buildings!'[15] Yet on his way to Baghdad in 1951, after a breakdown had delayed his aircraft for a day and a half in Rome, he wrote with a patriotic flourish: 'we were driven round for two hours on a sightseeing tour ... I went into St Peter's with a couple of Englishmen and when we came out one of them looked back at it and said, "Well I don't think it is a patch on St Paul's," which I thought was magnificently loyal.'[16]

He wrote from Kirkuk that as well as plant specimens, 'I have sent off another three rolls of film to Sinclair. I have been using the new large lens and don't know if I have got it right. It is said to be the best lens for portraits that there is.'[17]

In May 1951 he met Tahsin, the Amir of the Yazidis, at his village of Ba'adhava. 'He is a large fat stupid self-important young man,' he wrote, 'quite the least attractive person I have yet met in Iraq. He squanders all the funds of his sect in orgies in Baghdad. He is very unpopular and is almost certain to be murdered, the sooner the better. It is a pity that the Yazidis, who are an attractive people, should have such a rotten Amir.'[18] Thesiger had travelled in Iraqi Kurdistan 'to try to recapture the peace of mind I had known in the deserts of Southern Arabia'. But having been there, he wrote, 'I had no desire to go back. Travel was too restricted, rather like stalking in a Highland deer forest.' In contrast, the marshes of southern Iraq 'covered a smaller area than Iraqi Kurdistan, but they were a world complete in itself, not a fragment of a larger world to the rest of which I was denied access. Besides, being fond of Arabs, it was probable that I could never really like Kurds ... As people are more important to me than places I decided to return to the Arabs.'[19]

In October 1950, Thesiger and Dugald Stewart, the young British Vice-Consul at Amara, accompanied by a local Sheikh, rode their horses across a dusty, flat, grassy plain to an Al Essa encampment,[20] where they spent the night in a reed cabin, so close to the water that Thesiger could hear waves lapping the shore. 'As I came out into the dawn,' he wrote, 'I saw, far away across a great sheet of water, the silhouette of a distant land, black against the sunrise.'[21] 'For a moment I had a vision of Hufaidh, the legendary island, which no man may look on and keep his senses; then I realised that I was looking at great reedbeds. A slim, black, high-prowed craft lay beached at my feet – the Sheikh's war canoe, waiting to take me into the Marshes ... Five thousand years of history were here and the pattern was still unchanged.'[22] He later visited Abu Shajar, the island site of 'some forgotten city' where according to legend a hoard of gold was buried.[23] Here he learnt more of Hufaidh's palaces, palm groves, gardens of pomegranates and huge buffaloes, which Jinns kept hidden from sight.

R.S.M. Sturges, the Political Officer at Qurnah in 1920, whose wife knew Mrs S.E. Hedgcock, co-author with her husband under the *nom de plume* 'Fulanain' of *Haji Rikkan: Marsh Arab* (1927), told Thesiger about a possible connection between Hufaidh and the biblical Garden of Eden in 'the malarial swamps of the Qurnah district, where ... the mosquitoes were as big as bats and bit to the bone'. Sturges wrote: 'there was a local legend of a lost island in the marshes bearing luscious fruits and guarded by snakes and other animals. On certain nights it shone with a radiance visible for many miles. It seemed to move like some out-size will-o'-the-wisp and eluded all attempts to track it down ... I saw it myself once – a strong diffused glow as of the full moon just below the horizon.'[24]

Soon afterwards, Thesiger wrote giving his mother a brief description of this decisive first visit:

> I had a very enjoyable three weeks in the marshes of Southern Iraq. Stewart, the Consul from Amara, came with me. He was a Tug at Eton and then at Magdalen, but is about 10 years younger than I am. We started off hunting wild boars and killed two. One I managed to ride down after an exciting 2 mile chase, and kill it when it was under my horse's feet by shooting it one-handed in the back with a shotgun. I felt that if I had had a spear I could have stuck it. We started for two days on horses ... We then went right through the marshes in 'mashufs', the local canoes, each of which is punted by two Arabs. It seems desperately precarious at first but later you find that they don't seem to capsize. We went through endless swamps of bamboos, bullrushes and open water where the 'maidan' or marsh Arabs live in bamboo cabins, built on rotting piles of reeds and mud, like giant dabchicks' nests. They live by keeping buffaloes, fishing and rice growing. These swamps are alive with mosquitoes but there is very little malaria. The duck and geese were coming in from Siberia and Russia. One of our last days we saw skein after skein of geese, 70–100 strong, coming in, in unending wedges from the North ... I got to within 100 yards of a sandbank where they were coming in to rest. There must have been 2000 on it at one time. A marvellous sight.[25]

He enjoyed Stewart's company, and got on well with him and his wife. 'I had a delightful letter from Mrs Stewart,' he wrote, '... telling me she had had a son and asking me to be godfather. They are closing the Consulate [at Amara] and the Stewarts are being transferred to Cairo. Sad for I should have liked to have stayed with them again in October.'[26]

Thesiger's vivid thumbnail impressions show how much he was attracted by the Iraqi marshes and their inhabitants. He described in greater detail a second visit, in April 1951:

> I spent the whole month [of March] travelling by canoe and got right off the beaten track and among the real marsh Arabs who have seen few

Europeans. They lead an extraordinary life in the heart of these great swamps of bamboos and bullrushes, living either on small islands, which are probably the remains of ancient towns and villages which were here before the Mongols destroyed the irrigation works and turned Southern Iraq into a swamp, or on half-submerged platforms of accumulated buffalo dung and reeds ... The marsh Arabs are as self-contained as the Bedu. They live on fish, rice which they grow and buffalo milk. I found them very friendly and greatly enjoyed my time with them. I did a lot of doctoring and this got me their confidence. A sheikh's son was very ill with blood poisoning with a temperature of 105, but I got him well again with an injection of penicillin ... Most evenings after dinner there was singing and dancing which went on sometimes as late as two o' clock in the morning, and as everyone got up again at 6 this left one rather short of sleep. The fleas were appalling but luckily they don't seem to worry me though the Arabs were complaining about them bitterly most of the time. There were a lot of duck about and I got a bit of shooting but on the whole I was more interested in living with and seeing these Arabs than in shooting. However I did a certain amount of shooting for the pot ...[27]

Of the Marsh Arabs themselves, he wrote:

I can always get on with a simple people like them. The ones who get me uncomfortable, irritated and on the wrong foot are the semi-educated who wear European dress and try to do things in what they fancy is a civilised manner. In no time I am maddened by their poses and pretences whereas the hardships and discomforts of Bedu or marsh Arab life mean nothing to me. I was amused to find that I am immune to fleas, which swarm in the huts of the marsh Arabs. As we were always two or three under a blanket I used to be kept awake at night by the scratching and slapping of my bedfellows. As we always sat up till nearly two singing, dancing and talking and as they get up at 6 this meant I was rather short of sleep by the end.[28]

Over the years Thesiger compared his observations of the marshes with books written about the region, among them *Haji Rikkan: Marsh Arab* and Seton Lloyd's *Twin Rivers* (1943), a brief history of Iraq. *Marsh*

Dwellers of the Euphrates Delta (1962) by Dr S.M. Salim confirmed that the marshes and alternating stretches of barren desert covered about twenty thousand square miles, and that the depth of water was generally four or five feet, but as much as twenty feet in places. More than a decade passed before Thesiger wrote *The Marsh Arabs*, distilling from evocative glimpses in letters and diaries a hauntingly beautiful, poetic recreation of this now-vanished world:

> Memories of that first visit to the Marshes have never left me: firelight on a half-turned face, the crying of geese, duck flighting in to feed, a boy's voice singing somewhere in the dark, canoes moving in procession down a waterway, the setting sun seen crimson through the smoke of burning reedbeds, narrow waterways that wound still deeper into the Marshes. A naked man in a canoe with a trident in his hand, reed houses built upon water, black, dripping buffaloes that looked as if they had been calved from the swamp with the first dry land. Stars reflected in dark water, the croaking of frogs, canoes coming home at evening, peace and continuity, the stillness of a world that never knew an engine. Once again I experienced the longing to share this life, and to be more than a mere spectator.[29]

Whereas journeys were the theme of *Arabian Sands*, *The Marsh Arabs* described a settled communal life. 'Although I was almost continuously on the move,' Thesiger wrote, '[*The Marsh Arabs*] is not properly a travel book for the area over which I travelled was restricted.'[30] His photogenic, leisurely voyages from village to village by canoe linked the serial episodes in Thesiger's narrative of the years 1950–57, during most of which he spent February to August in the marshes. Its 'domesticated' drama,[31] in which he played a dominant role, involved a large supporting cast. He listed no fewer than thirty-five 'Chief Characters', of whom thirty-three were men or boys. Among the first Marsh Arabs, or 'Ma'dan', he met were Jasim al Faris, the 'tall gaunt' Sheikh of the Fartus,[32] and Falih, his handsome fourteen-year-old son. Sheikh Majid of the Al bu Muhammad was a powerful 'overlord'[33] whose son Falih presented Thesiger with a beautiful *tarada*, a 'sheikh's canoe',[34] thirty-six feet long with a high curved prow somewhat reminiscent of a Venetian gondola.

Hasan and Yasin, teenagers from Bu Mughaifat village, joined Thesiger

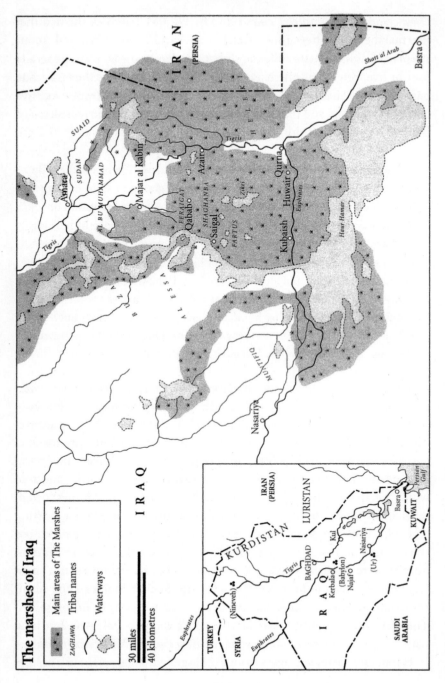

The marshes of Iraq

Main areas of The Marshes

ZAGHAWA Tribal names

Waterways

30 miles

40 kilometres

IRAN
(PERSIA)

HELBI

Shatt al Arab

Basra

Tigris

SUAID

SUDAN

Amara

AL BU MUHAMMAD

Majar al Kabir

Azair

Qurna

Huwair

Kubaish

Euphrates

Haur Haman

FERAIGAT

Qababo

SHAGHANBA

Saigal

Zikri

FARTUS

Tigris

B A Z

A L E S S A

MUNTIFIK

Nasariya

I R A Q

IRAN
(PERSIA)

LURISTAN

KURDISTAN

BAGHDAD

Kut

Tigris

Kerbala

(Babylon)

Najaf

(Ur)

Nasariya

Basra

Persian
Gulf

KUWAIT

(Nineveh)

TURKEY

SYRIA

Euphrates

Euphrates

I R A Q

SAUDI
ARABIA

314

as his canoeboys. Falih bin Majid found two more, Amara bin Thuqub and Sabaiti, who remained Thesiger's close companions during his seven years in Iraq. Much as Thesiger admired the Fartus, all four of his *tarada* crew were from other tribes. Amara (Thesiger's favourite), Hasan and Sabaiti were from the Feraigat, while Yasin was a Shaghanba. Amara was 'slightly built and remarkably handsome ... deft and self-possessed, a natural aristocrat'. In contrast, Sabaiti was 'rather clumsy and far from handsome, but obviously good-natured'; his family were shopkeepers, 'well off and very hospitable'.[35] Hasan was short and stocky, 'a keen wildfowler'. Sixteen years old (the same age as Hasan), Yasin was 'tall and gracefully built ... with the body of an athlete ... an attractive open face with a hint of Mongol blood'. Thesiger had thought 'disturbingly beautiful', the 'heavy, rather Mongolian face'[36] of a boy who remained on guard duty throughout the night at Falih's *mudhif*, or Sheikh's guest house. Yasin was a better waterman than Hasan, and 'already deemed exceptionally skilful, even by Madan standards'.[37]

Thesiger occasionally took with him Englishmen who wanted to see the Iraqi marshes and experience something of the Marsh Arabs' traditional way of life. These brief companionships included the author Gavin Maxwell, Gavin Young, then in his early twenties, a shipping clerk who became a successful travel writer, and Frank Steele, British Vice-Consul at Basra. Although his close friendship with Gavin Maxwell waned, Thesiger remained friends with Frank Steele and Gavin Young, and travelled with each of them years later in northern Kenya, Jordan and Indonesia. Of the four (including Thesiger himself), only Young returned to the Iraqi marshes after the revolution in Baghdad in 1958. He wrote two books about these experiences, *Return to the Marshes* (1977) and *Iraq: Land of Two Rivers* (1980). Thesiger praised them both, saying: 'Gavin did this well. He had a very personal [relationship] with the marshes and some of the people. He was very easy-going and he got on with everybody. *Return to the Marshes* is the finer of the two. I don't know why ... perhaps it [flows along] more easily than the other ... it gets it right ... To me, it's just a better book.'[38]

Gavin Maxwell's book *A Reed Shaken by the Wind* (1958), based on his journeys with Thesiger, was described by Thesiger as 'a brilliant piece of verbal photography'.[39] He and Maxwell travelled together in the marshes for more than two months, but at such close quarters Thesiger found him difficult, highly strung and demanding. Gavin Young, by contrast, 'had an instinctive understanding and affection for the Madan, and I always looked forward to his brief visits to me from Basra.'[40] Thesiger first mentioned Young in a letter to Kathleen from Kubaish in southern Iraq: 'Gavin Young who works with [Ralli Bros] a firm in Basra and is keen to see something of Arab tribal life has been with me for a week. He had a month's leave and gave up a week of it to travel in the marshes with me. He is a nice lad and I am always glad to help anyone who is keen on this sort of life. I think I have shown him an interesting side of Arab life and I hope he has enjoyed it. I also got him a bit of shooting.' Thesiger added: 'I have now got 132 pig [wild boar] in the past two months and am getting well known as a result.'[41] In *Return to the Marshes* Young described Thesiger as he was in 1952, when they first met: 'The man I saw at the consul's table in Basra all those years ago was tall and gaunt with a long, creased, sunburnt face, deep-set, probing eyes and large, sinewy, sunburnt wrists and hands. I found later that he was amazingly strong.'[42]

Thesiger ordered as many as two or three hundred cartridges at a time for his .275 Rigby-Mauser. By the time he left the marshes in 1958 he had killed approximately a thousand wild boar, and claimed that he was 'sick of slaughtering pig'.[43] At first he had ridden after boar, much as he had 'galloped down' lion in the Sudan. Sometimes he killed them by firing his rifle or shotgun one-handed from the saddle as if it were a pistol. He found this style of shooting difficult, as indeed it was, even though his twelve-bore shotgun and his Rigby each weighed little more than three and a half kilos. Gavin Young commented from personal experience in 1977: 'Anyone who has tried to aim such a relatively heavy rifle one-handed, let alone fire it accurately, will know what special strength of forearm and shoulder this feat requires.'[44] 'If I had a spear,' Thesiger wrote, 'I would try pig sticking … a spear … would be a handier weapon than a shotgun with one hand at full gallop.'[45] He had been chasing two full-grown sows near the Tigris when one of them 'whipped round' and charged. 'I just had time to get the gun over to my left side and shoot and I then felt her hit my horse. I had broken one of her front legs and killed her with another shot. My horse's front leg was covered with blood and I thought she had been gored but it was only blood from the pig.'[46]

Among the reed-fringed waterways, Thesiger shot wild boar as they swam using a 9mm Browning semi-automatic pistol, a weapon perhaps similar to the 'automatic' he had given his Kurdish companion and guide Nasser Hussain as a present.[47] Thesiger's best .275 rifle had been built for him by Rigby before the war. He gave his second-hand .275 Rigby to Amara in 1954, and that year he also gave an inexpensive but serviceable shotgun each to Sabaiti, Yasin and Hasan.

Four of the Fartus, Sheikh Jasim's tribe, brought Thesiger to Basra by canoe in November 1951. He wrote from the British Consulate: 'I had an interesting time in the marshes and came in here for a bath and to collect my letters. I brought four Fartus with me. They are my favourite tribe and real marshmen. None of these four had ever seen a town before or been in a car. One of them [Falih] is the sheikh's younger son, an attractive and very vivacious lad of 14 who very much rules the party.' The Fartus conformed to Thesiger's ideal of traditional people uncorrupted by towns, unused to modern transport:

They brought me down to Qurna where the Tigris and Euphrates meet by canoe from the Northern side of the marshes. It took us two days, the first day they were punting and paddling for 15 hours and the second for 12. It is a comfortable and agreeable if rather confined way of getting about. We have a mud fireplace in the bows and make tea and a very good hot lime drink at intervals as we go along. Ordinarily these marsh Arabs are very chary about quitting the sanctuary of their marshes so I was flattered when Jasim sent his younger son with me. The duck and geese are arriving from the North and I hope to get some really good shooting when I go back tomorrow. I have been very busy doctoring, often working almost without a stop from sunrise to sunset. I wish I knew more about it. It is not very easy when one is operating to have a dozen importunate old men and women plucking at one and demanding instant attention for bad eyes, leg sores, dysentery, deafness, stomach ache, toothache and God knows what else. There is so much that one could do for them if only I knew what to do. I have just bought another £25 worth of drugs to take up there with me. I find these marsh Arabs an attractive lot. They have practically no contact with the outside world and the Government on the whole leaves them very much alone. There is a curious fascination in these great

317

marshes. The thick reed-beds and the bamboos and the open lagoons whose surfaces are sometimes covered with water-lilies and at other times open water, where the small waves splash into our canoe. There is always something to look at, duck and geese, cormorants, pelicans, herons, coots, water rails, jumping fish, occasionally a pig and if you are lucky an otter. At present they are burning the reed beds to produce new shoots for their buffaloes and at night the red glare of the fires is reflected against the pall of smoke. I find their village life also of endless interest. It is fun to sit outside their huts at sunset and watch the canoes coming in, laden with bundles of bamboo shoots for the buffaloes to eat at night, and with the fish which they have caught during the day.[48]

By 'bamboo' Thesiger meant the thickest and toughest of the ubiquitous marsh reeds, the edible shoots of which were gathered daily by Ma'dan villagers as buffalo fodder. The Ma'dan used reeds to build coracles, to construct houses and their foundations, and to weave matting. The giant reeds, *Phragmites communis*, used for house-building, grew to a height of twenty-five feet. Thesiger took numerous photographs of the Marshmen's reed dwellings, including *mudhifs*. One large *mudhif* he saw in February 1951 stood on the promontory between two branches of a river. This was 'a barrel-vaulted building, roofed with honey-coloured matting. At either end four tapered pillars broke the roof line.' After being greeted by the *mudhif*'s owner, Sheikh Falih bin Majid, Thesiger was invited to enter. 'Kicking off my shoes,' he wrote, 'I passed between the pillars. Eight feet in girth, each pillar was formed by a bundle of giant reeds, the peeled stems bound so tightly together that the surface was smooth and polished.'[49] In *The Marsh Arabs* Thesiger gave a wonderfully atmospheric first impression of this vast building:

The great hall smelt acrid with smoke and the light was dim, after the bright sun outside. Shadowy figures stood along the walls. I called out, '*Salam alaikum*' and they answered together, '*Alaikum as salam*.' We seated ourselves on some gaudy rugs spread on the matting and the others settled themselves along the walls. Those that had rifles placed them in front of them. I noticed two lovely old rugs of blue and gold farther down the room, relegated there from the place of honour, in favour of the modern ones on which we sat. Against the wall at the far end was a wooden chest and near the entrance a large pitcher of porous clay filled with water and supported in a wooden frame. There was no other furniture. The hearth was a third of the way into the room and in the centre[50] ... The *mudhif*, which I later measured, was sixty feet long, twenty feet wide and eighteen feet high, but gave the impression of far greater size, especially when I first entered it. Eleven great horseshoe arches supported the roof. Like the entrance pillars, these were made of the stems of giant reeds, bound closely together, and were nine feet in circumference where they emerged from the ground, and two and a half feet at the top ... To complete the framework, further reed bundles, married so as to resemble two-inch cables, were lashed, one above the other, along the entire length of the building on the outside of the arches. The contrast between this horizontal ribbing and the shape of the vertical arches made a striking pattern seen from within. The roof itself was covered with overlapping reed mats, similar to those on the floor and sewn on to the ribs in such a way as to ensure a fourfold thickness. The sides of the room were the colour of pale gold but the ceiling was darkened by smoke to a deep chestnut and gave the effect of being varnished.[51]

As soon as he arrived at a village, Thesiger would be besieged by a crowd of men, women and children of all ages begging for medicine or treatment. He spent hours crouched in some stifling hut, or in a buffalo shelter swarming with flies, handing out pills, applying ointment, giving injections to the sick and wounded. The marsh dwellers' ailments and injuries ranged from boils, dysentery, eczema, ulcers and yaws to horrific wounds inflicted by wild boar. For years he dined out on the horrifying details of how he had taken out someone's eye. At the military hospital in Basra he learnt to perform minor surgical operations, including circumcisions, for which he was soon in great demand.

Before he arrived in Iraq Thesiger had never performed a circumcision, although he had often watched the operation in hospitals and among the tribes. In southern Iraq most circumcisions were done after puberty, and tribal circumcisers travelled from village to village in summer: 'Their traditional fee was a cock, but more often they charged five shillings'[52] (Thesiger couldn't help smiling as he read this aloud from

The Marsh Arabs). 'The examples of their work which I saw later were terrifying. They used a dirty razor, a piece of string and no antiseptics. Having finished, they sprinkled the wound with a special powder, made from the dried foreskins of their previous victims, and then bound it up tight with a rag ... One young man came to me for treatment ten days after his circumcision, and although I am fairly inured to unpleasant sights and smells, the stench made me retch.' In contrast, Thesiger operated using a sterilised scalpel, having injected a local anaesthetic, and treated the fresh wounds with sulphonamide powder and penicillin. He noted in his diary on 8 July 1952: 'Spent a busy day from dawn till after dusk doctoring. Injections, bad eyes etc and 112 circumcisions, 23 of them grown up, including 3 grown men. Did some 80 of the small ones without an anaesthetic.' His comment 'Tired by the evening'[53] was surely the apogee of understatement.

Not only were his operations relatively painless, Thesiger wrote: 'The rapidity with which mine heal, 4–8 days, has made me famous. When done by an Arab they may take a month or more to heal.'[54] Thousands of circumcisions are catalogued in the nine volumes of Thesiger's southern Iraq diaries. Most entries are brief, some almost casual: 'Sent a mashuf back for Amara and our kit. While I waited circumcised 6, two grown up';[55] 'Circumcised a grown up boy who had brought us to [Abd al Ridha's encampment]'; 'Circumcised one small boy before breakfast.'[56] Even a random selection of the daily totals of these operations is wincingly impressive: 'Circumcised 51, seventeen grown up [19 March 1955]' ... 'Circumcised 20, four grown up [14 June 1956]' ... 'Circumcised 27, five grown up [16 June 1956]' ... 'Circumcised 80. Thirteen grown up [6 April 1958].' According to Thesiger's southern Iraq diaries, in 1951 he performed sixty-seven circumcisions; in 1952–53 a total of 411; in 1954, 1365; in 1955, 1663; in 1956, 1238; and in 1958, 1394: making a total of 6138. Allowing a margin for error, this extraordinary number far exceeds Thesiger's modest estimate of 'hundreds' of circumcisions, quoted by Eric Newby in *A Short Walk in the Hindu Kush*.[57]

Thesiger's reputation for circumcising cleanly and almost painlessly spread far and wide throughout the Iraqi marshes. Circumcision became Thesiger's calling card, his introduction to unvisited tribes and his certain means of winning acceptance. He continued to circumcise boys

and men among the tribes of northern Kenya, and took many photographs illustrating the different methods of circumcision practised by the
Masai and Samburu.

Some of Thesiger's most dramatic photographs showed the Iraqi
marshes during the floods in May 1954. 'The rain half filled our *tarada*,'
he wrote, 'and I was afraid it would swamp us ... Many of these villages,
at this time of year, are below the level of the water, the floods being held
back by earthen walls, one or two feet high. If these break the village is
flooded.' He saw a village 'where there was 2' of water in the houses. They
were salvaging their things as we passed.'[58] On 3 May he noted in his
diary: 'The floods have risen a lot during the night ... Everywhere deep
water, palm trees and houses sticking up out of the water. Most of the
country abandoned.'[59] An image of palm trees in silhouette, bowed and
lashed by a gale, showed the desert bordering the western marshes under
six feet of water. Across the lagoon at Suq al Fuhud, 'Nearly all the *suq*
[was] under water and the mud houses collapsing one after the other.'[60]
He took many photographs of this 'extraordinary scene', and described in
The Marsh Arabs how 'As the shopkeepers [from the market at Fuhud]
climbed into boats, the mud walls of their shops collapsed behind them.'[61]
The floods caused Thesiger himself little inconvenience. 'A foot or so of
water more or less does not make any difference,' he wrote, 'if you are in
a boat. The Marsh Arabs are probably less affected by these quite exceptional floods than anyone else.'[62] He took advantage of the miles of
flooded country to visit by canoe people and tribes he had not met
previously, and had 'a very successful time'.[63] Many villagers, however, lost
their entire year's harvest. Thesiger commented shrewdly: 'they will
suffer, and any attempt to relieve their distress will founder on the
inevitable corruption. A lot of people will make a fortune and the
peasants will starve.'[64]

The floods drove 'enormous numbers' of wild boar onto higher
ground on the east side of the Tigris. Thesiger shot 205 of them in forty-
five days, and could have shot more had he not run out of cartridges. 'I
had an exciting time with two of them,' he wrote: 'We had dragged our
canoe through the mud, and I was sitting in it and the pig were about 100
yards off. I wounded the leading pig which promptly charged followed by
its companion. I hit the wounded pig with three more shots knocking it

over when it was about 5 yards off, and then had only one shot left for the other one which was close behind it. However the last shot in my rifle killed it when it was almost on us. Very unusual to be charged by two pigs at once. The Arabs with me stood very staunchly and never moved. Young Amara, who had the shotgun, fired at the first pig simultaneously with my last shot.'[65] Thesiger described these dangerous encounters in the same detail with which he had described lion hunts in the Sudan. He omitted nothing, though he assured friends, 'I never told my mother about these things because I knew it would worry her.'[66] Now he reassured Kathleen: 'Don't worry, I am not likely to see many pig from now on, and it would be a dull sport shooting them if one did not sometimes risk getting into trouble.'[67] Every Marsh Arab Sheikh interested in weapons was impressed by Thesiger's five-shot .275, and immediately wanted one for himself. 'I have got Rigby an order for three more rifles,' Thesiger wrote with amused satisfaction, 'gold inscribed, in cases with no expense spared.'[68]

For Thesiger 1954 proved yet another decisive year. His articles on 'The Marshmen of Southern Iraq' and 'The Madan or Marsh Dwellers of Southern Iraq' were published respectively in the journals of the Royal Geographical Society and the former Royal Central Asian Society. Gavin Maxwell read the article in the Royal Geographical Society's *Journal* at a moment when he 'had been searching for somewhere to go ... where there was still something left to see that had not already been seen and described'.[69] He wrote to Thesiger, who had returned to London that November after travelling for six weeks with his mother in Trans-Jordan, Syria, Lebanon, Turkey, Greece and Italy. (Wilfred had predicted: 'Trans-Jordan and Syria won't however be hot. The sort of weather when I wear a tweed suit. Rather like pleasant June weather in England but chilly in the evenings.'[70] It is unlikely, however, that Kathleen heeded this information. Thesiger felt miserable even in a draught. In Kenya, in a temperature of 90 degrees, he refused to discard even one layer of clothing: neither woollen vest, flannel shirt, cardigan nor Harris tweed jacket.)

When they lunched for the first time, at the Cavalry Club, Maxwell claimed he was taken aback by Thesiger's unexpectedly formal appearance. In *A Reed Shaken by the Wind*, he wrote: 'The bowler hat, the hard collar and black shoes, the never-opened umbrella, all these were a surprise to me.'[71] Although Maxwell's remarks exasperated Thesiger,[72] his cameo of Thesiger in London contrasted very effectively with images of him in the Iraqi marshes, and further dramatised Thesiger's more primitive second self, celebrated by a Marsh Arab war-chant: 'He does not want a buffalo/He does not want a hundred sheep/But his rifle and dagger are deadly.'[73]

Gavin Young, Thesiger's devoted friend and admirer, remembered him as he was in Iraq in the 1950s, a tall figure plodding barefoot through the mud and reeds. Beside him Amara, cool-headed, watchful, carried Thesiger's rifle. Thesiger wore an old tweed coat over a long Arab shirt which he had pulled up, exposing muscular legs and knee-length drawers. Young thought he looked like the ultimate Great White Hunter crossed with Widow Twanky. At other times, wearing his 'old-fashioned, hand-tailored, three-piece suit and gold watch-chain', Thesiger, according to Young, was 'the perfect reincarnation of Sherlock Holmes'. Thesiger parried Young's affectionate gibes with waspish good humour, scoffing: 'That's just the sort of thing a man who goes off with contracts for five books at a time *would* say!'[74]

Thesiger wrote in *The Marsh Arabs* that he took Gavin Maxwell round in his *tarada* for seven weeks when Maxwell came with him to the marshes in 1956, intending to write a book. Thesiger and Maxwell flew from London to Baghdad overnight on 30 January. By the time Maxwell left Thesiger on 30 March, they had been together for just over two months. Thesiger's 1956 southern Iraq diary needs to be read with care, since he uses 'Gavin' indiscriminately to mean either Maxwell or Young. His 19 April entry – 'Gavin went back to Jasim bin Faris [sic]. Sorry to see him go' – referred to Gavin Young, who joined him at Abd al Wahid's *mudhif* on 5 April, a week after Maxwell and Thesiger had parted at Basra. In *A Reed Shaken by the Wind* Maxwell portrayed Thesiger as dominating and impatient, spontaneously appreciative and unexpectedly compassionate; whereas in *Desert, Marsh and Mountain* Thesiger described Maxwell as 'trying, inclined to be querulous and neurotic'.[75] Yet according to Thesiger's diary and letters to his mother he had enjoyed Maxwell's company, even though Maxwell would write: 'I felt it strange that I could have travelled so far alone with one Englishman and known so little of him.'[76]

Having obtained on demand his permit to travel in the tribal areas, Maxwell was impressed by Thesiger's access to ambassadors and government ministers. At Basra they lodged in style with the Consul-General, Noel Jackson, whom Thesiger had known in Arabia.[77] The weather was perfect. 'Gavin loves the marshes,' Thesiger wrote, 'and thinks that they are the most beautiful place that he has ever seen ... at this time of year ... some of the sunsets and cloud effects during the day are very lovely.'[78] He shared Maxwell's enthusiasm for ornithology – 'He knows a lot about birds which is interesting, and the marshes were packed with wildfowl when we first arrived'[79] – and hoped he might prolong his visit: 'I have greatly enjoyed having him with me,' he wrote on 11 March, 'and wish he was staying longer ... I am hoping that [he] may be able to stay on for another month or so.'[80] Nowhere in his letters to Kathleen did he hint that he found Maxwell difficult; yet when Maxwell dismissed Kipling as a minor author, Thesiger sulked in angry silence.[81]

For much of the daytime Thesiger was busy dispensing medicines and performing circumcisions: twenty-five on 11 March, including four adults. Occasionally Maxwell complained of being ignored, but Thesiger felt this was unreasonable. 'I told Gavin to bring plenty of books, that I'd be busy doctoring them and talking to them. He didn't speak the Marsh Arabs' dialect. He couldn't help me hand out medicines because he didn't know what people needed ... Gavin got rather fed up after a while and said if he'd invited me to Scotland, he'd have looked after me better than I was looking after him. I said, "Damn it, Gavin, I warned you about this in London. You can't go on comparing the Marshes with a shooting party somewhere in the Highlands."'[82] Despite their differences, Thesiger wrote: 'Gavin has enjoyed himself thoroughly.'[83]

On 17 March Maxwell's journey nearly ended in tragedy. Thesiger wrote:

One day Gavin walked out across some wet ground to shoot some ducks while I sat in the canoe. Suddenly he was very nastily charged by a very large unwounded boar, which literally appeared from nowhere. He had only no 5's in his shotgun and I really gave up all hope for him. Our rifles were unloaded, and anyway we were too far away to help. The pig got to within about 4 yards of him and then sheered off. There was a small wet ditch between them and I think this turned it. Gavin was holding his fire to the last possible moment but could never have stopped it with no 5 shot. He had had a rather bad night with fleas and that morning had been rather gloomy. This escape cheered him up wonderfully and he was never in poor spirits again.[84]

Maxwell wrote in *A Reed Shaken by the Wind*: 'My encounter with the boar exercised a profound effect on my outlook ... From the beginning my idleness had irked me; I had been a passenger par excellence ... Now my narrow escape had at the same time satisfied a need of my own and made me the object of a more flattering interest.'[85] Thesiger attempted to mask his anxiety by chiding Maxwell – 'You really are a bloody fool!' – but showed pride and relief that he had stood his ground in the face of the charging boar. In a clumsy effort to calm Maxwell's nerves, Thesiger joked: 'Do you know I couldn't help wishing in a way that he'd got you? Nothing personal, I mean, but I've never seen that happen before, and I wanted to see what he'd do to you.'[86] In March 1953 Thesiger had been attacked at even closer range by a wounded boar. He 'chased it on a horse and came up where it was being bayed by dogs outside a village. Got off. Wounded it again. It charged and I got it at 4 yards through the heart ... it reached me and tried to gore me but I kept it off with the empty rifle in its face until it fell dead.'[87]

By the time Maxwell arrived in Iraq, he wrote, 'it had crossed my mind, though with no great emphasis, that I should like to keep an otter instead of a dog'.[88] He mentioned this to Thesiger, who replied that he had better get one in these Tigris marshes, where 'they were as common as mosquitoes, and were often tamed by the Arabs'.[89] This was no exaggeration. In his 1955 southern Iraq diary Thesiger noted: 'Saw 9 otters playing together. Raised themselves right out of the water to look at us. Swim very fast.'[90] On 20 March they found a baby female otter which Maxwell named Chahala, after a 'broad, slow-running, and dreamy' waterway 'reflecting a blue sky'.[91] 'He was absolutely delighted,' Thesiger wrote, 'and doted on it. We had it for 8 days and it was a delightful little thing and learnt to come when he called it. We made the mistake of giving it meat and this killed it. Gavin was heartbroken and reproaches himself bitterly for having been so foolish. We hope to get another one but it is getting late in the season.'[92]

Before Maxwell left Basra to return to England, Thesiger recorded in his Iraq diary: 'Two Feraigat from Qabab turned up [on 3 April, at Amara's father's *mudhif*] with a tame 5 months(?) old otter. It has been at a village somewhere near Daub [word almost illegible] for the past 3½ months. Produced it in a sack. When they were in a mashuf it followed them swimming. Tame and in good condition.'⁹³ On 4 April he wrote: 'Hired a car and sent off Ajram [a Marsh Arab youth] and the otter to Gavin in Basra.'⁹⁴ Maxwell named the otter Mijbil, after a Marsh Arab Sheikh whose name intrigued him.⁹⁵ Thesiger noted that Mijbil's *mudhif* was 'full of children which was pleasant. I like Mijbil. A 14 year old boy here, Mahdi, the best dancer I have ever seen. Wonderfully graceful and light on his feet. A curiously attractive mad looking lad.'⁹⁶

In May 1956 Dr Robert Hayman from the Natural History Museum in London examined Mijbil and the pelts of two similar otters that Maxwell had acquired in Iraq. He confirmed that Mijbil was a species new to science, and Maxwell alienated Thesiger by allowing it to be named *Lutrogale perspicillata maxwelli*, or Maxwell's otter. Thesiger told an interviewer in 1993: 'I thought at least he might have named it after me.'⁹⁷ Although he felt that Maxwell had treated him unfairly and ungenerously over naming the otter, he acknowledged that he also owed Maxwell a considerable favour. Before his trip to Iraq Maxwell had suggested to his literary agent, Graham Watson of Curtis Brown, that he might look at Thesiger's photographs with a view to publishing a selection of them in a book. Watson visited Thesiger at his mother's flat, and after some hours he was convinced that a marvellous book could be made of Thesiger's journeys in Arabia, if only Thesiger could be persuaded to write it. The next day Watson returned, bringing the publisher Mark Longman with him. Watson wrote: 'the same performance was repeated, disinterest and boredom slowly giving way to signs of warmth. By the time Mark and I left three hours later, Wilfred had promised, hedged by every conceivable qualification, to try his hand at writing a book. He seemed genuinely appalled at the prospect. The following day I returned yet again, this time with Elliott Macrae of Dutton, and an American publisher thus also became committed to the project.'⁹⁸ Watson amended this later: 'I first visited WT on a Thursday, taking Mark Longman back on Friday. And I know I collected Macrae after service at the Chapel in Chelsea Hospital. Thus the whole transaction took four days.'⁹⁹

Three weeks after Maxwell left the marshes, Thesiger wrote to Kathleen: 'You will I hope have seen Gavin Maxwell and got all the news from him. He stayed on a few days in Basra to wait for his mail intending to join me, but I found him another otter and sent it down to Basra before he turned up, and he took it back to London so I did not see him again. I was sorry about this for he was a very pleasant companion but I was delighted to have got him an otter.'[100] Thesiger's note to Maxwell accompanying Mijbil read: 'Here is your otter, a male and weaned. I feel you may want to take it to London – it would be a handful in the tarada.'[101] On the face of it Thesiger's advice made sense, even if his message lacked obvious warmth. Far from attempting to persuade him to stay on for a further month, using the otter as an excuse, Thesiger suggested quite openly that Maxwell should return to England. As a travelling companion Thesiger certainly preferred Gavin Young or Frank Steele to Maxwell, but he was alarmed when he learnt in late May that his mother had told Maxwell he had no business to profit from the experience he had gained with Wilfred by writing a book.

Thesiger appreciated that Kathleen had his best interests at heart, and was merely being protective, yet he resented her interfering in matters she did not fully understand. 'About Gavin and his book,' he wrote on 26 May 1956:

Remember that if it had not been for him I should not have signed a contract to write a book on the desert. When I first met him 2 years ago he asked me if I intended to write a book on the Marshes as I naturally had first rights to it as a subject. I said No and offered to help him if he came out to Iraq. That year he failed to get permission. This year he arranged with me to come before there was any talk of my writing a book. Anyway I am writing on the desert and if I do write on the Marshes it won't be for some years, and will be quite a different book to any Gavin can write. I have a great deal of knowledge and information on the marshes. Gavin has virtually none. He can perhaps make a readable book out of 6 weeks in the marshes but it will be very superficial. I see no reason why it should clash with any book I may write some years hence. I shall stand or fall by my book on the desert. If that is a success I can always sell a book on the marshes. Gavin saw Iraq for a few weeks as a tourist who does not speak the language. I have lived with the people for 7 years. Anyway I brought him out with me to collect information to write a book. You cannot reasonably blame him if he now writes it and if he does what he can to make it a success. You or I may not care for self advertisement but most people will always do it. Don't get up against him for I enjoyed having him with me. When he induced me to write a book he harmed himself, for had I not then thought about a later book on the marshes I should have given him a lot more information than I actually did ... I just write hurriedly to tell you not to worry about any book Gavin can write ...[102]

A few days later he wrote to Kathleen again:

I have just received a very distressed letter from Gavin Maxwell and an extremely nice one. He is very upset that you should feel about him as you do, but says none of the things, which he well might, to justify himself. I wrote to you a few days ago and said that I took Gavin out with me in order that he should write a book and take photos. He is now doing this and neither you nor I can blame him. If it had not been for him neither you nor I would have met Graham Watson and I should not now be under contract to write a book on the desert. As I said in my last letter my subject is the DESERT. If a book on that is a success, and no one can write this book except me, I might write a book on the Marshes. It would be quite a different book to any book Gavin writes. I really don't see how either you or I can resent Gavin writing a book on the Marshes, when I brought him out here so that he could do just that. I grew very fond of him during the 2 months we were together and value him as a friend so don't go on feeling bitter about him and thinking that he is trying to cut me out. I am afraid that Graham Watson was also very upset by your telephone conversation. Be careful with him for I don't want to get on the wrong side of him. He has done me more than proud so far, and contracts seem to be coming in from Holland etc.

Thesiger felt an urgent need to calm his mother's anger, yet he did not wish to further upset her by appearing ungrateful. 'Dearest one,' he continued, 'I know how you feel about it for my sake, but I do think that you have let yourself be carried away. I should hate stories to get round that I am jealous of Gavin, and that we are now on bad terms. This would not do me any good. Let Gavin have his book, and I hope that it is a good one. I am sure that he will acknowledge what he owes to me in the book. He would look rather a fool in a lot of people's eyes if he did not. Make your peace with him and Graham Watson. We can help each other and I like them a lot.' He concluded: 'Dearest Mother, don't feel that I don't understand how you have been feeling. I know how it has got on top of you and you have not had anyone to discuss it with, but I do know that Gavin has not in any way behaved unreasonably or badly, and also that a book on the Marshes by him won't prejudice the success of a book in a few years time by me, if I have made a success of a book on the desert.'[103]

Though a month had elapsed since Maxwell's otter had been identified and named, Thesiger's letter suggests that neither Kathleen nor he knew of this. When he found out about it some months later, he felt embittered and resentful. This marked the beginning of the end of his friendship with Maxwell. In March 1958 he advised Kathleen: 'Don't let Gavin worry you. I have no intention of seeing much of him again. I don't trust him an inch. However it is better not to avoid him completely nor to refuse to see him. If I meet him I shall be quite friendly, but hope not to see him.'[104] This was how Thesiger usually dealt with personal crises. He sat on the fence, no longer initiating involvement, yet refusing not to become involved. In the case of a young author who hoped to write about him in the early 1980s, Thesiger told his literary agent to 'Keep him at arm's length,' whilst at the same time he remained on friendly terms with his aspiring biographer and appeared to give him every encouragement.[105]

Thesiger didn't agree that he had damned *A Reed Shaken by the Wind* with faint praise: 'It's a brilliant piece of verbal photography. But it can only give a very superficial picture of the marshes. It reads easily, but it doesn't compare with Gavin's first book, *Harpoon at a Venture*, which I always think is his best one.'[106] Maxwell gave Thesiger a copy of *Harpoon at a Venture* (1952) soon after they first met, writing: 'Dear Thessiger [sic] … Don't feel bound to read it – I'm sure I couldn't if I hadn't written it.'[107] Thesiger's opinion of Maxwell's books became increasingly hostile as the two men gradually drifted apart. In the copy of Maxwell's enormously successful *Ring of Bright Water* (1960) given to Kathleen by Maxwell's mother, Lady Mary, Thesiger pencilled crabbed marginal notes criticising

Maxwell's unrestrained palette of adjectives – a 'shining enamelled sea', the 'plum-coloured distances' of Skye 'embroidered with threads and scrolls of snow'.[108] In particular, Thesiger found irritating and offensive Maxwell's preoccupation with 'Homeric', 'copious' and 'odiferous' evacuations by various animals, including Mijbil the otter.[109] Yet in his 1955 southern Iraq diary Thesiger had monitored his own bowel movements (information, admittedly, he never dreamt of publishing) and a painful boil on his bottom in no less forthright and sensory detail.[110]

Thesiger may well have envied Maxwell's ability to write rapidly and with apparent ease. *A Reed Shaken by the Wind*, for example, was published only a year after Maxwell had returned from Iraq, while Thesiger struggled to write his 'bloody book' about Arabia.[111] Unlike Maxwell, who understood how the most apparently trivial personal revelations could be of interest to the reader, Thesiger found great difficulty in letting himself go. His agent Graham Watson wrote: 'It required three things to set him off. (1) The feeling, previously unknown to him, which I was able to set off that the things which he had previously regarded as being of no interest to anyone but himself were of riveting interest to others. (2) This tiny root had to be guarded quickly by getting two publishers sufficiently interested to produce contracts. (3) In the early stages of his writing he had to be nurtured carefully along or the urge to write could easily have been killed.'[112]

Kathleen, who Thesiger described as his 'staunchest champion',[113] had influenced his decisions, monitored his friendships, and now played a significant part in this early stage of his literary career. The day Graham Watson brought Mark Longman to try to persuade him to write *Arabian Sands*, Thesiger recalled, 'Had it not been for my mother joining in, and insisting, "Wilfred, you must write a book," I probably never would have attempted it. After all, I didn't know either Graham Watson or Mark Longman in those days, and nothing they said influenced me as much as my mother persuading me to do it.'[114]

Among Thesiger's concerns while he was in the marshes had been Kathleen's health. She was now in her mid-seventies and had trouble with a leg, as well as chronic backache. She suffered from colds and influenza, and despite a still active life she lacked energy. 'The last letter I had from you,' Thesiger wrote in May 1956, 'said that you were not feeling at all well, and I am distressed and worried. My dearest one do take care of yourself and take things easy if you are feeling tired.'[115] In June he learnt that Kathleen had had an accident while driving despite the fact she had not been feeling well.[116] In 1953, aged seventy-three, she had bought a Rover saloon which she kept in a garage near the flat. 'I think of you so continuously,' he wrote, 'especially at night. This has brought it home to me more than ever what you mean to me.'[117] After ten days at St George's Hospital, opposite Hyde Park, Kathleen returned to the flat on 2 July. Thesiger wrote: 'You have made an amazing recovery for which I devoutly thank God. As you say it is due to your Irish fighting spirit.'[118]

Instinctively he felt that he should come home and be with Kathleen during her convalescence. If he did this, however, he would be unable to visit London that winter, unless, he wrote: 'I am willing to be put on the list for income tax for five years. If this happens I get the worst of both worlds for I cannot put in a claim for the expenses I incurred on my Arabian journeys, as I was then resident abroad, and yet must pay full income tax on what I make from my book. If I once get put on the English list for income tax I am on it for 5 years at least, even if I go abroad again next year. Ordinarily it would not matter, but it does at this moment if I am to make anything out of my book.'[119] Besides forfeiting his tax advantages as an overseas resident, Thesiger had planned to visit Nuristan. In the end, Thesiger and Kathleen decided to meet that October in Rome, and return to London together from Italy. This seemed sensible since 'in winter', he wrote, 'it is dark early and you will be more lonely'.[120] As an inducement, he added: 'October should be lovely in Rome and we would just lounge and enjoy ourselves there or nearby.'[121]

In July 1956 Thesiger wrote again, encouraging and praising his mother: 'What a wonderful recovery you are making. You are an amazing person and I bet you have astounded the doctors. But don't do too much, and do listen to their advice and not just go Bolshie when they talk to you. If you can just get your nerves quiet you will be all right. I know that it is no good telling you not to worry; but if only you could do this you would be all right.'[122]

Thesiger and Gavin Maxwell continued to meet, at increasingly in-frequent intervals, until 1965 when they saw one another for the last time in Morocco. Maxwell had been in Tangier, writing *Lords of the Atlas*. He appeared to have very little money, and had no car. Thesiger and his mother took him for drives and gave him lunch. Maxwell evidently enjoyed these brief excursions, writing to Wilfred: 'Please give my love to Kaye [i.e. Kathleen]; it was such a great pleasure to see you both again, and both looking so completely unchanged since ten years ago.'[123] Thesiger told Douglas Botting, Maxwell's biographer:

> Just before we left [Tangier], Gavin said to me, 'I do hope you and your mother can come and have lunch with me. I'd like to return your hospitality, and I've invited the Consul-General to join us. You'll find him interesting – he was a prisoner for a long time in China.' So we met up at the Rembrandt Hotel for drinks before lunch, and Gavin took me on one side and said, 'Can I have a word with you? As you know, I'm absolutely broke and I can't afford to pay for this lunch. Could you pay for it?' So like a bloody fool I said, 'Yes, all right, Gavin.' I thought the least he would do when the Consul-General came in would be to say, 'You owe this lunch to Wilfred – he's insisted on paying for it.' But he didn't. He just said, 'Well, now, pick yourself a very good lunch.' So we had a very expensive lunch at a very expensive restaurant, with wine and liqueurs, and at the end the Consul-General said, 'Thank you Gavin – you've just given me one of the best lunches I've ever had.' And then, when no one was looking, Gavin pushed the bill across to me and I said to myself, 'Well, you've had it, Gavin. I don't really want to see you again.' And I didn't.[124]

According to Gavin Young, Thesiger's friendship with Maxwell did not end with the episode in Tangier, but after a 'flaming row' between them in London.[125] Maxwell died at Raigmore Hospital in Inverness in 1969. Years later, Thesiger said: 'Gavin was interesting to talk to. Yet Mollie [Emtage, his mother's housekeeper] couldn't bear to be in the same room with him. If he'd turned up this afternoon, we'd have talked very easily and it would've been fun. But Gavin wasn't somebody I wanted to travel with ever again.'[126] Thesiger often praised Maxwell's writing (and indeed, his best work was superb), and even after their 'flaming row' he never entirely turned his back on him (as he'd turned his back on thieving villagers in Iraq in 'uncompromising ... righteous indignation'[127]). Certainly Thesiger had a vile temper, he was temperamental and prone to moods of black depression, he was prejudiced, occasionally vindictive, and vulnerable to influences – good and bad. But he seldom bore grudges; above all, he was not mean-spirited.

Though he mocked other people's attempts to analyse him, Thesiger was intensely introspective, and could be very self-critical, especially when he sensed he had hurt or offended someone he was fond of, notably his mother, to whom he once wrote: 'I regret so bitterly that I have not been a better son to you and that so often I have been cross or thoughtless or unkind.'[128] He never doubted for a moment that Kathleen's feelings for him were as intense as his for her: 'Brian [and] Roddy were desperately fond of her too, and she was fond of them; but they had wives and children and in that sense their affection was divided, whereas mine wasn't.'[129]

Thesiger's seven years among the Marsh Arabs embraced a wide spectrum of human experience. He had not been the first European to visit the marshes of southern Iraq: H. St John Philby and Gertrude Bell in 1916, R.S.M. Sturges in 1920, Mr and Mrs Hedgcock ('Fulanain'), who wrote *Haji Rikkan: Marsh Arab*, in 1927, and Freya Stark, who photographed the Marsh Arabs, their canoes and *mudhifs* in 1937 and 1943, were among those who travelled there before him. However, Thesiger's extensive sojourns in the marshes between 1951 and 1958, his contributions to the life of the Ma'dan, and the rich variety of information he gathered in the course of his journeys, viewed as a whole, raise him far above contemporaries and predecessors alike. His classic *The Marsh Arabs* describes 'times of excitement and hardship, accidents, pig hunts, blood feuds; there are episodes of tragedy and happiness, and moments of pure comedy. Not only does Thesiger evoke with great beauty the landscape and its teeming wild life, but we come to know the people, many of them individually, whose life he shares, the sheikhs who are his friends, his canoemen and their families.'[130]

TWENTY

Among the Mountains

While he was Political Adviser to the Abyssinian Crown Prince at Dessie in 1944, Thesiger had read with enormous pleasure Eric Shipton's book *Upon that Mountain*, published the previous year. 'Captivated by Shipton's personality',[1] he invited him early in 1952 to lunch at the Travellers Club in London. Shipton had written: 'the giant peak of Rakaposhi [in what in 1947 would become Pakistan] which rose from a belt of pinewoods in the gorge of the Hunza river ... presents one of the most stupendous mountain faces in the world'.[2] Thesiger listened with fascination as Shipton described Rakaposhi over lunch, and spoke with quiet modesty of his extraordinary life as a mountain explorer.

Shipton liked and admired Thesiger, but he could not resist poking fun at some of his camp and grandiloquent remarks: 'Once I gave him a lift from Pall Mall to his flat and on the way I said something like, "Wouldn't you find a car more convenient instead of relying on taxis?" He replied stiffly, "Gentlemen don't drive." I wondered if he'd ever speak to me again. As he got out, I noticed a red stain on his jacket, where he'd been sitting on a spoon covered with strawberry jam that somebody's child had left there after a picnic the day before. He must have been livid, but he never mentioned this when I saw him afterwards, and neither did I.'[3]

Shipton did not know that Thesiger had learnt to drive in 1928, and occasionally drove when he was abroad, and so, of course, he took seriously his remark about gentlemen not driving, which Thesiger said later he had intended as a joke.[4] Thesiger nevertheless did have a way of making oddly self-conscious statements about what made a 'gentleman'. John Verney referred to one when he wrote in March 1966 telling Thesiger: 'I shall vote Liberal as usual, just because it's such a futile thing to do and because Jo Grimond is an old Etonian – which (do you remember?) you once gave Tim White as the definition of a gentleman.'[5]

In July 1952 Thesiger flew from Baghdad to Karachi. From there he went by train, via Lahore and Rawalpindi, to Peshawar, where he hoped to get permission to visit Gilgit, Hunza and Chitral and to see Rakaposhi from Baltit, as Shipton had recommended. 'No one can say whether the Pakistan Government will give me the necessary permission or not,' he wrote. 'The trouble is that Gilgit and Hunza are in Kashmir and they are very sticky about allowing anyone to go there owing to the war with India. Chitral is near the Afghan border and diplomatic relations are strained with Afghanistan.'[6]

In Karachi Thesiger stayed with the British High Commissioner, Gilbert Laithwaite. He had known Laithwaite for some years, and had sent him offprints of his articles on the Empty Quarter published in the RGS *Journal*. In a letter accompanying 'Across the Empty Quarter' he had mentioned his interest in a pamphlet Laithwaite had written about weaving.[7] Thesiger was fascinated by textiles of many kinds. He had collected carpets and rugs while he was in the Sudan, and bought others in Persia, India and Morocco. His first (and favourite) carpet he had bought in Cairo in 1934. Hanging on the wall of a corridor in his mother's flat were several framed monochrome textiles by Kuba weavers, brought from the Congo by Wilfred Gilbert Thesiger in 1908. (Colonel Gilbert Drage, Kathleen's neighbour, who had taken Wilfred and his brothers rabbiting near The Milebrook, wrote a treatise on hand-loom weaving, and in 1941 The Studio published *Adventures in Embroidery* by Wilfred's cousin, the actor Ernest Thesiger. In his witty autobiography, *Practically True* (1927), Ernest described his fondness for needlework and lace-making. During a holiday in France he and a friend whiled away the long train journeys by doing embroidery. At one station a recently widowed woman in crêpe veils got into their compartment, sobbing into her handkerchief. But her tears, Ernest wrote, turned to fits of laughter as 'the sight of two grown men deep in embroidery had overcome her grief'.[8])

Thesiger looked forward to seeing Peshawar. 'Karachi,' he wrote to Kathleen, 'is a dull town, modern, ugly, and overgrown, in dull country.' He added a gently reproving postscript: 'For Heaven's sake put KARACHI, PAKISTAN, NOT INDIA. They are very touchy.'[9] He was

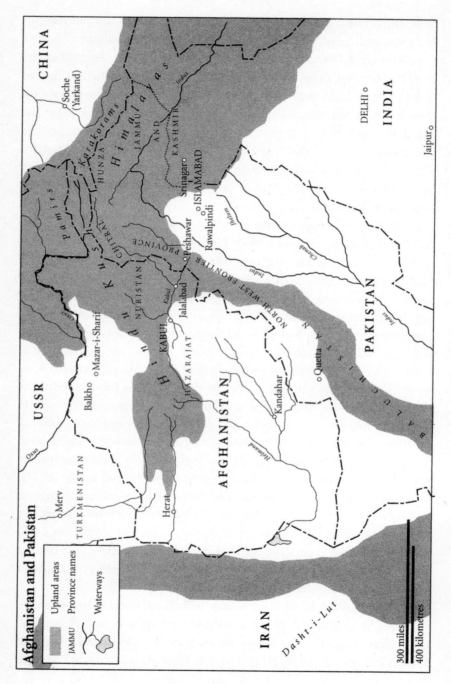

Afghanistan and Pakistan

Upland areas
JAMMU   Province names
Waterways

CHINA

Soche (Yarkand)

Karakorams

Himalayas

HUNZA

JAMMU

AND

KASHMIR

Srinagaro

ISLAMABAD

Pamirs

CHITRAL

KUSH

HINDU

NURISTAN

Peshawar

Rawalpindi

PROVINCE

NORTH WEST FRONTIER

DELHI o

INDIA

Jaipur o

Indus

Jhelum

Chenab

Kabul

Jalalabad

KABUL

Mazar-i-Sharif

Balkh o

USSR

HAZARAJAT

AFGHANISTAN

Quetta

PAKISTAN

Indus

BALUCHISTAN

Oxus

Merv o

TURKMENISTAN

Herat o

Kandahar

Helmand

300 miles

400 kilometres

IRAN

Dasht-i-Lut

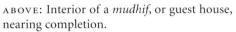

ABOVE: Interior of a *mudhif*, or guest house, nearing completion.

Suaid herdboy. This image was used for the frontispiece of the first edition of *The Marsh Arabs* in 1964.

BELOW: Kandari nomads coming down from Lake Shiva to the plains, 1965.

Thesiger in Copenhagen while
he was writing *The Marsh
Arabs*, 15 November 1961.

BELOW: Thesiger and Kathleen, about 1961.

Jan Verney,
Kathleen and
Thesiger on holiday
in Portugal in
June–July 1961.
The photograph
was probably taken
by John Verney.

Thesiger's portrait, painted in 1965 by Derek Hill.

BELOW: Outside the Travellers Club, Pall Mall, in 1973.

BELOW: Thesiger and David Niven at the Royal Geographical Society. Niven narrated a film, *The Forbidden Desert of the Danakil*, produced by Anglia Television, broadcast of 8 May 1973.

ABOVE: Aboard the *Fiona*, the 42-foot ketch on which Thesiger and Gavin Young sailed for five months round the Indonesian islands in 1977 in search of Joseph Conrad's eastern world.

BELOW: Thesiger and Gavin Young at Thesiger's flat in Chelsea, 1977.

BELOW: With Frank Steele on the Uaso Nyiro river, Kenya, in 1970. Steele accompanied Thesiger in 1960–61 travelling on foot with camels to Lake Turkana (then Lake Rudolf) in the former Northern Frontier District of Kenya.

ABOVE: Thesiger and Lokuyie, a Samburu *moran*, in northern Kenya.

BELOW: John Newbould with a pelican on the shore of Lake Natron.

BELOW RIGHT: Kisau, Thesiger's devoted companion, who died in 1974.

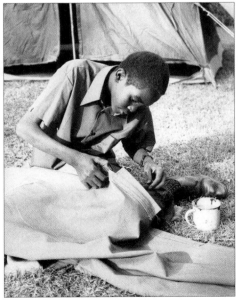

Lawi Leboyare, Thesiger wrote, 'was as dear to me as a son'.

Laputa Lekakwar, in whose house Thesiger lived during his last years at Maralal.

Ewoi Ekai, known as 'Kibiriti', in his garden near Maralal.

Thesiger and Erope on safari. Erope's name meant 'spring rains' in Turkana.

ABOVE: Looking out from 'The Viewpoint' on the edge of the escarpment at Malossa, near Maralal.

BELOW: Thesiger stroking the nose of 'Africano', greatest of the bulls on Robert Vavra's farm in Spain, near Seville, in July 1996.

Wilfred Thesiger leaving for Buckingham Palace with Alexander Maitland, on
2 November 1995, when Thesiger was knighted by HRH The Prince of Wales.

eventually allowed to travel in Swat and Chitral, thanks largely to a former Governor of the North-West Frontier province, Sir George Cunningham, who gave him a letter of introduction to the Chief Minister, Khan Abd al Quaiyun Khan, and spoke to the Governor, Khwaja Shahabud Din, on Thesiger's behalf. Not until the following year did Thesiger obtain a permit to travel in Hunza.

After a summer tramping over Swat and Chitral, he described this 'wonderful trip' to Kathleen: 'I think I covered about 500 miles on foot in a month through some of the biggest mountains in the world.'[10] (He had previously reassured her: 'Now don't get worried that I am going to do any mountaineering for I am not. I shall follow the tracks which the local shepherds use.'[11])

I went right up through the Hindu Kush to the edge of the Pamirs and looked down on the Oxus. I must be one of the few Englishmen who have seen the Oxus in the last half century. It is superb country. [Thesiger found the Pakistan borderlands and tribes so 'fascinating' that he wrote: 'Given my time over again I should have gone into the Indian Army and then transferred to the Political. However it was never a thing which occurred to me to do when I was at Oxford.'[12]] A lot of mountains are very sheer, towering great precipices too steep for snow to lie, but up round Barogil the mountains are more rolling. I liked this country best. It is very exhilarating. Great towering mountainsides across which the cloud shadows drift, and higher up the snows and glaciers very white and clear in the thin cold mountain air. There is the space and cleanliness of the desert and great heights and the clear blue sky of Central Asia. In the broad valleys are russet coloured bogs and patches of bog myrtle and groves of birch turning to gold in the autumn. Here we found Kirghiz, with Mongol faces and wispy beards, and Kazak and Wakikh and people from beyond Kashgar [where Eric Shipton later served as Consul].

During this journey Thesiger took a lot of photographs, using the ten rolls of Ilford 35mm film he had asked his mother to order from Mrs Cope at Sinclair's: '29 SHINER I think is the speed,' he scribbled laconically, 'but she will know.'[13] 'I only hope that they will come out well for the lighting is of course different to anything that I have been used to.'[14]

He had found 'a good Pathan bearer [Jahangir Khan] who speaks quite good English. But when we get up to Chitral they speak a curious language of their own. I wish I spoke Pushtu.'[15]

Thesiger précised the remainder of his journey:

From Mastuj I followed the River north to its source near Korumbar, on the Gilgit–Afghanistan border. I then came down it as far as LASHT and from there crossed a 14000' pass, the SHAH JIN ALI pass over the Hindu Kush to the RICH GOL. I went down this to Wandinkot, crossed it and went back up the TIRICH river, to the glacier, under TIRICH MIR, which is 25000' and the highest mountain in the Hindu Kush. I then crossed over another pass back into the Mastuj valley and down this to Chitral. From there I went into the country of the Black Kafirs, whom I have always wanted to see. A curious pagan survival. They are gradually being converted to Islam and in a few years time I don't suppose there will be any more of them left as pagans.[16]

Printing the names of mountains, passes, rivers and valleys in capital letters enabled Kathleen to identify them easily on a map, making Wilfred's letters more interesting for her.

Writing from Peshawar, he continued: 'I am now staying here for a day or two and am then off to Waziristan to see something of the Pathans. I hope to stay down there for about 20 days and then come back here and go up to Kabul'[17] – he had felt it would be a pity not to visit Kabul while he was so near to Afghanistan.[18] Before leaving Peshawar in August he had bought and sent off to his mother a handsome present: 'what I think is a rather attractive Shiraz carpet for your bedroom. I hope it will go with the other ones. I wish I had your gift for visualising how things will go together. I found it in a carpet shop here and fell in love with it when I saw it. It has a rather bold tribal pattern on a background of deep blue.'[19]

Thesiger kept a detailed record of his journey through Swat and Chitral in a ruled 'Century' pocket notebook, the first of a series which included journeys in Hunza, the Hazarajat in Afghanistan, Morocco, Nuristan and Ladakh. *Among the Mountains*, published in 1998, was drawn mostly from these diaries. The book excluded Morocco, and wasn't written by Thesiger, whose failing sight prevented him from

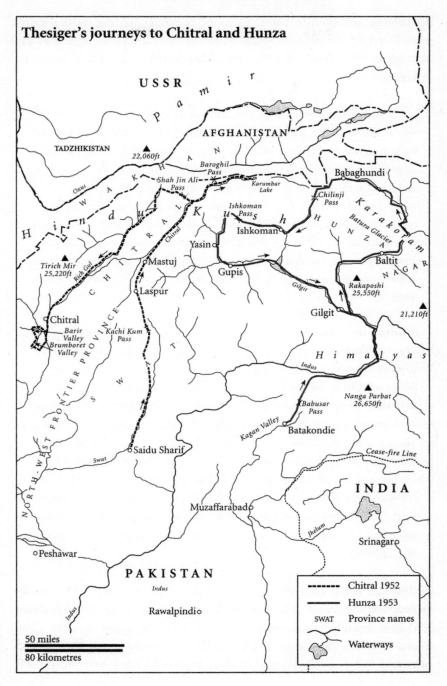

Thesiger's journeys to Chitral and Hunza

USSR

Pamir

TADZHIKISTAN

AFGHANISTAN

▲ 22,060ft

Oxus

W A K H A N

Baroghil
Pass

Shah Jin Ali
Pass

Karumbar
Lake

Babaghundi

H i n d u K u s h

C H I T R A L

Chilinji
Pass

K a r a k o r a m

▲ Tirich Mir
25,220ft

Rich Gol

Ishkoman
Pass

Ishkoman

H U N Z A

Batura Glacier

NAGAR

Yasin○

Baltit

Chitral

○Mastuj

Gupis

▲ Rakaposhi
25,550ft

Gilgit

▲ 21,210ft

○Laspur

Chitral

CHITRAL PROVINCE

*Barir
Valley*
*Brumboret
Valley*

Kachi Kum
Pass

Gilgit

H i m a l a y a s

Indus

S W A T

NORTH-WEST FRONTIER PROVINCE

▲ Nanga Parbat
26,650ft

○Saidu Sharif

Swat

*Babusar
Pass*

Kagan Valley

Batakondie

Cease-fire Line

INDIA

Muzaffarabad○

Jhelum

Srinagar○

○Peshawar

PAKISTAN

Indus

Rawalpindi○

▬ ▬ ▬	Chitral 1952
▬▬▬	Hunza 1953
SWAT	Province names
〰	Waterways

50 miles

80 kilometres

attempting any literary work. Some of his letters to his mother contained descriptions as fine as any in the diaries, and some material that was better still. Thus he summarised for Kathleen his three weeks in Waziristan:

I had a very interesting time. The Frontier has always been a bit of the world which I have wanted to see. Everyone was most kind to me and I thoroughly enjoyed myself. I got up to Razmak and am the first Englishman to have been there since we left the country. It was a very large military camp situated in the very heart of the Wazir country, and while our troops were there, there was almost constant fighting. We used to try and hold down Waziristan with a division of troops, and really never made any impression. The Pakistanis have moved all troops out of the area except for locally recruited Scouts, and since they have been administering it have had peace. A remarkable achievement for which one has to give them full credit. Of course the Mullahs can no longer whip up the tribes to fight against an infidel government. Even today however you can go nowhere without an escort and if you get out of the car to take a photo, even just outside one of the forts, the escort at once pickets the high ground around. Still you can go round in a pick-up with a dozen armed locals with you, whereas in the old days you would have been in an armoured lorry with an escort of armoured cars. I was glad they let me go to Razmak since the road goes through interesting country. They took a chance doing so and the officer with me half expected we should be shot up on the way back. Interesting. I thought the Pathan officers whom I met up there a magnificent lot of men and would enjoy to serve with them. They are extremely well educated and speak perfect English and are many of them far better read in English litterature [sic] than I am ... I shall go from Kabul to Kandahar and then to Quetta and spend a bit of time in Baluchistan.[20]

Thesiger returned to the Iraqi marshes in late February 1953. On the twenty-sixth he stopped at Falih bin Majid's *mudhif*. One of Falih's slaves had been married, and the party, entertained by gipsy dancing girls, lasted till two in the morning. The following morning, Falih, his son Abd el Wahid, Falih's cousin Abbas bin Mohamed and Thesiger went out, each in a separate canoe, to shoot wildfowl. As they were setting off, Thesiger noticed that Abbas's cartridge belt contained several cartridges marked 'LG' (Large Game) interspersed among the others. 'I said, "They are only for pig; for God's sake don't use them to shoot at duck or you will kill somebody." To prove my point I cut one open and showed him the seven large pellets, which I dropped into my pocket.'[21] Unfortunately, Abbas appears to have forgotten or ignored this warning, with fatal consequences, as Thesiger wrote to Kathleen:

> There has been a terrible tragedy. Falih bin Majid, the sheikh with whom I stay and who was my great friend, was shot the other day by his cousin while out shooting and died 36 hours later as a result of his wound … We were scattered among the reed beds and I heard a shot fired, from the sound straight at us. I shouted out to them to take care where they were firing and then on coming round a patch of reeds found Falih collapsed in his canoe and with one large buckshot apparently through his heart. We towed him for 7 hours to his house and then managed to get him to Basra by car and from there to Baghdad by air. I got up to Baghdad next day but he had died before I got there.

In his diary, Thesiger noted on 1 March: 'Heard that Falih died last night at 7.30. The pellet bruised his heart, collapsed his lung and cut the big nerves of the heart'. He continued in a letter:

> It really was a terrible tragedy for he was an outstanding person and we were great friends. I am sorry for his cousin. He was out of sight of Falih when he shot, he mixed up his cartridges and fired one loaded with buckshot and one of the pellets at 60 yards bruised Falih's heart, collapsed his lung and severed one of the big nerves. He died of shock. The doctor in Baghdad said it was a fatal wound and nothing I could have done would have saved him. He recovered consciousness after his first collapse and remained conscious to the end though very weak. I go back tomorrow to his house for the mourning. It is really very tragic and I am very upset. He had welcomed me so warmly the evening before when I arrived at his home. Abbas, in fear of his life, had fled through the reed-beds to the police-station at Qalit Salih, where he gave himself up. In doing so Abbas

not only disgraced himself and his family, in the eyes of the Ma'dan, but thwarted any attempt by Sheikh Majid to avenge the death of his son.[22]

After spending six weeks partly in the marshes, partly among the shepherd tribes to the north, Thesiger returned to the shepherd tribes for a further month. 'I have laid up my canoe,' he wrote, 'as I shall not be going back into the Marshes this year.' Laying up the canoe was also symbolic. Thesiger's *tarada*, a 'glistening, slim and high-prowed' craft, one of the finest ever built in the renowned boatyards at Huwair, had been a lavish present from Falih bin Majid.

Thesiger had not been able to visit England in time for Elizabeth II's coronation. From Basra he wrote on 29 June: 'I saw the film "Elizabeth the Queen" the other day. What an impressive ceremony it must have been. It seems to have gone off wonderfully well despite the bad weather and I am sure that the Queen was magnificent. I am taking three of my Marsh Arabs to see the film this evening with Gavin Young and wonder what they will make of it.'[23] Thesiger was delighted when someone told him that his club, the Travellers, had been praised as 'the best decorated Club in London'. 'I was also thrilled by the news of [Hillary and Tenzing's first ascent of] Everest,' he added. 'How very opportune it was. I do hope that they are not going to spoil it by squabbling over it. I gather that the Indians are out to make capital out of it. It is a sad thing that everything today is used for this sort of propaganda.' He went on: 'We have had some sticky weather in May which is always a rather unpleasant month out here, but now the North wind is blowing strongly and it is cool and pleasant. The hot weather comes in August but by then I shall be en route to Pakistan I hope.'[24]

From August until October 1953, Thesiger travelled in Hunza. He was rewarded with some magnificent views of Rakaposhi; views so fine he felt that they alone had made his arduous journey worthwhile. Although the Prime Minister had sanctioned Thesiger's proposed journey through Gilgit and Hunza, the Minister for Kashmir Affairs, whose office issued the necessary permits, was deliberately obstructive. 'He is I gather bitterly anti-British,' Thesiger observed. 'It needed practically a Cabinet row before I got it ... At any rate I have got it and I deserve it for I have shown exemplary patience for a month.'[25]

Thesiger's journey, among scenery he judged 'far more impressive' than anything he had seen in Chitral the previous year,[26] began and ended at Gilgit, and from there he wrote a marvellous long letter to his mother on 20 October, while the events he described were still fresh and vivid in his mind.

I have had a wonderful journey. From here I went up to BALTIT in HUNZA, and then followed the river up to the Afghan frontier, crossed the CHILINJI Pass (17000') into the top of the ISHKOMAN valley, followed this valley down to IMIT, then across the ISHKUMAN Pass (14000') to DARKOT, and from there back to Gilgit by YASIN and GUPIS. I was very lucky with the weather. The winter this year has been a month early but despite this we were across the Chilinji pass before the weather broke.

Thesiger was accompanied by Faiz Muhammad, an English-speaking Pathan, and a local ponyman with two packhorses. From Baltit he went with two ponies and two ponymen as far as Spanj in the Reshit valley; and from there, with two yaks and four porters, across the Chilinji Pass to Yasin.

I have never seen such country, it is indescribably magnificent ... From Baltit RAKAPOSHI (25000') rises absolutely straight from the valley bottom which is about 6000'. So you see about 20000' of mountain only a short distance away, without any foothills intervening, and what must be one of the most beautiful mountains in the world. I do hope my photos are a success. But it was not only Rakaposhi, seen above the terraced cultivations, orchards and poplars of the Hunza valley, but all the Karakoram mountains, some of them very grim and sheer. They seemed to hang there in the clouds right over one's head. This time I have really seen the big mountains and have been right through the heart of them.

He described how they had camped in some forest on the far side of the Chilinji Pass while it snowed for a whole night and a day. This was fortunate, since the Chilinji would have been impassable after such a heavy snowfall;

as it was it was a long steady grind but nowhere difficult ... When we got to the top I had a nasty moment for the other side was nearly vertical and with about 2 feet of snow on it. It would have been impossible if the snow had been frozen but was comparatively easy as it was soft, and we ploughed down 2000' pretty quickly with many a tumble. We had rather a grim time on the Ishkuman pass although it was only 14000', but it had all the fresh snow on it. The locals said we should never get across it. I took two extra porters and we camped near the top of the tree limit. Next morning the porters went badly stopping every ten minutes and wishing to camp for the day after 2 hours when we came to the last of the birch. It was then about 7.30 in the morning. I refused for I was afraid of the weather breaking again and the top of the pass only looked about 2 hours away. But almost at once we came to a flat plain about 3 miles across and deep in snow under a thickish crust. This took us about 4 weary hours to cross, and then there was a succession of steep ascents and shallow cups to cross. We toiled forwards foot by foot and every time we thought we were at the top there was another basin to get round or across and another ridge. Finally we reached the top at 5.30. The sun sets at 6 o'clock and there was no moon. Right across the topmost ridge of snow were the absolutely fresh tracks of a very large brown bear. This stimulated my porters but they were pretty done and my bearer was in tears. It was bitterly cold and all I could see below us was a large steep glacier covered with snow and the even steeper snow covered mountainside. We had to keep off the glacier for fear of crevasses. I went ahead with one of the two Hunza porters who were still with me, [an] excellent and untiring man. The Ishkuman porters, rather a poor crowd, and my hysterical bearer strung out behind. It was a brute of a descent, in places I went in up to my armpits, and very tiring work breaking trail for the porters through the thick ice crust on the snow. All the same we went too fast for the porters and after 2000' lost contact. We shouted and shouted; by then it was dark but got no answer. The porter with me kept insisting that we must go on down to the tree level, but I could not leave the others and anyway we had no matches with us. Eventually he slipped away and I was left by myself on the mountainside in the really freezing cold. I went on calling at intervals and I fancy about 2 hours later the 4 Ishkuman porters turned up. I was glad to see them for I was by then almost reconciled to spending the night in the open without any covering and losing my toes. They said my bearer had collapsed under a rock and refused to go on. However as the other Hunza porter had stayed with him and he had a large roll of bedding with him I was not worried about him. We went on downhill the porters going very slowly which meant long cold waits for me. The last bit was a very steep descent of about 500′ down a snow face. When we got to the bottom and found some scrub by the stream, I found that one of the four porters was missing. The others said he had stopped under a rock. I knew I could never get up the face we had just come down again in the dark so we made a bit of a fire and I got into my sleeping bags on the snow and spent a wet cold night as my warmth melted the snow through the sleeping bags. It was then 12.30 at night and we had been going without a stop since 5.30 of the morning before. Soon after it was light the missing porter turned up and after some tea I got them down to the edge of the villages in the valley below. These upper villages were deserted. I had another cup of tea and then leaving the porters to rest, the Hunza porter who had left me the night before was in this village with slightly frost bitten toes, I went back up the mountain to look for my bearer. It was heavy going as I was carrying a full pack. I was glad to run into them coming slowly down after about 2½ hours. My bearer's feet were slightly frost bitten. Meanwhile they had got word in the village that we were in trouble and all came up to help. After this it was all easy going to Gilgit.[27]

The Hazarajat region of Afghanistan where Thesiger travelled for five weeks in August and September 1954 was broken by gorges and stream-fed valleys; its parched terrain, and tawny ranges with few peaks, were quite different from the towering ice mountains, glaciers and torrents of the Karakoram or the Hindu Kush. He had intended to visit Nuristan, but found that permission to enter this virtually unadministered territory would be difficult to obtain. 'When I arrived in Kabul in July 1954,' he wrote, 'I therefore asked instead for permission to travel in the Hazarajat. This I knew would be more easily forthcoming. I hoped by first travelling in this region to establish my reputation in the eyes of the Afghan government so that another year they would give me a permit for Nuristan.'[28] This was how Thesiger prefaced his Hazarajat journey in *Among the Mountains* in 1998. In his article 'The Hazaras of Central

Afghanistan', printed in the Royal Geographical Society's *Journal* in September 1955, he had instead written: 'I went to Afghanistan in the summer of 1954 from southern Iraq, where I had been for six months among the marshmen. There I had been living in semi-submerged houses [doubtless a reference to the floods in May] and moving about in a canoe; now I was anxious to stretch my legs on the mountain tops. In 1952 and 1953 I had travelled in the Hindu Kush and Karakoram, in Chitral, Gilgit and Hunza, and had long wished to make a similar journey in the Hazarajat of Afghanistan.'[29]

Thesiger wrote to his mother from Basra on 1 June: 'I had a delightful letter from [Sir David] Lascelles our Ambassador in Kabul asking me to stay with him for as long as I liked and promising to do what he could to get me permission to wander about the country but warning me that the Afghans are very difficult. I shall go up there and stay with him and hope to get away into the country somewhere ...'[30] After six weeks spent with the Azairij, Al bu Daraj and Bazun shepherd tribes, much of the time 'among people whom I had not yet met', Thesiger wrote from Basra: 'I am off to Baghdad tomorrow evening by train and am taking Amara with me. I shall stay in Baghdad for four or five days and then fly to Karachi. I have heard that my visa will be given me there by the Afghan consulate. From Karachi to Peshawar and then by road to Kabul. I hope that I shall get permission to see something of the country.'[31]

Accompanied by Jan Baz, thirty-four years old, an interpreter provided by the Afghan government, Thesiger began his journey of nearly four hundred miles from the Unai Kotal range at the head of the Maidan. In *Among the Mountains* he outlined the route they followed:

crossing the Helmand river near Parakhulm, we worked our way upwards along the southern slopes of Kuh-i-Baba until we crossed this 17,000-foot-high range by the Zard Sang Pass. We then visited Naiak, recrossed Kuh-i-Baba to Panjao, and followed the Panjao river down to Sultan Ribat; here we were forced eastwards by impassable gorges and had some difficulty in getting back over the Helmand. We climbed up through some very broken country to the northern edge of the Dasht-i-Mazar, in Besud, which we skirted before descending the broad and fertile valley of the Kajao, to Kharbet. From there we went to Unai Kotal, down to Sar-i-Chashma and

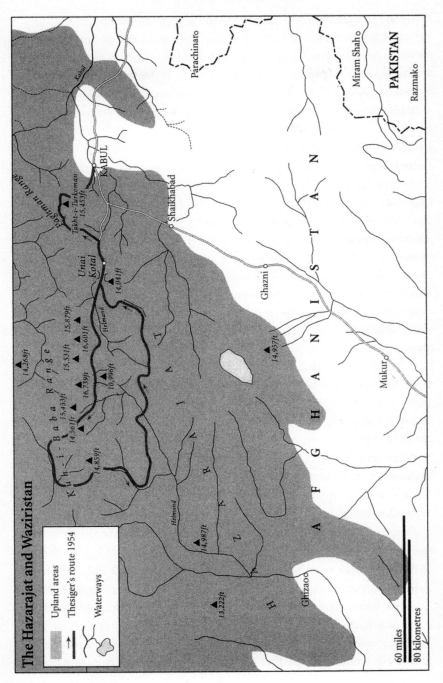

The Hazarajat and Waziristan

Upland areas
Thesiger's route 1954
Waterways

60 miles
80 kilometres

PAKISTAN

Razmako

Miram Shah

Parachinar

Kabul

KABUL

Shaikhabad

Paghman Range

Takht-i-Turkoman
15,453ft

Unai
Kotal

14,041ft

Ghazni

Mukur

14,957ft

Helmand

15,879ft

16,601ft

15,531ft

14,268ft

Kuh-i-Baba Range

15,453ft

16,739ft

10,396ft

14,561ft

14,859ft

H A Z A R A J A T

Helmand

14,987ft

13,222ft

Ghizao

H

A F G H A N I S T A N

347

up the Sanglakh valley. We then crossed the steep mountain range on the north side of the valley to Surkh-o-Parsa, recrossed this mountain range to the north of Takht-i-Turkoman, and descended from the holy pools of Hauz-i-Khas to Paghman and Kabul. During the six weeks [sic] Jan Baz and I travelled in the Hazarajat, of its four districts, Deh Kundi, Deh Zangi, Besud and Yakwalung, Deh Kundi was the only one I did not enter.[32]

The journey was uneventful, due to a large extent to Jan Baz, whose 'patience and tact' Thesiger praised: 'He was invariably cheerful, obliging and interesting, and his company was a constant pleasure.'[33] Thesiger's sketch of their route (like parts of the Hazarajat) is colourless and rather dry. His narrative, in contrast, sparkles with lively descriptions: of sleeping 'under a cold clear sky' on the flat roofs of domed houses; of women's clothes, 'red in colour' and 'often decorated with innumerable coins';[34] of a narrow gorge 'below jagged peaks where lammergeyers and ravens wheeled in the wind-torn sky';[35] of 'the featureless, dry, dusty downs below Kuh-i-Baba' and 'the varied colouring of hills, limestone rocks and fields'[36] – 'purple-greys, blues, off-white, yellow, orange and pale-green – softened by the hazy afternoon light'.[37]

Thesiger's brilliant black-and-white photographs do not merely illustrate the evocative descriptions (some rearranged or rewritten, others quoted directly from his diaries), but often bring the Hazarajat and its hardy inhabitants to life more vividly than words: weatherbeaten farmers; children with lovely wistful eyes; dwellings of rough stone among boulder-stubbled hills; tented encampments; heavy-laden camels led by nomads in turbans; women weaving *barak* cloth on makeshift looms; a track vanishing in shadow into the thinly wooded Koli Barit valley.

In October 1954 Thesiger met Kathleen in Amman, having proposed the itinerary for a tour of Trans-Jordan, Palestine, Syria and Lebanon by car. From Amman they visited Jerusalem, Damascus, Aleppo, Baalbek and Beirut, from where he suggested they fly to Istanbul and continue to Athens, Rome, Milan and London. Thesiger's former batman in the Druze Legion, Faris Shahin, joined them in Palestine. Kathleen loved every moment: 'the most wonderful 6 weeks', she wrote in her diary. 'A perfect memory to carry with me to the end of my days.' Faris, now in his mid-twenties, looked like the young Laurence Olivier. Anxious for promotion, he wrote several letters from Zerka, begging Thesiger to contact Brigadier [Sir] John Glubb ('Club-Pasha' or 'Clap Basha', was Faris's colourfully phonetic rendering of the name by which Glubb was known) on his behalf. Thesiger was sometimes slow in replying, and to one of Faris's letters Kathleen added in her expansive scrawl: 'Will you try to answer this or anyway keep his address for he seems to be so faithful.'[38]

On 31 March 1955 Thesiger informed his mother: 'I have heard from Lascelles in Kabul that the Afghan Government have given me permission to travel in Nuristan. He was convinced that they never would give me permission. I shall therefore go to Afghanistan at the end of July and spend August and September in Nuristan. It will be interesting since this part of the country is very little known.'[39] In March Thesiger learnt he had been awarded the Royal Central Asian Society's Lawrence of Arabia medal. He confided to Kathleen: 'I feel that it is more worthwhile getting than the RGS gold medal, which has been rather cheapened of recent years. [He later retracted this caustic reference to Freya Stark, who had been awarded the RGS Founder's Medal in 1942.[40]] I wrote to Sir Cecil Harcourt and thanked him for his letter. I told him I should be abroad and asked him that you should receive it on my behalf. I owe such a lot to your encouragement and help and I should like you to receive it for me.'[41]

'I am sorry that Roddy has had mumps,' he wrote from Basra. 'I have been lucky. There is an epidemic of mumps in this country and two months ago four of my canoeboys got it in turn. I was lucky to escape as we were sleeping side by side and the blankets always get mixed up.'[42] On 4 June, the day after Thesiger's forty-fifth birthday, one of his canoeboys, Hasan bin Maneti, was to be married. 'He comes from the first village I ever got to know,' Wilfred wrote, 'and I want to make sure he has a slap up wedding. I will fire off a lot of cartridges and we will go and collect the bride in my canoe.'[43] According to his diary, Hasan was married on 5 June and Thesiger fired off 'about 170 rounds with the revolver'.[44]

By June Thesiger feared that 'the trouble' between Afghanistan and Pakistan might prevent him travelling in Nuristan, 'right on the Pakistan border ... the mountainous country North of Jalalabad adjoining Chitral'. By 'the trouble' Thesiger meant Afghanistan's increasingly obvious resentment of the Durand Line, which from 1893 divided Afghanistan from the British Indian Empire. After the partition of British

India in 1947 into India and Pakistan, Afghanistan began openly to dispute the Durand Line's validity. The Afghans encouraged tribesmen living across the Line in Pakistan to form an independent state – 'Pushtunistan'[45] – which in due course would become integrated with Afghanistan. Thesiger wrote on 5 July: 'I am afraid Afghanistan is off for this year ... I shall go to Morocco and hope to get in touch with the Glaoui [the Pasha of Marrakesh, Hajj Tihami al Glawi] and then up into the High Atlas. This area is not anti French and is quiet. The trouble is in the towns and in the coastal plain.'[46]

On 19 July Thesiger flew from Baghdad to Casablanca via Paris. From Casablanca he went by CTM bus to Rabat, where he visited the British Consulate. Hartley, the Consul, struck him as 'a caricature of a FO type'; Dr Panouse, head of the Zoological Department, gave him useful advice.[47] In Marrakesh, Thesiger stayed at the Hôtel d'Atlas in the Arab quarter. He found the city little changed since 1937: 'the suqs ... the best from here to Pakistan. They sell what they make, not rubbish from Europe. Colourful and no sign of unfriendliness ... I was the only European there but no feeling of hostility. Story tellers, jugglers, snake charmers ... dancing boys, local dentists (with piles of teeth in front of them) etc.'[48]

During his visits to Marrakesh in 1937 and 1955 Thesiger might have met the French artist Jacques Majorelle, who had lived and worked in southern Morocco since 1917 and who made very popular a vivid cobalt pigment used by the Berbers, which became known as Bleu Majorelle. Majorelle was a gifted painter in the *fin de siècle* Orientalist tradition, to an extent mirrored by Thesiger's travel photography. However, the Orientalists' sensual voyeuristic preference for eastern bathing scenes and shapely odalisques had been replaced, for Thesiger, by tribal ceremonies and photogenic warriors. Besides remote peoples Thesiger also photographed landscapes, and buildings of many kinds, from mosques to Iraqi *mudhifs* to southern Arabia's mud-walled skyscrapers. Portraits were a favourite subject. In *Arabian Sands* he posed the rhetorical question of his 'perverse' attraction to the East – one which had already been answered by the Orientalists' formula: colour (that is, a rich variety of costume, customs and surroundings), danger, mystery, romance and, compared to Western Europe, a greater degree of sensual freedom. The later Orientalists used a camera to record detail, lighting and pose, just

as generations of artists have employed the camera lucida. Jacques
Majorelle would surely have found it ironic that Thesiger, an empathist
of Orientalism, identified himself with photography, since it had been
the camera's increasing precision and popularity that led to the decline of
Orientalist art towards the end of the nineteenth century. During his
visits to Morocco Thesiger photographed many of the *kasbahs* (in 1965
for example La Séguia in the Ourika valley) painted by Jacques Majorelle,
who included thirty of them in a portfolio, *Les Kasbahs de l'Atlas*, published in 1930.

Hajj Tihami al Glawi had arranged that Thesiger should have a letter,
in effect a pass, which allowed him to travel from one magnificent *kasbah*
to the next throughout his territory. This helped Thesiger to accomplish
more easily the arduous trek of three hundred miles he planned to make
from Telouet to Midett or Azrou, across the High Atlas. On 6 August, five
days after he had left Telouet, he noted in his diary: 'We were provided
with free transport from Telouet, from village to village. The *khalifa* at
Telouet told the retainer who he had sent with us to arrange for free
transport for us and accommodation. I hope this will go on to Azrou. We
are travelling in style with 3 riding mules and a baggage mule. I was given
letters at Telouet to 3 khalifas on our way, at Toundout, Qallat and a third
as yet unidentified.' The Glawi's letter may have read like another given to
Walter B. Harris by the Sultan in May 1888:

We give permission, by the help of God, to the ... Englishmen who are
bearers of this letter to travel in all parts of our Empire in which there is
no present danger ... And to those whose business it is, I give this
command, to the Kaids and Caliphas, that they take care of them and pay
all attention to their wants; that they accompany them, and supply a fitting
escort; and that they point out to them the dangerous places, and advise
them not to enter them.

'Without such a letter as this,' Harris affirmed, 'it would have been
impossible for us to have visited the mountains ... forbidden land to the
traveller.'[49]

At Taddert Thesiger encountered five members of an Oxford
University Exploration Society expedition who had arrived in southern

Morocco to study a remote Berber village at Ait Arbaa. He helped them to collect the twenty baggage mules they needed, and agreed that one of the undergraduates should join him on his long walk across the Atlas mountains. John Newbould, a botany student at Merton College and an officer in the Commandos, who had been his first choice, fell from a cliff the day after Thesiger arrived at Taddert and was taken to the hospital in Marrakesh with a fractured elbow. Instead it was agreed that Thesiger would take with him Colin Pennycuick, the expedition's zoologist. Pennycuick proved capable and enduring; however, he looked dirty and 'unkempt',[50] and irritated Thesiger by disputing his advice. Thesiger liked him, but noted abrasively in his diary: 'Colin is in many ways an opinionated young fool.'[51] By the time they arrived back at Taddert, Pennycuick had developed an abscess on the sole of his foot, and had to ride the baggage mule over a pass to the Ait Arbaa valley, where the Oxford expedition were camped.[52]

In Telouet on 2 August they hired a guide called Muhammed, 'a driver for the manganese mine' who spoke Arabic and a smattering of French. 'A bit of a corner boy,' Thesiger wrote, 'and I doubt if he can walk but I hope he will do.'[53] In fact Muhammed complained continually. At Amasin in the mountains they could find no riding mules, and 'Muhammed who hates walking kept up an incessant whine'.[54] Near Tighali, where the mountainside was very steep, 'Muhammed started up it on a mule,' Thesiger fumed, 'till I kicked him off it.'[55]

No doubt this was literally true. Bryan Clarke, the leader of the Oxford expedition, observed: 'The villagers were very impressed by Thesiger. He was more severe with them than we had ever been, and they concluded that he was an English Pasha.'[56] In March 1956, when a Marsh Arab youth 'pinched and hid'[57] their bamboo canoe-poles and a club, Gavin Maxwell described with loyal restraint how Thesiger 'boxed his ears',[58] whereas in his diary Thesiger wrote: 'I kicked him round his house and knocked him into a corner after which he went round the surrounding houses and produced the poles from where he had hidden them. When we were in the *tarada* [we] found our guide's club missing. Sent Hasan along to the house to tell the boy I would be along again in a minute if he did not produce it. Produced it at once from under a mat.'[59]

The great *kasbahs* like Tiourza, surrounded by high walls, were built for war; their high towers had very small windows screened by decorative wrought-iron grilles. Guest rooms at the Ghasat *kasbah* backed onto its outer wall around a courtyard with a deep well and some fruit trees. At Toundout, a brightly painted ceiling of intricate geometrical Islamic patterns caught Thesiger's eye.[60] When the *khalifa* of Toundout, Hajj Ibrahim, kept them waiting at the gate of his *kasbah*, instead of asking for the *khalifa*, Muhammed telephoned a complaint to the *khalifa* in Telouet – to the fury of Hajj Ibrahim, who overheard the guide's conversation. Thesiger wrote: 'Muhammed is bloody ... The *khalifa* [was] friendly despite this and ... said he must send someone with us as Muhammed was useless and half witted, with which I agreed.'[61] In general, Thesiger's small party fed well. Village headmen produced refreshing mint tea. In the *kasbahs* at dawn they had coffee with milk, heavily peppered; then bread, honey and mint tea; possibly a meat dish a little later. When they arrived at a village or a *kasbah* they would be given bread, honey and tea as 'elevenses'.[62] Then lunch. If they arrived somewhere in the evening, bread and honey, or kebab, were served with tea; dinner followed after dark.

Thesiger, renowned for his insatiably sweet tooth, noted with approval: 'They have good honey here.'[63] He adored chocolates, chocolate cake, puddings, sweet sherry, sweet liqueurs such as Drambuie and Kenya Gold, and almost any sort of jam. (He kept on his bedside table in London a supply of chocolate, which he plundered at intervals during the night – a habit perhaps acquired at school. Once, in his eighties, having lost his false teeth, he was amused and relieved when they turned up in a cupboard, firmly embedded in a thick slice of fruit cake he had been unable to finish eating, had put away and had promptly forgotten.) A 'very good lunch of bread and stew' served under a 'very fine walnut tree' at Tighali evoked nostalgic memories of Abyssinia: 'The bread like "injira" and the gravy very hot with pepper so that it was like "wat" [a highly seasoned sauce or meat dish]. Then kous-kous.'[64]

Though remote and wild, the High Atlas, Thesiger felt, was already tarnished by Western 'innovations'. A telephone line linked Toundout's *kasbah* with Telouet; the *khalifa* of Ai Qalat, Hajj Umr, drove Thesiger, Pennycuick and Muhammed, their idle, ineffectual, unwilling guide, in his car as far as the market town of Boumalne. When he first visited Morocco with his mother in 1937, Thesiger wrote that he 'was not disappointed: the cities still retained much of the romance associated with their past'. To reach Tangier from London, Thesiger and Kathleen had travelled by train across France and taken a boat from Marseilles. There were no passenger flights in those days from London to Morocco, and Marrakesh 'still seemed a long way off'.[65] In his 1937 *Times* article 'The Mind of the Moor', Thesiger remembered fifty years later, 'I described the resentment felt by the Moors for the French, who were competing with them on all levels, even as drivers of horse-drawn cabs in towns; the desperation of unemployed tribesmen starving in the shanty slums of Casablanca; and the inevitable growth of nationalism fostered by a frustrated intelligentsia'.[66]

At Boumalne, Thesiger wrote: 'Muhammed tried hard to leave us. I insisted on his coming on ... He is a bloody person, whining and lazy but better than nobody'.[67] Yet a day or two later, having paid off Muhammed at Samirir, he felt 'thankful to be quit of him'.[68]

Thesiger devoted much of his time in Morocco to photography. He took superb images of the *kasbahs*, including Ghasat, Asif Ougoun and Tabir Ait Zaghar,[69] the latter for 'the incised patterns on its walls'.[70] The sons of a Sheikh he photographed at Bon Duerar *kasbah*, 'bareheaded and close shaven', he noted wryly, 'will probably look rather like convicts'.[71] A fine landscape shot at Tafraout shows terraces of small, primitive mud-roofed houses on a hillside, beyond a grove of palms and some fruit trees. By the time he returned to Casablanca on 8 October, Thesiger had used twenty-one thirty-six-frame cassettes of Ilford film, a total of over 750 photographs. Although he felt occasionally unsure of his still relatively new Leica camera, it gave him almost no trouble; except on the summit of Toubkal, the highest peak in the Atlas range. Here, he wrote: 'Overwound my camera ... which was tiresome. The film came out of the cassette. Changed it inside my sleeping bag when we got back and I hope the film will be alright'.[72]

Birds had fascinated Thesiger since he was a boy. In the High Atlas he noted there were 'very few big birds. An occasional raven ... One lammergeyer above Taddert and a few Egyptian vultures.' Apart from these and 'one chickor [partridge], occasional choughs, red start, hoopoe, dipper, wagtail, chaffinch, bee-eaters, rock-pigeons, swallows, swifts', he observed 'little bird life, at any rate at this season'.[73]

Having promised Kathleen that he would do no mountaineering in Morocco,[74] Thesiger spent eleven hours roped to his companions climbing the high, sheer Aioui cliffs. 'My first climb,' he wrote, 'and I found it difficult in places. Astonishing how much confidence a rope gives you ... A heavy shower of rain and hail with thunder, made the rocks slippery. "Abseiled" down some of the way ... I often felt I should be glad to be off the mountain especially when anticipating the descent, but I am delighted to have done this climb which has given me a lot of confidence.'[75]

The Aioui cliffs made an impressive backdrop for Zaouia Ahansal, a village with several high-towered buildings. Thesiger and Pennycuick arrived there on 19 August, accompanied by Ernest Gellner, a lecturer from London University who was studying the Berbers,[76] and his wife Susan, whom they had met a week previously at Samirir. The Gellners had based themselves in one of Zaouia Ahansal's towers. Thesiger liked them, but found their servants 'very irritating': 'Said the mule boy is lazy and impertinent and Yusuf their 17 year old interpreter ... bone lazy. He wanders off each morning with his hands in his pockets while Ernest and Susan pack up. Neither of them lend a hand with fetching wood or cooking. They would be alright if Ernest chased them a bit.'[77] The Gellners seemed mildly overawed by Thesiger, whom Gellner described as 'a gentleman of the old style, intensely romantic', yet 'curiously intro-verted for one famous above all as a man of action'.[78]

During the ten days or so that Thesiger and Pennycuick spent with the Gellners, together they climbed Aioui's cliffs and the allegedly 'unclimbable' Taria gorge,[79] where they narrowly escaped being swept away by 'a terrible mass of yellow, muddy water' surging down in a flash flood.[80] Thesiger noted in his diary: 'Got some way up the gorge when it began to thunder. I pressed strongly that we should get out of the gorge before [the floodwater] came down. The others insisted on trying to get higher, through the roof of a cave down which the stream came. Bloody silly. They insisted that we should see the water rising ... However when it began to rain heavily we gave it up ... As we got to Taria village ['at the mouth of the gorge'[81]] the rain came down in sheets, and a little later both streams came down in a wall of water. What a hope if we had been in the gorge ... Four to five feet of raging water.'[82] On the way back to Zaouia

Ahansal the following morning, Thesiger reflected: 'There was probably 15 feet of water in the narrow part of the gorge yesterday so it was well we got out when we did.'[83] Years later, both the Gellners agreed that they had owed their lives to 'Wilfred's anxious warnings – which we derided at the time'.[84] Pennycuick, it appears, had been very reluctant to abandon the ascent through the cave, and even when confronted by the roaring flood and the debris of smashed bridges, to Thesiger's amazed exasperation he had still 'talked of wading the streams'.[85]

With a local muleman and a mule, Thesiger and Pennycuick left Zaouia Ahansal on 31 August and arrived two days later at Azilal. From there they travelled by bus to Marrakesh and Taddert, and on 4 September arrived back at the Oxford expedition's camp. John Newbould had long since recovered from his injuries, and he and Thesiger climbed the mountains in the neighbourhood of Ait Arbaa; from the 3600-metre summit of Tistouit they saw 'Toubkal rising up over the top of Bou Aurial, the Anti-Atlas, the desert and the coastal plain'.[86] Determined to climb Toubkal, they set off with a guide and two mules up the Ait Tadali valley to Iswan, where they slept in a village surrounded by maize. Thesiger lost his way among the maize in the dark, and had to be rescued by one of the villagers. He helped Newbould to collect specimens of flowers and plants one evening by a stream near Jabal Tifnaout; and later, crossing a spectacular, snow-flecked mountain pass, Newbould 'dallied' gathering plants in a grassy hollow.[87]

Setting off at 8 a.m. on 15 September, Thesiger and Newbould reached Toubkal's 4165-metre summit after what Wilfred judged an 'easy walk' of two and a half hours. Thesiger wrote: 'John felt the altitude for the last 1000'. I felt very fit and no effects of altitude at all.'[88] Despite the morning haze, there was 'a magnificent wild view over the precipices below us on all sides, and the sheer sided mountains leading off from Toubkal all round us. Sheer precipices below us to the S and E ... From the summit of Toubkal I could see into valley above *khalifa* Hajj Abd al Rahman's village. [Assareg, where Thesiger and Newbould spent a comfortable night in one of the *kasbah*'s inner courts.]'[89]

Climbing the Taria gorge in August, Thesiger had been hampered slightly by a 'very painful' boil on his bottom which lasted ten days and finally burst the day after he had climbed the gorge.[90] In Iraq in June he had been slightly run-down; he had developed large boils close to his rectum,[91] suffered from dysentery and become infected with round-worms, for which he was treated at the American Mission in Amara.[92] By the time he arrived at Toubkal, however, he was able to take the mountain – 'very steep in places', with 'loose scree near the top' – in his stride.[93] The ascent of Toubkal, the highest mountain in Morocco, had been one of the highlights of his long traverse of the High Atlas range. He had enjoyed helping Newbould to collect animal specimens and plants: 'John has got about 180 different [plant] species on this trip. Very good,' Thesiger noted in his diary,[94] a total which included an almost unknown variety of carnation.[95] He invited Newbould to come with him to Nuristan the following year. From Tizi-n-Test, on 21 September they went their separate ways: Newbould to Marrakesh, Thesiger to Taroudant and from there to Tiznit, Goulimine, Tafraout, Agadir, Mogador, Fez and Taza.

Thesiger's traverse of the High Atlas had been a worthwhile achievement, comparable with his journey in the Hazarajat the previous year. Despite this, he never thought of writing an article about Morocco for the RGS *Journal*, or of including his trek across the Atlas in *Desert, Marsh and Mountain*, published in 1979. *Among the Mountains*, published in 1998, described Thesiger's journeys in western Asia, prefaced by the highlands of Kurdistan. He had travelled in Morocco, he wrote, at 'the height of the conflict between the nationalists and the French'.[96] His first guide, Muhammed, had 'expected to be murdered' if he strayed too far away from his own country; another guide, Husain, had flatly refused to go further than Zaouia Ahansal. At Casablanca in July there had been a curfew; after Thesiger returned from the High Atlas in September, he found a curfew imposed on Marrakesh. A French military post south of Ahermoumou, near Fez, was attacked by insurgents; several French soldiers were killed. The elderly commandant at Ahermoumou, Captain André Jean Ithier, a 'very charming' old soldier 'who had risen from the ranks and served in the Riff campaign',[97] ordered an immediate evacuation of all French civilians to Fez. Thesiger was obliged to join the evacuation, having tried, but failed, to persuade Captain Ithier to let him stay on at Ahermoumou.[98] Taza, where he arrived by bus from Fez, was 'filled with refugee French and troops'.[99] There had been no curfew at Taza, despite reports of heavy fighting to the north and south of the town. Even so, Thesiger decided to take no unnecessary risks: 'Had a look round the Medina,' he wrote, 'but thought it silly to go too deep into the old town. I don't want to be killed in mistake for a Frenchman.'[100]

In October he joined his mother in Milan, and after travelling through Italy by train they returned to London in November. On 30 January 1956 Thesiger left London for his sojourn in the Iraqi marshes with Gavin Maxwell. By April he hoped that 'things [were] definitely fixed for my Afghan trip'.[101] He asked his mother to 'ring up Lillywhites and ask them to send 12 pairs of SNOW GLASSES (the cheap ones costing a few shillings such as were used by Shipton etc on Everest) to me c/o The UNITED KINGDOM HIGH COMMISSIONER, KARACHI and arrive there before the end of June'.[102]

After spending three weeks with Amara bin Thuqub among the Bani Lam shepherds, Thesiger arrived back in Basra. From there he went to Baghdad. 'I brought 52 bats up with me preserved in spirits,' he wrote. 'They had knocked them down with sticks in one of the "mudhifs" which I had been staying in, and I thought that the British Museum would be interested in them. This morning I put them into formalin inside the Embassy. I had no idea that formalin stinks as it does. Soon the smell had permeated into every corner of the Embassy, and HE came rushing out of his office to find out what had gone wrong with the drains. As far as I know they are still flushing them.'[103]

On 20 June Thesiger heard that Amara's first cousin, Bedai, had been attacked by three of his cousins from near Azair. He shot one of his attackers in self-defence, was himself wounded and escaped into the marshes, leaving Amara and his family, his nearest male relatives, at serious risk from the blood feud that was bound to follow. Thesiger helped to move Amara and his relatives deeper into the marshes, to a village inhabited by others of their tribe. He wrote to Kathleen: 'Amara and I had a lot of trouble persuading his old father to move, and then a very hard day's work actually moving them and their buffaloes. We had to tow the buffaloes an inch at a time and it took all day and was very hot. [Thesiger wrote in his diary: 'Thuqub said his 5 buffaloes are not used to the marsh and would never get to Bu M(ughafait) ... They refused to swim and ... Hassan and Muhammed spent most of the time swimming and whacking them with sticks. Tied one by its lower jaw and towed it behind the tarada ... I paddled all the way and found it very hard work].'[104] He went on: 'I then got in touch with the family of the dead man and after some trouble got them to agree to a three months truce. [In his diary on 28 June he wrote: 'fixed up a 6 months atwa'.] This is better than nothing and will give time for their blood to cool. Amara had unfortunately sold the rifle I gave him. (He got £140 for it. It was worth £12 in England.) He was of course without a weapon. I have however lent him my revolver.' While he was away in 1957 writing *Arabian Sands*, as extra protection for Amara, Thesiger left behind his own rifle and its remaining ammunition. Amara survived the blood feud, and was in Basra to greet Thesiger when he returned to Iraq in January 1958.[105]

From the beginning, John Newbould's plan to travel with Thesiger in Nuristan was fraught with difficulties. 'I mentioned Afghanistan to my tutors,' he wrote on 11 December 1955, 'and they are very strongly opposed to my going anywhere next summer on the grounds that I should spend the summer vac before my Schools reading. However I have some ideas of my own on this.'[106] Six months later, Newbould heard that the Afghan government had refused to grant him a visa for Nuristan. Thesiger updated Kathleen: 'The Afghans as you know have refused to allow Newbould to join me. Incomprehensible. I have a feeling that Lascelles mishandled them. Bitterly disappointing for Newbould. I had a very nice letter from him. He has taken it very well with no complaints. I am very sorry he won't be with me.'[107] Newbould was to have brought with him from England the plant-collecting material, aneroids and other instruments. Fortunately, Thesiger knew there were presses and blotting paper in Kabul, left over from his journey in the Hazarajat in 1954; however, 'there was ... no time to get the other things sent out from England'.[108]

Thesiger had been anxious to travel in Nuristan ever since he visited the Kafir tribes in Chitral in 1952. This little-known area of the Hindu Kush lay inside Afghanistan to the north of Jalalabad, along the Chitral border. Thesiger noted with obvious satisfaction that 'Comparatively few Europeans have travelled in Nuristan.'[109] Colonel Alexander Gardner, a soldier of fortune, passed twice through the former Kafiristan, 'Land of Unbelievers', accompanied by a priest, in 1826 and 1827; in 1883 W.W. McNair visited the Bashgul valley; this valley was explored more thoroughly in 1885 by Colonel Woodthorpe of the Indian Survey, accompanied by Sir William Lockhart. No other Europeans apparently visited Nuristan until Sir George Scott Robertson, a medical doctor from the Orkneys, lived for a year in 1890–91 in the Bashgul valley while serving as a British agent in Chitral. In 1888 Kipling wrote his powerful story 'The Man who Would be King' about the then independent Nuristan, or Kafiristan, based partly on Alexander Gardner's experiences. After visiting the Black Kafir valleys in Chitral, Thesiger had acquired a copy of Robertson's book *The Kafirs of the Hindu Kush* (1896), which Schuyler Jones has described as 'the book on the subject' and a model of 'pioneer fieldwork'.[110] In *Among the Mountains*, Thesiger described more fully the agreement between Sir Mortimer Durand and Abd er Rahman, the Amir of Afghanistan, about the frontier between Afghanistan and India, a source of the 'trouble' that prevented Thesiger from travelling in Nuristan in previous years: 'by this agreement the former Kafiristan fell almost entirely within Afghanistan. Only a small area remained inside Chitral, the area inhabited to this day by the Black Kafirs ... The other Kafirs (as the inhabitants of Kafiristan were known) were forcibly converted to Islam when Abd er Rahman overran their country in the winter of 1895–96, in a skilfully conducted campaign which lasted only four months. Two important German expeditions travelled extensively in Nuristan in 1928 and 1935, and more recently [in 1947–49] an expedition from Denmark[111] – when I went there in 1956 the Nuristanis referred to all Europeans as Germans.'[112]

Thesiger arrived on 18 July in Kabul, where he stayed with Ken Dulling at the British Embassy. A young Pathan student from the Faculty of Literature, Abd al Nawab, joined him as his interpreter. Clifford Jupp, an official at the Embassy in Kabul, drove him from Kabul to Kachu in the Panjshir valley, seventy miles north of Kabul, where he hired a cook-boy, two Tajik porters and two ponies, and set off north-east towards Nuristan.

At Shanaize in the Panjshir valley on 31 July Thesiger met Eric Newby and Hugh Carless, who had spent the previous three weeks attempting to climb Mir Samir, the twenty-thousand-foot peak that loomed at the head of the valley. 'They had got to within 700 feet of the top', Thesiger wrote in his diary, but were 'too small a party and the locals would not camp on the mountain'.[113] In *Among the Mountains*, Thesiger wrote: 'After a valiant but unsuccessful attempt to reach the summit, they had travelled down to Puchal in Nuristan, and come back to Panjshir over the Arayu pass. We spent a pleasant evening ... camped together in an orchard, and ... Newby later included an amusing description of our meeting in *A Short Walk in the Hindu Kush* [1958; always associated with this book is the story of Thesiger watching Carless and Newby blow up their airbags to sleep on a stony hillside, and his withering remark: 'God, you must be a couple of pansies'].[114] Newby sketched Thesiger as 'a great, long-striding crag of a man, with an outcrop for a nose and bushy eyebrows, forty-five years old and as hard as nails, in an old tweed jacket of the sort worn by Eton boys, a pair of thin grey cotton trousers, rope-soled Persian slippers and a woollen cap-comforter'.[115] These were the clothes Thesiger had worn in Morocco in 1955, including the light 'slippers' he had bought in Kurdistan some years before that.[116] Thesiger's tweed jacket was the same 'change coat' from Billings & Edmonds that he had worn at Eton. When Newby learnt this some years later, it occurred to him 'what a gigantically impressive schoolboy Thesiger must have been at Eton'.[117] The same year he left Eton, Thesiger had boxed as a welterweight (10st 7lbs). He had put on two stones by 1931; so it is reasonable to assume that he weighed about eleven stones when he left Eton in 1928. Over the years he had perhaps twenty suits made for him in London by tailors such as Dege or Tetley & Butler; but even in his eighties he could still wear quite comfortably a grey flannel suit which had been made to measure while he was at Oxford.

Thesiger and his small party crossed the 16,500-foot Chamar pass into Nuristan on 4 August and continued down towards Puchal, the main village in the Ramgul valley. On the way he met the first Nuristanis he had seen. 'In appearance,' he wrote, 'they were like handsome Europeans, light in colour, with brown hair and beards; several of them had grey eyes.'[118] In due course he found the Nuristanis were temperamental and erratic: 'they frequently raced about or flung themselves on the ground; they would ask innumerable questions, then suddenly lose interest. I sensed a streak of unpredictable violence in their nature.'[119] This was confirmed when a Nuristani who joined Thesiger's party near the Chamar pass started an argument with one of the Tajik ponymen, who

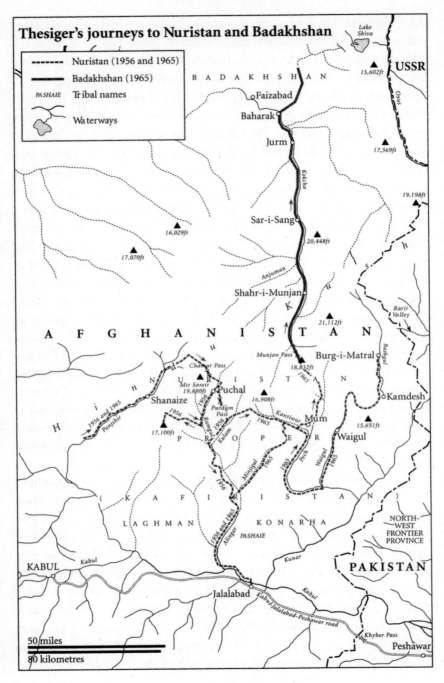

Thesiger's journeys to Nuristan and Badakhshan

owed him money from the sale of a cow – then suddenly attacked him.

Puchal, with its three mosques, was the religious centre of the area. Thesiger wrote: 'Nowhere have I heard so many calls to prayer as I did in these Nuristani villages, the words almost unintelligible, a strange travesty of the original Arabic.'[120] The mullahs in Puchal made no secret of their hostility to him as a Christian. When Thesiger returned there for the third time a fortnight later, after an unsuccessful attempt to get into the Kulam valley from Wanasgul, a mullah rushed down the hillside and poured out curses on him for defiling this stronghold of Islam with his presence. 'This was the fanaticism of the newly converted,' Thesiger observed. '[The mullah's] father must have been an infidel, for the country had only been converted to Islam sixty years before.'[121]

To Thesiger's surprise, when he visited Nuristan again in 1965, 'everyone in the village including the mullahs – even the mullah who had cursed me – was welcoming and friendly'. 'Unlike Robertson, I never had anything stolen by them, nor did I find them avaricious. They would drive a hard bargain, but many of them, especially in villages unused to Europeans, were exceedingly hospitable.'[122] Meals in Nuristani villages consisted of bread eaten with curds or cheese, eggs, chickens or fish. Once Thesiger was given corn cakes and mutton for dinner. He wrote: 'The meat tasted very good, but I suspected that it had come from a dying sheep as the animal had been slaughtered before we arrived.'[123] He admitted that he 'gorged' on grapes, apricots or peaches, and he was especially fond of white-heart cherries. He found it puzzling that the Nuristani villagers were lazy about gathering fruit, most of which was of poor quality: 'most of the mulberries were left to rot on the ground where they fell ... and I was often struck by the smell of fermenting mulberries when I walked through their orchards'.[124]

Thesiger found the scenery in the Kulam valley magnificent: 'the valley very narrow with the mountains rising above it, jagged and sheer'.[125] A land of great contrasts, Nuristan sometimes reminded him of Kurdistan, 'but on a vaster scale'.[126] As they edged along a narrow path above a rushing torrent, the pony carrying Thesiger's plant specimens, and everything he possessed except his bedding, snagged its load on a projecting rock and fell backwards into the river. A Nuristani boy who had come with them from Linar village jumped into the water and rescued the pony.

Thesiger's plant collection was reduced to a sodden mass of blotting paper, but he managed to dry the 'sopping-wet'[127] specimens in a gentle afternoon breeze, a task made more difficult by 'strings of women who came down the path carrying loads of wood'.[128]

Thesiger had replaced his Tajiks with Nuristani ponymen, who proved to be 'recalcitrant'. Crossing the Purdam pass into Kulam, he engaged instead four Nuristani porters, who carried 'magnificently'[129] but demanded about four times the going rate of pay. Thesiger vented his feelings in his diary: 'NEVER travel in Nuristan dependent on local transport. The locals will unscrupulously exploit you. Use porters, not horses and bring them from ... Panjshir.'[130]

The Pashaie villagers Thesiger met in southern Nuristan proved 'exceptionally friendly'.[131] In Korgal, he and his party stayed in a house with a carved entrance door and carved pillars inside. It was clean and tidy, the floor covered with fine grass. A room they were given turned out to be the local mosque. This would certainly never have happened anywhere else in Nuristan.[132] 'Very different to Puchal,' Thesiger wrote. 'No one came to pray in it and I heard no calls to prayer.'[133] Even in extreme old age, Thesiger still clearly remembered their host, the mullah, 'a Pathan gone Pashaie, who had the face of an elderly satyr with painted eyes and a bunch of herbs in his cap. He could not have been kinder or more helpful.'[134]

During the five weeks he spent in Nuristan, according to his diary Thesiger exposed sixteen cassettes of film. He wrote: 'I had already used up more than four spools of film coming up the Panjshir and Chamar valleys [on the way to Nuristan], and at this *ailoq* [summer pasture camp, above the source of the Ramgul river] I finished a fifth spool. These Nuristanis loved being photographed.'[135] A selection of Thesiger's photographs in *Among the Mountains* gives a brilliant visual summary of his journeys: Tajik shepherds resting in the Panjshir valley; the snow-flecked summit of Mir Samir; the Chamar valley, an awesome wilderness of boulders and scree; a Nuristani villager, in solemn profile, seated on a chair backed with ibex horns; inquisitive Nuristani boys, their eyes stained with a red juice; at Kulam, a boy lounging on his elbow; the winding Alingar river and its spacious valley, with fields, orchards and scattered forts.

On 4 September Thesiger and his companions started out while it was still dark, along the west bank of the Alingar river. They crossed the streams coming from two small side valleys, and shortly before 8 a.m. arrived at Kalatussiraj, the headquarters of Laghman, with its modern government buildings and a ruined palace set in a pleasure garden. Thesiger paid off his porters, and after an early lunch set off with Abd al Nawab in a horse-drawn tonga some twenty miles south-west from Kalatussiraj to Jalalabad. After three nights in a hotel, followed by two nights in Peshawar, Thesiger travelled by train to Karachi, and from there he flew to Baghdad.

Most of the following year, 1957, Thesiger devoted to writing *Arabian Sands*; in consequence he did not return to the Iraqi Marshes until January 1958. In Baghdad he lunched with the Ambassador, 'No one except the family, and we had a most interesting talk about the future of Iraq.'[136] A new Consul-General at Basra he dismissed as 'pompous and conventional ... a dull but pleasant little man'.[137] Instead of the Consulate, Thesiger stayed next door in a hotel overlooking the river, where there was 'in theory every modern convenience but in practice nothing works'.[138] As a result of the 1956 Suez crisis, he wrote, 'You need passes to travel away from the towns ... but otherwise the Iraqis seem as friendly as ever.'[139] Having obtained the necessary passes for travelling in the marshes, Thesiger kicked his heels in Basra, as impatient for Amara and Sabaiti to arrive as he felt 'delighted to be back'. In parenthesis, as it were, he added an amusing anecdote for Kathleen: 'I forgot to tell you that in the charter KLM plane to Baghdad they had a sweepstake to judge the number of hours that the plane we were in had flown in 9 years and the number of gallons she would use between Beirut and Basra, and guessing wildly I was first in both and won a very nice travelling clock.'[140]

He had found Baghdad 'very changed', unlike the marshes, which 'look very lovely at the moment'.[141] There were fewer duck about than there had been two years previously. The weather in January was bitterly cold; days of rain and brilliant sunshine, the water level very high 'after terrific storms in the Kurdish mountains'.[142] The water was thick with silt, a good omen for the villagers' rice crops. 'All goes well,' he wrote. '... I took my tarada down to the Euphrates to get it recoated with pitch, going there across the heart of the Marshes ... Everyone appears delighted to see me

... It is pleasant to feel wanted and to know that being here makes a difference to a lot of these people.'[143] Amara, Thesiger's favourite canoeboy, had been bereaved twice in four months. 'His old father died of cancer ... and three weeks later his wife whom he had married [only the year before] died in childbirth,'[144] leaving Amara with a baby son. 'However his new rifle is here,' Thesiger reported briskly, 'and also the one for Sabaiti and they are delighted with them.'[145] 'I found the one I had lent Amara in perfect condition although on one occasion the canoe in which he was travelling overturned in the stream near his village and it was the best part of an hour before he could find my rifle after diving and diving for it. I am sure his having it made the difference in stopping the other side from trying to murder him in the blood feud he is involved in.'[146] In a later version Thesiger wrote that 'the rifle was at the bottom of a muddy fast flowing river for several hours before he could recover it. He stripped it down, cleaned and oiled it thoroughly, and this ducking did it no harm ... Amara has shot about twenty pig with his [new rifle]. He insists on doing all the shooting now.'[147] As a precaution, Thesiger asked his mother to ask Rigby to send him two hundred .275-bore cartridges care of the British Consul-General in Basra. 'I am very short,' he explained, 'and I want to leave them with Amara when I leave, for his new rifle. This ammunition is not procurable in Iraq.'[148]

However improbable or naïve this may have been, it appears that Thesiger hoped his generous present of the new rifle might assuage Amara's grief, strengthen the already affectionate bond between them, and help to refocus the young Marsh Arab's attention on his benefactor, patron and friend. This would explain the otherwise jarring sequence of events Thesiger reported to Kathleen in his letter of 14 January: the death of Amara's father and young wife, followed soon afterwards by his apparently careless delight at receiving a new rifle. If indeed this were true, the episode did neither Thesiger nor Amara much credit. But it is more likely that Thesiger had written his letter spontaneously, never imagining that the ambiguous sequence of its contents might one day be 'misconstrued'.[149]

On 26 March he wrote telling his mother: 'I am busy trying to find Amara a new wife. I am also buying a bottle and patent foods for his son. It seems to be too small for its age but is always happy and laughing which I hope is a good sign. [Amara's] mother is devoted to it and looks after it.'[150] Amara's tragic bereavements had apparently affected Thesiger more than he cared to admit. Kathleen had been in bed with 'flu. 'I am distressed and worried that you have been ill for so long,' he wrote, 'and I do hope you are better now ... and not so exhausted. Take care of yourself for my sake for you know how much you mean to me and how utterly desolate I should be if anything happened to you. You are so completely all I have.'[151] His *tarada* crew of young Marsh Arabs were the latest in a lineage of tribal companions, friends and retainers who filled a role once occupied by Thesiger's younger brothers. He reported contentedly: 'The boys who are with me are well and happy and are I think genuinely glad to have me back with them. I find them very companionable and enjoy being with them.'[152]

From Amara, the provincial headquarters (after which Amara bin Thuqub was named), he wrote prophetically to Kathleen: 'I have a great affection for these people and only regret the changes which the next few years are likely to bring.'[153] Thesiger could of course have had no conception then of the suffering that would be inflicted on Shi'a Muslims in southern Iraq by Saddam Hussein's regime from the 1980s through the 1990s. Emma Nicholson has written in her moving, at times shocking, preface to *The Iraqi Marshlands* (2003), edited jointly with Dr Peter Clark: 'The Marsh Arabs were targeted specifically: villages were bombarded by artillery, and burned or demolished; chemical weapons were also employed. Concurrently, the Iraqi regime implemented a massive programme of drainage and damming of the marshes in a deliberate attempt to wipe out the indigenous population. In twenty years the marshes were reduced by 90 per cent, causing, according to the United Nations, "one of the world's greatest environmental disasters".'[154]

Thesiger had been accepted by the Marsh Arabs, and become more than a bystander, 'a mere spectator', in their ancient world.[155] 'I felt the urge to settle down,' he confided in a work-note, 'and to identify myself more closely with a society than I had been able when travelling in the past.'[156] By contrast, he felt little sympathy for 'an American student [of anthropology] from some American university ... living on the edge of the Marshes in one of the villages of rice cultivators, making a study of their way of life and social structure. He has been there for about seven months, and I gather finds the conditions very trying, and looks forward to finishing his thesis and getting back to America. He is appalled at their living conditions. I suppose it all depends by what standards you judge it.'[157] Tired of the book he had been writing about Arabia, Thesiger declared: 'I have got the Empty Quarter right out of my mind which I am sure is a good thing. I shall come back to it in June quite fresh. I wonder what John [Verney] will make of the chapters when he gets them.'[158]

Despite their past differences, he had promised, and still hoped, to find Gavin Maxwell another otter. He wrote: 'I have heard of two. One was very small and died a few days after they caught it. The other they had had for a month but some children killed it before I could get hold of it. I expect I will hear of some others.'[159] Towards the end of March, he noted despairingly: 'I have looked for an otter for him but have so far failed to find one.'[160] Finally, he wrote on 20 April: 'Will you tell Lady Mary [Maxwell] that I have I am afraid failed completely to find Gavin an otter.'[161] In an attempt to defuse any lingering tension between her and Maxwell, Thesiger pleaded with his mother: 'Don't get Gavin on your mind.'[162] He described how the marshes looked 'very lovely this last month', and suggested generously − yet with a surprisingly clumsy disregard for Kathleen's wounded maternal pride − 'Gavin's book will have enabled you to picture it all.'[163]

By the end of March, the Arabian book once again occupied his mind. 'I had a letter from Val [ffrench Blake],' he wrote to Kathleen from Basra on the twenty-sixth. 'I am glad that you saw him. Get onto John Verney and find out if he has read my chapters. Tell him I am counting on him to finish it before I get back so that I can incorporate his alterations into my final copy ... Get John to send his copy back and read this, and make notes for me on a separate piece of paper. I shall be very anxious to know how it reads to you as a whole.'[164] He continued two days later: 'I am sure that this real break when I have not once thought of my book will have done me good. I hope John will have read it through before I get home. I really must finish it off when I go to Ireland. I look forward to getting back there for I grew very attached to it during the time that I was there.'[165]

From Al bu Salih, where he had spent Eid with the Muntifiq, feasting for three days with their Sheikh on 'great dishes of rice and endless sheep',[166] he scribbled a note asking Kathleen to 'get in touch with Val and John and tell them both that I shall be in England from May 28th until June 6th and do very much want to see them both to talk about my book. It will be the last chance I get before I finish the book in Ireland ... My mind is beginning to run on the book again which I take to be a good sign, and sorry as I shall be to leave Iraq I am now looking forward to getting down to it again. When you get it back from John will you read it through conscientiously and make notes of what you think would improve it. I find your corrections very helpful and you will see that I have adopted practically every one you have made.'[167]

'Since lunch,' he wrote, 'I have just finished dealing with a swarm of patients, including 48 boys to be circumcised, and now am comparatively quiet except that the small room in which we are living is crowded with people all talking at once, and interrupting me to ask questions. It is not easy to write an intelligible letter under these circumstances.'[168] He concluded wearily: 'Two more boys have turned up to be circumcised and a bevy of women with colds and coughs and I don't know what else, so I must stop.'[169]

Two months later, in July, Thesiger was having tea with friends of his mother in Ireland. 'Someone entered the room. "Did you hear the four o'clock news? There has been a revolution in Baghdad and the Royal family have been murdered. The mob burnt the British Embassy ..."' Thesiger concluded his account of seven years among the Marsh Arabs: 'I realised that I should never be allowed back, and that another chapter in my life had closed.'[170]

TWENTY-ONE

A Winter in Copenhagen

Wilfred Thesiger invariably maintained that his books and photographs were mere 'by-products' of his journeys.[1] Although he had never travelled anywhere with the intention of writing about a journey, over two decades, from 1934 to 1957, he published more than twenty articles, including several describing his expeditions in Ethiopia and Arabia, which discreetly acknowledged their importance. Throughout his travels he had kept diaries and had photographed 'as a record' thousands of tribal people in their remote desert, marsh or mountain worlds. His diaries and photographs, together with letters he wrote to his mother and other members of his family, provided him with material for articles in *The Times*, the *Geographical Magazine* and the Royal Geographical Society's *Journal*. Years later they helped him to recall no less vividly much of the authentic detail he needed to write his books.

Thesiger's memories of his five years in Arabia remained, for him, almost as tangible as his actual experiences. Perhaps it is fortunate that when, in 1947, Laurence Kirwan, the Director and Secretary of the RGS, encouraged by Kathleen, urged him to write about his journeys in the Empty Quarter and other parts of Arabia, he refused. The decade between his second crossing of the Rub' al Khali and writing *Arabian Sands* allowed his memories to be sieved by a process of time, leaving behind only those things which had affected him most deeply. Even then, he had insisted: 'I had no desire to spend a year or more writing a book, when I could be off somewhere travelling in places that interested me.' Furthermore, he realised that writing would involve 'a great deal of hard work'.[2] John Verney remembered: 'Wilfred did work terribly hard on his books, but he would never have dreamt of slaving from nine to five in an office ... It would've been inconceivable ... I remember when a few of us met after the war, and we were talking about what we should do with our lives. Wilfred said rather airily: "Oh, I expect I shall just go on travelling." And I said: "You mean, you'll go on being the world's greatest spiv!"'[3]

Thesiger began to write *Arabian Sands* in London during November and December 1956. He admitted that he found this very difficult. 'I knew I couldn't begin to write a book, living here in the flat with my mother and Miss Emtage. I thought of places like Greece, Italy, Holland or Morocco. But I felt if I was in Morocco trying to describe the sunset, for instance, I should be describing what it looked like in Morocco instead of in Arabia. I decided then to spend the winter in Denmark. In Copenhagen there weren't any distractions. I didn't know anybody there, and so I was able to concentrate on reliving these all-important years in the desert.'[4]

For nearly four months, from February till May 1957, Thesiger lived in the Park Hotel in Jarmers Plads, near the Tivoli Gardens. 'I feel that this room will do me very well,' he wrote. 'It is small, up under the roof, but has two beds in it so there is room to spread my books and papers, and they have put in a large writing table. I pay £13 a month. It is right in the centre of the town which is convenient and has a good view out. It is very warm. I get my breakfast thrown in. Just round the corner there is a very good pub where they have excellent food. I can get a good meal there for about 6 shillings. I can get a light lunch in my room if I want it ... Copenhagen is cold and rather damp but not more so, at any rate so far, than London. I called on the Ambassador yesterday and am going there for a meal shortly.'[5]

As soon as Thesiger's friend from Eton, Valentine ffrench Blake, had read the first chapter of the typescript of what would become *Arabian Sands*, he wrote: 'I am writing to you immediately afterwards, so that first impressions, often most valuable, will be what you are getting.' He reassured Thesiger: 'There is some wonderful stuff here, and some passages of extremely fine writing which remind me of the spirit of John Buchan at his best.' But, he went on:

As a first chapter it is monstrously overweighted and I might have missed what you were trying to say, if you hadn't given me a clue beforehand. As a prologue to a description of the Weary Land, it is too long – and while of necessity autobiographical (because you are looking into yourself) – it reads too much like an autobiography in places, in other places too much like a guide book, – and in others like a history book. If you are to write a great work of art, which (having read this chapter) I can see you mean to do, and are capable of doing, you must have the self-discipline to limit your palette, as it were to the minimum colours essential to your theme. Which is, a) The hardness of the desert/ b) Your realisation of its attraction, by the paradox of discovering it when travelling in the Hejaz Mountains/ c) Looking back to your childhood to discover the clue which will explain your love of hardness in general/ d) Description of early travels and service in the Sudan and Abyssinia, as a young man, which led you towards the Arabian deserts.[6]

ffrench Blake drew Thesiger's attention to examples of 'mixed metaphor', 'overdone alliteration', 'cliché' and confused meanings, and to his tendency to 'rather biblical' turns of phrase, which may have resulted from a desire to emulate Lawrence's *Seven Pillars of Wisdom* and Doughty's *Arabia Deserta*. He had no doubt that Thesiger meant to write 'a work of art'[7] that expressed the intensity of the emotional and physical experience of his five years in the Arabian desert.

Thesiger had divided the opening chapter, 'Apprenticeship in Africa', between Abyssinia and the Sudan. It appears that, as well as Lawrence and Doughty, he was influenced by Essad-Bey's *Mohammed* (1938), of which the first two chapters, 'The Desert of the Prophet' and 'The People of the Desert', Thesiger's prologue is a poetical reworking, rather than a précis. Thesiger denied these influences, just as, years later, he dismissed much of the help he had been given by ffrench Blake and John Verney,[8] insisting that 'it was my book and I wrote it'.[9] His petulant and rather silly declaration (which was both unfair and ungrateful) had been provoked by Gavin Young's comment that Thesiger wrote his books 'by committee'.[10] In a creative sense this was untrue, but it did reflect Thesiger's habit of having the successive drafts of his manuscripts read by friends and members of his family as soon as they were written.

Thesiger's literary agent Graham Watson wrote to him in April: 'I think that my main criticism is that in general there is a lack of distinction.'[11] By this he meant that Thesiger was denying the reader information he felt 'passionately anxious to share'; 'lack of distinction' between the many different characters, 'names and people as familiar to you as a bus in Piccadilly is to me'; about where Thesiger's wanderings led and why; the lifestyle of the Bedu; most importantly, his impressions of the first crossing of the Empty Quarter. Watson added: 'One day succeeds another as I am sure it did on this trip without any distinction between one rising of the sun and its setting the next day but the reader gets no impression of the desperate isolation, the unendurable hardship, the burning heat of the day, the bitter cold of the night ... It seems to me that at the moment you are far too frightened of letting yourself go; far too frightened that people may say [of] you "this man is shooting a line", "is overemphasising the dangers of his trip", "is overemphasising the importance of what he wanted to do". To write a book in the first place is an egoistic activity. You must not be afraid of being an egoist.'

Watson's critique reached Thesiger in the midst of 'a sticky week'. He claimed to write instinctively, yet lamented having no 'framework on which to work'.[12] By the middle of May he had drafted ten chapters, more than half the book. 'I really have no comments to make on any of them,' Watson reported. 'The transformation between Chapter 10 and your earlier ones when you were still rather feeling your way to the correct formula is really quite astonishing ... If you can keep up the same standard I don't believe that you will have to do much further work from Chapter 9 onwards. I do think that it will require virtually a total rewrite on the first eight. However I don't think there is any doubt at all that at the end you will have a book of the very first importance. Don't you feel rather pleased with yourself?'[13]

Val ffrench Blake had been 'delighted to see Watson says exactly the same things as me', and joked, 'Perhaps I can become a literary agent with profit!'[14] He agreed with Watson that 'Chapter IX and X are really fine, very exciting, and very well told, and your style is really getting into gear and the characters are much clearer.' He encouraged Thesiger to 'Keep at it, you are really getting into your stride now; and most of the top-hamper of bad style is going overboard, to mix a few metaphors.'[15]

Shut away in his 'little snuggery' in Copenhagen, Thesiger worked rapidly. By 11 February he was 'deep into Chapter Four', satisfied that 'it is going quicker than the "Arabia is a desert and the Arabs live in Arabia"' phase he experienced in England.[16] This euphoria was short-lived. He wrote on 20 February: 'Here I alternate between moments of confidence and others of acute depression ... I am ... temporarily stuck. There is too much to say.'[17] He hoped that the first complete draft would be finished by the end of May. 'There are moments when I think it is going to come off, and others when I am filled with doubts.' If the book got written and was successful, he assured his mother, it would be due to her support: 'you have never doubted. You don't know what your faith in it has meant to me. I have a great story to tell but I do want to tell it well.'[18] He urged Kathleen: 'I am grateful for your criticisms which are a great help and are I know valid. Will you go on saying what you feel. Don't for Heaven's sake think that I shall be offended at anything you say. I want criticism from you and Val and Graham, and later I hope from Roddy.'

Every Friday he had 'a weekly mens lunch' at the English Club, which he enjoyed.[19] By the middle of March he had found a method that suited him. 'I am glad that the last two chapters seemed all right,' he wrote to Kathleen. 'I think they will be when I have revised them. It seems to me that the thing to do first is to get the stuff down. Graham is pleased with them. I struck a sticky patch but am over it.'[20] Faced with the prospect of having to rewrite much of what he had written until then, Thesiger accepted Watson's advice, but lost the thread of his narrative and the flow of ideas by spending too much time on the intricacies of grammar. He wrote: 'I feel my style is improving with practice,' but admitted, 'I spend a lot of time checking the meaning of words with a Dictionary to try and get the word I want. I know sometimes the sentences are too short. A lot of that can be got over with proper punctuation using semi-colons instead of full stops. Mark Longman will have to deal with that. I don't know enough about it.'[21] Criticisms from his mother, ffrench Blake and Watson, while intended to be constructive, damped Thesiger's spirits. He had asked for criticism, and realised the need for it, but he found it impossible to write fluently and at the same time view his writing with a coldly critical eye.

At Copenhagen's English Club Thesiger had met C.E. Montague-Evans, who had been a master at Eton while Thesiger was there. As a break from his unflagging routine he accepted an invitation to lunch with

Montague-Evans at Malmö in Sweden. He nearly missed the ferry: 'I thought it was Friday, and it was really Saturday and I was sitting in my room at 11.40 when the hall porter rang up to ask if I was not meant to be catching the boat at 12.'[22] Montague-Evans later read and praised Thesiger's manuscript: '"Enthralling" is the word. I could not put it down. It'll be a huge success!' But despite this, and praise from Val ffrench Blake and Graham Watson, for the moment Thesiger felt 'stale and fed up with the book and want[ed] to leave it and forget about it for a while'.[23] He thought of visiting Hamburg, but instead spent a night at Elsinore, followed by a night with Montague-Evans. 'I feel bored stiff with the book,' he wrote, 'and just cannot summon up enough energy to go on with it. It seems to me to be deadly dull as it is, and it should not be.' Kathleen had sent him James Morris's *Sultan in Oman* (1957), which he damned, writing: 'if people want that sort of chatty rubbish I hope they will never get it from me'.[24] He was out of the doldrums and working as hard as ever, after 'a very sticky week unable to write a word, and feeling very depressed about the book, but now I have got started again and hope that it will see me through to the end of the first draft'.[25] After a month at the Park Hotel he had been given another room with a larger window, which was not only lighter, but 'not being on the roof, the soot does not blow in which it did in a maddening way'.[26]

Soon after he arrived in Copenhagen, Thesiger heard from his mother that Gavin Maxwell had parted from Curtis Brown and Longman's. Thesiger wrote: 'Gavin is extraordinary and I am sorry for his Mother. He is unbalanced and will end up by committing suicide or in an asylum ... I don't think he can afford to chuck both his agent and his publisher. He has got to live, and wants the best terms he can get for his book [*Ring of Bright Water*].'[27] He wrote again two days later: 'I heard from Graham he says they have parted ostensibly because he says Graham won't get him enough for his otter book. I think Gavin is mental and will end in an asylum ... He may easily find that £sd drives him back to Graham'[28] '... Gavin left him in the sulks because he only got him £350 advance from Longmans for his book on the otter. Now he has accepted the same sum from Longmans through another agent. Graham says he is thankful to be quit of him. Longmans are still publishing the marsh book so Gavin has to accept Mark Longman's decision on what he can say about me.'[29] Two months later, Thesiger received the proofs of Maxwell's marshes book, *A Reed Shaken by the Wind*. He wrote telling his mother: 'I objected only to the representation of one incident and told Mark to cut it out. It is a well written but unpleasant book. Never a word of thanks or graciousness. However it is now harmless.' He added definitively: 'I don't really want to see Gavin Maxwell again.'[30] (Inexplicably, tactlessly, Longman's would advertise *Arabian Sands* on the dust jacket of Gavin Maxwell's book about Sicily *The Ten Pains of Death* (1959).) By the time of their last meeting in Tangier in 1965, as far as Thesiger was concerned any semblance of friendship between them was superficial – and virtually meaningless.[31]

Thesiger rewrote the first eight chapters of *Arabian Sands* in Ireland, in a room 'at the end of a long corridor' in Holloden, the O'Gradys' house near Bagenalstown.[32] Here he had as much or as little company as he wanted, whenever he wanted. In Watson's opinion, Thesiger was still inclined to be reticent, to under-describe events, places and people of intense interest to the reader: for example, he felt that Thesiger could have 'played up a good deal more' his journeys and researches for the Middle East Anti-Locust Unit; but he found the account of falconry in Chapter 15 'enormously interesting' and, apart from criticising its 'rather abrupt ending', wrote, 'this chapter seems to me to go very well indeed'.[33]

A reader's report written by a young woman of this 'extremely masculine book' commented that Thesiger came across as 'a delightful person' who 'conjured up the look and feel of the desert wonderfully – also the characters of his companions. He is especially good at describing camels ...' She felt the book was 'a little formless' and should be cut, but realised that its 'point is a way of life and not an achievement'. She concluded that it was 'a topping book', and her criticisms were 'minor compared to the toppingness of the book as a whole'.[34] By August the following year Watson felt able to praise the final chapter of *Arabian Sands* as 'a great improvement on the first version', and reported that Longman's were 'unreservedly enthusiastic'.[35] John Verney agreed that the last chapter was an 'unqualified improvement – in fact I think the tricky end, with leave-taking of Bin Kabina etc., is just right. Moving because terse. Bravo ...' He suggested some alterations, and added: 'But then, if I was you, I would have died of fatigue and despair years before and never been in a position to write a very wonderful book at the end! I really do think you've made a magnificent job of the book – Regard my few criticisms as sort of well-intentioned barnacles on the *Queen Mary*'s bottom.'[36] On 18 August 1958, Longman's literary adviser John Guest sent a telegram to Thesiger in Ireland congratulating him on his 'superb writing', and the same day wrote a letter describing *Arabian Sands* as 'a fine achievement and most beautifully written'.[37]

The prologue to *Arabian Sands*, scarcely altered since the day it was first written, over the years became identified with Thesiger as much as with his book; its stark perfection was his hallmark, its sense of challenge his epitaph:

A cloud gathers, the rain falls, men live; the cloud disperses without rain, and men and animals die. In the deserts of Arabia there is no rhythm of the seasons, no rise and fall of sap, but empty wastes where only the changing temperature marks the passage of the year. It is a bitter, desiccated land which knows nothing of gentleness or ease. Yet men have lived there since earliest times. Passing generations have left fire-blackened stones at camping sites, a few faint tracks polished on the gravel plains. Elsewhere the winds wipe out their footprints. Men live there because it is the world into which they were born; the life they lead is the life their forefathers led before them; they accept hardships and privations; they know no other way. Lawrence wrote in *Seven Pillars of Wisdom*, 'Bedouin ways were hard, even for those brought up in them and for strangers terrible: a death in life.' No man can live this life and emerge unchanged. He will carry, however faint, the imprint of the desert, the brand which marks the nomad; and he will have within him the yearning to return, weak or insistent according to his nature. For this cruel land can cast a spell which no temperate clime can match.[38]

From January to May 1959 Thesiger made the first of two journeys with mules in the former Abyssinia. At a private audience, the Emperor, Haile Selassie, welcomed him warmly and promised introductions to officials in the south. The Crown Prince, Asfa Wossen, who had refused Thesiger permission to travel freely in 1944, arranged a visit to Lalibela, prompted by the Emperor, to Thesiger's quiet satisfaction.[39] From the

Sandfords' farm at Mullu, to which they had now returned from England, Thesiger wrote informing his mother:

> I have had all the proofs [of *Arabian Sands*]. I think it reads well but I know it too well to be able to judge ... I had dedicated the book to bin Kabina and bin Ghabaisha. We discussed this when I was in London and you then said that you thought I should do this. You know that the book was written for you. I don't really care what anyone else thinks of it. That is why I wanted to and have put the passage in the Introduction about what you have meant to me. Now I feel distressed. You must know that it is your book and no one else's ... I think of you so often when I am in this country ... I have been working ten hours a day checking the proofs.[40]

Thesiger had had to correct the proofs both for Longman's and for his American publisher, E.P. Dutton. Kathleen acted as a go-between. At this critical stage, Thesiger's quixotic decision to travel again in Ethiopia, and the consequent difficulty in contacting him, meant that time became of 'the utmost urgency'.[41] Having heard from Kathleen that Thesiger wished 'to make an expedition into the depths of Abyssinia', John Guest of Longman's warned him: 'Since we are working full time ... I must ask you to lay aside any plans you may have in favour of completing work on your book. The position is, you must either do this or give us carte blanche to go ahead, so far as we can, using our own intelligence in meeting your wishes.'[42] Thesiger responded to Guest's perceptively worded ultimatum. On 6 March he wrote from Mullu to his mother: 'I hope to ... get away down south at the end of the month. I must stay to check the Index but I hope they will hurry up sending it.'[43]

Until he set off from Addis Ababa on 1 April 1959, Thesiger had stayed at the British Embassy (the former Legation) with Philip Mansfield, the First Secretary, and his wife Elinor. To his mother Thesiger wrote: 'I like being here in the compound. I think of you such a lot and of my childhood. The big shola tree is still there by the pond by the drive, and the pepper tree which was on the lawn outside Daddy's dressing room window, and in which I once shot a kite with the air rifle ... There are a lot of firs, I expect Daddy planted most of them, now fine big trees. Nowadays there is no view from the Legation steps ...'[44]

Night after night on the journey south to Lalibela, accompanied by Philip Mansfield, there was torrential rain, thunder and lightning. From Soddu, Thesiger tramped with baggage mules to Lake Margarita in the Rift Valley; then to Chenchia, and over the mountains to Gardula and the Kenya border. Farther south, the country was beautiful, 'green and pleasant and lots of wild flowers'. At one camp a lion chased and killed a mule. Mules, indeed, were the only difficulty. Since there were no longer muleteers prepared to travel for long distances, Thesiger had to go on from market to market, 'changing mules each time which is frustrating'. He resolved 'Next time [to] buy my own mules.'[45] He had looked forward to getting away, 'and to forgetting about the book for a while'.[46] Yet he was relieved to hear from Longman's and from Graham Watson that all was going well,[47] and later that his mother liked the dust jacket, since he had 'been wondering what they made of it'.[48]

He arrived at Mega on 8 May, the last five days marching over semi-desert country, camping near Boran villages at night. By then his shoes, which evidently had seen better days, were completely worn out. In order to find replacements, the Vice-Consul Ian Reeman drove Thesiger from Mega to Moyale, a British district headquarters on the Kenya border. Thesiger recalled: 'It was thanks to these worn out shoes that I thus met George Webb, District Commissioner at Moyale, a good linguist speaking Boran as well as Swahili, a widely read man, humorous and eminently civilised. George sent for the local cobbler and arranged for a pair of leather chapli sandals to be ready by breakfast time next day – which they were. Meanwhile he and his wife Jo put Reeman and myself up.'[49] As Thesiger was leaving, George Webb remarked: 'My heart sank when I saw you. I thought, "Oh God, another poor white come to bounce a cheque."'[50] Webb and his family became Thesiger's closest friends.[51] For years they looked after his affairs while he was abroad, and from 1961 until 1987 George Webb played an increasingly significant role as Thesiger's literary adviser and a meticulous unofficial editor of books such as *Desert, Marsh and Mountain* and *The Life of My Choice*.

Instead of September, as planned, *Arabian Sands* was published in October 1959, after a delay due to a strike by printers and binders. It was immediately successful, acclaimed enthusiastically by readers and reviewers alike. In *The Bookman*, Hammond Innes described it as 'that rare thing, a really great travel book'.[52] Warmly, if misleadingly, Lord Kinross claimed in the *Daily Telegraph*: 'Following worthily in the tradition of Burton, Doughty, Lawrence, Philby and Thomas, it is, very likely, the book about Arabia to end all books about Arabia.'[53] Sir John Glubb praised Thesiger in *The Times* as 'perhaps the last, and certainly one of the greatest, of the British travellers among the Arabs',[54] while St John Philby asserted that 'The crowning touches have been placed on this exploratory activity in Arabia by Wilfred Thesiger, who is probably the greatest of all the explorers.'[55] In the *New Statesman*, V.S. Pritchett observed that writing *Arabian Sands* had given Thesiger the opportunity 'to disclose the extraordinary experience, physical and mental [of being] shut up in himself with stern determination for half an active lifetime'.[56] Graham Watson suggested to Thesiger that 'the review by Pritchard [sic] ... I suspect ... has given you more real pleasure than any of the others, magnificent though the rest of the press has been. What I believe you must now accept is that this was a task which was well worth doing and was a task that you have carried out supremely well.'[57] In a moving letter, John Glubb thanked Thesiger for a signed copy of *Arabian Sands*: 'I have already read it from cover to cover in two days with immense absorption and enjoyment, not unmixed indeed with sadness and nostalgia, provoked by your vivid descriptions.' He ended with a query: 'What are you going to do now?'[58]

Graham Watson put this another way: *Arabian Sands* was 'in the nature of an uncompleted task'.[59] He took care to stress that Thesiger should not feel tied to 'active authorship', but that planning another book might be a pleasant occupation 'even if the execution was postponed for some two or three years':

What I am trying to say is that there are other subjects which cry out for treatment with almost the urgency of the Empty Quarter. We want the definitive book on the Marshes; we want a book about Abyssinia; we want a book – at least I feel there is one there – about your wanderings in Kurdistan and adjoining parts. I believe that you would now find that such writing would come much more easily and much more enjoyably now that you have mastered so superbly well the craft of writing. I can scarcely think of anything which would be more unselfishly worthwhile because you have a unique store of experience which, to put it pompously, I think it is your duty to pass on to others. As you know far better than I do, these particular parts of the world are suffering from change at such a speed that there is not much time left for someone to record them as you knew them.[60]

Thesiger did write eventually at length about Abyssinia in his best-selling autobiographical 'fragment'[61] *The Life of My Choice*, a work of 459 pages, published in 1987, which he always claimed to have based on the first chapter of *Arabian Sands*. In 1996 he returned to the theme of Abyssinia in *The Danakil Diary*, which described the day-to-day events of his Awash river expedition in 1933–34. A chapter on Thesiger's travels in Kurdistan in 1950–51 introduced the third postscript to his auto-biography *Among the Mountains*, published in 1998. These more detailed accounts of journeys in Ethiopia and western Asia had been preceded in 1979 by an elegant work, *Desert, Marsh and Mountain*, the first of five large-format books lavishly illustrated with Thesiger's superb photo-graphs.

John Verney had praised *Arabian Sands* as 'magnificent'.[62] Val ffrench Blake had been 'excited' by it, and by the experience of working on the manuscript. 'I do not see,' he wrote, 'how we could have established again any relationship so firmly, other than by a collaboration of this sort.'[63] After Eton, ffrench Blake and Thesiger, to an extent, had drifted apart. Working on *Arabian Sands* brought them together again after many years. 'Doing something, almost anything, together'[64] had been Laurens van der Post's sensible prescription for forging and maintaining close friendships. Grateful for their 'fragmentary' relationship, which he insisted had been 'one of the few really important ones in my life', ffrench Blake wrote to Thesiger:

I can't really analyze what has happened ... and I don't want to. I don't know why I said I'd help with your book, part (most) I think to repay what I had been unable to give before, part curiosity, part the vicarious traveller and adventurer, part the insatiable desire I have to put other people right, if given the chance. Doing it has been its own reward and has brought its own reward, because it has helped to break down what is a very thick barrier indeed, that of two rather strong characters being resolutely unemotional; the reward is that I now have a real friendship to look forward to, and not just a bit of work done to look back on.[65]

T.H. White, the author of *The Sword in the Stone*, *Mistress Masham's Repose* and *The Goshawk*, a friend of John Verney and Thesiger, added a deeply emotional tribute of his own, three years after *Arabian Sands* was first published:

Please will you let me kneel before you and scatter ashes on my miserable old head? It is far the best book I have ever read, it is worth ten times Doughty, a hundred times Freya Stark, and a thousand times that idiot Lawrence. Now I have got to lug it all the way back to Florence, to get you to sign it, when it will become my most valuable possession. Dearest Wilfred, you are a hopping genius, and I am bitterly, bitterly ashamed of not having seen it at once. I can't wait for the next volume, and I beg and implore God not to let you use more than your jokey number of 400 words. I am sending you my book of verses as a tribute. For you I feel nothing but hatred and envy, because I am a bad loser, and simply can't bear it that you should be a better writer than Verney or me. You are a god. Love and hugs of hatred and reverence from Tim White.[66]

Thesiger was flattered, but dismissed White's eulogy as 'preposterous', and his remark about Lawrence as 'utter nonsense'.[67] White's privately printed collection of poems (number 90 of a limited edition of 100, inscribed to Thesiger and signed by White) was among the two hundred books Thesiger asked the antiquarian book dealers Maggs Bros to sell on his behalf in April 1995.[68]

In 1960 Thesiger returned to Ethiopia, travelling on foot with mules from Mullu, north along the east side of the Abbai, or Blue Nile, to Lake Tana, Gondar and the Simien mountains. The long clockwise route took him south from there to Lalibela, Magdala and Addis Ababa. He remembered the two impressive, unrestored castles he saw beyond the 'shoddy setting of post-war Gondar with its ubiquitous tin roofs, ramshackle modern buildings, noise and fumes of motor transport'.[69] Fourteen thousand feet above sea level in the Simien mountains, a mule collapsed and had to be temporarily abandoned.[70] White patches on their highest slopes turned out to be formed by solid ice, not drifts of snow, as Thesiger had thought.

Alaqa Dessie, the elderly headman of a small community living on the grassy plateau of Magdala, told Thesiger that his father had been there when Napier's army captured Magdala in 1868. It was, Thesiger reflected in his diary, 'curious'[71] that the headman's father 'must have seen my grandfather here'.[72] Alaqa Dessie showed Thesiger the place where the besieged Emperor Theodore, Menelik's predecessor, shot himself with one of a pair of pistols given to him by Queen Victoria, at the top of a flight of stone steps leading to his palace on Magdala's summit. On the battlefield at Sagale, Thesiger found 'bones and skulls under great piles of rocks on the smaller of the two flat topped hills'[73] on which Negus Mikael made his final stand in 1916, 'where the dead were collected into heaps'.[74] Seated beside a nearby spring, Thesiger ate a meal of scrambled eggs and coffee before he continued on his way towards Addis Ababa.

He left Sagale on 15 May and reached Addis Ababa two days later, after exactly nineteen and a half hours on the road: he timed and logged these marches in his diary, and later, when writing *The Life of My Choice*; for some reason he added the daily totals in his diaries in red ink. At the British Embassy in Addis Ababa he stayed for a week with Sir Denis and Lady Wright. 'It is fun,' he wrote to his mother, 'being in this house again, the first time since my childhood. I have my old room at the back.'[75]

Thesiger and Kathleen had arranged to meet in Milan in July for a summer holiday on Lake Como. Aged eighty, Kathleen became easily flustered by travel preparations, and was now increasingly unsteady on her feet. Wilfred urged her: 'Be sure and get a Cook's agent to go with you to the airport and to put you on the plane. As you say it is only the start which fusses you.' He wrote affectionately, 'I look forward so enormously to seeing you again,' before adding a more prosaic reminder: 'Will you get Miss Emtage to check that there are no moths in my clothes.'[76] He gave Kathleen a summary of his forthcoming journey from Addis Ababa to Rome: 'I am staying until May 31st, when I fly to Khartoum to stay with Chapman Andrews. Then I plan to go to Benghazi to stay with Noel Jackson who was Consul-General in Basra and a great friend of mine.'[77] 'I have booked an air passage to Milan on June 30th [from Rome] ... I go [from Benghazi] to Tripoli to stay with our Ambassador from June 16th–18th – then to Catania, for Syracuse and Agrigento, till the 27th when I go to Rome ... I am longing to see you ... We will have such fun together.'[78]

TWENTY-TWO

Camel Journeys to the Jade Sea

Since he was a boy, Thesiger had been fascinated by the deserts of northern Kenya and the nomadic tribes that lived there. Visitors to the Legation at Addis Ababa, such as Arnold Hodson, had told him stories of big game hunting and tribal warfare. In the glass-fronted bookcases at his mother's flat in Chelsea were evocative titles he had read in his early teens: *Sun, Sand and Somals* and *The Ivory Raiders* by Major H. Rayne, *To Abyssinia Through an Unknown Land* by Captain C.H. Stigand; others, including A.H. Neumann's classic *Elephant Hunting in East Equatorial Africa*, A. Donaldson Smith's *Through Unknown African Countries* and *The Discovery by Count Teleki of Lakes Rudolf and Stefanie* by Lieutenant Ludwig von Höhnel, he had bought some years after he first started travelling in Kenya.

In November 1960, accompanied by Frank Steele, Thesiger set off from Kula Mawe, near Isiolo, to trek with camels to Lake Rudolf (later renamed Lake Turkana), and from there eastwards across the Chalbi desert to Mount Marsabit. The Northern Frontier District of Kenya, or NFD, was a restricted area where anyone other than government officials, district commissioners or game wardens was forbidden to travel without a special permit. George Webb, who had been transferred from Moyale to the Ministry of Defence in Nairobi, invited Thesiger to stay, and introduced him to the Governor of Kenya, Sir Patrick Renison, who gave Thesiger and Steele a permit to enter the NFD and travel wherever they wished. They had originally planned to retrace Thesiger's journey with mules in 1959, starting from Addis Ababa and approaching Lake Rudolf from the north. Thesiger wrote from Nairobi: 'I think [Frank] is quite happy to be going up to Rudolf from here and not from Addis Ababa, as indeed I am myself.'¹ In Nairobi he lunched with John Newbould, with whom he had travelled in 1955 in southern Morocco, who had been appointed Pasture Research Officer at Ngorongoro, the crater reserve adjoining the Serengeti National Park. Thesiger planned to stay at Ngorongoro with Newbould from early April until the end of May the following year.

From Archer's Post on the Uaso Nyiro river, Thesiger wrote ecstatically to Kathleen:

> This is the country I had read of as a boy and always wanted to see. Mountains all round on the horizon with [Mount] Kenya in the far distance white with snow. The country rolling open grass downs or thick scrub. A lot of animals. Zebra which let you up to within 50 yards, Grant's gazelle, gerenuk and a herd of eland. At our last camp we found the fresh droppings of an elephant 100 yards away where he had come to water at night. Lots of tracks of lion and buffalo and once of rhino. I hope we don't meet a rhino for we shall have real chaos if one charges our line of camels ... the tameness of the game here is extraordinary. In Isiolo giraffe and zebra constantly come onto the DC's lawn at night and sometimes elephant, and the other night two lion spent all night in the Vet's garden and would not go away though they banged trays and fired off shotguns. So different to Abyssinia.²

Newbould had whetted Thesiger's appetite for the Mathews range, 'forested with juniper and wild olive and full of elephant and buffalo'.³ At Archer's Post, Thesiger wrote, 'We are now in Samburu country, a section of the Masai. I have seen a few and they look very attractive. Still almost naked and smeared with red ochre.'⁴ The pastoral Samburu were destined to play a pivotal role in Thesiger's later life. Some of his closest relationships with tribal peoples were established among them, and during his last years at Maralal in northern Kenya he lived with one or other of his adoptive Samburu 'sons' in houses he had built for them and their extended families.

Travelling north along the west flank of the Mathews range, Thesiger wrote: 'there seem to be elephant everywhere. The first I saw, a big bull, was only 50 yards off the path to our right while we were going along with the camels.' In Ngaro Narok, 'a lovely valley' where they camped for Christmas, they found two elephant resting under the trees when they arrived: 'At night we heard elephant and rhino and of course hyena. One rhino coming down to water almost walked into our camp in the dark and made off with a loud snort. Looking for elephant the next morning I got within 30 yards of a black rhinoceros, the first I have seen ... I thought he looked very formidable as he went past peering suspiciously in every direction.'[5] Frank Steele, one of Thesiger's circle of close friends, proved 'a delightful companion'.[6] He helped Wilfred to learn enough Swahili to cope with the safari when Steele left him at Marsabit to return to London. For two years after the war, as a DC in northern Uganda, Steele had hunted elephant and other game fairly extensively. He noticed that 'to begin with, Wilfred was a bit on edge near elephant and rhino. He soon got used to them, but he hadn't had much experience of elephant, and until then he had only seen one white rhinoceros in the Sudan.'[7]

Tramping along the Ndoto mountains towards Lake Rudolf, Thesiger exulted: 'Looking north one feels that there is nothing there but hard, empty desert as far as the Abyssinian frontier and beyond; the great satisfaction of feeling that all the towns and civilisation are left behind, and that ahead are only scattered wells, and the encampments of nomads and wild animals. It is the wild animals that make this country so much more interesting than travelling in Abyssinia ... The mountains covered with forest and giant euphorbia give a background to the scene but I find that I want to get beyond them to the deserts which I can see to the north. Wonderful views of pale blue distance.'[8]

On 9 January 1961 they reached Lake Rudolf, 'a surprisingly beautiful place, very peaceful and with lovely lights over the lake and the islands in the middle' – yet the romance of arriving there seventy years after the lake's discovery by Teleki and von Höhnel in 1888 was spoilt by 'a fishing camp for enterprising sportsmen from Nairobi ... all pretty primitive but quite amusing when one has got over the initial shock of finding it here'.[9] Thesiger said: 'Of all the explorations done in Africa, I would soonest have done this journey. When I first reached Lake Rudolf ... I could understand what von Höhnel, Teleki, and their men had felt when they saw it there below them, stretching to the horizon.'[10]

Due to heavy going over thick sand (and the added strain of walking in shoes that once again had begun to fall apart), Thesiger 'tore a ligament',[11] which in fact was his Achilles tendon. Using a sailmaker's needle and copper wire, Frank Steele stitched together the detached sole and upper of Thesiger's worn-out shoes; but Thesiger was obliged finally to borrow the spare pair of desert boots that Steele, much to Thesiger's derision, had insisted on bringing with him. Steele recalled with admiration how, 'after weeks, Wilfred literally walked himself better'.[12] Thesiger noted: 'My foot has stood up well to a hard trek here from South Horr, no water on the way so we could not go slow and the going bad over lava. It still feels a little weak but will soon be all right. The few days rest here will do it good.'[13]

At Loiengalani, on the east shore of Lake Rudolf, they met George Adamson, the game warden there, whom they had met some weeks previously at Isiolo. He and his wife Joy were looking for somewhere to release Elsa, the lioness they had reared. The Adamsons and Elsa were already well known in Kenya, and after Joy wrote *Born Free* (1960), they became world famous. Thesiger and Joy took an instant dislike to one another. Thesiger wrote: 'I like Adamson very much but his wife is impossible. I wonder he has not taken her out into the bush and shot her long ago.'[14] When Thesiger deliberately provoked Joy by declaring, 'The only rational place for these animals is in Whipsnade,' she had risen, incandescent with rage, and screamed: 'You dare say a zing like zat to me!'[15] Thesiger said that he could never remember whether he had told Joy about the lion cubs he reared at Kutum and eventually felt obliged to shoot, but it appears that he hadn't; or else he may have divulged this information only to George Adamson, who wisely decided to keep it to himself.[16]

Thesiger and Steele circled Mount Kulal, fifteen miles east of Lake Rudolf, in blazing heat fanned by a tearing hot wind, across a desert of lava boulders that made cruel going for both men and camels. Yet in 1995 Thesiger played down the effects of the heat and the terrain, commenting: 'The country was certainly harsh, but I find Donaldson Smith's description [in *Through Unknown African Countries*] – "days of torment, marching through a fiery furnace"[17] – exaggerated.'[18] Far away, across the Chalbi desert, the 'cloud-capped' slopes of Marsabit rose from an empty landscape parched and wasted by drought. At waterholes they found

Rendille nomads and their camels, the men with distinctive earrings and bracelets, naked to the waist and armed with spears. Thesiger wrote later from Baragoi: 'The Rendille are a camel people, unlike the Samburu who own vast herds of cattle, and it was fun once more to see and hear great herds of camels.'[19] Among Marsabit's forests were volcanic craters, the largest of which, Lake Paradise, had been the base in 1924 for a four-year photographic safari by the Americans Martin and Osa Johnson, pioneer wildlife film-makers. As soon as Thesiger and Steele reached Marsabit, Frank left for England, much to Thesiger's regret, 'for [he] had found him an excellent companion, very equitable and full of pleasure in everything he saw'.[20]

From Marsabit Thesiger trekked to Lodwar, and Baragoi on the edge of Turkana country. At a Rendille encampment, 'the same sort of temporary villages you saw when travelling through the Danakil country',[21] he watched men and women dancing together at midnight under a full moon. He thought the scene was 'Very effective with the herds of camels couched all round and the dancers' spears stuck upright in the ground. The tunes were pleasing and the dancing very energetic in short bursts.'[22] By the time he reached Lodwar Thesiger's leg had practically recovered, and only felt 'a little weak at the end of a hard day's walking'.[23] He looked very fit and spare, his face, neck, arms and legs burnt dark ochre and reddened by sun and wind. He wrote: 'We usually started off each morning by moonlight, an hour or so before dawn. I now went on ahead of the camels to make sure they did not walk into buffalo or elephant. One morning, we found six buffalo in the middle of the riverbed and had to shout at them to get them to move.'[24] On the way from Marsabit his companions included Ekwar, a Turkana cookboy; two Somali camelmen; two Rendille camelmen to look after some hired Rendille camels; and Soiyah, a Turkana who, Thesiger wrote, 'had occasionally infuriated Frank and me by his oafishness'.[25]

On 24 March Thesiger's caravan reached Lake Baringo, where they camped for two days. From there they turned north-east to Maralal, headquarters of the Samburu district, a small township lying seven thousand feet or so above sea level on the Lorogi plateau. Thesiger wrote: 'Maralal is a most attractive station ... with the hills going up another 1000' behind the station and covered with forests of juniper all draped in moss. I arrived there for Easter. A good many people had come up there from neighbouring districts to spend the holiday but Eliot [sic] the game warden put me up and I spent a fascinating three days with him. He took me out one morning to show me rhinoceros. We found one, followed it for about three hours and it was very interesting to see Eliot and his tracker spooring, and eventually got up to within 5 yards of it in thick bush. It exploded from under our feet with a snort but I got a good though fleeting sight of it.'[26] In *My Kenya Days* Thesiger gave a more detailed description of his first meeting with Major Rodney Elliott, drawn partly from letters and partly from somewhat imperfect recollections.

> While I was unloading my camels among some trees outside Maralal, a Land Rover drew up nearby and a military-looking man got out and said abruptly, 'Are you Wilfred Thesiger?' I said, yes; and he went on, 'I am Rodney Elliott, the Game Warden. I understand you were given permission in Nairobi to shoot two animals a week in this division. Of course, had I known about this, you most certainly wouldn't have got permission to do so. Get in the car at once and come up to the office. I want you to fill in a form saying exactly what you have shot.'[27]

According to Thesiger, he made Elliott wait while he unloaded the camels and pitched camp. When Elliott found out that instead of a possible thirty-two head of game, Thesiger had shot only four – 'two Grant's gazelle, one Thomson's gazelle and one Burchell's zebra' for food[28] – he relaxed and invited him to stay in his house.[29] In September 1998, Elliott gave his 'corrected' version of these events. Then aged seventy-seven, six feet in height, his thick white hair and white moustache were offset by dark blue eyes and a reddish-fair complexion. He spoke quietly, with a fugitive, ready smile. In March 1961 Thesiger was almost fifty-one and Elliott was forty, yet Thesiger's description of him implied an older as well as an authoritative man. Thesiger insisted that he had dictated his description of Elliott exactly as he remembered him, adding the proviso: 'I'm hopeless guessing people's ages.'[30] According to Elliott, he told Thesiger to come up to his office when he was ready. He hadn't been informed by Major Ian Grimwood, Kenya's Chief Game Warden, that

Thesiger was travelling in the NFD: 'This was most unusual, quite unlike Grimwood who was very careful about these things, doing it by the book, protocol and so on ... I wasn't expecting Wilfred, a well-known man, here in my area.'[31]

In *My Kenya Days*, Thesiger gave a brief sketch of Maralal, 'a rectangle of wide streets planted with trees and small adjoining wooden shops painted in bright colours. In those days all the Samburu warriors, or *moran* as they were called, wore a length of red cloth knotted over one shoulder, their faces and chests often coloured with red ochre, their plaited hair long down their backs. The elders wore red blankets. All the women were draped with blue cloth. It was a peaceful and attractive place. You could spend a whole day in the town without seeing or hearing a car.'

Nevertheless, a garage specialising in Land Rover repairs had been established by Siddiq Bhola, a charming, cultivated Pakistani with a farm at Rumuruti, south of Maralal, whose family had lived in East Africa since the end of the nineteenth century. When Thesiger left Maralal for Nairobi, Bhola drove him the whole way in his car 'and absolutely refused to accept any payment [by which Thesiger meant, presumably, a contribution to the cost of petrol] for doing so'.[32] From then until Thesiger left Kenya in 1994, Siddiq Bhola and his sons gave him unstinting help and generous hospitality. Bhola even cleared an upstairs storeroom and built a lavatory so that Thesiger could write *The Life of My Choice* in relative peace and quiet. Bhola's compound was a Muslim enclave in a profoundly African setting, and the harmonious background to Thesiger's semi-permanent life at Maralal in future years resulted from the combined presence of these 'all-important' cultures.[33]

Thesiger travelled in April 1961 from Nairobi to Ngorongoro, where John Newbould lived in a three-roomed hut on a picturesque site above the crater. 'This is a wonderful place,' he wrote to Kathleen, 'and I do wish you could see it. From John's house you look right across the crater, a distance of about 12 miles, to the far rim. Below the house and about 2000 feet lower is the crater floor, a green grassy plain covered with game.'[34] Here were black rhinoceros, 'strange prehistoric looking beasts, very reptilian in appearance'.

When a male rhino attacked their car, Thesiger marvelled at how 'the bull got to his feet with incredible speed, spun round and charged. I have never seen anything so quick and vicious.'[35] In the crater he saw many kinds of game, including buffalo and several of Ngorongoro's famous black-maned lion. Yet these sights were eclipsed by the 'enormous herds of zebra, wildebeeste and gazelle' on the Serengeti plains. Having planned to trek for a month with donkeys, Thesiger and Newbould arranged to hire them from a Masai *boma* (a group of huts enclosed by a fence) in the crater. Thesiger hoped he had taken some good photographs of the Masai. 'I have always heard that the Masai are incredibly beautiful,' he wrote, 'and they certainly are ... They look so well with only a piece of cloth dyed a soft reddish brown, falling from one shoulder and with their heavy long bladed spears.' He and Newbould watched a Masai circumcision ceremony, something of peculiar interest to Thesiger. 'It was at dawn and was misty, wet and cold. The two boys were incredibly brave, for the way the Masai do the operation takes at least 3 minutes of cutting. Not a muscle twitched on either of their faces. Now they count as warriors.'[36] Some of the Masai carried buffalo-hide shields decorated with coloured heraldic designs. Later, when asked if he knew what these designs represented, Thesiger confessed that he did not. Much as he enjoyed living with primitive peoples, and respected their traditions, he never delved deeply into them. He observed: 'I'm not an anthropologist. I'm not going to go probing into the significance of their shields. I'm interested to see how they compete with their conditions and survive.'[37] Despite this, he collected books describing the tribes and tribal customs of every country he had visited. Among them were A.C. Hollis's celebrated study *The Masai* (1905) and *Some Notes on the Masai of Kenya Colony*, an important paper by Dr Louis S.B. Leakey, the anthropologist famed for his discovery of fossils of primitive man, related species and artefacts at Olduvai Gorge in Tanzania, north of the Ngorongoro crater. Thesiger always emphasised: 'I'm in no sense academic. I'm far more interested in individuals than in tribes. Studying people like butterflies under a microscope doesn't appeal to me. Instead, I want to be accepted by them ... to share the lives they're leading.'[38]

On 25 April Thesiger wrote to Kathleen: 'John Newbould and I are off today for a month's trek with donkeys, a circular journey round Ngorongoro.'[39] He continued: 'The more I see of the Masai the more I like them. They have scorned everything which the west has offered them, and how right they are. The tragedy is that the others who have not, like the Kikuyu, are bound to win in the modern world, though they lose their souls in the process.'[40]

In Maralal Thesiger had engaged Ibach, 'a powerfully-built young Turkana' who accompanied him that year to Ngorongoro and in 1963 when Thesiger and Newbould travelled on foot with fifteen donkeys across the Masai Steppe in northern Tanzania. The two Turkana, Ekwar and Ibach, and an 'impressively handsome' Samburu *moran* named Lokuyie, were among the first of Thesiger's tribal companions in Kenya from 1960 to 1963. Others joined him at various times.[41] He remained needlessly coy and evasive about the nature of these platonic, voyeuristic relationships, yet he enlisted only youths who caught his eye. A 'naked young Turkana who appeared to be about fourteen ... [a] powerfully-built, cheerful-looking lad with an engaging smile' joined Thesiger at Lodwar in October 1968. 'He said his name was Erope, which in Turkana means "spring rains";'[42] this poetic detail enhanced the story of their meeting, just as his classical allusion to Hadrian and Antinous in the Phrygian woods had transformed Thesiger's memorable first sight of Salim bin Ghabaisha.[43]

Before he left Kenya in June 1961, Thesiger visited Lamu with George Webb. 'It pleased me,' he wrote, 'to be back once more in this Muslim atmosphere ... seeing the town with its narrow streets separating the tall, whitewashed houses with their elaborately carved doors.'[44] During June and July John Verney and his wife Jan accompanied Kathleen to Portugal, where Wilfred eventually joined them. His delight at being with his mother was tempered by growing anxiety for her health. He had written from Ngorongoro: 'I am worried that your kidneys have been giving you trouble ... I know only too well that you have constant pain [from your back and your legs] and therefore have to accept an additional one as you did with your appendix ... You matter so terribly to me and I hate to think that you are suffering more pain.'[45] John Verney wrote that 'There was never any doubt of W's deep love of K (as she was always called) and indeed we were often struck by it. Nevertheless ... he was extremely on edge in her company. I daresay the two things are connected.'[46]

In November 1961 Thesiger returned to Copenhagen to begin writing

The Marsh Arabs. 'The book is underway,' he wrote. 'I have masses of stuff to put in it if I can make it interesting ... It took a long time to see a shape for the book but I may have it now.'[47] As always when on the threshold of anything new, he anticipated the worst: 'It is a difficult book to write for there is so much detail, and it is difficult to find a frame for it. The book could easily become cluttered up and unbearably dull. In the desert book the problem was to convey an impression of emptiness and monotony without making the book monotonous and boring, but it was all so stark that it was comparatively easy to highlight certain main features. Here the problem is to avoid loosing [sic] the wood in a jumble of trees, or rather the marshes in the reeds.'[48]

After a fortnight he moved to a quieter room at the back of the Park Hotel. 'The one I had,' he explained, 'was appallingly noisy and stopped me sleeping. This is much better.'[49] Of 'Copenhaven'[50] (an insightful slip) he wrote: 'I was right to come here where there is nothing to do but work.'[51]

Graham Watson had not attempted to read Thesiger's handwritten first chapter: 'I think that when you have to struggle with calligraphy it is almost impossible to reach any sort of critical opinion so I am now getting this chapter off to the typist.'[52] That accomplished, he reported: 'I really think you have started marvellously well and ... your hand has lost none of its professional cunning. The only basic criticism which occurs to me is that you are still rather tending to rush your fences and assume in your readers a knowledge which they do not possess ... Equally I think you have some terribly impressive writing ... and if you keep this level up, you need have no worries.'[53]

Kathleen's comments on early chapters Thesiger had sent to Curtis Brown to be typed echoed Watson's. Yet he was anxious to avoid at the start 'the sort of text book stuff like "The marshes cover 60,000 square miles. They are bordered by ... the tribes that live in the Marshes are X Y Z etc." Some of this will be necessary, but I want to try and fit it in later when I have caught the reader's attention. Anyway what you have seen is only a first rough draft. Do go on criticising. Criticism whether from you or Val or Graham is the only thing that is valuable.'[54] Watson commented: 'I think you are wise in trying to get the reader into the book by leading him gently by the ear and then giving him the necessary factual information later.'[55]

News that Kathleen had had two falls left Thesiger feeling very worried, on top of a 'thoroughly bad day' when the book wouldn't 'go right'. Otherwise, he noted dismally: 'I have nothing to tell you. I sit and try and work from 10 am till 10 pm and get about 1000 words done if I am lucky in twelve hours.'[56] Thesiger dined on Christmas Eve with the Danish translator of *Arabian Sands* and his family. On Christmas Day he lunched with 'Monty Evans' at Malmö.[57]

In February 1962 Thesiger climbed Mount Kilimanjaro with George Webb, and afterwards retraced his journey in northern Kenya, with camels, from Garba Tula to Lake Rudolf. Lokuyie, the Samburu *moran*, came with him on this journey; in June, from Mbalambala, together with Ekwar, Abakan (a thirteen-year-old Turkana who had recently joined Thesiger) and Ibach, they travelled by canoe down the Tana river as far as Walu, and from there trekked with donkeys for five days to the Boni Forest, and finally to Lamu. In August Thesiger and John Newbould travelled from Ngorongoro to Seronera in the Serengeti National Park, and east to Lake Natron on the border of Kenya and Tanganyika (as Tanzania was formerly known). 'When we were perhaps a mile from the lake,' Thesiger wrote, 'I began to hear a distant sound almost like an excited crowd at a football match, which grew louder and louder as we approached.'[58] Crowding the lake shore and the nearby islands were thousands of pelicans, many of them immature and as yet unable to fly. They were in no danger from man, unlike those in southern Iraq, which were shot by the Marsh Arabs, who used the loose skin of the bird's pouch as a tympan covering their drums.[59]

Thesiger wrote in *My Kenya Days*: 'My intention when I came to Kenya had been to make one, possibly two camel-journeys in the NFD.'[60] By July 1962 he felt that he had seen enough of the NFD 'and consequently of Kenya';[61] but he was anxious to see more of northern Tanganyika, the Masai and the abundant wildlife. At Ngorongoro, after some discussion, he and Newbould decided to travel the following year on foot with donkeys across the Masai Steppe, as far south as the Masai country extended.

In January 1963, after a holiday with his mother at Lake Como and Venice, Thesiger went to stay with the Verneys and their children in Florence, where they had taken a 'magnificent place ... very dark and gloomy when there is no sun! But splendid.' Jan Verney had written: 'John has a vast and beautiful studio with a massive ancient table to write on ... Of course we expect you here until we find you a suitable room near – wouldn't hear of anything else.'[62] John added: 'Of course you must come here on arrival – Meanwhile we're looking round for a pleasant billet nearby. It's a lovely quiet spot and I'm pretty sure you'll find it congenial for work. After all, I suppose more good books have been written in Florence than any other city! It will be great fun to have you around and personally I intend to walk a lot through the winter, if you ever want a companion. Bring warm clothes – these stone houses chill the marrow and though I *think* the heating is going to be excellent it's as well to over-insure.'[63] For Thesiger, who was always made miserable by the cold, the efficiency of the heating system was probably decisive. After his stay with the Verneys he moved to a room at the pensione Annalena nearby, in the via Romana, where he lived and wrote for the next three months. By February he could inform John Guest at Longman's: 'I hope to have my book on the Marsh Arabs finished by the end of March. It has gone better than I expected and John Verney assures me that it is better than *Arabian Sands*.'[64]

In April Kathleen, and Brian's younger daughter Philippa, joined Wilfred for a month at the pensione Annalena. Thesiger remembered T.H. White arriving for supper (no doubt bringing his treasured copy of *Arabian Sands* for him to sign), obviously tipsy, with an Italian youth in tow: 'Tim was good company when he'd had just the right amount to drink, but otherwise he said things to shock people, and that was tiresome. He started discussing penises with my mother, who let him go on and then said, "Tim, I really have no idea what you're talking about!"'[65]

Looking back, John Verney wrote affectionately to Thesiger:

The Florence winter of '62/63 was an enormous success – something unique and memorable and worthwhile – and that was as much due to your sharing it with us, as to Florence itself. As for my part in the Book: well, I can only say that I enjoyed helping and feel proud to have been able to help, simply because I have the greatest admiration for its subject matter, for your dedication to the Marsh Arabs. In short I knew it was something well worth helping with – since I was in a position to help – in much the same way that a midwife wants to help a mother. The child is entirely yours in everything that counts. But I am awfully glad that I could ease the delivery, help tidy up the umbilical cord and make a neat job of the navel! So let there be no more feelings of obligation on your part. Or mine. I'm pretty sure the book will be as great a success as it deserves; certainly it can never be bettered in its own way – and I thoroughly enjoyed every minute of the time we spent together on it!'[66]

Graham Watson believed that *The Marsh Arabs* would become a classic work on its 'neighbourhood', and if it did not quite reach the peaks of *Arabian Sands*, this was 'in the nature of the subject': 'The earlier book after all, contained sustained passages of prolonged physical danger and an epic of exploration, whereas *The Marsh Arabs* is just a marvellously perceptive account of a quite fascinating part of the world.'[67]

On 16 May Thesiger arrived back in Nairobi, where John Newbould met him at the airport. Three days later they drove to Arusha in northern Tanzania, then to Ngorongoro. At Seronera, Thesiger watched the vast annual migration of wildebeest, 200,000 animals massed 'like ants for 20 miles. Then many more scattered, perhaps another 100,000.' There were '19 lion in all following the wildebeeste',[68] and Thesiger noted four kills. At Ngorongoro, heavy downpours were accompanied by storms of thunder and lightning. Sometimes, in the evening, they heard the sound of lion roaring in the distance. British newspapers Thesiger saw at Arusha were devoted to the Profumo affair, a scandal involving the Secretary of State for War in Harold Macmillan's Conservative government. Also involved was Thesiger's first cousin Stephen Ward, whose mother Eileen had been Kathleen's younger sister. Thesiger commented on such headlines as '"Doctor Ward arrested" etc. Just what Roddy and I said would happen. I am glad Eileen is dead for nothing could be more squalid and humiliating. Somehow we always knew he would end in prison, but fancy an international scandal like this.'[69] Ward eventually committed suicide.

More than ever, Thesiger longed for the 'clean space' of the African plains.[70] He wrote: 'I expect we shall go back to Ngorongoro tomorrow and I hope we get off on our donkey trek soon.'[71] From 21 June to 3 September he trekked with Newbould across the Masai Steppe. Ibach came with them, and five others, including a Masai named Olais. Besides fifteen donkeys, they took with them Newbould's two riding ponies and 'Shillingi', a small black-and-white terrier they had bought for a shilling. Thesiger took many photographs of the Masai in their villages and at deep wells where they watered their cattle. Thirty years later, he used letters he had written to his mother, and brief notes scribbled in his diary, to give a fascinating description of this journey in *My Kenya Days*, the first of three postscripts to his autobiography, *The Life of My Choice*. For Thesiger, *My Kenya Days* was a *tour de force* in a very real sense. Until then he had never written anything by dictation; and at the age of eighty-two, he found great difficulty remembering words, phrases or sentences he was unable to read for himself and had to have read to him, over and over again. Before he began dictating he would listen attentively, sometimes for an hour or more, until he had fully grasped the sequence of events described in his letters and diaries. He wrote:

> There was always something to see. Though there was not the abundance of animal life found in the Serengeti, we did see occasional giraffe, oryx, zebra, gerenuk and duiker, and periodically the tracks and droppings of elephant and rhino. John was knowledgeable about the vegetation and gave me much interesting information about the plants, shrubs and trees along the way ... A month after we had left Ngorongoro, we arrived at the Namalulu wells. Here the wells had been excavated to a depth of thirty feet, and, inside, sloping trenches gave the cattle access to the water ... at Ngasumet ... three Masai stood in a well-shaft drawing water. One stood above the other ... naked, except for a skin-covering like a helmet which kept their plaited and ochred hair dry.[72]

In a letter from Kibaya, Thesiger wrote: 'This is about as far south as we are going. Now we turn east to Kijungu and then north back towards Arusha probably going along the Ruvu river.'[73] He expanded the brief jottings in his diary, giving Kathleen a charming sketch of Shillingi, the terrier, 'a very attractive little beast ... very independent', who 'will never come when he is called unless he wants to': 'He sleeps beside me at night and is useful for keeping the hyenas away ... He also drove off a lion at one of our camps.'[74] Elsewhere he described 'a most interesting encampment of Enderobo', south of Kibaya, living 'on what they shoot, on berries and wild honey. They use bows and poisoned arrows and keep no animals ... I think they must be very like the bushmen whom Van der Post wrote about in the Kalahari ... These were the apricot colour he describes.'[75]

By coincidence, Laurens van der Post's wife, Ingaret Giffard, had recently been invited to make an abridged version of *Arabian Sands* for Longman's 'The Heritage of Literature' series, intended for schools, which included such varied titles as *South* by Sir Ernest Shackleton and Gavin Maxwell's first book, *Harpoon at a Venture*. Fired with enthusiasm, she wrote to Thesiger while he was travelling in Tanzania that July: 'I am so delighted because for a long time now I have been wanting to do it, feeling it would make an immense contribution to the educational editions. You and I have discussed it more than once and, in consequence, I am taking your approval for granted!'[76] In September, at the end of his Masai journey, Thesiger wrote from Dar-es-Salaam to his mother: 'You will be amused to hear that *Arabian Sands* is to come out in "School Classics" so many school children will hate my name.' Half-serious, half-joking, he added: 'This might bring me in a bit of money.'[77]

Thesiger had taken a lot of photographs during this journey, including many of the Masai. 'Ordinarily,' he wrote, 'it is difficult to persuade Masai to let you photograph them.' Yet at Ngorongoro, when Newbould showed a group of Masai warriors copies of photographs Thesiger had taken the previous year, 'they were thrilled by them and all wanted to be photographed again'.[78] Thesiger described elsewhere how, 'On my journey in Tanzania with John Newbould in 1963, I was anxious to photograph some Masai we encountered, but they genuinely refused to be photographed. I therefore walked about, pointing my camera at nothing in an absorbed manner; after a while one of them asked if he could look through it. He did so and soon they were all looking at each other enthusiastically through the camera. After that there could be no further opposition to me doing the same. This was when I got some of my best results.'[79]

Before he returned to England on 20 October, Thesiger visited Zanzibar. He was curious to see it, he wrote, 'since it had been the starting point for the major nineteenth-century expeditions that explored East

Africa, including those by Burton and Speke, Thomson and Teleki with whose writings I was familiar'. Ibach, the young Turkana, came with him. Together they spent a day searching Zanzibar's forests without success for the indigenous red colobus monkeys, whose name derives from the Greek *kolobos*, meaning 'cut short', a reference to the animal's thumbs, which are either greatly reduced in size or else non-existent.[80]

From January to March 1964, Thesiger and his mother wintered in the Canary Islands, followed by Morocco in March, southern and central Spain in April, and Italy with the Verneys in Abruzzi in May. Visiting Abruzzi again after the war gave John Verney more background for his book *A Dinner of Herbs*, in which Thesiger featured as Matthew Prendergast, an eccentric English explorer with 'a passion for the untamed'.[81] In London, George Webb meanwhile checked the text proofs and index of *The Marsh Arabs*. John Guest wrote to Thesiger: 'I can, at last, say that there are no further problems on the book … You can, at any rate, congratulate yourself on having written a superb book which, I hope, will be faultless when it appears.'[82]

The Marsh Arabs gave further proof of Thesiger's latent genius as a writer and a photographer. Several of his friends, including Frank Steele, John Verney and Gavin Young, considered it in many ways to be a better book than *Arabian Sands*. In a review for the *Daily Telegraph*, H.D. Ziman hailed it as 'a masterpiece'. Raymond Mortimer in the *Sunday Times* called Thesiger the 'greatest of living explorers', and wrote: 'If readers already know something about this isolated people, it is because Mr Gavin Maxwell published in 1957 *A Reed Shaken by the Wind* – a brilliant account of his trip to the Marshes. This would have been impossible without the guidance of Mr Thesiger, who thus lost the virginity of the rare subject he had discovered. His own book, however, springs from incomparably greater knowledge' of the Ma'dan, 'among whom he became a legend'. In the *Observer*, Gavin Maxwell described *The Marsh Arabs* as a magnificent success and 'a more richly rewarding book than his first'. Thesiger himself always believed that *Arabian Sands* was the finest of his books. At the age of ninety he stated without a moment's hesitation: 'The books that have really mattered to me have been *Arabian Sands*, *The Marsh Arabs* and *The Life of My Choice*. When I sat down to write, I never thought: will this next book be as successful as the previous ones? I just wrote what I wanted, when I wanted and I said to myself – they can make of this what they like.'[83]

Although *Arabian Sands* and *The Marsh Arabs* – and indeed all Thesiger's other books – have remained continuously in print since they were first published, sales of both to begin with were comparatively modest. In July 1964 John Guest wrote informing Thesiger that a fire at one of Longman's warehouses outside London had destroyed the remaining stock of *Arabian Sands*. Guest's carefully worded letter had been intended to reassure Thesiger, but instead drew his attention to the book's waning sales. '*Arabian Sands*,' he wrote, 'is not, of course, selling very fast now so that the fire has not seriously affected its sale.'[84] Longman's immediately ordered a reprint, and also reported that *The Marsh Arabs* had been 'on all the lists of top selling books'. According to John Guest on 30 July: 'The last three weekly sales have been 140, 195 and 175, and the total sale a week ago was 7,013. I am sure it will keep going. In these difficult days for hardback books, this is a very nice sale.'[85]

Whereas *Arabian Sands* dealt with the constant physical and mental challenges of desert travel accompanied by small parties of nomadic tribesmen, *The Marsh Arabs* 'by converse, portrayed a settled communal life shared with the Marshmen in their photogenic wilderness of reeds, sky and water'.[86] In *Arabian Sands* Thesiger recreated not so much a literal impression as an intensely personal vision of Arabia. His ability to express or suppress intense emotion, to evoke atmosphere, to portray character and mood, to mine rich, complex veins of personal experience, raised an already engrossing narrative of exploration to the highest realms of modern travel literature. *Arabian Sands* could scarcely have differed more from the prosaic recollections of the Empty Quarter by Bertram Thomas and H. St John Philby, published in 1932 and 1933. As a literary phenomenon it can only be compared with classics of the genre such as C.M. Doughty's *Travels in Arabia Deserta* or T.E. Lawrence's *Seven Pillars of Wisdom*. Inevitably, every book Thesiger produced during the next forty years, including *The Marsh Arabs*, would be judged against the almost flawless perfection of *Arabian Sands*.

TWENTY-THREE

With Nomadic Tribes in Other Lands

In May 1964, using some of the money he had earned from *The Marsh Arabs*, Thesiger bought the rare 1926 subscribers' edition of Lawrence's *Seven Pillars of Wisdom*, a beautiful copy containing a letter handwritten by Lawrence and signed by him 'T.E. Shaw', the name by which he was known at that time. For the next thirty years this remained the undisputed 'jewel' of Thesiger's increasingly fine library.[1]

Thesiger flew from London to Athens on 15 June, and from there to Teheran. That year, between July and November, he did three journeys on foot in Iran. On the first of these, accompanied by an interpreter, a muleteer and two baggage mules, he travelled through the Elburz mountains from Meshed to the Valleys of the Assassins, whose evocative name Freya Stark adopted as the title of her second book in 1934, describing her travels in this region. Thesiger wrote: 'now I do feel that I have seen something of Persia. It is a great, bare, empty land with isolated villages wherever a spring comes out of a hillside. Then there is a little oasis of greenery – fruit trees, poplars, walnuts, and the Persian plane tree or "chenar", but always isolated dots or ribbons of green in the desert setting, for on the south side of the Elburz, and we have been travelling mostly on this side, even the high mountains are stark and bare, great faces of rock and bare scree.'[2] He disliked the villagers: 'One and all are unwelcoming, inhospitable and mean. When we arrive in a village in the evening there is always endless discussion and hanging about, with the loads still on the tired mules, before they will give us a house to stay in. If they were Arabs the first child we met would insist on taking us to his house. They then overcharge us for everything, often exorbitantly, and the owner of the house having made us pay for chickens, bread, milk,

402

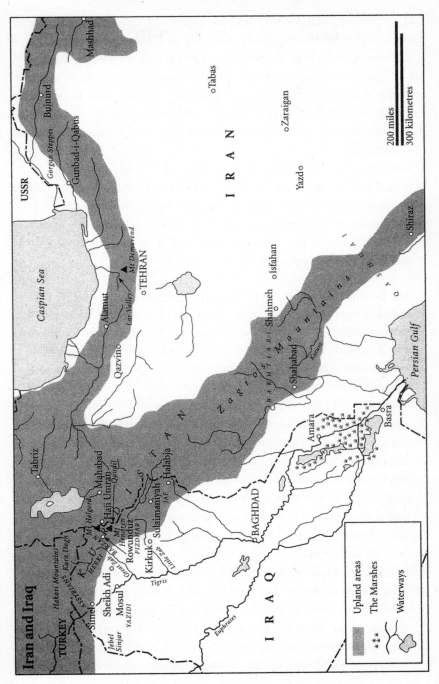

and everything, hangs about and expects to be fed by us. They never produce anything even fruit but later they demand payment. However it is interesting to have seen them.'³ Thesiger got on well with Moshirpur, his interpreter, who was 'easy to travel with', had 'a keen sense of humour' and, like Wilfred (except when in his blackest moods), was 'always ready to laugh at himself'. He concluded his letter impatiently: 'I will write again from Lar in a few days time. This is written under great difficulties in a tea shop.'⁴

On his second journey in Iran, this time using ponies, Thesiger travelled with the Bakhtiari nomads on their migration from the Zagros mountains to the coastal lowlands. A silent film, titled *Grass*, shot in 1925 by the producers of *King Kong*, recorded this colourful exodus of people and animals across the mountains. 'I had a wonderful time on the migration,' Thesiger wrote to his mother:

The country was superb, very like Iraqi Kurdistan, but on a bigger scale and far more of it. The trouble with Iraqi Kurdistan was that it was such a narrow strip between the Persian frontier and the desert. Here for fifteen days I crossed range after range and valley after valley. The mountains were of limestone and very steep and precipitous, great faces of bare rock along which the track would run on a narrow shelf. The country was well wooded on the lower slopes with large oaks, with the high bare mountain tops above the precipices. As I expected I would I liked the Bakhtiari. They still wear tribal dress. The men in a black felt cap, very wide black trousers and a white woollen coat, with a dark pattern woven on the back, reaching below the knees. The women's dress is very colourful in reds, blues and greens, often in velvet, and decorated with coins and ornaments. I took masses of photos. At first I only passed a straggle of families, but for the last half moved and lived with the proper migration. It was very impressive. The narrow track was choked for miles with a continuously moving string of beasts and people. Flocks of sheep and goats, the sheep white and the goats black, each in their separate herds, loaded donkeys and mules and cattle, for they load their cattle and some horses, usually ridden even on some of the worst bits of track. They hang bells round the necks of many of the sheep and goats, some large bells with a deep note, others smaller and with a lighter pitch. All day and all night one heard the sound of these bells. In camp after dark you would hear the flocks coming in, and often the sound of a pipe played by the shepherd boy. They camped at night in groups of fifteen or twenty fires, and all round the hillsides were the lights of other fires. Then with the first light or earlier they would be on the move. We climbed up one great mountain by the pale light of the last of the moon, starting at a quarter to four. Sunrise is at 6.30. Below us were the lights of many fires and above and below the press of many animals and men. The sound of the shouting, as they encouraged their animals, came up out of the dark below in an ebbing and flowing roar of sound, and everywhere was the sound of bells. Men passed in the dark, pale figures in their white cloaks, the women darker shadows in the dark, a flock of sheep, their fleeces strangely luminous, or a black flood of goats, and everywhere the scrambling, straining beasts of burden.[5]

These images Thesiger photographed magnificently; and described vividly in his diary on 1 October as: 'A continuous roar as men, boys and women shouted in [the] dark, encouragement to their animals'.[6] He continued his letter:

As the dawn came birds began to sing, and what had been indistinct became clear. Looking both back and forwards I could see the endless moving ribbon of men and animals. They stopped usually late in the morning, sometimes for the day but at other times went on again in the evening, this depending on the water and pasture. I stopped with a family, sometimes the same one for two or three days, sometimes a new one, but one and all made us welcome. I cannot tell you how much I enjoyed it all, and I only wish it had gone on for longer. In a normal year they would have started later and gone far more slowly, stopping for two or three days in the same place.[7]

At intervals between these journeys Thesiger stayed at the British Embassy in Teheran, where Sir Denis Wright had been transferred as Ambassador from Addis Ababa. The Embassy's summer residence was above the town, 'an attractive old fashioned [house] with a large open verandah ... in a large compound, very green with lawns, bushes and big chenar or plane trees', somewhat reminiscent of the Legation at Addis

Ababa. The Wrights' hospitable presence in Teheran[8] gave Thesiger a pleasant sense of continuity with his past, and made more tolerable these interludes in an unattractive capital city that was 'drab and trying to be modern'[9] in beautiful surroundings against its backdrop of snow-capped mountains.

In Teheran in June he had lunched with 'the General in charge of the Security Services'. Thesiger wrote ambiguously: 'I hope to make a good impression and convince him that my journeys have no sinister motive. Denis [Wright] could not be more helpful putting me in touch with all the people that matter.'[10] This could be interpreted to mean either that Thesiger was travelling in Iran for pleasure, or that his journeys indeed had some other motive (of course his mother would have known of this, even if she was unaware of what it entailed).

His third journey took him across the Dasht-i-Lut, literally, the 'Desert of Lot', a distance of two hundred miles, starting from Tabas, a town which was left in ruins after the massive Iranian earthquake in 1978. A Russian émigré, Lew Tamp, who knew Thesiger's diplomat friend Alexis Forter, had promised to take him up to the Russian border, south-east of the Caspian. Here was 'jungle country with possibly a few tigers in it and lots of other game, ibex, wild sheep, deer and wild boar'.[11] Tamp also drove Thesiger in his Land Rover to Tabas, four days' journey from Teheran, including a two-day crossing of the Dasht-i-Kevir desert by an old caravan route.[12]

Lieutenant Gohavi, commandant of the gendarmerie, arranged Thesiger's three-man armed escort, camels and a camelman, Abd el Ghani, from Falun village, with one spare camel. On 29 October Thesiger left Tabas and crossed the Dasht-i-Lut to Yazd. 'The distance is about 300 miles [sic],' he wrote, 'and I fancy it will take about 15 days to get there. I shall spend one day in Yazd, an interesting old town, and then get a bus to Teheran ... When I have done this trip I shall have done the three things I set out to do when I arrived in Persia. I feel a lot of people would have been satisfied with one of them.'[13]

One of Iran's 'wilder shores', the Dasht-i-Lut was a place Thesiger had always wanted to see. On 19 October, before he left Teheran for Tabas, he had met Lesley Blanch, the author of The Wilder Shores of Love (1954), a study of four nineteenth-century European women who became fascinated with the East, at a party at the British Embassy. He remembered her raising her arms above her head in rapture as she sighed: 'Ah! Teheran! Here, I can feel all around me the magic of the East!' Thesiger went on: 'I was damned if I was going to listen to more of this nonsense. I told her, rather curtly: "I think Teheran is appalling! I'd rather be on the Grand Canal in Venice, any day."' He wrote of her dismissively: 'A dull woman as I had expected. She is writing articles for Vogue which is about her level. I never thought much of "Wilder Shores".'[14] Blanch subsequently wrote a biography of the French romantic novelist Pierre Loti, who in the spring of 1900 had travelled along Thesiger's route across the Elburz mountains to the Caspian.

When the three gendarmes were ordered by their commandant to accompany Thesiger,[15] they had protested, 'What crime have we committed that you send us into the Dasht-i-Lut?'[16] According to Thesiger this had been 'much ado about nothing', since on seven days of their ten-day crossing to Yazd they found water that was drinkable, 'though sometimes brackish'.[17] Once the gendarmes tried to shoot a wild ass, even though for Muslims to eat donkey meat was unlawful; when Thesiger intervened (and in doing so frightened the animals away), the gendarmes sulked. The effort of reaching Yazd on foot enhanced for Thesiger the significance of this ancient and remote Muslim city. In Yazd by chance he met the Irish painter Derek Hill, an authority on Islamic architecture and decoration. Hill's informative company greatly increased Thesiger's appreciation of mosques such as the beautifully preserved fourteenth-century Masjid-i-Jumeh, or Friday Mosque,[18] whose 'lucid and precise' designs were extolled in 1937 by Robert Byron in *The Road to Oxiana*.[19]

Wilfred and his mother visited Morocco in January 1965, and returned in April to London. From 4 to 10 May they stayed in Ireland with Derek Hill at his house near Letterkenny. Hill wrote before their visit: 'So look forward to your visit. Do bring a rod ... I have a boat on the lake in front of the house. Tiny fish – but masses of them.'[20] He painted three portraits of Thesiger, one of which Kathleen bought for £300 and hung in her bedroom at the flat. Presumably she liked it. Or perhaps the trip to Ireland had stirred her 'Irish blood' and made her reckless.[21] After she died, Thesiger gave the portrait to his brother Roderic, and asked him to dispose of it.

Thesiger's versions of what happened to it next differed, but it appears that Roderic gave the painting to James Byam-Shaw, a former Chairman of the fine art dealers Colnaghi, of which Roderic was then a director. According to Thesiger: 'Roddy told Byam-Shaw he could give Derek's picture of me to one of the students [at the Byam-Shaw School of Art] so that they could either paint over it, or else throw it away and use the frame.'[22] His unpersuasive explanation for this astonishing act of vandalism was: 'My mother had thought that I liked it, and I thought she did. After my mother died, I didn't want to keep it. None of us liked it, and that's why I told Roddy to get rid of it.'[23] In Roderic Thesiger's opinion, Derek Hill was simply 'a dauber';[24] but setting these considerations aside, it is difficult to believe that anyone, whether an expert or a layman, would deliberately destroy the portrait of a well known subject painted by an acclaimed artist. The fate, if not the actual whereabouts, of Hill's portrait of Wilfred Thesiger remains a mystery, no less intriguing than the whereabouts of the original manuscript and typescripts of *The Marsh Arabs*, which have vanished, likewise, without trace.

Whereas Anthony Devas had painted a romantic portrait of Thesiger as a young man in his thirties filled with yearning, Derek Hill portrayed a hardened man of action, accustomed to extreme hardship and danger. It is hard to imagine Devas's Thesiger as a war hero, or confronted by bloodthirsty Danakil warriors in Aussa, or by charging lion in the Sudan, or fanatical tribesmen in the deserts of Arabia. Hill, on the other hand, exploited very suggestively Thesiger's defensive body language and emphasised trademark features, played down by Devas, such as his broken nose and disconcertingly baleful stare. Whereas Devas painted him swathed in a burnous, in Hill's portrait Thesiger wore an open-neck shirt, slacks and an old Harris tweed jacket, very like the clothes he had been wearing when they first met in Yazd. Hill painted Thesiger very much as he had been described no less forcefully or vividly by Gavin Maxwell in *A Reed Shaken by the Wind*. Devas had 'a passion for the quality of flesh', the 'luminosity of the skin',[25] which he painted superbly with a soft, glowing radiance.[26] Hill painted his portraits and landscapes energetically, with frenzied precision, imprinted by the rich texture of his brushwork.[27]

From June to September 1965, Thesiger once again travelled in

Nuristan. Baz Muhammad, an Afghan interpreter, and six Tajik porters accompanied him on this journey. From the high passes they gazed on mountain ranges crested with snow. Thesiger wrote: 'We scrambled down from those passes, sometimes into a defile so narrow that overshadowing precipices blocked out all but a strip of sky; we crossed icy torrents on snow bridges, and passed the first trees growing wherever roots could take a hold; we descended through forests of cedar and pine, juniper, holly-oak, wild walnut and olive, and came at last to the valley bottom.' He wrote lyrically of Chaman, in the Kantiwar valley, 'where the untroubled river idling past dragged at the overhanging willows; where black cattle, watched by boys with flutes, grazed on rich pasture among banks of lilac primulas, purple orchids, asphodel and grass of Parnassus; where bearded bare-footed men jogged past, carrying down from their camps glistening skins of butter weighing fifty pounds and more, tied to their backs in a frame of two crotched sticks'.[28] He noted in a letter: 'I found the country got more and more interesting the further I went to the east ... I hope my photos will be a success for I took masses, but views are difficult to photograph.'[29]

High on the cliffs were houses, propped precariously on wooden stilts, clinging like swallows' nests to the pale-coloured rock. In east Nuristan, at Burg-i-Matral in the Bashgul valley, Thesiger photographed woodwork intricately carved in varied patterns. Further south, at Waigul, he saw houses' entrances decorated with markhor horns, which he judged aesthetically yet with a hunter's experienced eye: 'Some of these horns were larger than any recorded by Rowland Ward [in *Records of Big Game*].'[30] On his way north to Faizabad he visited the still-active lapis lazuli mines at Sar-i-Sang. It appealed strongly to his romantic sense of history that 'All the lapis lazuli so extensively used in ancient Egypt, including the tomb artefacts of Tutankhamun, had come from this one valley in the remote mountains of Central Asia.'[31]

Among Thesiger's finest photographs were those he took that August of Kandari nomads winding down from Lake Shiva to the plains. On his way from Kabul to Mazar-i-Sharif and Herat in October, he saw for the last time the Kandaris camped in their black tents in sheltered valleys along the river. He ended the description of his second journey in Nuristan, published in *Desert, Marsh and Mountain*: 'I would gladly have gone back another year to Mazar-i-Sharif and done that journey on foot, but the opportunity has passed. Now that the main road is built, the lorries thunder by; the camel caravans are gone, their bells stilled for ever.'[32]

In 1965, when it still had been possible to do this journey, he had written to his mother from Teheran:

I should love to go back and see that country slowly on foot. It was frustrating to hurry through it by car, but even so it was very interesting. We went from Kabul to Pul-i-Kumri, and from there to Mazar-i-Sharif and Balkh and then to Herat. The country is quite different to the rest of Afghanistan. There you are in central Asia, endless open plains and in other places low rounded hills. The people too are different, Uzbeks and Turkomans. So far the country has been little affected by the changes which are going on elsewhere. The road from Mazar-i-Sharif to Herat is appalling and this of course has saved the country. You hardly meet another car, and everything is carried on long trains of camels tied head to tail, each lot with a single large bell, usually on the last camel, which has a wonderful deep note. We camped in the desert each night and in the darkness we heard these bells as the caravans went past.[33]

In October Thesiger and Frank Steele did a journey on foot from Tafileh to Petra in Trans-Jordan. 'I shall be home soon now,' Thesiger wrote from Teheran, 'but am looking forward to my time in Jordan and hope that Frank and I will do a fortnight's trip with donkeys through the mountains above the Dead Sea to Petra.'[34] They followed the Wadi Arabah and entered Petra from the north. Steele had obtained special permission from the Jordanian authorities for this journey through areas visited only by officials and others on duty.[35]

Every year from 1965 to 1969, in January or February, Thesiger took his mother to Morocco. In 1970–72, they stayed at Faro in southern Portugal. Thesiger said: 'I enjoyed my mother's company. Getting her away like that to the sun gave her and Miss Emtage, her housekeeper, a rest.'[36] On 27 April 1965 he wrote to a friend: 'My mother and I are back from Morocco where we had a wonderful time seeing nearly every corner of the country that was worth seeing. We covered 6000 miles, a lot of it in the Sahara, and stayed in 20 different hotels. Not a bad effort on my mother's part now she is 85!'[37]

In May 1966 Thesiger attended the celebrations marking the twenty-fifth anniversary of Haile Selassie's return to Addis Ababa. Thesiger's copy of a commemorative book, *Liberation Silver Jubilee*, produced by the Ethiopian Ministry of Information, was signed by twenty-five of the officers and sergeants who had served with Orde Wingate in the Gojjam campaign. Among them were Clifford Drew, Abraham Akavia, Laurens van der Post, Edwin Chapman-Andrews, Hugh Boustead and Neil McLean. Wingate's son Jonathan Orde Wingate also signed the book, although he had not taken part in the campaign. Thesiger used this list of signatures to help him describe the occasion in *The Life of My Choice*. Wearing a light grey three-piece suit, and looking distinctly ill at ease, he was photographed with van der Post at one of the many receptions.

Impressive though the celebrations had been, Thesiger 'could feel no enthusiasm about the adaptation to the modern world of this unique and fascinating country. What I saw now was all so different from the Abyssinia of just fifty years before when, as Ras Tafari, Haile Selassie had paraded past the Empress Zauditu after the battle of Sagale.'[38] After the celebrations he stayed with the Sandfords at Mullu. From Addis Ababa he flew to Jeddah, and from there he went on to Jizan and Qarra in the Yemen, now in its fourth year of civil war. He travelled extensively over much of the northern Yemen from June to November. Frank Steele wrote to him in December: 'What a journey. It must have been absolutely fascinating. I've just repeated what we did last year [in Jordan] ... taking Abdullah but not the terrible Khalil. Also an old Haji who skipped up the hills like a goat. Often thought of you on the journey.' He apologised that some Kodachrome photographs he had taken of Thesiger in Jordan had turned out 'very blue';[39] which supported Wilfred's criticism of colour photography, that 'until recently many of the colours were wrong and the pictures suffered in consequence'.[40]

Thesiger returned to Najran on 31 October 1967, and remained in the Yemen until 15 January 1968. During his years in Arabia, he wrote, 'the Yemen had for me the fascination of hostile and forbidden territory', the lure of a country the interior of which was seldom visited by Europeans. In 1962 Imam Badr, grandson of Imam Yahya, was deposed by a military coup after he had been in power only a week. He escaped from his ruined palace in Sana'a and rallied most of the north Yemen tribes to his support. He would soon have defeated the revolutionaries had not President Nasser of Egypt flooded the Yemen with Egyptian troops and heavy armaments. The royalists who joined together in support of the deposed Imam were armed and funded by King Faisal of Saudi Arabia. Despite the Egyptian forces' superior numbers and heavy armaments, including MiG fighter aircraft, by May 1966 the royalists had driven them out of most of the north and east of the country, and had detachments in the hills above Sana'a.[41]

At Qarra, in north-west Yemen, Thesiger met Prince Hasan bin Hasan, a cousin of Imam Badr and the royalist commander-in-chief in the north. To Thesiger's surprise, Prince Hasan gave him permission to travel wherever he wished in the country he controlled. Thesiger wrote of a three-day journey to Shahra, a fortress town in the Qarra mountains:

This ... was typical of later journeys. Nowhere have I experienced more strenuous travelling than in the Yemen; we would scramble down thousands of feet into a narrow valley, labour up the far side, then down and up again across another gorge, with yet more beyond. Often in the evening I would see our next day's destination apparently only four or five miles away across the plateau, and yet it would take all day to reach it ... The [rainwater] cisterns ... were infected with guinea-worm and many of the townsfolk suffered from it: they wound the worms out of their shins round matchsticks, taking days to extract them. As there was no other drinking water I was lucky to escape infection.[42]

In November 1967 Thesiger was less fortunate: he caught a bad cold, followed by sickness and diarrhoea. On 30 November, when the royalist headquarters camp near Sana'a was shelled in an air attack, he received a slight wound in his head from a splinter,[43] which drenched with blood a box of cigars another officer, Colonel Neil McLean, had brought with him for 'safe-keeping'.[44]

In May 1967 Thesiger had the cartilage removed from one knee at the King Edward VII Hospital in London, and in August he had the cartilage removed from his other knee. During one of these operations the

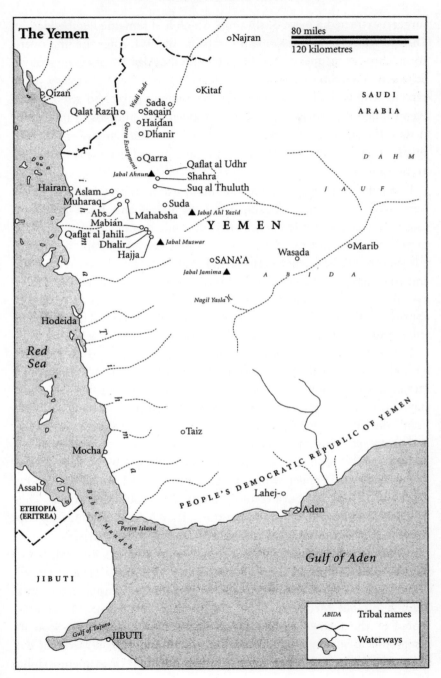

The Yemen

80 miles
120 kilometres

oNajran

oKitaf

oQizan

SAUDI
ARABIA

Qalat Razih o
Sada o
oSaqain
oHaidan
oDhanir

Wadi Badr

Qarra Escarpment

oQarra

DAHM

Qaflat al Udhr
Shahra
Suq al Thuluth

Jabal Ahnun ▲

JAUF

Hairan o
Aslam
Muharaq
Abs
Mabian
Mahabsha
oSuda

Jabal Ahl Yazid ▲

YEMEN

Qaflat al Jahili
Dhalir
Hajja

▲ Jabal Muswar

SANA'A o
Wasada

oMarib

Jabal Jamima ▲

ABIDA

Nagil Yasla

Hodeida o

Red
Sea

Taiz o

Mocha o

Assab o

ETHIOPIA
(ERITREA)

PEOPLE'S DEMOCRATIC REPUBLIC OF YEMEN

Lahej o
Aden

Bab el Mandeb

Perim Island

JIBUTI

Gulf of Aden

Gulf of Tajura
JIBUTI

ABIDA   Tribal names

Waterways

413

surgeon extracted a piece of shrapnel which had remained embedded in Thesiger's knee since the Gojjam campaign in 1941. After the first operation Thesiger recuperated in Madeira and the Algarve; after the second he spent September in southern Italy. His worn-out cartilages may explain why he had found crossing the Yemen's gorges so strenuous,[45] even though the previous year he had walked for hundreds of miles and crossed fifteen-thousand-foot-high passes in Nuristan, and after that had spent a fortnight trudging over the mountains and dry stony valleys of Trans-Jordan.

In northern Yemen, Thesiger took many excellent photographs. Some were of royalist forts or headquarters, at Sharaf and Kitaf; others of camps consisting of a few tents pitched beside gnarled ghaf trees, with camels couched nearby. A beautiful photograph of Haraja, a Tihama village, showed the finely woven conical straw hats worn by the tribesmen and the small thatched huts they lived in. When a republic was finally established, 'a dynasty which had endured a thousand years and was still approved by the majority of Yemenis, came to an end'. The northern tribes had fought, and many had died, for the royalist cause.[46]

In January 1968 Thesiger left the Yemen for England, and on 1 August he arrived back in Kenya, having been urged to return there by Frank Steele, who was now at the High Commission in Nairobi.[47] Thesiger stayed for three weeks with Steele, his wife Angela and their children Frank and Venetia (Wilfred's goddaughter) at 'their very attractive house with a stream going past under jacaranda trees and a lot of flowers'.[48] A weekend with the Steeles at Mombasa was followed by a visit to Lake Baringo. 'Later,' Thesiger wrote, 'Frank, his son and I are going to do a week's trek in the Samburu country (south of Rudolf) with camels. This will give me a chance to try out my knees. If all is well I shall then go up into the Turkana country for a couple of months with camels.'[49]

Before he left England Thesiger had been awarded a CBE. This latest honour paid tribute to his near-forty years of exploration and travel: achievements already acknowledged by the Royal Geographical Society's Founder's Gold Medal in 1948; the Lawrence of Arabia Medal presented by the former Royal Central Asian Society; the Royal Scottish Geographical Society's Livingstone Medal; and the Burton Medal of the Royal Asiatic Society. These awards joined other precious memorabilia displayed in his mother's flat, including silver-hilted Arab daggers, Arab swords in ancient scabbards encrusted with silver, rare travel books, pen-and-wash drawings and oil paintings by Edward Lear and Giovanni Battista Tiepolo. Aged seventy, Thesiger said: 'As such, possessions have meant very little to me. Those I cherish most are *Seven Pillars*, the albums of my photographs ... and Tiepolo's drawing of the angel ... I can't think what else.'[50]

At intervals, from 1 to 16 December 1966, Thesiger was filmed by BBC television. Richard Taylor's film *The Empty Quarter* was shown the following year. In her diary on Saturday, 26 August 1967, Kathleen wrote proudly: 'Wilfred's film on television 7.40',[51] marked with an enormous asterisk. Taylor's excellent, award-winning film was the first of many profiling Thesiger's life and journeys. To begin with, Thesiger was tense and rather wooden in front of the camera. After one interview broadcast live on the *Tonight* programme in 1964, he unclenched his fists and muttered quite audibly, 'Thank God that's over!' But when he became used to being filmed he appeared very natural and relaxed; he talked easily, but gave very little away. He had a strong visual presence and a convincing manner. Together with his books and photographs, films such as *The Last Explorer*, *The Forbidden Desert of the Danakil* and *Heart of a Nomad* helped to transform him from a respected explorer and traveller, honoured by learned societies, to a celebrity of international status.

In Nairobi Thesiger met John Seago, brother of the painter Edward Seago, whom he had first met in 1962 at Isiolo. 'After I get back from the Turkana country,' he wrote, 'he has asked me to join him in the forests, either on Mt Kenya or on the Aberdares where they are trying to catch a bongo. I have always wanted to see these forests and their camp will be in the remotest area they can find.'[52] In due course Seago's home in the Westlands suburb of Nairobi became Thesiger's base in Kenya, apart from Maralal, where he camped between his camel journeys in the north, until he settled eventually among the Samburu. After a week's safari with Frank Steele and his son, Thesiger wrote from Rodney Elliott's house at Maralal: 'All is well. My knees gave me no trouble at all and I walked all the time, about 15 miles a day over rough country ... It is such fun to be back and these parts have not changed at all.'[53]

On 5 September he wrote to his mother, who was approaching eighty-nine, and was increasingly frail, sketching the route of his camel journey from Maralal to Lake Rudolf and the Turkana country:

> I am off tomorrow for three months ... I have got Ibach, my Turkana servant who was with me from 1962–63, and a young Masai with me. I go up to Baragoi and then to Ilaut on the East side of the Ndoto mountains where I expect to be able to hire Rendille camels. I shall want 6 and two men to go with them. I shall spend some 20 days in the Samburu country, on the west side of the Ndotos, before crossing the Suguta, south of Lake Rudolf, and heading up into the Turkana country. I shall go up to Lodwar and will write to you again from there. I hope to get right up the west side of the lake before coming back here to Maralal.[54]

Thesiger had been greatly impressed by the Samburu, 'a very attractive tribe. They are very gracefully built and move superbly ... They have fine features with thin noses ... Most of them would make superb models for a Greek Hermes, the messenger of the Gods. They own large herds of cows and live in wigwams covered with cow dung and surrounded by thorn fences.'[55] He added significantly: 'It is fun to be back in the Africa of the past which today has vanished nearly everywhere else on the continent. The Turkana are even less affected by the changes elsewhere and most of them are still naked.'[56]

The journeys Thesiger made after 1968 in northern Kenya were still arduous, lengthy and purposeful, but inevitably they lacked the objectives that had motivated his expeditions in Abyssinia, the French Sahara and Arabia. Even in the Hazarajat, Nuristan and the northern Yemen, he had travelled in areas seldom visited by Europeans and almost unknown to the outside world. In northern Kenya, by contrast, the main geographical features had all been discovered and named by European explorers; many of them had since been renamed by the African administration after 1963, when Kenya achieved independence. Thesiger made his camel journeys for pleasure, and for peace of mind; that they tended to be repetitive did not concern him; even following an almost identical route there was always something new to see, something new to experience and to remember. He enjoyed the company of the tribesmen who came with him: Turkana, such as Ekwar, Ibach and Lowassa; and Neftali, 'a young Kikuyu who was energetic, enjoyed travelling and got on with the others'. For the journey to Lake Rudolf in September 1968, Rodney Elliott provided Thesiger with a game ranger called Longacha, a Samburu who was 'authoritative, intelligent and physically powerful'.[57] At Lodwar, Longacha found Erope, a fourteen-year-old Turkana who remained with Thesiger until about 1978, and was eventually killed in a skirmish on the Sudan border.

Thesiger's letters to his mother, written from Baragoi, Kangatet, Lodwar and Maralal from 18 September to 22 November 1968, give wonderfully detailed descriptions of this journey across northern Kenya. He wrote on 27 September from Kangatet on the Kerio river:

> We left Baragoi going west through the Samburu hills, broken volcanic country with thorn scrub and some big euphorbia. There was some water in the dry water courses and quite a lot of Turkana with camels, cattle, sheep and goats ... Then we came down to the Suguta valley ... Next day we struggled across the Suguta for four or five hours and were all pretty exhausted and thirsty when we got to the other side. The going was very soft and in places quite large sand dunes. There was a stream of brackish water 20 yards across and beyond this a tangle of dôm palms and bushes. There were quite a lot of Turkana here with their herds. We camped in a watercourse under a large acacia tree close to the hills on the far side and bought a goat for dinner.[58]

In *My Kenya Days*, he recollected: 'When we reached the far side, the others said, "We will go anywhere else with you, but never again across the Suguta." I was reassured by this since I had felt quite exhausted, but had attributed this to having had a cartilage removed from either knee before I went on my second journey to the Yemen. There, this had proved a handicap when I had to squat down as Arabs do to pee.'[59]

Two days later they reached the escarpment and saw the Kerio below them, a broad sparkling river that flowed through a valley filled with a forest of acacia trees. Thesiger wrote: 'Travelling in a car one would miss all the excitement of this, but after the Suguta and the volcanic wilderness we had been struggling across a few minutes before it was a wonderful sight.'[60] They camped under some lovely big acacias close to the river. The trees were full of birds. There was a constant cooing of doves and any number of different kinds of birdsong. 'One of the memorable things about Africa,' Thesiger noted, 'is the song of birds especially in the early morning.'[61] Birdsong and the hyena's eerie howl evoked Africa for him more vividly than any other sounds. He wrote: 'I do love this life. Here one is still in the Africa of the past and the Turkana still walk about naked, in a state of political innocence.' Tramping for hours over heavy sand, over low volcanic plains littered with stones 'the size of footballs', strengthened Thesiger's knees, which seemed 'as good as new'. He confided to Kathleen: 'It is a great relief to me for I was worried that they might cripple me for the rest of my life.'[62]

He gave her a sketch of this nomadic life. They started to load the camels before sunrise. The first thing was to get the headropes on the camels, which always caused an uproar. While this was being done, Ibach boiled water and made tea. Then the camels had their *herios* put on: hides and four poles which formed the baggage saddle. Richard (later Sir Richard) Dearlove, then 'a young man from the Foreign Office',[63] travelled with Thesiger and Frank Steele along the east side of the Mathews range, from Baragoi to Wamba, in October 1969. He recalled: 'Wilfred directs operations from his bedroll. One of the entourage serves him tea – the leaves are cooked in the kettle, copious quantities of sugar are added and a whole tin of evaporated milk. Wilfred has a prep school enthusiasm for the milk and licks the drops off the top of the tin.'[64] (At Maralal he used to scrape up with a clasp-knife honey that dripped onto the kitchen table, then lick the blade clean). By five-thirty the camels had been loaded and Thesiger's party set off by six o'clock, as the first birds began to sing in the trees around them. Along the banks of the Kerio, the trees were mostly large feathery acacias, tall, many-branched trees, quite unlike the flat-topped variety seen on the plains. Thesiger wrote: 'We usually travelled for about four hours. We could stop whenever it began to get unpleasantly hot and we felt inclined to do so, for even after the river had dried up there were wells every mile or so in the sandy river bed, and plenty of shade for us and food for the camels on either bank. Then if we felt like it we went on for another couple of hours in the evening.'[65]

At the mouth of the Kerio on the west shore of Lake Turkana, dense thickets of dôm palms and high reedbeds shut off any view of the open

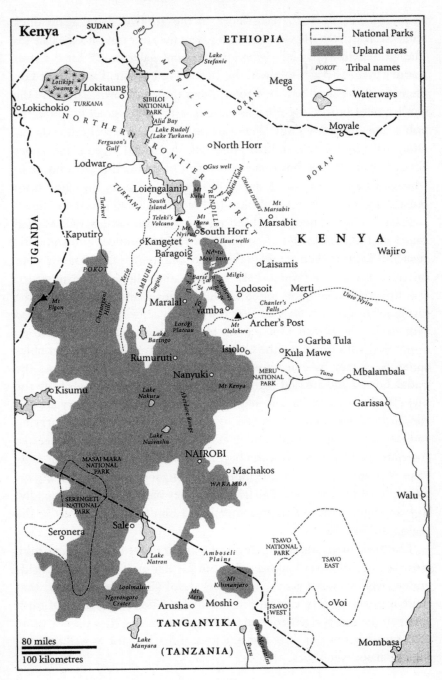

Kenya

SUDAN

Omo

ETHIOPIA

Lake Stefanie

Mega

Latikipi Swamp

Lokitaung

MERILLE

BORAN

Lokichokio

TURKANA

Moyale

N O R T H E R N

SIBILOI NATIONAL PARK

Alia Bay

Lake Rudolf (Lake Turkana)

North Horr

BORAN

Ferguson's Gulf

Lodwar

Gus well

Turkwel

CHALBI DESERT

Balesa Kulal

Loiengalani

Mt Kulal

South Island

Moyale

F R O N T I E R

Teleki's Volcano

Mt Mara

Mt Marsabit

Marsabit

TURKANA

Kangetet

Mt Nyiru

South Horr

Ilaut wells

K E N Y A

Wajir

Baragoi

Ndoto Mountains

Kerio

SAMBURU

Laisamis

PRENDILLE

National Parks
Upland areas
POKOT Tribal names
Waterways

UGANDA

Kaputir

POKOT

Suguta

Barsa...
Se...

Milgis

Lodosoit

Merti

Uaso Nyiro

Mt Elgon

Cherangani Hills

Maralal

Mathews Range

Wamba

Chanler's Falls

Archer's Post

Mt Ololokwe

Lordagi Plateau

Lake Baringo

Isiolo

Garba Tula

Kula Mawe

Rumuruti

Nanyuki

Lake Nakuru

Mt Kenya

MERU NATIONAL PARK

Tana

Mbalambala

Kisumu

Abardare Range

Garissa

Lake Naivasha

NAIROBI

Machakos

WAKAMBA

Walu

MASAI MARA NATIONAL PARK

SERENGETI NATIONAL PARK

Seronera

Sale

Amboseli Plains

TSAVO NATIONAL PARK

TSAVO EAST

Lake Natron

TSAVO WEST

Voi

Loolmalsin

Ngorongoro Crater

Mt Meru

Arusha

Moshi

Mt Kilimanjaro

TANGANYIKA

Lake Manyara

(TANZANIA)

Ruvu

Pare Mountains

Mombasa

80 miles

100 kilometres

water. Further along the lake shore, at the Turkwel delta, again thick reedbeds restricted the view – except where the river ran into the lake (as Thesiger noted in passing) 'when there is any water in it',[66] for the river was dry then. Thesiger followed the Turkwel to Lodwar. 'I am camped on the edge of the river bed,' he wrote, 'under the small town. There are the Government offices, the officials' houses, a prison, a small hospital, the police lines and a few shops. There are no Europeans here. I called on the DC, a friendly Kikuyu, and the police officer. No red tape or difficulties about permits. I miss however the comfort of an English DC's house in which to stay. The house I stayed in in the past looks the same from outside. I wonder what it is like inside. Everything looks smart and tidy.'[67]

From Lodwar, Thesiger trekked up the Turkwel (which W.D.M. Bell called in *The Wanderings of an Elephant Hunter* 'a queer and romantic river') to Kaputir, then across to the Kerio, and up that to Koloa. He went on from there to Kenyang, Lake Baringo and Maralal. The unsettled atmosphere in the region added a thrill of danger and excitement to the journey. Thesiger wrote: 'The Turkana country ... was never very settled even under the British. One section of the Turkana called the Ngorogo [Nyoroko] who live along the Uganda border, have always been trouble-some. Now they have acquired a lot of modern rifles from across the Sudan border and are raiding in every direction, taking animals from the other Turkana, as well as the neighbouring tribes.'[68] The country around the Turkwel was being patrolled by small bands of warriors carrying shields. For Thesiger, 'All this made it much more interesting. Rather like travelling in this country at the beginning of the century'[69] in the foot-steps of Major Rayne and Chauncey Hugh Stigand, who were among his favourite authors as a boy. The tribesmen they met were all very friendly; to his delight, many of them remembered him from his travels in the region in 1961–62.[70]

The thick forest along the Turkwel was very green from recent rain. Near Lodwar the river had been dry, but further up it became 'a consid-erable river, 40 yards across and 2 feet deep'.[71] Thesiger estimated that there were about fifty elephant in this forest. They found a lot of fresh spoor in the sandy riverbed; in a few hours' marching they usually came across tracks of two or three lion and four or five leopard, as well as sight-ing impala or waterbuck.

One morning, as they were moving along the dry bed of the Turkwel, Ibach noticed elephant in the long grass beside the river. Thesiger signed the camels to halt, while he and Ibach watched the herd from about 150 yards' distance. Twelve elephant were watering at an island covered with grass and reeds:

There was a big bull, with a smaller bull in attendance on him, and two young, one very small and perhaps only a month old. Now to move the elephant, so that we could pass, I blew a whistle and clapped my hands. They paid no attention. I then fired off the shotgun. The herd milled round for a second or two and then scrambled up the bank and disappeared into the forest. The big bull and the smaller one had disappeared into the long grass ... before this. They now reappeared and stood looking in our direction. The big bull then followed the others into the forest, but the smaller bull charged in our direction. He came about half way, then turned back into the long grass on the island, crossed it and stopped across the main river bed, keeping mostly out of sight behind a clump of grass growing in the middle of the sand ... We moved down towards him to see if we could spot him ... and saw him sneaking through the forest along the river bank ... It was lucky that Ibach had spotted these elephant. They were almost hidden from sight. If we had gone past them up the river bed they would have got our scent and this bull would have given us real trouble.[72]

Even so, Thesiger's party had to go back some four miles to reach a gap in the forest, which elsewhere was quite impenetrable for camels, in order to reach the bush country beyond it.

As far as Kaputir, the forest was 'stiff with buffalo', especially where the river was full of water. One morning they passed the tracks of a herd of forty-four; another of twenty-two; and a third of seventeen; as well as numerous smaller herds and single bulls. The buffalo usually withdrew into the forest before it got light, but on one occasion Thesiger saw a magnificent bull grazing in a clearing across the river. At Maralal the weather was 'filthy'. On the way there Thesiger was caught in two very heavy storms, both at night: 'There were 10 of us, and all we had was a tent 7 feet by 7 feet and 5 feet high. There was also a ground sheet which sufficed for 2 people. We also had to put our flour, rice, sugar, etc in the tent so you can imagine we were jammed tight when we were sitting in it.'[73] During the last two days, as they approached Maralal across high open country, eight thousand feet above sea level, it rained at intervals and they got thoroughly soaked and felt very cold. One of Thesiger's camels had grown progressively weaker, and he had given it away. Another went off its food, and was finally slaughtered and eaten. On cutting it up, Thesiger found that the animal had developed an abscess at the junction of its neck and chest. 'The other four arrived back in good shape.'[74]

In January 1969 Thesiger visited Tsavo East National Park, where he stayed with Phil Glover, a biologist who was studying the herds of elephant in the park and their habitat. Before he returned to London in February he drove to the Mara Reserve with Denis Zaphiro, a Kenya game warden whose father had been transferred in 1912 to Wilfred Gilbert Thesiger's staff in Addis Ababa. Thesiger remembered seeing Denis, aged about six, at Haile Selassie's coronation in 1930. When Denis came to dinner at John Seago's house in Nairobi, 'he said the only thing he remembered about the Coronation was his acute embarrassment at being dressed up in a kilt'.[75] Although he never regretted the years he spent hunting big game in Abyssinia and the Sudan, by the 1960s Thesiger's interest had shifted from hunting to conservation.[76] He always felt glad to have seen the Masai-Mara when he did, 'while it remained an unspoilt paradise of African wildlife'.[77]

Starting in August 1969, Thesiger did a two-month journey with camels to Alia Bay on the north-east shore of Lake Turkana. He drove from Nairobi to Maralal via Isiolo in his 'new' Land Rover,[78] a second-hand, long-wheelbase vehicle to which he had fitted two extra twenty-four-gallon tanks: one for petrol, the other for water. Before leaving Nairobi he took the Land Rover for a short drive 'to get the feel of it'.[79] Since the war he had done little if any driving; but in those days the roads in and around Nairobi were still relatively quiet, and of course there were even fewer cars and lorries further north – hardly any in the Eastern Province and Rift Valley Province, which comprised the area formerly known as the Northern Frontier District. In *My Kenya Days* Thesiger explained that although he had never previously owned a car (this was incorrect, since he owned a small car while an undergraduate at Oxford), he felt he must now buy one 'in order not to be dependent upon others to take me to the starting points of my journeys in Kenya'.[80] He wrote: 'I have been buying the various things which I need for my trip, medicines, food, a small tent and all the other oddments. Now I have more or less got everything together.' With some reluctance, he admitted: 'It is very convenient having my own car.'[81] Apparently Thesiger's eyes had been giving him trouble, presaging future problems with his sight. After treatment in London, he reassured Kathleen: 'Incredibly my eyes are ever so much better';[82] by the time he reached Loiengalani on 26 August, they had 'quite recovered'.[83]

When Thesiger and Frank Steele arrived there in 1961, Loiengalani was 'a rather nice empty oasis of dôm palms and acacia trees in very barren lava country with Mount Kulal rising up to the east and the very blue waters of the lake stretching out to the west towards the bare black mountains on the Turkana side of the lake'.[84] Now a Catholic mission had been built, which Thesiger felt 'spoilt the place'; and there were 'a lot of corner boys in an assortment of cast-off European clothes hanging about the place', whose presence seemed to him 'inseparable from Missions'. He resented these changes, but accepted that they were inevitable; the knowledge that in a few days he would be setting off into uninhabited country made them easier to bear.[85] The view of Lake Turkana was as magnificent as before: 'a great sheet of jade green water set in sur- roundings of utter desolation, black lava rocks and stones and no sign of vegetation'. Night and day, this country was blasted by 'a tearing wind' – which prompted Thesiger to warn his mother: 'You would not like this place.'[86]

On 29 August Thesiger went on from Loiengalani to Alia Bay, through country that was 'very exciting' and 'full of game'.[87] Except for bands of Merille and Boran raiders, the region was uninhabited. Thesiger noted with relief: 'There was no moon which helped as the Merille raid round the time of the full moon in order to have its light to drive the looted stock with [sic] during the night. They surround any encampment they attack and make a point of massacring everyone in it, so that no one is left to give the alarm.'[88] In 1973, when Thesiger visited the area north of Alia Bay, he saw the body of a naked youth lying beside the track. He had been speared by Merille, who had removed the dead boy's navel as proof of their kill. Thesiger compared this ritual unfavourably with the Danakil practice of castrating their victims, which, he wrote, 'to me seemed a more rational method of mutilation than excising someone's navel'.[89]

Guinea fowl were plentiful, and Thesiger shot a lot of them, as well as sandgrouse and an occasional Grant's gazelle. Whenever possible they bought a goat and fed off that. Otherwise they carried rice, white flour to make chapattis for Thesiger, tins of tomato purée – the only tinned food he had brought – maize flour, or *ugali*, to make *posho*, a large quantity of sugar and plenty of tea, salt ghee and onions to feed the whole caravan. Thesiger recalled: 'All I had to drink was tea and water flavoured sometimes with powdered lemon. The water of Lake Turkana, though drinkable, tastes unpleasantly brackish. At intervals on the journey ... we had found fresh water to drink.'[90]

From Alia Bay, Thesiger's party crossed to North Horr, then south to Guss, and down the west side of Mount Kulal and east of El Donyo Mara to Baragoi. 'There are several maneating lions on the east side of Kulal,' he noted casually, 'that is why we came down the west side ... Near El Donyo Mara we found constant tracks of lion, and were not too happy that they were not maneaters. One night we had one in our camp at 9.30. The Game Scout saw it go past my bed about 30 yards away. There was a lot of shouting and running about, and the lion just stood and looked at us, so I fired a shot over his head. He grunted and made off, but we found in the morning that he had come back and lain down about 40 yards off and watched our camp.'[91]

In January 1969 in Nairobi, Thesiger had met Gavin Maxwell's aunt, Lady William Percy, who had recently been widowed. Thesiger liked her, but in a letter to Kathleen he could not resist remarking: 'Gavin has I see just published another book ... "Raven seek thy Brother" a title he has taken from *Arabian Sands*. I wonder if he acknowledges it.'[92] In November he heard that Maxwell had died (he learnt later of throat cancer[93]). Thesiger wrote wistfully and without rancour: 'What a sad life he had, everything going wrong. I feel sad to hear he is dead.'[94]

After a holiday in March with his mother in Portugal, Thesiger flew back to Kenya via Ghana, where he stayed from 10 to 24 July with George and Josephine Webb and their children. Although the country did not appeal to him as much as East Africa, he enjoyed the 'shabby, squalid, down-at-heel towns, alive with cheerful, colourful, laughing crowds'. He had imagined that 'the natives here would be very black with squashed noses and thick lips'; instead, many of them, he wrote, 'are brown with good features, and on the whole they do not seem to be blacker than the crowds in the markets in Nairobi'.[95]

In August Rodney Elliott proposed that the Kenya Game Department should make Thesiger an Honorary Game Warden, which, Thesiger wrote approvingly, 'would give me official status'.[96] From September to December 1970 he led anti-poaching patrols with camels in the country north and west of Isiolo, along the Uaso Nyiro river. In January 1971, at the suggestion of Peter Jenkins, the Park Warden, he led foot patrols in Meru National Park, and in July, using camels, he patrolled the area of Mount Marsabit. 'There are a lot of Somali and Boran "shifta" in the area [round Isiolo],' he wrote.

> These armed bands started as guerillas fighting against the Kenya government ... Four or five years ago the Kenya Government reached an agreement with the Somali Government and the Somali Government dropped their claims to [land inhabited by Somalis in] Northern Kenya. Many of the armed bands then withdrew from the area, but some remained on and became poachers. They trap leopard and shoot rhinoceros for their horns, which sell at a high price in the Far East as an aphrodisiac. Rodney Elliott ... has been waging a continuous campaign against them for several years. He and his men have shot 60 or more of them but they still go on. I should have an interesting time hunting round for them in interesting country.[97]

Thesiger, the hunter turned conservationist, found 'dangerous men' a quarry no less challenging than dangerous big game.[98] He wrote in *My Kenya Days*: 'Rodney Elliott had told me that if we did encounter Shifta, who were utterly ruthless, we should shoot them on sight. I had been hoping on this journey that we should do so. At Kom Galla [a favourite hideout for poachers in the area], we left the camels some distance away and approached the wells prepared to fight if we met anybody there; but to our disappointment we failed to do so. Four days later, at Kauro, we were again disappointed not to find any Shifta and only their stale tracks.'[99] In February 1971, accompanied by Erope and two other young Turkana named Kibo and Lowassa, Thesiger made a circuit of Mount Kenya, including an ascent of Lenana (16,355 feet), the third highest peak on the mountain, giving Thesiger, who was now sixty, 'a personal sense of achievement'.[100]

The following April, he and Kathleen spent what was to be their last holiday together, in Portugal. By then Kathleen 'was ninety-one and getting frail; she could ... hardly recognise anybody or remember anything. Two years earlier in Morocco her memory had been surprisingly good.'[101] In April and May 1973, Thesiger saw his mother for the last time before her death. He recalled that 'time and again she had repeated, "I just wish that I could die quietly ... I just wish that I could die quietly."'[102] Later that summer she was admitted to a private nursing home in Kensington, where she died on Sunday, 28 October, at the age of ninety-three.

Thesiger heard the news when he arrived from Maralal at John Seago's house in Nairobi: 'John said to me, "So, you got my telegram?" I said, "No, I left Maralal a week ago." He told me that my mother had died three days before, very peacefully in her sleep. I said: "Thank God for that."'[103] Thesiger wrote: 'Now that this had finally happened I could only feel thankful. She had not been in any pain, but her mind had gone completely and in a way I think she had been conscious of this. Such a tragic, lingering end to a life that had meant so much to many, and especially to me, had distressed me enormously. We had always meant so much to each other.'[104]

In a letter to Kathleen from Accra in July 1970, Thesiger had confided:

I have thought of you a great deal. I remember with such pleasure the times we have spent together – the drives and walks at the Milebrook. Do you remember when you and I got into the car one morning and drove across Wales to St David's, and then stopped on the way back at a farm house on Tregaron bog and watched the geese come in at dawn. And in London our shopping expeditions, morning coffee at Fortnum and Mason's and lunch at the Guards Club, or hors d'oeuvres at the Causerie in Claridges. And all the places we have visited abroad – Jordan, Jerusalem,

Damascus, Constantinople, and how you introduced me to Florence and showed me the boy David in the Museum there, and how we used to drive round Rome after dark in a horse cab, and the Greek temples which we visited together in Sicily, and the lights of the fishing boats putting out to sea, below our windows at Amalfi, Delphi and the Acropolis. And the passes of the high Atlas and the Kasbahs on the edge of the Sahara, and the crowds round the dancers, and jugglers and snake charmers in the Jama al Fana in Marrakesh, and our first sight of Fez in 1936, and Telouet when we went there to lunch with the Glawi's son, and so much more. Spain and the Balearic Islands, and the visit we made to the volcanoes on Tenerife, and this year the flowers under the pine trees near Faro, and the cottages in the hills, so clean and gay, and the geraniums and the irises along the roads, and the view over the town and out across the marshes from the hotel terrace. And so much more.

He left until last the memory he treasured most of all: 'Your voice calling out "Is that you Wilfred?" as I come back in the afternoon to the flat.' In conclusion, he wrote: 'You don't need to be told what you have meant to me.'[105]

This affectionate long paragraph, flooded with exotic images and place names, was typical of a literary style Thesiger had evolved during the months he spent writing *Arabian Sands* and *The Marsh Arabs*. Here were the credentials of his love for Kathleen; the renewed assurance of the pleasure her company always gave him; the proofs of his gratitude to her for everything she had done for him and his brothers; the reminder that, however insignificant, no detail of their time together had been ignored or forgotten. Over-anxious, eloquent, it made a determinedly lavish tribute to his mother, a celebration of his unfailing devotion, which others rarely saw expressed – except by the briefest of caresses, sidelong glances, barely perceptible gestures, signalling that Thesiger was 'on edge',[106] adoring, protective, watchful, in Kathleen's presence. As much as he needed his mother, he needed Kathleen to need him. Kathleen understood perfectly the complexity of her son's emotions. They were alike in so many ways. Yet Wilfred, more than his brothers, embodied the polarised emotional identities of both parents: his mother's spontaneous Celtic passion, his father's longings frustrated by his inability to articulate, or perhaps even to physically express, them.[107] Kathleen, like Wilfred, liked to tease. Both were natural delegators. A visitor to the flat remembered Kathleen asking: 'Wilfred, will you hand me my glasses?' And when the visitor said, 'K, your glasses are on the table beside you,' Kathleen had replied, 'Let Wilfred get them for me.'

His mother's death freed Thesiger of the responsibility he had felt for her ever since his father died. But still he missed her desperately. Since he was nine, Kathleen had been the centre and focus of his world, an emotional crutch in times of crisis, who understood his craving for savagery and colour, and encouraged even his most dangerous ventures. By setting him free, she had ensured that she would never lose him. Now that he had lost her, Thesiger felt disorientated, isolated and very lonely. When he returned to London that autumn, he felt Kathleen's presence 'everywhere in the flat. I'd go into a room and expect to find her there.'[108]

The year before his mother died, in July 1972, Thesiger took on 'a very intelligent and likeable young Samburu' named Joseph Kisau.[109] He became very attached to Kisau, and was heartbroken when on 1 September 1974 the boy died of hepatitis B. 'He had been such a happy, cheerful and enterprising lad and he seemed to have identified himself completely with me. His sudden and unexpected death shook me badly.'[110] Thesiger said that he had not wept (outwardly) when his mother died, but when Kisau died, he did shed tears, 'something I hadn't done for a long time';[111] perhaps in a sense he had wept for them both: for Kisau and Kathleen, for Kathleen and Kisau.

Thesiger's correspondence with his mother had spanned more than half a century. After she died, he stopped writing the long, descriptive letters which had complemented and expanded upon the notes he jotted in his travel diaries. He said: 'My mother wrote to me constantly, and I wrote to her whenever I could. I loved getting a pile of letters from her, and she was interested in everything I had to tell her about my journeys. She kept all my letters, just as she had kept my father's letters to her and the letters my father had written to his mother and father before that.'[112] He regretted that he had kept only a few of the letters his mother wrote. In his last letter to her, dated 21 September 1973, Thesiger thanked her for 'five letters from you which I was delighted to get', and explained that he was off the next day to the Mara river, where 'The wildebeeste migration is passing through … and I am told there are about a million wildebeeste there now. I have seen the migration before on the Serengeti and it is an extraordinary sight.' He looked forward to a journey north to Alia Bay and Siboloi, 'the new Game Park'. He wrote: 'I can help Peter Jenkins who is in charge by being up there. It should be exciting as it is on the route used by tribes raiding down out of Ethiopia. They come down in bands 100–200 strong armed with rifles. I hope we shall be allowed to have Bren guns and 2″ mortars … I think of you so often and remember the journeys we have done together. Your loving son, Wilfred.'[113] His affectionate last words summarised his lifelong devotion to Kathleen, and their generally harmonious, mutually rewarding relationship as mother, son and inseparable friends.

Thesiger had always been glad that he hunted big game before the war in the Sudan, where unlike Kenya there were no white hunters and he was allowed to hunt by himself. Ironically, in July 1972, he agreed to accompany a safari led by René Babault, a professional guide employed by White Hunters International in Nairobi. Babault's clients were Lord Airlie and Lord Hambleden, Airlie's cousin. In *My Kenya Days* Thesiger wrote: 'I had known Lord Airlie's father when I was an Honorary Attaché to the Duke of Gloucester's mission to Haile Selassie's coronation at Addis Ababa. Lord Airlie's father had then been Comptroller to the Duke. I was only just twenty at the time, and he had been kind and helpful to me in this unfamiliar company and setting. I was now anxious to meet his son.'[114] Starting from Lodosoit, they travelled for ten days along the east side of the Mathews Range, and then along the east side of the Ndoto mountains as far as Ngoronet. In September 1972 Thesiger wrote: 'I very much enjoyed the fortnight [sic] I spent on safari with Lord Airlie and Lord Hambleden. I liked them both enormously and hope to see them again when I get back [to England]. Airlie had his eldest son and a daughter with him, and Hambleden had three sons and his Italian wife … Rennie [sic] Babault … asked me to go along and lend him a hand in running the safari and in looking after the others while they were shooting … In all we had 40 camels and 12 horses so you can imagine what a party it was!'[115] Thesiger admitted he had 'enjoyed the novelty of this extraordinary safari'.[116]

In August 1972, an encounter at Baragoi, fifty miles north of Maralal, was to have a permanent effect on Thesiger's future life in Kenya. He wrote in *My Kenya Days*:

> There was a small primary school at Baragoi and most of the boys in it were aged between seven and twelve. On my way through Baragoi I used to stop my car under some trees near the school and the boys would come over and ask if they could play boxing. One small boy in particular caught my attention and he invariably came over to greet me whenever I stopped near the school. Once, when I looked about for him, I couldn't see him anywhere. Feeling anxious in case something had happened to him, I went over and asked one of the children, 'Where is Lawi?' The boy replied, 'He's in your car.' I went back to it and found Lawi sitting in the front seat. I said, 'What are you doing in the car, Lawi?', to which he replied, 'I don't know. I'm leaving school and I'm going to stay with you,' and so we drove off together ... Lawi was perhaps eleven or twelve years old at the time.[117]

Thesiger realised the obvious implications of this story, and took care to add that Lawi's parents were in Maralal, 'and seemed quite happy that he should join me. He had until then been living at Ololokwe with his grandmother, to whom he was devoted.'[118] Some years after he wrote this, Thesiger explained that he had given Lawi's parents a sum of money at the time Lawi joined him: 'They didn't have much, and I felt I was helping them. Among the Samburu it was quite normal for children to live with relatives, or with friends of the family. Anyone who was well-off was expected to help the poorer members of his tribe. I gradually became involved with certain individuals and their families, and it gave me pleasure to do what I could for them.'[119]

Samburu circumcision ceremonies marking a new age-set began on 6 July 1976, after the Lmasula clan had killed a bull on Nyiru, the sacred mountain. Thesiger's young protégé Gabriel Lawi Leboyare belonged to the Lkuwono, or the blacksmiths' clan, always the first of these Samburu clans to be initiated. Lawi was now aged sixteen, and was old enough to be circumcised. Since Thesiger had by then become so closely involved with Lawi's family, 'as one of them I witnessed not only the circumcisions of the initiates but the ceremonies which went with them'.[120]

Thesiger described these ceremonies in some detail in *My Kenya Days*, but did not include detailed descriptions of the actual circumcisions; these he reported with clinical exactness in an unpublished essay, justifying himself by writing: 'Although I have no anthropological training it seemed to me worth recording what I saw and what I was told.'[121] (Paul Spencer, an anthropologist, author of two books on the Samburu, had to leave Kenya to write his thesis before these ceremonies took place. They were described in greater detail, however, by Thesiger's friend Nigel Pavitt in *Samburu*, a fascinating book, illustrated with Pavitt's colour photographs.[122]) Circumcisions took place every fourteen years or so; according to Thesiger:

> Previous age sets had been circumcised in 1960–62, 1948, 1936 and 1921. Almost certainly ... when the next age set should be circumcised, these ceremonies will have been much modified or even abandoned[123] ... I have lived for long periods with the Samburu over the past 10 years and, even although I do not speak their language, many of them speak Swahili and a number of the younger ones speak English. One of my companions in particular spoke excellent English, and he was at pains to point out everything which he thought would interest me. He and my other two companions, as well as a large number of my Samburu friends, were circumcised at this time. I was thus able to participate in the ceremonies and to take whatever photographs I wanted ... female circumcision (clitoridectomy), which men may not watch ... went on at the same time.[124]

After the white bull, or 'boys' ox', had been killed on Mount Nyiru, the Lkuwono and other clans chose a site for their circumcision camp near woodland where there was also water and grazing. Each *lorora*, or circumcision camp, was enclosed by a thorn fence, and inside it the women of each family built a hut of wattle and daub, roofed with grass. Two months before the circumcisions, Lawi and the other initiates put on dyed-black goatskin capes and set off to gather sticks from which they fashioned bows and arrows. After they had been circumcised, the boys used their bows and arrows to shoot small birds – which they stuffed with grass and hung down behind their heads – and at the ankles of uncircumcised girls, who either fled or else ransomed themselves with beads. *Lmuget loolbaa*, the ceremony of casting away the arrows, followed a

431

month later, after which Lawi and his contemporaries became warriors and were known thenceforth as *moran*. 'No ceremony in their lives,' Thesiger wrote, 'would ever have a comparable significance.'[125] Thesiger described other details of this extended ritual: shaving the initiates' heads; singing the *lebarta*, the circumcision song, which he thought was 'immensely moving and impressive in the dark';[126] collecting blood from an ox by shooting a blocked arrow into its jugular vein; the initiates handing roasted oxmeat stuck on a knifeblade to their mothers, saying to them, 'Never give me food again';[127] each boy handing over the strings of beads he had worn until then. Finally the young *moran* were rubbed all over with red ochre. From that day onwards they might never eat in the presence of women, or anywhere women could be seen; nevertheless, the *moran* in Thesiger's households occasionally ignored this restriction.

Having performed thousands of circumcisions in the Iraqi marshes, it was only natural that Thesiger was interested to see how the operation was carried out among tribes such as the Masai and the Samburu. 'In the 1976–77 ceremonies,' he wrote, 'many of the initiates, who may have numbered 7000 in all, were as old as 25 to 28 ... They were well aware how agonisingly painful the operation would be, but despite this they were desperately anxious to be circumcised. Only thus would they cease to be mere boys without any standing in their tribe and society.'[128] Thesiger observed the proceedings from close quarters, and took a great many photographs. He would never allow these to be published or exhibited, and insisted that they were of interest only to anthropologists and researchers, and 'weren't meant for just ordinary people to come and gawp at'.[129] He wrote: 'The morning circumcisions start soon after dawn, and I sometimes wondered how the operators, who in a big camp might number as many as four or five, could see what they were doing ... Two different methods of circumcision were used during these ceremonies. I had previously seen one of them used by the Masai in Tanzania, and it was this method which was now used by a Masai circumcising among the Samburu.'

Thesiger described the bloodcurdling procedure with a delicacy and precision worthy of his cousin Ernest's *Adventures in Embroidery*:

> He pulled the foreskin back as far as it would go; his assistant then held the head of the penis and turned it as required. The operator severed the inner

skin from round the base of the glans, and peeled it back a little. Next he pulled the foreskin forward, felt inside it for the severed end of the inner skin and tried to pull this inner skin from under the outer skin. Generally he failed at the first attempt, and had to retract the foreskin and do some more cutting. The tugging, retracting, cutting and more tugging generally went on for four or five minutes, in one case for twelve. Finally he would succeed in drawing out the inner skin, thereby doubling the original length of the foreskin. He then put a finger inside, felt for the glans and made a small slit in the dorsal skin, through which he eventually forced the glans. The double length of foreskin now hung down under the base of the glans. He cut off some of this skin, but left an inch or so hanging down to form the distinctive tie, which is so peculiar to the Samburu and the Masai … The other method used by the Ndorobo operators is quicker, but generally causes far greater swelling afterwards. The operator, after retracting the foreskin, pinched up and cut off the inner skin in half a dozen pieces. If he left even a small piece of skin attached to the glans, this was pointed out and he removed it … He then pulled the foreskin forward as far as it would go, made a small slit in the dorsal side and forced the glans through it. It was generally unnecessary to trim the tie. In the case of a short foreskin, there would hardly be a tie, in contrast to the Masai method … [The boys] remained absolutely motionless, staring straight ahead while they were being circumcised. The expression on their faces never altered and not a muscle twitched in their bodies. They could have been anaesthetised for all the sign of pain they showed. In the case of one 14 year old boy, I did notice that the muscles of his thighs tightened as he was cut. Three boys disgraced themselves at a *lorora* near Maralal, but this was the only instance of which I heard during the 1976–77 ceremonies. A school teacher circumcised at the end of the previous cycle near Mount Nyiru had tried to jump up and run away.

Thesiger's knowledge and experience now proved invaluable. He wrote:

A Kikuyu, named Mowra, also turned up and at first carried out a number of circumcisions. He performed the operation with a series of quick slashes, but refused to allow anyone to hold the head of the penis, often

433

with disastrous results. At first he was much sought after, since the parents felt that their sons were less likely to disgrace them by wincing with pain in the minute or so that it took Mowra to circumcise them. Mowra had collected his thirty shillings for each boy and moved on before it became evident that in many cases he had slashed off part of the glans. In one camp I treated 69 of his patients and of these he had maimed 29. In one case he had cut off nearly half the glans, resulting in severe haemorrhage. As a result of numerous complaints he was heavily fined and put in prison.[130]

Thesiger never heard of anyone dying from loss of blood either during these ceremonies or in the past. 'I treated one boy,' he wrote however, 'who appeared to have lost about 2 pints of blood when I arrived, and I wondered what would have happened to him had I not been there.'[131]

The circumcision ceremonies concluded with a feast, when a hundred or more oxen were slaughtered near the camp and the meat roasted over innumerable fires. Smoke from these fires partly obscured the scene, while vultures circled overhead. After the feast, the newly-initiated *moran*, together with the older generation of warriors, the girls from the *lorora* and any visitors who stayed on, danced outside the camp till sunset. They then dispersed, but assembled again after dusk and danced for hours to the incessant trumpeting of a kudu horn, working themselves into a frenzy. The next day, the *moran* washed the red ochre off their bodies and each of them repainted his head (except for his face), neck, shoulders and breast, and decorated himself with strings of beads. That done, Thesiger wrote: 'They and their families now leave the *lorora*, which is burnt down to prevent it being used to impose curses.'[132]

Thesiger always felt proud to have been able to witness these 'all-important' ceremonies,[133] and, more than this, to have participated in them. Among the tribes in Northern Darfur, the Middle East, Arabia and the Iraqi marshes, he had wanted above all 'to share this life, and to be more than a mere spectator'.[134] He had felt the same desire to live among the pastoral Samburu, 'as one of them'.[135] However, since his mother's death he had become depressed, restless, unfocused and unsettled. He had inherited her flat in Chelsea and everything it contained. Now Kathleen's faithful housekeeper, Mollie Emtage, returned every year from her home in Stratford-upon-Avon to look after him; she continued to do this devotedly until the year before she died, aged ninety-one, in March 1989.

In March 1975, and again in January 1977, Thesiger visited Addis Ababa and the Danakil country. In 1975 he stayed with the Sandfords at Mullu and drove for a week along the Awash to Sardo and Tendaho, turning back 126 kilometres beyond Sardo. In 1977 he stayed briefly with Dick and Anne Sandford and visited Batie on the Awash before flying from Addis Ababa to Sana'a in the Yemen. The diplomat Hugh Leach remembered travelling with him in the Tihama, 'happy days shooting for the pot and peaceful nights under the stars'.[136] But as time went by Leach noticed how Thesiger had become increasingly withdrawn. He had made up his mind to leave Kenya, and now regretted making this decision. He had found Lawi a job with a safari outfitter in Nairobi, and had given Erope his tent and some money to buy livestock. He also gave Kisau's mother a generous present of £500, and sold his Land Rover to Siddiq Bhola.

Yet, Leach observed astutely: 'At sixty-seven he was too young to [give up his life in Africa] and was already making plans to go back to Kenya and resurrect, so far as he could, his Samburu companions, which he subsequently did.'[137] Thesiger had considered alternatives, such as India and Egypt; but these proved to be no more than temporary distractions. Both countries were 'crowded and impersonal';[138] and they lacked the close companionships which Thesiger had already established, and now realised how much he had begun to miss, among the Samburu in northern Kenya.

TWENTY-FOUR

Kenya Days

In early February 1977 Thesiger went from north Yemen to Muscat, Salala, Nazwa and Ibri in Oman, before returning in April to London. He enjoyed travelling as he had done in the past with donkeys, among the villages of the Tihama. But even in the remotest villages he had been aware of a prevailing mood of discontent, which he felt resulted from the wealth remitted to their families by Yemeni labourers working in Saudi Arabia. Everywhere he found changes. The noise of motorcycles reverberated in the narrow streets of old Sana'a, and the streets in its New Town were jammed by traffic. Salala, 'once a straggling Arab village, [was] now a town with traffic lights'.[1]

Thesiger was flown by helicopter to bin Kabina's tents in the desert, where he also met bin Ghabaisha. He remembered them as they had been more than a quarter of a century before; now the teenage boys from whom he had parted at Dubai were middle-aged men with grey beards. Thesiger wrote sadly: 'I was moved to be among them once again, but I knew that our old relationship was irrevocably gone.'[2] Of the Rashid assembled there to greet him, none rode camels any longer; instead an assortment of four-wheel-drive vehicles were parked behind the tents. A television crew filmed Thesiger and the Rashid as they feasted on meat from a camel that bin Kabina had slaughtered.

Thesiger felt dismayed and dislocated by the changes he had seen. Having boasted for years that he was out of step with his times, he found it strangely disquieting that his companions adjusted effortlessly to this new Arabian world, something he himself had been unable to do. 'We parted,' he wrote, 'before I went to Abu Dhabi, which I found an Arabian Nightmare, the final disillusionment.'[3] He wrote in 1979: 'The values of the desert have vanished: all over Arabia the transistor has replaced the tribal bard.'⁴ He later modified these criticisms, yet he never ceased to mourn the Bedu, 'a cheerful, courageous, dignified people whose spirit once lit the desert like a flame'.⁵ Just as he mourned them, he mourned his own irretrievable past.

In July 1977 Thesiger spent a fortnight in India, visiting Delhi, Agra, Fatapur and Sikri. On 17 July he flew to Singapore, and from there to Bali, where he joined Gavin Young and his godson for a five-month cruise round the Indonesian islands. Inspired by Norman Sherry's brilliant study *Conrad's Eastern World* (1966), Young planned to write *In Search of Conrad*, documenting his quest 'for scenes and ghosts known to that heavily accented foreigner from Eastern Europe'⁶ made familiar to countless readers of Joseph Conrad's novels, including *Almayer's Folly*, *An Outcast of the Islands* and Thesiger's favourite, *Lord Jim*. To do this, Young chartered *Fiona*, a forty-two-foot ketch built in Poole in 1912, and her part-owner Brian McGarry, 'an expert navigator'.⁷ Pamela, Lady Egremont, a friend of Thesiger and Young, gave Wilfred Cyril Connolly's *The Unquiet Grave: A Word Cycle by Palinurus* to read during the voyage. She begged him: 'Please avoid all eastern equivalents of the Strophades, the Harpies and the Lucanian shore – above all avoid the fate of Palinurus.'⁸ (According to the legend, Palinurus piloted the ship of the Trojan prince Aeneas. While he slept Palinurus fell into the sea, and after three stormy days and nights was washed ashore near Velia. He was murdered, stripped of his clothing and left unburied on the seashore.)

On 31 July *Fiona* sailed from Bali, by the Lombok Straits, to the island of Pulo Laut, then along the east coast of Kalimantan (Borneo) to Tandjong Redeb on the Berau river. Thesiger noted on the half-title of his worn copy of *Conrad's Eastern World* that they sailed from there across to the Celebes and Dongala, down the coast of the Celebes to Macassar, round the south coast of Kalimantan, through the Carimata Straits to Kuching in Sarawak. Thesiger spent a fortnight in Sarawak with the Royal Geographical Society Mulu expedition led by Robin Hanbury-Tenison, with Nigel Winser as deputy leader. He took some wonderful photographs there, among them one of a young tribesman possibly at the mouth of the Santibong estuary, or further upstream at Kuching, on the Sarawak river.⁹ One morning a villager emerged from the forest with a small cardboard box in which there were some forty dead butterflies.[10] The largest had a wingspan of five inches, and their colours ranged from turquoise to chocolate, scarlet and silver. Thesiger bought the collection as a memento, and later put it away in a cupboard at the flat. The butterflies were thus much better preserved than his beautiful Old Master drawings, which to his brother Roderic's dismay Wilfred left hanging, exposed to direct sunlight, all year round on the sitting room walls.[11]

From Sarawak they sailed to Brunei. On the way *Fiona*'s engine broke down:

There had been a hurricane before we set out and the sea was still running high. Mac [McGarry] had mentioned ten-foot waves. One night, as we approached Singapore, I was on watch, and very early I thought I saw an island ahead of us. I shouted down to Mac who came on deck. By now we could make out a line of reefs in the distance to the south with the surf breaking high into the air. Mac checked our position on his chart and said, 'Thank God, we're just where we should be. Go down and get some sleep. I'll call you as soon as we're round the point and then we'll have some breakfast.' A couple of hours later Mac woke me with a flood of obscenities as he came down the companionway. I said, 'Christ, what's the matter now, Mac?'

He replied, 'The only thing that's certain is fucking death!', a nice way to be woken up in the morning. He went on, 'The wind has failed completely and we're drifting on to the reefs.' From the deck I could see that they were much closer. I asked him how long *Fiona* would last when we struck them. He said, 'She'll be gone in two minutes.' From time to time, the wind would get up, only to die away all too soon. It took us eight hours to get round the point which Mac had hoped to weather in time for breakfast. By then the reefs were very close.[12]

Gavin Young's godson had left *Fiona* at Kuching, and Young had sailed from Brunei aboard the *Rajah Brooke*, leaving Thesiger and Brian McGarry to take *Fiona* back to Singapore. Thesiger recorded this near-disastrous crossing in two diaries. On Tuesday, 29 November there was a strong south-easterly gale and rough seas. He wrote: 'Mac thrown twice across the cabin and then onto the floor. In great pain. I thought he had been incapacitated and the ship in a gale. Very heavy torrential rain.'[13] After a day of calm weather, there was a big north swell which lasted for two days. On 3 December he noted: 'Waves 20 feet high. 200 yards apart'; on 5 December, Subi Basar, one of the Natuna islands, was visible at dawn. By midday *Fiona* was off the point, and Thesiger saw a 'very big swell breaking on reefs 1 mile away'. He scribbled: 'Strong wind against us. Then wind failed. Mac and I thought we had had it. Luckily the wind picked up and then almost inch by inch we edged past the point but it took till 4 to be clear of it. Anxious all the time the wind would fail again. Very heavy torrential rain … ' Pamela Egremont's caution, 'avoid the fate of Palinurus', now seemed like a prophecy. Thesiger marked with large crosses in pencil a passage in *The Unquiet Grave*: 'Palinurus still clutching the tiller of his improvised craft, tosses on the pallid wastes of the heaving Sicilian. Three times the red sun sinks and the sheen of opal darkens on the cold and ancient gristle of the sea, three times the cloud-swept Pleiades glimmer from the rainy South before at last the creaming and insouciant surf relinquishes its prey.'[14]

They finally arrived back in Singapore on 8 December. 'This had been a fascinating experience,' Thesiger wrote. 'For me the challenge of the sea had always had a rather distant appeal … on *Fiona* with only three of us on board [for the first time] I was really close to the sea in an exotic tropical setting.'

On 22 June 1978 Thesiger flew from London to Nairobi; on 27 June he drove back to Maralal. Lawi Leboyare came with him. Except on anti-poaching safaris, Thesiger had by then given up using camels for his journeys in northern Kenya. 'I still much preferred travelling with camels,' he wrote, 'but now it would have been ridiculous to do so when I could equally well use a Land Rover.'[15]

In his late sixties, Thesiger looked very fit, and showed remarkably few signs of ageing. Photographed in 1977 at John Seago's compound in Nairobi, he appeared at least fifteen years younger than he was. In Seago's colour photograph Thesiger's skin is deeply sunburnt, his hair still dark. He was twenty years older than Salim bin Kabina and Salim bin Ghabaisha, yet now he appeared almost to be their contemporary. Other photographs of Thesiger in 1977 confirm this, including one taken by Gavin Young aboard *Fiona* and another by Nigel Winser in Sarawak.[16] But in February, while he was at Nazwa in Oman, he noted on successive days: 'cartilage of knee troublesome after we stopped' and 'knee giving trouble'.[17] On 1 March a Major-General K. Parkins had flown Thesiger by helicopter to Muscat, where his knees were examined by a local doctor. A friend observed: 'Wilfred is not quite as tough as of old. Now, he sometimes wears dark glasses, and I notice how he casts covetous glances at my sleeping bag.'[18]

For several years before he took part in the big Samburu circumcision ceremonies in July 1976 to December 1977, Thesiger had based himself increasingly at Maralal, where he camped in a variety of places on the outskirts of the town. A day or two after they returned to Maralal in July 1978, Lawi suggested that instead of living in tents, Thesiger should build a house. When Thesiger replied that he owned no land, Lawi said: 'I can put one anywhere I like.'[19] The next day they walked up a hill above the valley where they had camped, about a mile to the east of Maralal, and found a site with a fine view shaded by wild olives. Thesiger wrote in *My Kenya Days*:

> We levelled a small patch of ground under some of the trees and dug a shallow trench outlining the house. In the trench, we set up nine-foot high cedar poles adjacent to each other, for the outer wall, and divided the house into three rectangular rooms of roughly equal size, ten feet by twelve, each with a window but with only one door in the central room. We obtained the roof timbers from Siddiq Bhola, and employed a local builder to put on a pitched roof of corrugated iron which was admittedly unsightly but conveniently weathertight. We concreted the floor and plastered the inside walls with a mixture of mud and cow-dung. We then bought some basic furniture in the town and put up a shelter outside the house for the kitchen, where we cooked on three stones. We also fastened gutters to the roof to catch water in drums when it rained. We built a verandah in front of the house and after that started to plant a garden.[20]

Apart from its concrete floor and corrugated iron roof, the house Thesiger built for Lawi and himself was similar to others round Maralal. A few years later, corrugated iron had replaced the traditional thatched roofs which Thesiger much preferred.

Gavin Young was first visitor to Lawi's house above the valley, with thatched huts nearby on smooth green hillsides, where the clanking cowbells echoed and Samburu neighbours greeted Thesiger with cries of 'Jambo! Jambo, mzee juu!' (The tribesmen around Maralal invariably addressed Thesiger, who was by then as famous in Kenya as he had become in England, Europe and countries further afield, as mzee juu.) The garden was hedged round with prickly cactus; around a water tank were morning glory, bougainvillaea and jacaranda, and further on a patch of maize and a few drills of potatoes. At night zebra foraged noisily among the maize. 'A path leading to the house wound and split and reunited between low, tough shrubs and seedlings, thorn bushes armed with long white spikes; among scattered, nameless, tiny purple, red, white and yellow flowers; past the triple spires of candelabra cactus and cypress trees with trunks fantastically entwined. Jagged blue hills shimmered in the distance, with scrolls of cloud massed white and blue at the horizon beneath an infinity of sapphire sky.'[21] Coming back to this beautiful, tranquil place, little wonder that Thesiger exclaimed: 'Thank God, we're home.'[22]

Gavin Young remembered Thesiger's entourage as it was then: 'Kendawa, aged nineteen, a plumpish, easy-going Samburu came from a buffalo-infested clearing near Maralal ... Chugana [Erope's brother], was shy and dreamy; a short, tubby sixteen-year-old, who cooked and clowned in equal measure, was nicknamed variously Bonzo, Charlie (after Chaplin), and the Hobbit. Lawi, the most remarkable of this quartet, one of those special people who had been endowed with an extra ration of warmth, sense and goodness. About a year younger than Kendawa, he was six feet tall, quick-witted, humorous, endlessly good natured.'[23] Thesiger commented that Lawi was also 'a naturally good driver and used to maintain that, whereas I was quite the worst driver in Kenya, I had been a very good instructor'.[24] When Phil Snyder trained Thesiger, Erope, Lawi and Kibo, a Turkana youth, in mountain-rescue techniques on sheer cliffs above the Athi river, 'Erope had hated it,' Thesiger wrote, 'and would not go near a precipice. But Phil Snyder said of Lawi, "He is one of the best natural rock-climbers I have met."'[25] Thesiger had also taught Lawi to box. Besides this he could sew, shoot and cook well. When Thesiger teased him: 'In fact, there's very little you are not – in your own estimation, Lawi,' the young Samburu would reply in a gently mocking tone: 'Now then, *mzee juu*, don't be unkind like dees.'[26] If Lawi had been a naturally adept driver, Erope certainly was not. Thesiger approved of and was amused by Erope's contempt for cars. Once, when Thesiger's Land Rover had broken down, Erope jumped out and gave it a kick. He jeered: 'Now you can't even eat it.'

Lawi was Thesiger's 'creation', his pride and joy: 'even in his late teens he had an air of self-possession and quiet authority'.[27] When he came to stay with Thesiger in London in 1981, Thesiger was delighted to hear another member of the Travellers Club ask Lawi which school in England he had attended. 'Not bad,' said Thesiger, 'for someone who had left the village school at Baragoi when he was twelve, and until then had never been anywhere else but Kenya.'[28] Thesiger paid no heed to later suggestions that Lawi's questioner had been making fun of him.

In 1982 Thesiger was made an Honorary Fellow of both the British Academy and of Magdalen College, Oxford. These, and honorary DLitts from the Universities of Bath and Leicester, acknowledged his out-standing achievements as an explorer and a traveller, the superb books he had written, and his photographs, which testify to his sense of a perfect subject, and his superlative gift for composition. He had been a Fellow of the Royal Society of Literature since 1965, when *The Marsh Arabs* had won him the prestigious Heinemann Award. *Desert, Marsh and Mountain* had been published in 1979, and he was already working on *The Life of My Choice*, which he wrote over six years in London, Hyderabad, Maralal and Belgrade, where Mark Allen, an expert in Middle Eastern affairs for the Foreign Office, described how Thesiger had taken over his study: 'His method was to use lined paper and write in black biro in his awkward and anything but cursive hand – just a few lines at a time. Very often he would screw up the page after only a line or two. When I got back from the embassy, the study floor would look like a snowfall ... His own lean and taut style cost him great effort ... He always wanted the pages read and would listen to and easily implement changes suggested.'[29]

George Webb, who acted as Thesiger's unofficial editor of *Desert, Marsh and Mountain* and *The Life of My Choice*, felt that he had 'a surer talent as a photographer than as a writer – in which capacity, though endowed with real fondness for expressive language, he never found it easy to draft elegantly'.[30] In his tireless pursuit of 'brevity, clarity and flow (or rhythm)',[31] Thesiger pruned ruthlessly and subjectively to avoid diluting his material and to attain the literary 'pitch' he sought.[32] Sometimes there were subjects, such as the death of his brother Brian, that he chose to exclude.[33] Brian Thesiger Doughty-Wylie retired from the Royal Welch Fusiliers in 1957 with the rank of lieutenant-colonel. He died, aged seventy-one, in 1982, while Thesiger was writing *The Life of My Choice*; yet save for an opaque comment, 'I just didn't want to,' Wilfred refused to explain why he made no mention of this in the book.[34]

While he was in India in 1978 writing *Desert, Marsh and Mountain*, Thesiger met Sir Robert ffolkes on several occasions: twice in Delhi in January, again in February in Hyderabad. Aged thirty-five, ffolkes was in charge of the Save the Children Fund in Ladakh. In September 1983 Thesiger met him in Srinagar and drove with him by way of the Zoji-la pass, Drass and Kargil, over the Namikula and Fatula passes, to Leh. From then until the end of October he did his last serious journeys with ffolkes, travelling in Ladakh with yaks and ponies through some of the world's most spectacular mountain scenery. A description of these journeys, based on notes jotted in his Ladakh diary, was published in *Among the Mountains* in 1998: 'We set off from Leh on 17 September and for the next six weeks we travelled with ponies or yaks from one village to another. We crossed many passes, among them the Sisir-la, Kupa-la and the 17,000-foot-high Sengyyi-la where a little snow still lingered.'[35] In fact the visit to Ladakh nearly had to be abandoned. In July 1983 Wilfred and Mark Allen had travelled together in Bosnia and Montenegro. Allen wrote: 'After we returned to Belgrade, Wilfred's back went. This was awful. He was in bed, being visited by doctors and nurses ... There was a lot of shaking of heads and an anxious, hobbling farewell at the airport. A little while later, we got a postcard from Leh. Wilfred had walked [sic] over a 17,000 ft pass and loved it.'[36]

Thesiger wrote:

After descending from [a pass] in the bitter cold we sometimes arrived in a village after dark. Only in the Tibesti mountains in the Sahara had I seen a landscape as barren. We travelled incessantly over rocks and stones where the only vegetation was an occasional artemesia plant. Sometimes we crossed two passes a day, or skirted tremendous gorges. At last we would reach a small village with some cultivation along a stream, perhaps bordered by tamarisk and willow. Many of the villages had such strange, yet evocative names: Photoksar, Yulchung, Linkshet, Hanupata. Everywhere we were welcomed, for Robert ffolkes had done much to help these people. We would stay in a village for a day or two, and each night sit round a hearth in the increasing cold and drink their buttered tea. Some of these people, especially the old women, had striking faces. I was happy to be accepted by them, able to take what photographs I wanted with no feeling of restraint.[37]

On 25 September Thesiger had crossed the Kupa-la pass heading for Gougma, which he reached a week later. While Robert ffolkes made a detour on the way, Thesiger stayed for two nights at Amchi, near Gompa monastery, with the headman, a 'doctor' who still used traditional medicines. At Gompa he photographed monks harvesting; and he remembered a steep, cold climb beyond the monastery which he attempted on 1 October, three days after ffolkes had rejoined him. They returned briefly to Leh and visited the great monastery of Hemis, then travelled through more of Ladakh's spectacular mountain valleys until, in the last week of October, they arrived back near Leh, at the impressive Spituk monastery.

From Ladakh Thesiger went on to Jaipur, Pushkar and Jaisalmer in Rajasthan, Bandhavgarh in Bhopal, and Hyderabad. At the Pushkar fair, he noted in his diary on 16 November 1983: 'Huge crowd [150,000], with cows, camels [and] horses, camped everywhere. Wonderful.'[38] From 11 to 22 December he stayed at Bandhavgarh jungle camp, where on his first day, travelling with elephants, he got to within fifteen yards of a large tiger on its kill. Over the next ten days he saw fresh tiger tracks, and heard monkeys calling, disturbed by a tiger's presence. On three occasions he saw tigers again: once a tiger and a tigress, each on its kill; and another tigress as she joined her three cubs. This had been an exciting experience, but to Thesiger's disappointment he was unable to get a closer view of the tigress and her cubs as they were higher up on a hill that was inaccessible to his elephant.[39]

Before he returned to England in 1984, Thesiger visited Bandhavgarh, accompanied by Pamela Egremont, and afterwards spent a month in Nepal. He went there intentionally in March and April, since he was anxious to see the rhododendrons, but for some reason, that year, they were not in flower. This was not a good time to see the Himalayas, which were then usually obscured by haze. Once, however, he caught a glimpse of the Annapurna range, clearcut and beautiful after the rain. 'This was the vision,' Thesiger wrote, 'I took away with me from the Himalayas.'[40]

At Maralal, Thesiger's quartet of young Samburu had been replaced by a trio, of whom Lawi remained the undisputed leader. Lawi found another promising teenager, who said his Samburu family name was Lekakwar, and that he was known as 'Tommy Gun'. Thesiger renamed the boy Laputa after the Zulu leader in John Buchan's novel *Prester John*. A year after he joined Thesiger's entourage Laputa produced Ibrahim Ewoi Ekai, a Turkana about the same age as himself, who had trained as a mechanic at Siddiq Bhola's garage in Maralal. Since he proved both deft and intelligent, Bhola had nicknamed Ewoi Ekai 'Kibiriti', the Swahili word for 'match'. Kibiriti was over six feet tall, with broad shoulders and a distinctive hoarse voice which Thesiger always claimed he could recognise anywhere as soon as he heard it.[41] Lawi and Laputa had spent five years at a primary school and could read and write, whereas Kibiriti had never been to school and could do neither. Despite this handicap, he had been elected as chairman of a primary school in Maralal, and according to Thesiger he was 'not only industrious but has a head for business'.[42]

Ever since he was a child, Thesiger had been interested in gardening. His parents had been keen gardeners, he and his brother Brian each cultivated a small garden at their preparatory school, and in the Sudan, at Kutum, in Northern Darfur, Thesiger had tended flowers and vegetables. It fascinated him that Kibiriti 'proved to be a surprisingly knowledgeable, practical gardener', able to give advice on what to plant and how to prune.[43] This seemed all the more extraordinary since the Turkana country where Kibiriti had been brought up was too arid for cultivation. Just as he had helped to build the first house for Lawi, in due course Thesiger gave Kibiriti and Laputa money to build houses for themselves and their families. Kibiriti laid out very attractive gardens round his house, built on a level plain within sight of Lawi's house, only a short distance from the town.

'Prester John' Laputa, as he came to be known, had a sombre, rather wistful expression, and spent much of his time immersed in thought; but what his thoughts were, nobody really knew. Soon after Lawi got married, Thesiger moved into Laputa's house, and one evening Laputa remarked that he wanted to try to draw, something he had always wanted to do, but had never accomplished. Thesiger wrote: 'I gave him a large sheet of paper and went off to bed while he sat there starting to work by the light of a hurricane lamp. In the morning he showed me a pencil drawing he had made based on photographs of three lion. I was astonished not only by their life-like realism and accurate proportions, but also by the originality with which he had drawn details such as the lion's mane.'[44] Thesiger exaggerated wildly the often mediocre abilities of anyone he cared for. His friends, including his publisher Adrian House and Frank Steele, who stayed with him for short periods at Maralal, agreed that Laputa was an able copyist, but a less accomplished artist. Laputa's younger brother Rupalen, on the other hand, in his gold-embroidered baseball cap, gold-and-silver-embroidered T-shirt and shorts, riding a dazzling chromium-plated bicycle with an enormous chromium-plated bell, was a work of 'performance art' in his own right. He was very talented, and drew excellent portraits in pastels of the Samburu; but, Rupalen sighed: '*Mzee juu* won't help me, and he thinks only of Laputa.'[45]

Laputa was inclined to be very vague, a tendency which Thesiger ascribed to his 'strongly artistic temperament'.[46] Whereas Lawi and Kibiriti, each in his own impermeable way, had been competent and in control of their lives, Laputa appeared fragile, vulnerable and at the mercy of fate. In 1988 he married a Samburu girl called Margaret Namitu, whom Thesiger described as 'tall and placid, unfailingly cheerful and always eager to help'.[47] Thesiger, who seldom lapsed into political correctness, went on: 'She herself keeps the house clean and tidy and, unlike so many of these educated women [this chauvinistic remark was perhaps aimed at Lawi's pretty Kikuyu wife, who was a schoolteacher] is prepared to turn her hand to anything, such as fetching water or wood.'[48] Laputa and Namitu had two children: a boy called Sandy and a daughter, Rosanna. Namitu had a younger brother, Samuel, known as 'Bushbaby' or 'Bushboy', and three half-brothers: Talone, Lechiin and Sepiri, nicknamed 'Sungura' ('hare') by Thesiger because of his speed and agility.

Laputa's house was built on a hillside, overlooking a wide valley about half an hour's walk from the town. The layout was similar to that of the houses Thesiger had had built for Lawi and Kibiriti. Each had three adjacent rooms, the middle one serving as a sitting room and bedroom. Thesiger had a bedroom to himself, furnished with a double bed, a chest of drawers and a wardrobe. He shared it with Julius Lopego, a sixteen-year-old cousin of Namitu, whom Thesiger described rather implausibly as his 'bodyguard'.[49] 'I don't care a damn what people think,' he said. 'I like having somebody near me ... it's this thing of not wanting to be on my own if I can avoid it ... Sex doesn't come into it ... If I'm seized and I need to get to the *cho* [a ramshackle dry closet with a nine-foot-deep pit, thirty yards from Laputa's house] at night, I'll need somebody to steady me ... to hold the torch and the mug [of water he used to clean himself] and guide me back.'[50] After Thesiger had his prostate gland removed, he found that he was impotent. He said: 'Someone told me that when Socrates was seventy, he thanked the gods that he didn't need to bother about sex any more. Well, I thought, he sounds pretty dull. When the surgeon took out my prostate, he never said all that would be in the past. But, after a while, with nothing very obvious happening, I realised that I was in the same boat as Socrates.'[51]

Like Robert Louis Stevenson in Samoa, or Gauguin in Tahiti, the romance of a famous English explorer living with African tribespeople in the wilds of northern Kenya added an exotic lustre to Thesiger's already lambent image in his declining years. He was well aware of this, and played his part to perfection. He liked to tell his visitors in London about his operation for hernia in February 1982 at Wamba, near Mount Warges, east of Maralal, and how 'they just cut me open with a spear'.[52] While in the past his friends had never been quite certain how Thesiger would behave – whether, in the words of Dorothy Middleton, editor of the RGS *Journal*, he would be 'charming or *farouche*'[53] – as he grew older he enjoyed being lionised (in small doses), even though he dismissed most of the praise lavished upon him as 'rubbish'.[54] Deeply tanned and distinguished-looking in a handmade suit from Savile Row, Thesiger was once greeted at a drinks party by an elderly dowager who remarked,

'What fun you must be having! I don't expect you go to many parties in the back of beyond where you live?' Thesiger replied indulgently: 'In fact, it's just the opposite. We had a marvellous party last month. All the guests arrived naked, and we ate one of them afterwards.'[55]

Thesiger's long-awaited autobiography, *The Life of My Choice*, was published on 5 May 1987, the same year as *Visions of a Nomad*, which he always regarded as the finest work devoted to his photographs. On 8 June he was admitted to the London Clinic for an operation to remove part of his colon, which had become afflicted with cancer. While he was discussing the details of the operation with the surgeon, George Webb, who was with him, joked: 'Wilfred, after this you'll be a semi-colon'; to which the surgeon added: 'Surely that is better than being a full stop.'[56]

When he first settled at Maralal, Thesiger dominated his younger Samburu and Turkana companions, just as he had dominated tribal companions wherever he lived or travelled, in Abyssinia, the Sudan, Arabia or southern Iraq. Ever since his boyhood when he took charge of his younger brothers, he had been a natural leader. A 'gang-leader' was how his oldest friends often described him.[57] With age came infirmity. He grew increasingly dependent on those around him, and more than ever willing to give in to his adoptive 'sons' and their frequently extravagant demands. Thesiger insisted:

Looking back over my life I have never wanted a master or servant relationship with my retainers. Even in the Sudan as an Assistant DC when I travelled with camels, I instinctively slept and sat on the ground and shared my food with those who were travelling with me. This, of course, is what I did in Arabia and in the Marshes of Iraq and I have continued to do so in Kenya ... Here in Kenya the people among whom I am living are involved in my life and I am involved in theirs. I pay them no wages and have never regarded them as servants, but as part of my family. I have endeavoured to help them establish themselves and this has often involved me with considerable expense; it has, however, been my pleasure to do this.[58]

The trouble, said Frank Steele, was that 'Wilfred's Samburu and Turkana "sons" did not treat him in the same family spirit, certainly not as "sons" should treat their "father" who has been so incredibly generous towards them.'[59] As in the film *The Servant*, where the distinction between master and servant becomes blurred, and gradually their roles are reversed, in Kenya Thesiger's older Samburu companions steadily usurped his authority, and began to drain him at an alarming rate of increasingly large sums of money. Though in close harmony with their surroundings and often highly intelligent, few Samburu and Turkana in Thesiger's 'family' circle showed any aptitude for business, nor had they any idea of the value of money. Thesiger admitted that he had probably been mistaken in encouraging young Samburu to harbour business aspirations that were almost inevitably doomed to failure. By giving away large sums over the years he had made their lives too easy, had raised their level of expectations too abruptly. As someone remarked: 'However well-intentioned, it was a case of the blind misleading the blind.' When Thesiger returned to Kenya in June 1978, after eighteen months' absence, he had been joined immediately by Lawi and Kendawa. A note in the cash account section of his 1978 pocket diary shows that at that time he paid Lawi five hundred Kenyan shillings a month (roughly £5 sterling), and Kendawa three hundred. Apart from place names – Baragoi, Barsaloi, Maralal and so on – which he printed in capital letters and underlined, almost all the day-to-day entries in this diary concern the small sums of money Thesiger advanced to Lawi, Kendawa and any other Samburu who were with him.

Until 1978 Thesiger's eyesight, though slightly imperfect, was still mainly unimpaired by age. But in February of that year, while he was writing *Desert, Marsh and Mountain* at the Rock-Castle Hotel in Hyderabad, he had experienced 'something like flashing lights ... like flashes of lightning' in front of his eyes.[60] When he got back to London in March he underwent laser surgery at Moorfields Eye Hospital to repair a separating cornea.[61] As his sight began to grow weaker, he became increasingly unable to distinguish between Kenyan banknotes, and would sometimes unknowingly hand one of his 'sons' a thousand shillings instead of a hundred to pay for a day's food and any other shopping at Maralal.

The following examples taken from Thesiger's External Account at his London bank, Child & Co. in Fleet Street, provide a dramatic illustration of the downward slide which, had it continued, would have left him virtually penniless.[62] On 28 July 1989 he made five withdrawals totalling £12,700. On 21 August he made five more withdrawals, totalling £5700. On 29 December four cash withdrawals amounted to £7150; on 17 January 1990 five withdrawals came to £10,900; and on 23 January five for cash, totalling £16,900: a total of £34,950 in cash withdrawals in less than a month. From 27 November to 19 December 1990, at Maralal, Thesiger paid out sums varying from £4000 to £15,038. All this, in and around a remote African township where a family of six or more could live quite comfortably on £3 a day, or (depending on the rate of exchange) two or three hundred Kenyan shillings. These dates and figures are selected at random, and of course Thesiger dispensed considerable quantities of money during the years before and after 1989–90. His brother Roderic felt certain that Wilfred had spent at least half a million pounds on the Samburu from 1978 to 1994. Some of this money was used to purchase plots of land and to build houses or shops. Large sums were also spent on four-wheel-drive cars, lorries and a sixty-five-seater single-decker bus, the 'Samburu Express', which Thesiger purchased for Lawi. Maintaining the bus proved to be very expensive; in the end Lawi abandoned it after a jealous rival allegedly filled its petrol tank with sand, and the 'Samburu Express' was left to rot, shored up on bricks, a strangely apt memorial to the combustion engine Thesiger so detested, and a blight on Lawi's otherwise attractive garden.

In all these ventures, Thesiger admitted he had been a more or less willing accomplice: 'They would tell me why they needed the money, and I'd give it to them, knowing that it was very likely a ramp – either a pack of lies, or at best only half-true. I sort of accepted that half of anything they told me was sheer nonsense. But their standards are different from ours and you can't begin to compare them ... I was an utter fool, I suppose, but I don't regret any of it ... The only thing, perhaps, was having to sell my copy of *Seven Pillars of Wisdom* to buy more cars and pay off their gambling debts in Nairobi.'[63]

Thesiger had been very proud when one of his 'sons' assured him that he had arranged to sell thousands of cattle for slaughter to provide meat for the Kenyan army. He told his friends: 'He is going to be Maralal's first millionaire.'[64] But he did not reveal how many thousands of pounds he had given the youth to buy cows which never materialised. This scheme, like so many others, had been a mere fantasy, and a farce.

As well as a man of action, all his life Thesiger was a dreamer. His *raison d'être* had been his dream of living a life of 'savagery and colour', a life he pursued without compromise, often at great cost and with no small degree of risk. This life of sometimes inconceivable hardship had given him an abnormally acute perception of reality. Yet he also lived in a quixotic parallel universe of his own creation. For Thesiger no less than for 'Prester John' Laputa, being a dreamer had been both his strength and his weakness. Like Don Quixote, Thesiger had tilted at windmills. Cars, aeroplanes, modern communications were among the giants he relentlessly attacked, yet espoused discreetly for his own purposes. For months or years, a succession of young tribesmen in many lands had shared his self-imposed and restless existence; some, no doubt, like Sancho Panza hopeful of improving their lot, others attractive, aimless wanderers who had caught Thesiger's eye. Though Quixote's squire never became the governor of an island, with Thesiger's help Lawi Leboyare did become chairman of Maralal's urban council.

The days at Laputa's house followed a pleasant, simple routine. Each morning the nightwatchman, who had slept in the kitchen, carried outside a small kitchen stove known as a *jiko*, and having replenished the charcoal set it alight with paraffin and matches and left it to burn for half an hour on the terrace immediately in front of the verandah. He then carried it back into the kitchen, filled a saucepan from one of the rainwater drums and boiled water for Thesiger to shave with, and to make tea and coffee. Zebra sauntered, coughing and snorting, among the acacias. As soon as he woke, Thesiger yelled for shaving water. A sixteen-year-old would respond sleepily, '*Oyee!*' or '*Ndio!*' and come running from the kitchen gloom, carrying a black plastic basin.[65] Clad in a green *kikoi*, a bulky garment shaped like an artichoke, Thesiger would shuffle unsteadily from his bedroom to a settee, where he shaved with long, slow, careful strokes and washed his face and neck with a soft facecloth. Somewhere in the background a wireless played dance music interspersed with the 'English news'.

The mornings were usually very still, windless, silent except for doves clattering and cooing in the trees, or a cockerel crowing in one of the *manyattas.* For breakfast Thesiger would have either porridge with plenty of sugar and milk, or else two or three eggs, or sometimes 'Morning Gold' cornflakes, and drank one or two cups of coffee or tea. Sandy, Laputa and Namitu's little boy, often fetched and carried his breakfast things – plates, cup and saucer, cereals, coffee and teapot – in relays, each time he appeared standing stiffly to attention and greeting Thesiger with a garbled, emphatic, 'Good moloning to *you!*' in near-perfect mimicry of Thesiger's voice and manner.

Until he became unable to do so, Thesiger would walk to Maralal, using a walking stick and leaning on someone's arm. A steep path led from the house down to the *luggah* – the dry watercourse at the bottom of the valley – up the other side, through some open forest and across a plain, covered with bushes and withered grass, to the town. Thesiger would spend the morning at Bhola's garage, which served as a *poste restante* and a meeting point for some of his followers. Bhola and his sons were courteous, patient, and never seemed to mind these intrusions. On the contrary, they were invariably welcoming and hospitable. Thesiger sometimes lunched at Bhola's compound, but more often Kibiriti gave him lunch at his house, or less frequently he lunched at Lawi's house. Afterwards he was driven back to Laputa's, where he sat in a deckchair on the verandah until sunset.

One night, when Thesiger's 'bodyguard' Julius Lopego was staying with friends in Maralal, some men broke into Laputa's house and attacked Thesiger in his bedroom with sticks.[66] Thesiger wrote: 'The whole thing was an interesting experience but one which I have no desire to repeat. This was the first of such attacks here in Maralal ... nine such thugs broke into Laputa's younger brother Rupalen's shop and stole everything in it including the money, after severely beating up Rupalen ... When they interviewed me the police said they were sorry I had not killed one of my attackers so that they would know who they were. Lopego never ceases to regret that he was away and was unable to kill at least one. Had he been there I am sure that he would have succeeded, using his iron-shod club.'[67] Lopego was seldom away from the house overnight, and the fact that the attack occurred on a night when he was sleeping in the town suggested that someone knew his movements in advance. The nightwatchman was locked up in the kitchen, where he usually spent the night, and the dogs never barked, perhaps indicating that they had been fed with drugged meat by the intruders. Strangely, Thesiger's attackers were able to lock Laputa's bedroom door from the sitting room side, whereas this door was normally locked after Laputa and Namitu had gone into their bedroom, an understandable precaution in a small house with five or six other people living in it.

After he was attacked, Thesiger barricaded the front door at night with a heavy settee. When he went into the kitchen after dark to watch Namitu and the children as they cooked dinner, he now ordered someone to bring his spear. The weapon rested against the wall behind an armchair near the kitchen door where he always sat. The spear-carrier made a colourful addition to a line of children who followed Thesiger in and out of the kitchen every night: one child carrying a jar of honey, another a pot of Marmite, a third with Thesiger's spear in one hand, in the other hand a bottle of tomato ketchup. Any friend of Thesiger who stayed at the house was given a long-bladed, razor-sharp Samburu dagger and instructed how to use it. This was no doubt more effective than the lilting *ilkoronkoi* (pronounced 'gorongoy') sung by herdsmen at night in the valley to protect their cows from being attacked by wild animals.

Thesiger ended *My Kenya Days*: 'When I first came to Kenya, I intended to spend perhaps two years in the country travelling with camels in the Northern Frontier District, but since then I have come to regard Maralal as my home. It is here, among those whose lives I share today, that I hope to end my days.'[68] When he wrote these words, in April 1993, he could never have guessed that less than two years later Lawi and Laputa would both be dead, and that he would be alone and living permanently in England.

One night, when there was a full moon and the African sky was glittering with stars, a child had pointed to the moon and asked: 'Are we as far from you in London?'

Thesiger replied: 'When I'm in London, you seem much further away than the moon.'

EPILOGUE

In February 1990, Thesiger flew from Nairobi to the United Arab Emirates to attend the opening of the first exhibition of his photographs, arranged by Peter Clark, the director of the British Council in Abu Dhabi. In October 1991 he returned to the UAE for the publication by Motivate, his Middle East publisher, of the first edition of *Arabian Sands* in Arabic. His sight had begun to deteriorate rapidly; Motivate's director, Ian Fairservice, noted that he appeared frailer than the previous year.[1] Despite his failing sight and his increasing infirmity, Thesiger continued to visit the UAE at intervals, and he always looked forward immensely to his sojourns in Dubai with Ian and Janice Fairservice and their children. He had begun to mellow with age. On his departure from Abu Dhabi in 1990 he praised the 'dignity' of this modern city,[2] which in 1979 he had condemned in *Desert, Marsh and Mountain* as 'an Arabian Nightmare'. In 1990 and 1991 he travelled to Zimbabwe, Malawi and the Okavango Swamps in Botswana.

A book about Thesiger's life in Kenya based on his recollections had been proposed in 1985, but failed to materialise. By 1992 he could no longer see well enough to read or write without assistance, but in June of that year he began to dictate *My Kenya Days* in London, and later at Maralal in October and November. He found dictation far from easy, having been accustomed always to write in longhand,[3] but he completed the book in April 1993. In November 1992 Thesiger decided to give up photography, since the magnifying viewfinder attached to his Leicaflex camera no longer compensated sufficiently for the effects of cataract in both eyes and astigmatism in his right eye.

After he returned to Kenya from Indonesia in 1978, Thesiger had lived a mainly sedentary life at Maralal, first with Lawi Leboyare, then with Laputa Lekakwar, in one or other of the cedar houses he had helped them to build on the outskirts of the town. In September 1994 Laputa died, aged only thirty-two, after a short illness. Thesiger was affected deeply by the young Samburu's tragic end: he could not bear to go on living in the house they had shared for more than a decade. On 10–11 October he flew back to London, and for the next few months he remained undecided whether or not to spend the rest of his life among his Samburu 'families' in northern Kenya.

Lawi meanwhile had been in poor health. He had high blood pressure and had suffered a small stroke. On Good Friday, 14 April 1995, Thesiger received a telephone call from Siddiq Bhola telling him that Lawi had died.[4] Thesiger had been very fond of Laputa, and in *The Life of My Choice* he had written that Lawi was 'as dear to me as a son'.[5] Now that both Laputa and Lawi had gone, Thesiger said, 'That's all finished now'[6] – meaning that his days in Kenya were finally over. And he reflected grimly on his mother's words: 'I hope that in your old age you'll never feel as lonely as I do.'[7]

On 17 October 1994 Thesiger visited his oculist, Patrick Trevor-Roper, who assured him that his sight, though imperfect, was good enough for him to drive a car legally (whether he could have driven safely, Trevor-Roper added, was quite another matter[8]). Thesiger complained of headaches, which his doctor felt might be connected with his failing sight. On 29 November his eyes were examined by an ophthalmic surgeon at Moorfields Eye Hospital, who told him there was a 95 per cent chance that the sight in his left eye could be restored enough for him to read with comparative ease, using reading glasses, but the sight in his right eye could not be improved significantly, if at all.

At Moorfields on 19 December 1994 a cataract was removed by microsurgery and Thesiger's left eye was fitted with a new lens. That evening he took off the eyeshield the hospital had given him and went to a dinner party with Lady Egremont and Major-General and Mrs Charles Vyvyan.[9] On 15 June 1996 he had a further eye operation, at the Cromwell Hospital in Kensington. At Whipps Cross Hospital on 26 June 1996 a cataract on his right eye was removed by laser surgery. Thesiger was now able to tell the time and read the smallest lettering on the face of his Rolex wristwatch. As a result of the first operation his long-range vision was slightly impaired; otherwise his sight was much improved.

In July 1996, however, while he was in Spain, staying with his close friend the photographer Robert Vavra on his farm near Seville, he saw 'bright flashes and circles of light', but could not tell which eye was causing them.[10] He liked being among the bulls, the horses and the mounted *vaqueros* on Vavra's farm, where a magnificent bull known as 'Africano' delighted everyone by allowing Thesiger to stroke his nose. Thesiger said: 'Too many people are living second-hand lives, instead of creative lives. Farmers are like remote peoples. They live life as they always have. What I think is so damaging isn't the loss of identity or the loss of purpose, but the loss of interest in life caused by the machine age. The machine age creates tension and this diminishes people's lives. Aeroplanes and motorized transport rob journeys of any sense of achievement. People like the Bedu in Arabia, who use cars instead of camels, forfeit their original character.'[11]

Telling how he had stroked Africano's nose reminded Thesiger of how his own nose, perhaps his best-known physical feature, had come to be broken no fewer than three times: 'The first time was when Roddy or someone threw a stone at me. This was at The Milebrook, when we were children, playing a game we called "defending the pig-sty". My nose was broken again at Eton, when somebody threw a cricket ball. The third time I was boxing for Oxford against Cambridge. My nose got broken ... my ear was torn, and my mouth all messed up. I remember going to London from Eton to have the second break set.'[12] Staying with friends in the Cotswolds in May 1997, Thesiger had two 'fairly nasty' falls. He found he had dislocated his right thumb, and promptly reset it: 'It was sticking out,' he explained, 'and I pushed it back [until] it clicked.'[13]

On Thursday, 2 November 1995, Thesiger was knighted at Buckingham Palace by HRH The Prince of Wales. In 1984, Sir Anthony Rumbold had 'tried very hard to get Wilfred a knighthood, but for some reason it hadn't come off'.[14] Frank Steele, who drafted one of the 1995 citations, felt that this time it had succeeded because of Thesiger's iconic status as one of the twentieth century's greatest explorers and travellers, and his worldwide fame due to his books, photographs and the films made about him, and their inspirational effect on young people.[15]

Thesiger's popular fame had increased quite dramatically over the quarter of a century since 1970. His books had been translated into French, Spanish, German, Italian, Danish, Swedish, Norwegian, Dutch, Hungarian, pictorial Chinese, Japanese and Arabic. His legacy was rich and varied. He had inspired generations of young men and women to retrace his footsteps or to make their own way following his example. His books were immensely influential, and had given pleasure to countless thousands of readers all over the world. His writing delighted the most critical of experts no less than the general public; indeed, his appeal was almost universal.

Popularity alone, however, is no proof of greatness. It was Thesiger's stature as a man, added to the extraordinary combination of his accomplishments and his personality, that ensured his lasting worldwide fame. Visitors from all over the world were given a warm welcome, and they found Thesiger in his old age very ready to talk about his adventurous past. Forty years previously, such visitors might well have found him unforthcoming and difficult to talk to. While it is true that he was inclined to be temperamental, the fact remains that had he been less determined, ruthless or self-centred, it is unlikely that he would have achieved his greatest objectives as an explorer and a traveller.

Among Thesiger's rarer pleasures had been the Shikar Club's annual dinner, held at the Savoy Hotel in early December. Spending so much of each year abroad, he was seldom able to attend, and the occasions when he did so meant even more to him in consequence. Thesiger became a member of the club in 1939, and later served for some years on its committee. Founded by Lord Lonsdale and J.G. Millais in 1907, the club's objects, which included maintaining 'the highest standards of sportsmanship', appealed strongly to Thesiger. The club also promoted the belief that 'hunting big game, as distinct from simply shooting wild animals, enables men to test themselves under conditions of hardship and sometimes of real danger. There is a sense of achievement in cleanly killing an outstanding trophy, sometimes after weeks of hunting and a true sportsman only shoots selectively.' Thesiger always maintained that he had shot 'selectively and seldom'.[16]

Accompanied by Pamela Egremont, on 31 May 1996 Thesiger travelled to Addis Ababa for the celebrations marking the centenary of the

Ethiopian capital's foundation by Menelik II. They stayed with the British Ambassador, Robin Christopher, at the Embassy – the former Legation where Wilfred had been brought up until he was almost nine. Lady Egremont recollected how it had been 'touching and wonderful' watching Thesiger as he 'held court', and that he had been obviously moved to meet friends he had known in the past, and descendants of people who had worked for his father and mother.[17]

In early April 1995 Thesiger's right hand had begun to shake so much that he could hardly write. He had little appetite, and complained that food had no taste.[18] He was convinced that he had Parkinson's disease, and a medical examination in July 1997 confirmed that rudimentary Parkinson's had caused elliptical tremors in his right hand, made even more apparent due to the extraordinary length of his fingers and his long, curving thumb. (During tests at Francis Galton's Anthropometric Institute on 15 April 1889, the length of Wilfred Gilbert Thesiger's left middle finger was recorded as 5.2 inches.[19] This was among the physical characteristics inherited from his father by the younger Wilfred.) X-rays showed wear and tear on Thesiger's bones and joints – in particular in his upper right leg, his pelvis and his lower back – but of the sort commonly found among former athletes aged between forty and fifty, rather than men who were closer to ninety. Apart from his sight and the effects of Parkinson's disease, Thesiger also now suffered from arthritis. Over the years he had dispensed many thousands of pills to ailing tribesmen. Now the position was reversed, and much to his disgust he had to accustom himself to taking daily dosages of pain-killer as well as pills to control the Parkinson's and its side effects.

An old friend, William Delafield, would arrive at Thesiger's flat laden with delicacies from Partridge's the grocers in Sloane Street. In June 1991 they had visited the Pitt Rivers Museum in Oxford, where Delafield recommended that Wilfred's large archive of photographs should be conserved and housed, and after his death be gifted outright to the museum. In October 1993 Thesiger's photograph albums and negatives (except for items he intended to give to his family and friends) were removed from his flat and taken to the museum, followed in March 1997 by a further collection of artefacts, daggers and swords, mainly from Africa and Arabia. Instead of the estimated twenty-five thousand, in due course there were found to be some thirty-eight thousand negatives in Thesiger's photographic archive.

From his return to London in October 1994 until May 1997, Thesiger had lived alone. Although his mind remained clear and sharp, he was occasionally troubled late at night by inexplicable noises and visions of intruders.[20] Despite visits to Abu Dhabi and Dubai, Addis Ababa, Seville and Fugitive's Drift in Zululand, working on *The Danakil Diary* and seeing many visitors, like his mother Thesiger complained continually that he felt lonely. In order to give him company in the evenings and to help with domestic affairs such as cooking, shopping and laundry, a succession of young men lived in one of the flat's spare bedrooms rent free, and received a small monthly allowance. When Thesiger was asked why he did not engage a housekeeper to look after him as Mollie Emtage had done, he said: 'I could never hope to find Mollie's like again. Living here, in this flat, without my mother or without Mollie, feels like living in a prison. Even if I did find someone satisfactory, it would still feel like a prison – except that I'd be living with my gaoler.'[21]

Thesiger was determined to move from his flat to a retirement home, where he would be looked after day and night and would find the companionship he craved.[22] In January 1997 Julian Lush (whose father, Brigadier Maurice Lush, was Dan Sandford's brother-in-law) took Thesiger to lunch at the Charterhouse, near Smithfield and the Barbican, where a small brotherhood of single elderly men of slender means lived in retirement. For a number of reasons, sadly, neither the Charterhouse nor another excellent home at Blackheath felt able to accept him. But with the enthusiastic help of Sir Iain Mackay-Dick, Governor of Morden College, and Thesiger's staunch friend William Barlow of the Chelsea Royal Hospital, a comfortable room was found at Orford House, near Coulsdon in Surrey, one of several outstanding retirement homes owned and managed by Friends of the Elderly. Thesiger moved into Orford House on 23 June 1998. Facing it across a wide lawn was Woodcote Grove House, and after a few months Thesiger moved to a room there. From this first room at the back of the house he later moved to a brighter one on the first floor, overlooking the lawn, Orford House and the fields beyond, and there he remained.

John Shipman, a close friend for almost forty years, had seen Thesiger at frequent intervals in London, and continued to visit him regularly at Coulsdon. He wrote:

> From the spacious inner hall of Woodcote Grove House rose an elegant staircase, its gleaming mahogany banister bleached to a pale amber by decades of filtered sunlight. Wilfred would ascend the stairs with surprising agility until a few months before his death. At the top, a long, brightly decorated corridor led to his room. Modestly proportioned, this had space enough for the few pieces of furniture which he had brought with him from London: a desk, a table, two armchairs, a stool and a chest of drawers. The walls were hung with pictures; other mementoes of people and places were displayed here and there. An alcove of shelves contained some of his favourite books, including all of his own authorship. When his eyesight failed, it delighted him to be read to; and he would generally choose to hear passages from his own work ... On the table by the window a brilliant blue lump of polished lapis lazuli, a cherished talisman from his journey through Badakhshan in 1956, did service as a paperweight. If one picked it up to admire its colour and texture, one was conscious of being the focus of a watchful eye until one put it down. Among the pictures in Wilfred's room, perhaps the most striking was a portrait of his mother by Simon Elwes, painted [in 1960] while she and her son, during one of his infrequent visits to Europe, were on holiday in Spain ... Also striking was a profile of Wilfred himself sketched by Laputa ... But the picture to which my own eye always returned was the black and white photograph of the Kathiri Sultan's Palace in Seiyun, Wadi Hadhramaut, which hung above Wilfred's desk, close to a photograph of charging Moroccan horsemen taken some years later.[23]

In January 2001 Thesiger began to be treated for Alzheimer's as well as Parkinson's disease. By the end of the year, Parkinson's was causing a progressive loss of memory, renewed shaking (particularly of his hands), stooping gait and (to his exasperation) a tendency to dribble. By March 2002 his sight had deteriorated so much that he could no longer read or tell the time, except by looking at a page, or at his watch, from certain angles – and then only very imperfectly. Once again he began to experience hallucinations. Orford House, across the lawn, appeared to expand and contract; men in uniforms came out on horses; carriages with people in them moved across in front of the building. Thesiger talked about his life, sometimes with an almost desperate urgency, as if he were doing so for the first time. He seemed more than ever anxious and determined that every detail of his life history, his aspirations, his deeply held convictions should be made known, discussed and accurately recorded.

A friend observed at this time:

Thesiger's legendary mystique is all the more extraordinary, since he fails to satisfy the ultimate definition of a popular hero. In other words, unlike Scott at the South Pole, or Malory trying to reach the summit of Everest, he hadn't died a hero's death while pursuing a great objective. Instead, Thesiger survived his many life-threatening journeys across desert, marsh and mountain, not to mention big game hunting adventures in the Sudan and wartime escapades in Abyssinia, Syria and North Africa. Thesiger's character, and his rugged appearance, were certainly cast in the heroic mould. He possessed unusual reserves of courage and impregnable self-belief, besides a highly developed instinct for opportunity and a compelling, fugitive charm. When compared to others, Thesiger's life seemed to follow a remarkably straight path free of distraction and misadventure. He had succeeded brilliantly in all his chosen pursuits ... Thesiger set very little store by material things, but did value certain possessions such as his collection of books and his travel photographs ... He was never commercially minded. He never travelled with the intention of writing a book, any more than he made money, deliberately, by writing, in order to travel.

Everyone who made the pilgrimage to Coulsdon carried away a memory of enduring personal significance. Many visitors either joined Thesiger for lunch at Woodcote Park Golf Club (of which, as a resident of Woodcote Grove House, he became a non-playing member) or drove him to lunch at one of the quieter hotels or country pubs in the neighbourhood. Even when his memory for recent events had begun to fail, Thesiger conjured often vivid memories prompted by association. A Fortnum's cake, for instance, reminded him how as a boy at Eton he had been asked what relation he was to Ernest Thesiger the actor. Now Thesiger said: 'I only met him twice – once when he came down to lunch at Magdalen and once in my mother's flat. And then there was the time when Ernest was having morning tea at Fortnum's and somebody said to him, "What relation are you of Wilfred Thesiger?" And I felt that now this had cancelled the other out.'[24]

Towards the end of April 2003, Thesiger began to look very frail indeed. For the first week of May he was confined to bed. On 16 May, after a fall, he was X-rayed at St Helier Hospital for a suspected hip fracture. He had broken no bones, but suffered much pain for several days, and after that continued to have difficulty in walking even aided by one of his heavy African walking sticks. For some time he had needed help with dressing, and it was becoming evident that he could no longer fend for himself in other ways. On 11 August he was moved to the Selkirk Nursing Wing, adjoining Woodcote Grove House, where he had a room on the ground floor with a view of the garden. He still preferred, however, to walk (with assistance) the short distance to the main house and have lunch and supper with the other residents. Even this he viewed coura- geously, and without resignation, as a challenge: 'I daresay, not much of a challenge; but a challenge all the same.'[25]

At Woodcote Grove House on Sunday, 17 August, just before lunch, Thesiger fell, but apparently without injuring himself seriously. Later he complained of a severe pain in his thigh, and that evening he was taken by ambulance to the Mayday Hospital in Croydon. He had fractured his left femur, but due to his age and frailty, the doctors were reluctant to subject him at once to the trauma of surgery that required a general anaesthetic.

Thesiger seemed to be aware that his life had almost ended. Once again, he stood at the frontier of an undiscovered country. He demanded of someone at his bedside: 'What is your tribe?' And suddenly weary, he cried out with impatience: 'For God's sake, let me go.'[26] At five minutes past four on the afternoon of Sunday, 24 August 2003, Wilfred Thesiger died, peacefully and with great dignity, at the age of ninety-three.

A funeral service was held on 8 September at Putney Vale Crematorium in south-west London, attended by members of Thesiger's family and a few friends. This was followed on 7 November by a memorial service at Eton College chapel. Some time after his funeral, Thesiger's ashes were scattered on Stowe Hill above the Teme Valley, close to The Milebrook, where so many of his happiest childhood days were spent.

ACKNOWLEDGEMENTS

Sir Wilfred Thesiger discussed very openly his life and journeys, and gave me unrestricted access to his archive of diaries, letters, manuscripts and notebooks. He authorised this biography in July 1992, eleven years before his death, and at intervals over the ensuing decade I read and discussed its contents and the drafts of various chapters with him. I wish to take this opportunity to acknowledge Wilfred Thesiger's tireless endeavours to clarify for me the background and detail of successive stages in his long life. His guidance was not only invaluable, but in countless instances absolutely essential.

It gives me great pleasure to thank the following people for their advice and generous assistance during the preparation of this biography. HE Fisseha Adugna, the Ethiopian Ambassador; the Earl of Airlie; Sir Mark and Lady Allen; Mrs Robert Arguille; the late St John Armitage; Mr and Mrs Michael Asher; Mrs Philip Astley; the late Mrs Reginald Astley; Mrs Samantha Aves-Duffell and staff at Woodcote Grove House, Coulsdon; Robin Baird-Smith; Nick Baker; Mr and Mrs William Barlow; Mr and Mrs Julian Barrow; Air Vice-Marshal Sir Erik Bennett; Hugh Bett; the late Siddiq Bhola and his family; the late Miss Mary Buckle; John Butterwick; Miss Juanita Carberry; Mrs Jeremy Case; the late Viscount Chelmsford and the Dowager Viscountess Chelmsford; the Viscount and Viscountess Chelmsford; Dr Charles Claouie; Peter Clark; Ronald Clark; Justin Codrai; the late Ronald Codrai; Mr and Mrs James Cook; Simon Courtauld; Peter Danby-Smith; William Delafield; Sir Richard Dearlove; Mrs Sydney Downey and Miss Margaret Downey; Dr Elizabeth Edwards; Pamela, Viscountess Egremont; Ibrahim Ewoi Ekai (Kibiriti); Major Rodney Elliott; the late Miss Mollie Emtage; Mr and Mrs Jasper Evans;

Mr and Mrs Ian Fairservice; Mark Farrer; Sir Matthew Farrer; Maggie Fergusson; Lt Col R.L.V. and the late Mrs ffrench Blake; Mrs John Fletcher; Robert Floyd; Sir Edward Ford; Dr Rita Gardner CBE, Director and Secretary, the Royal Geographical Society; Miss Gillian Gibbins; the late John Guest; Robin Hanbury-Tenison; Mrs John Harvey; Valerie Hemingway; Dr John Hemming; John Hewitt; the late Ross Higgins; Adrian House; Bruce Hunter; the late Mrs Elspeth Huxley; the late Mr and Mrs Ralph Hammond Innes; the Earl Jellicoe; Bruce Johnson; Richard Johnson; the late Quentin Keynes; Jeffrey King; the late Sir Laurence Kirwan; Robert Lacey; Hugh Leach; the late Gabriel Lawi Leboyare; Matthew Leeming; Mrs Sarah Lee-Uff and staff at Orford House, Coulsdon; the late Laputa Lekakwar, Mrs Margaret Namitu Lekakwar and their family; Martin Lloyd-Elliott; Mrs Sheila Lloyd-Elliott; Mrs Stephen Lockhart; Gwen Lowman, Managing Editor, the Royal Geographical Society; Alexander Luce; the Lord and Lady Luce; Mr and Mrs Julian Lush; Brian MacDermot; Paul McDermott; Sir Iain Mackay-Dick; Dr Ian MacLennan; Lucinda McNeile; John Maggs; Mr and Mrs Harry Marshall; the late General Jacques Massu; Michael Meredith; the late Mrs Dorothy Middleton; the late Raoul Millais; the late John Grey Murray; Francis Nation-Dixon; Mr and Mrs Eric Newby; the Baroness Nicholson of Winterbourne; Michael O'Hanlon; the late Miss Sheila Parish; Nigel Pavitt; Jonathan Pegg; Miles Previtt; Mrs Florence Rossetti; Trevor Royle; the late Sir Anthony Rumbold and Lady Rumbold; Tahir Shah; Michael Shaw; Len Sheen; Andrew Sheepshanks; Mr and Mrs Robin Sheepshanks; John Shipman; the late Eric Shipton; Anthony Smith; the late Dame Freya Stark; the late Frank Steele and Mrs Frank Steele; Venetia Steele (Mrs Gavin Simmonds); Dr Deborah Stinson; the late Colonel David Stirling; Michael Street; Mrs Dorothy Tantrum; the late Roderic M.D. Thesiger and Mrs Roderic Thesiger; Colin Thubron; Dr Patrick Trevor-Roper; the late Sir Laurens van der Post; Robert Vavra; the late Sir John Verney and Lady Verney; Sebastian Verney; the late Tim Vigors; the late Mrs Majorie Villiers; the late Hamish Wallace; the late Graham Watson; Mr and Mrs George Webb; Miss Helen Webb; Miss Gritta Weil; Mr and Mrs Nigel de N. Winser; the late Gavin Young.

To my dear father and mother, the late Mr and Mrs William Maitland, I owe an immense debt of gratitude for everything they have done for me.

ACKNOWLEDGEMENTS

My wife Margaret, as always has given me invaluable advice, enthusiastic encouragement and constant support.

For their kind permission to quote from published and unpublished material, I wish to thank: Sir Mark Allen; Douglas Botting; Virginia Cowles; Curtis Brown Group Ltd; Sir Richard Dearlove; Pamela, Viscountess Egremont; Faber & Faber Ltd; Lt Col R.L.V. ffrench Blake; Hugh Leach; Longmans Ltd; Middle East Centre, St Anthony's College, Oxford, and the family of H. St John Philby; the Baroness Nicholson of Winterbourne; the Royal Geographical Society; the Seven Pillars of Wisdom Trust; John Shipman; Lady Verney; Sebastian Verney; Chisholm Wallace; George Webb; Gritta Weil.

I also wish to thank the College Librarian and the Archivist, Eton College Library, for their courteous and helpful assistance.

I gratefully acknowledge the advice and assistance of the Pitt Rivers Museum, University of Oxford, which now owns Sir Wilfred Thesiger's photographic archive.

Alexander Maitland
London, December 2005

NOTES

ABBREVIATIONS

BPT: Brian Peirson Thesiger
DVT: Dermot Vigors Thesiger
KMA: Kathleen Mary (Mrs Reginald)
    Astley (after October 1931)
KMT: The Hon Kathleen Mary Thesiger
    (until October 1931)
RMDT: Roderic Miles Doughty Thesiger
WGT: The Hon Wilfred Gilbert Thesiger
WT: Sir Wilfred Patrick Thesiger

ALIP: *Wilfred Thesiger: A Life in Pictures*
AS: *Arabian Sands*
ATM: *Among the Mountains*
AVW: *A Vanished World*
DD: *The Danakil Diary*
DMM: *Desert, Marsh and Mountain*
MKD: *My Kenya Days*
MLAT: *My Life and Travels*
TLMC: *The Life of My Choice*
TMA: *The Marsh Arabs*

INTRODUCTION
  1. WT verbatim: 1980
  2. KMA verbatim: 4 June 1964
  3. WT verbatim: 4 June 1964
  4. WT verbatim: October 1993. There
     were, eventually, more than seventy
     albums
  5. WT verbatim: 4 June 1964

ONE: *The Emperor Menelik's 'New Flower'*
  1. H. Vivian: *Through Lion Land to the
     Court of the Lion of Judah*, 1901: 168–9

  2. TLMC, 1987: 13
  3. H. Vivian: *Through Lion Land...*: 175
  4. Lord Hindlip: *Sport and Travel*, 1906:
     55
  5. Augustus B. Wylde: *Abyssinia*, 1901:
     416
  6. TLMC: 43
  7. WT North Abyssinia diary: 13 May
     1960
  8. TLMC: 43
  9. ibid.: 44
 10. ibid.

TWO: *Hope and Fortune*
  1. WGT to KMT: letter dated 1 March
     1911
  2. TLMC: 29
  3. Ernest Thesiger: *Practically True*,
     1927: 'From my father's family I
     inherited a love for music': 15. Lord
     Chelmsford played the clarinet,
     Ernest's father played the violin, his
     brothers 'both played stringed
     instruments' and his sister Sybil
     played the piano. Ernest took up the
     violin. He wrote: 'I have frequently
     regretted my choice, for a slight
     knowledge of the piano is always
     useful, whereas a violinist, unless he
     can devote plenty of time to practise,
     is a public nuisance': 15. Ernest's
     father, The Hon. Sir Edward Peirson
     Thesiger, was Clerk Assistant to the
     House of Lords and a member of the

orchestra of the Wandering Minstrels

4. Timothy Green: *The Adventurers*, 1970: 30–1
5. TLMC: 28, 30
6. WT verbatim: 1990
7. WGT archive: letter dated St Petersburg, 7 April 1907: 'My dear Mother ... You did not tell me what Percy arranged about the graves at St Peter le Poor's [sic]. I wonder there was no trace of John Andrew's grave.'
8. TLMC: 58
9. Sir John Verney to Alexander Maitland: letter dated 24 October 1983; and verbatim: Suffolk, 1984
10. TLMC: 80
11. ibid.
12. WT to KMA: letter dated 4 January 1940
13. WT verbatim: April 1997
14. ibid.
15. TLMC: 68
16. WGT archive
17. ibid.
18. TLMC: 68
19. WGT archive: 22 July 1896
20. ibid.: 19 April 1896
21. ibid.: 20 'somethingth' August 1896
22. ibid.: 24 September 1896; 20 May 1896
23. TLMC: 21
24. WGT archive: 5 February 1896
25. WGT archive
26. ibid.
27. DVT: 'Isis Idol' 812, *Isis* no. 867, 1 March 1933: 5
28. TLMC: 27–8
29. WGT archive: letter dated 17 July 1904
30. ibid.: letter dated 15 September 1904
31. ibid.: letter dated 20 January 1907
32. ibid.: letter dated 10 June 1907
33. WT verbatim: 1995
34. WT verbatim: October 1994
35. KMA archive
36. TLMC: 30
37. WT verbatim: October 1994
38. TLMC: 64
39. Tim Vigors, obituary, *The Times*
40. Lucinda McNeile verbatim: July 1992

THREE: *Gorgeous Barbarity*

1. WGT archive: 27 October 1909
2. TLMC: 24
3. ibid.
4. WGT archive: 11 November 1909
5. TLMC: 95
6. WT verbatim: 1995
7. TLMC: 25
8. WGT archive: letter dated 14 November 1909
9. ibid.: letter dated 29 November 1909
10. ibid.
11. KMA archive: ms memoir, nd (1910)
12. ibid.
13. ibid.
14. WGT archive: letter dated 23 December 1909
15. ibid.
16. TLMC: 27; and cf Chapter 1, note 7, re the palace and its hills
17. ibid.: 49
18. WGT archive: letter dated 18 December 1909
19. KMA archive: ms memoir nd (1910)
20. WGT archive: letter dated 18 December 1909
21. ibid.
22. KMA archive: ms memoir nd (1910)
23. C.F. Rey: *The Real Abyssinia*, 1927: 63
24. TLMC: 56
25. WGT archive: letter dated 14 May 1910
26. ibid.

FOUR: *'One Handsome Rajah'*

1. WGT archive: 4 June 1910
2. WGT archive: date 15 July 1910
3. Frank Champain to WT: letter dated 12 October 1927
4. TLMC: 45
5. ibid.: 45–6
6. Timothy Green: *The Adventurers*, 1970: 33

7. WT often used this phrase when he spoke of his early youth
8. TMA: 43–4
9. WT verbatim: 1964
10. ibid.
11. Green, 1970: 26
12. ibid.
13. C.H.M. Doughty-Wylie to KMT: letter dated 18 April 1915. The meaning is not quite clear, however, and it is possible that Doughty-Wylie might have been referring to one of Kathleen's ponies, 'Firecrest' or 'Redpoll', rather than Brian's reddish-fair hair
14. WT verbatim: 1979
15. TLMC: 61
16. Green, 1970: 33
17. MKD: 208
18. WT verbatim: 1995
19. KMA archive: ms memoir
20. MKD: 188
21. WT verbatim: c.1992
22. MKD: 1
23. TLMC: 46
24. ibid.
25. Pamela, Lady Egremont verbatim: 1997
26. TLMC: 62
27. ibid.: 295
28. WT verbatim: 1990
29. AS: 17
30. DMM, 1979: prelims
31. TLMC: 63
32. ibid.
33. WGT archive:
34. John Verney, *A Dinner of Herbs*, 1966: 31
35. TLMC: 47
36. WT verbatim: nd, but early to mid-1980s
37. E.S. Turner in the *London Review of Books*; Geoffrey Moorhouse in the *Daily Telegraph*
38. AS: 40
39. TLMC: 62
40. ibid.: 63
41. Letter in WT's copy of *Jock of the Bushveld*, 1907 (private collection)
42. ibid. In 1959 WT received a letter from G.M. Castle-Smith, who wrote: 'I met your father on the Sidamo frontier when I was DC Moyale, early in 1914. I was deputed to take him down to Nairobi. He had with him a fellow called Saphiro [sic] (a really terrific shot with a .450) and a Baroness Eschwega (I was told not to let the latter out of my sight!) I was myself due for leave and when we got to England I stayed with your father in South Wales. I later heard from my brother who was governor of Mongala province that the Baroness had been expelled from the Soudan [sic] and that she was the wife of a major in the German Emperor's bodyguard. She was an attractive girl and had long fair hair which she used on Safari to sew up any tears she might have in her clothing from thorns etc! At Lysamis [sic] I got your father his first Rhino and tried to catch her young one for him but without success as he was too strong and we couldn't hold him.' Letter dated 30 August 1959
43. A.W. Hodson: *Where Lion Reign*, 1927: 7

FIVE: *Passages to India and England*
1. TLMC: 48
2. WGT archive
3. TLMC: 48
4. ibid.: 51
5. ibid.: 53
6. ibid.: 56
7. ibid.
8. ibid.: 58
9. Geoffrey Archer: *Personal and Historical Memoirs of an East African Administrator*, 1963: 115
10. DMM: 19
11. WGT archive: letter dated 4 January 1918

12. ibid.
13. WT archive
14. TLMC: 59
15. ibid.: 61
16. DMM: 18
17. TLMC: 61
18. WGT archive: letter dated 12 March 1918
19. ibid.
20. ibid.
21. TLMC: 62
22. WGT archive: dated 20 December 1918
23. TLMC: 64
24. WT verbatim: 1965
25. TLMC: 64

SIX: *The Cold, Bleak English Downs*
1. WT verbatim: 1995
2. TLMC: 65
3. WGT archive: letter dated 20 June 1919
4. ibid.
5. WT verbatim: 30 October 1994
6. WGT archive: letters dated 29 July and 15 August 1919
7. ibid.: letter dated 29 July 1919
8. ibid.: letter dated 15 September 1919
9. ibid.: letter dated 24 September 1919
10. WT verbatim: 27 October 1994
11. TLMC: 68
12. Gavin Maxwell: *A Reed Shaken by the Wind*, 1957: 3
13. WT verbatim: 1964
14. DMM: 19
15. WT verbatim: 1994
16. ibid.
17. TLMC: 66
18. DMM: 19
19. TLMC: 67
20. DMM: 19
21. Ernest Thesiger: *Practically True*, 1927: 3
22. E.M. Lang to KMT: dated 4 June 1920
23. TLMC: 63
24. ibid.

25. WT verbatim: 27 October 1994
26. WT to KMT: letter dated March 1920
27. BPT to KMT: letter dated 30 January 1921
28. TLMC: 67
29. ibid.
30. DMM: 6,7
31. Green, 1970: 35
32. TLMC: 67
33. BPT to KMT: letter dated November 1922
34. BPT to KMT: letter undated (but c.1921)
35. R.C.V. Lang to WGT: letter dated 17 December 1919
36. R.C.V. Lang to KMT: letter dated 20 March 1920
37. R.C.V. Lang to KMT: letter dated 9 December 1920
38. R.C.V. Lang to KMT: letter dated 21 April 1920
39. R.C.V. Lang to KMT: letter dated 24 October 1921
40. WT to KMT: letter postmarked 10 February 1921
41. WT verbatim: 18 January 1995
42. WT verbatim: 13 November 2000
43. TLMC: 67
44. Green, 1970: 35
45. WT ms archive; TLMC: 68
46. TLMC: 79; and MCC membership certificate (private collection)
47. TLMC: 65
48. WT Milebrook diary: entry dated 8 August 1922 (private collection)
49. ibid.: entry dated 26 August 1922; Sir John Verney to Alexander Maitland, letter dated 25 June 1984: 'Dear Alex … I'm pleased you visited Roddy & saw the early environment. Stow [sic] Hill … what memories of 50 years ago! love John'

SEVEN: *Eton: Lasting Respect and Veneration*
1. TLMC: 69
2. WT verbatim: 9 February 1995

3. ibid.
4. ibid.
5. TLMC: 73
6. ibid.: 72
7. ibid.: 73
8. ibid.
9. Lt Col R.L.V. ffrench Blake verbatim: May 1984
10. WT verbatim: 1994
11. ibid.
12. On 5 October 1949 'Cob' Bevan wrote a letter praising Thesiger's wireless broadcast, published in the *Listener*
13. TLMC: 72; and WT verbatim: 1995
14. Green, 1970: 36
15. TLMC: 97
16. WT to KMT: letter postmarked 15 February 1924
17. TLMC: 71
18. ibid.: 60
19. WT verbatim: 1995
20. WT to KMT: letter postmarked 19 November 1923
21. WT to KMT: letter postmarked 27 November 1923
22. ibid.
23. WT to KMT: letter dated 7 July 1924
24. TLMC: 23
25. ibid.
26. WT to KMT: letter dated 7 July 1924
27. WT verbatim: 1979

EIGHT: *Shrine of my Youth*
1. TLMC: 76, 98
2. ibid.: 77
3. ibid.: 295; Aldington, 1960: 31
4. W. Bynner: *Journey with Genius*, 1953: 281
5. D.H. Lawrence: 'Assorted Articles', in ibid.: 245
6. WT verbatim: 30 October 1994
7. TLMC: 80
8. ibid.: 79
9. TLMC: 79
10. ibid.: 80
11. Corbin, 1978: 4, in G. Marvin: *Bullfight*, 1988: 144

12. WT verbatim: 11 September 1995
13. DVT, 'Isis Idol', *Isis* 867, 1933: 5; in Green, 1970: 41
14. WT archive
15. TLMC: 79
16. ibid.
17. WT to KMT: nd (but October 1930): 'The Rampura is the last word in luxury ... There are a good many celebrities ... on board including Clara Butt, her husband Hobbs Sutcliffe and a Rajah or two ... HRH had Clara Butt and her husband to dinner one night.' Writing in 1927, Ernest Thesiger described seeing Dame Clara Butt for the first time. One night he was leaning against the door of the music room in a house in Kensington, staring at a tall girl with a chain of coloured stones in her hair, who was standing opposite him. He was wondering who she was when his host came to lead her to the piano. He heard him turn to someone standing near and whisper, '"A new discovery!" The tall girl stood by the piano and shut her eyes, then started to sing Somervell's Shepherd's Lullaby. I don't think that anyone who heard Clara Butt that night will ever forget it, and never since had her glorious voice thrilled me more than it did when she sang that simple song' (*Practically True*: 22–3). Instead, WT had been fascinated by the view from the Suez Canal and beyond. He wrote: 'You really feel you have got East at last ... rather a lovely sunset over the marshes and desert. The next morning ... the Red Sea Hills and the Arabian coast ... grim and forbidding but rather alluring' (WT to KMT: nd but Saturday, October 1930)
18. DD: 1
19. WT verbatim: October 1992

20. DVT, 'Isis Idol', *Isis* 867, 1933: 5
21. DD: 2, entry dated 27 October 1930
22. WT to KMT: letter dated 5 November 1930 (Guy Fawkes Night)
23. TLMC: 93
24. WT to BPT: letter dated 12 November 1930
25. TLMC: 93
26. WT to KMT: letter dated 10 November 1930
27. WT verbatim: 13 November 2000
28. WT verbatim: c.1993
29. WT to KMT: letter dated 30 October 1930
30. WT to KMT: letter dated 12 November 1930
31. WT to KMT: letter dated 30 October 1930
32. Sir S.P. Barton, press cuttings: *Birmingham Post*, 30 September 1930 (private collection)
33. TLMC: 91
34. WT to KMT: letter dated 30 October 1930
35. WT to KMT: letter dated 10 November 1930
36. E. Waugh: *Remote People*, 1931: 47
37. TLMC: 92
38. Waugh, 1931: 29
39. ibid.: 64
40. ibid.: 38
41. WT to KMT: letter dated 15 November 1930
42. WT verbatim: 1995; cf DD: 14
43. WT to KMT: letter dated 15 November 1930
44. WT to KMT: letter dated 10 November 1930
45. ibid.
46. *Geographical Journal* CXIII, June 1949: 45
47. WT verbatim: 1994
48. ibid.
49. DD: 37
50. ibid.
51. WT to KMT; and cf letter dated 10 November 1930
52. WT to KMT: letter dated 15 November 1930
53. WT to KMT: letter dated 10 November 1930
54. DD: 37
55. WT to KMT: letter dated 15 November 1930
56. ibid.
57. DD: 15, entry dated 17 November 1930
58. ibid.: 28, 29, entry dated 5 December 1930

NINE: *The Mountains of Arussi*
1. WT verbatim: 1995
2. Geoffrey Moorhouse: *The Fearful Void*, 1974: 31. WT always laughed at DVT's favourite story about the MP who had been awarded a VC in the First World War. Asked who was the bravest man he had ever known, the MP replied: 'My batman. He was never more than a yard behind me.'
3. Green, 1970: 40
4. WT verbatim: 17 October 1994
5. WT: *Visions of a Nomad*, 1987: 12
6. WT verbatim: 1995
7. TLMC: 98
8. ibid.: 98–9
9. ibid.: 295
10. R.P. Ross to WT, letter dated 28 July 1931 (private collection)
11. WT Milebrook diary: entries dated 20 and 21 August 1931 (private collection)
12. ibid.: entry dated 6 October 1931
13. ibid.: entry dated 7 October 1931
14. WT verbatim: 24 January 1995. He added: 'I think [Reggie] felt rather swamped by all of us.'
15. ibid.
16. TLMC: 100
17. WT verbatim: 1965
18. TLMC: 199
19. ibid.: 102
20. Sir Anthony Rumbold verbatim: 1984

21. WT verbatim: 1979
22. ibid.
23. WT verbatim: 1994
24. ibid.
25. ALIP: 17
26. Aldington, 1960: 33
27. TLMC: 101
28. ibid.
29. Green, 1970: 37
30. WT verbatim: 1989
31. TLMC: 97
32. ibid.: 78
33. ibid.
34. TLMC: 103
35. WT verbatim: 1995
36. WT archive
37. Dr S.A. Neave to WT: letter dated 23 August 1933
38. Sir Sidney Barton to WT: letter dated 6 June 1933
39. Secretary of the RGS to Sir Sidney Barton: letter dated 23 August 1933
40. TLMC: 97
41. ALIP: 19
42. TLMC: 92
43. WT verbatim: 1979
44. Robert Robertson talking to Mr and Mrs William Maitland: Pitlochry, c.1996
45. Col Dan Sandford to WT: letter dated 8 June 1933
46. DD: 39. WT wrote 'Omar', 'Umr', or 'Umar'. Sandford's headman signed himself 'Omar'. See his letter to WT dated 8 August 1934 (private collection)
47. Sandford to WT: letter dated 8 June 1933
48. Sandford to Omar Ibrahim: letter dated 13 July 1933
49. Sandford to WT: letter dated 14 July 1933
50. DD: 41
51. WT Milebrook diary: entry dated 18 April 1933 (private collection)
52. WT verbatim: c.1995
53. DD: 34
54. ibid.: 42
55. ibid.: 41
56. WT: 'Notes on the Blue Winged Goose', unpub. ms, 1933 (private collection)
57. David Haig-Thomas's diary 1933: entry dated 3 October (private collection)
58. ibid.: entry dated 5 October
59. DD: 44–5
60. David Haig-Thomas's diary 1933
61. DD: 45
62. ibid.: 44
63. WT: Abyssinia 'Mammals', 1933 (private collection)
64. WT: Abyssinia 'Plants', 1933 (private collection)
65. DD: 47
66. ibid.: 117
67. ibid.: 118
68. ibid.
69. DD: 64
70. Oxford University Exploration Club: Sixth Annual Report, 1933–1934: 3–4

TEN: *Across the Sultanate of Aussa*
1. WT verbatim: 1995
2. DMM: 23
3. TLMC: 120
4. ibid.: 167
5. ibid.: 168
6. WT verbatim: c.1996
7. WT to KMA: letter dated 26 November 1933
8. ibid.
9. WT to BPT: letter dated 23 January 1934
10. WT to DVT: letter dated 27 November 1933
11. WT to KMA: letter dated 26 November 1933. WT's 'trusty .450', given to him by his mother, was a double-barrelled, sidelock .450 Nitro Express by John Rigby, London. He used this rifle to hunt dangerous big game, such as elephant and lion, in the Sudan

12. WT to KMA: letter dated 26–27 November 1933
13. WT to KMA: letter dated 26 November 1933
14. WT to KMA: letter dated 27 November 1933
15. WT's review of *Desert and Forest* by L.M. Nesbitt, *Geographical Journal*, 1934: 527–8
16. WT verbatim: 1969
17. 'The Awash River and the Aussa Sultanate', *Geographical Journal* LXXXV, 1935: 1–19
18. *Ibis*, October 1935: 774
19. ibid.
20. WGT to Lady Chelmsford: letter dated 7 November 1909
21. WT to KMA: letter dated 8 December 1933
22. *Geographical Journal* LXXXV, 1935: 1–19
23. TLMC: 125
24. *Geographical Journal* LXXXV, 1935: 1–19
25. WT verbatim: 1994
26. WT to KMA: letter dated 23 December 1933
27. ibid.
28. WT to KMA: letter dated 22 January 1934
29. WT to KMA: letter dated 30 January 1934
30. WT to KMA: letter dated 22 January 1934
31. ibid.
32. WT to KMA: letter dated 5 February 1934
33. WT to KMA: letter dated 7 February 1934
34. WT to KMA: letter dated 31 January 1934
35. *Geographical Journal* LXXXV, 1935: 1–19
36. ibid.
37. TLMC: 135
38. ibid.; and WT to George Gordon (President of Magdalen College

Oxford): letter dated 24 January 1934
39. TLMC: 135
40. WT to BPT: letter dated 23 January 1934
41. AS, reprint 2000: 11
42. WT to KMA: letter dated 15 April 1934
43. ibid.
44. WT to Sandford: letter dated 30 April 1934
45. WT to KMA: letter dated 15 April 1934
46. TLMC: 145
47. AS, reprint 2000: 12–13
48. TLMC: 154
49. DD: 178
50. *Geographical Journal* LXXXV, 1935: 18
51. WT to RMDT: letter dated 27 November 1933
52. *Geographical Journal* LXXXV, 1935: 19
53. ibid.
54. Sandford to KMA: letter dated 17 February 1934
55. ibid.
56. Sandford to KMA: letter dated 12 March 1934
57. Sandford to KMA: letter dated 17 February 1934
58. DD: 204
59. *Geographical Journal* LXXXV, 1935 (discussion): 22
60. WT to KMA: letter dated 5 May 1934
61. ibid.
62. DD: 204
63. ibid.: 230
64. Alan Houghton Brodrick: *The Abbé Breuil, Prehistorian*, 1963: 177
65. ibid.
66. DD: 204
67. Brodrick, 1963: 179–80
68. DD: 204
69. Omar Ibrahim to WT: letter dated 8 August 1934 (private collection)
70. *Geographical Journal* LXXXV, 1935 (discussion): 20

71. ibid.: 1–19
72. WT to KMA: letter dated 5 May 1934
73. DD: 204
74. ibid.: 198

ELEVEN: *Savage Sudan*
1. WT verbatim: c.1995; and cf WT to RMDT: letter dated 27 June 1935: 'I have been reading Rupert Brooke a great deal lately and the more I read of his the more attracted I am. He must have been a fascinating person to have known.'
2. WT verbatim: c.1979
3. TLMC: 66–7
4. ibid.: 67
5. WT verbatim: 1994
6. TLMC: 67
7. WT verbatim: c.1995
8. WT verbatim: 1965; and cf AS: 2: 'The Empty Quarter offered me the chance to win distinction as a traveller ...' (reprint 2000)
9. WT verbatim: 1993
10. Michael Asher: *Thesiger*, 1994: 112
11. TLMC: 70. (In 1968 Sir Julian Hall remembered WT at Eton, but did not mention that he had caned him.)
12. DD: 203
13. Odette Keun: *A Foreigner Looks at the British Sudan*, 1930: 49–50
14. ibid.: 51–2
15. WT verbatim: 1965
16. WT to KMA: letter dated 24 March 1935: 'Could you order 6 pairs of khaki stockings from Fortnum and Masons for me'
17. WT verbatim: 1995
18. WT undated ms (private collection)
19. WT verbatim: to John Guest at the Travellers Club: 1965
20. WT ms note (private collection)
21. TLMC: 191
22. K.D. Henderson: *The Making of Modern Sudan*, 1953: 112
23. TLMC: 171
24. ibid.: 187
25. ibid.
26. TLMC: 172
27. ibid.: 182
28. WT to KMA: letter dated 14 January 1935
29. WT to KMA: letter dated 20 January 1935
30. J.G. Millais: foreword to H.C. Brocklehurst: *Game Animals of the Sudan*, 1931: xviii
31. ibid.: xix
32. WT verbatim: 1979
33. A.B. Percival: *A Game Ranger's Notebook*, 1924: 56
34. TLMC: 175
35. WT verbatim: 1993
36. TLMC: 183
37. WT to KMA: letter dated 20 January 1935
38. WT to KMA: letter dated 20 June 1935
39. TLMC: 183
40. ibid.: 186
41. WT to KMA: letter dated 8 February 1935
42. WT to KMA: letter dated 21 February 1935
43. WT to KMA: letter dated 15 March 1935
44. WT verbatim: 9 February 1995
45. WT verbatim: 1979
46. A. de Saint-Exupéry: *Wind, Sand and Stars*, 1941: 36
47. P. Cabanne: *Dialogues with Marcel Duchamp* (trans. R. Padgett), 1987
48. Green, 1970: 48
49. TLMC: 186
50. WT to KMA: letter dated 19 July 1935
51. WT verbatim: nd but an emphatic expression he often used
52. WT to KMA: letter dated 10 July 1935
53. ibid.
54. TLMC: 187
55. WT to KMA: letter dated 14 February 1935

56. TLMC: 190
57. ibid.
58. WT to KMA: letter dated 14 February 1935
59. WT verbatim: 1993
60. Lion skulls shown to Alexander Maitland by Daphne M. Hills, Curator Mammal Group, Dept of Zoology, Natural History Museum, South Kensington, 4 October 2004
61. TLMC: 193
62. WT to RMDT: letter dated 15 March 1935
63. WT to KMA: letter dated 15 March 1935
64. TLMC: 193
65. WT to KMA: letter dated 9 August 1935
66. ibid.
67. WT to KMA: letter dated 30 May 1935
68. WT to KMA: 9 June 1935
69. WT verbatim: 1993
70. WT to KMA: letter dated 31 December 1935
71. Green, 1970: 48
72. TLMC: 295
73. WT to KMA: letter dated 30 May 1935
74. TLMC: 199
75. ibid.
76. ibid.: 198
77. WT to KMA: letter dated 30 May 1935
78. TLMC: 198
79. ibid.
80. WT to KMA: letter dated 30 May 1935
81. TLMC: 200
82. WT to BPT: 30 May 1935
83. ibid.
84. TLMC: 201
85. ibid.
86. WT to KMA: 9 June 1935
87. WT verbatim: 1965
88. Verney: *A Dinner of Herbs*, 1966: 88

89. WT to KMA: letter dated 30 May 1935
90. ibid.
91. WT to KMA: letter dated 19 July 1935
92. WT to KMA: letter dated 19 June 1935
93. TLMC: 193
94. WT verbatim: 1964
95. WT to KMA: letter dated 13 August 1935
96. WT to KMA: letter dated 16 September 1935
97. WT to KMA: letter dated 30 January 1935
98. WT to KMA: letter dated 16 September 1935
99. WT to KMA: letter dated 20 January 1935
100. WT to KMA: letter dated 16 September 1935
101. ibid.
102. WT to KMA: letter dated 20 January 1935
103. WT to KMA: letter dated 13 August 1935
104. WT to KMA: letter dated 20 September 1935
105. WT to KMA: letter dated 31 December 1935
106. TLMC: 210
107. ibid.
108. ibid. 398
109. WT to KMA: letter dated 31 December 1935
110. ibid.
111. ibid.
112. TLMC: 213
113. ibid.: 214
114. WT to KMA: letter dated 31 December 1935
115. TLMC: 214
116. ibid.: 207
117. ibid.
118. MKD: 132
119. WT to RMDT: letter dated 15 July 1936

120. TLMC: 207
121. WT's Samburu adoptive 'son', Lawi Leboyare, talking to WT at Laputa Lekakwar's house, near Maralal, Kenya, April 1993
122. TLMC: 216
123. WT verbatim: 1988
124. WT to KMA: letter dated 31 December 1935
125. ibid.
126. WT to KMA: letter dated 24 November 1935
127. WT verbatim; and *Visions of a Nomad*, 1987: 10
128. WT to KMA: letter dated 24 November 1935
129. ibid.
130. *Sudan Notes and Records* XXII (i), 1939: 157
131. TLMC: 239
132. WT to KMA: letter dated 13 June 1936
133. TLMC: 239
134. WT to KMA: letter dated 13 June 1936
135. ibid.
136. TLMC: 240
137. WT to R.B. Astley: letter dated 15 July 1936; Vyvyan Richards: *Portrait of T.E. Lawrence*, 1936: 12–13
138. WT to KMA: letter dated 21 June 1936
139. TLMC: 240
140. Major C.S. Jarvis: *Arab Command* (4th imp), 1943: 6
141. TLMC: 240
142. ibid.: 241
143. ibid.: 242
144. WT verbatim: 1979
145. TLMC: 205
146. ibid.: 208
147. WT to KMA: letter dated 12 April 1937
148. Vivienne de Watteville: *Speak to the Earth*, 1935 (reprint 1985, Introduction by Alexander Maitland: xxiii)
149. WT to KMA: letter dated 3 November 1938
150. TLMC: 293
151. WT to KMA: letter dated 8 June 1937
152. TLMC: 257
153. WT to KMA: letter dated 21 July 1937
154. WT to KMA: letter dated 25 August 1937
155. WT verbatim: 2001; cf MLAT, Introduction by Alexander Maitland: 7
156. WT to KMA: letter dated 15 March 1935
157. WT to KMA: letter dated 3 September 1936
158. WT to KMA: letter dated 21 July 1937
159. TLMC: 216
160. ibid.: 217
161. WT verbatim: c.1994
162. WT to KMA: letter dated 20 November 1936
163. WT verbatim: cf August 2002 (see Epilogue)
164. TLMC: 249–50
165. WT to KMA: letter dated 5 June 1937
166. WT to DVT: letter apparently misdated 29 April 1937, corrected by WT to 29 May 1937
167. WT ms report (private collection)
168. TLMC: 217–18
169. WT ms report (private collection)
170. WT to KMA: letter dated 30 March 1937
171. WT to KMA: letter dated 25 August 1937
172. WT verbatim: 1977
173. TLMC: 248
174. WT verbatim: 1997
175. WT to KMA: letter dated 6 April 1937
176. TLMC: 248–9
177. Guy Moore to KMA: letter dated 20 December 1937

178. WT to KMA: letter dated 25 August 1937
179. WT to KMA: letter dated 10 September 1936
180. TLMC: 251
181. Mark Leather: ms dated 19 August 1937 (private collection)
182. WT to KMA: letter dated 19 August 1937
183. TLMC: 258
184. ibid.: 257
185. ibid.: 257–8

TWELVE: *The Nuer*
1. DD: 1
2. WT verbatim: 1995
3. WT to KMA: letter dated 8 February 1938
4. Captain V.H. Fergusson *et al.*: *The Story of Fergie Bey*, 1930: 295
5. WT verbatim: 1995
6. E. Evans-Pritchard: *The Nuer*, 1940: 3
7. ibid.: 55
8. ibid.: 3
9. TLMC: 273
10. ibid.: 266
11. WT to KMA: letter dated 10 July 1938
12. TLMC: 266
13. Michael Shaw verbatim: c.1998
14. DVT, 'Isis Idol', *Isis* 867, 1933: 5
15. TLMC: 259
16. WT to KMA: letter dated 26 December 1937
17. TLMC: 260–1
18. ibid.
19. WT to KMA: letter dated 26 December 1937
20. WT to KMA: letter dated 19 December 1937
21. WT to KMA: letter dated 8 January 1939
22. WT to RMDT: letter dated 19 January 1939
23. WT to KMA: letter dated 16 January 1938
24. TLMC: 268
25. ibid.
26. ibid.: 272–3
27. ibid.: 273
28. ibid.: 268
29. ibid.
30. WT to KMA: letter dated 2 March 1938
31. ibid.
32. WT to DVT: 1 April 1938
33. WT to DVT: 8 February 1938
34. WT to KMA: letter dated 17 July 1938
35. WT to DVT: letter dated 1 April 1938
36. WT verbatim: c.1998
37. TLMC: 275
38. ibid.
39. WT verbatim: 1995. Alexander Maitland helped WT to search for the stock of the .350 Rigby-Magnum. WT sold his .350 Magnum for £30 and his .450 Nitro Express for £120, both to Rigby, on 3 July 1969
40. WT to KMA: letter dated 11 April 1938
41. ibid.
42. WT to KMA: letter dated 3 June 1938 (WT's twenty-eighth birthday)
43. ibid.
44. WT to KMA: 16 July 1938
45. WT verbatim: c.1965
46. WT to KMA: letter dated 16 July 1938
47. WT to KMA: letter dated 1 April 1938
48. WT to KMA: letter dated 16 July 1938
49. ibid.
50. WT to KMA: letter dated 7 June 1938
51. ibid.
52. ibid.
53. WT to KMA: letter dated 5 May 1938
54. TLMC: 276
55. ibid.
56. ibid.
57. WT to KMA: letter dated 18 May 1938

58. WT to KMA: letter dated 5 May 1938
59. WT to KMA: letter dated 8 February 1938
60. WT to KMA: letter dated 18 May 1938
61. ibid.
62. WT to DVT: letter dated 30 November 1938
63. Gustav Nachtigal: *Sahara and Sudan*, vol 1, 1879 (trans. A.G.B. Fisher and H.J. Fisher, new edn 1974), quoted in ALIP: 29
64. *Geographical Journal* XCIV (6)
65. TLMC: 246
66. WT to KMA: letter dated 19 August 1938
67. WT to KMA: letter dated 30 July 1938
68. ibid.
69. WT to KMA: letter dated 19 August 1938
70. WT Tibesti diary 1938: entry dated 7 August
71. TLMC: 294
72. ibid.: 291
73. ibid.: 295
74. ibid.: 294
75. WT verbatim 1995: and cf TLMC: 358
76. WT to KMA: letter dated 19 August 1938
77. ibid.
78. WT undated ms (private collection)
79. Bynner, 1953: 281
80. WT to KMA: letter dated 19 August 1938
81. TLMC: 282
82. *Geographical Journal* XCIV (6), 1939: 437
83. ibid.: 437–8
84. ibid.: 438–9
85. ibid.: 439
86. ibid.: 438
87. WT to KMA: letter dated 19 August 1938
88. WT to KMA: letter dated 6 November 1938
89. ibid.
90. WT Tibesti diary 1938: entry dated 21 September
91. ibid.: entry dated 14 September
92. ibid.: entry dated 15 September
93. TLMC: 288
94. WT Tibesti diary 1938: entry dated 16 September
95. TLMC: 289
96. WT Tibesti diary 1938: entry dated 16 September; and TLMC: 288
97. WT Tibesti diary 1938: entry dated 16 September
98. TLMC: 289
99. WT to KMA: letter dated 6 November 1938
100. ibid.
101. *Geographical Journal* XCIV (6), 1939: 443
102. ibid.
103. WT to KMA: 6 November 1938
104. General Jacques Massu to Alexander Maitland: letter dated 8 June 1998
105. WT verbatim: 1998
106. TLMC: 290
107. WT Tibesti diary 1938: entry dated 11 October
108. ibid.: entry dated 12 October
109. WT to KMA: letter dated 6 November 1938
110. ibid.
111. TLMC: 294
112. de Saint-Exupéry, 1941: 21
113. AS (reprint 2000): 20
114. WT to KMA: letter dated 28 December 1938
115. WT to RMDT: letter dated 28 November 1938
116. WT verbatim: c.1988
117. WT to DVT: letter dated 30 November 1938
118. WT verbatim: c.1988
119. WT to KMA: letter dated 19 November 1938
120. WT to KMA: letter dated 23 November 1938
121. TLMC: 432

122. WT verbatim: 13 November 2000
123. WT to KMA: letter dated 30 November 1938
124. TLMC: 261
125. WT to KMA: letter dated 30 November 1938
126. WT to KMA: letter dated 22 December 1938
127. TLMC: 258
128. WT to KMA: letter dated 22 February 1939
129. TLMC: 302
130. WT to KMA: letter dated 12 April 1939
131. WT to KMA: letter dated 3 June 1939 (WT's twenty-ninth birthday)
132. TLMC: 101
133. WT to DVT: letter dated 30 November 1938
134. WT to KMA: letter dated 23 November 1938
135. WT to KMA: letter dated 12 April 1939
136. WT to KMA: letter dated 19 November 1938
137. WT to KMA: letter dated 4 April 1939
138. WT to KMA: letter dated 23 March 1939
139. ibid.
140. WT to KMA: letter dated 8 January 1939
141. TLMC: 302
142. WT to KMA: letter dated 8 January 1939
143. WT to KMA: letter dated 7 February 1939
144. TLMC: 301
145. WT verbatim: c.1965
146. WT to KMA: letter dated 7 February 1939
147. WT to KMA: letter dated 22 February 1939
148. WT to KMA: letter dated 7 February 1939
149. ibid.
150. WT verbatim: he varied this sometimes, saying that he 'craved the past, resented the present and dreaded the future'
151. WT to KMA: letter dated 7 February 1939
152. TLMC: 306

THIRTEEN: *Rape of my Homeland*
1. TLMC: 305
2. WT verbatim: 1965
3. WT to KMA: letter dated 10 May 1939
4. WT to KMA: letter dated 3 June 1939
5. WT to DVT: letter dated 4 October 1939
6. WT to KMA: letter dated 16 September 1939
7. TLMC: 305
8. WT to KMA: letter dated 4 October 1939
9. TLMC: 235
10. WT to KMA: 2 December 1939
11. ibid.
12. Anthony Mockler: *Haile Selassie's War*, 1984: 338
13. Col Sir Hugh Boustead: *The Wind of Morning*, 1972: 149
14. MKD: 170
15. WT to KMA: letter dated 12 January 1940
16. WT to KMA: letter dated 27 March 1940
17. Sir David Attenborough: 1976
18. WT verbatim: 1992
19. WT verbatim: 1992
20. WT to KMA: 1 May 1940
21. ibid.
22. Mockler, 1984: 217
23. TLMC: 311
24. ibid.: 345
25. ibid.: 323
26. Mockler, 1984: 217
27. TLMC: 313
28. WT to KMA: letter dated 31 May 1940
29. Frank Steele verbatim: 1992. Steele

described an incident during his trek
with WT in 1961 to Lake Rudolf and
Marsabit in the former Northern
Frontier District of Kenya

30. Christine Sandford: *The Lion of
Judah Hath Prevailed*, 1955: 79
31. TLMC: 235
32. ibid.
33. ibid.
34. Green, 1970: 53
35. TLMC: 314
36. ibid.: 183
37. WT to KMA: letter dated 27 July
1940
38. WT to KMA: letter dated 11 October
1940
39. *The Abyssinian Campaigns*, HMSO
1942: 28
40. WT archive: unidentified newspaper
report
41. WT to KMA: letter dated 10 July
1940
42. WT archive: unidentified newspaper
report
43. TLMC: 314
44. ibid.: 315
45. Mockler, 1984: 195
46. TLMC: 315
47. ibid.
48. WT ms undated (private collection)
49. WT to KMA: letter dated 5
November 1940
50. WT verbatim: c.1988
51. TLMC: 235
52. WT verbatim: c.1988
53. WT verbatim: 1995
54. TLMC: 237
55. ibid.: 92
56. WT verbatim: 20 February 1995:
'Evelyn Waugh is a bastard'
57. TLMC: 318
58. ibid.
59. Mockler, 1984: 195
60. Christopher Sykes: *Orde Wingate*,
1959: 271
61. TLMC: 318
62. ibid.: 334

63. ibid.: 330
64. ibid. 353
65. WT verbatim: 1979
66. TLMC: 320
67. ibid.: 333
68. WT verbatim: 1988
69. TLMC: 333
70. Sykes, 1959: 110
71. Judges VII.6
72. Leonard Mosley: *Gideon goes to War*,
1955: 67
73. ibid.: 69
74. TLMC: 333
75. ibid.: 326
76. ibid.: 321
77. ibid.
78. AS (reprint 2000): 21–2
79. WT verbatim: c.1988
80. WT to KMA: letter dated 3
September 1940
81. ibid.
82. TLMC: 332
83. ibid.: 350
84. Mosley, 1955: 69
85. Julian Prichard to KMA: letter dated
6 April 1941
86. Green, 1970: 54
87. ibid.: 55
88. ibid.
89. WT verbatim: c.1996
90. TLMC: 339
91. ibid.: 345
92. ibid.: 344
93. Green, 1970: 56
94. TLMC: 346–7
95. ibid.: 347
96. ibid.
97. WT ms archive: review by W.E.D.
Allen, nd (1955) (private collection)
98. ibid.
99. TLMC: 348
100. ibid.

FOURTEEN: *Among the Druze*
1. TLMC: 349
2. WT to KMA: 18 January 1942
3. TLMC: 351

4. ibid.: 351

5. ibid.: 352

6. ibid.: 355

7. WT to KMA: letter dated 17 August 1941

8. WT to KMA: letter dated 27 July 1941

9. ibid.

10. ibid.

11. TLMC: 360

12. WT to KMA: letter dated 17 August 1941

13. TLMC: 358

14. Lt Col R.L.V. ffrench Blake verbatim: May 1984

15. TLMC: 361

16. WT verbatim: c.1996

17. WT verbatim: c.1965

18. WT to KMA: letter dated 12 May 1941

19. TLMC: 367

20. WT to KMA: letter dated 17 August 1941

21. WT to KMA: letter dated 25 November 1941

22. TLMC: 364

23. ibid.: 368

24. WT to KMA: letter dated 8 November 1941

25. TLMC: 365

26. WT to KMA: letter dated 25 December 1941

27. TLMC: 365

28. WT to KMA: letter dated 27 December 1941

29. MKD: 8

30. ibid.: 207

31. WT verbatim: 1964

32. KMA Syria diary 1954: entry dated 27 October (private collection)

33. WT verbatim: an often repeated remark, no specific date

34. WT to KMA: letter dated 27 December 1941

35. ibid.

36. WT to KMA: letter dated 10 January 1942

37. TLMC: 368

38. WT to KMA: letter dated 10 January 1942

39. WT to KMA: letter dated 10 April 1942

40. WT to KMA: letter dated 9 March 1942

41. WT to KMA: letter dated 10 April 1942

42. TLMC: 367

43. WT to KMA: letter dated 10 April 1942

44. AS (reprint 2000): 22

45. George Washington Chasseaud: *The Druses of Lebanon*, 1855: 384, 385

46. WT to KMA: letter dated 25 February 1942

47. WT to KMA: letter dated 16 September 1941

48. WT to KMA: letter dated 14 December 1941

49. WT to KMA: letter dated 8 November 1941

50. TLMC: 101

51. Nicolette Devas: *Two Flamboyant Fathers*, 1966: 234

52. WT to KMA: letter dated 4 June 1942

53. WT to KMA: letter dated 14 May 1942

54. WT to KMA: letter dated 4 June 1942

55. ibid.

56. WT to KMA: letter dated 2 July 1942

57. TLMC: 101

58. WT to KMA: 13 July 1942

59. WT verbatim: 1995

60. WT to KMA: 13 July 1942. The text introducing Dermot's memorial service, Isaiah 32:1.2, contains the phrase the 'weary land', later one of many titles suggested by WT as a title for *Arabian Sands*

61. Humphrey Brooke to KMA: letter dated 2 May 1942 (private collection)

62. TLMC: 368

63. ibid.: 360–1

FIFTEEN: *The Flowering Desert*

1. WT to KMA: letter dated 21 June 1942
2. TLMC: 369–72
3. WT to KMA: letter dated 27 June 1942
4. ibid.
5. TLMC: 372
6. WT to KMA: letter dated 4 September 1942
7. WT to KMA: letter dated 25 September 1942
8. WT to KMA: letter dated 5 October 1942
9. ibid.
10. ibid.
11. WT to KMA: letter dated 9 September 1942
12. WT to KMA: letter dated 8 November 1942
13. TLMC: 373–4
14. WT to KMA: letter dated 8 November 1942
15. TLMC: 374
16. WT to KMA: letter dated 15 November 1942
17. WT to KMA: letter dated 21 November 1942
18. WT to KMA: letter dated 18 October 1942
19. WT to KMA: letter dated 8 November 1942
20. Virginia Cowles: *The Phantom Major*, 1958: 23
21. TLMC: 375
22. WT to KMA: letter dated 18 November 1942
23. ibid.
24. WT verbatim: 1992
25. WT to KMA: letter dated 15 November 1942
26. TLMC: 374
27. WT to KMA: letter dated 18 November 1942
28. Col David Stirling verbatim: August 1983 and 6 June 1990
29. Asher: *Thesiger*, 1994: 224
30. WT verbatim: 1994
31. WT to KMA: letter dated 21 November 1942
32. TLMC: 376
33. ibid.
34. WT to KMA: letter dated 15 November 1942
35. TLMC: 382
36. WT to KMA: letter dated 18 February 1943
37. Asher, 1994: 218
38. ibid.
39. TLMC: 377
40. ibid.: 378
41. ibid.: 379
42. ibid.
43. WT verbatim: 1995
44. TLMC: 381
45. Cowles, 1958: 278–9
46. WT to KMA: letter dated 19 February 1943
47. WT to KMA: letter dated 7 May 1943
48. TLMC: 382
49. WT to KMA: letter dated 7 May 1943
50. TLMC: 383
51. WT to KMA: letter dated 7 May 1943
52. TLMC: 384
53. WT to KMA: letter dated 7 May 1943
54. ATM: 3
55. ibid.: 182
56. WT to KMA: letter dated 21 April 1943
57. WT to KMA: letter dated 10 May 1943

SIXTEEN: *Palestine: Shifting Lights and Shades*

1. WT to KMA: letter dated 15 July 1943
2. TLMC: 387
3. WT to KMA: letter dated 15 July 1943
4. WT to KMA: letter dated 19 May 1943
5. ibid.
6. WT verbatim: phrases repeated by him in books and in conversation

7. WT to KMA: letter dated 21 April 1943
8. WT to KMA: letter dated 20 May 1943
9. WT to KMA: letter dated 29 May 1943
10. TLMC: 387
11. ibid.
12. WT to KMA: letter dated 20 May 1943
13. WT verbatim: 1996; cf WT's reply to a question after an RGS lecture on DD: Tuesday, 19 November 1996
14. TLMC: 350
15. ibid.
16. WT verbatim: 1990
17. WT to KMA: letter dated 29 June 1943
18. WT to KMA: letter dated 22 June 1943
19. WT to KMA: letter dated 7 October 1943
20. WT to KMA: letter dated 23 September 1943
21. TLMC: 389
22. ibid.
23. WT verbatim: 1965
24. Asher: *Thesiger*, 1994: 211
25. Sir Laurens van der Post to WT: 30 May 1990 (private collection)
26. J.D.F. Jones: *Storyteller: The Many Lives of Laurens van der Post*, 2001: 444
27. ibid.
28. TLMC: 389
29. WT to KMA: letter dated 7 October 1943
30. TLMC: 390
31. WT to KMA: letter dated 14 October 1943
32. WGT to Lady Chelmsford: letter dated 2 November 1909
33. WT to KMA: letter dated 14 October 1943
34. TLMC: 393

SEVENTEEN: *Prelude to Arabia*
1. WT unpublished ms (private collection)

2. WT to KMA: letter dated 12 December 1944
3. ibid. Owen Bevan Lean was a cousin of David Lean, who directed the film *Lawrence of Arabia*. Information given to Alexander Maitland by John Hewitt; and by O.B. Lean's secretary, Mrs Florence Rossetti, 19 May 2005
4. AS (reprint 2000): 22–3
5. DMM: 32
6. TLMC: 396
7. Asher: *Thesiger*, 1994: 234
8. WT to KMA: letter dated 12 September 1945
9. WT to KMA: letter dated 8 January 1945
10. WT to KMA: letter dated 6 February 1945
11. ibid.
12. TLMC: 395
13. WT archive, unpublished ms
14. ibid.
15. WT to KMA: letter dated 1 October 1944. Travelling in Aussa in 2004, Michael Street met descendants of the Sultan, Mohammed Yayu, and an eyewitness of WT's meeting with the Sultan at Gurumudli in 1934
16. WT unpublished ms (private collection)
17. TLMC: 396

EIGHTEEN: *Arabian Sands*
1. WT to KMA: letter dated 30 March 1945
2. Bertram Thomas: *Alarms and Excursions in Arabia*, 1931: 289
3. WT to KMA: 30 March 1945
4. *Geographical Journal* CXVII (1), March 1951: 118
5. TLMC: 397
6. ibid.
7. ibid.: 398
8. AS (reprint 2000): 1
9. ibid.: 2
10. TLMC: 398
11. WT to KMA: letter dated 20 March 1945

12. ibid.
13. WT to KMA: letter dated 30 March 1945
14. WT to KMA: letter dated 5 December 1947
15. AS (reprint 2000): 25
16. WT to KMA: letter dated 15 May 1945
17. WT to KMA: letter dated 6 May 1945
18. Based on WT verbatim: 1 February 1995
19. AS (reprint 2000): 38
20. *Geographical Journal* CXVII (1), March 1951: 118
21. TLMC: 46
22. WT verbatim: 1988
23. WT archive, Rub' al Khali ms diary 1945–46
24. ibid.
25. WT to KMA: letter dated 18 September 1945
26. ibid.
27. TLMC: 75
28. WT verbatim: 5 January 1965
29. WT to KMA: letter dated 27 December 1944
30. WT to KMA: 7 October 1945
31. WT to KMA: 4 October 1945
32. WT verbatim: c.1995
33. WT to KMA: letter dated 2 November 1945
34. AS (reprint 2000): 35
35. ibid.: 36–7
36. WT to KMA: letter dated 8 January 1946
37. ibid.
38. AS (reprint 2000): 156
39. ibid.
40. WT to KMA: letter dated 13 January 1946
41. AS (reprint 2000): 53
42. WT to KMA: letter dated 11 March 1946
43. ibid.
44. ibid.
45. AS (reprint 2000): 54–5
46. ibid.: 55–6
47. WT archive, Rub' al Khali ms diary 1945–46: entry dated 1 February 1946
48. ibid.: entry dated 2 February 1946
49. WT to KMA: letter dated 26 February 1946
50. See AS (reprint 2000)
51. ibid.: 56
52. WT to KMA: letter dated 30 June 1946
53. WT archive, Hijaz [sic] ms diary 1946: entry dated 25 June 1946
54. Sir Laurence Kirwan to KMA: letter dated 25 March 1947
55. WT to KMA: letter dated 24 October 1946
56. WT to KMA: letter dated 19 March 1946
57. WT verbatim: c.1996
58. TLMC: 399
59. AS (reprint 2000): 112–13
60. WT to KMA: letter dated 26 February 1947
61. ibid.
62. *Geographical Journal* CXI (1), 1948: 1
63. ibid.: 3
64. ibid.: 15
65. ibid.: 3
66. ibid.: 4
67. Asher: *Thesiger*, 1994: 301
68. *Geographical Journal* CXI (1), 1948: 6
69. AS (reprint 2000): 136
70. *Geographical Journal* CXI (1), 1948: 10
71. ibid.: 11
72. AS (reprint 2000): 169
73. *Geographical Journal* CXI (1), 1948: 5
74. AS (reprint 2000): 151
75. ibid.: 150
76. ibid.: 154–5
77. ibid.: 166
78. ibid.: 170
79. ibid.: 2
80. Verney, *A Dinner of Herbs*, 1966: 150
81. WT verbatim: 1964; and cf AS (reprint 2000): 16
82. AS (reprint 2000): 192

83. WT to KMA: letter dated 14 May 1947
84. AS (reprint 2000): 176–7
85. ibid.: 177
86. WT to KMA: letter dated 17 May 1947
87. ibid.
88. AS (reprint 2000): 175
89. *Geographical Journal* CXI (1), 1948: 18
90. (Sir) Laurence Kirwan to KMA: 25 March 1947
91. *Geographical Journal* CXI (1), 1948: 20
92. AS (reprint 2000): 192
93. *Geographical Journal* CXIII, 1949: 21
94. WT to KMA: letter dated 5 December 1947
95. WT verbatim: 1992
96. WT to KMA: letter dated 5 December 1947
97. *Geographical Journal* CXIII, 1949: 22
98. WT to KMA: letter dated 5 December 1947
99. ibid.
100. AS (reprint 2000): 202–3
101. ibid.: 192–3
102. *Geographical Journal* CXIII, 1949: 30
103. ibid.
104. WT to KMA: letter dated 6 February 1948
105. ibid.
106. AS (reprint 2000): 227
107. ibid.: 229–30
108. ibid.: 230
109. ibid.: 232
110. ibid.: 236
111. ibid.
112. H. St John Philby to KMA: letter dated 27 January 1948 (private collection)
113. H. St John Philby to KMA: letter dated 20 February 1948 (private collection)
114. WT to KMA: letter dated 1 May 1948
115. WT to KMA: letter dated 13 May 1948

116. AS (reprint 2000): 240
117. ibid.
118. ibid.: 242
119. ibid.
120. AS (reprint): 247
121. *Geographical Journal* CXIII, 1949: 38
122. WT to KMA: letter dated 16 March 1948
123. ibid.
124. AS (reprint 2000): 263
125. ibid.: 141
126. ibid.: 238
127. ibid.: 172
128. ibid.: 264
129. ibid.: 265
130. ibid.
131. WT Oman ms diary 1948
132. AS: (reprint 2000): 272
133. ibid.
134. WT to KMA: letter dated 4 January 1949
135. AS (reprint 2000): 283
136. WT to KMA: Arabia ms archive 1945–50
137. AS (reprint 2000): 291
138. WT Oman ms diary 1949: entry dated 16 February
139. *Geographical Journal* CXVI (4), 1950: 147
140. ibid.: 169
141. ibid.: 148
142. ibid.: 152
143. ibid.
144. ibid.: 156
145. ibid.
146. WT to KMA: letter dated 7 January 1950
147. *Geographical Journal* CXVI (4), 1950: 157
148. ibid.: 158
149. AS (reprint 2000): 267
150. WT to KMA: letter dated 11 January 1950
151. WT to KMA: letter dated 12 January 1950
152. WT to KMA: letter dated 26 February 1947

153. AS (reprint 2000): 170
154. ibid.: 303
155. ibid.: 320
156. ibid.: 317
157. ibid.: 318
158. ibid.: 321
159. ibid.: 318
160. ibid.: 321
161. C.H. Inge to WT: 4 December 1948
162. AS (reprint 2000): 321
163. T.E. Lawrence, *Seven Pillars of Wisdom*, 1935: 660
164. ibid.: 31–2

NINETEEN: *Marsh and Mountain*
1. WT to KMA: letter dated 26 June 1949
2. ATM: 1
3. ibid.: 2
4. WT to KMA: letter dated 26 June 1949
5. ATM: 2
6. ibid.
7. ibid.: 4
8. WT to KMA: letter dated 31 May 1950
9. WT to KMA: letter dated 11 May 1951
10. WT to KMA: letter dated 7 May 1951
11. WT to KMA: letter dated 9 October 1950
12. ibid.
13. WT to KMA: letter dated 11 May 1951
14. ibid.
15. WT verbatim: 4 June 1964
16. WT to KMA: letter dated 26 February 1951
17. WT to KMA: letter dated 11 May 1951
18. WT to KMA: letter dated 7 May 1951
19. TMA: 2,3
20. WT South Iraq diary 1950: entry dated 23 October
21. TMA: 5
22. ibid.
23. ibid.: 69

24. R.S.M. Sturges to WT: letter dated 9 November 1965 (private collection)
25. WT to KMA: letter dated 14 November 1950
26. WT to KMA: letter dated 7 May 1951
27. WT to KMA: letter dated 6 April 1951
28. WT to KMA: letter dated 8 April 1951
29. TMA: 5–6
30. ibid.: xiii
31. WT verbatim: c.1964
32. TMA: 99
33. ibid.: 119
34. ibid.: 212
35. ibid.: 123
36. ibid.: 16
37. ibid.: 119
38. WT verbatim: 1980. WT himself said he aimed at achieving 'brevity, clarity and flow (or rhythm)' in his writing; cf the American poet Nicholas Vachel Lindsay, who spoke of having 'a working grip on prose. Brevity and sharp edges' (quoted in Edgar Lee Masters's 1935 biography *Vachel Lindsay*: 167). Lindsay also remarked that 'Hardship gave me the gift of understanding,' a comment very relevant to WT's ethos of desert travel
39. DMM: 174
40. ibid.
41. WT to KMA: letter dated 11 May 1952
42. Gavin Young: *Return to the Marshes*, 1977: 12
43. TMA: 199. On 28 March 1954 WT noted: 'This makes 102 pig since we left Basra. 590 in all.' On 12 June 1954 he noted '251 pig this year'. If we add 149 pig to the 590 WT counted in March 1954, this gives a total of 739, to which must be added the numbers he shot between 1955 and 1958. He may not have listed every 'pig', i.e. wild boar, he shot; and

indeed part of his 1954 South Iraq diary appears to be missing. The total number is probably close to a thousand

44. Young, 1977: 12
45. WT to KMA: letter dated 2 March 1951
46. ibid.
47. WT to KMA: letter dated 8 April 1951
48. WT to KMA: letter dated 29 October 1951
49. TMA: 9
50. ibid.: 9–10
51. ibid.: 12
52. TMA: 91
53. WT South Iraq diary 1952: entry dated 8 July
54. ibid.
55. WT South Iraq diary 1956: entry dated 10 June
56. WT South Iraq diary 1952: entry dated 9 July
57. Eric Newby: *A Short Walk in the Hindu Kush*, 1958: 247
58. WT South Iraq diary 1954: entry dated 2 April
59. ibid.: entry dated 3 May
60. ibid.
61. TMA: 180
62. WT to KMA: letter dated 14 April 1954
63. WT to KMA: letter dated 1 June 1954
64. ibid.
65. WT to KMA: 14 April 1954
66. WT verbatim: 1979
67. WT to KMA: letter dated 14 April 1954
68. ibid.
69. Gavin Maxwell: *A Reed Shaken by the Wind*, 1957: 2
70. WT to KMA: letter dated 1 June 1954
71. Maxwell, 1957: 3
72. WT verbatim: 4 June 1964. (Sir) Bernard Miles wrote to WT from the Mermaid Theatre on 3 May 1965: 'It was a great pleasure to meet you, though I was rather perturbed to see you so conventionally dressed!' (private collection)
73. Maxwell, 1957: 164
74. WT verbatim: 1993
75. DMM: 174
76. Maxwell, 1957: 223
77. WT to KMA: letter dated 4 February 1956
78. WT to KMA: letter dated 11 March 1956
79. ibid.
80. ibid.
81. Ross Higgins verbatim: Glasgow, 1958
82. WT verbatim: June 1964
83. WT to KMA: letter dated 29 March 1956
84. ibid.
85. Maxwell, 1957: 180, 181
86. ibid.: 179
87. WT South Iraq diary 1953: entry dated 20 March; see also WT to KMA: letter dated 5 September 1953
88. Gavin Maxwell: *Ring of Bright Water*, 1960: 74
89. ibid.: 75
90. WT South Iraqh; see also WT to KMA: letter d diary (i) 1955: entry dated 4 April
91. Maxwell, 1957: 193
92. WT to KMA: letter dated 29 March 1956
93. WT South Iraq diary 1956: entry dated 3 April
94. ibid.: 4 April
95. Maxwell, 1960: 83
96. WT South Iraq diary (i) 1956: entry dated 9 March
97. Asher: *Thesiger*, 1994: 420
98. Graham Watson: *Book Society*, 1980: 139
99. Graham Watson to Alexander Maitland: letter dated 8 November 1983
100. WT to KMA: letter dated 25 April 1956

101. Maxwell, 1957: 224
102. WT to KMA: letter dated 26 May 1956
103. WT to KMA: letter dated 30 May 1956
104. WT to KMA: letter dated 26 March 1958
105. Michael Shaw verbatim: December 1993
106. WT verbatim: June 1964
107. Gavin Maxwell to WT: letter dated 1 December 1954 (tipped into WT's copy of *Harpoon at a Venture*) (private collection)
108. Maxwell, 1960: 10
109. ibid.: 26, 91, 206
110. WT South Iraq diary 1955: entries dated 8, 9, 10 June
111. WT verbatim: 1964
112. Graham Watson to Alexander Maitland: letter dated 8 November 1983
113. WT to KMA: letter dated 10 February 1958
114. WT verbatim; and cf ALIP: 9–10
115. WT to KMA: letter dated 31 May 1956
116. WT to KMA: letter dated 30 May 1956
117. WT to KMA: letter dated 20 June 1956
118. WT to KMA: letter dated 2 July 1956
119. ibid.
120. ibid.
121. ibid.
122. WT to KMA: letter dated 9 July 1956
123. Gavin Maxwell to WT: printed card, nd but c.1965 (private collection)
124. Asher: *Thesiger*, 1994: 421; and Douglas Botting: *Gavin Maxwell: A Life*, 1993: 476 (Thesiger told Alexander Maitland this story, almost word for word, more than twenty years before it was published by Botting)
125. Gavin Young verbatim: 23 September 1993
126. WT verbatim: 1979
127. Maxwell, 1957: 219
128. WT to KMA: letter dated 20 June 1956
129. WT verbatim: c.1998
130. TMA 1964: Longmans, 1st edition, front jacket blurb

TWENTY: *Among the Mountains*

1. ATM: 1
2. Eric Earle Shipton: *Upon that Mountain*, 1943: 219–20
3. Shipton verbatim: 1969
4. WT verbatim: 1970
5. Sir John Verney to WT: 18 March 1966
6. WT to KMA: 2 August 1952
7. WT to Sir Gilbert Laithwaite: letter dated 8 October (c.1948)
8. Ernest Thesiger: *Practically True*, 1927: 40–1
9. WT to KMA: letter dated 2 August 1952
10. WT to KMA: letter dated 5 October 1952
11. WT to KMA: letter dated 20 August 1952
12. ibid.
13. ibid.
14. WT to KMA: letter dated 5 October 1952
15. WT to KMA: letter dated 20 August 1952
16. WT to KMA: letter dated 5 October 1952
17. ibid.
18. WT to KMA: letter dated 20 August 1952
19. ibid.
20. WT to KMA: letter dated 18 October 1952
21. TMA: 130
22. WT to KMA: letter dated 4 March 1953
23. WT to KMA: letter dated 29 June 1953
24. ibid.
25. WT to KMA: letter dated 2 September 1953

26. WT to KMA: letter dated 20 October 1953
27. ibid.
28. ATM: 91
29. *Geographical Journal* CXXI (3), September 1955: 312
30. WT to KMA: letter dated 1 June 1954
31. WT to KMA: letter dated 13 July 1954
32. ATM: 92
33. ibid.: 116
34. ibid.: 94, 98
35. ibid.: 99
36. ibid.: 102
37. ibid.: 108
38. KMA ms: added to Faris Shahin's letter dated 12 March 1949 (private collection)
39. WT to KMA: letter dated 31 March 1955
40. WT verbatim: 1990
41. WT to KMA: letter dated 2 April 1955
42. WT to KMA: letter dated 31 May 1955
43. ibid.
44. WT South Iraq diary 1955: entry dated 5 June
45. Bijan Omrani and Matthew Leeming: *Afghanistan: A Companion and Guide*, 2005: 105
46. WT to KMA: letter dated 5 July 1955
47. WT Morocco diary 1955: entries dated 22–26 July
48. ibid.: entry dated 28 July
49. Walter B. Harris: *The Land of an African Sultan*, 1889: 228
50. Asher: *Thesiger*, 1994: 440
51. WT Morocco diary 1955: entry dated 21 August
52. ibid.: entry dated 4 September
53. ibid.: entry dated 2 August
54. ibid.: entry dated 6 August
55. ibid.: entry dated 7 August
56. Bryan Clarke: *Berber Village*, 1959: 118
57. WT South Iraq diary 1956: entry dated 28 March
58. Maxwell, 1957: 219
59. WT South Iraq diary 1956: entry dated 28 March
60. WT Morocco diary 1955: entry dated 5 August
61. ibid.
62. ibid.: entry dated 7 August
63. ibid.
64. ibid.
65. TLMC: 257
66. ibid.: 258
67. WT Morocco diary 1955: entry dated 10 August
68. ibid.: entry dated 12 August
69. ALIP; and cf photographs pages 153–4
70. WT Morocco diary 1955: entry dated 6 August
71. ibid.: entry dated 9 August
72. ibid.: entry dated 15 August
73. ibid.: entry dated 7 August
74. WT to KMA: letter dated 20 August 1952
75. WT Morocco diary 1955: entry dated 27 August
76. ibid.: entry dated 12 August
77. ibid.: entry dated 20 August
78. Asher: *Thesiger*, 1994: 443
79. ibid.: 442
80. ibid.
81. WT Morocco diary 1955: entry dated 21 August
82. ibid.
83. ibid.: entry dated 22 August
84. Asher: *Thesiger*, 1994: 442
85. WT Morocco diary 1955: entry dated 21 August
86. ibid.: entry dated 6 September
87. ibid.: entry dated 14 September
88. WT Morocco diary 1955: entry dated 15 September
89. ibid.: entry dated 12 September
90. ibid.: entry dated 22 August
91. WT South Iraq diary 1955: entries dated 8, 25 June

92. ibid.: entry dated 29 June
93. WT Morocco diary 1955: entry dated 15 September
94. ibid.: entry dated 21 September
95. Asher: *Thesiger*, 1994: 443
96. ibid.: 440
97. WT Morocco diary 1955: entry dated 3 October
98. ibid.
99. ibid.: entry dated 4 October
100. ibid.
101. WT to KMA: letter dated 25 April 1956
102. WT to KMA: letter dated 30 May 1956
103. WT to KMA: letter dated 6 July 1956
104. WT South Iraq diary: entries dated 23–24 June
105. WT to KMA: letter dated 6 July 1956
106. John Newbould to WT: letter dated 11 December 1955 (private collection)
107. WT to KMA: letter dated 9 July 1956
108. *Geographical Journal* CXXIII (4), December 1957: 457
109. ATM: 131
110. Dr S. Jones: *Bibliography of Nuristan*, 1966: 84
111. ibid.
112. ATM: 131–2
113. WT Nuristan diary 1956: entry dated 31 July
114. ATM: 135
115. Newby, 1958: 246
116. Asher: *Thesiger*, 1994: 438
117. Eric Newby: *A Traveller's Life*, 1982
118. ATM: 138
119. ibid.: 143
120. ibid.: 141
121. ibid.
122. ibid.: 179
123. ibid.: 144
124. ibid.
125. ibid.: 141
126. ibid.: 181
127. ibid.: 149
128. ibid.
129. ibid.: 152
130. WT Nuristan diary 1956: entry dated 28 August
131. ATM: 155
132. ibid.
133. WT Nuristan diary 1956: entry dated 31 August
134. ATM: 155
135. ibid.: 139
136. WT to KMA: letter dated 12 January 1958
137. ibid.
138. ibid.
139. ibid.
140. WT to KMA: letter dated 26 January 1958
141. WT to KMA: letter dated 1 February 1958
142. WT to KMA: letter dated 26 January 1958
143. ibid.
144. WT to KMA: letter dated 14 January 1958
145. ibid.
146. WT to KMA: letter dated 26 January 1958
147. WT to KMA: letter dated 10 February 1958
148. ibid.
149. WT verbatim: c.1997
150. WT to KMA: letter dated 26 March 1958
151. ibid.
152. WT to KMA: letter dated 10 February 1958
153. ibid.
154. Emma Nicholson and Peter Clark (editors): *The Iraqi Marshlands*, 2003: ix–x
155. TMA: 6
156. WT ms nd (but c.1961) (private collection)
157. WT to KMA: letter dated 10 February 1958
158. WT to KMA: letter dated 1 February 1958
159. ibid.

160. WT to KMA: letter dated 26 March 1958
161. WT to KMA: letter dated 20 April 1958
162. ibid.
163. WT to KMA: letter dated 26 March 1958
164. ibid.
165. WT to KMA: letter dated 28 March 1958
166. WT to KMA: letter dated 20 April 1958
167. ibid.
168. ibid.
169. ibid.
170. TMA: 208–9

TWENTY-ONE: *A Winter in Copenhagen*

1. WT verbatim
2. WT verbatim
3. Sir John Verney verbatim; and John Verney to Alexander Maitland: letter dated 24 October 1983, giving a different version: 'I told his mother that I'd called him a spiv – after his lecture at the Asian Society [sic] when a Colonel (retired) or whatever had grumbled that WT appeared to wander about Arabia with no proper job'
4. WT verbatim: 1964
5. WT to KMA: letter dated 7 February 1957
6. Val ffrench Blake to WT: letter dated 28 December 1956
7. ibid.
8. Asher: *Thesiger*, 1994: 450
9. WT verbatim: 1980
10. Gavin Young verbatim
11. Graham Watson to WT: letter dated 2 April 1957
12. WT to KMA: letter dated 6 April 1957
13. Graham Watson to WT: letter dated 13 May 1957
14. Val ffrench Blake to WT: letter dated 19 April 1957
15. Val ffrench Blake to WT: letter dated 11 May 1957

16. WT to KMA: letter dated 11 February 1957
17. WT to KMA: letter dated 20 February 1957
18. ibid.
19. WT to KMA: letter dated 7 March 1957
20. WT to KMA: letter dated 10 March 1957
21. WT to KMA: letter dated 13 March 1957
22. WT to KMA: letter dated 22 March 1957
23. WT to KMA: letter dated 29 March 1957
24. WT to KMA: letter dated 6 April 1957
25. ibid.
26. WT to KMA: letter dated 13 March 1957
27. WT to KMA: letter dated 26 February 1957
28. WT to KMA: letter dated 28 February 1957
29. WT to KMA: letter dated 7 March 1957
30. WT to KMA: letter dated 6 May 1957
31. WT verbatim: January 1965
32. WT verbatim: 1993
33. Graham Watson to WT: letter dated 30 September 1957
34. Unidentified reader's report sent by Graham Watson: 25 October 1957
35. Graham Watson to WT: letter dated 21 August 1958
36. Sir John Verney to WT: letter dated 19 August 1958
37. John Guest to WT: letter dated 18 August 1958
38. AS (reprint 2000): xxi
39. WT verbatim
40. WT to KMA: letter dated 6 March 1959
41. John Guest to WT: letter dated 3 February 1959
42. ibid.
43. WT to KMA: letter dated 6 March 1959

44. WT to KMA: letter dated 28 January 1959
45. WT to KMA: letter dated 30 May 1959
46. WT to KMA: letter dated 26 March 1959
47. WT to KMA: letter dated 30 March 1959
48. WT to KMA: letter dated 30 May 1959
49. TLMC: 409–10
50. ibid.: 410
51. WT verbatim: 1979; and cf TLMC: 410
52. Ralph Hammond Innes, *The Bookman*, vol. 1 no. 4, November 1959
53. Lord Kinross, *Daily Telegraph*, 1959
54. Brigadier Sir John Glubb, *The Times*, 1959
55. H. St John Philby, 1959
56. V.S. Pritchett, *New Statesman*, 1959
57. Graham Watson to WT: letter dated 30 October 1959
58. Brigadier Sir John Glubb to WT: letter dated 11 October 1959 (private collection)
59. Graham Watson to WT: letter dated 30 October 1959
60. ibid.
61. WT verbatim: c.1982
62. Sir John Verney to WT: letter dated 19 August 1958
63. Lt Col R.L.V. ffrench Blake to WT: letter dated 9 February 1959
64. Sir Laurens van der Post verbatim: 13 Cadogan Street, London SW3, 1963
65. Lt Col R.L.V. ffrench Blake to WT: letter dated 26 August 1959
66. T.H. White to WT: letter dated 13 March 1963 (private collection)
67. WT verbatim: 1995
68. Maggs Bros 'Thesiger Library' catalogue no. 1193, 1995: 38
69. TLMC: 418
70. WT Northern Abyssinia diary 1960: entry dated 6 April
71. ibid.: entry dated 27 April
72. ibid.
73. ibid.: entry dated 15 May
74. WT to KMA: letter dated 19 May 1960
75. ibid.
76. WT to KMA: letter dated 1 June 1960
77. WT to KMA: letter dated 23 May 1960
78. WT to KMA: letter dated 14 June 1960

TWENTY-TWO: *Camel Journeys to the Jade Sea*

1. WT to KMA: letter dated 2 December 1960
2. WT to KMA: letter dated 16 December 1960
3. WT to KMA: letter dated 5 December 1960
4. WT to KMA: letter dated 16 December 1960
5. WT to KMA: letter dated 27 December 1960
6. ibid.
7. Frank Steele verbatim: 1993
8. WT to KMA: letter dated 27 December 1960
9. WT to KMA: letter dated 11 January 1961
10. Maggs Bros 'Thesiger Library' catalogue no. 1193, 1995: 36
11. WT to KMA: letter dated 11 January 1961
12. Frank Steele verbatim: 1991
13. WT to KMA: letter dated 11 January 1961
14. ibid.
15. MKD: 6, 62
16. WT verbatim: 1993
17. Maggs Bros 'Thesiger Library' catalogue no. 1193, 1995: 33
18. MKD: 21
19. WT to KMA: letter dated 11 February 1961
20. MKD: 31

21. WT to KMA: letter dated 11 February 1961
22. ibid.
23. WT to KMA: letter dated 2 March 1961
24. MKD: 37
25. ibid.: 32
26. WT to KMA: letter dated 6 April 1961
27. MKD: 38
28. ibid.
29. Major Rodney Elliott verbatim: London, 29 September 1998
30. WT verbatim: Coulsdon, September 1998
31. Major Rodney Elliott verbatim: London, 29 September 1998
32. MKD: 40
33. WT verbatim: 1992
34. WT to KMA: letter dated 21 April 1961
35. ibid.
36. ibid.
37. WT verbatim: 1979
38. WT verbatim
39. WT to KMA: letter dated 25 April 1961
40. ibid.
41. WT verbatim: a term which he used frequently
42. MKD: 104
43. AS (reprint 2000): 177
44. MKD: 57
45. WT to KMA: letter dated 25 April 1961
46. Sir John Verney to Alexander Maitland: letter dated 7 November 1983
47. WT to KMA: letter dated 7 November 1961
48. WT to KMA: letter dated 10 November 1961
49. WT to KMA: letter dated 17 November 1961
50. WT ms nd (but 1961) (private collection)
51. WT to KMA: letter dated 7 November 1961
52. Graham Watson to WT: letter dated 15 November 1961
53. Graham Watson to WT: letter dated 24 November 1961
54. WT to KMA: letter dated 29 November 1961
55. Graham Watson to WT: letter dated 7 December 1961
56. WT to KMA: letter dated 7 December 1961
57. WT to KMA: letter dated 27 December 1961
58. MKD: 87
59. WT South Iraq diary ms note
60. MKD: 86
61. ibid.
62. Jan (Lady) Verney to WT: letter dated 10 November 1962
63. Sir John Verney to WT: letter dated 6 November 1962
64. WT to John Guest: letter dated 16 February 1962
65. WT verbatim: January 1965
66. Sir John Verney to WT: letter dated 21 May (nd but c.1964)
67. Graham Watson to WT: letter dated 9 April 1963
68. WT Kenya diary 1963: entry dated 31 May
69. WT to KMA: letter dated 15 June 1963
70. WT verbatim: 1992
71. WT to KMA: letter dated 15 June 1963
72. MKD: 98–9
73. WT to KMA: letter dated 5 August 1963
74. ibid.
75. WT to KMA: letter dated 26 August 1963
76. Ingaret Giffard to WT: letter dated 25 July 1963 (private collection)
77. WT to KMA: letter dated 9 September 1963
78. WT to KMA: letter dated 26 May 1963
79. MKD: 205
80. MKD: 101
81. Verney: *A Dinner of Herbs*, 1966: 30

82. John Guest to WT: letter dated 21 January 1964
83. MLAT: 7
84. John Guest to WT: letter dated 17 July 1964
85. John Guest to WT: letter dated 30 July 1964
86. MLAT: 5–6

TWENTY-THREE: *With Nomadic Tribes in Other Lands*
1. WT verbatim: January 1965
2. WT to KMA: letter dated 10 August 1964
3. ibid.
4. ibid.
5. WT to KMA: letter dated 8 October 1964
6. WT Iran diary 1964: entry dated 1 October
7. WT to KMA: letter dated 8 October 1964
8. WT to KMA: letter dated 21 June 1964
9. ibid.
10. ibid.
11. ibid.
12. WT Iran diary 1964: entry dated 26 October
13. WT to KMA: letter dated 27 October 1964
14. WT to KMA: letter dated 20 October 1964
15. ibid.
16. DMM: 123
17. ibid.
18. ibid.
19. Robert Byron: *The Road to Oxiana*, 1937: 202
20. Derek Hill to WT: letter dated 9 April 1965 (private collection)
21. WGT to Lady Chelmsford: letter dated 2 November 1909
22. WT verbatim: 1982
23. ibid.
24. RMDT verbatim: Lucton, 1984
25. Nicolette Devas: *Two Flamboyant Fathers*, 1966: 223

26. ibid.: 213
27. Derek Hill observed by Alexander Maitland: Hampstead, 1984
28. DMM: 231
29. WT to KMA: letter dated 11 August 1965
30. DMM: 232
31. ATM: 187
32. DMM: 233
33. WT to KMA: letter dated 16 October 1965
34. ibid.
35. MKD: 102
36. WT verbatim: 1965
37. WT to Alexander Maitland: letter dated 27 April 1965
38. TLMC: 434
39. DMM: 270
40. Frank Steele to WT: letter dated 16 December 1966
41. WT: *Visions of a Nomad*, 1987: 10
42. DMM: 271
43. WT Yemen diary 1967: entry dated 30 November
44. DMM: 274
45. ibid.: 271
46. ibid.:275
47. MKD: 102
48. WT to KMA: letter dated 1 August 1968
49. WT to KMA: letter dated 7 August 1968
50. WT verbatim: 1980
51. WT ms (private collection)
52. WT to KMA: letter dated 21 August 1968
53. WT to KMA: letter dated 2 September 1968
54. WT to KMA: letter dated 5 September 1968
55. ibid.
56. ibid.
57. MKD: 103
58. WT to KMA: letter dated 27 September 1968
59. MKD: 103
60. WT to KMA: letter dated 27 September 1968
61. ibid.

62. ibid.
63. WT to KMA: letter c.November 1969
64. Sir Richard Dearlove in 'The Ultimate Traveller', October 2003: 28–9
65. WT to KMA: letter dated 12 October 1968
66. ibid.
67. ibid.
68. WT to KMA: letter dated 22 November 1968
69. ibid.
70. ibid.
71. ibid.
72. ibid.
73. ibid.
74. ibid.
75. WT to KMA: letter dated 14 December 1968
76. WT verbatim: 1965
77. MKD: 107
78. ibid.: 115
79. WT to KMA: letter dated 13 July 1969
80. MKD: 115
81. WT to KMA: letter dated 28 July 1969
·82. WT to KMA: letter dated 18 July 1969
83. WT to KMA: letter dated 28 August 1969
84. ibid.
85. ibid.
86. ibid.
87. WT to KMA: letter 9 October 1969
88. ibid.
89. MKD: 153
90. ibid.: 119
91. WT to KMA: letter dated 9 October 1969
92. WT to KMA: letter dated 2 January 1969
93. WT to KMA: letter dated 4 January 1970
94. WT to KMA: letter dated 14 November 1969
95. WT to KMA: letter dated 20 July 1970
96. WT to KMA: letter dated 14 August 1970
97. WT to KMA: letter dated 25 August 1970
98. WT verbatim: 1993
99. MKD: 136–7
100. ibid.: 147
101. ibid.
102. MKD: 153
103. ibid.
104. ibid.
105. WT to KMA: letter dated 20 July 1970
106. Sir John Verney to Alexander Maitland: letter dated 7 November 1983
107. WGT to KMT: undated note (c.1911) written in pencil: 'After 35 years of being absolutely alone ones power of engrossing oneself is all frozen up even when one feels most & perhaps more then.'
108. WT verbatim: 1975
109. MKD: 147
110. ibid.: 154
111. WT verbatim: 1993
112. WT verbatim: 1975
113. WT to KMA: letter dated 21 September 1973
114. MKD: 148
115. WT to KMA: letter dated 1 September 1972
116. MKD: 148
117. ibid.: 151–2
118. ibid.: 152
119. WT verbatim: 1982
120. MKD: 161
121. WT ms 'Samburu Circumcision Ceremonies': nd (but c.1976) (private collection)
122. MKD: 165
123. WT ms 'Samburu Circumcision Ceremonies' (c.1976)
124. ibid.
125. ibid.

126. MKD: 162
127. ibid.: 163
128. WT ms 'Samburu Circumcision
Ceremonies' (c.1976)
129. WT verbatim: 1995
130. WT ms 'Samburu Circumcision
Ceremonies' (c.1976)
131. ibid.
132. ibid.
133. WT verbatim: 1993
134. TMA: 6
135. WT verbatim: 1992
136. Hugh Leach in 'The Ultimate
Traveller', October 2003: 17
137. ibid.
138. WT verbatim: 1979

TWENTY-FOUR: *Kenya Days*
1. DMM: 296
2. ibid.
3. AS (reprint 2000): xv
4. DMM: 298
5. WT verbatim: 1990
6. Gavin Young: *In Search of Conrad*,
1991: 3
7. ibid.: 144
8. Pamela, Lady Egremont, ms note to
WT: 20 June 1977
9. ALIP: 209
10. WT verbatim: 1997
11. RMDT verbatim: 1983
12. MKD: 165–6
13. WT Indonesia ms: 1977 (private
collection)
14. 'Palinurus' (Cyril Connolly): *The
Unquiet Grave* (reprint),1946: 100–1
15. MKD: 161
16. ALIP: 49
17. WT diary 1977
18. Gavin Young verbatim: 1993
19. MKD: 167
20. ibid.: 168
21. Alexander Maitland ms Kenya
notebook: 1992
22. GavinYoung verbatim: 1993
23. ibid.
24. MKD: 182

25. ibid.
26. Gavin Young verbatim: 1993
27. MKD: 183. One of WT's friends saw
him as a Professor Higgins recreating
'My Fair Lawi'
28. WT verbatim: 1982
29. Sir Mark Allen in 'The Ultimate
Traveller', October 2003: 9–10
30. George Webb in ibid.: 6
31. WT verbatim: 1992
32. WT verbatim
33. WT verbatim: 1987
34. ibid.
35. ATM: 229
36. Sir Mark Allen in 'The Ultimate
Traveller', October 2003: 11
37. ATM: 229–30
38. WT Ladakh diary 1983: entry dated
16 November
39. ibid.: entry dated 22 December
40. ATM: 40
41. MKD: 41
42. ibid.
43. ibid.: 186
44. ibid.
45. Rupalen Lekakwar verbatim: 1993
46. MKD: 184
47. ibid.: 187
48. ibid.
49. ibid.: 189
50. WT verbatim: 1992
51. ibid.
52. WT verbatim: 1982
53. Dorothy Middleton verbatim:
1970; and Paul Bowles: *The
Sheltering Sky*, 1949: 60: 'Because
he was accustomed to imposing his
will without meeting opposition, he
had a highly developed and very
male vanity which endeared him,
strangely enough, to almost
everyone.' cf Ernest Thesiger:
Practically True, 1927: 63: 'I have
always found that people who are in
the habit of being flattered and
fawned upon rather enjoy an
occasional insult.'

54. WT verbatim
55. WT verbatim: 1965
56. WT verbatim: 1987
57. Lt Col R.L.V. ffrench Blake verbatim: May 1984
58. MKD: 208
59. Frank Steele verbatim: 1991
60. WT verbatim: 1992
61. ibid.
62. WT ms archive
63. WT verbatim: 1993
64. WT verbatim: 1988
65. WT often summoned help using English and Swahili: e.g. '*Kuja!* [Come here!] Bring me my hot water!'
66. MKD: 189
67. ibid.: 189–90
68. ibid.: 210

EPILOGUE

1. Peter Clark: *Thesiger's Return*, 1992: 71
2. ibid.: 65; and AS (reprint 1991): Preface
3. WT verbatim: 1992
4. WT telephone call to Alexander Maitland: 14 April 1995
5. TLMC: 432
6. WT telephone call to Alexander Maitland: 14 April 1995
7. WT verbatim: 1969
8. Patrick Trevor-Roper to WT verbatim: 17 October 1994
9. Alexander Maitland, ms notebook: 19 December 1994
10. Robert Vavra telephone call to Alexander Maitland: 2 July 1996
11. WT verbatim: 17 February 1997
12. WT verbatim: 11 September 1995
13. WT verbatim: 29 May 1997
14. Sir Anthony Rumbold verbatim: 1984
15. Frank Steele verbatim: 1995
16. WT verbatim: 1965; Shikar Club members' list
17. Pamela, Lady Egremont and WT verbatim; telephone call from Addis Ababa to Alexander Maitland: 12 June 1996
18. Alexander Maitland observing WT: 3 April 1995
19. WGT archive: Francis Galton's laboratory report dated 15 April 1889
20. WT verbatim: 1993; and apparition described to Margaret and Alexander Maitland, 1 January 1996
21. WT verbatim: 1996
22. WT verbatim: 1997
23. John Shipman in 'The Ultimate Traveller', October 2003: 35–6
24. WT verbatim: 27 October 1994
25. WT verbatim: August 2003
26. WT verbatim: 18, 20 August 2003 (RMDT died 5 March 2005)

BIBLIOGRAPHY

Unless otherwise stated, all titles listed were published in London and are first editions.

ARTICLES BY WILFRED THESIGER

'An Abyssinian Quest: I Finding a Lost River', *The Times*, 31 July 1934

'An Abyssinian Quest: II The Customs of the Dankali', *The Times*, 1 August 1934

'An Abyssinian Quest: III Fauna near Aussa', *The Times*, 2 August 1934

'An Abyssinian Quest: IV Salt as Currency', *The Times*, 3 August 1934

'The Awash River and the Aussa Sultanate', *Geographical Journal* LXXXV: 1–19, 1935

'A Collection of Birds from Danakil, Abyssinia', *The Ibis*, 774–807, October 1935

'The Mind of the Moor', *The Times*, 21 December 1937

'A Camel Journey to Tibesti', *Geographical Journal* XCIV (6): 433–46, 1939

'Galloping Lion', *Sudan Notes and Records* XXII (1): 155–7, 1939

'A New Journey in Southern Arabia', *Geographical Journal* CVIII: 129–45, 1946

'A Journey Through the Tihama, the 'Asir, and the Hejaz Mountains', *Geographical Journal* CVIX: 188–200, 1947

'Empty Quarter of Arabia', *The Listener*, 4 December 1947

'Studies in the Southern Hejaz and Tihama', *Geographical Magazine*, May 1948

'Across the Empty Quarter', *Geographical Journal* CXI (1): 1–21, 1948

'Sands of the Empty Quarter', *Geographical Magazine*, December 1948

'Wolves of the Desert', *Geographical Magazine*, February 1949

'Travel on the Trucial Coast', *Geographical Magazine*, July 1949

'A Further Journey across the Empty Quarter', *Geographical Journal* CXIII; 21–44, 1949

'Hawking in Arabia', *The Listener*, 10 November 1949

'The Badu of Southern Arabia', *Journal of the Royal Central Asian Society*, 39: 53–61, 1950

'Desert Borderlands of Oman', *Geographical Journal* CXVI (4): 137–68, 1950
'Bertram Sidney Thomas CMG OBE' (obituary), *Geographical Journal* CXVII
   (1): 117–19, March 1951
'The Marshmen of Southern Iraq', *Geographical Journal* CXX (3): 272–81, 1954
'The Madan or Marsh Dwellers of Southern Iraq', *Journal of the Royal Central
   Asian Society*, 41: 4–25, 1954
'The Marsh Arabs of Iraq', *Geographical Magazine*, July 1954
'The Hazaras of Central Afghanistan', *Geographical Journal* CXXI (3), 1955
'The Ma'dan or Marsh Dwellers of Southern Iraq' (trans, Baqir al Dujaili),
   Arrabita Printing & Publishing Ltd, 1956
'A Journey in Nuristan', *Geographical Journal* CXXIII (4), 1957
'Marsh Dwellers of Southern Iraq', *National Geographic Magazine* CXIII (2):
   205–39, February 1958

BOOKS BY WILFRED THESIGER
Arabian Sands, Longmans 1959
The Marsh Arabs, Longmans 1964
Desert, Marsh and Mountain, Collins 1979
The Life of My Choice, Collins 1987
Visions of a Nomad, Collins 1987
My Kenya Days, HarperCollins 1994
The Danakil Diary, HarperCollins 1996
Among the Mountains, HarperCollins 1998
Crossing the Sands, Motivate 1999
A Vanished World, HarperCollins 2001
My Life and Travels (edited by Alexander Maitland), HarperCollins 2002

BOOKS WITH A FOREWORD OR AN INTRODUCTION BY WILFRED THESIGER
Allen, M.: *Falconry in Arabia*, 1980 (foreword)
Crewe, Q: *In Search of the Sahara*, 1962 (preface)
ffrench Blake, N. St J.: *Handbook for Adventure*, nd (introduction)
Hook, H: *Home from the Hill*, 1987 (foreword)
Keay, J. (editor): *Exploration*, 1993 (foreword)
Kirkby, B.: *Sand Dance*, 2000 (foreword)
Lawrence, T.E.: *Seven Pillars of Wisdom*, reprint 2000 (foreword)
Pavitt, N.: *Kenya, The First Explorers*, 1989 (foreword)
Pavitt, N.: *Samburu*, 1991 (introduction)
Taylor, S.: *The Mighty Nimrod*, 1989 (introduction)
Trench, R: *Arabian Travellers*, 1986 (introduction)

BOOKS, ARTICLES AND ESSAYS INCLUDING PROFILES OF WILFRED THESIGER
Asher, M.: *Thesiger*, Viking 1994

Clark, J.: *Everest to Arabia*, Azimuth Inc., Calgary 2000

Clark, P.: *Thesiger's Return*, Motivate 1992

Green, T.S.: 'Wilfred Thesiger', in *The Adventurers*, Michael Joseph 1970: 23–93

Kirkby, B.: *Sand Dance*, McClelland & Stewart Inc., Toronto 2000

Maitland, A.: 'Wilfred Thesiger: Traveller from an Antique Land', *Blackwoods Magazine*, vol. 328 no. 1980: October 1980

Maitland, A.: 'An Explorer's Insight', *Geographical Magazine*, August 1990

Maitland, A.: *Wilfred Thesiger: A Life in Pictures*, HarperCollins 2004

Maxwell, G.: *A Reed Shaken by the Wind*, Longmans 1957

Newby, E.: *A Short Walk in the Hindu Kush*, Secker & Warburg 1958

Verney, J.: *A Dinner of Herbs*, Collins 1966

Young, G.: *Return to the Marshes*, Hutchinson 1977

Young, G.: 'The Last Explorer', in *Worlds Apart*, Hutchinson 1987: 276–85

Young, G.: *In Search of Conrad*, Hutchinson 1991

GENERAL

Adamson, J.: *Born Free* (3rd impression), 1960

Aldington, R.: *Lawrence of Arabia*, 1955 (reprint 1960)

Allen, M.: *Falconry in Arabia*, 1980

Allen, W.E.D.: *Guerilla War in Abyssinia*, 1943

Andersson, C.J.: *Lake Ngami*, 1856

Archer, Sir G.: *Personal and Historical Memoirs of an East African Administrator*, 1963

Armbruster, C.H.: *Initia Amharica* (2 vols), Cambridge 1908–10

Badoglio, P.: *The War in Abyssinia*, 1937

Bagnold, R.: *Libyan Sands* (5th edn), 1942

Baker, Sir S.: *The Nile Tributaries of Abyssinia*, 1867

Baldwin, W.C.: *African Hunting and Adventure from Natal to the Zambesi* (1st US edn), 1863; and (3rd edn) 1894

Barker, A.J.: *The Civilizing Mission: The Italo–Ethiopian War 1935–36*, 1968

Barton, Sir S.P.: *Abyssinia* (newspaper cuttings etc., 7 vols), 1929–42

Bates, D.: *The Abyssinian Difficulty*, 1979

Baum, J.E.: *Savage Abyssinia*, 1928

Beech, M.W.H.: *The Suk, Their Language and Folklore*, Oxford 1911

Beke, C.T.: *The Sources of the Nile*, 1860

Beke, C.T.: *The British Captives in Abyssinia* (2nd edn), 1867

Bell, G.: *The Desert and the Sown*, 1907

Bell, G.: *Amurath to Amurath*, 1911

Bell, Sir G.: *Shadows on the Sand*, 1983

Bell, W.D.M.: *The Wanderings of an Elephant Hunter*, 1923

Bennett, E.: *The Downfall of the Dervishes*, 1898

Bent, J.T.: *The Sacred City of the Ethiopians*, 1893

Berkeley, G.: *The Campaign of Adowa* (2nd edn), 1935
Blackwood: *Tales from the Outposts* (12 vols), 1934
Blanc, H.: *A Narrative of Captivity in Abyssinia*, 1868
Bland-Sutton, J.: *Man and Beast in Eastern Ethiopia*, 1911
Blanford, W.T.: *Observations on the Geology and Zoology of Abyssinia*, 1870
Blixen, K.: *Out of Africa*, 1937
Blunt, Lady A.: *Bedouin Tribes of the Euphrates* (2 vols), 1879
Blunt, Lady A.: *A Pilgrimage to Nejd* (2nd edn, 2 vols), 1881
Blunt, W.: *Desert Hawk*, 1947
Boswell, C. & Moore, H.: *Field Observations on the Birds of Iraq*, Baghdad 1956–57
Boustead, Sir H.: *The Wind of Morning* (2nd impression), 1972
Boyes, J.: *The Company of Adventurers*, 1928
Brocklehurst, H.C.: *Game Animals of the Sudan*, 1931
Brodrick, A. Houghton: *The Abbé Breuil, Prehistorian*, 1963
Browne, Major G. St J. Orde: *The Vanishing Tribes of Kenya*, 1925
Bruce, J. of Kinnaird: *Travels to Discover the Source of the Nile* (5 vols), 1790
Buchanan, A.: *Sahara*, 1926
Budge, W.: *The Queen of Sheba and her Only Son, Menyelek* (2nd edn), 1922
Bulpett, C.W.L.: *John Boyes, King of the Wa-Kikuyu*, 1911
Burckhardt, J.L.: *Travels in Nubia*, 1819
Burton, Captain R.F.: *First Footsteps in East Africa*, 1856
Buxton, D.: *Travels in Ethiopia* (2nd edn), 1967
Bynner, W.: *Journey with Genius*, 1953
Byron, R.: *The Road to Oxiana*, 1937
Cabanne, P.: *Dialogues with Marcel Duchamp* (trans. R. Padgett), 1987
Cagnolo, Father C.: *The Akikuyu*, Nyeri 1933
Camerer, A.: *Essaie sur l'Histoire Antique d'Abyssinie*, Paris 1926
Campbell, M.: *A Short History of the British Embassy Addis-Ababa*, Addis Ababa 1972
Carruthers, D.: *Arabian Adventure*, 1935
Carruthers, D.: *Beyond the Caspian*, 1949
Chanler, W.A.: *Through Jungle and Desert*, 1896
Chapman, A.: *On Safari*, 1908
Chapman, A.: *Savage Sudan*, 1921
Chapman, A.: *Retrospect*, 1928
Chasseaud, G.W.: *The Druses of Lebanon*, 1855
Cheesman, R.E.: *In Unknown Arabia*, 1926
Cheesman, R.E.: *Lake Tana and the Blue Nile*, 1936
Churchill, W.S.: *The River War* (2 vols), 1899
Clarke, B.: *Berber Village*, 1959
Codrai, R.: *The Seven Shaikhdoms*, 1990

Codrai, R.: *Abu Dhabi*, 1992

Codrai, R.: *Faces of the Emirates*, 2001

Coffey, T.M.: *Lion by the Tail*, 1974

Colenso, F.E. & Durnford, E.: *History of the Zulu War and its Origin* (2nd edn), 1881

Conrad, J.: *Works* (22 vols), Gresham ('Medallion' edn), 1925

Coulbeaux, J.B.: *Histoire Politique et Réligieuse d'Abyssinie* (3 vols), Paris 1929

Cowles, V.: *The Phantom Major: The Story of David Stirling and the SAS Regiment*, 1958

Crayon, G. (Washington Irving): *The Alhambra* (2 vols), 1832

Cromer, The Earl of: *Modern Egypt* (2 vols), 1908

Cunninghame Graham, R.B.: *Mogreb-El-Acksa*, 1898

de Gaury, G.: *Rulers of Mecca*, 1951

de Monfreid, H.: *Secrets of the Red Sea*, 1934

de Monfreid, H.: *Hashish*, 1935

de Monfreid, H.: *Sea Adventures*, 1937

de Saint-Exupéry, A.: *Wind, Sand and Stars* (1st edn 1939), 1941

Devas, N.: *Two Flamboyant Fathers*, 1966

de Watteville, V.: *Out in the Blue*, 1927

Dickson, H.R.P.: *The Arab of the Desert* (3rd edn), 1959

Dollman, J. & Burlace, J.: *Rowland Ward's Records of Big Game* (8th edn), 1922

Doughty, C.M.: *Travels in Arabia Deserta* (2 vols), Cambridge 1888

Dracopoli, I.I.: *Through Jubaland to the Lorian Swamp* (2nd edn), 1914

Dufton, H.: *A Narrative of a Journey Through Abyssinia, 1862–63* (2nd edn), 1867

Dugmore, A. Radclyffe: *The Vast Sudan* (2nd edn), 1926

Dutton, E.A.T.: *Kenya Mountain*, 1930

Dutton, E.A.T.: *Lillibullero* (2nd edn), Zanzibar 1946

Edelberg, L. & Jones, S.: *Nuristan*, Graz 1979

Essad-Bey: *Mohammed*, 1938

Evans-Pritchard, E.E.: *The Nuer*, Oxford 1940

Farrer, J.A.: *Zululand and the Zulus* (3rd edn), 1879

Fergusson, B.: *Eton Portrait* (photographs by L. Moholy-Nagy), 1937

Fergusson, Captain V.H. *et al.*: *The Story of Fergie Bey*, 1930

Fitzpatrick, (Sir) J.P.: *Jock of the Bushveld* (1st edn, 4th impression), 1907

Fitzroy, Sir A.: *A History of the Travellers Club*, 1929

Flecker, J.E.: *Hassan*, 1924

French, Major The Hon. G.: *Lord Chelmsford and the Zulu War*, 1939

Fulanain (Hedgcock, S.E.): *Haji Rikkan, Marsh Arab*, 1927

Geddes, M.: *The Church History of Ethiopia*, 1696

Gleichen, Count: *With the Mission to Menelik*, 1898

Glubb, J.B.: *The Story of the Arab Legion*, 1948

Grabham, G.W. & Black, R.P.: *Report on the Mission to Lake Tana*, Cairo 1925
Graves, R.: *Lawrence and the Arabs*, 1927
Graziani, R.: *Fronte Sud*, Milan 1938
Grey, R.F.: *The Sonjo of Tanganyika*, 1963
Gruhl, M.: *Abyssinia at Bay*, 1935
Guarmani, C.: *Northern Nejd*, 1938
Guest, E.: *Notes on Plants and … Their Names in Iraq*, 1933
Haile Selassie: *The Autobiography, 1892–1937*, 1976
Hallpike, C.R.: *The Konso of Ethiopia*, 1972
Harlan, H.: 'A Caravan Journey through Abyssinia', *National Geographical Magazine* XLVII.: (6), 613–63, June 1925
Harris: *Guerilla Warfare in Gojjam*, 1941
Harris, W.B.: *The Land of an African Sultan*, 1889
Harris, W. Cornwallis: *The Highlands of AEthiopia* (3 vols, 2nd edn), 1844
Hassanein, A.M.: *The Lost Oases*, 1925
Hayes, A.J.: *The Source of the Blue Nile*, 1905
Henderson, E.: *This Strange Eventful History*, 1988
Henderson, K.D.D.: *The Making of Modern Sudan*, 1953
Henty, G.A.: *The March to Magdala*, 1868
Herbert, Agnes: *Two Dianas in Somaliland*, 1908
Hindlip, Lord: *Sport and Travel*, 1906
Hodson, A.W.: *Seven Years in Southern Abyssinia*, 1927
Hodson, A.W.: *Where Lion Reign*, nd (c.1928)
Hogarth, D.G.: *The Penetration of Arabia*, 1905
Hogarth, D.G.: *Arabia*, Oxford 1922
Hollis, A.C.: *The Masai, Their Language and Folklore*, Oxford 1905
Hooker, J.D. & Ball, J.: *Journal of a Tour in Marocco and the Great Atlas*, 1878
Hotten, J.C.: *Abyssinia and its People*, 1868
Howarth, D.: *The Desert King: A Life of Ibn Saud*, 1964
Ingrams, H.: *Arabia and the Isles*, 1942
Izzard, M.: *Freya Stark: A Biography*, 1993
Jackson, H.C.: *Osman Digna*, 1926
Jacob, H.: *Kings of Arabia*, 1923
James, F.L.: *Wild Tribes of the Sudan*, New York 1883
Jardine, D.: *The Mad Mullah*, 1923
Jarvis, Major C.S.: *Arab Command* (4th impression), 1943
Jennings, Major J.W. & Addison, C.: *With the Abyssinians in Somaliland*, 1905
Johnston, C.: *Travels in Southern Abyssinia* (2 vols), 1844
Johnston, Sir H.: *The Kilima-Njaro Expedition*, 1886
Jones, A. & Monroe, E.: *The History of Ethiopia* (late edn), Oxford 1970
Keun, Odette: *A Foreigner looks at the British Sudan*, 1930
Kinglake, A.W.: *Eothen: Traces of Travel Brought Home from the East*, 1844

Lawrence, T.E.: *Seven Pillars of Wisdom: A Triumph* (1926), 1935

Lawrence, T.E.: *Crusader Castles* (2 vols), 1936

Leese, A.S.: *A Treatise on the One-Humped Camel in Health and Disease*, Stamford 1933

Leonard, Major A.G.: *The Camel, its Uses and Management*, 1894

Lloyd, S.: *Twin Rivers: A Brief History of Iraq* (2nd edn), 1947

Lloyd-Jones, Major W.: *Havash! Frontier Adventures in Kenya*, 1925

Lobo, J.: *Voyage Historique d'Abyssinie*, Paris 1728

Lobo, J.: *A Short Relation of the River Nile*, 1791

MacFie, J.W.S.: *An Ethiopian Diary*, 1936

MacMichael, H.: *Brands Used by the Chief Camel-Owning Tribes of Kordofan*, Cambridge 1913

MacMichael, H.: *A History of the Arabs in the Sudan* (2 vols), Cambridge 1922

Mack, J.E.: *A Prince of Our Disorder*, 1976

Maitland, A.: *Speke, and the Discovery of the Source of the Nile*, 1971

Maitland, A.: *A Tower in a Wall: Conversations with Dame Freya Stark*, 1982

Maitland, A.: *Wilfred Thesiger: A Life in Pictures*, 2004

Mansur, A.: *Land of Uz*, 1911

Markham, C.: *A History of the Abyssinian Expedition*, 1869

Martelli, G.: *Italy against the World*, 1937

Marvin, G.: *Bullfight*, 1988

Maxwell, G.: *Harpoon at a Venture* (3rd edn), 1953

Maxwell, G.: *A Reed Shaken by the Wind*, 1957

Maxwell, G.: *Ring of Bright Water*, 1960

Maydon, Major H.C.: *Simen, its Heights and Abysses*, 1925

Maydon, Major H.C. *et al.*: *Big Game Shooting in Africa*, 1932

Meakin, B.: *The Land of the Moors*, 1901

Meakin, B.: *The Moors*, 1902

Merrild, K.: *A Poet and Two Painters*, 1938

Miles, Col S.B.: *Countries and Tribes of the Persian Gulf* (2nd edn, 2 vols), 1920

Millais, J.G.: *Far Away up the Nile*, 1924

Mockler, A.: *Haile Selassie's War*, 1984

Monod, T.: *L'Adrar Moritanien (Sahara Occidental)*, Dakar 1952

Montbard, G.: *Among the Moors*, 1894

Moorehead, A.: *African Trilogy*, 1944

Moorhouse, G.: *The Fearful Void*, 1974

Mosley, L.: *Gideon goes to War*, 1955

Musil, A.: *The Middle Euphrates*, New York 1927

Musil, A.: *The Manners and Customs of the Rawala Bedouins*, New York 1928

Naval Intelligence Division: *A Handbook of Arabia*, 1916

Naval Intelligence Division: *Geographical Handbook Series: Iraq and the Persian Gulf*, 1944

Naval Intelligence Division: *Geographical Handbook Series: Western Arabia and the Red Sea*, 1946

Nesbitt, L.M.: *Desert and Forest: The Exploration of the Abyssinian Danakil*, 1934

Neumann, A.H.: *Elephant Hunting in East Equatorial Africa*, 1898

Newby, E.: *A Short Walk in the Hindu Kush*, 1958

Niebuhr, C. (trans. R. Heron): *Travels through Arabia* (2 vols), 1792

O'Balance, E.: *The War in Yemen*, 1971

Omrani, B. & Leeming, M.: *Afghanistan: A Companion and Guide*, 2005

Pakenham, T.: *The Mountains of Rasselas*, 1959

Palinurus (Cyril Connolly): *The Unquiet Grave* (reprint), 1946

Pallme, I.: *Travels in Kordofan*, 1844

Parkyns, M.: *Life in Abyssinia ... Three Years Residence and Travels* (2 vols), 1853

Pavitt, N.: *Kenya: The First Explorers*, 1989

Pavitt, N.: *Samburu*, 1991

Pavitt, N.: *Turkana*, 1997

Pease, Sir A.E.: *Travels and Sport in Africa* (3 vols), 1902

Pease, Sir A.E.: *The Book of the Lion*, 1913

Percival, A.B.: *A Game Ranger's Notebook*, 1924

Philby, H. St J.: *The Heart of Arabia*, 1922

Philby, H. St J.: *Arabia of the Wahabys*, 1928

Philby, H. St J.: *The Empty Quarter*, 1933

Philby, H. St J.: *Harun Al-Rashid*, 1933

Philby, H. St J.: *Sheba's Daughters*, 1939

Philby, H. St J.: *Pilgrim in Arabia*, 1943

Philby, H. St J.: *The Background of Islam*, 1947

Phillips, W.: *Oman: A History*, 1967

Playfair, Captain R.L.: *The History of Arabia Felix, or Yemen*, 1859

Portal, Sir G.: *My Mission to Abyssinia*, 1892

Powell-Cotton, Major P.H.G.: *A Sporting Trip Through Abyssinia*, 1902

Powell-Cotton, Major P.H.G.: *In Unknown Africa*, 1904

Raswan, C.: *The Black Tents of Arabia*, 1935

Rayne, Major H.: *Sun, Sand and Somals*, 1921

Rayne, Major H.: *The Ivory Raiders*, 1923

Rey, C.F.: *Unconquered Abyssinia as it is Today*, 1923

Rey, C.F.: *In the Country of the Blue Nile*, 1927

Rey, C.F.: *The Romance of the Portuguese in Abyssinia*, 1929

Rey, C.F.: *The Real Abyssinia* (2nd edn), 1935

Rich, C.J.: *Narrative of a Residence in Koordistan* (2 vols), 1836

Richards, F.: *A Persian Journey*, 1931

Richards, V.: *Portrait of T.E. Lawrence*, 1936

Richardson, J.: *Travels in the Great Desert of the Sahara* (2 vols), 1848
Riefenstahl, L.: *The People of Kau*, 1976
Rihani, A.: *Ibn S'aud: His People and His Land*, 1928
Robertson, Sir G.: *The Kafirs of the Hindu Kush*, 1896
Rodd, F.J.R.: *People of the Veil*, 1926
Salim, S.: *Marsh Dwellers of the Euphrates Delta*, 1962
Salt, H.: *Twenty Four Views*, 1809
Salt, H.: *A Voyage to Abyssinia*, 1814
Sandford, C.: *The Lion of Judah Hath Prevailed*, 1955
Schmidt, D.: *Yemen: The Unknown War*, 1968
Scott, H.: *In the High Yemen*, 1942
Seligman, C.G.: *Pagan Tribes of the Nilotic Sudan* (2nd edn), 1965
Selous, Captain F.C.: *African Nature Notes and Reminiscences*, 1908
Shah, T.: *In Search of King Solomon's Mines*, 2002
Sherry, N.: *Conrad's Eastern World* (1st pbk edn), 1976
Shipton, E.E.: *Upon that Mountain*, 1943
Sim, K.: *Desert Traveller: The Life of Jean Louis Burckhardt*, 1969
Skinner, R.P.: *Abyssinia Today*, 1906
Smiley, D.: *Arabian Assignment*, 1975
Smith, A.D.: *Through Unknown African Countries*, 1897
Soane, E.B.: *To Mesopotamia and Kurdistan in Disguise*, 1912
Spencer, P.: *The Samburu*, 1965
Stark, F.: *The Valleys of the Assassins*, 1934
Stark, F.: *The Southern Gates of Arabia*, 1936
Stark, F.: *Seen in the Hadhramaut*, New York 1939
Stark, F.: *Letters from Syria*, 1942
Stark, F.: *Beyond Euphrates* (autobiography vol. II, 1928–33), 1951
Stark, F.: *Rivers of Time* (compiled by Freya Stark and A. Maitland;
    introduction by A. Maitland), 1982
Steele, P.: *Eric Shipton: Everest and Beyond*, 1998
Steer, G.L.: *Caesar in Abyssinia*, 1936
Steer, G.L.: *Sealed and Delivered*, 1942
Stern, H.A.: *Wanderings Among the Falashas in Abyssinia*, 1862
Stevens, E.S.: *Folk Tales of Iraq*, 1931
Stigand, Captain C.H.: *To Abyssinia Through an Unknown Land*, 1910
Stigand, Captain C.H.: *Hunting the Elephant in Africa*, New York 1913
Stigand, Captain C.H.: *The Land of Zinj*, 1913
Stoddard, L.: *The New World of Islam*, 1921
Storrs, R.: *Orientations* (2nd edn), 1937
Sutherland, J.: *The Adventures of an Elephant Hunter*, 1912
Swayne, Captain H.G.C.: *Seventeen Trips Through Somaliland*, 1895
Sykes, C.: *Orde Wingate*, 1959

Sykes, Sir M.: *The Caliph's Last Heritage*, 1915
Talbot, D.A.: *Ethiopia: Liberation Silver Jubilee, 1941–66*, Addis Ababa 1966
Taylor, S.: *The Mighty Nimrod*, 1989
Tellez and Knapton: *Travels of the Jesuits in Ethiopia*, 1710
Thesiger, E.: *Practically True*, 1927
Thesiger, E.: *Adventures in Embroidery*, 1941
Thomas, B.: *Alarms and Excursions in Arabia*, 1931
Thomas, B.: *Arabia Felix*, 1932
Thomas, B.: *The Arabs* (1st impression Keystone Library), 1940
Thomson, J.: *Travels in the Atlas and Southern Morocco*, 1889
Tilman, H.: *Snow on the Equator*, 1937
Treat, I.: *Pearls, Arms and Hashish*, 1930
Tristram, H.B.: *The Great Sahara*, 1860
Ullendorf, E.: *The Ethiopians* (2nd edn), Oxford 1973
van der Post, L.: *The Heart of the Hunter*, 1961
Villiers, A.: *Sons of Sinbad*, 1940
Vivian, H.: *Through Lion Land to the Court of the Lion of Judah*, 1901
von Höhnel, Lieut L.: The *Discovery by Count Teleki of Lakes Rudolf and Stefanie* (2 vols), 1894
Walker, C.H.: *The Abyssinian at Home*, 1933
Watson, G.: *Book Society*, 1980
Waugh, E.: *Remote People*, 1931
Waugh, E.: *Black Mischief*, 1932
Wavell, A.J.B.: *A Modern Pilgrim in Mecca*, 1912
Wellsted, J.R.: *Travels to the City of the Caliphs* (2 vols), 1840
White, T.H.: *The Goshawk* (2nd edn), 1960
White, T.H.: *Verses* (limited edn of 100 copies), Alderney 1962
Wienholt, A.: *The Story of a Lion Hunt*, 1922
Wilmot, A.: *History of the Zulu War*, 1880
Wilson, Sir A.: *The Persian Gulf*, 1928
Wilson, Sir A.: *South West Persia*, 1941
Wingate, O.: *Appreciation of the Ethiopian Campaign*, (after) 1941
Wylde, A.B.: *Abyssinia*, 1901
Wyndham, R.: *The Gentle Savage: A Sudanese Journey ...*, 1936
Young, G.: *Return to the Marshes*, 1977
Young, G.: *Iraq: Land of Two Rivers*, 1980
Young, G.: *In Search of Conrad*, 1991
Young, Sir H.: *The Independent Arab*, 1933
Zulfo, I.H.: *Karari*, 1980

INDEX

WT = Wilfred Thesiger

Ababdah (tribe): 238, 239
Abakan: 395
Abd al Nawab: 360, 365
Abd el Ghani: 406
Abdi Awad (Khartoum tailors): 126
Abdullahi: 97
Aberdare Mts: 415
Abhebad, Lake: 107, 116, 261
Abu Dhabi: 165, 293, 296, 297, 298, 299, 436,
    455, 460
'Abu Higl' (lion): 154
Abu Shajar: 310
Abu Tayyi: 226
Abyssinia: 3, 7, 17, 20–2, 24, 30, 31, 33, 37–40,
    42, 44, 46, 49, 50, 52, 54, 55, 60, 64, 67–9, 72,
    74, 76, 77, 88, 89, 91, 94, 96, 97, 107, 109,
    119, 122, 127, 140, 153, 162, 168, 194–8, 200,
    201–3, 205, 207–9, 211, 214, 219, 220, 229,
    232, 233, 239, 241, 242, 245, 251, 255,
    257–60, 264, 269, 274, 285, 372, 377, 378,
    380, 391, 387, 411, 416, 422, 448, 462; (*see
    also* Ethiopia)
Abyssinians: 26, 27, 50, 66, 79, 110, 124, 200,
    206, 208, 209, 215, 216, 221, 255, 257
Accra: 426
Adamson, George (1906–89): 388
Adamson, Joy (1910–80): 388
Addis Ababa: 5, 6, 7, 11, 17–19, 21, 23, 29, 31,
    32, 34, 35, 37, 39, 40, 43, 44, 46, 49, 50, 54, 56,
    62, 65, 72, 74, 76–9, 82, 88, 91, 94, 97, 98, 100,
    101, 103, 107, 109, 119, 132, 134, 150, 153,
    168, 201, 203, 204, 209, 211, 214, 217, 220,
    221, 253, 255–8, 260, 261, 265, 268, 378, 382,
    383, 385, 405–6, 411, 422, 429, 435, 458, 460
Aden: 46, 49, 74, 204, 305
Adoiamara (Danakil tribe): 102, 108
Adventures in Embroidery (Ernest Thesiger):
    335

Afar (tribes): *see* Danakil
Afdam: 82, 107, 113, 116
Afghanistan: 174, 308, 335, 338, 345, 346, 349,
    350, 359, 360, 410
Afghans: 286, 335, 359, 409
Africa: 2, 146, 165, 174, 181, 193, 202, 241, 264,
    391, 418, 435, 447, 450, 453, 459, 462
'Africano' (bull): 457
Agadir: 357
Agedabia: 242, 243, 246
Agheila: 243, 246
Agibar: 218, 219
Agra: 437
Agrigento: 384
Ahamado (chief): 110
Ahermoumou: 357
Ai Qalat: 353
Ain Diyar: 253
Aioui (cliffs): 355
Airlie, David George Ogilvy, 13th Earl of, DL:
    429
Airlie, 12th Earl of, KT GCVO MC: 74, 79, 80,
    429
Ait Arbaa: 352, 356
Aiyun: 286
Aizamale (tribe): 117
Ajram: 326
Akarit: 248
al-Atrash, Sultan Pasha: 236
al Auf, Muhammad: 278, 281, 284
al bu Daraj: 346
al bu Muhammed, Sheikh Majid of the: 313,
    342
al bu Salih: 368
al Essa: 310
al Faris, Jasim: 313, 317, 323
al Glawi, Thami: 156, 350, 351, 427
al Kadar, Emir Abd: 224
al Qaiyun Khan, Khan Abd: 337
al Ridah, Abd: 320

511

al Shalan, Nuri: 231, 236
al Wahid, Abd: 323, 340
Alaqa Dessie: 383
Ali (Sultan of Aussa): 261
Alia Bay: 423, 424, 429
Alingar river: 364, 365
Alawites: 229
Aleppo: 152, 348
Alexander, King of Serbia: 17
Alexander, Mrs Cecil Frances: 18
Alexandria: 238
Algarve: 414
Algeria: 224, 248
Algiers: 16
Ali Wali: 110
Alice in Wonderland (Lewis Carroll): 78
Alington, Dr C.A.: 66
Allen, (later Sir) Mark, CMG: 442, 443
Allen, W.E.D.: 210, 218, 219
Alresford: 85
Alston, Lt Gordon: 243–7
Amman: 152, 225, 348
Amritsar: 201
Amundsen, Roald (1872–1928): 192
Anka wells: 138
Aosta, Duke of: 201, 218
Altair (dhow): 118–19
Among the Mountains (WT): 308, 338, 345,
    346, 357, 360, 361, 364, 381, 443
Annapurna: 445
Antinous: 393
Anzio: 241
Aouzou: 184, 185
Arab Legion: 152
Arabia: 2, 126, 146, 153, 164, 165, 167, 174, 176,
    178, 180, 181, 202, 257, 258, 262–4, 266, 272,
    274, 275, 285, 286, 295, 298, 301, 304, 307,
    308, 310, 324, 326, 331, 350, 368, 370, 372,
    374, 380, 401, 408, 411, 416, 434, 436, 437,
    448, 457, 459
Arabian Sands (WT): 40, 114, 115, 119, 152,
    178, 188, 213, 232, 258, 267, 269, 272, 274,
    277, 282, 285, 286, 289, 293, 300, 304, 305,
    313, 330, 350, 359, 365, 370, 371, 376,
    377–82, 395–7, 399–401, 424, 427, 455
Arabs: 229, 242, 245, 251, 253, 260, 264, 271,
    277, 279, 283, 284, 286, 292, 301, 306, 310,
    316, 320, 322, 374, 402, 415, 417
Arami (of the Tedda): 184
Archer, Sir Geoffrey F., KCMG OBE: 46, 52, 95,
    154
Archer, Olive (Lady): 46, 52, 111, 154
Archer's Post: 386
Armenia: 254
Armenian massacres: 16
Armenians: 16, 253

Arnah: 252
Arnhem: 241
Arusha: 397, 398
Arussi Mts: 36, 79, 96, 98, 99, 100, 101
Asaimara (Danakil tribe): 102, 108, 110, 113
Asba Tafari: 110
Aseila: 118
Asfa Wossen, Crown Prince of Ethiopia: 38, 44,
    90, 204, 255, 257, 259–61, 377
Asia: 76, 181, 202, 357, 381, 409, 410
Assal, Lake: 116, 147
Assareg: 356
Assir: 273, 289
Assyrians: 253
Athens: 348, 402
Athlit: 250, 253, 255
Astley (*née* Vigors), Kathleen Mary (Mrs
    Reginald), CBE (WT's mother): 1, 2, 6–10,
    18–24, 27–32, 34, 37, 38, 40, 41, 43, 46, 47,
    49–56, 58–63, 67, 68, 71, 76, 80, 81, 86, 87,
    89, 93, 94, 96, 101, 103–5, 107, 109, 110, 114,
    117, 128, 132, 134–7, 140, 145, 147, 149, 150,
    152, 154–6, 159–61, 163, 166, 167, 176, 179,
    181, 184, 187, 189–92, 194, 196, 198, 203,
    204, 207, 208, 215, 216, 220–2, 224, 227–9,
    232–5, 237, 239–41, 245, 249–51, 253, 255,
    256, 259, 263, 265, 267, 268, 270, 271, 273–5,
    278, 286, 289–94, 296, 299, 303, 309, 311,
    316, 322, 324, 326–33, 335, 337, 338, 340,
    341, 343, 346, 348, 349, 353–5, 358, 359,
    365–71, 374–6, 378, 383, 384, 386, 392–400,
    404, 407, 408, 410, 415, 417, 418, 423, 424,
    426–9, 434, 445, 456, 459, 460, 461, 463
Astley, Reginald Basil (WT's stepfather): 85, 86,
    87, 104, 232, 233, 240, 241, 243, 267
Aswan: 130
Atbara river: 202
Atlas Mts: 156, 160, 187, 350, 351, 352, 353,
    354, 356, 357, 427
Auchinleck, Field-Marshal Sir Claude, GCB:
    238
Audas, Major R.J.: 135
Aussa: 91, 93, 101, 103, 110, 112, 113, 115, 120,
    122, 187, 408
Awash river: 40, 79–82, 90, 91, 94–6, 100, 102,
    103, 105–7, 109, 110, 112, 116, 120–2, 211,
    219, 261
Ayelu, Mt: 102
Azairij: 346
Azilal: 356
Azraq: 152
Azrou: 351

Ba'adhava: 309
Baalbek: 152, 228, 348
Babault, René: 429

Backhouse, Olive: 29, 79, 86
Badakhshan: 461
Badayat (tribe): 153, 179
Badogale (tribe): 112
Badoglio, General Pietro: 209
Bagenalstown: 18, 376
Baggara (Arabs): 180
Baghdad: 222, 307, 309, 315, 323, 335, 341, 346, 350, 358, 365, 369
Bagnold, Brigadier Ralph Ager, OBE FRCS: 264, 301
Bahdu: 102, 107–10, 115, 122
Bahr al Jabal: 168, 171, 190
Bahr dar Giorgis: 214
Bahr el Ghazal: 163
Bahrain: 266, 296, 298, 300, 303
Baï: 284, 285
Bait Kathir (tribe): 266, 269–71, 277, 280, 281, 283, 284, 291
Baker, Florence (Lady): 101
Bakhtiari (nomads): 404
Balaia (Belayia), Mt: 197, 198, 213
Balcha, Dedjazmatch: 22
Bale: 96, 103
Bali: 437
Balkh: 410
Ballynoe: 51, 52
Baltit: 335, 343
Baluchistan: 340
Bandhavgarh: 49, 444
Bani Hussain (tribe): 140–3, 148, 151, 153, 154, 155, 164, 169
Bani Lam (tribe): 358
Bani Sakhr (tribe): 153
Baragoi: 389, 416–18, 424, 429, 430, 442
Barbary sheep: 138, 160
Bardai: 179, 183, 185
Baring, Evelyn: (see Cromer, 1st Earl of)
Baringo, Lake: 389, 414
Barker, 'Pongo': 130
Barlow, William: 460
Baro river: 195
Barton, Sir Sidney P.: 77, 79–81, 91, 94, 95, 110, 114, 117, 120
Bashgul: 359, 360, 409
Basra: 106, 280, 315–17, 319, 323–7, 342, 346, 349, 358, 359, 365, 366, 368, 383
Basso: 179
Bath: 442
Bawden, Edward, RA: 205
Baz Muhammad: 409
Bazun: 346
BBC (British Broadcasting Corporation): 290, 415
Beachley Rectory: 32, 51
Beaudesert House (school): 61

Beethoven, Ludwig van (1770–1827): 224
Beirut: 152, 232, 348, 365
Beitz (German engineer): 115
Belayia, Mt: (see Balayia)
Belgrade: 17
Bell, Gertrude Margaret Lowthian (1868–1926): 228, 333
Bell, Walter Dalrymple Maitland (1880–1954): 420
Benghazi: 384
Bentinck, Count Arthur: 72, 131, 200, 205, 239
Berbera: 46, 154
Beriforo: 108
Besud: 346, 348
Bevan, Reverend C.O.: 65, 66
Bhola, Siddiq: 391, 435, 440, 445, 452, 456
Bhopal: 444–5
Bianchi, Gustavo: 93
Biglieri, Signor: 93
Bilen: 80, 81, 103, 106, 107, 108
Billings & Edmonds (tailors): 361
bin Duailan, of the Manahil tribe ('The Cat'): 294
bin Ghabaisha, Salim: 65, 180, 273, 277, 286, 288, 290, 291, 294, 298, 299, 304, 378, 393, 436, 439
bin Hasan, Prince Hasan: 412
bin Kabina, Salim: 65, 180, 272, 273, 277–81, 283, 284, 287, 288, 290, 293, 294, 298, 299, 304, 376, 378, 436, 439
bin Majid, Falih: 313, 315, 318, 340–2
bin Maneti, Hasan: 313, 315, 317, 349, 352, 358
bin Mohamed Abbas: 340, 341, 342
bin Tafl, Musallim: 281, 284, 287
bin Thuqub, Amara: 65, 180, 315, 317, 320, 322, 323, 326, 358, 359, 365, 366, 367
bin Zaltin: 243
Bir Natrun: 145, 146, 147, 150, 167, 178
'Black Hand': 17
Black Kafirs: 338, 359, 360
Blackheath: 460
Blanch, Lesley: 406, 407
blue-winged geese: 96, 98, 120
Boer War: 17
Boma: 20
Bond, James: 1
Bookman, the (magazine): 379
Boran (tribe): 39, 379, 423, 425
Borkou: 179
Born Free (Joy Adamson): 388
Bosra eski Sham: 226
Botswana: 455
Botting, Douglas: 332
Bou Aurial: 356
Bou Duerar: 354
Bouerat: 243, 246, 248

Boumalne: 353, 354

Boustead, Colonel (later Sir) Hugh, KBE CMG DSO MC: 198, 211, 213, 216, 217, 219, 411

Bowcock, Philip: 169

Breuil, Abbé Henri: 119

British Academy: 442

British Legation (Addis Ababa): 5, 8, 29, 32–4, 36, 43, 44, 56, 58, 62, 63, 72, 76, 77, 102, 132, 150, 204, 267, 378, 385, 405, 459

British Ornithological Union: 127

Brittany: 70, 72

Brocklehurst, Captain Henry Courteney: 129, 130, 138

Brondy, Matteo: 161

Brooke, Rupert Chawner (1887–1915): 83

Brooke, Thomas Humphrey, CVO: 235

Browning (small-arms manufacturer): 317

Brunei: 438

Bu Mughaifat: 313, 358

Buchan, John, 1st Baron Tweedsmuir (1875–1940): 65, 71, 89, 90, 114, 120, 371, 445

Buckingham, Bishop of: 67

Buckingham Palace: 457

Buckle, Mary ('Minna'): 35, 46, 49, 50, 51, 61, 62, 88, 132, 151, 154, 199, 233, 265

Buraimi: 298, 299, 303

Burckhardt, Jean Louis (1784–1817): 226

Burg-i-Matral: 409

Burma: 262, 263, 266

Burton, Isobel (Lady) (1831–96): 10

Burton, Captain (later Sir) Richard Francis, KCMG (1821–90): 22, 380, 400, 414

Burye: 211, 214

'Bushbaby' (also 'Bushboy'), Samuel Ngarientim Lepushirit (Samburu): 446

Bushire: 307

Buthelezi, Chief Mangosuthu: 14

Butler, Colonel: 225

Buxton, David: 259

Byam-Shaw, James: 408

Byam-Shaw School of Art: 408

Byron, Robert: 407

Cairo: 46, 49, 130, 188, 197, 221, 225, 237, 238–42, 246, 248, 250, 256, 259, 263, 265, 266, 268, 275, 311, 335

Calabria: 16

Caldwell, Edmund: 40, 63

Cambridge, University of: 72, 93, 457

Camel Corps: 200

Campbell, Robin Francis, CBE DSO: 70, 83, 84, 87, 122

Campbell twins: 61

Canary Islands: 400

Carless, Hugh Michael, CMG: 360, 361

Casablanca: 350, 354, 357

Caspian Sea: 307, 406, 407

Castlemaine, Lord: 19

Catania: 384

Catherine II, Empress of Russia, ('Catherine the Great', 1729–96): 12

Cavalry Club: 322

Cecil, Reverend William Gascoigne: 9

Cederquist, Reverend Karl: 29

Celebes: 437

Central Asia: 337

Chad: 147, 148, 164, 179

Chalala: 325

Chalbi desert: 385, 388

Chaman: 409

Chamar pass: 361

Chamar valley: 364

Chamberlain, Arthur Neville (1869–1940): 194, 196

Champain, Frank: 29

Chance, Ronnie: 63

Chapman, Abel (1851–1929): 129

Chapman-Andrews, Sir Edwin, KCMG OBE: 205, 383, 411

Chapon Baisac: 124

Charles I, King: 18

Charterhouse, the: 460

Charteris, Mary Rose: 275

Chasseaud, George Washington: 232

Cheesman, Colonel Robert Ernest, CBE: 79, 81, 205, 296, 297

Chelalo, Mt: 98, 111

Chelmsford, The Hon Frederic Augustus Thesiger, 2nd Baron (WT's grandfather): 9, 11, 12, 13, 14, 90, 383

Chelmsford, Sir Frederic Thesiger, 1st Baron (WT's great-grandfather): 13, 89

Chelmsford, 2nd Baroness (née Adria Fanny Heath, WT's grandmother): 14, 29, 61

Chelmsford, The Hon Frederic John Napier Thesiger, 1st Viscount, PC GCSI GCMG GCIE GBE (WT's uncle): 11, 15, 47, 66, 74, 90, 94, 201

Chelmsford, 1st Viscountess (née The Hon Frances Charlotte Guest): 90

Chelmsford, The Hon Andrew Charles Gerald Thesiger, 2nd Viscount: 61

Chelsea: 1, 132, 243, 267, 385, 434

Cheltenham College: 15, 16

Chenchia: 379

Chercher Mts: 21, 22, 110

Cheshire Regiment: 197, 198, 199

Child & Co.: 449

Chilinji pass: 343

Chindits: 262

Chitral: 335, 337, 338, 343, 346, 349, 359, 360

Christie, Dame Agatha Mary Clarissa, Lady Mallowan (1890–1976): 309
Christopher, Robin: 459
Churchill, (later Sir) Winston Leonard Spencer (1874–1965): 133, 239
Cipressi, Villa: 87
Circassians: 229, 231, 253
Claridge's Hotel: 120, 426
Clark, Dr Peter: 367, 455
Clarke, Bryan: 352
Clarke, Brigadier Dudley: 241
Clun: 235
Clyde river: 196, 197
Codrai, Ronald (1924–2000): 304, 306
Collins (Captain W.G. Thesiger's batman, later manservant): 17, 21
Colnaghi & Co. Ltd, P. & D. (fine art dealers): 275, 408
Como, Lake: 85, 87, 383, 395
Congo: 2, 17, 20, 154, 181, 335
Connolly, Cyril Vernon (1903–74): 437
Conrad, Joseph (1857–1924): 133, 134, 437
Constantinople: 427
Constanza: 73
Cope, Mrs: 337
Copenhagen: 370, 371, 373, 374, 375, 393
Corbett, Edward James ('Jim', 1875–1955): 57
Coryton, George: 190
Coulsdon: 460, 461, 462
Coward, (later Sir) Noël Pierce (1899–1973): 224
Cowles, Virginia: 245
Cox, Major-General Sir Percy (former President of the RGS): 120
Cromer, Evelyn Baring, 1st Earl of (1841–1917): 124
Croydon: 463
Cunningham, Sir George, GCIE KCSI OBE: 337
Curre, Mrs (WT's godmother): 29, 52
Curtis Brown Group Ltd (WT's literary agents): 326, 375, 394
Cyrenaica: 242

Dadi: 180, 273
Dahm: 271, 287, 288
Daily Telegraph: 380, 400
Dair: 226
Danakil (tribes): 2, 21, 38, 39, 45, 74, 79–81, 84, 91, 93, 95, 99, 100, 102, 104, 105, 107–15, 117, 122, 123, 125, 127, 130, 132, 140, 141, 157, 162, 167, 171, 179, 184, 187, 189, 190, 193, 229, 244, 264, 269, 389, 408, 424, 435
Danakil Diary, The (WT): 80, 82, 98, 99–101, 119, 121, 162, 274, 381, 460
Dangila: 79, 214
Daoud: 77

Darkot: 343
Darley, Major Henry: 40
Dasht-i-Lut: 406, 407
Dasht-i-Mazar: 346
Daud, Idris: 65, 132, 147–9, 153, 155, 158, 164, 169, 176, 179, 180, 182, 184, 185, 187–9, 194, 201, 202, 224, 273, 277
Davidson, W.J.: 205
Dawson, Geoffrey: 190
de Chardin, Pierre Teilhard: 119
de Gaury, Colonel Gerald: 3, 213, 221, 222, 225, 226
de Halpert, Frank: 97, 109
de Henriques, Fiore: 4
de Monfreid, Daniel: 118
de Monfreid, Henri: 22, 31, 111, 118, 119, 138, 184
de Watteville, Bernard Percival (1877–1924): 154–5
de Watteville, Vivienne (1900–57): 154–5
Dearlove, Sir Richard: 418
Debra Lebanos: 209, 221
Debra Markos: 214, 216–18
Dege & Co. (tailors): 361
Deh Kundi: 348
Deh Zangi: 348
Delafield, William: 459
Dembecha: 214, 215, 216
Denmark: 360, 371
Denmark, Crown Prince of: 12
Derra: 218
Dervishes: 224–5
Desert, Marsh and Mountain (WT): 46, 57, 73, 88, 101, 114, 179, 258, 323, 357, 379, 381, 409, 442, 443, 449, 455
Dessie: 45, 198, 245, 255, 257, 258, 260–2, 266, 334
Devas, Anthony: 2, 3, 4, 233, 408
Devas, Nicolette: 233
Dhaufar: 271, 285, 291, 305
Dhiby well: 297
Diana, Signor: 93
Dickson, Harold: 266
Din, Khwaja Shahabud: 337
Dinka (tribe): 162, 164, 177
Dire Dawa: 21, 22, 31, 40, 44, 82
Dodds, Hugh: 34
Donatello (1386–1466): 167
Doughty, Charles Montagu (1843–1926): 133, 192, 372, 380, 382, 401
Doughty-Wylie, B.P. Thesiger: (see Thesiger, Brian Peirson)
Doughty-Wylie, Col Charles Hotham Montagu: 32, 87
Doughty-Wylie, Lillian Oimara ('Judith'): 32, 87, 268, 269

Doughty-Wylie, Philippa: 396
Draga, Queen of Serbia: 17
Drage, Colonel Gilbert: 335
Dresden: 11
Drew, Clifford ('Pansy'): 411
Druses of Lebanon, The (G.W. Chasseaud): 232
Druze (people): 34, 180, 220–3, 225, 229–32, 236, 238, 252, 260, 269
Druze Legion: 225
Dubai: 299, 302, 304, 436, 455, 460
Dulling, Ken: 360
Durand, Sir Mortimer: 360
Durand Line: 349, 350
Duru' (tribe): 283, 291, 300–3
Dutton, E.P. (publishers USA): 326, 378

East Africa Corps: 200, 202
Edward VII, King (1841–1910): 28
Egremont, Pamela, Viscountess: 35, 437, 439, 445, 456, 458, 459
Egypt: 124, 130, 146, 196, 238, 239, 250, 412, 435
Ekwar: 389, 393, 395, 416
Elburz Mts: 307, 402, 407
elephant hunting: 171–5
Elizabeth II, Queen: 342
Ellesmere Land: 100
Elliott, Major Rodney: 390, 391, 415, 417, 425
'Elmi' (camel): 116
Elwes, Simon: 461
Emi Koussi, Mt: 179, 183
Empty Quarter: (see Rub' al Khali)
Emtage, Mollie: 265, 332, 371, 410, 434, 435, 460
Enfidaville: 248, 250
Ennedi: 179, 181
Ennedi Mts: 147
Entomology, Imperial Institute of: 91
Equatorial Corps: 200
Erbi: 184
Erbil: 307
Eritrea: 208
Erope (Turkana): 148, 393, 417, 435, 441, 442
Essad-Bey: 372
Essex Regiment: 199, 210
Ethiopia: 115, 119, 120, 196, 218, 255, 257, 261, 370, 381, 382, 411, 429; (see also Abyssinia)
Eton College: 33, 53, 55, 57, 61, 63–8, 70–3, 87, 88, 112, 113, 122, 124, 132, 151, 178, 193, 200, 223, 228, 246, 311, 335, 361, 371, 381, 457, 462, 464
Euphrates river: 317, 365
Evans-Pritchard, E.E.: 164
Everest, Mt: 342, 358, 462

Fada: 179, 182

Fairservice, Ian: 455
Fairservice, Janice: 455
Faisal, King: 412
Faiz Muhammed: 343
Faizabad: 409
Falih: (see bin Majid)
Fara: 118
'Faraj Allah' (camel): 87, 153, 157, 158, 171
Faris Shahin: 180, 223, 224, 228, 252, 273, 277, 348, 349
Farsan Isles: 119
Fartus tribe (southern Iraq): 313, 315, 317
'Farur' (camel): 116
Fasher (Fascia, Fasquia), El: 131, 147, 149, 150, 158–60, 180, 188, 190, 243, 244, 246
Fata Burnu: 134
Fawwaz, Captain: 223
Faya: 179, 181, 182, 186, 187
Feraigat (tribe): 315, 326
Fergusson, Captain Vere Henry ('Fergie Bey'), OBE (1891–1927): 162, 163, 190
Ferri, Signor: 16
Fez: 155, 160, 357
Fezzan: 178
ffolkes, Sir Robert Francis Alexander, 7th Bart: 443, 444
ffrench Blake, Lt Col Robert Lifford Valentine, DSO: 63–5, 84, 223, 368, 369, 371–5, 381, 394
Fiche: 45, 219, 220
Fiona (ketch): 437, 438, 439
Fitzgerald, Vesey: 266, 267
Fitzpatrick, Sir J. Percy: 40
Flecker, James Elroy (1884–1915): 222
Fleming, Ian Lancaster (1908–64): 1
Florence: 252, 382, 395, 396, 427
Foley, Lieutenant Tim: 239
Fontainebleau: 70
Forchi (gorge): 185, 186
Ford, (later Sir) Edward William Spencer, KCB KCVO ER DDL: 87
Forodone (lake): 187
Forter, Alexis, OBE: 406
Fortnum & Mason Ltd: 97, 126, 139, 157, 426, 462, 463
Frazer, Sir James George (1854–1941): 133
French, Major The Hon Gerald, DSO: 14
French Somaliland: 21, 91, 107
Fur (tribe): 142, 155, 190

Galabat: 200, 201, 202, 205–8, 210
Galifage: 113
Galla (tribe): 39, 82, 98, 108, 162
Galla Itu (tribe):80
Galton, Sir Francis (1822–1911): 15, 459
Gambeila: 195

Garchegan: 16
Gardner, Colonel Alexander: 359, 360
Gardula: 379
Garkek (Nuer chief): 164
Gauguin, Paul (1848–1903): 447
Gedaref: 201, 202
Gellner, Ernest: 355, 356
Gellner, Susan: 355, 356
Geographical Journal: 93, 266
George V, King (1865–1936): 32, 74
Germans: 235, 238, 244, 246, 247, 288, 360
Ghana: 424
Ghanim: 270, 278, 280
Ghasat: 353, 354
Gibbon, Edward (1737–94): 133
Gibson, Sarah (Mrs John Andrew Thesiger): 11
Gibson-Watt, J.M.: 128
Gibson-Watt, Mrs: 128
Gideon (Hebrew judge): 213
'Gideon Force': 213, 214
Giffard, Ingaret, Lady van der Post: 399
Gilgit: 335, 342, 343, 345, 346
Gillan, J.A. (later Sir Angus), KBE CMG: 128, 159, 190, 191
Gillan, Lady: 128
Giulietti, Signor (explorer): 93
Glasgow: 196
Gloucester, HRH The Duke of: 74, 77, 78, 80, 95, 429
Glover, Phil: 422
Glubb, Lt Colonel Sir John Bagot ('Glubb Pasha'), CMG DSO OBE MC (1897–1986): 152, 153, 221, 349, 380
Gogh, Vincent van (1853–90): 126
Gohavi, Lieutenant: 406
Gondar: 50, 239, 382
Goran (tribe): 147, 177
Gordon, General Charles George (1833–85): 124
Gordon, George (President of Magdalen College, Oxford): 70, 90, 113
Goulimine: 357
Goumarri: 103
Gouro: 179
Goutama: 97
Grass (film): 404
Graziani, Marshal Rudolfo: 201, 221
Greece: 161, 322, 371
Green, Timothy S.: 33, 57, 216
'Grey Pillars' (Cairo): 237–40
Gridiron Club, Oxford: 84
Grimond, Rt Hon Joseph T.D. ('Jo'), PC LLD : 335
Grimwood, Major Ian: 390, 391
Guards Club: 426
Guest, The Hon Frances Charlotte, 1st Viscountess Chelmsford: 90

Guest, John: 377, 378, 396, 400, 401
Guildford Cathedral: 200
Gupis: 343
Gurmuz (tribe): 203
Gurumudli: 114

'Habib' (camel): 135, 157
Habta Giorgis: 39
Habta Mariam: 97
Habta Wold (Legation *syce*): 35, 77
Hadhramaut: 265, 271, 274, 290–4, 461
Hadrian, Emperor (76–138AD): 393
Haggard, Sir Henry Rider (1856–1925): 72, 114, 194
Haig-Thomas, David: 94, 95–104, 106, 107, 111, 117, 118, 120, 121
Haig-Thomas, Peter: 96
Hail: 266
Haji Rikkan: Marsh Arab ('Fulanain'): 310, 312, 333
Hajj Ibrahim: 353
Hajj Umr: 353
Hall, (later Sir) Julian: 124
Hama: 228
Hambleden, William Herbert Smith, 4th Viscount: 429
Hamid: 224
Hamilton, John: 130
Hammond Innes, Ralph: 379–80
Hanbury-Tenison, Robin: 437
Handcock, Charlotte Elizabeth: 10
Handcock, Henrietta: 9
Handcock, Colonel The Hon Robert French: 19
Hanks, Bimbashi Arthur: 200–2
Harar: 22, 26, 44, 45, 67, 82, 119
Harari people: 82
Harcourt, Sir Cecil: 349
Harod river: 213
harpooning (hippo): 169–70
Harris, Bimbashi W.: 197, 198
Harris, W.B.: 351
Harrison, Reverend Prebendary J.: 235
Hart-Davis, Rupert: 66
Hasan bin Hasan, Prince: (*see* bin Hasan)
Hasan bin Maneti: (*see* bin Maneti)
Hassa oasis: 266
Hatfield: 61
Haurar: 229
Hauz-i-Khas: 348
Havell, H.L.: 45
'Hawiya' (camel): 116
Hayman, Dr Robert: 326
Hazarajat: 338, 345, 346, 348, 357, 359, 416
Heath, Adria Fanny (2nd Baroness Chelmsford): 14, 29, 61
Heath, Major-General: 14

Hedgcock, Mr and Mrs S.E.: 310, 333
Hejaz: 273, 289, 372
Helgord, Mt: 307
Henderson, Edward Firth, CMG: 226, 228, 229, 231, 299, 304
Hendren, Mt: 307
Herat: 409, 410
Herbert, Agnes: 80
Herefordshire: 62, 132
Hermon, Mt: 229
Hervey, Lord Herbert: 23, 26, 32
Hill, Arthur Derek: 4, 407, 408
Hillary, Sir Edmund, KBE: 342
Himalayas: 445
Hindlip, Lord and Lady: 6
Hindu Kush: 337, 338, 345, 346, 359
Hodson, (later Sir) Arnold Wienholt, KCMG: 41, 42, 60, 62, 168, 200, 385
Hofuf: 266
Höhnel, Lt Ludwig von: 199, 385, 387
Holland: 371
Holloden: 376
Homs: 227, 228
Hon: 246
Horsham: 52, 61
House, Adrian: 447
Hoyos, Count Alexander: 10, 29
Huddleston, Sir Hubert: 260
Hufaidh: 310
Hule, lake: 229
Hull: 70, 85
Humphreys, Dr Noel: 100
Hunza: 334, 335, 337, 338, 342–5, 366
Husain (guide, Morocco): 357
Hussein, Saddam: 367
Huwair: 342
Hyderabad: 442–4, 449

Ibach: 393, 395, 400, 416, 421
Ibis, The (magazine): 107, 127
Ibn Saud, King: 291–6, 304
Ibrahim, Omar: 95, 97–9, 102, 108, 110, 115, 117, 119
Iceland: 70, 85
Illustrated London News: 73
Imam Badr: 411, 412
Imam Yahya: 411
Imit: 343
India: 47, 51, 66, 72, 74, 106, 174, 191, 201, 241, 335, 350, 360, 437
Indonesia: 286, 315, 455
Inge, C.H.: 305
Ingebara: 214
Ingleson, Philip, CMG MBE MC: 147, 158–9
Iran: (*see* Persia)
Iraq: 65, 106, 134, 140, 196, 253, 307, 309, 311, 316, 319, 320, 325–8, 330, 332, 333, 350, 367, 369, 448
Iraqi Kurdistan: 248, 255, 307, 308, 310, 357, 361, 363, 365, 380, 404
Iraqi marshes: 53, 54, 104, 106, 310, 311, 323, 327, 329, 358, 365, 380, 400, 432, 434, 448
Iraqi Petroleum Company: 299
Ireland: 18, 19, 51, 52, 369, 376, 377, 407
Isa Adam (guide): 182
Isandhlwana: 13, 14, 118
Isfahan: 307
Ishkoman pass: 343, 344
Ishkoman valley: 343
Isiolo: 385, 386, 388, 425
Israelis: 212, 251
Istanbul: 73, 160, 348
Italian Legation (Addis Ababa): 51
Italians: 150, 195, 201, 204, 205, 208–10, 212, 214, 216–18, 220, 221, 251, 286
Italy: 161, 194, 201, 202, 208, 219, 322, 371, 414
Ithier, Capitaine André Jean: 357

Jabal al Akhdar: 293, 298, 302, 303
Jabal Bishgara: 181
Jabal Druze: 152, 221–3, 225, 226, 229, 241
Jabal Maidob: 137–9, 145, 146, 157, 158, 160, 178
Jabal Salur: 160
Jabal Singhar (Sinjar): 254, 308
Jabal Tifnaout: 356
Jabrin oasis: 293, 296, 297
Jackson, Gordon Noel, CMG MBE: 324, 383
Jaipur: 33, 47, 49, 88, 444
Jaipur, Sir Sawai Madho Singh Bahadur, Maharajah of, GCSI GCIE GCVO: 48, 49
Jaisalmer: 444
Jalalabad: 349, 359, 365
Jan Baz (interpreter): 346, 348
Jan Meda (Addis Ababa): 45
Janin: 250
Jarvis, Major C.S., CMG OBE: 152
Jeddah: 266, 293
Jeffery, W.J. & Co. Ltd (gun and rifle makers): 79
Jenkins, Peter: 425, 429
Jerusalem: 153, 160, 196, 250, 251, 348
Jews: 153
Jibuti: 21, 31, 32, 40, 46, 49, 74, 82, 97, 110, 118, 119, 124, 132, 184
Jock of the Bushveld (J.P. Fitzpatrick): 40, 63, 207
Johnson, Bimbashi: 217
Johnson, Martin: 389
Johnson, Osa: 389
Johnson, Dr Samuel (1709–84): 27

Jones, J.D.F.: 254
Jones, Dr Schuyler: 360
Jordan: 106, 152, 196, 221, 225, 315, 322, 348, 410, 411, 414
Jupp, Clifford Norman, CMG: 360

Kababish (tribe): 137, 147
Kabrit: 241, 245
Kabul: 338, 340, 345, 346, 348, 349, 359, 409, 410
Kada (spring): 183
Kafir tribes: 338, 359, 360
Kafiristan: 359, 360
Kajao: 346
Kalahari desert: 399
Kalamantan: 437
Kalatusseraj: 365
Kandahar: 340
Kandari (nomads): 409
Kangatet: 417
Kantiwar valley: 409
Kaputir: 421
Karakoram Mts: 343, 345, 346
Karnak: 152
Kasbahs de l'Atlas, Les (Jacques Majorelle): 351
Kashgar: 337
Kashmir: 335, 342
Kassala: 206
Kassimi: 97, 100
Kathir (of the Badayat tribe): 179, 183
Kazak: 337
k'ebero (wolf): 96, 99
Kebkabia: 140, 141, 144, 148
Kendawa: 441, 449
Kennet, Lady (formerly Mrs Robert Falcon Scott): 93–4
Kenya: 106, 129, 130, 132, 136, 149, 162, 165, 189, 198, 199, 203, 210, 315, 321, 322, 379, 385, 388, 393, 395, 414–17, 423–5, 429–31, 435, 441, 442, 447–50, 453, 455, 456
Kenya, Mt (17,058ft): 386, 415, 426
Kereri (paddle-steamer): 165, 166, 191, 195
Kerio river: 417, 418, 420
Keun, Odette: 124–5, 129
Kharbet: 346
Khartoum: 128–30, 136, 142, 148, 150, 158, 159, 176, 189, 190, 192, 194, 197, 199, 204, 210, 211, 214, 253, 383
Khayyam, Omar: 188
Khazna, the (Petra): 226
'Kibiriti' (Ibrahim Ewoi Ekai): 445, 446, 447, 452
Kibo: 426, 441
Kikuyu (tribe): 393, 417, 420, 433, 446
Kilimanjaro, Mt (19,340 ft): 106, 395
Kilwal: 170

King Kong (film): 404
Kinnear, N.B.: 117, 120
Kinross, Lord: 380
Kipling, Joseph Rudyard (1865–1936): 48, 133, 134, 360
Kirghiz (tribe): 337
Kirkuk: 308, 309
Kirwan, Sir Archibald Laurence Patrick, KCMG TD: 274, 289, 370
Kisau, Joseph: 428, 435
Kitchener, Horatio Herbert, Field Marshal Lord, KG etc. (1850–1916): 124
Knighton: 131, 216
Kobé-Zaghawa (tribe): (see Zaghawa)
Kodak: 94, 112, 192
Koli Barit: 348
Korgal: 364
Kosti: 197
Krak des Chevaliers: 226–8
Krim, Abdel: 119
Kuba (tribe): 335
Kubaish: 316
kudu (antelope): 96
Kuh-i-Baba: 346, 348
Kulal, Mt: 388, 423
Kulam valley: 363, 364
Kulzikuma, Mt: 116
Kurdish people: 16, 253, 308, 310, 317
Kutum: 126, 128, 130–6, 138–41, 147, 148, 150, 153, 158, 159, 165, 167, 171, 174, 177, 192, 196, 197, 445
Kuwait: 266

Ladakh: 106, 338, 443, 444
Laghman: 365
Lahore: 335
Laila: 295, 296, 297, 298
Laisamis: 40, 41
Laithwaite, Sir John Gilbert GCMG KCB KCIE CSI: 335
Laja, the: 229, 235
Lalibela: 261, 377, 379, 382
Lambie, Dr: 96
Lamu: 393, 395
Lamy, Fort: 179
Lang, E.M.: 55, 59
Lang, R.C.V.: 45, 53, 55, 57–61, 64, 65
Lascelles, Sir David: 346, 349, 359
Lasht: 338
Laurie, Ran: 202
Lawi Leboyare, Gabriel: 149, 189, 430, 432, 435, 439–42, 445–7, 449–53, 456
Lawrence, David Herbert (1885–1930): 71
Lawrence, Geoffrey (Lord Oaksey): 191, 233
Lawrence, Colonel Thomas Edward ('Lawrence of Arabia', 1888–1935): 66, 71, 77, 89, 127,

133, 151, 152, 178, 231, 248, 277, 306, 372, 377, 382, 401, 402, 414
Leach, Hugh R., OBE: 435
Leakey, Louis Seymour Bazett (1903–72): 392
Lean, (later Sir) David (1908–91): 258
Lean, Owen Bevan: 257, 258
Lear, Edward (1821–88): 415
Leather, Bimbashi Mark: 160
Lebanese: 252
Lebanon: 196, 228, 229, 235, 322, 348
Lechiin (Samburu): 446
Leclerc, General P.F.: 248
Leh: 443, 444
Leica (cameras): 94, 171, 194, 267, 275, 308, 354, 455
Leicester, University of: 442
Lekakwar, Laputa: 445–7, 451–3, 456, 461
Lekakwar, Margaret Namitu: 446, 447, 452, 453
Lekakwar, Rosanna: 446
Lekakwar, Rupalen: 446, 452
Lekakwar, Sandy (Alessandro): 446, 452
Lenana, Pt (16,355 ft, third highest peak of Mt Kenya): 426
Lettauré, Commandant: 70
Libya: 164, 167, 177, 201, 239, 243
Libyan desert: 139, 145, 146, 264
Liddell Hart, Sir Basil Henry (1895–1970): 248
Life of My Choice, The (WT): 20, 35, 36, 39, 46, 47, 57, 63, 64, 67, 68, 70, 75, 77, 84, 88, 90, 93, 108, 114, 128, 131, 133, 134, 138, 146, 147, 149, 150, 152, 154, 156, 168, 170, 172, 176, 179, 182, 185, 186, 188, 196, 201, 206, 207, 216, 219, 225, 226, 233, 239, 242, 245, 248, 252, 253, 258–60, 268, 379, 381, 383, 391, 398, 400, 411, 442, 443, 448, 456
Lij Belai Zaleka: 216, 217
Lij Yasu: 24, 26, 35, 38, 39, 44, 45
Linnean Society: 18, 90
lion hunting (Northern Darfur): 129, 130, 135, 136, 140–5, 151, 153–5
lion hunting (Western Nuer District): 167, 174, 175
Livingstone, David (1813–73): 414
Liwa oasis: 279, 280, 282, 290, 293, 297, 299–301
Lkwono (Samburu clan): 430, 431
Lloyd, Seton: 312
Lmasula (Samburu clan): 430
Lock & Co. (hat makers): 150
Lockhart, W.S.A. (later General Sir William): 360
Lodosoit: 429
Lodwar: 389, 393, 416, 417, 420
Loiengalani: 388, 423
Lokuyie: 393, 395
London: 40, 53, 54, 61, 67, 72, 74–7, 86, 97, 126,

127, 142, 150, 156, 158, 160, 172, 182, 186, 203, 204, 241, 243, 253, 256, 257, 267, 271, 273, 284, 289–91, 308, 309, 322, 323, 326, 327, 331, 332, 334, 342, 348, 354, 358, 387, 402, 407, 412, 436, 439, 442, 447–9, 453, 455–7, 460, 461, 463
Long Range Desert Group (LRDG): 239, 264
Longman, Mark: 326, 330, 374, 376
Longmans (publishers): 375–9, 396, 399, 401
Lonsdale, Hugh Cecil Lowther, 5th Earl of (1857–1944): 458
Lopego, Julius (Samburu): 447, 452
Lorogi plateau (Kenya): 389
Loti, Pierre (Louis Marie Julien Viaud, 1850–1923): 70
Lowassa: 416, 426
Lucas (schoolboy): 55, 58
Lurs (tribe): 222
Lush, Julian: 460
Lush, Brigadier Maurice Stanley, CB CBE MC: 460
Lutyens, Sir Edwin (1869–1944): 47
Luxor: 130, 152, 196
Lydekker, Richard: 109
Lyttleton, George: 66

McGarry, B.: 437, 438, 439
Mackay-Dick, Major-General Sir Iain C., MBE: 460
McLean, Lt-Col Neil, LD DSO: 411, 412
Macmillan, Maurice Harold, 1st Earl of Stockton (1894–1986): 397
McNair, W.W.: 359
McNeile, A.M.: 63, 66
Macrae, Elliott (publisher): 326
Maan: 225
Mad Mullah of Somaliland, the (Mohammed bin Abdullah Hassan): 44
Madeira: 414
Maffey, Sir J.L. (later Lord Rugby), GCMG KCB KCVO CSI CIE: 74, 78, 79, 162
Mafraq: 226
Magdala: 45, 96, 382, 383
Maggs Bros Ltd: 66, 382
'Maguer' (elephant): 171–2
Mahdi, the (Mohammed Ahmad): 124, 142, 155
Mahler, Gustav (1860–1911): 234
Mahomet (Legation servant): 77
Mahra: 280
Maidan: 346
Maidob (tribe): 137, 138, 147, 160, 164, 184, 194
Majorelle, Jacques (1886–1962): 350, 351
Malakal: 165, 166, 176, 197–9
Malawi: 455

Malha village: 223, 236, 252
Malik, Sayyah: 138
Mallowan, Sir Max: 309
Malmö: 375, 395
Malo (Nuer): 164, 169
Malory, George: 462
Malossa: 76
Mansfield, Elinor: 378
Mansfield, Philip Robert Aked, CMG: 378, 379
Manz: 219
Mara river: 422, 428
Marada: 246
Maralal: 76, 132, 136, 149, 150, 165, 199, 284, 386, 389, 390, 391, 393, 415, 416, 417, 418, 420, 421, 422, 426, 429, 430, 433, 440, 441, 442, 445, 446, 447, 448, 449, 450–3, 455, 456
Maraventano, General: 217, 218, 220
Mareuge, Capitaine: 186
Margarita, Lake: 379
Marrakesh: 155, 160, 161, 350, 352, 354–7, 427
Marsabit, Mt: 385, 387–9, 425
Marseilles: 74, 97, 119, 160, 354
Marsh Arabs: 106, 162, 164, 180, 311–13, 318, 321–6, 333, 342, 346, 352, 366, 367, 369, 395
Marsh Arabs, The (WT): 30–1, 252, 313, 318, 320, 321, 323, 333, 394, 397, 400–2, 408, 427, 442
Martin, Dr: 110
Martin, Lieutenant: 244
Masai (tribe): 163, 321, 386, 392, 395, 398, 399, 416, 432, 433
Masai steppe: 393, 397
Mashakezey: 183
Masjid-i-Jumeh (Friday Mosque): 407
Maskal: 27
Massey, Sir Vincent, PC DCL: 233
Massu, General Jacques: 186
Mastuj: 338
Mataka: 108
Mathews Range (Kenya): 386, 418, 429
Maufe, (later Sir) Edward Brantwood, RA: 200
Maurice, G.K.: 135
Maxwell, Gavin (1914–69): 53, 54, 104, 106, 268, 315, 316, 322–32, 352, 358, 368, 375, 376, 399, 400, 408, 424
Maxwell (née Percy), Lady Mary: 268, 329, 368
Mayday Hospital (Croydon): 463
Mayfair: 129
Mayne, Major Blair ('Paddy'): 243
Mazar-i-Sharif: 409, 410
MCC (Marylebone Cricket Club): 61
Mecca: 189
Mega: 379
Meknes: 160
Mellor, F.H.: 192
Melton Constable: 85

Menelik II, Emperor of Abyssinia: 5, 6, 7, 8, 22, 24, 35, 39, 44, 78, 459
Mercury (driver): 251
Merille (tribe): 423, 424
Meru: 425
Meshed: 402
Metemma: 200, 202, 205, 206, 210
Meulen, Dan van der: 274
Meynell, Lt-Col Hugo Francis, OBE: 229
Meynell, Mark: 112, 229
Michelangelo Buonarotti (1475–1564): 167
Midett: 351
Middle East: 2, 153, 176, 202, 211, 240, 241, 434, 455
Middle East Anti-Locust Unit (MEALU): 258, 265, 271, 280, 285, 289, 295, 376
Middleton, Dorothy (1909–99): 447
Midji lake: 187
'Mijbil' (otter): 326, 327, 330
Milan: 348, 358, 383
Milebrook, The: 13, 34, 62, 71, 76, 81, 85, 86, 96, 101, 104, 131, 132, 136, 137, 145, 156, 176, 191, 196, 208, 215, 216, 233–5, 243, 249, 251, 267, 335, 426, 457, 464
Miles, Major A.T., DSO OBE MC: 74
Millais, Captain Hesketh Raoul le Jarderay (1901–99): 129
Millais, Sir John Everett (1829–96): 129
Millais, John Guille (1865–1931): 69, 129, 458
Minchinhampton: 61
Mir Samir: 360, 364
Miski valley: 183
Modra valley: 183, 184
Mogador (Essaouira): 357
Mohammed, prophet: 306
Mohammed Yayu: 103, 112, 114–16, 219, 261
Mombasa: 414
Monari, Signor: 93
Mongalla: 131
Mongol (people): 315, 337
Montagu-Evans, C.E.: 374, 375, 395
Montgomery of Alamein, Field-Marshal Bernard Law, 1st Viscount (1887–1976): 239
Moore, Major Guy M., MC: 127, 130–5, 137–40, 145, 147, 148, 151–3, 157, 159, 160, 165, 166, 168, 178, 182, 187, 190, 194, 227
Moorfields Eye Hospital: 449, 456
Moorhead, Dr: 52
Morden College: 460
Morocco: 76, 106, 118, 152, 155, 156, 161, 166, 181, 190, 196, 208, 335, 338, 350, 351, 353–5, 357, 361, 371, 386, 400, 407, 410, 426, 461
Morris, Jan (James): 375
'Moses' (monkey): 34
Mosley, Leonard: 218, 219
Mosul: 253, 307, 308, 309

Motivate Ltd (publishers): 455
Mount of Olives: 160
Mourina: 17
Moussa Hamma: 80, 84
Mowra (Kikuyu): 433, 434
Moyale: 379, 385
Mozart, Wolfgang Amadeus (1756–91): 224
Mughshin: 270, 271, 278–81
Muhammed (guide): 352–4, 357
Muhammed (Iraq): 358
Muhammed (orderly): 202, 218
Muhammad Ali: 124
Muhsin, Sheikh: 281
Mukalla: 280, 285, 286, 287, 288, 291, 299
Mullu: 79, 94, 97, 98, 153, 200, 378, 382, 411, 435
Munich crisis: 188
Munich pact: 194
Muntifiq (tribe, Iraq): 368
Munzinger, J.A. Werner ('Munzinger Pasha'): 93
Murray, John Grey ('Jock'), CBE: 274
Murray & Co. Ltd, John (publishers): 274
Muscat: 274, 293, 298, 436, 440
Muscat, Sultan of: 279, 303, 394, 305
Mussolini, Benito (1883–1945): 140, 201, 203, 209, 221
Muwaiqih: 298, 301, 302, 304
My Kenya Days (WT): 33, 34, 198, 227, 274, 390, 391, 395, 398, 417, 422, 425, 430, 440, 453, 455

Nachtigal, Dr Gustav: 178, 183
Naiak: 346
Nairobi: 40, 385, 386, 391, 397, 414, 415, 422, 424–6, 429, 435, 439, 450, 455
Najran: 289, 293
Nanamsena gorge: 184
Napier, General Sir Robert Cornelis (1810–90): 96, 383
Napoleon Bonaparte, Emperor Napoleon I, (1769–1821): 296
Nasser, Gamel Abdel, President of Egypt (1918–70): 412
Nasser Hussain (Kurdistan): 308, 317
Natural History Museum (South Kensington): 90, 91, 96, 98, 120, 135, 154, 173, 257, 286, 289, 308, 326, 358
Naver, Loch: 74
Ndoto Mts: 387, 416, 429
Neftali: 416–7
'Negadras' (camel): 116
Negus Mikael: 44, 45, 383
Nelson, Rear-Admiral Horatio, Viscount (1758–1805): 12, 13, 18
Nepal: 445

Nesbitt, Ludovico Mariano: 93, 103, 105
Neumann, Arthur Henry: 385
Newbold, Douglas: 127, 191, 192, 197, 198, 201
Newbould, John: 106, 352, 356, 357, 359, 391–3, 397–9
Newby, George Eric, MC: 320, 360, 361
New Statesman: 380
New York: 52, 53
New Zealand Divisional Cavalry: 248
Ngaro Narok: 387
Ngorongoro crater (Tanzania): 386, 391–3, 395, 397–9
Nicholson, Emma (Baroness Nicholson of Winterbourne): 367
Nigeria: 69, 201
Nile, Blue (Abbai): 128, 213, 216, 218, 220, 382
Nile, White: 162, 163, 171, 173, 192, 197, 238, 253
Nimrud: 309
Nineveh: 309
'Norah' (cheetah): 137
Norfolk: 61, 85
Northern Frontier District of Kenya, former (NFD): 199, 385, 391, 395, 422, 453
Nott, Brigadier Donald, DSO OBE MC (1908–96): 217, 219, 220
Nuba (tribes): 192, 193, 199
Nuer (tribe): 126, 159, 162–72, 174–7, 189, 190, 193, 194
Nuremberg: 191
Nuristan: 106, 249, 308, 331, 338, 345, 349, 359–61, 363, 364, 409, 414, 416
nyala (antelope): 36, 96, 99
Nyiru, Mt: 430, 431

Oaksey, Lord: (see Lawrence, Geoffrey)
Obeid, El: 197
Observer: 400
O'Gradys, the (relatives of WT's mother): 376
Okavango swamps: 455
Okehampton: 51, 55
Olduvai gorge: 392
Olivier, Laurence Kerr, Baron Olivier of Brighton (1907–89): 348
Ololokwe: 430
Oman: 280, 285, 300–3, 305, 307, 436, 440
Omdurman: 142, 157, 158, 204
Orford House: 460, 461
Orientalists (artists): 285, 350, 351
Orkney Islands: 360
Otash: 143
Otterburn: 90
Ouaita: 179
Oudai: (see Wadai)
Oude: 179
Ouga, Hamdo (Danakil chief): 112

Ouma lake: 187
Ounianga Kebir: 179, 187
Owen, Richard: 192, 194
Oxford (city): 152, 459
Oxford, University of: 16, 61, 63, 71–3, 81, 83, 87–90, 94, 96, 121–3, 125, 132, 156, 186, 191, 208, 224, 226, 233, 275, 337, 361, 423, 442, 457
Oxford University Exploration Society: 351, 352, 356
Oxus river: 337

Paghman: 348
Pakistan: 308, 334, 335, 337, 340, 342, 349, 350, 391
Palestine: 106, 149, 151, 153, 161, 174, 211, 225, 226, 244, 250, 251, 273, 348
Pamirs, Mts: 337
Panjao: 346
Panjshir valley: 360, 361, 364
Pankhurst, Sylvia (1882–1960): 268
Panza, Sancho: 451
Paradise, Lake: 389
Parakulm: 346
Paris: 49, 72, 186, 187
Park, Bertram: 10
Park Hotel (Copenhagen): 371, 394
Parkins, Major-General K.: 440
Parsons, Desmond: 63
Pashaie (tribe): 364
Pathans: 338, 340, 343, 360
Patriots, Abyssinian: 216–19
Pavitt, Nigel: 431
Peake, Lieutenant-Colonel F.G. ('Peake Pasha'), CMG CBE : 152
Peat, Bill: 87
Pennycuick, Colin: 352, 353, 355, 356
Pera: 160
Percival, A. Blayney: 129
Percy, Lady William: 424
Persia (Iran): 196, 222, 258, 307, 335, 361, 402, 404, 406
Persian Gulf: 298
Peshawar: 335, 338, 346, 365
Peter I, King: 17
Petra: 225, 226, 253, 410
Philby, Harry St John Bridger, CIE (1885–1960): 264, 267, 293–7, 304, 333, 380, 401
Phillimore, Harry (later Lord): 63, 87
Phipps, Mervyn: 231
Pitt Rivers Museum, Oxford: 459
Platt, Major-General Sir William: 200, 206, 210, 211
Plowman, C.H.F.: 82
Poland: 249

Polo, Marco: 16
Port Said: 197
Port Sudan: 111
Portugal: 161, 393, 410, 424, 426
Post, (later Sir) Laurens van der (1906–96): 253, 254, 381, 399, 411
Powell-Cotton, Major P.H.G.: 50, 66
Powys (Radnorshire): 62
Practically True (Ernest Thesiger): 55, 335
Prichard, Julian: 216
Profumo, John Dennis: 397
Puchal: 361, 363
Purdey, James & Co. Ltd (gun and rifle makers): 51
Pushkar: 444
Putney Vale Crematorium, London: 463

Qabab: 326
Qalit Salih: 341
Qallat: 351
Qamashlia: 253
Qandil Mts: 307
Qarra Mts: 271, 411, 412
Qasr Rhilana: 248
Quetta: 340
Quixote, Don: 451

Rabadh: 282–4
Radnorshire: 2, 13, 62, 227
Raffles, Sir Thomas Stamford (1781–1826): 18
Rahazian, Wadi: 272
Rahman, Abd er: 360
Rajasthan: 444
Rakaposhi, Mt (25,550 ft): 334, 335, 343
Raleigh Club: 84
Ramgul river: 364
Ramgul valley: 361
Ramlat al Ghafa: 278, 280, 281, 285
Ras Ababa Aregai: 219
Ras Desta: 221
Ras Hailu: 216, 217
Ras Kassa: 219, 221
Ras Mulugeta: 208
Ras Tafari: (see Selassie, Haile)
Ras Tasamma: 24, 26
Rashid (tribe): 180, 271, 277, 280, 282–6, 288, 291, 293, 297–9, 302, 304, 436
Ratta (Legation servant): 77
Ravensdale, Lady: 78
Rawalpindi: 335
Rayne, Major Henry: 40, 66, 199, 385, 420
Razmak: 340
Reed Shaken by the Wind, A (Gavin Maxwell): 53, 315, 322, 323, 325, 329, 330, 376, 400, 408
Reeman, Ian: 379

Rendille tribe (Kenya): 389, 416
Renison, Sir Patrick: 385
Reshit: 343
Return to the Marshes (Gavin Young): 315, 316
Revolt in the Desert (T.E. Lawrence): 66, 226
Rey, Colonel Sir C.F., CMG: 27–8
Rich Gol: 338
Riefenstahl, Leni (1902–2003): 199
Rigby, John & Co. Ltd (gun and rifle makers): 130, 157, 172, 308, 316, 317, 366
Rimbaud, Arthur (1854–91): 22
Ring of Bright Water (Gavin Maxwell): 329, 375
Riyadh: 266, 283, 294, 296
Robertson, Sir George Scott, KCSI MP: 360, 363
Robertson, Robert: 94
Robertson, Sir William: 94
Rodd, Francis James Rennell: 243, 271, 280
Rodger, George: 199
Rodgers, Guy: 131
Rodney, George Brydges, Admiral and 1st Baron (1719–92): 12
Rome: 49, 221, 309, 331, 348, 383, 384, 427
Romilly, H.A.: 168, 253
Rommel, Field-Marshal Erwin (1891–1944): 238, 239, 248, 254
Ross, F. & T. (steam trawler company): 85
Ross, R.P.: 85
Rottingdean: 53
Roughton: 62
Rousillon: 118
Rowe, Lt: 217, 218
Rowunduz: 307, 308
Royal Academy: 93
Royal Academy Schools: 93
Royal Asiatic Society: 414
Royal Central Asian Society (Royal Society for Asian Affairs): 274, 322, 349, 414
Royal Geographical Society (RGS): 91, 105, 107, 112, 114, 120, 123, 127, 183, 243, 271, 274, 280, 288, 290, 291, 293, 300, 322, 335, 346, 349, 357, 370, 414, 437, 447
Royal Hospital, Chelsea: 326, 460
Royal Scottish Geographical Society: 414
Royal Society of Literature: 442
Royal Zoological Society of London: 18, 173
Ruallah (tribe): 231, 236
Rub' al Khali (Empty Quarter): 262–6, 269–75, 278–82, 285, 288, 290–4, 297, 298, 303–5, 335, 368, 370, 373, 380, 401
Rudolf, Lake: (*see* Turkana, Lake)
Rumbold, (later Sir) H.A.C., KCMG KCVO CB: 87, 457
Rumuruti: 391
Rupalen (Lekakwar): 446, 452

Sa'ar (tribe): 290, 291, 292, 293
Sabaiti (WT's canoeboy): 315, 317, 365, 366
Sabeans (inhabitants of ancient Saba): 254
Sacred Squadron, Greek (SAS): 248, 250, 251
Sade Malka: 106
Safartak bridge: 216, 217
Sagale: 44, 113, 134, 221, 383, 411
Sahara: 127, 137, 167, 178, 179, 188, 193, 257, 411, 427, 443
Sahara, French: 85, 137, 152, 171, 211, 416
Said Munge: 97, 98
St Aubyn's (school): 53–61, 63–6, 68, 70, 72, 84, 88, 122, 123, 150, 212
St-Exupéry, Antoine de: 188
St George's Hospital: 331
St Helena: 18, 296
St Paul's Cathedral: 309
St Peter's, Rome: 309
St Peter's Church, London SW1: 9, 86
St Peter's Church, London SW7: 86
St Petersburg: 17
Sakela (Sakalla): 198, 207, 213, 214
Salala: 269–71, 273, 278, 280, 281, 285–7, 298, 304, 436
Salih Ma'z: 252
Salim, Dr S.M.: 313
Samburu (tribe): 132, 149, 162, 165, 199, 321, 386, 389, 391, 393, 395, 414–17, 428, 430–5, 440–2, 445, 446, 448–50, 456
Samirir: 354, 355
San Remo: 222
Sana'a: 412, 435, 436
Sanderson, Paul: 143–5, 148
Sandford, Anne: 435
Sandford, Christine: 97, 109, 153, 200, 203, 265, 378, 411, 435
Sandford, Colonel (later Brigadier) D.A., CBE DSO: 79, 93, 94, 96, 97, 109, 114, 117, 127, 153, 200, 204–7, 210, 211, 214, 255, 260, 265, 378, 411, 435, 460
Sandford, Dick: 435
Sanglakh valley: 348
Sar-i-Chasma: 346
Sar-i-Sang: 409
Sarawak: 437, 438, 439
Sardo: 435
Saudi Arabia: 291, 294, 305, 412, 436
Savoy Hotel: 458
School of Oriental and African Studies: 127, 158
Schuster, John: 87, 156
Scott, (later Sir) Peter Markham (1909–89): 93
Scott, Captain Robert Falcon (1868–1912): 93, 462
Seago, Edward: 415
Seago, John: 415, 426, 439

Seaton Delaval: 85
Seen in the Hadhramaut (Freya Stark): 167, 194
Seiyun: 461
Selassie, Haile, Emperor of Abyssinia (Ras
    Tafari): 38, 44, 45, 50, 67, 68, 69, 74–8, 83,
    90, 91, 97, 108, 113, 162, 200, 203–5, 208,
    210–12, 214, 215, 217, 220, 221, 253, 255,
    260, 261, 377, 411, 422, 429
Selous, Captain Frederick Courteney
    (1851–1917): 66, 206
Senussi, the: 201
Serengeti: 386, 392, 395, 398, 429
Seronera: 395, 397
Seven Pillars of Wisdom (T.E. Lawrence): 66,
    133, 140, 152, 226, 277, 306, 372, 377, 401,
    402, 415, 450
Seville: 457, 460
Shackleton, Sir Ernest Henry (1874–1922): 399
Shaganba (tribe): 315
Shah jin Ali: 338
Shamba: 190
Shammar (tribe): 231, 254
Shanaize: 360
Shankalla (people): 203
Sharja: 298, 299, 303, 306
Sheikh Adi: 309
Shepherd's Hotel (Cairo): 237
Sherry, Professor Norman: 437
shifta (brigands): 98, 425, 426
Shikar Club: 458
'Shillingi' (dog): 398
Shilluk (tribe): 164
Shipman, John: 460–1
Shipton, Eric Earle, CBE (1907–77): 334, 335,
    337, 358
Shiraz: 307, 388
Shiva, Lake: 409
Shoa province: 216, 219
Short Walk in the Hindu Kush, A (Eric Newby):
    320, 361
Siboloi: 429
Sicily: 241, 376, 427, 439
Sinclair, James, & Co. Ltd (photographic
    dealers): 275, 291, 300, 309, 337
Sindia wells: 153
Singapore: 437–9
Skye, Isle of: 330
Sladen, Percy, Memorial Trust: 90
Slaney river: 51
Slim, Field-Marshal William Joseph, 1st
    Viscount (1891–1970): 207, 210
Smith, A. Donaldson: 385, 388
Snyder, Phil: 441
Sobat river: 195
Socrates (c.470–399BC): 447
Soddu: 379

Soemering's gazelle: 81
Soiyah (Turkana): 389
Somalis: 21, 108, 425
Soubouroun (hot springs): 185
South (Ernest Shackleton): 399
South Horr (Kenya): 388
Spain: 400, 427, 457, 461
Spanj: 343
Special Air Services (SAS): 240–2, 244, 245,
    248, 250, 262, 264
Special Operations Executive (SOE): 206, 225,
    237–42
Speke, John Hanning (1827–64): 400
Spencer, Dr Paul: 431
Srinagar: 443
Stanford, Edward & Co. Ltd: 182
Stanyforth, Major: 74
Stark, Dame Freya Madeline (1893–1993): 105,
    152, 167, 194, 222, 228, 274, 333, 349, 382,
    402
Steele, Angela: 414
Steele, Frank Fenwick, OBE: 106, 315, 327, 385,
    387–9, 400, 410, 411, 414, 415, 418, 423, 446,
    448–9, 457
Steele, Frank jnr: 414, 415
Steele, Venetia (WT's goddaughter): 414
Steer, G.L.: 205
Stevenson, Robert Louis (1850–94): 447
Stewart, D.L.L. (later Sir Dugald), of Appin,
    KCVO CMG: 310, 311
Stewart, Mrs Dugald: 311
Stewart, Major-General J.M. (later Sir James),
    KCMG CB: 46
Stigand, Captain Chauncey Hugh: 199, 385,
    420
Stirling, Colonel Archibald David, DSO OBE:
    213, 240, 241, 243, 245
Stirling, Peter: 242
Stowe Hill: 62, 76, 464
Stroud (Gloucestershire): 61
Sturges, R.S.M.: 310, 333
Sudan: 33, 34, 69, 72, 78, 87, 95, 96, 106,
    124–31, 133, 135, 138, 142, 143, 147, 150,
    154, 162, 163, 166–9, 171, 173, 174, 176, 177,
    181, 190–2, 194, 196, 200–4, 210, 214, 254,
    260, 265, 266, 269, 288, 316, 322, 335, 372,
    408, 417, 420, 422, 445, 448
Sudan Defence Force: 160, 181, 197, 198, 200,
    202, 205, 221
Sudan Notes and Records (periodical): 151, 192
Sudan Political Service: 117, 123–5, 127, 128,
    159, 175, 178, 197, 261
Suez Canal: 241, 365
Suguta: 417
Sultan (of the Bait Kathir tribe): 269, 278, 281
Sulaiyil (and Amir of): 291–5

Sunday Times: 400
'Sungura' (Sepiri; Samburu): 446–7
Suq al Fuhud: 321
Susannah (WT's nurse): 21, 30, 31, 43, 88
Sutherland, county of: 81
Swayne, H.G.C.: 80
Sweden: 375
Sykes, Christopher: 212, 252
Symes, Lt-Col Sir George Stewart, GBE KCMG
  DSO: 201, 204
Syracuse: 384
Syria: 34, 106, 149, 151, 152, 161, 196, 221, 225,
  226, 229, 233, 235, 237, 238, 241, 253, 254,
  260, 269, 279, 283, 299, 322, 348, 462
Szek, Count Samuel Teleki von: (*see* Teleki)

Tabas: 406
Tabir Ait Zaghar: 354
Tabriz: 307
Taddert: 351, 352, 354, 356
Tafileh: 410
Tafraout: 354, 357
Tagabo Hills: 135, 137
tahr, Arabian (wild goat): 298
Tajiks: 361, 363, 364, 409
Tajura: 31, 93, 107, 116–19
Takht-i-Turkoman: 348
Talone (Samburu): 446
Tamp, Lew: 406
Tana, Lake: 382
Tanganyika: 106, 130, 392, 393, 397, 399,
  432
Tangier: 160
Tanzania: (*see* Tanganyika)
taradas (canoes): 310, 313, 315, 321, 323
Taranto: 16, 49
Taria gorge: 355, 356
Taroudant: 160, 357
Taum, Sheikh Ali (of the Kababish): 137
Taylor, Richard: 415
Taza: 357
Teheran: 307, 402, 405, 406, 407, 410
Teleki, Count Samuel (von Szek): 199, 387, 400
Telouet: 351–3
Teme Valley: 62, 249, 464
Ten Pains of Death, The (Gavin Maxwell): 376
Tendaho: 435
Tenerife: 427
Tenzing, Sherpa: 342
Ternouth, J.: 12
Tetley & Butler (tailors): 221, 361
Theodore II, Emperor of Abyssinia: 383
Thesiger, The Hon Alfred Henry: 9, 11
Thesiger, Charles: 13
Thesiger, The Hon Charles Wemyss: 10
Thesiger, Dermot Vigors (WT's brother): 32,

40, 44, 50, 61, 62, 73, 74, 86, 89, 103, 121,
  151, 156, 158, 166, 171, 178, 191, 197, 208,
  215, 233–5, 251, 256, 259, 267
Thesiger, Lt-Col The Hon Eric Richard, DSO
  (WT's uncle): 15
Thesiger, Ernest Frederic Graham, CBE
  (1879–1961) (WT's cousin): 12, 55, 219, 335,
  432, 463
Thesiger, The Hon Harold Lumsden (WT's
  uncle): 15
Thesiger, John Andrew: 11, 12
Thesiger (*née* Vigors), Kathleen Mary (WT's
  mother): (*see* Astley, Kathleen Mary)
Thesiger, The Hon Percy Mansfield (WT's
  uncle): 10, 14, 15, 51, 61, 86
Thesiger, The Hon Mrs P.M. (WT's aunt): 61
Thesiger, Roderic Miles Doughty (1915–2005)
  (WT's brother): 32, 43, 44, 50, 61, 62, 86, 89,
  151, 156, 166, 167, 188, 191, 192, 208, 215,
  233, 235, 240, 241, 246, 250, 273–5, 333, 349,
  374, 397, 407, 408, 438, 450, 457
Thesiger, Sybil Adeline, MBE (WT's cousin):
  128
Thesiger, Captain The Hon Wilfred Gilbert,
  DSO (WT's father): 2, 6, 8–11, 14–17, 20–4,
  26–32, 34, 37–41, 43, 45–58, 72, 77, 79, 86,
  88–90, 102, 105, 112, 119, 156, 168, 190, 193,
  200, 203, 207, 256, 335, 378, 422, 427, 428,
  445, 459
THESIGER, SIR WILFRED PATRICK,
  KBE DSO (1910–2003): family
  background, parents, 9–28, 37–8; birth, 29;
  childhood (Abyssinia), 30–50; childhood
  (Ireland, England), 51–3, 61–2; preparatory
  school, 51–61; father's death, 55–6; Eton,
  63–7; Oxford, 70–3, 83–90; Abyssinia (Haile
  Selassie's coronation), 74–82; mother
  remarries, 85–6; Sudan (Darfur) 129–60,
  (Western Nuer) 162–177, 190–5; big game
  hunting, 33, 47–9, 64, 78–82, 99, 113,
  129–30, 138, 140–5, 150–1, 153–5,
  166,168–76, 308, 316–7, 321–5, 390; Tibesti,
  178–88; WWII Abyssinian campaign,
  196–219; Druze, 220–36, 252–5; Western
  desert, 237–49; Dessie, 255–62; Arabia,
  263–306; Kurdistan, 307–10; Iraqi marshes,
  310–33, 358–9, 365–9; mountains of Asia,
  52–65, 334–48, 359–65; Morocco, 350–8;
  Ethiopia 377–9, 382–3: Kenya, 385–93,
  397–400, 415–35, 440–2, 445–53; Yemen,
  411–14; mother's death, 426; later journeys,
  402–11, 436–40, 443–5; England, 456–64;
  death, 463; appearance, 1, 3, 4, 29–30, 167–8;
  characteristics, 1, 2, 3, 30–4, 45;
  photography, 3, 84, 91, 94, 112, 118, 150,
  166–7, 194, 199, 320–1, 326, 337, 348, 350–1,

354, 364, 370, 399, 414, 415, 437, 455, 457;
writing, 3, 370–7, 379–82, 393–5, 396–7,
400–1, 442–3 (*see also individual books*)
Thesiger Doughty-Wylie, Brian Peirson, MC
(WT's brother): 32, 33, 35, 36, 38, 40, 41, 44,
46, 47, 49, 51–4, 56–64, 66, 73, 74, 86–9, 94,
113, 130, 137, 150, 156, 157, 191, 199, 208,
215, 233, 241, 266, 268, 269, 275, 333, 396,
443, 445
Thomas, Bertram Sidney, CMG OBE
(1892–1950): 263–7, 269, 279, 280, 290, 297,
304, 380, 401
Thompson, J.M.: 72
Thomson, Joseph (1858–95): 400
Tibbu (Tebu, Tedda) (tribe): 177, 180, 183, 184,
185, 186, 273
Tiepolo, Giovanni Battista (1696–1770): 415
Tieroko: 183, 184
Tigris river: 254, 316, 317, 321, 325
Tihama: 267, 273, 289, 414, 435, 436
Tikah (tribe): 180
Tilho, Lt-Col.: 179, 187
Timkat: 67
Tini: 148, 153, 159, 179, 187–9, 202
Tiourza: 352
Tirano pass: 184
Tirich Mir: 338
Tirich river: 338
Tistouit: 356
Titley: 62
Titley House: 61, 71
Tito, Marshal (Josip Broz, 1892–1980): 261
Tivoli Gardens: 371
Tiz-n-Test: 357
Tizmit: 357
Tolodi: 192, 199
Tonight (BBC television programme): 415
Toubkal, Mt: 354, 356, 357
Toundout: 351, 353
Trafalgar, Battle of: 13
Trafalgar Square: 12
Trans-Jordan: (*see* Jordan)
Travellers Club: 54, 84, 334, 342, 442
Travels in Arabia Deserta (C.M. Doughty): 372
Trevor-Roper, Patrick Dacre, FRCS: 456
Trinity College, University of Cambridge: 93
Tripoli: 227, 246, 248, 384
Tsavo National Park: 422
Tunisia: 181, 241, 242, 248, 249
Turkana (tribe): 39, 148, 198, 199, 203, 389,
393, 395, 400, 415–18, 420, 423, 426, 441,
445, 448, 449
Turkana, Lake (Lake Rudolf): 198, 385, 387,
388, 395, 414, 416–18, 422, 424
Turkey: 161, 322
Turkoman (people): 253, 410

Turks: 229, 231, 237, 253
Turkwel river: 420, 421
Tutankhamun: 409

Uaso Nyiro river: 40
Uganda: 106, 387, 420
Ulundi: 14
Umm al Hait: 272
Umm al Samim: 270, 300, 301
Unai Kotal: 346
United Arab Emirates: 455
United Nations: 367
Upon that Mountain (Eric Shipton): 334
Uruq al Shaiba: 281–2, 284
Uvaroff, Dr (later Sir) Boris P., KCMG FRS:
259, 271, 286, 289
Uzbeks: 410

Valley of the Kings: 196
Valleys of the Assassins: 402
Van, Lake: 15, 16
Vasseur, Olivier le: 119
Vavra, Robert: 457
Venice: 395, 407
Verney, Jan (Lady): 393, 395, 396, 400
Verney, Sir John, 2nd Bart (1913–93): 11, 38,
139, 223, 241, 286, 334, 369–72, 376, 381,
382, 393, 395–7, 400
Verney, Sir Ralph, 1st Bart: 84
Victoria, Queen: 383
Vigors, Edward (WT's uncle): 19, 84
Vigors, Eileen Edmée: (*see* Ward, Eileen
Edmée)
Vigors, General Horatio Nelson Trafalgar: 18
Vigors, Reverend Louis: 18
Vigors, Ludlow Ashmead (WT's uncle): 19, 61,
94
Vigors (*née* Handcock), Mary Louisa Helen
(WT's grandmother): 10, 19, 53, 68
Vigors, Captain Nicholas Aylward, DCL: 18
Vigors, Thomas Mercer Cliffe (WT's
grandfather): 19
Villa Cipressi: 87
Villon, François (1431–?): 37
Vincent's Club: 84
Visions of a Nomad (WT): 448
Vivian, Herbert: 5, 6
Vyvyan, Major-General Charles: 456
Vyvyan, Mrs Charles: 456

Wad Medani: 128, 159
Wadai: 179
Wadi Arabah: 410
Wadi Halfa: 130
Wadi Hawash: 179
Wadi Howar: 130, 146, 147, 153

Wahiba (sands): 301
Wagidi fort: 218
Waigul: 409
Wakeman, Dr: 23, 26
Wakikh: 337
Wales: 72, 426
Wales, HRH The Prince of: 457
Wamba: 418, 447
Wanasgul: 363
Wanderobo (tribe): 433
Ward, Reverend Arthur Evelyn: 9
Ward (née Vigors), Eileen Edmée (WT's aunt): 9, 19, 397
Ward, Dr Stephen (WT's cousin): 397
Ward & Co. Ltd, Rowland (publishers and taxidermists): 109, 191, 192, 409
Warges, Mt: 447
Wark: 90
Watson, Graham: 289, 326, 328–30, 372–6, 379–81, 394, 397
Watson-Wentworth, Lord Charles, 2nd Marquess of Rockingham (1730–82): 11–12
Watt, James (1736–1819): 128
Waugh, Evelyn Arthur St John (1903–66): 78, 93, 209, 210
Wavell, Field-Marshal Archibald Percival, 1st Earl (1883–1950): 200, 207, 211
Waziristan: 338, 340
Webb, George Hannam, OBE: 106, 149, 379, 385, 393, 395, 400, 424, 442, 448
Webb, Josephine ('Jo'): 379, 424
Wedderburn-Maxwell, Henry Godfrey, MBE (1895–1971): 126, 165, 166, 168, 175, 190, 195, 253
Weir House: 85, 104
Wellington College: 87
Wellsted, James: 301
Wernert, Dr Paul: 119
Western Arab Corps: 149–50, 160, 200
Westley Richards & Co. Ltd (gun and rifle makers): 79, 80
Whipps Cross Hospital: 456
White, Terence Hanbury ('Tim', 1906–64): 3, 335, 382, 396
Whitworth, Ursula Joan (Mrs Roderic Thesiger): 275
Wienholt, Arnold: 200, 206, 207
Wilder Shores of Love, The (Lesley Blanch): 406, 407
Williams, Mary Anne (Mrs Charles Thesiger): 13
Williams, Major W.A.: 15–16

Wind, Sand and Stars (Antoine de Saint-Exupéry): 188
Wingate, Jonathan Orde: 411
Wingate, Major-General Orde Charles, DSO (1903–44): 207, 210–21, 241, 252, 262, 411
Wingate, Sir Reginald: 46
Winser, Nigel de N.: 437, 439
Wollo: 255, 257, 260, 261
Woodcote Grove House: 460, 461, 462, 463
Woodcote Park Golf Club: 462
Woodthorpe, Colonel R.G., CB: 360
Woolwich: 212
Wright, Sir Denis Arthur Hepworth, GCMG: 383, 405, 406
Wright, Iona, Lady: 383, 406
Wylde, Augustus: 6

Yakwalung: 348
Yasin (place): 343
Yasin (WT's canoeboy): 313, 315, 317
Yazd: 406, 407, 408
Yazidis (people): 254, 309, 310
Yazidis, Amir of the: 309–10
Yemen: 178, 258, 267, 271, 273, 411, 412, 414, 416, 417, 435, 436
Yoa, lake: 187
Young, Gavin David (1928–2001): 106, 315, 316, 323, 327, 332, 342, 372, 400, 437–9, 441
Yusuf (interpreter): 355

Zaghawa-Kobé tribe: 134, 147, 148, 151, 153, 155, 164, 169, 176, 177, 183,189, 194, 224
Zagros Mts: 404
Zaltin: (see bin Zaltin)
Zanzibar: 67, 300, 399, 400
Zaouia Ahansal: 355–7
Zaphiro, Denis: 422
Zaphiro, Philip: 422
Zard Sang pass: 346
Zauditu, Waizero, Empress of Abyssinia: 44, 45, 67, 74, 411
Zayid, Sheikh bin Sultan al Nahyan: 165, 298–300, 302, 304
Zella: 246
Zem Zem, Wadi: 246
Zerka: 349
Ziman, H.D.: 400
Zimbabwe: 455
Zouar: 179, 185, 186
Zulu War: 13, 14, 72
Zululand: 460
Zulus: 13, 14, 72, 118, 162, 445